KB186204

한국의 토익 수험자 여러분께,

토익 시험은 세계적인 직무 영어능력 평가 시험으로, 지난 40여 년간 비즈니스 현장에서 필요한 영어능력 평가의 기준을 제시해 왔습니다. 토익 시험 및 토익스피킹, 토익라이팅 시험은 세계에서 가장 널리 통용되는 영어능력 검증 시험으로, 160여 개국 14,000여 기관이 토익 성적을 의사결정에 활용하고 있습니다.

YBM은 한국의 토익 시험을 주관하는 ETS 독점 계약사입니다.

ETS는 한국 수험자들의 효과적인 토익 학습을 돕고자 YBM을 통하여 'ETS 토익 공식 교재'를 독점 출간하고 있습니다. 또한 'ETS 토익 공식 교재' 시리즈에 기출문항을 제공해 한국의 다른 교재들에 수록된 기출을 복제하거나 변형한 문항으로 인하여 발생할 수 있는 수험자들의 혼동을 방지하고 있습니다.

복제 및 변형 문항들은 토익 시험의 출제의도를 벗어날 수 있기 때문에 기출문항을 수록한 'ETS 토익 공식 교재'만큼 시험에 잘 대비할 수 없습니다.

'ETS 토익 공식 교재'를 통하여 수험자 여러분의 영어 소통을 위한 노력에 큰 성취가 있기를 바랍니다.

감사합니다.

Dear TOEIC Test Takers in Korea,

The TOEIC program is the global leader in English-language assessment for the workplace. It has set the standard for assessing English-language skills needed in the workplace for more than 40 years. The TOEIC tests are the most widely used English language assessments around the world, with 14,000+ organizations across more than 160 countries trusting TOEIC scores to make decisions.

YBM is the ETS Country Master Distributor for the TOEIC program in Korea and so is the exclusive distributor for TOEIC Korea.

To support effective learning for TOEIC test-takers in Korea, ETS has authorized YBM to publish the only Official TOEIC prep books in Korea. These books contain actual TOEIC items to help prevent confusion among Korean test-takers that might be caused by other prep book publishers' use of reproduced or paraphrased items.

Reproduced or paraphrased items may fail to reflect the intent of actual TOEIC items and so will not prepare test-takers as well as the actual items contained in the ETS TOEIC Official prep books published by YBM.

We hope that these ETS TOEIC Official prep books enable you, as test-takers, to achieve great success in your efforts to communicate effectively in English.

Thank you.

입문부터 실전까지 수준별 학습을 통해 최단기 목표점수 달성!

ETS TOEIC® 공식수험서
스마트 학습 지원

www.ybmbooks.com에서도 무료 MP3를 다운로드 받을 수 있습니다.

ETS 토익 모바일 학습 플랫폼!

ETS 토익기출 수험서 어플

구글플레이　앱스토어

교재 학습 지원	• 교재 해설 강의
	• LC 음원 MP3
	• 교재/부록 모의고사 채점 분석
	• 단어 암기장
부가 서비스	• 데일리 학습(토익 기출문제 풀이)
	• 토익 최신 경향 무료 특강
	• 토익 타이머
모의고사 결과 분석	• 파트별/문항별 정답률
	• 파트별/유형별 취약점 리포트
	• 전체 응시자 점수 분포도

ETS 토익 학습 전용 온라인 커뮤니티!

ETS TOEIC® Book 공식카페

etstoeicbook.co.kr

강사진의 학습 지원	토익 대표강사들의 학습 지원과 멘토링
교재 학습관 운영	교재별 학습게시판을 통해 무료 동영상 강의 등 학습 지원
학습 콘텐츠 제공	토익 학습 콘텐츠와 정기시험 예비특강 업데이트

*toeic®

토익 정기시험
기출문제집 4
1000 RC

토익 정기시험
기출문제집4
1000 RC

발행인 허문호

발행처 YBM

편집 이태경, 박효민, 오유진

디자인 강상문, 이미화, 이현숙

마케팅 정연철, 박천산, 고영노, 김동진, 박찬경, 김윤하

초판발행 2023년 12월 18일

6쇄발행 2025년 1월 2일

신고일자 1964년 3월 28일

신고번호 제 1964-000003호

주소 서울시 종로구 종로 104

전화 (02) 2000-0515 [구입문의] / (02) 2000-0563 [내용문의]

팩스 (02) 2285-1523

홈페이지 www.ybmbooks.com

ISBN 978-89-17-23950-8

*toeic.

토익® 정기시험 기출문제집 4
1000

RC

PREFACE

Dear test taker,

English-language proficiency has become a vital tool for success. It can help you excel in business, travel the world, and communicate effectively with friends and colleagues. The TOEIC® test measures your ability to function effectively in English in these types of situations. Because TOEIC scores are recognized around the world as evidence of your English-language proficiency, you will be able to confidently demonstrate your English skills to employers and begin your journey to success.

The test developers at ETS are excited to help you achieve your personal and professional goals through the use of the TOEIC® 정기시험 기출문제집 1000 Vol. 4. This book contains test questions taken from actual, official TOEIC tests. These questions will help you become familiar with the content and the format of the TOEIC test. This book also contains detailed explanations of the question types and language points contained in the TOEIC test. These test questions and explanations have all been prepared by the same test specialists who develop the actual TOEIC test, so you can be confident that you will receive an authentic test-preparation experience.

Features of the TOEIC® 정기시험 기출문제집 1000 Vol. 4 include the following.

- Ten full-length test forms all accompanied by answer keys and official scripts
- Specific and easy to understand explanations for learners
- The very same ETS voice actors that you will hear in an official TOEIC test

By using the TOEIC® 정기시험 기출문제집 1000 Vol. 4 to prepare for the TOEIC test, you can be assured that you have a professionally prepared resource that will provide you with accurate guidance so that you are more familiar with the tasks, content, and format of the test and that will help you maximize your TOEIC test score. With your official TOEIC score certificate, you will be ready to show the world what you know!

We are delighted to assist you on your TOEIC journey with the TOEIC® 정기시험 기출문제집 1000 Vol. 4 and wish you the best of success.

최신 기출문제 전격 공개!

유일무이 **출제기관이 독점 제공한 기출문제가 담긴 유일한 교재!**

이 책에는 정기시험 기출문제 10세트가 수록되어 있다. 시험에 나온
최신 기출문제로 실전 감각을 키워 시험에 확실하게 대비하자!

국내최고 **기출 포인트를 꿰뚫는 명쾌한 해설!**

최신 출제 경향을 가장 정확하게 알 수 있는 기출문제를 풀고 출제
포인트가 보이는 명쾌한 해설로 토익을 정복해 보자!

독점제공 **ETS 제공 표준점수 환산표!**

출제기관 ETS가 독점 제공하는 표준점수 환산표를 수록했다. 채점
후 환산표를 통해 자신의 실력이 어느 정도인지 가늠해 보자!

스마트 학습 **동영상 강의, 단어장, 채점서비스 무료 제공!**

ETS 토익기출 수험서 어플 다운로드 및 실행 ▶ 토익(상단 메뉴)
▶ 실전서(좌측 메뉴) ▶ ETS 토익 정기시험 기출문제집 1000 Vol. 4
RC를 클릭해 무료 제공하는 자료로 스마트하게 학습하자!

* ybmbooks.com에서도 단어장 MP3파일, 단어장 PDF, 정답 PDF,
  토익 연습용 답안지 PDF 제공

TOEIC 소개

Test of English for International Communication(국제적 의사소통을 위한 영어 시험)의 약자로, 영어가 모국어가 아닌 사람들이 일상생활 또는 비즈니스 현장에서 꼭 필요한 실용적 영어 구사 능력을 갖추었는가를 평가하는 시험이다.

시험 구성

구성	PART		유형	문항 수	시간	배점
Listening	Part 1		사진 묘사	6	45분	495점
	Part 2		질의 응답	25		
	Part 3		짧은 대화	39		
	Part 4		짧은 담화	30		
Reading	Part 5		단문 빈칸 채우기	30	75분	495점
	Part 6		장문 빈칸 채우기	16		
	Part 7	독해	단일 지문	29		
			이중 지문	10		
			삼중 지문	15		
Total	**7 Parts**			**200문항**	**120분**	**990점**

평가 항목

LC	RC
단문을 듣고 이해하는 능력	읽은 글을 통해 추론해 생각할 수 있는 능력
짧은 대화체 문장을 듣고 이해하는 능력	장문에서 특정한 정보를 찾을 수 있는 능력
비교적 긴 대화체에서 주고받은 내용을 파악할 수 있는 능력	글의 목적, 주제, 의도 등을 파악하는 능력
장문에서 핵심이 되는 정보를 파악할 수 있는 능력	뜻이 유사한 단어들의 정확한 용례를 파악하는 능력
구나 문장에서 화자의 목적이나 함축된 의미를 이해하는 능력	문장 구조를 제대로 파악하는지, 문장에서 필요한 품사, 어구 등을 찾는 능력

※ 성적표에는 전체 수험자의 평균과 해당 수험자가 받은 성적이 백분율로 표기되어 있다.

수험 정보

시험 접수 방법

한국 토익 위원회 사이트(www.toeic.co.kr)에서 시험일 약 2개월 전부터
온라인으로 접수 가능

시험장 준비물

신분증	규정 신분증만 가능 (주민등록증, 운전면허증, 기간 만료 전의 여권, 공무원증)
필기구	연필, 지우개 (볼펜이나 사인펜은 사용 금지)

시험 진행 시간

09:20	입실 (9:50 이후 입실 불가)
09:30 ~ 09:45	답안지 작성에 관한 오리엔테이션
09:45 ~ 09:50	휴식
09:50 ~ 10:05	신분증 확인
10:05 ~ 10:10	문제지 배부 및 파본 확인
10:10 ~ 10:55	듣기 평가 (LISTENING TEST)
10:55 ~ 12:10	독해 평가 (READING TEST)

**TOEIC
성적 확인**

시험일로부터 약 10-11일 후, 인터넷 홈페이지와 어플리케이션을 통해 성적을 확인할 수 있다.
TOEIC 성적표는 우편이나 온라인으로 발급받을 수 있다(시험 접수 시 양자택일).
우편으로 발급받을 경우는 성적 발표 후 대략 일주일이 소요되며, 온라인 발급을 선택하면
유효기간 내에 홈페이지에서 본인이 직접 1회에 한해 무료 출력할 수 있다. TOEIC 성적은
시험일로부터 2년간 유효하다.

토익 점수

TOEIC 점수는 듣기 영역(LC)과 읽기 영역(RC)을 합계한 점수로 5점 단위로 구성되며 총점은
990점이다. TOEIC 성적은 각 문제 유형의 난이도에 따른 점수 환산표에 의해 결정된다.

토익 경향 분석

PART 1 사진 묘사 Photographs

1인 등장 사진

주어는 He/She, A man/woman 등이며 주로 앞부분에 나온다.

2인 이상 등장 사진

주어는 They, Some men/women/people, One of the men/women 등이며 주로 중간 부분에 나온다.

사물/배경 사진

주어는 A car, Some chairs 등이며 주로 뒷부분에 나온다.

사람 또는 사물 중심 사진

주어가 일부는 사람, 일부는 사물이며 주로 뒷부분에 나온다.

사람 또는 사물 중심 사진 **33**%

1인 등장 사진 **33**%

사물/배경 사진 **17**%

2인 이상 등장 사진 **17**%

PART 1 최신 출제 경향

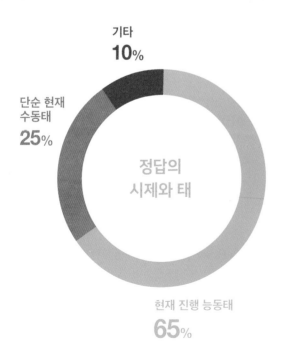

기타 **10**%

단순 현재 수동태 **25**%

현재 진행 능동태 **65**%

정답의 시제와 태

현재 진행 능동태

<is/are + 현재분사> 형태이며 주로 사람이 주어이다.

단순 현재 수동태

<is/are + 과거분사> 형태이며 주로 사물이 주어이다.

기타

<is/are + being + 과거분사> 형태의 현재 진행 수동태, <has/have + been + 과거분사> 형태의 현재 완료 수동태, '타동사 + 목적어' 형태의 단순 현재 능동태, There is/are와 같은 단순 현재도 나온다.

평서문
질문이 아니라 객관적인 사실이나 화자의 의견
등을 나타내는 문장이다.

의문사 의문문
각 의문사마다 1~2개씩 나온다. 의문사가
단독으로 나오기도 하지만 What time ~?,
How long ~?, Which room ~? 등에서처럼
다른 명사나 형용사와 같이 나오기도 한다.

명령문
동사원형이나 Please 등으로 시작한다.

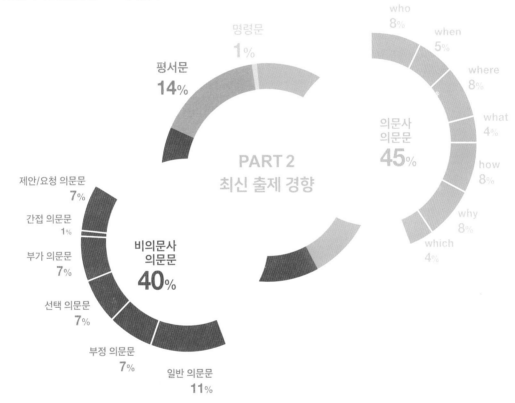

비의문사 의문문
일반(Yes/No) 의문문 적게 나올 때는 1~2개, 많이 나올 때는 3~4개씩 나오는 편이다.
부정 의문문 Don't you ~?, Isn't he ~? 등으로 시작하는 문장이며 일반 긍정 의문문보다는 약간 더 적게 나온다.
선택 의문문 A or B 형태로 나오며 A와 B의 형태가 단어, 구, 절일 수 있다. 구나 절일 경우 문장이 길어져서 어려워진다.
부가 의문문 ~ don't you?, ~ isn't he? 등으로 끝나는 문장이며, 일반 부정 의문문과 비슷하다고 볼 수 있다.
간접 의문문 의문사가 문장 처음 부분이 아니라 문장 중간에 들어 있다.
제안/요청 의문문 정보를 얻기보다는 상대방의 도움이나 동의 등을 얻기 위한 목적이 일반적이다.

PART 3 짧은 대화 Short Conversations

- 3인 대화의 경우 남자 화자 두 명과 여자 화자 한 명 또는 남자 화자 한 명과 여자 화자 두 명이 나온다. 따라서 문제에서는 2인 대화에서와 달리 the man이나 the woman이 아니라 the men이나 the women 또는 특정한 이름이 언급될 수 있다.

- 대화 & 시각 정보는 항상 파트의 뒷부분에 나온다.

- 시각 정보의 유형으로 chart, map, floor plan, schedule, table, weather forecast, directory, list, invoice, receipt, sign, packing slip 등 다양한 자료가 골고루 나온다.

PART 3
대화 유형

2인 대화 & 시각 정보 **23%**
2인 대화 **63%**
3인 대화 **14%**

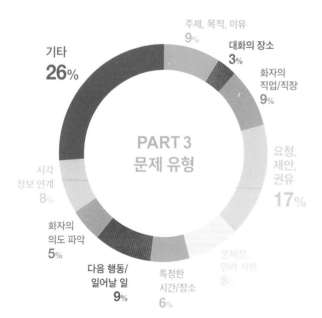

PART 3
문제 유형

주제, 목적, 이유 **9%**
대화의 장소 **3%**
화자의 직업/직장 **9%**
요청, 제안, 권유 **17%**
문제점, 염려 사항 **8%**
특정한 시간/장소 **6%**
다음 행동/일어날 일 **9%**
화자의 의도 파악 **5%**
시각 정보 연계 **8%**
기타 **26%**

- 주제, 목적, 이유, 대화의 장소, 화자의 직업/직장 등과 관련된 문제는 주로 대화의 첫 번째 문제로 나오며 다음 행동/일어날 일 등과 관련된 문제는 주로 대화의 세 번째 문제로 나온다.

- 화자의 의도 파악 문제는 주로 2인 대화에 나오지만, 가끔 3인 대화에 나오기도 한다. 시각 정보 연계 대화에는 나오지 않고 있다.

- Part 3에서 화자의 의도 파악 문제는 2개가 나오고 시각 정보 연계 문제는 3개가 나온다.

PART 4 짧은 담화 Short Talks

총 10담화문 30문제 (지문당 3문제)

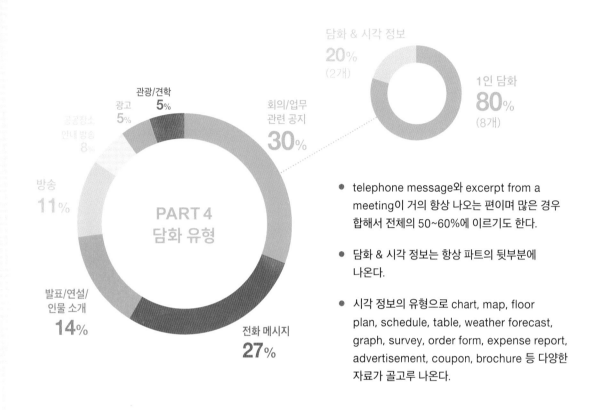

- telephone message와 excerpt from a meeting이 거의 항상 나오는 편이며 많은 경우 합해서 전체의 50~60%에 이르기도 한다.

- 담화 & 시각 정보는 항상 파트의 뒷부분에 나온다.

- 시각 정보의 유형으로 chart, map, floor plan, schedule, table, weather forecast, graph, survey, order form, expense report, advertisement, coupon, brochure 등 다양한 자료가 골고루 나온다.

- 문제 유형은 기본적으로 Part 3과 거의 비슷하다.

- 주제, 목적, 이유, 담화의 장소, 화자의 직업/직장 등과 관련된 문제는 주로 담화의 첫 번째 문제로 나오며 다음 행동/일어날 일 등과 관련된 문제는 주로 담화의 세 번째 문제로 나온다.

- Part 4에서 화자의 의도 파악 문제는 3개가 나오고 시각 정보 연계 문제는 2개가 나온다.

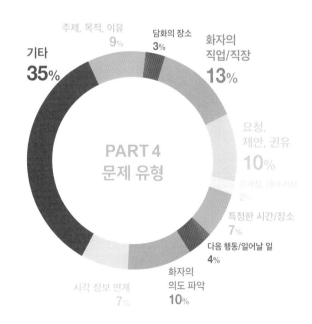

문법 문제

시제와 대명사와 관련된 문법 문제가 2개씩,
한정사와 분사와 관련된 문법 문제가 1개씩
나온다. 시제 문제의 경우 능동태/수동태나
수의 일치와 연계되기도 한다. 그 밖에 한정사,
능동태/수동태, 부정사, 동명사 등과 관련된
문법 문제가 나온다.

어휘 문제

동사, 명사, 형용사, 부사와 관련된 어휘
문제가 각각 2~3개씩 골고루 나온다.
전치사 어휘 문제는 3개씩 꾸준히
나오지만, 접속사나 어구와 관련된 어휘
문제는 나오지 않을 때도 있고 3개가
나올 때도 있다.

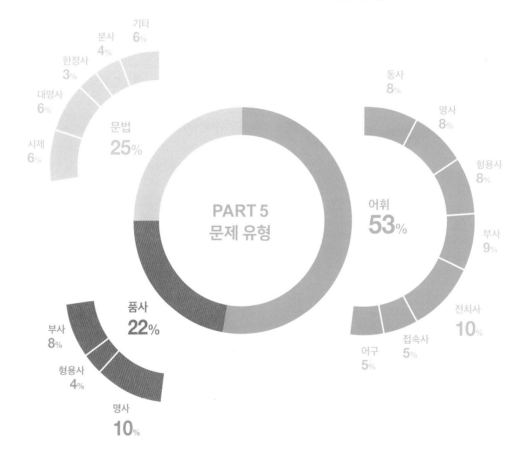

품사 문제

명사와 부사와 관련된 품사 문제가
2~3개씩 나오며, 형용사와 관련된 품사
문제가 상대적으로 적은 편이다.

PART 6 장문 빈칸 채우기 Text Completion

총 4지문 16문제 (지문당 4문제)

한 지문에 4문제가 나오며 평균적으로 어휘 문제가 2개, 품사나 문법 문제가 1개, 문맥에 맞는 문장 고르기 문제가 1개 들어간다. 문맥에 맞는 문장 고르기 문제를 제외하면 문제 유형은 기본적으로 파트 5와 거의 비슷하다.

어휘 문제

동사, 명사, 부사, 어구와 관련된 어휘 문제는 매번 1~2개씩 나온다. 부사 어휘 문제의 경우 therefore(그러므로)나 however(하지만)처럼 문맥의 흐름을 자연스럽게 연결해 주는 부사가 자주 나온다.

문맥에 맞는 문장 고르기

문맥에 맞는 문장 고르기 문제는 지문당 한 문제씩 나오는데, 나오는 위치의 확률은 4문제 중 두 번째 문제, 세 번째 문제, 네 번째 문제, 첫 번째 문제 순으로 높다.

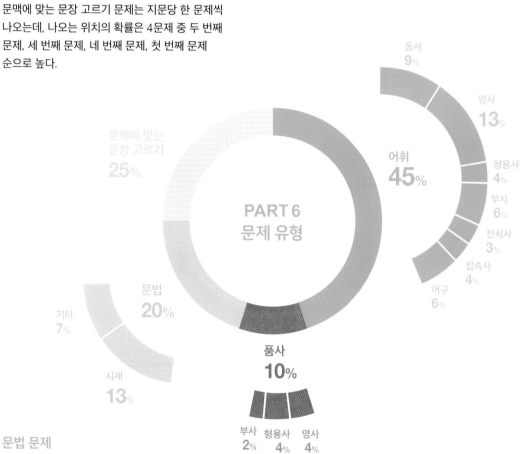

문법 문제

문맥의 흐름과 밀접하게 관련이 있는 시제 문제가 2개 정도 나오며, 능동태/수동태나 수의 일치와 연계되기도 한다. 그 밖에 대명사, 능동태/수동태, 부정사, 접속사/전치사 등과 관련된 문법 문제가 나온다.

품사 문제

명사나 형용사 문제가 부사 문제보다 좀 더 자주 나온다.

PART 7 독해 Reading Comprehension

지문 유형	지문당 문제 수	지문 개수	비중 %
단일 지문	2문항	4개	약 15%
	3문항	3개	약 16%
	4문항	3개	약 22%
이중 지문	5문항	2개	약 19%
삼중 지문	5문항	3개	약 28%

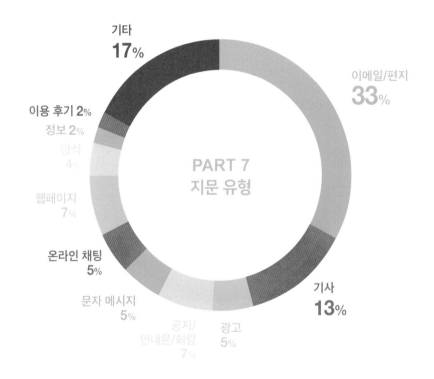

- 이메일/편지, 기사 유형 지문은 거의 항상 나오는 편이며 많은 경우 합해서 전체의 50~60%에 이르기도 한다.

- 기타 지문 유형으로 agenda, brochure, comment card, coupon, flyer, instructions, invitation, invoice, list, menu, page from a catalog, policy statement, report, schedule, survey, voucher 등 다양한 자료가 골고루 나온다.

(이중 지문과 삼중 지문 속의 지문들을 모두 낱개로 계산함 - 총 23지문)

총 15지문 54문제 (지문당 2~5문제)

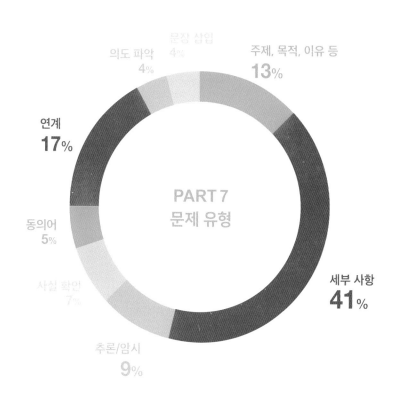

의도 파악
4%

문장 삽입
4%

주제, 목적, 이유 등
13%

연계
17%

PART 7
문제 유형

동의어
5%

세부 사항
41%

사실 확인
7%

추론/암시
9%

- 동의어 문제는 주로 이중 지문이나 삼중 지문에 나온다.
- 연계 문제는 일반적으로 이중 지문에서 한 문제, 삼중 지문에서 두 문제가 나온다.
- 의도 파악 문제는 문자 메시지(text-message chain)나 온라인 채팅(online chat discussion) 지문에서 출제되며 두 문제가 나온다.
- 문장 삽입 문제는 주로 기사, 이메일, 편지, 회람 지문에서 출제되며 두 문제가 나온다.

점수 환산표 및 산출법

점수 환산표 이 책에 수록된 각 Test를 풀고 난 후, 맞은 개수를 세어 점수를 환산해 보세요.

LISTENING Raw Score (맞은 개수)	LISTENING Scaled Score (환산 점수)	READING Raw Score (맞은 개수)	READING Scaled Score (환산 점수)
96-100	475-495	96-100	460-495
91-95	435-495	91-95	425-490
86-90	405-470	86-90	400-465
81-85	370-450	81-85	375-440
76-80	345-420	76-80	340-415
71-75	320-390	71-75	310-390
66-70	290-360	66-70	285-370
61-65	265-335	61-65	255-340
56-60	240-310	56-60	230-310
51-55	215-280	51-55	200-275
46-50	190-255	46-50	170-245
41-45	160-230	41-45	140-215
36-40	130-205	36-40	115-180
31-35	105-175	31-35	95-150
26-30	85-145	26-30	75-120
21-25	60-115	21-25	60-95
16-20	30-90	16-20	45-75
11-15	5-70	11-15	30-55
6-10	5-60	6-10	10-40
1-5	5-50	1-5	5-30
0	5-35	0	5-15

점수 산출 방법   아래의 방식으로 점수를 산출할 수 있다.

STEP 1

자신의 답안을 수록된 정답과 대조하여 채점한다. 각 Section의 맞은 개수가 본인의 Section별 '실제 점수(통계 처리하기 전의 점수, raw score)'이다. Listening Test와 Reading Test의 정답 수를 세어, 자신의 실제 점수를 아래의 해당란에 기록한다.

	맞은 개수	환산 점수대
LISTENING		
READING		
총점		

Section별 실제 점수가 그대로 Section별 TOEIC 점수가 되는 것은 아니다. TOEIC은 시행할 때마다 별도로 특정한 통계 처리 방법을 사용하며 이러한 실제 점수를 환산 점수(converted[scaled] score)로 전환하게 된다. 이렇게 전환함으로써, 매번 시행될 때마다 문제는 달라지지만 그 점수가 갖는 의미는 같아지게 된다. 예를 들어 어느 한 시험에서 총점 550점의 성적을 받는 실력이라면 다른 시험에서도 거의 550점대의 성적을 받게 되는 것이다.

STEP 2

실제 점수를 위 표에 기록한 후 왼쪽 페이지의 점수 환산표를 보도록 한다. TOEIC이 시행될 때마다 대개 이와 비슷한 형태의 표가 작성되는데, 여기 제시된 환산표는 본 교재에 수록된 Test용으로 개발된 것이다. 이 표를 사용하여 자신의 실제 점수를 환산 점수로 전환하도록 한다. 즉, 예를 들어 Listening Test의 실제 정답 수가 61~65개이면 환산 점수는 265점에서 335점 사이가 된다. 여기서 실제 정답 수가 61개이면 환산 점수가 265점이고, 65개이면 환산 점수가 335점임을 의미하는 것은 아니다. 본 책의 Test를 위해 작성된 이 점수 환산표가 자신의 영어 실력이 어느 정도인지 대략적으로 파악하는 데 도움이 되긴 하지만, 이 표가 실제 TOEIC 성적 산출에 그대로 사용된 적은 없다는 사실을 밝혀 둔다.

토익®정기시험
기출문제집 4
1000

TEST 01
무료 동영상 강의

RC

기출 TEST

01

READING TEST

In the Reading test, you will read a variety of texts and answer several different types of reading comprehension questions. The entire Reading test will last 75 minutes. There are three parts, and directions are given for each part. You are encouraged to answer as many questions as possible within the time allowed.

You must mark your answers on the separate answer sheet. Do not write your answers in your test book.

PART 5

Directions: A word or phrase is missing in each of the sentences below. Four answer choices are given below each sentence. Select the best answer to complete the sentence. Then mark the letter (A), (B), (C), or (D) on your answer sheet.

101. Former Sendai Company CEO Ken Nakata spoke about ------- career experiences.

    (A) he
    (B) his
    (C) him
    (D) himself

102. Passengers who will be taking a ------- domestic flight should go to Terminal A.

    (A) connectivity
    (B) connects
    (C) connect
    (D) connecting

103. Fresh and ------- apple-cider donuts are available at Oakcrest Orchard's retail shop for £6 per dozen.

    (A) eaten
    (B) open
    (C) tasty
    (D) free

104. Zahn Flooring has the widest selection of ------- in the United Kingdom.

    (A) paints
    (B) tiles
    (C) furniture
    (D) curtains

105. One responsibility of the IT department is to ensure that the company is using ------- software.

    (A) update
    (B) updating
    (C) updates
    (D) updated

106. It is wise to check a company's dress code ------- visiting its head office.

    (A) so
    (B) how
    (C) like
    (D) before

107. Wexler Store's management team expects that employees will ------- support any new hires.

    (A) enthusiastically
    (B) enthusiasm
    (C) enthusiastic
    (D) enthused

108. Wheel alignments and brake system ------- are part of our vehicle service plan.

    (A) inspects
    (B) inspector
    (C) inspected
    (D) inspections

109. Registration for the Marketing Coalition Conference is now open ------- September 30.
(A) until
(B) into
(C) yet
(D) while

110. Growth in the home entertainment industry has been ------- this quarter.
(A) separate
(B) limited
(C) willing
(D) assorted

111. Hawson Furniture will be making ------- on the east side of town on Thursday.
(A) deliveries
(B) delivered
(C) deliver
(D) deliverable

112. The Marlton City Council does not have the authority to ------- parking on city streets.
(A) drive
(B) prohibit
(C) bother
(D) travel

113. Project Earth Group is ------- for ways to reduce transport-related greenhouse gas emissions.
(A) looking
(B) seeing
(C) driving
(D) leaning

114. Our skilled tailors are happy to design a custom-made suit that fits your style and budget -------.
(A) perfect
(B) perfects
(C) perfectly
(D) perfection

115. Project manager Hannah Chung has proved to be very ------- with completing company projects.
(A) helpfulness
(B) help
(C) helpfully
(D) helpful

116. Lehua Vacation Club members will receive double points ------- the month of August at participating hotels.
(A) onto
(B) above
(C) during
(D) between

117. The costumes were not received ------- enough to be used in the first dress rehearsal.
(A) far
(B) very
(C) almost
(D) soon

118. As a former publicist for several renowned orchestras, Mr. Wu would excel in the role of event -------.
(A) organized
(B) organizer
(C) organizes
(D) organizational

119. The northbound lane on Davis Street will be ------- closed because of the city's bridge reinforcement project.
(A) temporarily
(B) competitively
(C) recently
(D) collectively

120. Airline representatives must handle a wide range of passenger issues, ------- missed connections to lost luggage.
(A) from
(B) under
(C) on
(D) against

GO ON TO THE NEXT PAGE

121. The meeting notes were ------- deleted, but Mr. Hahm was able to recreate them from memory.

(A) accident
(B) accidental
(C) accidents
(D) accidentally

122. The current issue of *Farming Scene* magazine predicts that the price of corn will rise 5 percent over the ------- year.

(A) next
(B) with
(C) which
(D) now

123. Anyone who still ------- to take the fire safety training should do so before the end of the month.

(A) needing
(B) needs
(C) has needed
(D) were needing

124. Emerging technologies have ------- begun to transform the shipping industry in ways that were once unimaginable.

(A) already
(B) exactly
(C) hardly
(D) closely

125. The company handbook outlines the high ------- that employees are expected to meet every day.

(A) experts
(B) accounts
(C) recommendations
(D) standards

126. Because ------- of the board members have scheduling conflicts, the board meeting will be moved to a date when all can attend.

(A) any
(B) everybody
(C) those
(D) some

127. The project ------- the collaboration of several teams across the company.

(A) passed
(B) decided
(C) required
(D) performed

128. We cannot send the store's coupon booklet to the printers until it ------- by Ms. Jeon.

(A) is approving
(B) approves
(C) has been approved
(D) will be approved

129. ------- the closure of Verdigold Transport Services, we are looking for a new shipping company.

(A) In spite of
(B) Just as
(C) In light of
(D) According to

130. The ------- information provided by Uniss Bank's brochure helps applicants understand the terms of their loans.

(A) arbitrary
(B) supplemental
(C) superfluous
(D) potential

PART 6

Directions: Read the texts that follow. A word, phrase, or sentence is missing in parts of each text. Four answer choices for each question are given below the text. Select the best answer to complete the text. Then mark the letter (A), (B), (C), or (D) on your answer sheet.

Questions 131-134 refer to the following announcement.

Come to the Maxley Heights Center for Horticulture and learn how to create a beautiful, eco-friendly garden for your home or business. ------- . We will teach you how to plant a rain
131.
garden, which is simply a shallow sunken garden ------- a special soil mix to filter pollutants from
132.
rainwater flowing from nearby roads and rooftops. These gardens can be landscaped with native plants and flowers. ------- , rain gardens are always beneficial to the local environment. Among
133.
other things, ------- improve drainage and protect rivers and streams.
134.

To register, visit www.maxley-horticulture.org.

131. (A) Children of all ages will enjoy the new exhibits.
   (B) Learn about rainfall patterns across the region.
   (C) Build a set of simple patio furniture with easy-to-acquire materials.
   (D) Next Saturday at 4 P.M., we are hosting a free workshop for the public.

132. (A) to use
   (B) used to
   (C) by using
   (D) that uses

133. (A) Best of all
   (B) For example
   (C) In any event
   (D) As a matter of fact

134. (A) we
   (B) they
   (C) both
   (D) yours

GO ON TO THE NEXT PAGE

31 July

Akwasi Dombo
Fourth Avenue
GA 105
Accra, Ghana

Dear Mr. Dombo,

Thank you for your ------- support in helping me to plan the opening gala for Tokyo's fashion
        135.

week. The event was a huge success, and I was honored to work with you. I know that our

attendees follow your work closely, and they loved the designs you contributed for this event.

Your designs received a lot of ------- on social media. Shows like this will keep Tokyo on the map
          136.

as a premier fashion centre. ------- . I realize that the multiple delays made the planning no easy
         137.

task. The auction ------- our Young Designers Award program is coming up soon and I look
     138.

forward to working with you on that as well.

Sincerely,

Asahi Ishioka
Director, Japanese Guild of Fashion Designers

135. (A) amazed
(B) amazement
(C) amazing
(D) amazingly

136. (A) attention
(B) proposals
(C) innovation
(D) criticism

137. (A) Several other events have gone
    surprisingly well.
(B) Thank you also for your flexibility in
    planning the event.
(C) Please stop by our office the next
    time you are in the city.
(D) Tokyo is a top tourism destination for
    many reasons.

138. (A) will benefit
(B) to benefit
(C) has benefited
(D) benefits

From: Patron Services <patronservices@menachinlibrary.org>
To: Edgar Hughes <hughese98@villachesta.com>
Subject: Card expiration date approaching
Date: December 3

Dear Mr. Hughes,

Please be advised that your Mena Chin Library card will expire one month from today.

------- must be renewed if you intend to keep your membership for the coming year.
139.

------- . This can be done at the information desk at any branch location.
140.

------- you decide to close your account, no action is necessary. Failure to complete your renewal
141.

by the ------- date will result in the expiration of your library privileges.
142.

If you have any questions about this notice, or about general library services, you may reply

directly to this e-mail.

Sincerely,

Patron Services

139. (A) It
(B) You
(C) Our
(D) Each

140. (A) To sign up for a card, visit your local
library branch.
(B) For questions about library membership,
please visit our Web site.
(C) Renewal must be completed at least one
week before your card expires.
(D) You may opt out of this program at any
time.

141. (A) Also
(B) Should
(C) Because
(D) Although

142. (A) specifically
(B) specifics
(C) specified
(D) specificity

GO ON TO THE NEXT PAGE

April 7

Naomi Burwell
43 Waymire Road
South Portland, ME 04109

Dear Ms. Burwell,

I am Omar Ridha, the manager of Droplight Studio. ------- . We offer a full range of photography
                                                      143.
services for real estate professionals like you. We take pride in composing interior and exterior

shots that make a property look its best. Droplight Studio spares no effort in ------- superior
                                                                                144.
digital images. ------- , our professional-grade equipment, lighting, and staging techniques allow
                 145.
us to highlight the best features of a property. And once the photo shoot is over, every image

------- expert editing. All these services come standard in every package.
146.

Please visit our Web site to view our work as well as our pricing and scheduling information. We

are happy to work with you to customize orders.

Sincerely,

Omar Ridha, Droplight Studio

---

143. (A) I would like to introduce you to our
           business.
       (B) Great photographs can make your
           property stand out.
       (C) We are looking forward to your visit.
       (D) It was the first studio of its kind to
           open in this area.

144. (A) researching
       (B) creating
       (C) purchasing
       (D) displaying

145. (A) If not
       (B) By comparison
       (C) Otherwise
       (D) Indeed

146. (A) receives
       (B) is receiving
       (C) had received
       (D) had to receive

PART 7

Directions: In this part you will read a selection of texts, such as magazine and newspaper articles, e-mails, and instant messages. Each text or set of texts is followed by several questions. Select the best answer for each question and mark the letter (A), (B), (C), or (D) on your answer sheet.

Questions 147-148 refer to the following information.

STOP! PLEASE READ FIRST.

Thank you for purchasing this item.

As you do the unpacking, please verify that all components are included and place them in a safe area to avoid loss or damage. Assemble the item on a soft surface or on the flattened empty box.

Follow the pictures and begin the assembly by placing the main part on its side. Never overtighten any screws or bolts, or you may damage the wood or cushioning. Please visit our Web site to obtain maintenance tips and register your product for warranty coverage: www.indoordelight.com.

---

147. Where is the information most likely found?

(A) On a door
(B) On a receipt
(C) In a box
(D) On a Web site

148. What kind of item is most likely discussed?

(A) A desktop computer
(B) A piece of furniture
(C) A household appliance
(D) A power tool

GO ON TO THE NEXT PAGE

We are asking all Winnipeg staff to keep a copy of this schedule at their desks as a quick reference tool for scheduling interoffice meetings. Whenever possible, please schedule these meetings during one of the underlined hours, that is, after 7:00 A.M. but before 11:00 A.M.

Winnipeg		Toulouse
<u>7:00 A.M.</u>	—	2:00 P.M.
<u>8:00 A.M.</u>	—	3:00 P.M.
<u>9:00 A.M.</u>	—	4:00 P.M.
<u>10:00 A.M.</u>	—	5:00 P.M.
11:00 A.M.	—	6:00 P.M.
12:00 noon	—	7:00 P.M.

149. What is suggested by the schedule?

(A) A conference has been scheduled.
(B) A firm has offices in two time zones.
(C) Administrative assistants make travel plans.
(D) Some meeting times have been changed.

150. What is indicated about 11:00 A.M. Winnipeg time?

(A) It is when the Winnipeg office closes for lunch.
(B) It is when staff in Toulouse begin their workday.
(C) It is not a preferred time to schedule a meeting.
(D) It has just been added to the schedule.

The Bryant Foyer is one of the premier event spaces in our area. Set on a hill, it has expansive windows that provide sweeping views of the adjacent botanical gardens and the river. Built in 1897, it was the home of the Francona Charitable Trust until its renovation just over a year ago. Today, the space can accommodate up to 200 guests and is ideal for wedding receptions, office parties, and panel presentations. With its marble floors, cathedral ceiling, and stunning artwork, the Bryant Foyer is the ideal location for your next gathering.

The on-site restaurant, Andito's, caters our events and also operates as its own business. This farm-to-table restaurant, headed by chef Michaela Rymond, meets all dietary needs and has revolutionized the local food scene. Area residents know to plan far in advance to get a seat.

To reserve the event space or to make a dinner reservation, give us a call at 216-555-0157.

151. What is indicated about the Bryant Foyer?

(A) It is located on the shores of a lake.
(B) It has recently been renovated.
(C) It will build a botanical garden for guests.
(D) It is reserved solely for corporate events.

152. What is suggested about Andito's?

(A) It was started by an international chef.
(B) It offers limited menu options.
(C) It is now funded by a charitable organization.
(D) It is very popular with local residents.

GO ON TO THE NEXT PAGE

Questions 153-154 refer to the following text-message chain.

Joan Chi (12:39 P.M.)
Hello Mina. Are you almost finished with the field measurements? I'm getting hungry.

Mina Evers (12:40 P.M.)
Sorry, Joan. I'm afraid you and Ms. Lim will have to go to lunch without me today. There's a problem with the site coordinates. This is going to take some time.

Joan Chi (12:51 P.M.)
Oh no. Should we bring something back for you?

Mina Evers (12:59 P.M.)
Get me a chicken sandwich.

Joan Chi (1:00 P.M.)
Sure thing, Mina. See you in a while.

153. At 1:00 P.M., what does Ms. Chi most likely mean when she writes, "Sure thing, Mina"?

(A) She will bring lunch for Ms. Evers.
(B) She can provide a tool that Ms. Evers needs.
(C) Some site coordinates are correct.
(D) Some measurements must be double-checked.

154. What will happen next?

(A) Ms. Chi will get new site coordinates.
(B) Ms. Chi and Ms. Lim will be out for a while.
(C) Ms. Evers will share a recipe.
(D) Ms. Lim will begin taking measurements.

Questions 155-157 refer to the following notice.

This season's excellent weather has yielded a substantial harvest of fruits and vegetables, in many cases more than growers may find buyers for. Those of you wishing to donate surplus produce to community organizations can do so by visiting Vosey Farm and Garden's Web site (www.vfgrdn.org), where you will find our list of drop-off locations.

If you need us to come to you instead, please contact us. We will reach out to one of the many independent truck drivers who have kindly volunteered to transport and quickly distribute your food donations to vetted groups that need it. Check our Web site for more information about this service as well as for insights into topics related to farming and gardening in the Northern Great Plains region.

155. For whom is the notice most likely intended?

(A) Farmers
(B) Professional chefs
(C) Truck drivers
(D) Supermarket managers

156. What does the notice indicate about the weather?

(A) It caused transportation delays.
(B) It included heavier rain than usual.
(C) It was frequently a topic in the local news.
(D) It was beneficial for crops.

157. What service does the notice mention?

(A) Staffing for local businesses
(B) Food collection and distribution
(C) Farm machinery repair
(D) Gardening workshops

GO ON TO THE NEXT PAGE

Questions **158-160** refer to the following notice.

We are delighted that you are joining us for today's event. — [1] —. We ask that you adhere to the following guidelines to ensure that all attendees have an enjoyable experience.

Upon entering the venue, please put any and all electronic devices in silent mode. Ringtones and lit screens are very distracting to both the performers and your fellow audience members. — [2] —. Moreover, audience members are not allowed to make an audio or visual recording of the performance.

Bags and other items in the aisles pose a safety concern. — [3] —. If your bag is too big to fit properly under a seat, consider storing it in a locker for just $2. — [4] —. One of our attendants will gladly assist you with that.

Thank you for your cooperation.

158. Where most likely is the notice posted?

(A) In an airplane
(B) In a concert hall
(C) At a restaurant
(D) At a post office

159. What is stated about large bags?

(A) They can be put in a locked box for a fee.
(B) They must be left outside the building.
(C) They will be inspected by an attendant.
(D) They must be stored under a seat.

160. In which of the positions marked [1], [2], [3], and [4] does the following sentence best belong?

"Please refrain from making phone calls or texting at all times."

(A) [1]
(B) [2]
(C) [3]
(D) [4]

```
======================== *E-mail* ========================

To:            Camille Ayala <ayala@esplinelectronics.com>

From:          Masae Adachi <madachi@sweeterspecialties.com>

Date:          February 12

Subject:       Event order

Attachment:    📎 Sweeter Specialties Request Form
```

Dear Ms. Ayala,

Thank you for selecting our business to provide baked goods for the Esplin Electronics conference event in March. We are honored that you chose us for a fourth year in a row! On March 29, we will provide a large vanilla cake for each of the ten venues you indicated, and we will deliver a custom-baked multilayer cake on the following day. You will be billed on March 28. Please review the attached order form and return it to me within seven days.

Regarding the cake you ordered for March 30, our head pastry chef will produce it according to your specifications. In fact, he created a sample of the complete recipe earlier today—almond crème cake with fresh raspberry filling. We have judged it to be a delectable treat, and we are sure that you will be pleased.

If you have any concerns, just send me an e-mail. As always, we value your business.

Masae Adachi, Owner
Sweeter Specialties

---

161. What is the main purpose of the e-mail?

(A) To request confirmation of an order
(B) To adjust some delivery dates
(C) To announce the expansion of a business
(D) To promote new dessert products

162. What is suggested about Ms. Ayala?

(A) She is receiving a professional award.
(B) She has worked as a pastry chef.
(C) She has been a Sweeter Specialties client in the past.
(D) She received a positive recommendation about a chef.

163. What is indicated about the multilayer cake?

(A) It has been a best-selling product with clients.
(B) It is the most expensive cake at Sweeter Specialties.
(C) It is baked for Esplin Electronics annually.
(D) It is a new flavor combination for Sweeter Specialties.

164. The word "judged" in paragraph 2, line 3, is closest in meaning to

(A) criticized
(B) settled
(C) determined
(D) described

GO ON TO THE NEXT PAGE

Great Dishwasher!

I never had a dishwasher before. After remodeling my kitchen, I finally had room for a compact dishwasher. I did a lot of research, and the Dish Magic 300 seemed to be the best choice. It was pricier than other models, but all of the reviews were excellent. So, I decided to spend the extra money. I have had the dishwasher for one month now, and I could not be happier with my decision. Most importantly, the dishes come out sparkling clean, no matter how dirty they were going in. Also, the machine is so quiet, you do not even know it is running. Lastly, it is designed to use water efficiently, which is very important to me. Overall, I am very pleased with this dishwasher.

– Anna Yakovleva

165. Why did Ms. Yakovleva choose the Dish Magic 300 dishwasher?

(A) It was less expensive than most models.
(B) It was the largest model available.
(C) It was rated very highly.
(D) It was the same brand as her other appliances.

166. The word "running" in paragraph 1, line 7, is closest in meaning to

(A) adjusting
(B) controlling
(C) moving
(D) operating

167. What is indicated about Ms. Yakovleva?

(A) She cares about saving water.
(B) She recently moved to a new home.
(C) She bought the dishwasher a year ago.
(D) She remodels kitchens professionally.

Questions 168-171 refer to the following information.

Skyler Airlines employs more than 20,000 people from all over the world. We're growing fast and have many positions available. — [1] —. So regardless of your background, there's probably a place for you on our team. Skyler employees enjoy many perks. — [2] —. For example, our discount program enables them to fly to any of our destinations for a fraction of the average ticket price. — [3] —. We offer upward and global mobility, tuition reimbursement, a mentorship program, and a generous compensation package. — [4] —. Annual paid vacations enable a comfortable work-life balance. It's no wonder that Skyler Airlines was named "Best Airline to Work For" by *Travel Vista Journal* three years in a row.

168. For whom is the information intended?

(A) Skyler Airlines employees
(B) Skyler Airlines customers
(C) Potential journal subscribers
(D) Current job seekers

169. In the information, what is NOT mentioned as being offered to employees?

(A) Payment for educational expenses
(B) Free airline tickets
(C) Opportunities for mentoring
(D) Paid days off

170. What is mentioned about Skyler Airlines?

(A) It flies to the most destinations around the world.
(B) It is planning to merge with another airline.
(C) It has been praised by a trade publication.
(D) It has replaced its seats with more comfortable ones.

171. In which of the positions marked [1], [2], [3], and [4] does the following sentence best belong?

"Our openings cover a broad range of skill sets."

(A) [1]
(B) [2]
(C) [3]
(D) [4]

GO ON TO THE NEXT PAGE

Susan Gowan 9:16 A.M.
Good morning. The presentation slides about the new line of headphones are almost ready for distribution to our many partner stores. We are on track to send them out next Monday.

Maggie Lorenz 9:17 A.M.
How do they look?

Susan Gowan 9:20 A.M.
There are still some missing elements.

Alan Woodson 9:21 A.M.
We mainly need the information from the user studies that reviewed the headphones for sport use. We should have that report from the research and development office by Wednesday.

Maggie Lorenz 9:22 A.M.
Yes, let's not overlook that. And if you're concerned about the report not arriving by Wednesday, please contact Matt Harven and remind him to expedite a summary to us.

Susan Gowan 9:23 A.M.
Assuming we receive that summary soon enough to incorporate its findings into the slides, should the three of us schedule a trial run through the presentation on Thursday or Friday?

Maggie Lorenz 9:24 A.M.
Let's try for Thursday afternoon. Then we will still have Friday to make any necessary changes.

Alan Woodson 9:25 A.M.
Fine by me. I'm free after 2 P.M.

172. What is indicated about a presentation?

(A) It will be expensive to produce.
(B) It will highlight some best-selling products.
(C) It will be Ms. Gowan's first project.
(D) It will be sent to multiple locations.

173. At 9:22 A.M., what does Ms. Lorenz imply when she writes, "let's not overlook that"?

(A) More staff should attend a meeting.
(B) Information from the user studies is important.
(C) The presentation must run smoothly.
(D) Partner stores must be notified about an upcoming report.

174. Who most likely is Mr. Harven?

(A) A store manager
(B) An amateur athlete
(C) A product researcher
(D) An advertising executive

175. When do the writers plan to meet to review a slide presentation?

(A) On Monday
(B) On Wednesday
(C) On Thursday
(D) On Friday

GO ON TO THE NEXT PAGE

Aparna Kothari, Media Contact
Kitchen Swifts
akothari@kitchenswifts.com.au

FOR IMMEDIATE RELEASE

SYDNEY (4 June)—Kitchen Swifts and Chef Darius Cordero are joining together to give home cooks a new culinary experience. The award-winning chef is the owner of restaurants in both the Philippines and Australia, including the recently opened Enriqua's. He says his cooking reflects his Filipino heritage, which is a blend of many cultures.

"I've designed these simplified recipes for Kitchen Swifts so that cooks at home can enjoy new and exciting flavours with ease," he said. "While preparing and eating these meals, you can feel like you are travelling the world with me."

Zahra Chambers, vice president of Kitchen Swifts, says she is pleased to work with Chef Cordero and to offer delicious new recipes to their customers. Kitchen Swifts supplies menus, recipes, and ingredients for two people, four people, or six people, including a range of vegetarian selections. Customers choose the most appropriate meal options, and then a box is delivered weekly. Current customers will see no price increase with the partnership. To find out more, visit the Kitchen Swifts Web site at www.kitchenswifts.com.au.

---

https://www.sydneyrestaurants.com.au

A colleague arranged for us to eat at Enriqua's while I was at a conference in Sydney. It is usually fully booked for dinner; you may need to call months in advance for a table. We had a wonderful lunch there instead. Everything was delicious, and the bread and desserts are baked on-site! It was a worthwhile treat before I flew back to Hong Kong.

—Meili Guan

176. What is the purpose of the press release?

(A) To promote the opening of a restaurant
(B) To announce a business partnership
(C) To introduce a travel program
(D) To congratulate an award recipient

177. In the press release, the word "reflects" in paragraph 1, line 4, is closest in meaning to

(A) results in
(B) changes
(C) shows
(D) thinks about

178. What is indicated about Kitchen Swifts?

(A) It raised its prices for all customers.
(B) It revised its delivery schedule.
(C) It offers several meal options.
(D) It has a new vice president.

179. What is most likely true about Ms. Guan?

(A) She went to Mr. Cordero's restaurant.
(B) She recently went to Sydney for a vacation.
(C) She is a colleague of Ms. Chambers.
(D) She regularly orders from Kitchen Swifts.

180. What did Ms. Guan suggest about Enriqua's in the review?

(A) It has a limited lunch menu.
(B) It takes dinner reservations.
(C) It serves bread from a local bakery.
(D) It has a location in Hong Kong.

GO ON TO THE NEXT PAGE

To:	laura.savard@orbitmail.scot
From:	cboyle@ceoleire.co.uk
Date:	25 May
Subject:	RE: Some suggestions

Dear Ms. Savard,

Thank you for your kind offer to either pick up your online order from my shop or to pay extra for air or train transport. Neither arrangement is necessary, as I am happy to deliver your items to you in Stranraer myself. It so happens that my sister and her children live nearby in Kirkcolm. Before seeing them, I will drive my rental car to your house and hand deliver the items to you.

As you know, my merchandise is 100 percent handcrafted. If any damage occurs in transit, the repair turns into an expensive, time-consuming ordeal. Over the years, I've seen too much damage done by inattentive baggage handlers. My policy is to deliver items personally whenever feasible or hire a ground- or sea-based courier service I trust.

I look forward to meeting you on 5 June. I expect to arrive at your house no later than 5 p.m.

Sincerely,

Conor Boyle
Ceoleire Classics

Northern Ireland Ferry Service

Date of Issuance: 26 May
Passenger Name: Conor Boyle

Departing Belfast: Friday, 5 June, 1:05 PM
Docking at Cairnryan: Friday, 5 June, 3:20 PM

Baggage: 1 suitcase (small), 2 instrument cases
(1 mandolin, 1 guitar)
Vehicle transport: No

Adult Standard Class: £55.00

Please arrive 30 minutes prior to departure.

181. What is the purpose of the e-mail?

(A) To finalize a plan
(B) To accept an invitation
(C) To promote a new service
(D) To request feedback on a policy

182. Why will Mr. Boyle travel from Stranraer to Kirkcolm?

(A) To make a delivery
(B) To attend a meeting
(C) To drop off a rental car
(D) To visit with family members

183. What is indicated in the e-mail?

(A) Mr. Boyle's sister is a cofounder of Ceoleire Classics.
(B) Mr. Boyle has been disappointed by air- and train-freight companies.
(C) Ms. Savard has purchased items from Mr. Boyle in the past.
(D) Ms. Savard prefers a specific brand of luggage.

184. What is most likely true about Ms. Savard?

(A) She often travels for her job.
(B) She paid extra to have items hand delivered.
(C) She recently purchased musical instruments.
(D) She will meet Mr. Boyle at the rental car office.

185. How is Mr. Boyle traveling to Cairnryan on June 5 ?

(A) By car
(B) By train
(C) By boat
(D) By plane

GO ON TO THE NEXT PAGE

Train to Achieve (TTA)—Our classes prepare you to succeed!

Profiled in the latest *Business Directions Nigeria* newsletter, Train to Achieve (TTA) is one of the most innovative training providers in West Africa. By offering our classes entirely in online format, we bring the classroom to your home. All classes include individualized instruction and are taught by recognized professionals in their respective fields. Upon successful completion of a class, you will receive an official Certificate of Training, a valuable addition to any résumé. For a complete list of class fees and schedules, visit our Web site at www.traintoachieve.org.ng. The following are some of our most popular classes.

Introduction to Social Media Marketing (TTA1504): Taught by marketing consultant Marcus Akpan, the class equips you with the know-how to promote your business online.

Become a Successful Freelance Writer (TTA3283): Business writer Brenda Akande gives you expert guidance on how to hone your writing skills and sell your writing services.

Starting an Internet Radio Station (TTA7629): Online radio host Natalie Kabiru shows you how to appeal to your target market and gives practical tips for setting up your broadcast service.

Basics of Graphic Design (TTA7633): Veteran graphic designer Doug Umaru helps you acquire the basic skills needed to start a graphic design business.

Discussion forum for students enrolled in Train to Achieve Class TTA1504

Posted on: 21 May, 9:41 A.M.　　**Posted by:** Joseph Egbe　　**Subject:** Presentations

Viewing the list of students enrolled in this class, I remembered chatting with some of you on the forum for January's poster design class. I look forward to sharing our learning experiences again for this class. Yesterday I was the second student to meet with Mr. Akpan for an individual videoconference about my business. I own a food truck from which I sell baked goods, and when I shared with Mr. Akpan the outline for my Web site, he suggested that I add a section with vivid images of all my baked goods. It was helpful advice.

Egbe's Bakery—Unique baked-in flavours in every bite!

- **Section 1:** Explore our menu and price list
- **Section 2:** Browse photos of our delicious treats
- **Section 3:** Learn about our catering services
- **Section 4:** View lists of ingredients

186. What is indicated about TTA?

(A) It was founded by a graphic designer.
(B) It publishes its own online newsletter.
(C) It offers classes led by industry professionals.
(D) It has classroom facilities in cities across West Africa.

187. According to the advertisement, what does TTA provide to students who finish a class?

(A) A résumé-writing workshop
(B) A discount on a follow-up class
(C) A list of current job postings
(D) A certification document

188. What is most likely true about Mr. Egbe?

(A) He helped design a discussion forum.
(B) He has previously taken a TTA class.
(C) He develops videoconferencing software.
(D) He recently sold a bakery food truck.

189. What TTA class is Mr. Egbe enrolled in?

(A) Introduction to Social Media Marketing
(B) Become a Successful Freelance Writer
(C) Starting an Internet Radio Station
(D) Basics of Graphic Design

190. What section did Mr. Egbe most likely add to the outline after speaking with Mr. Akpan?

(A) Section 1
(B) Section 2
(C) Section 3
(D) Section 4

GO ON TO THE NEXT PAGE

Caribbean Flavours Abound

By Rebecca Roats

NOTTINGHAM (1 August)—Orange Bay Kitchen has been serving up an infusion of Jamaican flavours in a laid-back Caribbean atmosphere for six months now. Managed by Keron Deslandes, the 150-seat restaurant is an aromatic jewel amid the bustling shops and eateries in Wester Square. The servers are always happy to help diners select from the variety of delights on the extensive menu, which includes curried goat, oxtail soup, and red snapper. The restaurant is most famous for its jerk chicken. Marinated for 24 hours prior to grilling and served with sides of stewed cabbage and coconut rice, the dish is a good deal at £12.

If you stop in on any Friday night between 7 and 11 P.M., you will enjoy live reggae music.

---

https://www.dinerreviews.co.uk/orangebaykitchen

Posted on 22 August by Tamika Peterkin, tpeterkin@sunmail.co.uk

Orange Bay Kitchen: 2/5 Stars

After reading a glowing article about Orange Bay Kitchen by Rebecca Roats, I was eager to give this place a try. My husband and I arrived there at 7 P.M. yesterday, keen to enjoy live music with our dinner. Unfortunately, the band's performance that night had been cancelled. Undeterred, we stayed and both ordered the jerk chicken. While the chicken's smoky flavour was outstanding, the stewed cabbage was lacking in flavour. Also, the portion size was smaller than we had anticipated, so we ordered another appetiser to avoid going home hungry. The head chef came out to apologise and was extremely nice, but we will probably not go back anytime soon.

```
========================= E-Mail Message =========================

    To:          tpeterkin@sunmail.co.uk
    From:        vsmith@orangebaykitchen.co.uk
    Date:        24 August
    Subject:     Your review
    Attachment:  📎 0258

    Dear Ms. Peterkin,

    Thank you for visiting Orange Bay Kitchen and leaving a review. Our manager, Keron
    Deslandes, told me more about your visit and our failure to live up to your expectations
    that evening. Please accept the attached £20 gift certificate; I do hope that you will give
    us another try.

    During your visit, our band had an equipment malfunction, which is what led to the
    last-minute cancellation. However, the band will be back performing weekly beginning
    in September. Also, I want you to know that Head Chef Adio Brown has changed the
    spices he uses in the stewed cabbage. I am sure you will find them delightful.

    Sincerely,

    Vea Smith, Owner
    Orange Bay Kitchen
```

191. What does the article mention about Orange Bay Kitchen?

(A) It is currently hiring servers.
(B) It is located on a quiet street.
(C) It has another location in Jamaica.
(D) It opened six months ago.

192. According to the article, what is the most popular menu item at Orange Bay Kitchen?

(A) Red snapper
(B) Oxtail soup
(C) Jerk chicken
(D) Curried goat

193. What is suggested about Ms. Peterkin's visit to Orange Bay Kitchen?

(A) She was there on a Friday.
(B) She dined alone.
(C) She requested extra rice.
(D) She ordered dessert.

194. What is a purpose of the e-mail?

(A) To answer a question
(B) To offer an apology
(C) To ask for feedback
(D) To confirm a reservation

195. Whom did Ms. Peterkin meet at Orange Bay Kitchen?

(A) Ms. Roats
(B) Mr. Deslandes
(C) Mr. Brown
(D) Ms. Smith

GO ON TO THE NEXT PAGE

Orbys Distributors

Client: Green Canyon   **Date:** June 10
Account: 4352-0

Item	Price
Garden soil, 33 cubic meters	$1,170.00
Crushed gravel, 30 metric tons	1,710.00
Decorative stone, 20 metric tons	1,140.00
70 paving stones, .6 x .6 meters	630.00
Subtotal	4,650.00
Discount (10%)	465.00
Delivery charge	350.00
Grand Total	4,535.00

Please see the enclosed notice outlining important changes to your billing.

Orbys Distributors

To our valued customers:
Our current invoicing system has been in use since Orbys Distributors was founded over twenty years ago. As a much-needed upgrade, we are switching to electronic invoicing. Starting August 1, invoices will be generated automatically each month and will be sent to the e-mail address associated with your company's account.

Rest assured that our long-standing incentives remain in place:

- A 10% discount for orders of more than $4,000
- A 20% discount for charitable organizations
- Free deliveries to locations within 5 miles of one of our supply centers
- Free samples for members of our Frequent Buyer Club

More information about our transition to electronic invoicing is available on our Web site. Thank you for your support. Orbys Distributors appreciates your business.

```
┌─────────────────────────────────────────────────────────────────┐
│                          *E-mail*                                 │
├─────────────────────────────────────────────────────────────────┤
│  To:      │ Mary Peterson, Billing Department                     │
│  From:    │ Tanvir Singh, Account Manager                         │
│  Date:    │ September 12                                          │
│  Subject: │ Account 1012-4                                        │
└─────────────────────────────────────────────────────────────────┘
```

Hello Mary,

I received a query today from William Tesoriero at Tesoriero Remodeling. His monthly invoice for August never arrived.

As you know, Mr. Tesoriero was one of our very first customers. Since we first opened for business, he has made purchases from us on a regular basis. He is also a member of the Frequent Buyer Club. This is a customer we absolutely do not want to lose. I explained to him that the rollout of our electronic invoicing system did not go as smoothly as we had hoped and promised that this would not happen again.

I would appreciate it if you could please investigate the problem without delay and send the invoice for August to Mr. Tesoriero.

Tanvir

---

196. What does the invoice suggest about Green Canyon?

(A) It does landscaping projects.
(B) It designs highways.
(C) It repairs old houses.
(D) It operates a farm.

197. Why most likely did Green Canyon receive a discount on its order dated June 10 ?

(A) It is a charitable organization.
(B) It belongs to the Frequent Buyer Club.
(C) It spent more than $4,000 on merchandise.
(D) It is located near an Orbys Distributors supply center.

198. According to the notice, what is changing at Orbys Distributors?

(A) Its e-mail address
(B) Its list of incentives
(C) Its invoicing system
(D) Its delivery schedule

199. What is suggested about Mr. Tesoriero?

(A) He asked to meet with Mr. Singh.
(B) He is interested in employment at Orbys Distributors.
(C) He recently placed an order for some construction machinery.
(D) He has been a customer of Orbys Distributors for about twenty years.

200. What does Mr. Singh ask Ms. Peterson to do?

(A) Make a bill payment
(B) Solve a problem
(C) Confirm an order
(D) Update an account number

Stop! This is the end of the test. If you finish before time is called, you may go back to Parts 5, 6, and 7 and check your work.

토익®정기시험 기출문제집 4 1000

TEST 02
무료 동영상 강의

RC

기출 TEST
02

READING TEST

In the Reading test, you will read a variety of texts and answer several different types of reading comprehension questions. The entire Reading test will last 75 minutes. There are three parts, and directions are given for each part. You are encouraged to answer as many questions as possible within the time allowed.

You must mark your answers on the separate answer sheet. Do not write your answers in your test book.

PART 5

Directions: A word or phrase is missing in each of the sentences below. Four answer choices are given below each sentence. Select the best answer to complete the sentence. Then mark the letter (A), (B), (C), or (D) on your answer sheet.

101. Before operating your handheld device, please ------- the enclosed cable to charge it.
(A) plan
(B) remain
(C) use
(D) finish

102. Safile's new external hard drive can ------- store up to one terabyte of data.
(A) secure
(B) security
(C) securely
(D) secured

103. Mr. Peterson will travel ------- the Tokyo office for the annual meeting.
(A) to
(B) through
(C) in
(D) over

104. Yong-Soo Cosmetics will not charge for items on back order until ------- have left our warehouse.
(A) them
(B) they
(C) themselves
(D) their

105. Our premium day tour takes visitors to historic sites ------- the Aprico River.
(A) onto
(B) since
(C) inside
(D) along

106. Eighty percent of drivers surveyed said they would consider buying a vehicle that runs on -------.
(A) electricity
(B) electrically
(C) electricians
(D) electrify

107. Xinzhe Zu has ------- Petrin Engineering as the vice president of operations.
(A) attached
(B) resigned
(C) joined
(D) combined

108. Next month, Barder House Books will be holding ------- third author's hour in Cleveland.
(A) it
(B) itself
(C) its own
(D) its

109. Chester's Tiles ------- expanded to a second location in Turnington.

(A) severely
(B) usually
(C) recently
(D) exactly

110. Tabrino's has ------- increased the number of almonds in the Nut Medley snack pack.

(A) significant
(B) significance
(C) signifies
(D) significantly

111. ------- she travels, Jacintha Flores collects samples of local fabrics and patterns.

(A) Wherever
(B) In addition to
(C) Either
(D) In contrast to

112. Most picture ------- at Glowing Photo Lab go on sale at 3:00 P.M. today.

(A) framer
(B) framing
(C) framed
(D) frames

113. All students in the business management class hold ------- college degrees.

(A) late
(B) developed
(C) advanced
(D) elated

114. We hired Noah Wan of Shengyao Accounting Ltd. ------- our company's financial assets.

(A) to evaluate
(B) to be evaluated
(C) will be evaluated
(D) evaluate

115. Ms. Charisse is taking on a new account ------- she finishes the Morrison project.

(A) with
(B) going
(C) after
(D) between

116. Cormet Motors' profits are ------- this year than last year.

(A) higher
(B) high
(C) highly
(D) highest

117. In its ------- advertising campaign, Jaymor Tools demonstrates how reliable its products are.

(A) current
(B) relative
(C) spacious
(D) collected

118. Remember to submit receipts for reimbursement ------- returning from a business trip.

(A) such as
(B) when
(C) then
(D) within

119. Patrons will be able to access Westside Library's ------- acquired collection of books on Tuesday.

(A) instantly
(B) newly
(C) early
(D) naturally

120. Please ------- any questions about time sheets to Tabitha Jones in the payroll department.

(A) direction
(B) directive
(C) directed
(D) direct

GO ON TO THE NEXT PAGE

121. Before signing a delivery ------, be sure to double-check that all the items ordered are in the shipment.

(A) decision
(B) announcement
(C) receipt
(D) limit

122. Funds have been added to the budget for expenses ------ with the new building.

(A) associated
(B) association
(C) associate
(D) associates

123. Ms. Bernard ------ that a deadline was approaching, so she requested some assistance.

(A) noticed
(B) obscured
(C) withdrew
(D) appeared

124. Mr. Moscowitz is ------ that Dr. Tanaka will agree to present the keynote speech at this year's conference.

(A) hopes
(B) hoped
(C) hopeful
(D) hopefully

125. Two Australian companies are developing new smartphones, but it is unclear ------ phone will become available first.

(A) if
(B) which
(C) before
(D) because

126. Corners Gym offers its members a free lesson in how to use ------ properly.

(A) weighs
(B) weights
(C) weighty
(D) weighed

127. ------ the rules, overnight parking is not permitted at the clubhouse facility.

(A) Prior to
(B) Except for
(C) Instead of
(D) According to

128. Once everyone ------, we can begin the conference call.

(A) arrived
(B) is arriving
(C) to arrive
(D) has arrived

129. Each summer a motivational video that highlights the past year's ------ is shown to all company employees.

(A) preferences
(B) accomplishments
(C) communications
(D) uncertainties

130. Employees who wish to attend the retirement dinner ------ Ms. Howell's 30 years of service should contact Mr. Lee.

(A) honor
(B) to honor
(C) will honor
(D) will be honored

PART 6

Directions: Read the texts that follow. A word, phrase, or sentence is missing in parts of each text. Four answer choices for each question are given below the text. Select the best answer to complete the text. Then mark the letter (A), (B), (C), or (D) on your answer sheet.

Questions 131-134 refer to the following e-mail.

To: Myung-Hee Hahn
From: Dellwyn Home Store
Date: January 15
Subject: Order update

Dear Ms. Hahn,

Your ------- order of a red oak dining table and six matching chairs arrived at our store this morning.
    131.
We would now like to arrange for the delivery of the ------- . Please call us at 517-555-0188 and
                                                          132.
ask ------- to Coleman Cobb, our delivery manager. ------- .
     133.   **134.**

Customer Service, Dellwyn Home Store

131. (A) specially
     (B) specialize
     (C) special
     (D) specializing

132. (A) furniture
     (B) appliances
     (C) refund
     (D) tools

133. (A) speak
     (B) spoken
     (C) is speaking
     (D) to speak

134. (A) He can schedule a convenient time.
     (B) He began working here yesterday.
     (C) He can meet you at 11:00 A.M.
     (D) He recently moved to Dellwyn.

GO ON TO THE NEXT PAGE

Keep Cool Service Contractors:
67 Main Road, Edinburgh Village
Chaguanas, Trinidad and Tobago

Keep Cool Service Contractors can bring you peace of mind. As part of an annual contract, we will service your air-conditioning system, ensuring your ------- and comfort. This includes inspecting
135.
the system, making repairs as needed, and professionally cleaning your air ducts. ------- , if
136.
necessary, we can replace your old air-conditioning system with a new, cost-efficient one.

Our workers are highly qualified licensed technicians who stay up-to-date with ongoing training.
------- . We promise you fair prices and professional work, ------- by our Keep Cool guarantee.
137.   138.
Call 1-868-555-0129 for a free quote today.

135. (A) safe
     (B) safely
     (C) safest
     (D) safety

136. (A) On one hand
     (B) Nonetheless
     (C) Furthermore
     (D) And yet

137. (A) Take advantage of dozens of useful
         online tools.
     (B) Moreover, the air conditioner you
         chose is very popular.
     (C) Plus, they are friendly, clean, and
         knowledgeable.
     (D) Thank you for visiting our contractor
         showroom.

138. (A) backed
     (B) backs
     (C) backing
     (D) back

To: All Customers

From: asquires@lightidea.com

Date: March 6

Subject: Information

Dear Light Idea Customers,

Light Idea is enacting a price increase on select energy-efficient products, effective April 17.

Specific product pricing will ------- . Please contact your sales representative for details and

139.

questions.

The last date for ordering at current prices is April 16. All orders ------- after this date will follow the

140.

new price list. ------- . Customers will be able to find this on our Web site.

141.

We will continue to provide quality products and ------- service to our valued customers. Thank you

142.

for your business.

Sincerely,

Arvin Squires

Head of Sales, Light Idea

---

139. (A) agree
(B) vary
(C) wait
(D) decline

140. (A) receiving
(B) having received
(C) received
(D) will be received

141. (A) The updated price list will be available on
March 20.
(B) We apologize for this inconvenience.
(C) Your orders will be shipped after April 17.
(D) We are increasing prices because of
rising costs.

142. (A) exceptionally
(B) exception
(C) exceptional
(D) exceptionalism

GO ON TO THE NEXT PAGE

To: Jang-Ho Kwon <jkwon@newart.nz>
From: Kenneth Okim <k.okim@okimjewelry.nz>
Subject: Good news
Date: 30 August

Dear Jang-Ho,

Thank you for the shipment last month of 80 units of your jewelry pieces. I am happy to report that they have been selling very well in my shop. My ------- love the colourful designs as well as
143.
the quality of your workmanship. ------- .
144.

I would like to increase the number of units I order from you. Would you be able to

------- my order for the September shipment?
145.

Finally, I would like to discuss the possibility of featuring your work exclusively in my store. I

believe that I could reach your target audience best and that the agreement would serve

------- both very well. I look forward to hearing from you.
146.

Best regards,

Kenneth Okim
Okim Jewelry

143. (A) patients
     (B) students
     (C) customers
     (D) teammates

144. (A) If you need more time, please let me
         know.
     (B) Unfortunately, I do not have adequate
         shelf space at this time.
     (C) I would like to show you some of my
         own designs.
     (D) The reasonable prices also make
         your pieces a great value.

145. (A) include
     (B) double
     (C) repeat
     (D) insure

146. (A) us
     (B) you
     (C) we
     (D) these

PART 7

Directions: In this part you will read a selection of texts, such as magazine and newspaper articles, e-mails, and instant messages. Each text or set of texts is followed by several questions. Select the best answer for each question and mark the letter (A), (B), (C), or (D) on your answer sheet.

Questions 147-148 refer to the following invitation.

Focus Your Social Media Presence

For small-business owners, it can be a challenge to stand out in a competitive social media environment. Successfully reaching your target market involves knowing how and where to promote your products in a way that is effective and memorable. The Savan Business Center offers support for business owners who need a boost in doing just that. For over 50 years, we've been helping entrepreneurs grow their sales through insight of current industry trends and understanding of our clients' unique needs.

Let us help you get more organized in creating effective and far-reaching social media content. Our latest webinar, Focus Your Social Media Presence, will cover topics related to making your business stand out. You can sign up on our event Web page.

Date: February 5
Time: 10:00 A.M. to 11:00 A.M.
Event Web page: https://www.savanbusinesscenter.com/socialmedia

---

147. What is true about the Savan Business Center?

(A) It works with small businesses.
(B) It publishes a weekly newsletter.
(C) It recently launched a new Web site.
(D) It is seeking suggestions for webinar topics.

148. What is indicated about the webinar?

(A) It begins at 11:00 A.M.
(B) It features advice on creating promotional content.
(C) It is being offered every month.
(D) It requires a small fee to attend.

GO ON TO THE NEXT PAGE

Dine Out Darville Is Back!

Dine Out Darville, which runs this year from June 22 to 28, is the perfect chance to try a restaurant in Darville for the first time or revisit one of your favorite restaurants in town. You might even visit multiple restaurants during the weeklong event! Twelve popular restaurants will offer special four-course dinners—including a cup of soup, a salad, a main course, and a dessert—all for a reduced price of $30. Reservations are highly recommended. Dine Out Darville welcomes hundreds of locals and tourists each year, and you do not want to miss your opportunity to get a great meal at a great price.

Visit www.darvillebusinesscouncil.org/dineout for a list of participating restaurants.

---

149. What is mentioned about Dine Out Darville?

(A) It lasts for one week.
(B) It is held in a different location each year.
(C) It is being held for the first time.
(D) It includes both lunch and dinner.

150. What is NOT included in the reduced-price meals?

(A) A cup of soup
(B) A salad
(C) A dessert
(D) A beverage

Rainsy To Move Headquarters

DADE (July 11)—Rainsy LLC announced yesterday that it is moving its headquarters to Dade.

A data storage and analytics firm currently based in Salt Creek, Rainsy has clients that include some of the country's largest credit card companies, online retailers, and software providers. Rainsy helps these businesses manage and understand their customer data.

Rainsy is not planning to close its current offices in Salt Creek. However, the Dade location will become its new base of operations, as several members of its executive team will work there. The company's chief executive officer and chief financial officer will relocate to Dade along with approximately 50 percent of the company's workforce.

The office of Rainsy's chief technology officer will remain in Salt Creek, as will the account management team. The company's new Dade offices are located at 12 Glacier Parkway.

151. What does Rainsy LLC do?

(A) It stores and analyzes consumer information.
(B) It sells technology products online.
(C) It processes credit card payments for retailers.
(D) It develops computer software programs.

152. Who will be based in Dade?

(A) Rainsy's chief technology officer
(B) The entire Rainsy executive team
(C) About half of Rainsy's employees
(D) The Rainsy account management team

Questions 153-154 refer to the following text-message chain.

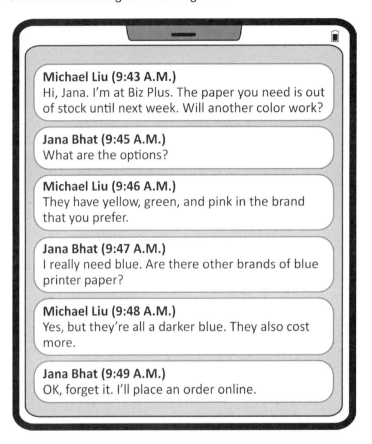

Michael Liu (9:43 A.M.)
Hi, Jana. I'm at Biz Plus. The paper you need is out of stock until next week. Will another color work?

Jana Bhat (9:45 A.M.)
What are the options?

Michael Liu (9:46 A.M.)
They have yellow, green, and pink in the brand that you prefer.

Jana Bhat (9:47 A.M.)
I really need blue. Are there other brands of blue printer paper?

Michael Liu (9:48 A.M.)
Yes, but they're all a darker blue. They also cost more.

Jana Bhat (9:49 A.M.)
OK, forget it. I'll place an order online.

153. What is suggested about the paper Mr. Liu is shopping for?
(A) It is light blue.
(B) It is expensive.
(C) It is sold exclusively at Biz Plus.
(D) It has been discontinued.

154. At 9:49 A.M., what does Ms. Bhat most likely mean when she writes, "OK, forget it"?
(A) She wants to check her budget.
(B) She thinks Mr. Liu should not purchase paper at Biz Plus.
(C) She believes Mr. Liu should not place an order this week.
(D) She plans to cancel her order.

Questions 155-157 refer to the following letter.

20 May

Neil Croft, Director
Queensland Libraries
13 Hummocky Road
Brisbane QLD 4003

Dear Mr. Croft,

— [1] —. I have read your inquiry about offering financial management courses at libraries across Queensland. The Society for Financial Management Advisors (SFMA) welcomes the opportunity to partner with the libraries to make basic financial management information more widely available.

You proposed that SFMA members could lead introductory courses at several library branches. — [2] —. SFMA members have offered similar courses to recent graduates, people changing careers, and first-time investors in the past.

— [3] —. If you have a list of library branches that would host the first series of events, I can suggest facilitators who work near those libraries or would be willing to travel to them. Do you have a general profile of the expected attendees? — [4] —. That information would help us tailor the courses to audience needs and interests.

I look forward to meeting with you to develop a plan. Please contact me by telephone at 07 5550 1344 to set up a time to discuss the courses.

Sincerely,

Roberta Otney
Roberta Otney
Chairperson, Society for Financial Management Advisors

155. Why did Ms. Otney write the letter?

(A) To welcome a new library director
(B) To register for an SFMA finance course
(C) To confirm some educational credentials
(D) To reply to a question from Mr. Croft

156. What is one thing Ms. Otney requested?

(A) A library membership
(B) A list of course instructors
(C) The locations of some libraries
(D) Mr. Croft's telephone number

157. In which of the positions marked [1], [2], [3], and [4] does the following sentence best belong?

"This is something I would be happy to arrange."

(A) [1]
(B) [2]
(C) [3]
(D) [4]

Claro Vision

The difference is clear.

Take advantage of our limited-time offer:
50% off all eyeglass frames through 30 September

Other advantages available today and every day:

● Free eyeglass fittings and adjustments

● Money-back guarantee if you are not completely satisfied

● More than 500 locations in shopping malls throughout Canada

● Low-cost vision checkups by licensed opticians

To find a store near you, visit www.clarovision.ca/locations,
or call 416-555-0122 today!

---

158. Why most likely was the advertisement created?

(A) To draw attention to an underused professional service
(B) To publicize the benefits of a warranty policy
(C) To announce the opening of new store locations
(D) To promote a temporary price discount

159. What is stated about Claro Vision stores?

(A) They are larger than competitors' stores.
(B) They accept all major credit cards.
(C) They are located next to shopping malls.
(D) They provide eyeglass fittings at no cost.

160. What is stated about vision checkups?

(A) They are completed by a partner company.
(B) They are performed by a certified professional.
(C) They should be done every ten months.
(D) They are offered on a limited number of days.

Rossery Building Corporation
2710 South Exmouth Drive
Singapore 188509

1 April

Elizabeth Balakrishnan
Bala Home Furnishings
416 Holliton Drive C2
Singapore 793801

Dear Ms. Balakrishnan,

This is a reminder that the one-year lease for your space will end on 30 April. Please contact my office at 1555 0124 to make an appointment to renew your lease. There will be a small increase in rent and fees because of rising operating costs.

Updated charges upon lease renewal:

Monthly rental	S$1,800.00
Parking space fee	S$50.00
Cleaning service	S$10.00
Security fee	S$35.00
Total monthly charge	S$1,895.00

If you are not renewing your lease, please notify our office by 15 April. Plan to vacate the property by 5 P.M. on 30 April. There will be an inspection of the property, and there may be charges for repairs or damages beyond normal usage.

Kind regards,

Alexis Tan
Alexis Tan

161. What is the purpose of the letter?
(A) To explain the fees for equipment installation
(B) To offer a discount on a service
(C) To provide information about a lease agreement
(D) To request a change to a property amenity

162. According to the letter, what must Ms. Balakrishnan pay for each month?
(A) Furniture rental
(B) Office supplies
(C) An inspection fee
(D) A parking space

163. Who most likely is Ms. Tan?
(A) A repair person
(B) A property manager
(C) A cleaning person
(D) A security company employee

GO ON TO THE NEXT PAGE

Questions 164-167 refer to the following e-mail.

```
*E-mail*

To:       lkhoury@britelyauto.co.uk
From:     khagel@qualiview.co.uk
Date:     14 April
Subject:  Your proposed changes

Dear Ms. Khoury,

Thank you for forwarding your proposed revisions to the contract for Qualiview Ltd. to
be your wholesale supplier of automotive window glass.

First, we will gladly agree to an extension of the contract term from one to three years.
Secondly, I am not sure what more we can do to address your concerns about packaging
materials. We use custom-built crates and innovative packaging to reduce the risk of
breakage during shipping. While we will replace any goods that may be damaged in
transit, we do not agree to pay an additional penalty fee in the event of such damage.

I would like to discuss this further with you next week; however, I will be out of the
office through Tuesday afternoon. Would you be available to meet before 11:00 A.M. on
either Wednesday or Thursday? Friday is also possible. Please let me know a convenient
date and time for you.

Best regards,

Karl Hagel
Qualiview Ltd.
```

164. Why did Mr. Hagel write the e-mail?

(A) To report damage to an item
(B) To finalize a purchase
(C) To request a product sample
(D) To negotiate a contract

165. What is indicated about Qualiview Ltd.?

(A) It sells its products online.
(B) It makes windows for cars.
(C) It has paid penalty fees in the past.
(D) It recently redesigned its shipping
    crates.

166. The word "address" in paragraph 2, line 2,
is closest in meaning to

(A) respond to
(B) think about
(C) greet
(D) deliver

167. When is Mr. Hagel available next week?

(A) On Monday morning
(B) On Tuesday afternoon
(C) On Wednesday morning
(D) On Thursday afternoon

Questions 168-171 refer to the following article.

Shipping Disruptions

SINGAPORE (6 June)—Recently, the demand for international freight space has been outpacing the availability of shipping containers. This container shortage has led to higher costs for goods being shipped out of Asian ports. A drop in the production of rolls of steel, the raw material that containers are made from, has further complicated the situation. — [1] —.

Some exporters have considered the more expensive option of air freight, but companies are still faced with a difficult choice. — [2] —. They must either ask their customers to accept shipment delays, or substantially raise customer prices to cover the costs of expedited shipping. Either way, suppliers risk triggering customer dissatisfaction.

"We are working with business partners, investors, and government officials to discuss solutions to this problem," said Henry Lam, a spokesperson for the household goods producer QET Group. — [3] —. "It's going to take total cooperation of all stakeholders to find a solution."

Not all companies are suffering, though. For example, Fezker, the producer of athletic apparel and footwear, has implemented strategies to better overcome this situation. Fezker has successfully refocused its efforts away from exports to western countries and toward expanding its domestic and regional markets. — [4] —.

"We moved quickly, so the shipping container shortage has not caused a significant impact on our profits," said Fezker CEO Nuwa Lee.

---

168. What is mentioned about shipping containers?

(A) They come in different sizes.
(B) They are in short supply.
(C) They are made from a variety of materials.
(D) They can be used for long-term storage.

169. What does Mr. Lam say is needed to resolve the situation?

(A) A sharp increase in the number of customers
(B) A relaxation of government restrictions
(C) The development of new technologies
(D) Communication between affected groups

170. What type of clothing does Fezker produce?

(A) Rain jackets
(B) Sportswear
(C) Business suits
(D) Work uniforms

171. In which of the positions marked [1], [2], [3], and [4] does the following sentence best belong?

"These markets are supplied using more readily available truck and train transportation."

(A) [1]
(B) [2]
(C) [3]
(D) [4]

GO ON TO THE NEXT PAGE

Gary Wendel (7:40 A.M.)
Good morning, team. Can you share the current status of your projects, please?

Jing Yu (7:42 A.M.)
I met with the client last week to confirm the start date for Phase B of the Palisade project.

Robbie Zuniga (7:43 A.M.)
I am headed to the job site now for the Riverview project. The rain last week delayed pouring the concrete for the sidewalks. I will check the conditions this morning to see if the situation has improved.

Gary Wendel (7:44 A.M.)
When will Phase B of the Palisade project begin?

Jing Yu (7:46 A.M.)
We will break ground in March and plan to have the building completed by November.

Gary Wendel (7:47 A.M.)
That's good news about the March start date. I am sure the client is happy about that.

Gary Wendel (7:50 A.M.)
Robbie, let me know what you find out about the site conditions. Perhaps Nathan Burry can help at the site. He's our most knowledgeable concrete finisher.

Robbie Zuniga (7:55 A.M.)
Actually, I'm meeting Nathan at the site this morning, so I'll get his opinion on when we can pour the concrete. The rest of the project is on hold until we can do this.

Gary Wendel (7:57 A.M.)
Keep me posted. I don't want to rush it if it's still too wet. At the same time, the Riverview project is already behind schedule because of equipment problems and late delivery of building materials.

Robbie Zuniga (7:58 A.M.)
Will do.

172. In what industry do the writers most likely work?

(A) Construction
(B) Energy
(C) Manufacturing
(D) Travel

173. Why did Mr. Wendel begin the discussion?

(A) To plan a client meeting
(B) To discuss a weather forecast
(C) To obtain an update on some work
(D) To change the start date of an event

174. What is indicated about the Riverview project?

(A) It has had several delays.
(B) It is being managed by Ms. Yu.
(C) It will be completed in November.
(D) Its clients are happy with the progress.

175. At 7:58 A.M., what does Mr. Zuniga most likely mean when he writes, "Will do"?

(A) He will revise a delivery schedule.
(B) He will purchase more equipment.
(C) He will hire workers to help at a site.
(D) He will share the outcome of a meeting.

GO ON TO THE NEXT PAGE

From:	Madalyn Kerluke <mkerluke@karabel.ca>
To:	Omar Niklaus <oniklaus@karabel.ca>, Jay Toncic <jtoncic@karabel.ca>
Date:	Friday, 3 February 2:16 P.M.
Subject:	Taste-test results
Attachment:	Fatior Labs survey results

Hi, Team.

I just received the 24–26 January survey results from Fatior Labs for our new ice-cream taste test. As you can see from the attached document, the results are very disappointing. We sent the four flavours that we considered to be the best, but none of them received high enough ratings to advance to the next stage of development. Most of the reviews were consistent among the 92 taste-test participants in our target market of consumers ages 25 through 40. It's not a big problem if a product gets low scores in colour in the testing phase, since we can easily adjust that in the laboratory. But we should never be sending out samples that are getting scores lower than 3 in the taste category.

I would like to meet at 9 A.M. on Monday (6 February) to figure out how to proceed. There is one flavour we may be able to work with if we make a few adjustments, as suggested by most of our taste testers. We will also need to get some new flavours to Fatior Labs no later than 1 March if we are going to get a new ice cream on the Preston Grocers freezer shelves by the beginning of June.

Madalyn Kerluke

Fatior Labs Consumer Taste-Testing Survey

Date: 24 January

Company: Karabel Industries

Participant number: 54

Directions: You will be given a 45 g sample of 4 different ice creams. Please rate the taste, texture, sweetness, and colour of each ice cream on a scale of 1 (very unpleasant) to 5 (very pleasant). Please write any additional comments below.

Flavour	Taste	Texture	Sweetness	Colour
Lemon	2	3	2	4
Mango	3	3	2	1
Salted Caramel	2	1	1	5
Peanut Brittle	3	4	2	2

Comments: The fruit-flavoured ice creams were surprisingly sour. I did not care for them at all. I think the Peanut Brittle has the most potential, but it's missing something. I bet that adding chocolate swirls or brownie bits would make it a winner.

176. What does the e-mail indicate about Karabel Industries ice cream?

(A) It is currently sold in four flavors.
(B) Its coloring can be changed easily.
(C) Its popularity has declined recently.
(D) It is sold in Karabel Industries stores.

177. What does Ms. Kerluke state that she wants to do?

(A) Visit a laboratory
(B) Hold a team meeting
(C) Contact a grocery store
(D) Write new survey questions

178. What is suggested about Fatior Labs?

(A) It has 92 employees.
(B) It manufactures food colorings.
(C) It will perform another taste test for Karabel Industries.
(D) It supplies ice cream to Preston Grocers.

179. Based on the survey form, what flavor will Karabel Industries most likely make adjustments to?

(A) Lemon
(B) Mango
(C) Salted Caramel
(D) Peanut Brittle

180. What can be concluded about participant number 54 ?

(A) The participant purchased several containers of ice cream.
(B) The participant is between the ages of 25 and 40.
(C) The participant regularly takes consumer surveys.
(D) The participant prefers fruit-flavored ice cream.

GO ON TO THE NEXT PAGE

https://www.creategreat.ca/openings

Create Great, an Ontario-based creative agency with a diverse range of global clients in the fashion industry, is seeking a copywriter who is passionate about fashion, understands market trends, and handles digital tools with ease.

The ideal candidate will be someone who works well in a fast-paced environment with team members from international backgrounds. The copywriter will collaborate with the creative team to develop brand strategies that suit customer needs and with the marketing team to ensure the success of brand-based publicity campaigns for current and prospective clients. As remote work is permitted for copywriters, residence in Canada is not required.

To apply, send your cover letter and résumé to the director of our creative team, Fran Benjamin, Create Great, 838 Colbert Street, London, ON N6B 3P5. Application deadline: August 5.

Annie Smith
4810 South Bryant Street
Portland, OR 97206

August 6

Fran Benjamin
Create Great
838 Colbert Street
London, ON N6B 3P5

Dear Ms. Benjamin,

I am writing to apply for the copywriter position at Create Great. As an expert fashion designer who also has writing experience, I believe I would be a valuable addition to your team. Enclosed please find my résumé.

I have a decade of experience as the lead designer for women's collections at MODA, a clothing line in Portland. I oversee the design production process from initial market research to finished product. In my role, I work in close partnership with the marketing and production teams.

In addition, for the last five years, I have been maintaining my own blog. My posts focus on trends in women's fashion and how to make clothing and cosmetics more sustainable. What started as a hobby has now attracted paying advertisers and over 15,000 followers. Visit www.medesheen.com for examples of my writing.

Thank you for considering my application.

Sincerely,

Annie Smith
Annie Smith

Enclosure

181. According to the Web page, what will the job recipient be able to do?

(A) Work remotely
(B) Manage a team
(C) Travel internationally
(D) Relocate to Canada

182. On the Web page, the word "suit" in paragraph 2, line 4, is closest in meaning to

(A) adapt
(B) determine
(C) invest
(D) satisfy

183. What is indicated about Ms. Smith?

(A) She has already met Ms. Benjamin.
(B) She has worked as a copywriter.
(C) She missed an application deadline.
(D) She forgot to submit a required document.

184. According to the letter, what is one of Ms. Smith's responsibilities at MODA?

(A) Hiring fashion designers
(B) Writing drafts of advertisements
(C) Managing a production process
(D) Researching sustainable clothing options

185. What most likely is Medesheen?

(A) A brand of cosmetics
(B) A fashion blog
(C) An online magazine
(D) An advertising agency

GO ON TO THE NEXT PAGE

```
======= E-Mail Message =======
```

From: Akihito Nakashima <a.nakashima@gilchristshipping.com>
To: Fowler Office Supplies <support@fowlerofficesupplies.com>
Subject: Order B19849
Date: August 19

To Whom It May Concern,

Yesterday, I purchased some office supplies on your Web site. I received an e-mail receipt, but the costs are not itemized on it. To satisfy a new company policy, I must give my supervisor a receipt with the charges for each item listed separately. Could you e-mail me such a receipt? If not, is it possible for me to get this information myself from your Web site? Finally, can confirmations for future orders possibly be sent to more than one e-mail address? It would be ideal for my supervisor to automatically receive one.

Thank you,

Akihito Nakashima, Executive Assistant
Gilchrist Shipping

```
======= E-Mail Message =======
```

From: Fowler Office Supplies <support@fowlerofficesupplies.com>
To: Akihito Nakashima <a.nakashima@gilchristshipping.com>
Subject: RE: Order B19849
Date: August 19
Attachment: ⬚ B19849

Dear Mr. Nakashima,

Attached is the receipt you requested. In apology for the inconvenience, we will provide you with 10 percent off the total price of your next order. To view a full description of any previous order, first log in to your account on our Web site, go to the "My Orders" tab, and then click on any order number.

I noticed that included in each of your last few orders was an identical order for ten of a particular item. You should know that we will reduce the price for that item by 5 percent if you mark this as a recurring order. To do this, simply check the "Recurring Order" box on the online order form.

As for your final query, this is not possible right now. However, I will share the idea with our technical team.

All the best,

Cameron Higgins, Customer Relations
Fowler Office Supplies

Fowler Office Supplies

Receipt for Order: B19849
Order Date: August 18

Item	Price	Quantity	Total
Printer paper	$8.00/500 sheets	10	$ 80.00
Toner (black)	$50.00/cartridge	1	$ 50.00
Gel pens (blue)	$5.00/8-pack	3	$ 15.00
Staples	$3.50/box	2	$ 7.00
GRAND TOTAL			**$152.00**

Return Policy: Unopened merchandise may be returned by mail or in one of our stores within 60 days of purchase. For returns by mail, log in to your www.fowlerofficesupplies.com account to print a shipping label. For in-store returns, bring the item and the order number to any Fowler Office Supplies location.

186. Why did Mr. Nakashima send the e-mail?

(A) He did not receive an item he ordered.
(B) He was mistakenly charged twice for an item.
(C) He received a receipt that was not detailed enough.
(D) He did not get a confirmation e-mail for a purchase he made.

187. According to the second e-mail, what will Mr. Nakashima receive with his next order?

(A) A catalog
(B) A free pen
(C) A printed receipt
(D) A price discount

188. For what item does Mr. Higgins suggest that Mr. Nakashima select "Recurring Order"?

(A) Printer paper
(B) Toner
(C) Gel pens
(D) Staples

189. What will Mr. Higgins ask the technical team to look into?

(A) Improving the Web site's response rate
(B) Providing an option to send receipts to multiple e-mail addresses
(C) Placing a link to customers' order history on the home page
(D) Making return labels printable from any device

190. What is needed to return an item at a Fowler Office Supplies store?

(A) The original receipt
(B) A credit card number
(C) A confirmation e-mail
(D) The order number

GO ON TO THE NEXT PAGE

Questions 191-195 refer to the following article, Web site, and receipt.

Crawford and Duval Opens Brick-and-Mortar Stores

HONG KONG (18 February)—Crawford and Duval, the online retailer known for its handcrafted blankets, decorative pillows, and other household goods, has established four brick-and-mortar stores in Hong Kong. Last Monday, the company celebrated the grand opening of boutique stores in Causeway Bay, Discovery Bay, and Sheung Wan in addition to a large department store in Central District. While the boutique stores carry the most popular of the small household goods for which Crawford and Duval is famous, the Central District location also boasts an indoor plant department and an on-site café that features specialty coffees, teas, and light snacks. Moreover, it has a much more extensive selection of the merchandise than what is available through the company's Web site.

| https://www.crawfordandduval.com.hk |

| **Home** | Best Sellers | Full Catalogue | Shopping Cart |

Crawford and Duval comes to our loyal shoppers in Hong Kong!

Crawford and Duval is pleased to announce the opening of its first brick-and-mortar stores in the following locations: Causeway Bay, Discovery Bay, Sheung Wan, and Central District.

Since the launch of our online store five years ago, we have helped you to create the living space of your dreams. Now we make it even easier to decorate your home. Each location has an interior designer on staff, so you can consult with an expert in person while you browse our popular items.

All locations are convenient to public transportation. Our Central District location offers free parking in its attached car park.

As part of our grand-opening celebration, shoppers who visit one of our stores before 1 March will receive a gift card for HK$70 to use during their visit.

Members of our online Frequent Purchase Club will receive the same benefits in our stores, including a 10 percent discount on purchases of HK$500 or more.

Crawford and Duval

Customer Receipt

Date: 23 February

Item	Price
Bamboo table lamp	HK$1,450.00
Decorative cushions, set of two	HK$750.00
Aloe plant in a 7.5-litre planter	HK$300.00
Machine-washable wool blanket	HK$2,000.00
Sub Total	HK$4,500.00
Less 10%	HK$450.00
TOTAL	HK$4,050.00

☐ **Cash**

☐ **Gift card number:**

☑ **Credit card number:** ************5598

Name on the credit card: Mei-Lin Fong

Stop at our in-store café for a treat!

---

191. What is the purpose of the article?

(A) To compare locally made products
(B) To announce store openings
(C) To list changes to a Web site
(D) To review a café

192. What does the Web site indicate about Crawford and Duval?

(A) It has store locations around the world.
(B) It has been in business for ten years.
(C) It employs interior designers.
(D) It offers free parking at all of its stores.

193. According to the receipt, what is indicated about the blanket?

(A) It can be washed by machine.
(B) It is made of cotton.
(C) It is queen-sized.
(D) It comes in a set with pillows.

194. Where most likely did Ms. Fong make her purchase?

(A) On a Web site
(B) In a boutique shop
(C) At a café
(D) In a department store

195. What is suggested about Ms. Fong?

(A) She often buys food from Crawford and Duval.
(B) She is a member of the Frequent Purchase Club.
(C) She applied a gift card to her purchase.
(D) She shopped during a grand-opening event.

GO ON TO THE NEXT PAGE

---

https://www.osawacorporateteambuilding.com/home

| Home | Requests | Reviews | Contact Us |

Osawa Corporate Team Building

Bring your team together to promote cooperation while having fun! Our activities increase job satisfaction and engagement. We do all the planning so you can relax. Simply choose the event that is right for your team.

Scavenger Hunt—An outdoor game in which teams are given a list of objects to find and photograph with their phone or camera. Group size: 10–50 people. Time: 3 hours.

Game Day—This is a high-energy game day with fun team activities. This event builds team strength, communication, and problem-solving skills. Group size: 20–500 people.
Time: 2 hours.

Team Painting—Each team member creates a painting outdoors based on a predetermined theme. The paintings are linked together at the end. Group size: 6–30 people. Time: 1–2 hours.

Robot Building—Your group will be broken into teams. Each team builds a robot to be used in challenges against the others. Group size: 10–30 people. Time: 2–3 hours.

All Chocolate—Your group will have the chance to use engineering skills to build a tower of chocolate. Then you learn how to make chocolate from a local chocolatier.
Group size: 8–150 people. Time: 2 hours.

Book an event in October and receive 15 percent off.

---

https://www.osawacorporateteambuilding.com/requests

| Home | Requests | Reviews | Contact Us |

Name (Alexandra Peterson)
Company name (Whitten Tech)
E-mail address (apeterson@whittentech.com)
Phone (617-555-0123)

Location and date of event (Downtown Boston, October 15)

What events are you interested in? Choose your top three.
1 (Game Day) 2 (Scavenger Hunt) 3 (Team Painting)

Number of participants (28 people)

Additional information
(We are interested in a fun activity for our sales team before the busy selling season begins. We spend a lot of time in the office, so we want an outdoor event.)

We will contact you within three business days with a quote and confirmation.

https://www.osawacorporateteambuilding.com/reviews

| Home | Requests | **Reviews** | Contact Us |

What Our Customers Are Saying

Posted by Whitten Tech on October 20

Our team hired Osawa Corporate Team Building to lead an activity for the sales staff at Whitten Tech. The facilitator of the Scavenger Hunt, Lorenzo Benford, was excellent. The 28 members of our sales team all had positive feedback. They reported that they loved exploring the city, learning about its history, and finding new local attractions, even on a cold and cloudy day. I highly recommend this activity. The only downside was that we did not realize how far we would be walking. It would have been helpful to have an idea of the walking distances so we could have been fully prepared.

196. What does the first Web page indicate about the Scavenger Hunt?

(A) It requires participants to rent a camera.
(B) It concludes with prizes for participants.
(C) It is a suitable activity for indoors.
(D) It takes three hours to complete.

197. What event is best for a group of more than 200 people?

(A) Game Day
(B) Team Painting
(C) Robot Building
(D) All Chocolate

198. What is suggested about Ms. Peterson?

(A) She has joined the Building Robots event in the past.
(B) She will receive a discount on an event.
(C) She recently started a job at Whitten Tech.
(D) She used to be an event planner.

199. What can be concluded about Whitten Tech?

(A) It changed its number of event participants.
(B) It provided its staff with free passes to museums.
(C) It was unable to schedule its first-choice activity.
(D) It was not able to hold its event outside.

200. According to the review, what was disappointing about the event?

(A) The focus on local history
(B) The lack of information about walking distances
(C) The difficulty in keeping the group together
(D) The uninteresting facilitator

Stop! This is the end of the test. If you finish before time is called, you may go back to Parts 5, 6, and 7 and check your work.

토익®정기시험
기출문제집 4
1000

TEST 03
무료 동영상 강의

RC

기출 TEST
03

READING TEST

In the Reading test, you will read a variety of texts and answer several different types of reading comprehension questions. The entire Reading test will last 75 minutes. There are three parts, and directions are given for each part. You are encouraged to answer as many questions as possible within the time allowed.

You must mark your answers on the separate answer sheet. Do not write your answers in your test book.

PART 5

Directions: A word or phrase is missing in each of the sentences below. Four answer choices are given below each sentence. Select the best answer to complete the sentence. Then mark the letter (A), (B), (C), or (D) on your answer sheet.

101. ------- your order is being processed, please call customer service with any questions.

(A) Still
(B) Either
(C) While
(D) Also

102. ABC Truck Supplies has the ------- selection of mufflers in the state.

(A) natural
(B) widest
(C) overall
(D) positive

103. Sharswood Landscaping has received dozens of five-star ------- for its work.

(A) reviews
(B) reviewer
(C) reviewed
(D) reviewing

104. Dr. Cho will visit the Teledarr Lab during the annual open house, since ------- may not have another chance to see it.

(A) hers
(B) she
(C) her
(D) herself

105. Dorn Department Store decided to ------- its already large selection of housewares.

(A) create
(B) enforce
(C) apply
(D) expand

106. We ------- that you bring a portfolio of work samples to the interview.

(A) was asking
(B) having asked
(C) ask
(D) asks

107. Members of the Bold Stone Farm Store receive ------- discounts on all purchases.

(A) depth
(B) deepen
(C) deep
(D) deeply

108. If your plans change, please contact us at least 24 hours before the time of your -------.

(A) reserved
(B) reservation
(C) reservable
(D) reserve

109. Hold the tomato seedling gently by the stem in order to avoid harming ------- roots.

(A) its
(B) at
(C) that
(D) in

110. At the registration table, be sure to collect your name tag ------- entering the conference.

(A) very
(B) often
(C) always
(D) before

111. Maihama vehicles include an extended ------- to cover engine repairs.

(A) record
(B) operation
(C) budget
(D) warranty

112. The hotel's new Web site features an ------- collection of high-quality images.

(A) absolute
(B) efficient
(C) impressive
(D) undefeated

113. On behalf of everyone at Uniontown Bank, we ------- thank you for your continued patronage.

(A) deservedly
(B) commonly
(C) sincerely
(D) perfectly

114. Fragile equipment must be stored in a secure location so that nothing is ------- damaged.

(A) accident
(B) accidents
(C) accidental
(D) accidentally

115. Ms. Sampson will not arrive at the convention ------- after our team's presentation.

(A) until
(B) lately
(C) from
(D) when

116. The community picnic will be held ------- the park behind the Seltzer Public Library.

(A) in
(B) all
(C) for
(D) here

117. The new hires ------- for an orientation on May 10 at 9:00 A.M.

(A) to be gathering
(B) will gather
(C) gathering
(D) to gather

118. When Mr. Young approached the desk, the receptionist ------- offered him a seat in the waiting room.

(A) politely
(B) polite
(C) politeness
(D) politest

119. Members of the Marvale marketing team claimed that ------- was the best design for the new corporate logo.

(A) they
(B) them
(C) theirs
(D) their

120. The new Kitsuna video camera is currently on sale for $375, not ------- tax.

(A) excepting
(B) alongside
(C) within
(D) including

GO ON TO THE NEXT PAGE

121. All associates are ------- to follow the standard operating procedures outlined in the handbook.

(A) concerned
(B) tended
(C) maintained
(D) expected

122. This month Framley Publishing House is embarking on its ------- expansion so far.

(A) ambitiously
(B) most ambitiously
(C) ambition
(D) most ambitious

123. After months of collaboration, Matricks Technology's software developers ------- released a top-quality product.

(A) profoundly
(B) overly
(C) finally
(D) intensely

124. Tickets are valid for one-time access and do not allow for ------- into the venue.

(A) duplication
(B) reentry
(C) permission
(D) turnover

125. We hired Okafor Construction to do the renovation ------- it was not the lowest bidder on the project.

(A) if only
(B) alternatively
(C) whereas
(D) even though

126. The first ------- of the training will introduce staff to certain workplace responsibilities.

(A) part
(B) parted
(C) parting
(D) partial

127. According to industry -------, Ghira Company plans to relocate its headquarters to Australia.

(A) reported
(B) reportedly
(C) reporter
(D) reports

128. Next month, the Kneath House will host an exhibition of ------- furniture and clothing from the eighteenth century.

(A) authentic
(B) authentically
(C) authenticate
(D) authenticity

129. PKTM's regional managers serve ------- the direction of the vice president.

(A) among
(B) under
(C) behind
(D) opposite

130. ------- a recent surge in demand, Vanita's Catering is hiring four additional servers.

(A) Everywhere
(B) Possibly
(C) In total
(D) Owing to

PART 6

Directions: Read the texts that follow. A word, phrase, or sentence is missing in parts of each text. Four answer choices for each question are given below the text. Select the best answer to complete the text. Then mark the letter (A), (B), (C), or (D) on your answer sheet.

Questions 131-134 refer to the following e-mail.

To: All Staff
From: Yoreli Costa
Date: February 15
Subject: Florence Shawn

Hi Everyone,

I have news to share about a ------- in the human resources department. After nearly twenty
                                131.
years with Cometti Creative, Florence Shawn has decided to retire from the position of director of

human resources.

Our current senior manager of human resources, Makoto Ichise, will replace Ms. Shawn when

she retires. Ms. Shawn ------- Mr. Ichise since he joined the company five years ago.
                         132.

Ms. Shawn's ------- day will be February 22. A retirement party will be held for her on that day
             133.
at 4:00 P.M. in the Terey Lobby. ------- .
                                  134.

Best,

Yoreli Costa
Director of Operations, Cometti Creative

131. (A) difference
     (B) strategy
     (C) change
     (D) practice

132. (A) mentors
     (B) is mentoring
     (C) will mentor
     (D) has been mentoring

133. (A) last
     (B) original
     (C) flexible
     (D) alternate

134. (A) Cometti Creative will hire a replacement
         soon.
     (B) We hope that you can all attend to wish
         her well.
     (C) Ms. Shawn was the first director of human
         resources at Cometti Creative.
     (D) The first project will be the creation of a
         talent development program.

GO ON TO THE NEXT PAGE

Lovitt Real Estate

Helping Manitoba Families Find their Dream Homes

Manuel Lovitt, ------- of Lovitt Real Estate, has been selling real estate for over 17 years. Mr. Lovitt
      135.

and his award-winning team ------- in homes for families in the Winnipeg, Brandon, and Dauphin
      136.

areas. They know about the schools, parks, services, transportation, and activities that enhance

family life in the area where you want to reside. ------- .
      137.

Contact Lovitt Real Estate today and let the team guide you ------- the home of your dreams.
      138.

They will listen to your needs, negotiate on your behalf, and get you the best home for your

hard-earned money.

Call 431-555-0168 to speak to an agent or visit www.lovittrealestate.ca for more information.

---

135. (A) own
(B) owned
(C) owner
(D) owning

136. (A) practice
(B) specialize
(C) report
(D) purchase

137. (A) They can arrange transportation for your
local elementary school.
(B) That is because they live in the
communities they serve.
(C) They will be closed for the summer but
will be back soon.
(D) Therefore, they can help you with all
your banking needs.

138. (A) toward
(B) fixing
(C) because
(D) along

Welcome to "Distributing Your Savings." This slide ------- is the third of a twelve-segment
139.

educational series called "Preparing for Retirement." ------- .
140.

This series provides only ------- advice. It should not replace the guidance of your investment
141.

planner. The series has been developed as background material to help you ask key questions

when ------- with your investment planner. We hope you find this information helpful.
142.

Swainson-Gray Investments

---

139. (A) presenting
(B) presents
(C) presentation
(D) presented

140. (A) You are encouraged to visit our office
for a free portfolio review.
(B) The series is designed to help you
make informed financial decisions.
(C) Please fill out the paperwork before
your appointment.
(D) Your responses will help us serve you
better in the future.

141. (A) regional
(B) expensive
(C) supplemental
(D) playful

142. (A) consulting
(B) prescribing
(C) listing
(D) following

Questions 143-146 refer to the following e-mail.

To: Dana Paulwell
From: Silas Laveau
Date: August 22
Subject: My input
Attachment: Article

Dear Dr. Paulwell,

This message is in response to yesterday's staff meeting, particularly the discussion on how certain aspects of the clinic may affect our work and mission. ------- .
143.

Currently, the vending machines in the hall outside our waiting room are stocked with sugary and salty products such as soft drinks and chips. As a health care provider, we -------
144.
beverages and snacks that show our commitment to wellness. ------- , our mission is focused
145.
on good health.

I have attached an article about actions that medical centers like ours are taking to improve their hospitality stations. I hope you find it ------- . It details some easy and cost-effective
146.
changes we could consider.

Kind regards,

Silas Laveau

---

143. (A) I thought it went on longer than was necessary.
(B) I wish we had been informed about it sooner.
(C) I would like to make a suggestion on this topic.
(D) I would be honored to lead a follow-up session.

144. (A) will offer
(B) have offered
(C) were offering
(D) should be offering

145. (A) After all
(B) By the way
(C) In the meantime
(D) On the other hand

146. (A) useful
(B) eventful
(C) profitable
(D) comfortable

PART 7

Directions: In this part you will read a selection of texts, such as magazine and newspaper articles, e-mails, and instant messages. Each text or set of texts is followed by several questions. Select the best answer for each question and mark the letter (A), (B), (C), or (D) on your answer sheet.

Questions 147-148 refer to the following advertisement.

Medillo Shoes Celebrates Twenty Years in Cape Town!
246 Breda Place, Wynberg, Cape Town 7800
021 555 0149 | www.medilloshoes.co.za

Does your job require you to stand all day long? Get the support you need! At Medillo Shoes, we specialise in comfortable, supportive footwear that is stylish and suitable for any business or medical setting.

Visit us on 10 May to receive 20 percent off your purchase of one or more pairs of shoes during this anniversary event. Should you need assistance finding the best shoes for your professional needs, our footwear specialists will be on hand to help. Schedule a free consultation at www.medilloshoes.co.za to avoid a long wait.

---

147. What will happen at Medillo Shoes on May 10 ?

(A) All shoes will be discounted.
(B) Shop assistants will be hired.
(C) A shoe style will be discontinued.
(D) Operational hours will be extended.

148. What is indicated about Medillo Shoes?

(A) It has been in business for ten years.
(B) It specializes in athletic footwear.
(C) It is located next to a medical center.
(D) It allows customers to make appointments.

GO ON TO THE NEXT PAGE

To:	Sales Team
From:	Neil Cullen
Date:	10 April
Subject:	My schedule next week

Dear Team,

I will be out of the office next week, from 15 to 19 April, attending the conference of the National Technology Alliance in Glasgow. While away, I will check e-mail and voice mail infrequently. For any urgent matters, please contact my assistant, Christina Choo. If you have a specific question about the Ezenx Industries account, please e-mail Mya Soroka. I will be back in the office on 22 April and will see all of you then.

Best,

Neil Cullen, Director of Sales and Marketing
Shallok Technology

149. What is the purpose of the e-mail?

(A) To register for a conference
(B) To announce a new account
(C) To schedule a meeting
(D) To inform colleagues of an absence

150. What is most likely true about Ms. Soroka?

(A) She will be traveling with Mr. Cullen.
(B) She works on the Ezenx Industries account.
(C) She is Ms. Choo's supervisor.
(D) She will be out of the office until April 22.

Questions 151-152 refer to the following notice.

CITY OF BRYANTON
Building Permit Office

Notice for residents and contractors working in Bryanton

Beginning on Monday, July 1, the City of Bryanton's Building Permit Office, located at 912 Fir Avenue, will be open from Monday to Thursday, 9:00 A.M. to 5:00 P.M. Applications for permits will no longer be accepted on Fridays or Saturdays. The average processing time for permit applications will remain three business days. With this change, the city will lower its operating costs while maintaining its high standards of service for residents.

151. What change is the Building Permit Office making?

(A) It is moving to a new location.
(B) It is simplifying the permit application process.
(C) It is reducing the number of days it will accept permit applications.
(D) It is increasing the processing time for permit applications.

152. According to the notice, why is the change being made?

(A) To save the city money
(B) To attract more residents
(C) To improve the quality of service
(D) To decrease the number of new permit applications

GO ON TO THE NEXT PAGE

https://www.riverthamestours.uk/order/confirmation

River Thames Tours

Thank you for reserving a River Thames tour with us. We are eager to welcome you aboard. Each tour lasts 3 hours. Your tour includes a luncheon served at 1:00 p.m. Please consult our Web site for a menu. Should you have any dietary restrictions and like to request a special meal, please contact our customer experience manager, Martin Torma, at least 48 hours prior to your tour.

This reservation also entitles you to a 10 percent discount on a walking tour by Edgerton Walking Tours—just provide your confirmation code when booking.

Name:	Lewis Califf
Purchase Date:	18 April
Confirmation Code:	H102057
Tour Start:	1 May, 11:30 a.m.
Quantity:	4
Total:	£180.00
Payment:	Credit card ending in 1037

Please note: Boarding ends 10 minutes before departure time. Tours cannot be rescheduled.

153. What is indicated about the river tour?

(A) It is one hour long.
(B) It comes with a meal.
(C) It can be rescheduled.
(D) It sells out quickly.

154. How many tickets did Mr. Califf purchase?

(A) 1
(B) 3
(C) 4
(D) 7

155. How can customers receive a discount on a walking tour?

(A) By making a reservation online
(B) By paying with a credit card
(C) By requesting a coupon from the captain
(D) By mentioning a confirmation code

Questions 156-157 refer to the following text-message chain.

Michiko Saunders [8:06 A.M.]
Hi, Jacob. Are you on your way to the office?

Jacob Kwon [8:08 A.M.]
Yes. I should be there in about 25 minutes.

Michiko Saunders [8:10 A.M.]
OK. I was just starting to print out the design proposal for the Dansby Group, but we've run out of paper. And we don't have another delivery of it coming until Wednesday.

Jacob Kwon [8:12 A.M.]
I see an office supply store across the street. It just opened for the day.

Michiko Saunders [8:13 A.M.]
Fantastic. Three packs of paper should be enough.

Jacob Kwon [8:15 A.M.]
OK. By the way, when will the representatives from the Dansby Group be coming to our office? I could also pick up some coffee and snacks for that meeting.

156. At 8:12 A.M., what does Mr. Kwon most likely mean when he writes, "I see an office supply store across the street"?

(A) He needs help finding a building.
(B) He can purchase some paper.
(C) He will look for a new printer.
(D) He is going to negotiate a delivery schedule.

157. What will Ms. Saunders most likely do next?

(A) Reschedule a meeting
(B) Prepare some refreshments
(C) Check on an arrival time
(D) Revise a design proposal

GO ON TO THE NEXT PAGE

Questions 158-160 refer to the following letter.

Kipbank Business Services
548 Sycamore Lake Road
Green Bay, WI 54301

April 2

Madeline Omar
Passionflower Interior Design
1556 Deer Run Road
Green Bay, WI 54301

Dear Ms. Omar,

A business owner's days are filled with juggling the wants, needs, and demands of customers, staff, and suppliers. — [1] —.

Let Kipbank find the right solutions for your small business so that you can focus on your products and people. Kipbank offers checking accounts, corporate credit cards, business loans, and payroll and bookkeeping services. — [2] —. This fall, we will also add financial planners to our team to help you and your employees plan for your futures.

With our corporate credit cards, Kipbank customers can take advantage of money-saving offers from selected hotel, office supply, and air travel partners. — [3] —. These deals are automatically applied to qualified purchases. And the business owner can place spending limits on each card. — [4] —.

Please call us at 920-555-0122 to set up an appointment or just stop by when it is convenient. We look forward to meeting you and providing your enterprise with superior service.

Sincerely,

Thomas Piskorksi

Thomas Piskorksi, Kipbank Customer Concierge

158. What is suggested about Ms. Omar?

(A) She is an accountant.
(B) She works for Mr. Piskorksi.
(C) She operates a small company.
(D) She is a Kipbank customer.

159. What is stated about the credit cards?

(A) They come in a variety of colors.
(B) They require an annual fee.
(C) They include discounts on certain purchases.
(D) They can be used to buy personal items.

160. In which of the positions marked [1], [2], [3], and [4] does the following sentence best belong?

"Everyday financial details only add more distractions."

(A) [1]
(B) [2]
(C) [3]
(D) [4]

Questions 161-163 refer to the following article.

OTTAWA (22 May)—*Waldenstone Business Review* has added a new category to its esteemed international business awards this year. The Waldenstone Corporate Prize is awarded to a business with the foresight to develop strategies that help ensure the company's long-term viability.

This year's award was presented to Carila Corporation, a major player in the electronics sector. Under the direction of CEO Atsak Kakar, Carila Corporation went from near bankruptcy to a high level of profitability in just three years.

"Winning this award was very gratifying, not just for me but for the entire company," Mr. Kakar said upon receiving the award. "Everyone has worked extremely hard to get this company back on solid financial ground. The long-term solution has brought exceptional value to our shareholders."

161. What is the purpose of the article?

(A) To profile a newly opened business
(B) To analyze a trend in the electronics industry
(C) To highlight a company's achievement
(D) To discuss changes to an employment contract

162. What is suggested about Carila Corporation?

(A) It no longer develops electronics.
(B) It was once a struggling business.
(C) It has been unable to attract more clients.
(D) It is seeking to replace its CEO.

163. The word "solution" in paragraph 3, line 6, is closest in meaning to

(A) mixture
(B) proof
(C) statement
(D) answer

GO ON TO THE NEXT PAGE

Commbolt is for Everyone!

As a Commbolt customer, you've come to expect the best in reliable high-speed Internet, straightforward pricing options, and top-notch customer service from friendly professionals who are responsive to your every need. — [1] —. Unlike the competition, we promise to never lock you into inflexible contracts or suddenly raise your monthly bill without notice.

At Commbolt, we know you have options when it comes to choosing an Internet service provider. — [2] —. To show our gratitude for your loyalty, we are offering a special limited-time referral bonus.

The way it works is simple. — [3] —. You can use e-mail, social media, or even text messages to tell everyone about Commbolt. When a new user signs up using your code, each of you will receive a monetary credit. Receive $10 when new referrals sign up for a monthly plan at $45, and receive $20 for a plan costing $60 per month. The best news? — [4] —. There is no limit to the credits; the more people you sign up, the more money you get.

Your unique code is **XA4R177**.

---

164. What Commbolt benefit does the advertisement mention?

(A) Its low prices
(B) Its excellent customer service
(C) Its lifetime contracts
(D) Its convenient installation schedule

165. What is the maximum amount a customer can earn when one referred person signs up for service?

(A) $10.00
(B) $20.00
(C) $45.00
(D) $60.00

166. What is true about the Commbolt promotion?

(A) It may not be posted on social media.
(B) It does not provide credit for more than three referrals.
(C) It is expected to run for a full year.
(D) It rewards both new and existing customers.

167. In which of the positions marked [1], [2], [3], or [4] does the following sentence best belong?

"Just share your unique referral code with friends and family."

(A) [1]
(B) [2]
(C) [3]
(D) [4]

---

https://www.sarahscatering.com

Sarah's Catering—What You Serve Matters

Sarah's Catering is a family-owned-and-operated company. The company was founded ten years ago with a mission to provide the highest quality catering services in our community. We work closely with local growers and use only the freshest ingredients. Our menu items can be adapted to the client's taste or dietary needs. For example, we can prepare vegetarian, vegan, and gluten-free options.

We provide catering for birthday parties, wedding receptions, corporate meetings, business holiday parties, and many other types of events. From planning the menu and preparing your food to engaging servers and cleanup staff for the event, Sarah's Catering has it covered.

Sarah's Catering can cater lunches in your office for a minimum of twenty people. We offer delicious options to make your group's meal a satisfying experience.

We're here to serve you! Ordering is fast and simple. Visit www.sarahscatering.com/quote to request a cost estimate for your next event.

What people are saying

"Sarah's Catering was very easy to work with, and the food was delicious! Everyone in the office commented on how good the food was." — Glen Liu, Perkins Real Estate

"All the food was perfect, and the staff was the best." — Annie Pierce, Kania Marketing, Inc.

---

168. What is indicated about Sarah's Catering?

(A) It uses locally sourced products.
(B) It is twenty years old.
(C) It specializes mainly in weddings.
(D) It has an on-site dining room.

169. The word "taste" in paragraph 1, line 4, is closest in meaning to

(A) preference
(B) sample
(C) experience
(D) flavor

170. What is mentioned as a service provided by Sarah's Catering?

(A) Entertainment planning
(B) Cooking demonstrations
(C) Cleanup after meals
(D) Rentals of tables and chairs

171. Who most likely is Mr. Liu?

(A) An employee of Sarah's Catering
(B) A professional event manager
(C) A customer of Sarah's Catering
(D) An assistant at a marketing firm

GO ON TO THE NEXT PAGE

Questions **172-175** refer to the following online chat discussion.

Marcus Steuber [10:41 A.M.] Are we still planning to have the author video conference today? I haven't yet received a meeting invitation.

Brinda Rajan [10:42 A.M.] I do have the meeting on my calendar. Let me forward it to you; it appears our editorial assistant didn't include you.

Marcus Steuber [10:43 A.M.] Thanks, I just received it. The timing doesn't work for me, though. I have an appointment with Hazel Luong to discuss the printing issues at our Singapore plant.

Brinda Rajan [10:44 A.M.] Could you postpone that? The new author we're working with really needs your guidance on the final book design and formatting. You're our most knowledgeable production editor.

Marcus Steuber [10:45 A.M.] Let me check with my supervisor. I'll add Mr. Borg to our chat.

Joshua Borg [10:47 A.M.] Hi, team. Marcus, you should prioritize your appointment with Hazel. I'll be visiting the plant next week, and we need to have some viable solutions before then.

Brinda Rajan [10:48 A.M.] OK, I'll contact Ms. Benoit to find out if she can meet later in the day, then.

Marcus Steuber [10:48 A.M.] That would work. I'm free between 4 and 6 P.M.

172. Why does Mr. Steuber write to Ms. Rajan?

(A) To invite her to a professional event
(B) To check on the status of a meeting
(C) To make travel plans for a business trip
(D) To ask about an assistant's performance

173. At 10:45 A.M., what does Mr. Steuber most likely mean when he writes, "Let me check with my supervisor"?

(A) He needs final approval on a book design.
(B) He would like advice on changing an appointment.
(C) He requires access to the corporate calendar.
(D) He is uncertain how to add team members to the chat.

174. Who most likely is Ms. Benoit?

(A) A writer
(B) A designer
(C) A production editor
(D) A printing plant supervisor

175. What will Ms. Rajan probably do next?

(A) Suggest solutions to a printing issue
(B) Arrange to visit the Singapore plant
(C) Attend a meeting with Ms. Luong
(D) Reschedule a video conference

GO ON TO THE NEXT PAGE

Rambling River Festival
Schedule of Musical Events

Friday, September 8
- 3:30 P.M.   Johanna Greenblatt
- 8:00 P.M.   Bethesda Radio Show featuring the Blass Brothers Band
               (to be recorded at the Bramley Theater)

Saturday, September 9
- 6:30 P.M.   The Rolling Dozen
- 7:45 P.M.   Jefferson Cage

All events take place at the Bethesda Park Open-Air Stage unless otherwise noted. Feel free to bring picnic blankets.

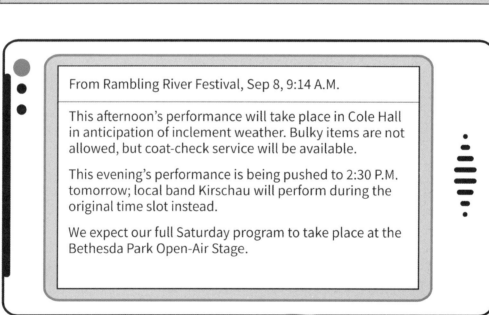

From Rambling River Festival, Sep 8, 9:14 A.M.

This afternoon's performance will take place in Cole Hall in anticipation of inclement weather. Bulky items are not allowed, but coat-check service will be available.

This evening's performance is being pushed to 2:30 P.M. tomorrow; local band Kirschau will perform during the original time slot instead.

We expect our full Saturday program to take place at the Bethesda Park Open-Air Stage.

176. Who was originally scheduled to perform at the Bramley Theater?

(A) Johanna Greenblatt
(B) The Blass Brothers Band
(C) The Rolling Dozen
(D) Jefferson Cage

177. What does the schedule suggest about the Rambling River Festival?

(A) It takes place annually.
(B) It requires a ticket for entry.
(C) It features local food vendors.
(D) It is mainly an outdoor event.

178. According to the text message, what can audience members do at Cole Hall?

(A) Check coats
(B) Store bulky items
(C) Buy concert tickets
(D) Pick up a schedule of events

179. In the text message, the word "pushed" in paragraph 2, line 1, is closest in meaning to

(A) moved
(B) extended
(C) managed
(D) pressured

180. When will Kirschau perform?

(A) At 3:30 P.M. on Friday
(B) At 8:00 P.M. on Friday
(C) At 2:30 P.M. on Saturday
(D) At 6:30 P.M. on Saturday

GO ON TO THE NEXT PAGE

Questions 181-185 refer to the following e-mail and article.

To:	All Branch Managers
From:	Fran Corliss
Subject:	Survey results on mobile banking
Date:	April 7

Hello all,

Ogden Bank recently conducted a survey of its customers concerning mobile banking. Here are some key takeaways.

Over 95 percent of our customers own a mobile device. However, although interest in mobile banking is high, only 39 percent of our customers use our application. Some customers cite security concerns (23 percent), but a majority (78 percent) say that they simply do not think the app works well.

A mandatory meeting for all branch managers will be held at our headquarters on April 12 at 4:00 P.M. to brainstorm strategies for responding to this challenge.

Best,

Fran Corliss
Director of Mobile Banking, Ogden Bank

Boost for Mobile Banking

By Edward Panzius

FLEMINGTON (May 25)—Ogden Bank has rolled out major improvements to its mobile banking application. It has expanded the variety of tasks that can be accomplished through the app and made it much easier to use.

"Many of our account holders have been frustrated in the past by a clunky, limited app," said Alys DeFreese, manager of the Flemington branch of Ogden Bank. "They can now do just about any task with the app that they could over the phone or by visiting a branch in person. This is just another example of how we support our customers in any way we can."

According to Ms. DeFreese, in the few weeks since the upgrade, 20 percent of account holders have switched to depositing checks and paying bills online. She anticipates that number will rise as more customers learn about the easy-to-use app.

"The convenience made a big difference for me," said account holder Yair Baum. Another customer, Maria Reed, added, "I appreciate the flexibility of being able to do my banking whenever and wherever I want."

181. What is one purpose of the e-mail?

(A) To provide details on a new privacy policy
(B) To propose a survey of banking habits
(C) To ask bank staff to test a mobile app
(D) To inform managers of a company problem

182. According to the e-mail, what percentage of the bank's customers use the mobile app?

(A) 23 percent
(B) 39 percent
(C) 78 percent
(D) 95 percent

183. In the article, the word "anticipates" in paragraph 3, line 5, is closest in meaning to

(A) considers
(B) waits for
(C) prepares for
(D) expects

184. Who most likely attended a meeting at Ogden Bank headquarters on April 12 ?

(A) Mr. Panzius
(B) Ms. DeFreese
(C) Mr. Baum
(D) Ms. Reed

185. What is suggested about Ogden Bank's management?

(A) It prefers that account holders do their banking in person.
(B) It is considering offering free checking to new account holders.
(C) It is in the process of hiring more staff.
(D) It prioritizes improvements in customer experience.

TEST 3

GO ON TO THE NEXT PAGE

Questions 186-190 refer to the following notice, Web page, and e-mail.

Attention, Library Members

The Westwood Library is excited to announce the start of a book club, which is open to all library members. The club will meet on the last Thursday of each month, from 7:00 to 9:00 P.M. in the Harrison Meeting Room, to discuss a book chosen by one of our professional staff. From January to June, we will read recently published nonfiction works, and from July to December, we will focus on contemporary fiction titles. For more information, visit www.westwoodlibrary.org or speak with the staff at the circulation desk.

---

https://www.westwoodlibrary.org/bookclub

We hope you will join us for the book club on the last Thursday of each month at 7:00 P.M.! Below are the titles selected for the first half of the year.

January:	*Wild Open Range* by Jaxon McDonald
February:	*The Journey of a Song* by Lucy Xi
March:	*Due North: Adventures in Alaska's Northern Territory* by Isabel Beck
April:	*The Art of Mindful Carpentry* by Peter Landers
May:	*Mary Swan: A Legend Before Her Time* by Kai Noble
June:	To Be Announced

To:	Lisa Calle <lcalle@worldmail.com>
From:	Gail Frey <gfrey@myemail.com>
Date:	March 27
Subject:	Book club

Dear Ms. Calle,

It was delightful to see you leading the book club yesterday evening. Ms. Beck's *Due North* is lengthy, and it was a challenge to finish it before the meeting. However, I have to thank you for choosing that book because it revived my childhood interest in traveling to Alaska. In fact, I've already looked up some tours!

The club meeting was packed, and I hardly got to talk to you. We should catch up sometime soon. Perhaps we might try the new French restaurant on Looper Street. I hear it is amazing and reasonably priced.

Sincerely,

Gail Frey

186. What is the purpose of the notice?

   (A) To highlight some books in the library
   (B) To announce a change in library hours
   (C) To promote an activity at the library
   (D) To introduce a new librarian

187. What is suggested about the book *Wild Open Range* ?

   (A) It is a best-selling title.
   (B) It is a work of nonfiction.
   (C) It was published ten years ago.
   (D) It is available at a discount for library members.

188. What author most likely wrote about a famous person?

   (A) Jaxon McDonald
   (B) Lucy Xi
   (C) Peter Landers
   (D) Kai Noble

189. What can be concluded about Ms. Calle?

   (A) She is a library staff member.
   (B) She has written book reviews.
   (C) She is Ms. Frey's supervisor.
   (D) She favors historical fiction.

190. What does Ms. Frey indicate about the book she read?

   (A) It discussed a topic that was unfamiliar to her.
   (B) It had parts that she thought were inaccurate.
   (C) It was easy to read in the time available.
   (D) It inspired her to explore an old interest.

GO ON TO THE NEXT PAGE

From:	Tatiana Schwartz <orders@georgestreetsweets.co.uk>
To:	Alejandro Ordaz <aordaz@brooksidestationery.co.uk>
Date:	28 April
Subject:	Confirmation of order number 47892
Attachment:	🗋 Order receipt

Dear Mr. Ordaz,

Thank you for placing an order with George Street Sweets. This e-mail is to confirm that we have received your request. Your receipt has been attached to this e-mail.

If you have any questions or need to make any changes to your order, please reply to this message or phone us at (091) 498 0172. Note that we are unable to accommodate order changes that are submitted less than 48 hours before your scheduled pickup time.

If picking up your order, we are located at 29 George Street. Parking is available next door, directly behind Spike's Cycle Shop. We offer delivery to customers within 10 kilometres of our shop for a fee of £2.50. Please note that cancellations within 24 hours of your pickup or delivery time will not be refunded.

Sincerely,

Tatiana Schwartz

George Street Sweets

Order: 47892

Date of Order: 28 April

Pickup Date and Time: N/A

Delivery Date and Time: 2 May, 11:30 A.M.

Delivery Location: 2 Spen Lane, Business Suite 202

Payment Method: Credit Card—Alejandro Ordaz

Customisation Instructions: None

Item	Cost
18-inch round cake (chocolate with vanilla icing)	£32.00
1 set of candles	£5.00
Delivery	£2.50
Total	**£39.50**

From:	Alejandro Ordaz <aordaz@brooksidestationery.co.uk>
To:	Tatiana Schwartz <orders@georgestreetsweets.co.uk>
Date:	29 April
Subject:	RE: Confirmation of order number 47892

Dear Ms. Schwartz,

I received my order confirmation e-mail and receipt, and I noticed an error. It seems that the person to whom I spoke on the phone while placing my order did not copy down the message I requested. The customisation I specified was that "Happy Retirement" be written on top.

I hope it will still be possible to include this message despite the timing. Please respond to this e-mail to confirm. Also, there will be more guests than I originally expected, so I might contact your business again to place an additional order.

Best,

Alejandro Ordaz

191. What is a policy of George Street Sweets?

(A) Orders cannot be changed.
(B) Orders placed less than 48 hours before pickup incur an extra fee.
(C) Orders must be paid for when they are placed.
(D) Orders cannot be refunded within 24 hours of pickup.

192. What is suggested about the building at 2 Spen Lane?

(A) It has parking spaces behind a bicycle shop.
(B) It is located within 10 kilometers of George Street Sweets.
(C) It is a residential apartment building.
(D) It is owned by Ms. Schwartz.

193. What can be concluded about the cake?

(A) It has not been paid for yet.
(B) It will have only chocolate icing.
(C) It was ordered over the phone.
(D) It contains ice cream.

194. In the second e-mail, what does Mr. Ordaz request?

(A) A full refund
(B) A different flavor
(C) A response to an e-mail
(D) An additional candle

195. What does Mr. Ordaz mention about the event in his e-mail?

(A) It will take place on April 29.
(B) It is an anniversary party.
(C) Its start time has changed.
(D) It will be larger than expected.

GO ON TO THE NEXT PAGE

To:	Undisclosed Recipients
From:	iqbal_grewal@woolfflooring.com.au
Date:	12 June
Subject:	Cost-savings survey

Dear Colleagues,

At Woolf Flooring we are looking for ways to reduce day-to-day costs without sacrificing product quality, customer service, or staff morale. To this end, we are seeking input from select staff members in a variety of departments via an online survey that can be found at www.surveyquest.com.au/109820. Everyone who has been chosen to take part in the survey has been with the company for at least ten years and, therefore, is very familiar with our processes.

The deadline for completing the survey is 19 June. Note that this survey is for recipients of this e-mail only. Please do not forward this e-mail to others or post the link to the survey elsewhere.

We also plan to hire outside consultants to review our operations and write a report of their findings. We understand that some colleagues disagree with this approach to cutting costs; however, we have determined that getting an outside perspective is a worthwhile investment that will be likely to save us money in the long run.

Best,

Iqbal Grewal, Director of Business Transformation
Woolf Flooring

---

https://www.surveyquest.com.au/109820

Woolf Flooring Cost-Savings Survey

Based on your experience as an employee of Woolf Flooring, please provide one idea for a change that could be implemented to improve productivity and cut costs. Thank you.

Date: 18 June

Name and role: Beth Mair, sales manager

I have noticed that some employees grab a new pair of disposable gloves every time they return from a break. They could be using the same ones throughout the whole day. By limiting the use of gloves to one pair per day, Woolf Flooring would save thousands of dollars per year. Doing so would also reduce waste. A new policy regarding the use of personal protective items would be easy to implement immediately and would simply require sending a company-wide e-mail to explain it.

TEST 3

**Miyoko Consulting
Woolf Flooring Report Summary**

Thank you for allowing us to spend the last few weeks reviewing your operations. You will find a detailed expense-reduction report with projected savings in the pages that follow. Here is a list of our main recommendations.

1. Employees do not always use wood stains and other materials as efficiently as possible. More training time could be dedicated to this.

2. Employees could be more mindful of electricity costs—for instance, turning off all lights and machines when not in use.

3. Several Internet service providers are offering special pricing right now. Switching to one of these providers could save a considerable amount of money in the long run.

4. More effort could be made to reuse supplies—for example, some basic personal protective equipment could be used more than once.

---

196. In his e-mail, what does Mr. Grewal indicate about the survey?

(A) It does not have an end date.
(B) It requires the use of a password.
(C) It can be completed on paper.
(D) It should not be shared with others.

197. According to the e-mail, what do some Woolf Flooring employees disagree with?

(A) The plan to hire consultants
(B) The way a survey is structured
(C) The way a budget report is presented
(D) The departments selected to provide feedback

198. What can be concluded about Ms. Mair?

(A) She regularly provides ideas for change.
(B) She has worked at Woolf Flooring for many years.
(C) She will be helping to collect feedback.
(D) She works in the production department.

199. In the survey, what does Ms. Mair note about her suggestion?

(A) It may require some new equipment.
(B) It has worked well at other companies.
(C) It could be implemented right away.
(D) It has been suggested to management before.

200. What recommendation made by Miyoko Consulting corresponds with Ms. Mair's suggestion?

(A) Recommendation 1
(B) Recommendation 2
(C) Recommendation 3
(D) Recommendation 4

Stop! This is the end of the test. If you finish before time is called, you may go back to Parts 5, 6, and 7 and check your work.

토익˚정기시험
기출문제집 4
1000

TEST 04
무료 동영상 강의

RC

기출 TEST
04

READING TEST

In the Reading test, you will read a variety of texts and answer several different types of reading comprehension questions. The entire Reading test will last 75 minutes. There are three parts, and directions are given for each part. You are encouraged to answer as many questions as possible within the time allowed.

You must mark your answers on the separate answer sheet. Do not write your answers in your test book.

PART 5

Directions: A word or phrase is missing in each of the sentences below. Four answer choices are given below each sentence. Select the best answer to complete the sentence. Then mark the letter (A), (B), (C), or (D) on your answer sheet.

101. Mr. Barrientos has worked at the company ------- six years.

(A) for
(B) since
(C) with
(D) lately

102. The staff cafeteria stops ------- lunch at 2:00 P.M.

(A) taking
(B) buying
(C) serving
(D) working

103. The annual report will be ready after ------- make the necessary revisions.

(A) I
(B) me
(C) myself
(D) my

104. Mr. Louden was offered a full-time position at Fortelio Corporation ------- a division manager.

(A) about
(B) as
(C) after
(D) around

105. Kennedy Sports will ------- its end-of-season sale through the month of January.

(A) continuing
(B) continued
(C) continues
(D) continue

106. Ms. Najjar is going to give a presentation ------- workplace regulations at noon.

(A) near
(B) to
(C) past
(D) on

107. Mr. Telguld submitted the ------- surveys before the monthly board meeting.

(A) completely
(B) completed
(C) completing
(D) completes

108. Travel funds are available to student presenters coming to the conference from a significant -------.

(A) location
(B) amount
(C) reason
(D) distance

109. Ms. Okada is ------- a new social media campaign at the request of our office manager.
(A) organize
(B) organized
(C) organizing
(D) organization

110. The speaker will offer five tips for making wise purchasing -------.
(A) items
(B) decisions
(C) values
(D) remedies

111. Please log on to your online checking account ------- the next 30 days in order to keep it active.
(A) within
(B) how
(C) whether
(D) and

112. The Bradyville Inn ------- live jazz music in the dining area on Friday evenings.
(A) features
(B) marks
(C) sounds
(D) collects

113. Leeann's Organic Fruit Spreads can be purchased ------- from the company's Web site.
(A) direction
(B) directly
(C) directness
(D) directed

114. ------- the event organizers' best efforts, they have been unable to attract enough volunteers this spring.
(A) Behind
(B) Versus
(C) Among
(D) Despite

115. Mr. Perez ------- as an industrial engineer at Gaberly Logistics for almost twenty years.
(A) employs
(B) to be employed
(C) is employing
(D) has been employed

116. Soon after Ms. Manilla was hired, the sales department's productivity began to increase -------.
(A) mainly
(B) respectively
(C) noticeably
(D) closely

117. Small businesses ------- participate in the Get Ahead program will receive marketing tools to help them attract customers.
(A) that
(B) they
(C) what
(D) whoever

118. Our copy editors will review the manuscript ------- will not return it until the end of next week.
(A) or
(B) once
(C) either
(D) but

119. Mira Kumar was probably the ------- of all the interns at Kolbry Media last summer.
(A) ambitious
(B) most ambitious
(C) ambitiously
(D) more ambitiously

120. Orbin's Fish Company expanded to a total of 26 stores ------- its takeover of a rival chain.
(A) whenever
(B) toward
(C) following
(D) usually

GO ON TO THE NEXT PAGE

121. Ms. Cartwright told her team members that she wanted ------- to streamline the company's assembly process.

(A) theirs
(B) they
(C) them
(D) themselves

122. Rupert's Food Service uses ------- technology to track all of its shipments.

(A) strict
(B) numerous
(C) advanced
(D) crowded

123. Our app includes a ------- so that users can determine whether they are within their budget goals.

(A) calculator
(B) calculated
(C) calculating
(D) calculations

124. To ------- that its facilities are cleaned every day, the Selboa Company has hired more janitors.

(A) ensure
(B) affect
(C) provide
(D) secure

125. During his term as a legislator, Jeremy Moran ------- promoted public awareness of the need for infrastructure improvements.

(A) act
(B) action
(C) active
(D) actively

126. Pyxie Print's business is so new that we need to explain the full range of our services to ------- clients.

(A) trained
(B) potential
(C) elected
(D) paid

127. Phone orders that are ------- to local stores by 11:00 A.M. are eligible for same-day pickup.

(A) submitted
(B) submission
(C) submitting
(D) submits

128. An Oswald Hardware associate will ------- place an order for customers who need larger quantities than what is in stock.

(A) slightly
(B) wholly
(C) busily
(D) gladly

129. Mia Daushvili performed with the Bayhead Orchestra on Monday evening, ------- her virtuosic skills on the piccolo.

(A) displays
(B) had displayed
(C) displaying
(D) was displayed

130. When reviewing applicants for the clerk position, Ms. Ng will consider both education and ------- experience.

(A) prior
(B) quick
(C) lean
(D) calm

PART 6

Directions: Read the texts that follow. A word, phrase, or sentence is missing in parts of each text. Four answer choices for each question are given below the text. Select the best answer to complete the text. Then mark the letter (A), (B), (C), or (D) on your answer sheet.

Questions 131-134 refer to the following notice.

D-Zine Pop

D-Zine Pop is your source for information about the latest ------- in the world of fashion. What
                                                   131.

started as a social media experiment ------- into a content platform with subscribers in seventeen
                                                      132.

countries worldwide. We are constantly adding features to improve our user experience and share

what apparel and clothing accessories are popular right now. We also make periodic updates to

our terms of service. Subscribers' ------- access to content is contingent upon consenting to these
                                                  133.

terms; therefore, we encourage you to review and accept them at dzinepop.com/privacy. Contact

our customer service team at support@dzinepop.com if you have any questions. ------- .
                                                              134.

131. (A) controversies
(B) consumers
(C) trends
(D) versions

132. (A) evolving
(B) evolution
(C) will be evolving
(D) has evolved

133. (A) continue
(B) continued
(C) continuation
(D) continues

134. (A) Representatives are available 24 hours a day to assist you.
(B) The changes made to our user privacy policy are no longer effective.
(C) Fresh content is accessible through phone and desktop apps.
(D) We are no longer offering a discounted rate if you renew your subscription.

GO ON TO THE NEXT PAGE

Rescue your device with Phone Tune-Up

Is your smartphone screen scratched or cracked? ------- ? Do your apps freeze or crash? The
                                                    135.

experts at Phone Tune-Up can help! We use nothing but the best quality parts to ------- your
                                                                                136.

mobile phone. Let our certified technicians save you the time and expense involved in replacing

your phone with a new one. When we are ------- , you will think your old phone is brand new. To
                                        137.

make an appointment, call 604-555-0198 or visit www.phonetuneup.com. Same-day service is

often available ------- needed parts are in stock.
                138.

---

135. (A) Does your printer need frequent ink
        refills?
    (B) Does it take all day for your battery to
        recharge?
    (C) Do you want to complete a short
        survey?
    (D) Do you pay too much for your data
        plan?

136. (A) remove
    (B) borrow
    (C) examine
    (D) repair

137. (A) trained
    (B) available
    (C) done
    (D) dismissed

138. (A) whose
    (B) must
    (C) if
    (D) of

FOR IMMEDIATE RELEASE

SACRAMENTO (July 28)—The Sacramento-based supermarket chain Hsing Market announced today that it is opening a branch ------- in San Jose in October. It will occupy the building that
139.
once housed the Watson Office Superstore located at 1539 West Oak Street, which closed last year.

Hsing Market CEO Alice Tran said, "We are very excited to ------- open a store in San Jose. -------.
140.   **141.**
When the Watson building became available, we jumped on the opportunity to move in."

As a neighborhood grocery store, Hsing Market prides itself on hiring applicants from the local community. Approximately 75 percent of all employees live within two miles of the store where they ------- .
142.

---

139. (A) location
(B) locate
(C) to locate
(D) locating

140. (A) finally
(B) instead
(C) likewise
(D) suddenly

141. (A) The store features a variety of fresh and prepared foods.
(B) We hope that you will be able to join us at our grand-opening celebration.
(C) We have had our eyes on the city for quite some time.
(D) Our corporate headquarters will be renovated soon.

142. (A) save
(B) work
(C) shop
(D) register

GO ON TO THE NEXT PAGE

Questions 143-146 refer to the following Web page information.

About Leafi Cloth

Tropick Textiles recently expanded the ------- of fabrics available on the market. In its quest to
                                   143.

introduce environmentally friendly alternatives to cotton and other traditional fibers, the company

------- a new fiber made from materials that are typically discarded. Tropick Textiles takes banana
144.

and pineapple leaves and combines them with bamboo fibers to create Leafi Cloth. The plants'

leaves are ordinarily disposed of ------- the fruit is harvested. Tropick Textiles' process prevents
                          145.

many leaves from entering a landfill, converting them instead into usable material. ------- .
                                                              146.

---

143. (A) range
     (B) expense
     (C) strength
     (D) appearance

144. (A) are developed
     (B) has developed
     (C) will develop
     (D) to develop

145. (A) now
     (B) thus
     (C) even
     (D) once

146. (A) The resulting durable fabric is a suitable
         substitute for cotton cloth.
     (B) Inquiries regarding Leafi Cloth were
         directed to the sales department.
     (C) Tropick Textiles will celebrate its
         one-hundredth anniversary this year.
     (D) Manufacturing costs have been
         increasing for Tropick Textiles lately.

PART 7

Directions: In this part you will read a selection of texts, such as magazine and newspaper articles, e-mails, and instant messages. Each text or set of texts is followed by several questions. Select the best answer for each question and mark the letter (A), (B), (C), or (D) on your answer sheet.

Questions 147-148 refer to the following receipt.

Zippy Petrol Mart
M64 Motorway
Leicester
0113 4960423
23 May

Biscuits	£2.00
Fruit cup	£0.95
Crisps	£1.10
VAT	**£0.81**
Inclusive	
Total	**£4.86**

Sign up for our Zippy Club rewards card.
You could have earned 4 Zippy Club points on this transaction.
Points can be used for discounted merchandise, car products,
phone accessories, and more!

---

147. What was purchased on May 23 ?

(A) Fuel
(B) Snacks
(C) Auto parts
(D) Phone accessories

148. What does the receipt indicate about Zippy Petrol Mart?

(A) It has multiple locations.
(B) It accepts most major credit cards.
(C) It has a customer rewards program.
(D) It reduced the prices of all its merchandise.

GO ON TO THE NEXT PAGE

Questions 149-150 refer to the following notice.

Coming Soon: The Best of PBQ Radio

During the week of April 21–27, PBQ Radio will be hosting a best-of-the-decade program. The most popular tunes by recording artists from the past decade will be played all day long. Both well-known and lesser-known recording artists will be featured. We plan to showcase each artist's top works.

In addition to featuring the best music of the decade, we would like to highlight our region's businesses. Advertising time is available for purchase. Let our listeners know that your business is one of the best in the community! You can request a shout-out for your company from a program host, or our professional marketing team can write and record a 30-second advertisement.

Visit www.pbqradio.com/advertise for details and pricing.

---

149. For whom most likely was the notice written?

(A) Radio-show hosts
(B) New recording artists
(C) Business owners
(D) Sound technicians

150. What is true about PBQ Radio?

(A) It has been in business for ten years.
(B) It is looking for experienced musicians.
(C) It was voted the best station in the community.
(D) It has its own marketing department.

Questions 151-152 refer to the following text-message chain.

> **Frank Jabati [11:12 A.M.]**
> Hi, Maxine. I'm running late with this delivery today. Could you contact Ms. Dibello to let her know?
>
> **Maxine Larsen [11:13 A.M.]**
> Sure! I know that she is eager to get those new items. She says she needs to set up her kitchen properly so that she can prepare a special meal tonight. What time do you think you will arrive there?
>
> **Frank Jabati [11:15 A.M.]**
> I'm not sure—the road I was taking was closed for repairs. The detour road has heavy traffic.
>
> **Maxine Larsen [11:17 A.M.]**
> Sorry to hear that. What's your estimate?
>
> **Frank Jabati [11:19 A.M.]**
> Maybe around 1 P.M.
>
> **Maxine Larsen [11:20 A.M.]**
> OK, great. I will get in touch with Ms. Dibello to confirm that she will be home at that time. Then I'll get back to you.
>
> **Frank Jabati [11:22 A.M.]**
> Thanks!

151. What most likely has Ms. Dibello purchased?

(A) Linens
(B) Bookshelves
(C) Gardening tools
(D) Appliances

152. At 11:17 A.M., what does Ms. Larsen most likely mean when she writes, "What's your estimate"?

(A) She must verify the distance of a route.
(B) She wants to know how much traffic there is.
(C) She wants to know a delivery time.
(D) She has to calculate a delivery charge.

GO ON TO THE NEXT PAGE

Questions 153-154 refer to the following e-mail.

To:	Janet Hubschmann
From:	customerservice@readymadeofficesupplies.net
Date:	September 3
Subject:	Thank you

Dear Ms. Hubschmann,

We here at Readymade Office Supplies are excited to welcome you to our Customers Count rewards program. Your account number 41120 is now registered.

Be sure to enter your account number to earn points on all your purchases from our Web site. You will earn one point for every dollar you spend on qualifying purchases. Redeem your points on your account page for rewards, including free two-day expedited shipping, special discounts, and more. You can still order via mail from our print catalog, over the telephone from one of our helpful representatives, or by visiting our retail locations across the United States and Canada. However, those purchases do not currently qualify for the rewards program.

Have questions? Please visit https://www.readymadeofficesupplies.net/customerservice.

153. What types of purchases earn reward points?

(A) Those made online
(B) Those made by mail
(C) Those made by phone
(D) Those made in a store

154. What is a benefit of the program?

(A) Invitations to retail events
(B) Free samples
(C) Faster shipping
(D) Extended product warranties

Questions 155-157 refer to the following letter.

Native Plant Society Headquarters
161 Sussex Street
Sydney, NSW 2001

15 April

Yasmine Harabi
247 Kooljak Road
Perth, Western Australia 6280

Membership number 4290

Dear Ms. Harabi,

Thank you for your continued support as a society member. Given your recent move, your membership has been transferred to the chapter located in the city of Perth. We will be mailing a replacement member identification card within a few days.

Unlike the chapter in the city of Canberra, the Perth branch meets the first Saturday of every month, so your next meeting will be in three weeks. If you have any questions, please contact us weekdays between 8:00 a.m. and 4:00 p.m. at (08) 5555 0145.

Sincerely,

Leticia Davis

Leticia Davis
Membership Department

155. What is the purpose of the letter?

(A) To announce a special event
(B) To explain changes based on a
    relocation
(C) To propose a new meeting time
(D) To request updated contact information

156. What is suggested about the city of Canberra?

(A) It is famous for its many gardens.
(B) It houses the headquarters of
    Ms. Davis' organization.
(C) It is where Ms. Harabi previously lived.
(D) It is home to some of Australia's rarest
    plants.

157. What can be concluded about the Native Plant Society?

(A) It is under new leadership.
(B) Its membership is growing.
(C) It is raising membership dues.
(D) Its chapters hold monthly meetings.

GO ON TO THE NEXT PAGE

Questions 158-160 refer to the following Web page.

---

https://www.greenroofplus.com

| **Basics** | Photos | Resources | News |

What Are Green Roofs?

Green roofs are an energy-saving option for office buildings and homes. A green roof is one that's covered with grasses, flowers, or other plants. It lowers heating and cooling costs while increasing a structure's aesthetic appeal. This Web site is designed for sharing ideas, photos, and resources to create and maintain a green roof.

Planting a rooftop garden is a rewarding do-it-yourself project, but special waterproofing and other preparations require the services of an experienced contractor. Costs vary widely by region, roof size, and complexity of the garden you want to create. Be sure to get estimates from at least two contractors.

If your contractor determines that your roof can handle the extra weight of soil, plants, and irrigation, ask about the project's timeline. Small, simple rooftop gardens may take only one week to complete.

---

158. According to the Web page, what can visitors to the Web site do?

(A) Discuss how to create a garden
(B) Learn how to maximize vegetable production
(C) Seek advice about landscaping problems
(D) Help contractors calculate costs

159. What is NOT mentioned about green roofs?

(A) They decrease energy bills.
(B) They remove pollution from the air.
(C) They make a structure more beautiful.
(D) They can be installed on commercial and residential buildings.

160. In paragraph 3, line 1, the word "handle" is closest in meaning to

(A) touch
(B) control
(C) deliver
(D) support

Questions 161-163 refer to the following advertisement.

Martino Technical has been providing live sound-mixing services for more than 30 years. We use the latest technology to produce the best sound.

The majority of our clients are heavy-metal and classic-rock musicians. Before they go on tour, we rehearse with them to ensure that the sounds are perfectly blended and balanced. In addition, we create recordings for them that they can post on social media to promote their shows.

Our sound-mixing engineers are known for their experience and professionalism and have an impressive track record working on tours worldwide. They have worked with many popular music groups, including The Peakes, Firebrand, and Cellar Cats, and make bands sound just as good during live performances as they do on their records.

Contact us by e-mailing information@martinotechnical.ie.

---

161. What is indicated about Martino Technical?

(A) It acquires most clients through social media.
(B) It was founded over 30 years ago.
(C) It has received many industry awards.
(D) It has offices throughout the world.

162. The word "promote" in paragraph 2, line 4, is closest in meaning to

(A) encourage
(B) schedule
(C) publicize
(D) advance

163. What is NOT stated about the live sound-mixing engineers?

(A) They create promotional materials.
(B) They have considerable expertise.
(C) They travel abroad frequently.
(D) They have degrees in music.

GO ON TO THE NEXT PAGE

Questions 164-167 refer to the following e-mail.

To:	Employees <employees@bonahoomenterprises.com>
From:	Marcia Noh <mnoh@bonahoomenterprises.com>
Date:	November 14
Subject:	November 28 event

Dear all,

On the evening of November 28, there will be a formal dinner to honor our company president and founder, Mr. Bonahoom. At the dinner, we will express our appreciation for his leadership over these past twenty years in making Bonahoom Enterprises a successful company and a great place to work. — [1] —.

This event will be held in the private banquet room at Chez Bistro and is intended to be a surprise, so please avoid mentioning it to him. Those few who are involved with the setup will arrive at 5 P.M. All other attendees should come no later than 6:15 P.M. in anticipation of Mr. Bonahoom's arrival at 6:30 P.M. We expect the celebration to wrap up no later than 8 P.M. — [2] —.

There is no need to bring a gift. — [3] —. We do ask, though, that you find time this week to sign a card for him. It can be found at Ms. Mueller's desk, inside an envelope marked "November 28."

Finally, you are welcome to bring one guest with you to the event if you wish. — [4] —. Kindly RSVP to this e-mail so we can get a complete count of the number of attendees.

All the best,

Marcia Noh

---

164. What is the main purpose of the e-mail?

(A) To ask staff to sign up to give speeches at a celebration
(B) To find people willing to bring various items to a dinner
(C) To invite workers to a surprise party
(D) To look for volunteers to help plan an event

165. According to the e-mail, when are most people expected to arrive?

(A) At 5:00 P.M.
(B) At 6:15 P.M.
(C) At 6:30 P.M.
(D) At 8:00 P.M.

166. What should people do if they want to sign a card?

(A) They should request it from Mr. Bonahoom.
(B) They should e-mail Ms. Noh.
(C) They should wait for it to be passed around the office.
(D) They should go to Ms. Mueller's desk.

167. In which of the positions marked [1], [2], [3], and [4] does the following sentence best belong?

"The senior staff will be presenting a commemorative plaque on behalf of the whole office."

(A) [1]
(B) [2]
(C) [3]
(D) [4]

Questions 168-171 refer to the following online chat discussion.

Colin Wikander (10:23 A.M.) I have reviewed the draft of the new client questionnaire, and it looks great overall. I would make the question about bookkeeping strategies more open-ended, though. As written, it may lead respondents to give simple yes or no answers.

Midori Sakai (10:24 A.M.) That's a good point. We'll need to fix that. I also want to add a couple of questions about how financial and tax reports have been handled in the past.

Ela Hamidah (10:24 A.M.) I could look at the bookkeeping question to see what I can come up with.

Colin Wikander (10:25 A.M.) Well, it's four pages already.

Midori Sakai (10:27 A.M.) That's true. I'll just wait for Ela's revision of the third question. Then Jack Neligan can put a draft of the form up on our Web site.

Colin Wikander (10:28 A.M.) Is it true that we are not planning to collect any paper forms?

Midori Sakai (10:30 A.M.) We might do that, but digital collection is preferable to avoid the lag time of waiting for our clients to print, fill out, and scan the forms to send them back.

168. What type of company do the writers most likely work for?

(A) Publishing
(B) Accounting
(C) Retail
(D) Design

169. What does Mr. Wikander suggest about a question?

(A) It is mislabeled.
(B) It is difficult to read.
(C) It should be reworded.
(D) It should be made optional.

170. At 10:25 A.M., what does Mr. Wikander most likely mean when he writes, "Well, it's four pages already"?

(A) He is surprised by the long answers clients gave.
(B) He is impressed with how quickly the questionnaire is coming along.
(C) He thinks information in the first four pages should be cut out.
(D) He thinks the questionnaire should not be any longer.

171. Why does Ms. Sakai think that paperless forms will be preferable?

(A) They allow for faster data collection.
(B) They reduce the number of errors.
(C) They are good for the environment.
(D) They do not take up space in an office.

GO ON TO THE NEXT PAGE

https://www.trehospitalityassociation.com/discussion/tunisia

I have been a member of the TRE Hospitality Association for many years, but until now, I have posted messages only on the Greece and Egypt forums. — [1] —. This is my first post on the Tunisia forum.

I am looking for recommendations for a janitorial service on the island of Djerba. My company is opening a hotel there. Our hotel will offer 80 rooms with two restaurants on-site. — [2] —. I would like to contract with a company that can provide about four full-time custodial workers and housekeepers, plus an additional five workers on an as-needed basis for large events on our property. — [3] —.

I may have met some of you previously at one of our hospitality conferences. If so, please remind me. In fact, I attended the most recent one in Rabat. — [4] —. I would like to reconnect!

John Karikas, Director of Development

Synecdoche Hotel Group

172. Why did Mr. Karikas write the post?

(A) To promote a job fair
(B) To request referrals to a service provider
(C) To recommend a tourist destination
(D) To invite colleagues to a grand opening

173. What is suggested about the TRE Hospitality Association?

(A) It is based in Egypt.
(B) It was recently expanded to include hotel owners.
(C) It is an international organization.
(D) It offers janitorial services.

174. What is indicated about Mr. Karikas?

(A) He teaches a hospitality course.
(B) He lives in Rabat.
(C) He is a former restaurant owner.
(D) He attended at least one hospitality conference.

175. In which of the positions marked [1], [2], [3], and [4] does the following sentence best belong?

"It will also have a large meeting room."

(A) [1]
(B) [2]
(C) [3]
(D) [4]

GO ON TO THE NEXT PAGE

To:	Manuel Torres <m.torres@opalmail.co.uk>
From:	Anya Patel <a.patel@support.harlund.co.uk>
Date:	3 May
Subject:	Auto insurance

Dear Mr. Torres,

Welcome to Harlund Ltd. We are pleased to provide you with comprehensive automobile insurance for your new vehicle. We have received your first payment of £36.00, and your coverage is now in effect. Your policy number is M413927.

Your billing schedule is based on an annual premium of £432.00. The remaining payments of £36.00 per month are due on the fifteenth day of each month starting in June.

You can visit us online at www.harlund.co.uk to pay bills and manage your policy. Our Web site offers easy options for managing your account information and for making payments with scheduled transfers directly from your bank.

Should you have any questions or wish to change your policy, call the customer support centre at 020 7946 0516. In the event of a vehicle incident, please contact an agent as soon as possible at 020 7946 0520. Be sure to have your policy number at hand. Thank you for trusting Harlund Ltd. We look forward to providing you with superior service.

Best regards,

Anya Patel, Harlund Ltd. Customer Support Agent

E-mail

To:	Anya Patel <a.patel@support.harlund.co.uk>
From:	Manuel Torres <m.torres@opalmail.co.uk>
Date:	4 May
Subject:	RE: Auto insurance

Dear Ms. Patel,

Thank you for the confirmation. I'm happy to have insurance from a trustworthy company. For your reference, the new car is now registered in my name.

Although I made the initial payment to you by credit card, I plan to follow the process outlined in your e-mail for future payments.

I also wanted to let you know that I have not yet received the insurance certificate. I looked for one that I could download from your Web site, but I could not find anything. Could you please send me a copy of the certificate?

Sincerely,

Manuel Torres

176. What can be inferred about Mr. Torres?

    (A) He is moving to a new home.
    (B) He recently bought a car.
    (C) He will be retiring soon.
    (D) He recently opened a bank account.

177. In the first e-mail, the word "coverage" in paragraph 1, line 3, is closest in meaning to

    (A) measurement
    (B) information
    (C) commentary
    (D) protection

178. What does Ms. Patel recommend that Mr. Torres do?

    (A) Call an agent if needed
    (B) Register at a local office
    (C) Place an order promptly
    (D) Revise an agreement

179. How does Mr. Torres intend to make future payments?

    (A) By cash
    (B) By credit card
    (C) By electronic transfer
    (D) By personal check

180. What does Mr. Torres state that he looked for?

    (A) Directions to an office
    (B) A document to download
    (C) Reviews from customers
    (D) Contact information

TEST 4

Tour Schedule for Book Launch by Andrew Darr

At each appearance, Mr. Darr will read an excerpt from his new novel, *Down the Mountainside*, followed by a question-and-answer session. Afterward, Mr. Darr will be available to autograph copies of his books.

Venue	City	Date	Time
Neighbourhood Books	Toronto, Ontario	18 May	6:00 P.M.
Weinstock Books and Stationery	Ottawa, Ontario	27 May	7:00 P.M.
Portage Avenue Books	Winnipeg, Manitoba	6 June	6:30 P.M.
Downtown Books and Café	Regina, Saskatchewan	15 June	7:00 P.M.

Book Review: *Down the Mountainside*

Reviewer: Camile Lin
Date: 15 May

Andrew Darr, the author of the best-selling series about detective Charles Martin, will be visiting our city this week, appearing at Neighbourhood Books to promote his new novel, *Down the Mountainside*. The new work sees Martin investigating mysterious events at a ski resort in the French Alps.

Darr's storytelling has come a long way since readers first met Charles Martin in *The Doorbell*, and this installment is Darr's strongest work to date. Fans of the stories will welcome the return of Darr's wit after a three-year wait, and newcomers to the Martin series are sure to find themselves captivated.

The story includes the right balance of suspense and humour, with an ending that is unpredictable, even to the most devoted Darr reader. I highly recommend this book to all mystery fans. You won't be disappointed.

181. According to the schedule, what is NOT mentioned as an activity for Mr. Darr?

(A) Reading from his book
(B) Answering questions
(C) Signing books for individuals
(D) Taking photos with participants

182. What city is the book reviewer from?

(A) Toronto
(B) Ottawa
(C) Winnipeg
(D) Regina

183. What is most likely true about *Down the Mountainside*?

(A) It is the author's first book.
(B) It is a collection of short stories.
(C) It is part of a series.
(D) It is being translated into French.

184. Who is Mr. Martin?

(A) A fan of the author's
(B) A character in the book
(C) The writer of the review
(D) The owner of a bookstore

185. According to the review, who would most likely read *Down the Mountainside*?

(A) People who like to read mysteries
(B) People who enjoy novels based on true stories
(C) People who travel frequently
(D) People who prefer science fiction

TEST 4

GO ON TO THE NEXT PAGE

Annual Citrus Production in Yuma County

- 82 tons of citrus fruit
- Over 120,000 boxes of lemons
- 15,000 boxes of oranges
- 9,000 boxes of grapefruit
- $190 million in revenue

Employing close to 3,000 workers and contributing nearly $2 million in taxes to fund public services for the county

—Arizona Agriculture Division

City West Bank
455 Canyon Avenue
Phoenix, Arizona 85007

March 21

Domingo Ramirez, Director
Arizona Agriculture Division
55 Sixth Avenue
Yuma, Arizona 85364

Dear Mr. Ramirez,

I read the recent report from the Arizona Agriculture Division summarizing Yuma County's success in the citrus industry. City West Bank wants to help the Arizona Agriculture Division you lead by expanding this industry further. We offer low-interest loans and provide expert advice through our connections to area chambers of commerce and to agricultural researchers at Arizona's state universities.

We recognize that agritourism in southwest Arizona is growing as a result of the popularity of farm tours, bird-watching, and scenic country lodging, but tourism is unlikely to surpass the strength of this region's agriculture production. We support farmers in many counties in Arizona and are poised to help the citrus growers in Yuma County. Together, we can accomplish great things.

Cordially,

Bianca Schreiber

Bianca Schreiber
Industry Investment Programs

Schreiber Named Vice President of National Investment Strategies

PHOENIX (January 19)—City West Bank announced today that Ms. Bianca Schreiber will be promoted to vice president of National Investment Strategies effective February 1. Ms. Schreiber currently oversees City West Bank's Industry Investment Programs, serving businesses throughout Arizona.

Bank President William Dolle cited

Ms. Schreiber's record of successful investment in the agricultural sector. "Ms. Schreiber's efforts in working with the director of the Arizona Agriculture Division have significantly boosted citrus production. Yuma County now produces as many grapefruit as it does oranges. Ms. Schreiber's keen insight will make her even more valuable to us in her new role," remarked Mr. Dolle.

186. What does the report indicate about the Yuma County region?

(A) It does not tax fruit that is sold there.
(B) Several types of fruit are cultivated there.
(C) More workers are needed for agricultural jobs.
(D) New types of fruit are being produced there.

187. What is one reason Ms. Schreiber writes to Mr. Ramirez?

(A) To explain the benefits of doing business together
(B) To clarify information in the report
(C) To remind him to make a loan payment
(D) To offer him advice from university agricultural researchers

188. According to the letter, why do tourists visit Yuma County?

(A) To shop at farmers markets
(B) To take pictures
(C) To enjoy theme parks
(D) To observe wildlife

189. What is suggested about Mr. Ramirez?

(A) He accepted Ms. Schreiber's proposal.
(B) He used to be employed by City West Bank.
(C) He is a member of the Yuma Chamber of Commerce.
(D) He recently bought a citrus farm.

190. For what accomplishment does Mr. Dolle praise Ms. Schreiber?

(A) Arranging the shipping of agricultural products
(B) Opening many City West Bank branch offices
(C) Helping to increase grapefruit production to 15,000 boxes
(D) Promoting Yuma County as a vacation destination

GO ON TO THE NEXT PAGE

https://www.unetcon.org/messages_audreysmith80

Unetcon – Message Center

Pending Invitations

From: Don Fitzpatrick
Branch Manager, Wilsonville Financial

To: Audrey Smith

Dear Audrey,

Please accept this invitation to connect professionally on Unetcon. I am a fellow Stonerook University graduate and am always looking to expand my network. In this case, I am also reaching out to see if you would be interested in joining the private Stonerook alumni group page to stay current with everything that our fellow graduates are up to. https://www.unetcon.org/private/stonerookugrads.

Kind regards,
Don Fitzpatrick

Accept Invitation	Ignore Invitation	Reply to Don

https://www.unetcon.org/private/stonerookugrads

Stonerook University Graduates

Check out the continued success and latest updates from Stonerook graduate Jonah Hilliard.

Current	Education	Professional
Director, Albright School of Business Founder and Director, Clear Path Contact Phone: 843-555-0139 E-mail: jhilliard@mccleese.edu Office: 403 Cordon Hall 530 N Kensington St. Charleston, SC 29425	Master of Business Administration – Turnbull University Bachelor of Arts in Education Studies – Stonerook University	Mr. Hilliard has led the Albright School of Business since 2017. Between 2007 and 2017, he carried out extensive research on emerging markets in West Africa while teaching business management in Lagos, Nigeria. Two years ago, he founded Clear Path, a business that advises students from around the globe who wish to pursue studies in the United States.

```
┌─────────────────────────────────────────────────────────────────┐
│                          *E-mail*                                 │
├─────────────────────────────────────────────────────────────────┤
│  From:      │ Audrey Smith <audrey_smith80@rapidonet.co.uk>       │
│  To:        │ Jonah Hilliard <jhilliard@mccleese.edu>             │
│  Date:      │ 19 September                                        │
│  Subject:   │ Referral                                            │
└─────────────────────────────────────────────────────────────────┘
```

Dear Jonah,

It has been a long time since we last talked. I recently came across your profile on Unetcon and saw that you are now leading the business school at McCleese! My research in Lagos ended last year, when I accepted a position as lead consultant at Pryor and Martell. I have been based here in Manchester ever since.

Congratulations to you on your most recent business venture—Clear Path already has quite an impressive reputation! I have a nephew who is interested in pursuing a degree in management information systems in the United States, and I was hoping I could put you both in touch so that he can take advantage of your new company's expertise in this area.

Best,

Audrey Smith

191. What does the invitation indicate about Unetcon?

(A) It is a business consulting firm.
(B) It is a financial services company.
(C) It is an employment agency.
(D) It is a professional networking Web site.

192. According to the Web page, where is Mr. Hilliard currently working?

(A) In Lagos
(B) In Charleston
(C) In Wilsonville
(D) In Manchester

193. What is suggested about Ms. Smith?

(A) She taught at Stonerook University.
(B) She works at Wilsonville Financial.
(C) She accepted Mr. Fitzpatrick's invitation.
(D) She plans to visit Lagos this year.

194. What do Ms. Smith and Mr. Hilliard have in common?

(A) They cofounded Clear Path.
(B) They are colleagues at Pryor and Martell.
(C) They were classmates at Turnbull University.
(D) They both conducted research in Nigeria.

195. What is one purpose of Ms. Smith's e-mail to Mr. Hilliard?

(A) To request his professional services
(B) To provide a professional reference
(C) To conduct an informational interview
(D) To apply for a position at Albright School of Business

GO ON TO THE NEXT PAGE

Modern Salon Academy
www.modernsalonacademy.ca

Established more than twenty years ago, Modern Salon Academy is Toronto's most recognized beauty school. The school offers hands-on training, small class sizes, and individualized instruction from leading industry professionals in the following programs.

• Cosmetology I: Gain foundational knowledge of haircutting and styling.

• Cosmetology II: Learn techniques in haircutting, styling, and colouring.

• Skin Care: Learn techniques in providing advanced skin-care treatments.

• Leadership: Study salon management, business operations, and compliance.

Modern Salon Academy is a winner of the International Cosmetology Society's prestigious Award of Excellence. It is no surprise, then, that over 95 percent of our graduates have gone on to successful careers in both the beauty and fashion industries.

Modern Salon Academy Expands in Ontario

TORONTO (23 August)—Modern Salon Academy, a highly regarded beauty school here in Toronto, is opening a regional campus in Oshawa. The school is already admitting students for classes that are scheduled to begin on 4 October.

Modern Salon Academy has had a substantial rise in enrollment over the past few years. Francine Dupuis, educational director of Modern Salon Academy, notes, "More than half our students live outside the city limits, so having a satellite campus makes perfect sense."

Modern Salon Academy offers professional training and certification for careers in a variety of areas, including hair care, skin care, and makeup. For more information about Modern Salon Academy, including admission requirements, fees, and academic calendars, visit www.modernsalonacademy.ca.

—Chrissy Jellen for the *Ontario Daily Times*

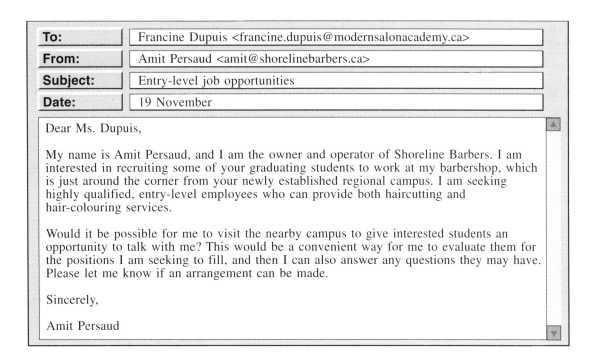

To:	Francine Dupuis <francine.dupuis@modernsalonacademy.ca>
From:	Amit Persaud <amit@shorelinebarbers.ca>
Subject:	Entry-level job opportunities
Date:	19 November

Dear Ms. Dupuis,

My name is Amit Persaud, and I am the owner and operator of Shoreline Barbers. I am interested in recruiting some of your graduating students to work at my barbershop, which is just around the corner from your newly established regional campus. I am seeking highly qualified, entry-level employees who can provide both haircutting and hair-colouring services.

Would it be possible for me to visit the nearby campus to give interested students an opportunity to talk with me? This would be a convenient way for me to evaluate them for the positions I am seeking to fill, and then I can also answer any questions they may have. Please let me know if an arrangement can be made.

Sincerely,

Amit Persaud

196. How does Modern Salon Academy teach its students?

(A) Through online courses
(B) Through academic lectures
(C) Through individualized training
(D) Through large-group discussions

197. According to the article, what has increased at Modern Salon Academy?

(A) The cost of tuition
(B) The number of students
(C) The requirements for admission
(D) The hours needed for certification

198. What is most likely true about Shoreline Barbers?

(A) It is located in Oshawa.
(B) It is opening a shop in Toronto.
(C) It was sold to Francine Dupuis.
(D) It has very affordable services.

199. Who would best meet Mr. Persaud's needs?

(A) Students in Cosmetology I
(B) Students in Cosmetology II
(C) Students in Skin Care
(D) Students in Leadership

200. According to the e-mail, what does Mr. Persaud want to do?

(A) Establish another business
(B) Retrain staff members
(C) Teach some classes
(D) Interview some students

Stop! This is the end of the test. If you finish before time is called, you may go back to Parts 5, 6, and 7 and check your work.

토익® 정기시험
기출문제집 4
1000

TEST 05
무료 동영상 강의

RC

기출 TEST
05

READING TEST

In the Reading test, you will read a variety of texts and answer several different types of reading comprehension questions. The entire Reading test will last 75 minutes. There are three parts, and directions are given for each part. You are encouraged to answer as many questions as possible within the time allowed.

You must mark your answers on the separate answer sheet. Do not write your answers in your test book.

PART 5

Directions: A word or phrase is missing in each of the sentences below. Four answer choices are given below each sentence. Select the best answer to complete the sentence. Then mark the letter (A), (B), (C), or (D) on your answer sheet.

101. After upgrading to Pro Data Whiz, our clients began ------- problems with spreadsheets.

    (A) has
    (B) had
    (C) have
    (D) having

102. Requests for additional days off are ------- by Ms. Chung in Human Resources.

    (A) approved
    (B) dropped
    (C) reached
    (D) reminded

103. The programmers have a list of changes ------- the next software update.

    (A) between
    (B) of
    (C) for
    (D) above

104. Let Farida Banquet Service ------- professional catering for your important corporate events.

    (A) providing
    (B) provide
    (C) provides
    (D) to provide

105. Using various innovative techniques, Boyd Industries has improved the ------- of its tiles.

    (A) closure
    (B) product
    (C) quality
    (D) method

106. ------- of all cosmetics are final, and refunds will not be given under any circumstances.

    (A) Sale
    (B) Sales
    (C) Sells
    (D) Selling

107. If you have already submitted your response, no ------- action is required.

    (A) bright
    (B) further
    (C) previous
    (D) average

108. Ms. Sieglak stated that the app design was based on ------- own research.

    (A) she
    (B) hers
    (C) her
    (D) herself

109. ------- the organization has doubled its outreach efforts, it has yet to see an increase in new clients.

(A) Until
(B) Because
(C) Although
(D) Therefore

110. Starting on October 8, ------- board of education meetings will be streamed live on the school district's Web site.

(A) all
(B) so
(C) that
(D) to

111. The hairstylists at Urbanite Salon have ------- experience working with a variety of hair products.

(A) considers
(B) considerable
(C) considerate
(D) considering

112. Both candidates are ------- suitable for the assistant manager position.

(A) permanently
(B) promptly
(C) equally
(D) gradually

113. With the acquisition of Bloom Circuit, Wellstrom Hardware has ------- expanded its offerings and services.

(A) greater
(B) greatness
(C) great
(D) greatly

114. Please note that file names should not ------- capital letters or spaces.

(A) differ
(B) contain
(C) match
(D) pick

115. The Sun-Tech ceiling fan has received more than 15,000 five-star reviews from ------- customers.

(A) satisfied
(B) checked
(C) adjusted
(D) allowed

116. Please ------- the Returns section of our Web site if you are unhappy with any part of your order.

(A) visit
(B) visits
(C) visited
(D) visiting

117. Ito Auto Group is offering excellent ------- on pre-owned vehicles this month.

(A) trips
(B) reasons
(C) customs
(D) deals

118. Product prices are influenced ------- such factors as consumer demand and retail competition.

(A) by
(B) under
(C) those
(D) nearly

119. Monmouth Enterprises will be ------- prefabricated houses online starting on April 1.

(A) predicting
(B) passing
(C) retaining
(D) marketing

120. All employees should familiarize ------- with the company's policies and procedures.

(A) their
(B) them
(C) theirs
(D) themselves

GO ON TO THE NEXT PAGE

121. Custom furniture orders require a 50 percent deposit ------- the time of the order.

(A) as
(B) off
(C) into
(D) at

122. We are planning a ------- for the Klemner Corporation's twentieth anniversary.

(A) celebration
(B) celebrated
(C) celebrity
(D) celebrate

123. Though she lacks political experience, Ms. Diaz has been ------- impressive in her first term as mayor.

(A) quite
(B) soon
(C) ever
(D) next

124. The university library usually acquires ------- copies of best-selling books to meet students' demand.

(A) multiply
(B) multiple
(C) multiples
(D) multiplicity

125. This year's conference tote bags were ------- donated by Etani Designs.

(A) generous
(B) generosity
(C) generously
(D) generosities

126. We will be holding a ------- on Friday to honor the 30-year engineering career of Mr. Kuan.

(A) record
(B) share
(C) reception
(D) place

127. Groove Background creates soothing playlists of instrumental music, ------- classical and jazz.

(A) instead
(B) including
(C) in addition
(D) indeed

128. Members of the finance department ------- to Mr. Chua's lecture on risk avoidance.

(A) to be invited
(B) inviting
(C) invite
(D) are invited

129. The board of trustees debated for hours ------- the revised hiring policies.

(A) during
(B) above
(C) over
(D) across

130. The participants closely ------- the fitness instructor's movements tend to learn the proper technique more quickly.

(A) imitate
(B) imitations
(C) imitative
(D) imitating

PART 6

Directions: Read the texts that follow. A word, phrase, or sentence is missing in parts of each text. Four answer choices for each question are given below the text. Select the best answer to complete the text. Then mark the letter (A), (B), (C), or (D) on your answer sheet.

Questions 131-134 refer to the following article.

Grocery Chain to Host Event

LEIGHTON (October 8)—Ohale Foods, one of the region's largest supermarket chains, is seeking to fill almost 100 open positions. For that reason, the company is holding a ------- event on October
131.
20. Job opportunities exist at all fourteen of Ohale's current stores. ------- , Ohale is seeking
132.
employees for its new Westside location, which is still under construction. ------- .
133.

Those who ------- the event should bring copies of their résumé to the Grand Ballroom of the
134.
Palace Suites Hotel between 10 A.M. and 7 P.M. No appointment is required.

131. (A) manufacturing
(B) hiring
(C) political
(D) sporting

132. (A) If not
(B) After all
(C) Additionally
(D) For example

133. (A) Its grand opening is scheduled for
mid-November.
(B) Most applicants had prior experience.
(C) Its appointment of Linda Okumu as
its CEO has surprised analysts.
(D) Local competitors cannot match its
prices.

134. (A) attending
(B) to attend
(C) attended
(D) are attending

GO ON TO THE NEXT PAGE

Questions 135-138 refer to the following instructions.

Thank you for your purchase of an Ajaz Water Filter Pitcher. It is a wonderful solution for water that tastes great! To improve the effectiveness of the Ajaz Water Filter Pitcher, we ------- priming the
   135.
filter before the first use. ------- . Then screw the filter clockwise into the lid of the pitcher until it fits
   136.
------- . As you use the pitcher, remember that ------- water flow is a signal that the filter is becoming
137.   **138.**
clogged and will need to be replaced soon.

135. (A) tried
     (B) recommend
     (C) consider
     (D) started

136. (A) Our filtration system will be
         redesigned within the next year.
     (B) Water use may be reduced by
         running your dishwasher less
         frequently.
     (C) To do this, run cool tap water through
         the filter for three minutes.
     (D) There are 150 liters of water in the
         main storage tank at all times.

137. (A) extremely
     (B) highly
     (C) tightly
     (D) steadily

138. (A) diminished
     (B) diminishes
     (C) diminish
     (D) diminishable

Returning merchandise

Abney Home Products is committed to providing outstanding service, and we guarantee the

------- of all the products in our catalog. If you are not satisfied with a purchase, call our customer
139.

service line at 339-555-0177 to request a return authorization code. The service agent

------- you for the invoice number from the package insert. ------- . Please be aware that Abney
140.   **141.**

Home Products is not ------- for postage on merchandise returns.
                      142.

---

139. (A) condition
    (B) object
    (C) explanation
    (D) preview

140. (A) asked
    (B) is asking
    (C) has asked
    (D) will ask

141. (A) Our employees have software training
        and are skilled at resolving problems.
    (B) To cancel a furniture delivery, please call
        within 24 hours of ordering.
    (C) When you send back the product, be
        sure to include the authorization code.
    (D) The catalog has sections for kitchen
        goods, lighting, appliances, and more.

142. (A) responsibly
    (B) responsible
    (C) responsibility
    (D) responsibleness

TEST 5

GO ON TO THE NEXT PAGE

Questions 143-146 refer to the following memo.

To: All Employees
From: Marina Papantonio, Safety Liaison
Date: November 12
Subject: Safety Training

It is time once again for our annual safety training workshop. This year, training will focus on digital safety measures, like avoiding scams and protecting against cyberattacks. Our technology experts already have installed new programs throughout our company's information system to reduce risk. ------- , we all need to understand how the programs work and what to do when a
143.
problem arises.

To accommodate ------- , several workshops will be conducted throughout the upcoming week.
144.
You can register for any one of these ------- on our company's intranet page. Just click on the link
145.
for "Safety Training."

------- . If you are unable to take part in any of the scheduled workshops for any reason, you must
146.
inform your supervisor.

143. (A) If so
     (B) However
     (C) Otherwise
     (D) In that case

144. (A) itself
     (B) his
     (C) whose
     (D) everyone

145. (A) sessions
     (B) positions
     (C) conferences
     (D) competitions

146. (A) Cyberattacks are on the rise.
     (B) The training is held each summer.
     (C) Please make every effort to sign up.
     (D) Last year's program was canceled.

PART 7

Directions: In this part you will read a selection of texts, such as magazine and newspaper articles, e-mails, and instant messages. Each text or set of texts is followed by several questions. Select the best answer for each question and mark the letter (A), (B), (C), or (D) on your answer sheet.

Questions 147-148 refer to the following advertisement.

Owl and Moon

Buy one mattress, and choose one of our beautiful rugs for free!

Use the following coupon code when you check out at owlandmoon.co.uk: ESSZRS4T.

Our mattresses are shipped directly to your home and usually arrive within one week. Try out a mattress for 90 days, and if you are not happy with it, send it back for a full refund. We also offer low-interest financing for two years on all our furniture.

---

147. What types of products are being advertised?

(A) Camping gear
(B) Household items
(C) Office equipment
(D) Automobile accessories

148. What is indicated about the company?

(A) It has been in business for two years.
(B) It accepts product returns.
(C) It has same-day delivery.
(D) It has a yearly sale.

GO ON TO THE NEXT PAGE

Questions 149-150 refer to the following e-mail.

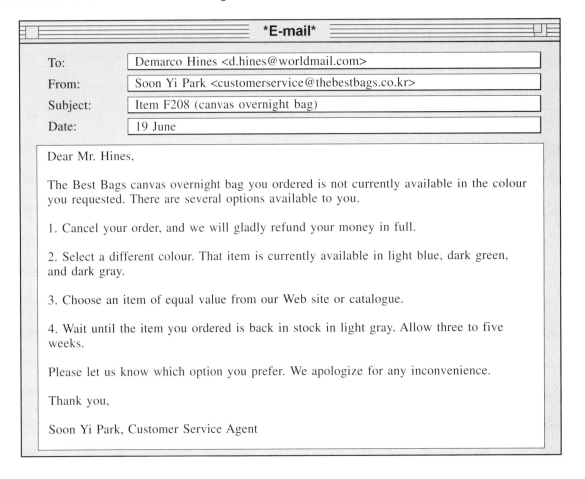

Dear Mr. Hines,

The Best Bags canvas overnight bag you ordered is not currently available in the colour you requested. There are several options available to you.

1. Cancel your order, and we will gladly refund your money in full.

2. Select a different colour. That item is currently available in light blue, dark green, and dark gray.

3. Choose an item of equal value from our Web site or catalogue.

4. Wait until the item you ordered is back in stock in light gray. Allow three to five weeks.

Please let us know which option you prefer. We apologize for any inconvenience.

Thank you,

Soon Yi Park, Customer Service Agent

---

149. What is the purpose of the e-mail?

(A) To confirm shipment of an order
(B) To acknowledge the return of an order
(C) To provide alternatives for an order
(D) To thank a customer for placing an order

150. What color bag is currently NOT available?

(A) The light blue one
(B) The dark green one
(C) The dark gray one
(D) The light gray one

Questions 151-152 refer to the following text-message chain.

Christie Moroff (9:47 A.M.)
Good morning, Ren. I just stopped by your office.

Ren Nomura (9:48 A.M.)
Then you already know that I am not there today.

Christie Moroff (9:48 A.M.)
Yes, your new office mate—I can't remember her name—told me that you just started working remotely on Tuesdays. I was looking for some empty binders.

Ren Nomura (9:49 A.M.)
That's Cheryl. I thought you had already met her. Are there any binders in the supply closet?

Christie Moroff (9:50 A.M.)
No, I just looked. Frank has ordered some more, but they won't be in until next week. I need two or three of them now.

Ren Nomura (9:51 A.M.)
Check with Cheryl. She is really helpful.

Christie Moroff (9:52 A.M.)
OK. I will.

151. What is suggested about Mr. Nomura?

(A) He does not usually work on Tuesdays.
(B) He shares an office with Ms. Moroff.
(C) He recently purchased office supplies.
(D) He works off-site one day a week.

152. At 9:51 A.M., what does Mr. Nomura most likely mean when he writes, "Check with Cheryl"?

(A) Cheryl may have extra binders.
(B) Cheryl must approve a purchase.
(C) Cheryl will be able to locate Frank.
(D) Cheryl knows when a delivery will arrive.

GO ON TO THE NEXT PAGE

Cortica Bank

Please fill out the following form to open a new bank account.

Is this your first account with Cortica Bank? __ Yes **X** No

Existing account number (if applicable): 190-37580

New account type: __ Chequing **X** Savings __ Investment

Name: Frances Wilkes

Mailing address: 17 Jones Street
North Sydney NSW 2060

Phone number: (02) 7010 8624

E-mail address: fwilkes@myemail.com.au

Initial deposit amount (minimum $500): $1,500

Would you like to sign up for electronic communications? __ Yes **X** No

If you select "Yes," we will contact you via voice mail, e-mail, or text.
If you select "No," you will receive monthly paper statements in the mail.

Please note that accounts take up to two business days to be established. Your funds will be available after this period. You will receive your debit card in the mail in up to five business days.

---

153. What is indicated about Ms. Wilkes?

(A) She has another account with Cortica Bank.
(B) She plans to open an investment account.
(C) She has lost a debit card.
(D) She placed an order for checks.

154. How will the bank most likely contact Ms. Wilkes?

(A) By e-mail
(B) By text message
(C) By telephone
(D) By letter

Construction Superintendent
Jones-Richmond Construction (JRC)

Founded 25 years ago, JRC is a full-service general contractor serving clients throughout Winnipeg and the surrounding area.

Responsibilities:
- Report to senior project manager
- Manage on-site construction activities
- Ensure compliance with safety regulations
- Negotiate purchases and contracts
- Establish construction schedules

Qualifications:
- Minimum five years of commercial construction experience
- Willingness to travel to job sites daily (usually within a 50-kilometre radius)
- Strong written communication skills

To apply, submit a résumé and cover letter through www.jrc.ca/apply.

155. What is suggested about Jones-Richmond Construction?

(A) It is a new company.
(B) It has won industry awards for its work.
(C) It is based in Winnipeg.
(D) It specializes in home construction projects.

156. What is NOT listed as a responsibility of the construction superintendent?

(A) Setting schedules
(B) Training inexperienced workers
(C) Participating in contract discussions
(D) Ensuring worker safety

157. According to the advertisement, what must a successful job applicant have?

(A) A technical certification
(B) A reference letter from a former employer
(C) Senior management experience
(D) The ability to visit construction sites each workday

GO ON TO THE NEXT PAGE

To:	All Sledgehammer Gym Staff
From:	Lucas Sledge
Date:	September 15
Subject:	Payroll changes
Attachment:	📎 Form

Dear Staff,

Thanks to your dedicated work, word of our little gym has spread. Over the past twelve months, enrollment has significantly increased and so has our teaching staff. Although this growth is wonderful, having to process the payroll by myself has become rather burdensome. Therefore, I have contracted Trumbull and Company to provide direct deposit of your wages into your bank accounts. — [1] —. Consequently, you no longer need to deposit your paycheck yourself. Also, you will now be able to get your pay stubs and tax information online. — [2] —.

To allow for these changes, I am asking everyone to provide me with the necessary banking details. Please complete the attached form and bring it to the office with a voided check no later than September 25. — [3] —. The new process will take effect in October. — [4] —. Please let me know if you have any questions.

Take care,

Lucas

158. What is mentioned as a benefit of the new payment system?

(A) It will reduce Mr. Sledge's workload.
(B) It will include more staff involvement.
(C) It will simplify tax collection.
(D) It will result in fewer payment errors.

159. What does Mr. Sledge ask employees to do?

(A) Update their contact information
(B) Submit ideas on how to improve the gym
(C) Provide information about their bank account
(D) Sign up for a professional development class

160. In which of the positions marked [1], [2], [3], and [4] does the following sentence best belong?

"If I am not around, please see my assistant."

(A) [1]
(B) [2]
(C) [3]
(D) [4]

Questions 161-163 refer to the following article.

Aussie Coffee Fair This Weekend

SYDNEY (4 June)—Coffee will be the main attraction this weekend at the Aussie Coffee Fair hosted by Homewares, the country's top kitchen appliance manufacturer. The event will be held at the Harbour Expo Centre.

The two-day event will feature a variety of coffee-oriented presentations by coffee growers and roasters, food writers, makers of kitchen equipment, and chefs. Foods and beverages will be available to view, taste, and buy at booths throughout the centre.

Sessions will feature demonstrations on cooking with coffee and tips for brewing the best cup of coffee, as well as information on nonfood uses for coffee. In addition, culinary experts will be on hand to meet with coffee enthusiasts for discussions designed to help them create a true coffeehouse experience in their own homes.

Entry to the Aussie Coffee Fair is free. However, registration is required as space is limited. For information and to register online, go to www.aussiecoffeefair.com.

161. The word "top" in paragraph 1, line 3, is closest in meaning to

(A) only
(B) leading
(C) highest
(D) modern

162. Who will NOT be conducting informational presentations at the fair?

(A) Chefs
(B) Coffee growers
(C) Equipment makers
(D) Coffeehouse owners

163. What must people do to attend the fair?

(A) Sign up on a Web site
(B) Call to make a reservation
(C) Buy a ticket at the event location
(D) Present a Homewares product receipt

GO ON TO THE NEXT PAGE

Questions 164-167 refer to the following e-mail.

From:	melissa@grandgrainsbakery.com
To:	elinorotero@webmail.com
Date:	October 28
Re:	Desserts

Dear Ms. Otero,

I just followed up with our baker about your request to have an assortment of desserts instead of one large cake for the party you are hosting at your home on November 7. We suggest ordering three dessert pieces per person. The cost for three desserts is between $10 and $12 per person. Our most popular desserts are the mini cheesecakes, the berry tartlets, and the brownies.

I know you are using a separate caterer for the lunch, and they will help serve and clean up after the party. You also mentioned that you were considering whether to put the dessert table in your backyard or inside your house. Just keep in mind that if you order the cheesecakes, they should not be left out for more than two hours. If you give us very specific instructions about where to set up the desserts, our staff can leave them in the appropriate place without disturbing the party.

Once you make your dessert choices, simply let us know how many guests you expect, and we can take care of the rest.

Melissa Luhya
Grand Grains Bakery

164. What is the purpose of the e-mail?

(A) To advertise some new pastries
(B) To present options for an event
(C) To recommend serving a larger cake
(D) To request payment on an order

165. What does Ms. Luhya indicate about the mini cheesecakes?

(A) They are the most expensive dessert.
(B) They are available in several flavors.
(C) They should not be unrefrigerated for a long time.
(D) They cannot be ordered in larger sizes.

166. The word "disturbing" in paragraph 2, line 6, is closest in meaning to

(A) interrupting
(B) frightening
(C) rearranging
(D) moving

167. What information does Ms. Luhya request from Ms. Otero?

(A) A street address
(B) An approximate budget
(C) The name of a caterer
(D) The number of guests

To:	Cheryl Futrel <cfutrel@zephyrmail.com>
From:	Lydia Matsuda <service@candella.com>
Date:	June 9
Subject:	Home decorating

Dear Ms. Futrel,

Thank you for your interest in Candella Interior Design. — [1] —. We are proud to claim that we are the oldest and most successful online design consulting company in the region. We welcome you as a new client. — [2] —. From modest country homes to urban apartments, we do it all.

We understand from your original inquiry that you intend to sell your apartment soon and are primarily interested in how best to present it to prospective buyers. Here's how our design services work: the first step is completing an online questionnaire. — [3] —. Next, you will be matched with an online professional interior designer who can help you with all choices for paint colors, window treatments, and floor coverings. You will receive a room layout plan and a personalized list of ideas for furniture and accessories, with all products available for purchase online. — [4] —. As a special bonus, from now until July 1 our online retail partners have agreed to offer a 10 percent discount on products purchased through our links.

Finally, you will be glad to learn that we charge not by the hour but by the room for our design ideas, with the average price being about $275 per room.

We look forward to hearing from you and working with you soon.

Sincerely,

Lydia Matsuda

168. What is indicated about Candella Interior Design?

(A) Its main office is located in a major city.
(B) Its staff members visit clients' houses.
(C) It has been in business longer than its competitors have been.
(D) It is a family-run business.

169. Why does Ms. Futrel want to redecorate her apartment?

(A) To prepare for a visit from relatives
(B) To make it attractive to potential buyers
(C) To replace furniture that she dislikes
(D) To use it as an example for her clients

170. What will happen on July 1 ?

(A) Room accessories will be distributed.
(B) Work will begin on a new project.
(C) The client list will be expanded.
(D) A special offer will end.

171. In which of the positions marked [1], [2], [3], and [4] does the following sentence best belong?

"The answers will give us a sense of your taste and requirements."

(A) [1]
(B) [2]
(C) [3]
(D) [4]

GO ON TO THE NEXT PAGE

TEST 5

Questions 172-175 refer to the following text-message chain.

Darius Wilkins (11:09 A.M.)
Hi, Ms. Clarke. This is Darius from Roto Bicycle. I promised to check with you before servicing your bicycle.

Lauren Clarke (11:14 A.M.)
Thanks. So, what do you think?

Darius Wilkins (11:15 A.M.)
In addition to the regular maintenance service, I suggest a drivetrain cleaning and new brake mechanisms.

Lauren Clarke (11:16 A.M.)
OK. What does that come to?

Darius Wilkins (11:18 A.M.)
An extensive maintenance service, which includes the same gear and brake adjustments as a regular maintenance service, plus the drivetrain cleaning, is $140. Add $70 for two new brake mechanisms and pads and another $30 for labor charges. So it should come to around $240 altogether. Shall I move forward?

Lauren Clarke (11:21 A.M.)
Wow! That much?

Darius Wilkins (11:22 A.M.)
Especially with that major bicycle race you have ahead of you.

Lauren Clarke (11:24 A.M.)
I know. I guess we have to do it. Please let me know when it's ready.

172. Why did Mr. Wilkins contact Ms. Clarke?

    (A) To recommend a new product
    (B) To discuss a scheduling problem
    (C) To confirm that a bicycle part has been ordered
    (D) To request permission to do some work

173. What most likely cost about $30 ?

    (A) New braking mechanisms
    (B) Labor charges
    (C) Basic maintenance service
    (D) Drivetrain cleaning

174. At 11:21 A.M., what does Ms. Clarke imply when she writes, "That much"?

    (A) She did not realize how busy Mr. Wilkins is.
    (B) The pressure in her tires was surprisingly low.
    (C) The cost of repairs seems high.
    (D) Repairing the bike will take more time than she expected.

175. What is suggested about Ms. Clarke?

    (A) She prefers to pay with cash.
    (B) She is shopping for a new bicycle.
    (C) She is unhappy with the quality of a repair.
    (D) She will soon compete in a bicycle race.

GO ON TO THE NEXT PAGE

E-Mail Message

To: Cassie Raferty <cassie@mailcurrent.ie>
From: Youssef Zimri <zimri@zimrimechanical.ie>
Subject: Following up
Date: 12 September
Attachment: cmcclinic

Dear Ms. Raferty,

I am very happy with your work so far. Your suggestion to add photos from our archive certainly dressed up the "Company History" page. The help-wanted pop-up bubble on the home page also looks good. Hopefully, it will attract applicants with mechanical experience.

I'd like you to add one more project to our "Portfolio" page. We have finally finished replacing the plumbing and heating systems at Clary Medical Centre's satellite clinic in Galway. It was a challenging job, and I'm proud of our results. The attachment contains photos and a short description of what we did there.

Sincerely,

Youssef Zimri
Owner, Zimri Mechanical

---

https://www.clarymedicalcentre.ie

| About | **News** | Staff | Contact Us |

Clinic opening soon

We have repurposed 47 High Street, Galway, into a satellite medical clinic and will celebrate with a grand opening party on Friday, 28 October. Remarks by Medical Director Dr. Celia O'Leary and local elected officials will begin promptly at 1:00 P.M., followed by a ribbon-cutting ceremony and tours until 4:30 P.M.

Thirty miles from the Clary Medical Centre's main campus, the Clary Clinic is housed in the historic Brandmore shoe factory, which closed more than two decades ago. During renovations, care was taken to maintain the exterior's nineteenth-century architectural features. The clinic's interior boasts eighteen examination rooms, a state-of-the-art x-ray facility, private offices for patient consultations, and a lab for processing patient samples.

Clinic staff will begin seeing patients on Tuesday, 1 November. To make an appointment, please call 020 915 1424.

176. Who most likely is Ms. Raferty?

(A) A job recruiter
(B) A plumbing contractor
(C) A Galway historian
(D) A Web-site designer

177. What is indicated about Mr. Zimri?

(A) He is trying to recruit an assistant architect.
(B) He is a member of Clary Medical Centre's board of directors.
(C) He is pleased with his firm's work at a former shoe factory.
(D) He is waiting for Dr. O'Leary's feedback on a portfolio.

178. According to the Web page, what will happen at the grand opening event?

(A) Government officials will be in attendance.
(B) Sandwiches will be served.
(C) New building plans will be revealed.
(D) Former patients will be interviewed.

179. On the Web page, the word "maintain" in paragraph 2, line 3, is closest in meaning to

(A) assert
(B) heal
(C) support
(D) preserve

180. According to the Web page, what is NOT part of the Clary Clinic?

(A) A medical laboratory
(B) A pharmacy
(C) Medical imaging equipment
(D) Offices for clinicians

GO ON TO THE NEXT PAGE

Questions 181-185 refer to the following form and e-mail.

PURCHASE ORDER

Pirate's Bounty Seafood
11 Harbor Street
Charlottetown, Prince Edward Island, C1A 0A5

2 October
Purchase Order: 5338

VENDOR	SHIP TO
Rochette's Commercial Refrigeration 2175 Lyons Avenue Guelph, Ontario, N1C 0A1 519-555-0112	Pirate's Bounty Seafood 11 Harbor Street Charlottetown, Prince Edward Island, C1A 0A5 Attn: Lenore Okiya 782-555-0145

ITEM NUMBER	DESCRIPTION	QUANTITY	PRICE	TOTAL
BF550	Blizzard walk-in freezer	1	$6,400.00	$6,400.00
	Features: 1.5m x 2m x 2.5m, adjustable shelves, aluminum flooring, galvanized steel panels			

COMMENTS OR SPECIAL INSTRUCTIONS		
Restaurant expanding. Need unit by 17 November.	SUBTOTAL	$6,400.00
	TAX	$960.00
	GRAND TOTAL	$7,360.00

To:	Lenore Okiya <l.okiya@piratesbounty.ca>
From:	Shaliya Umuma <customerservice@rochettesrefrigeration.ca>
Date:	3 October
Subject:	Purchase Order 5338

Dear Ms. Okiya,

We received your purchase order for the Blizzard walk-in freezer. Unfortunately, the model you requested is on back order and will not be available for three months. We regret the inconvenience and would like to offer you some options.

I can offer you the Blizzard BF600, which measures 2m x 2.5m x 3m, at the discounted price of $6,900 plus tax. It comes with the same features as the item you ordered. Alternately, we have a refurbished BF400 in stock. It's the same size as the BF550; however, while the BF550 includes a remote control for setting the temperature, the BF400 has a wall-mounted device for that purpose. The BF400 unit comes with a two-year warranty. It is priced at $5,600 plus tax.

Please let me know how you wish to proceed. Just reply to this e-mail.

Shaliya Umuma, Customer Service Manager

181. Why does Pirate's Bounty Seafood need to purchase new equipment?

(A) Its current refrigerator stopped working.
(B) The warranty on its current refrigerator has expired.
(C) The restaurant is increasing in size.
(D) The restaurant is moving to a new location.

182. What is the problem with the item Ms. Okiya ordered?

(A) It was lost during shipping.
(B) It has been discontinued.
(C) It is temporarily out of stock.
(D) It has a damaged control panel.

183. What is NOT a feature of the Blizzard BF600 ?

(A) It has a fast-freeze switch.
(B) It has adjustable shelves.
(C) It has aluminum flooring.
(D) It has galvanized steel panels.

184. According to the e-mail, what does the BF400 model come with?

(A) A user manual
(B) A remote control
(C) A warranty
(D) A tax waiver

185. In the e-mail, the word "Just" in paragraph 3, line 1, is closest in meaning to

(A) immediately
(B) kindly
(C) shortly
(D) simply

GO ON TO THE NEXT PAGE

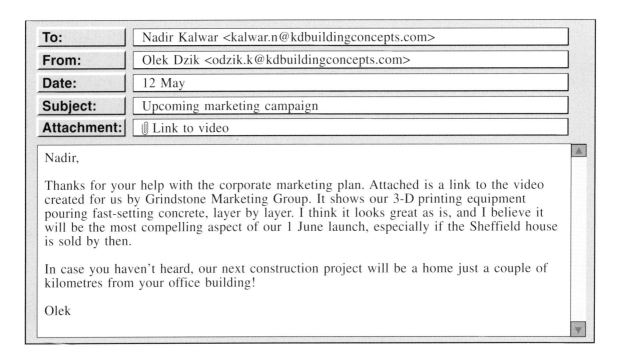

Fifth Annual International Marketing Society Conference
23–25 October, Grant Hotel and Conference Centre, London

Day 1:

Time	Description	Venue
7:00 A.M. to 8:00 A.M.	Morning Social: Complimentary omelets, pastries, coffee, tea	Mezzanine
8:30 A.M. to 10:00 A.M.	Marcos Secada, founder and CEO, Grindstone Marketing Group	Room 2
10:30 A.M. to noon	Claire Song, business columnist and best-selling author	Room 10
12:30 P.M. to 2:00 P.M.	Lunch (ticket purchase required)	Alexander Ballroom

To:	Nadir Kalwar <kalwar.n@kdbuildingconcepts.com>
From:	Olek Dzik <odzik.k@kdbuildingconcepts.com>
Date:	12 May
Subject:	Upcoming marketing campaign
Attachment:	📎 Link to video

Nadir,

Thanks for your help with the corporate marketing plan. Attached is a link to the video created for us by Grindstone Marketing Group. It shows our 3-D printing equipment pouring fast-setting concrete, layer by layer. I think it looks great as is, and I believe it will be the most compelling aspect of our 1 June launch, especially if the Sheffield house is sold by then.

In case you haven't heard, our next construction project will be a home just a couple of kilometres from your office building!

Olek

House Constructed Using 3-D Technology For Sale

SHEFFIELD (15 May)—An international construction firm specializing in innovative building technologies has completed one of Britain's first 3-D printed houses. The new structure is located on Morgan Road in Sheffield.

KD Building Concepts took less than two weeks to execute the first phase of the project, which entailed printing the concrete walls and installing the electrical and plumbing systems, according to company president Olek Dzik. In just two months, the fully landscaped house with two bedrooms and two bathrooms was ready for market.

"Labour costs were cut in half thanks to 3-D printing technology," said Mr. Dzik, whose company has offices in France and Germany, as well as in Sheffield. "At KD Building Concepts, we are committed to building homes that are both affordable and luxurious."

The house was listed for sale this week by a local real estate broker. The asking price is £150,000.

Next on the horizon for KD Building Concepts is the construction of a home in Hamburg, Germany.

186. What is mentioned on the schedule?

(A) Free breakfast is available for conference participants.
(B) The conference is five days long.
(C) A keynote address will be delivered at the end of the first day.
(D) A featured speaker has been replaced.

187. According to the schedule, what will happen at 10:30 A.M.?

(A) A writer will give a presentation.
(B) Coffee will be served in the lobby.
(C) Lunch tickets will be sold in room 10.
(D) A revised schedule will be distributed.

188. What can be concluded about Mr. Dzik?

(A) He wants a marketing video to be shortened.
(B) He has asked Mr. Kalwar for a new marketing plan.
(C) He organized a conference in London.
(D) He hired Mr. Secada's firm for a project.

189. What is suggested about Mr. Kalwar?

(A) He is a videographer.
(B) He works in Germany.
(C) He is planning to buy a house in Sheffield.
(D) He specializes in construction materials.

190. What does the article indicate about the house created with a 3-D printer?

(A) It cost £150,000 to build.
(B) It was finished in two months.
(C) It will be landscaped next week.
(D) Its bedrooms are all the same size.

GO ON TO THE NEXT PAGE

Questions 191-195 refer to the following job posting, flyer, and article.

Gallery manager at Richard Lahiri Gallery in Cromwood

Applicants for this full-time position must have experience in retail art with an established history of successfully attracting patrons interested in purchasing original works of art. Experience managing a social media account is also desired. The position will be primarily on-site; however, some remote hours can be scheduled. Candidates must be available to start work on or before April 1. Qualified applicants should contact gallery director Richard Lahiri at rlahiri@richardlahirigallery.com.

Summer Scene Arts Program

Starting on May 1, five art galleries in Cromwood will be hosting open houses every Friday from May through August. Come enjoy live music, refreshments, artist talks, and more on the Cromwood boardwalk. Activities start at 4:00 P.M. and continue until 9:30 P.M., rain or shine. Participating galleries are listed below.

**Rita Blake Art • Siitva Gallery • Richard Lahiri Gallery
Patricia Dolivo Painting • Ashland Pottery and Crafts**

Funded by the Cromwood City Council and Regents Bank

Summer Activities in Middleton County
Compiled by Lisa Yu-Seaver

Cromwood Art Nights
Residents of Elmhurst, Melbridge, and Cromwood are invited to explore the local art scene in Cromwood this summer. The five galleries on the boardwalk overlooking the Wye River are holding special events each Friday as part of the Summer Scene Arts Program. This Friday, Richard Lahiri and his gallery manager, Geetu Gelang, will use a giant screen to demonstrate software for creating virtual art. The event will also feature craft vendors, food trucks, and live music. See www.cromwood.gov/things-to-do for more information.

Movies in Brady Park
The popular summer movie series in Herrontown returns on June 16! Each Saturday evening, a classic film will be projected on Brady Park's Grand Lawn. Bring your picnic basket and a blanket and get comfortable! The schedule of films is available at www.bradypark.org/activities.

191. What is stated in the job posting about the managerial position?

(A) It is fully on-site.
(B) It is Mr. Lahiri's current job.
(C) It requires sales experience.
(D) It will be part-time until April 1.

192. According to the flyer, what will happen on May 1 ?

(A) A public arts program will begin.
(B) A city council meeting will take place.
(C) A new art gallery will hold a grand opening.
(D) Regents Bank will be closed for the day.

193. What is suggested about Ashland Pottery and Crafts?

(A) It is located near the Wye River.
(B) It specializes in virtual art.
(C) It hosts pottery workshops every Saturday.
(D) It is sponsoring a summer movie series.

194. What is suggested about Geetu Gelang?

(A) She is a local musician.
(B) She will be selling her crafts on May 1.
(C) She plans to start a social media account.
(D) She was recently hired by the Richard Lahiri Gallery.

195. According to the article, where is Brady Park located?

(A) In Cromwood
(B) In Elmhurst
(C) In Herrontown
(D) In Melbridge

GO ON TO THE NEXT PAGE

Senano Designs Buys Gendalla in $60 Million Deal

LOS ANGELES (March 20)—Fashion powerhouse Senano Designs announced on Wednesday that it had acquired Gendalla, an up-and-coming luxury brand. The acquisition is part of Senano's plan to supplement its clothing products with a line of designer watches. Over the next two years, the company has further plans to expand its offerings to include fragrances and luggage. Lina Pacheco, Senano's chief executive officer, said that such expansion is necessary to keep up and compete with other international fashion houses. Although based in Los Angeles, in recent years Senano has opened offices in Philadelphia, Chicago, and Miami. Ms. Pacheco says she was unfamiliar with Gendalla products until a year ago, when she saw one of their ads in an automobile magazine. "The products have a distinctive, modern style," Ms. Pacheco said, "which will go well with Senano's trendsetting clothes."

MEMO

From: Oscar Johansen, Accounting department
To: All Gendalla employees
Date: March 22
Subject: Travel expense policy
Attachment: Policy

I have attached a copy of Senano's policy on travel expenses, which will go into effect when we officially become employees of Senano on March 31.

Note that Senano's policy is more restrictive than Gendalla's policy in several ways. For example, employees will no longer have one month to submit expense reports. However, the new policy will make some processes much easier: specifically, Senano's requirements for submitting expenses under $50 are simpler than those under current Gendalla policy.

Carlie Dawson, an accounting director who works at Senano's headquarters, will come to our New York office to lead an information session about this and other policy-related changes on Thursday, March 28, at 2:00 P.M. I strongly encourage you to attend.

```
┌──────────────────────────────────────────────────────────────┐
│                     Senano Designs                            │
│                   Travel Expense Policy                        │
│                                                                │
│  • To be reimbursed for work-related travel, employees must    │
│    submit a travel request at least two weeks before a trip,   │
│    listing the reason for travel and estimating all expenses.  │
│  • Original receipts must be submitted for expenses above $50. │
│    Any expenses below that do not require the submission of    │
│    original receipts.                                          │
│  • All receipts and expense reports must be submitted within   │
│    three weeks after a trip is completed. Expenses submitted   │
│    after this time will require the approval of the department │
│    head.                                                       │
│                                                                │
│                                                      Page 1    │
└──────────────────────────────────────────────────────────────┘
```

196. What does Gendalla mainly produce?

(A) Watches
(B) Luggage
(C) Clothing
(D) Fragrances

197. According to the article, why is Senano Designs acquiring Gendalla?

(A) To sell products at a lower price
(B) To expand its social media presence
(C) To offer a more diverse range of products
(D) To address declining sales in some cities

198. What are Gendalla's employees invited to do on March 28 ?

(A) Suggest changes to a travel policy
(B) Attend a meeting in the afternoon
(C) Tour Senano's corporate headquarters
(D) Make an appointment with an accountant

199. Where is Ms. Dawson's office?

(A) In New York
(B) In Chicago
(C) In Philadelphia
(D) In Los Angeles

200. How is Gendalla's current travel expense policy likely different from Senano's?

(A) A receipt must be submitted for every expense.
(B) Preapproval must be obtained for expenses over $50.
(C) The expense report must be signed by a manager.
(D) Employees can submit their expense reports jointly.

Stop! This is the end of the test. If you finish before time is called, you may go back to Parts 5, 6, and 7 and check your work.

토익®정기시험
기출문제집 4
1000

TEST 06
무료 동영상 강의

RC

기출 TEST
06

READING TEST

In the Reading test, you will read a variety of texts and answer several different types of reading comprehension questions. The entire Reading test will last 75 minutes. There are three parts, and directions are given for each part. You are encouraged to answer as many questions as possible within the time allowed.

You must mark your answers on the separate answer sheet. Do not write your answers in your test book.

PART 5

Directions: A word or phrase is missing in each of the sentences below. Four answer choices are given below each sentence. Select the best answer to complete the sentence. Then mark the letter (A), (B), (C), or (D) on your answer sheet.

---

101. The new policy allows employees to set ------- own working hours under certain conditions.

(A) they
(B) their
(C) theirs
(D) themselves

102. Based on last year's data, Paik Company increased its sales projections ------- the current year.

(A) when
(B) for
(C) if
(D) or

103. Harbison's Department Store interviews applicants ------- standard business hours.

(A) among
(B) beside
(C) during
(D) onto

104. Takealong Industries' commercial propane heaters deliver more warmth to ------- areas.

(A) wideness
(B) widen
(C) wider
(D) widely

105. By switching to new project-management software, the editorial team has ------- improved its publication processes.

(A) great
(B) greatly
(C) greater
(D) greatest

106. The search committee ------- three candidates for the chief executive position.

(A) nominating
(B) nomination
(C) has nominated
(D) has been nominated

107. ------- a two-month delay, new carpeting was installed in the east conference room.

(A) Additionally
(B) Although
(C) After
(D) Furthermore

108. To boost -------, the Makeup Artist Academy is offering a free starter kit to new students.

(A) enroll
(B) enrolled
(C) enrolling
(D) enrollment

109. Because Lectula Furniture Company ------- its delivery times, we were able to set a firm opening date for the new hotel.

(A) guarantees
(B) advises
(C) requires
(D) delays

110. The computer technician was very ------- but was not able to solve my problem.

(A) friendly
(B) neutral
(C) possible
(D) frequent

111. To make room for conference attendees, ------- visitors to the office building should use the rear parking area tomorrow.

(A) regular
(B) regularly
(C) regularize
(D) regularity

112. Employees must wear their security badge in a way that is ------- visible when in the building.

(A) clearly
(B) recently
(C) evenly
(D) secretly

113. Ms. Phon wanted to attend the gallery opening; -------, the inclement weather made that impossible.

(A) therefore
(B) following
(C) however
(D) for example

114. Giving leadership tasks to warehouse package handlers often ------- them to work more productively.

(A) adopts
(B) reinforces
(C) motivates
(D) attracts

115. Kaybing Construction works ------- on large commercial projects in the Newfoundland area.

(A) exclusively
(B) exclusive
(C) exclusivity
(D) exclusives

116. Carly Logan plans -------, so Alan Zill has volunteered to be the stamp club's next treasurer.

(A) resigning
(B) to resign
(C) resigns
(D) to have resigned

117. Although the housing market slowed ------- the summer months, sales began to pick up again in the autumn.

(A) apart
(B) even
(C) only
(D) over

118. To remain fully functional, the exercise machines need to be cleaned -------.

(A) rather
(B) almost
(C) routinely
(D) openly

119. The extended warranty is good for ten years or 100,000 miles, ------- comes first.

(A) whoever
(B) either
(C) whichever
(D) another

120. Atlantic Grocers must offer online shopping options or ------- losing customers to other supermarkets.

(A) risk
(B) protect
(C) cancel
(D) hold

GO ON TO THE NEXT PAGE

121. ------ client is assigned to a personal financial adviser to whom inquiries should be addressed.

(A) Each
(B) All
(C) Some
(D) Most

122. Mr. Singh wants to form a ------ to explore some employee reward programs.

(A) supervisor
(B) suggestion
(C) notification
(D) committee

123. Please provide your phone number ------ the delivery driver needs to contact you.

(A) whereas
(B) despite
(C) if not
(D) in case

124. ------ of Pondview Tower are required to make rent payments on or before the first day of every month.

(A) Owners
(B) Buyers
(C) Tourists
(D) Tenants

125. Likoni Hospitality Group, one of Mombasa's largest employers, has a ------ impact on the local economy.

(A) considerably
(B) considerable
(C) considering
(D) consideration

126. ------ best sellers, Booksters offers a wide selection of classics and biographies.

(A) Besides
(B) Somewhat
(C) Whose
(D) Becoming

127. New food regulations require all Dean's Burgers packaging to contain the notice that ------ undercooked meat can be harmful.

(A) consumer
(B) consumption
(C) consumes
(D) consuming

128. Each Genutria snack bar contains as much protein as two eggs, with none ------ the fat and cholesterol.

(A) of
(B) by
(C) out
(D) minus

129. Fisko eyeglass frames come in various ------, including round, square, and oval.

(A) sights
(B) methods
(C) shapes
(D) materials

130. The CEO wants a greater portion of next year's budget ------ to research and development.

(A) allocated
(B) imprinted
(C) economized
(D) rationalized

PART 6

Directions: Read the texts that follow. A word, phrase, or sentence is missing in parts of each text. Four answer choices for each question are given below the text. Select the best answer to complete the text. Then mark the letter (A), (B), (C), or (D) on your answer sheet.

Questions 131-134 refer to the following advertisement.

Estella Guitar Lessons: Play with the Best

Whether you play acoustic guitar ------- electric, taking lessons with an Estella Guitar teacher is the
          131.

best way to improve your ability. With years of experience crafting playing techniques, -------
           132.

qualified instructors can tailor lessons to focus on the skills you want to fine-tune. Receive a

customized learning plan to set goals and overcome the challenges that cause many players to

get discouraged. ------- . An Estella Guitar teacher will help boost your confidence.
    133.

At Estella Guitar, we believe that playing music is a way of expressing yourself. ------- , we will help
           134.

you go beyond the familiar chords and riffs to develop your own identity as a musician. Ready to

get started? Visit www.estellaguitar.com/lessons to get matched with the right instructor for you!

---

131. (A) is
    (B) or
    (C) likely
    (D) from

132. (A) our
    (B) ourselves
    (C) ours
    (D) us

133. (A) Contact a technician for questions
        about repairs.
    (B) A high-quality instrument will help you
        to perform at your best.
    (C) The best resource for you as a
        learner is an expert to guide your
        progress.
    (D) It took them several years to master
        their instruments.

134. (A) So far
    (B) With that in mind
    (C) On a different note
    (D) At that point

GO ON TO THE NEXT PAGE

Questions 135-138 refer to the following policy.

In-home delivery takes approximately one week after an order is shipped from our warehouse.

The actual time may vary based on the location of your ------- and your availability for accepting the
                                                            135.

item. Vernico Furniture will work with a carrier ------- an appointment that is convenient for you.
                                                    136.

Typical hours are Monday through Friday between 8 A.M. and 5 P.M., ------- evening appointments
                                                                      137.

can often be arranged. Upon arrival at your home, the item will be placed in the location you

desire. ------- . Assembly is included as well.
        138.

135. (A) garden
     (B) records
     (C) residence
     (D) organization

136. (A) to schedule
     (B) is scheduling
     (C) as a schedule
     (D) that scheduled

137. (A) if so
     (B) when
     (C) though
     (D) in the meantime

138. (A) When buying a home, location is
         extremely important.
     (B) Refinishing furniture is a form of art.
     (C) Furnished apartments can be found
         online.
     (D) All packing materials will be removed.

Questions 139-142 refer to the following e-mail.

To: Thao Pham <thaopham@amail.com>
From: Leena Montoya <lmontoya@academemedia.com>
Date: April 17
Subject: Subscription

Dear Mr. Pham,

------- . Your subscription to *Medical Innovations Quarterly* has been canceled. ------- May 1, you
139. **140.**
will no longer receive the print edition.

We hope that you will consider once again becoming a ------- of our publications. Academe Media
141.
publishes many high-quality scientific journals in addition to *Medical Innovations Quarterly*. Should

you wish to subscribe to one by May 31, we can offer you a two-year subscription at the annual

rate. Visit www.academemedia.com/shop and enter the code DOUBLE ------- checkout.
142.

If you have any feedback that could help us improve our products or services, please call me

directly at 212-555-0122.

Sincerely,

Leena Montoya
Customer Service Manager, Academe Media

139. (A) Thank you for your timely order.
(B) We have processed your request.
(C) This is a payment reminder.
(D) Please contact us to update your
    information.

140. (A) Starts
(B) Started
(C) Starter
(D) Starting

141. (A) distributor
(B) producer
(C) reader
(D) teacher

142. (A) until
(B) upon
(C) without
(D) next

GO ON TO THE NEXT PAGE

Questions 143-146 refer to the following information.

In a commercial kitchen, all refrigerators are required to have a thermometer that ------- from
143.
0°F (-18°C) to 220°F (104°C). To prevent the growth of bacteria, refrigerated foods must be

stored at 41°F (5°C) or below. The head chef is responsible for checking these thermometers

throughout the day to ensure that the kitchen is in compliance at all times.

Also important to consider is ------- . Thermometers should always be located in the warmest
144.
spot in the refrigerator. ------- . This location is also appropriate because it allows the
145.
thermometer to be easily ------- as soon as the door is opened.
146.

143. (A) ranges
     (B) ranger
     (C) ranged
     (D) ranging

144. (A) size
     (B) safety
     (C) reliability
     (D) placement

145. (A) Remove them carefully.
     (B) This is typically inside the door.
     (C) It should be kept cool at all times.
     (D) They can also be purchased in
         bulk.

146. (A) sold
     (B) seen
     (C) repaired
     (D) removed

PART 7

Directions: In this part you will read a selection of texts, such as magazine and newspaper articles, e-mails, and instant messages. Each text or set of texts is followed by several questions. Select the best answer for each question and mark the letter (A), (B), (C), or (D) on your answer sheet.

Questions 147-148 refer to the following e-mail.

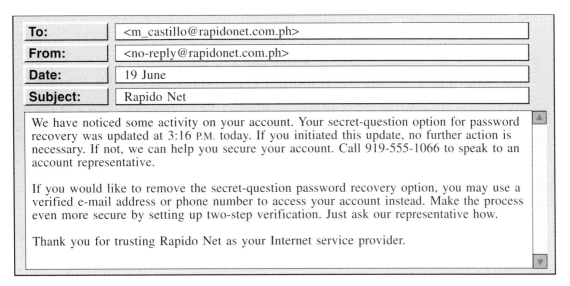

To:	<m_castillo@rapidonet.com.ph>
From:	<no-reply@rapidonet.com.ph>
Date:	19 June
Subject:	Rapido Net

We have noticed some activity on your account. Your secret-question option for password recovery was updated at 3:16 P.M. today. If you initiated this update, no further action is necessary. If not, we can help you secure your account. Call 919-555-1066 to speak to an account representative.

If you would like to remove the secret-question password recovery option, you may use a verified e-mail address or phone number to access your account instead. Make the process even more secure by setting up two-step verification. Just ask our representative how.

Thank you for trusting Rapido Net as your Internet service provider.

147. What is the purpose of the e-mail?

(A) To welcome a new user to Rapido Net
(B) To remind a user about a forgotten password
(C) To confirm that a change was made to a user's account
(D) To inform a user about new company policies

148. What is indicated about Rapido Net?

(A) It provides faster Internet speeds than its competitors.
(B) It offers extra security through two-step verification.
(C) It automatically generates complex passwords for customers.
(D) It has increased its monthly user fee.

GO ON TO THE NEXT PAGE

To:	<lduberville@futuremail.co.uk>
From:	<support@globaltech.co.uk>
Date:	23 March
Subject:	Residential service

Dear Ms. Duberville,

Thanks for your order. We are very pleased to have you as a new customer and are contacting you to request that you set up an appointment for one of our representatives to install a Global Tech modem at your home. Please go online and select a 30-minute window out of the four we have posted to your account.

In preparation for our visit, please clear the area on the wall where you would like us to install the modem. Setting up the modem will take just a few minutes, after which you will be able to enjoy our service.

We will use the phone number listed on your account the morning of the appointment to confirm the visit. Let us know at this time if you have any questions for us.

Sincerely,

Gordon Mackey
Customer Service, Global Tech

149. What kind of service has Ms. Duberville
    most likely contracted?

    (A) Window installation
    (B) House cleanup
    (C) Wall-to-wall carpeting
    (D) Internet access

150. What will happen at the time selected by
    Ms. Duberville?

    (A) She will pick up some equipment at an
        office.
    (B) She will receive a new Global Tech
        mobile phone.
    (C) She will be visited by a Global Tech
        representative.
    (D) She will be e-mailed a customer
        satisfaction survey.

Katrina Finton (1:46 P.M.)
Hey, Steven. I am hoping to move into a new apartment soon, and the landlord requires a letter verifying my place of employment and my income. I have written up the letter. Would you be willing to sign it today as proof that I work here at Carrino Agency?

Steven Khen (1:48 P.M.)
Double-check with Ariana Seltzer first. The human resources department usually has a form they can provide for you.

Katrina Finton (1:49 P.M.)
I tried that. They don't have a set form.

Steven Khen (1:50 P.M.)
No problem then. Bring your document over.

Steven Khen (1:51 P.M.)
By the way, the meeting about the Zaine Company Web site was moved to 3:00 P.M. You already have all your designs for their Web site ready, right?

Katrina Finton (1:52 P.M.)
I'm all set.

TEST 6

151. At 1:49 P.M., what does Ms. Finton most likely mean when she writes, "I tried that"?

(A) She signed a rental agreement.
(B) She submitted proof of income.
(C) She contacted Ms. Seltzer.
(D) She filled out a form.

152. What most likely is Ms. Finton's position?

(A) Apartment manager
(B) Office administrator
(C) Human resources director
(D) Web designer

GO ON TO THE NEXT PAGE

Questions 153-155 refer to the following Web page.

---

http://www.marilisprofessionalcoaching.com

Marilis Professional Coaching: January Events

January 15 at 4:30 P.M.—Job Search Support
Learn about the latest tools and techniques to help you find a rewarding entry-level job. Topics include the best Web sites for job announcements and how to use professional organizations to get job leads.

January 16 at 4:30 P.M.—How to Market Yourself
To set yourself apart from other job candidates, you have to effectively communicate the value you'll bring to the company. This session will help you successfully promote yourself to potential employers, both in person and through social media.

January 17 at 4:30 P.M.—Interview Strategies
Get tips on interview rules, common questions, and the process for what you need to do before, during, and after a job interview. This session will be interactive, featuring mock interviews with attendees.

Go to www.marilisprofessionalcoaching.com/register to sign up for any of these low-cost events. Note that all January events are virtual.

---

153. What is the purpose of the Web page?

(A) To promote career-assistance services
(B) To announce a local job fair for recent graduates
(C) To advertise open positions at social media companies
(D) To describe rewarding careers in Web design and creation

154. According to the Web page, what will happen on January 17 ?

(A) Companies will post job opportunities.
(B) Employers will make hiring decisions.
(C) Job candidates will attend a group interview.
(D) Participants will practice responding to interviewers.

155. What is indicated about the events?

(A) They occur each month.
(B) They take place online.
(C) They are for senior professionals.
(D) They are free of charge.

Eston Development Worth a Look

by Marcus Watanabe

"Ideal residential developments combine twenty-first-century convenience with small-town charm." That is the philosophy found in the brochure of the Homestead at Eston, a recently completed housing development just outside the town of Eston. — [1] —.

The community has wide streets, sidewalks, and three small parks surrounding a central square. The square features a café, a restaurant, and several shops. In the northeast corner of the development, there is an activity complex that includes a gym, theater, and swimming pool. — [2] —. "This means you never have to leave the community unless you want to," said Marjorie Solomon, sales director. "Once you visit, you'll realize why so many people are purchasing homes here."

While never leaving your development struck me as an odd idea, the Homestead planners deserve praise for creating a very attractive place to live. — [3] —. The planners have obviously prioritized the environment. Natural habitats have been carefully preserved, and homes and other structures have been designed to conserve water and energy.

Model homes are currently available for tours. — [4] —. Open houses take place 12:30–4:00 P.M. Saturdays and Sundays. Alternatively, appointments can be made by calling 856-555-0129.

156. What is indicated about the activity complex?

(A) It has a variety of desirable features.
(B) It is currently under construction.
(C) It has low membership fees.
(D) It is located in the central square.

157. How can a prospective resident learn more about Homestead at Eston?

(A) By viewing a model home online
(B) By requesting a brochure
(C) By visiting the community
(D) By calling a current homeowner

158. In which of the positions marked [1], [2], [3], and [4] does the following sentence best belong?

"Homestead, however, is more than just a pretty place."

(A) [1]
(B) [2]
(C) [3]
(D) [4]

GO ON TO THE NEXT PAGE

From:	Stefan Fonsman <sfonsman@kaybunconstruction.ca>
To:	Rita Palore <rpalore@palorecement.ca>
Subject:	Palore Cement
Date:	March 2

Dear Ms. Palore,

Thank you for sending your estimate for the cement work on our apartment project in Smithville. The narrative accompanying your bid answered all of our questions, and my team was impressed by your firm's previous work and references. Your company is my first choice to take on the project.

Nonetheless, I still need budget approval from my director, Anita Cho. Your proposed price is a bit steeper than anticipated. I will be speaking with Ms. Cho about this tomorrow morning. Based on your company's reputation for outstanding work, I am confident that she will sign off on your bid.

I expect to get back to you by March 4.

Regards,

Stefan Fonsman
Kaybun Construction

159. What is one purpose of the e-mail?

(A) To introduce a new owner
(B) To acknowledge receipt of an estimate
(C) To invite team members to
    a presentation
(D) To ask for additional work references

160. When will Mr. Fonsman meet with Ms. Cho?

(A) On March 2
(B) On March 3
(C) On March 4
(D) On March 5

City of Altamesa seeks election workers

<u>Who is qualified to be an election worker?</u> Almost anyone, including homemakers and professionals, as well as those who are unemployed, self-employed, or retired.

<u>Requirements:</u>
- Available 6 A.M. to 1 P.M. or 1 P.M. to 8 P.M. on March 5, June 7, and November 1
- Is not a politician and does not live with or work for a politician
- Is 18 years of age or older
- Is comfortable interacting with the public
- Is organized and detail-oriented

Workers must attend a four-hour pre-election training workshop on March 4 and will be compensated based on their title:
Election Assistant, $18/hour
Election Clerk, $20/hour
Election Chief, $22/hour

For details or to apply, visit www.altamesaelections.gov/apply.

161. What information is included in the announcement?

(A) Rates of pay
(B) Work site locations
(C) The application deadline
(D) The training workshop's start time

162. What does the announcement suggest is a requirement for being hired?

(A) Interest in politics
(B) A high school diploma
(C) A voter registration card
(D) Good communication skills

163. What is mentioned about the training workshop?

(A) It is offered three times a year.
(B) It is led by an experienced election official.
(C) It is required for all election workers.
(D) It is available both online and in person.

GO ON TO THE NEXT PAGE

```
┌─────────────────────────────────────────────────────────────────┐
│                            *E-mail*                               │
├─────────────────────────────────────────────────────────────────┤
│  To:        Jihyang Lee <jlee@myemail.com>                        │
│  From:      Robert Wang <rwang@frontstreetbank.com>               │
│  Date:      April 7                                               │
│  Subject:   Is VIS for you?                                       │
└─────────────────────────────────────────────────────────────────┘
```

Dear Ms. Lee:

You are now able to enroll in Front Street Bank's new Voice Identification System (VIS). VIS is a fast, convenient, and secure way to access and control your bank accounts by phone. — [1] —. For example, you can make a payment on a Front Street Bank loan by saying "loan payment." You can check your credit-card transactions by saying "recent transactions." You can even transfer money between accounts by saying "transfer." Discover all the ways VIS can simplify your banking life at www.frontstreetbank.com/VIS. — [2] —.

Your voice identification is stored securely by Front Street Bank and can be used only with Front Street Bank. Call 615-555-0189 to set up VIS for your accounts. — [3] —. If in the future you no longer wish to use VIS to access your account, simply call to have one of our customer-service representatives delete your identification file.

— [4] —. Thank you for being a valued Front Street Bank customer.

Sincerely,

Robert Wang, Branch Manager

---

164. What is the purpose of the e-mail?

(A) To welcome a new customer
(B) To report an account error
(C) To confirm approval of a loan
(D) To promote a new service

165. What is indicated about VIS?

(A) It provides voice access to accounts.
(B) It can be used at various financial institutions.
(C) It requires customers to pay a fee.
(D) It is available only during designated hours.

166. What should a customer do to cancel VIS?

(A) Visit a local bank branch
(B) Make a telephone call
(C) Complete an online form
(D) Send an e-mail to customer service

167. In which of the positions marked [1], [2], [3], and [4] does the following sentence best belong?

"You can perform numerous specific tasks."

(A) [1]
(B) [2]
(C) [3]
(D) [4]

Thumbnail Publishing Ltd.

Four new titles in the Enterprise series have just been released. Buy one, get one 50 percent off when you purchase from our Web site by November 30 (excludes shipping). Order your copies today!

Maestro by Christine Menon
A biography of famous executive Haruto Yamada, with insight into how his career influenced business governance. Paperback €14.99

Working Under Moonbeams by Chang-Ho Jin
Commerce in twentieth-century Korea as illuminated through interviews with former trade company employees. Hardcover €22.99, Audiobook €8.99

The Connections Unseen by Mai Quang Vinh
A collection of transcribed lectures and archival photos from Gloria de Leon's 40-year career as a professor of business administration. Hardcover €25.99

Flashback by Jack Olivier
A former Australian trade commissioner recalls the highs and lows of his diplomatic career in this engaging memoir. Paperback €14.99, Downloadable e-book €9.99

TEST 6

168. What is the company offering to customers?

(A) A coupon for a specific author's books
(B) A discount for ordering two books online
(C) A reduced price for shipping
(D) A free copy of the publisher's catalog

169. Who is Mr. Yamada?

(A) A government agent
(B) A career counselor
(C) A biography writer
(D) A company leader

170. What feature is shared by all of the books described in the advertisement?

(A) They were written by the same author.
(B) They can be read in digital formats.
(C) They focus on business topics.
(D) They were translated into several languages.

171. What book includes historic images?

(A) *Maestro*
(B) *Working Under Moonbeams*
(C) *The Connections Unseen*
(D) *Flashback*

GO ON TO THE NEXT PAGE

Questions 172-175 refer to the following text-message chain.

Priyanka Kapoor [9:41 A.M.]
We need to talk about the upcoming family physicians conference in London. Where do we stand?

Alonso Gonzalez [9:44 A.M.]
I've already purchased airline tickets for all of us.

Priyanka Kapoor [9:47 A.M.]
Great. Scott Harris will arrange our shuttle from the London airport to the conference venue. Will our mobile phones be functional outside of the Wi-Fi zones?

Alonso Gonzalez [9:50 A.M.]
I've researched our mobile phone provider's international plan. It offers the ability to call and text but provides limited data options with slow download speeds.

Brian Kim [9:53 A.M.]
Let's buy international SIM cards before we leave. We can get the prepaid cards with high-speed data and unlimited calling and texting. We won't have to worry about being connected to Wi-Fi.

Priyanka Kapoor [9:57 A.M.]
That will solve the problem.

Alonso Gonzalez [9:57 A.M.]
Good idea, Brian. Thanks. Now let's discuss meeting up for our meals.

Priyanka Kapoor [9:59 A.M.]
Each day of the conference begins with a continental breakfast in the lobby. Let's meet there in the morning. I know of a great place for dinner, so let's plan on 6:00 P.M. the first evening. We'll decide about the other meals later.

172. Where do the writers most likely work?

(A) At a travel agency
(B) At a medical office
(C) At a transportation company
(D) At a telecommunications firm

173. At 9:41 A.M., what does Ms. Kapoor most likely mean when she writes, "Where do we stand?"

(A) She is requesting an update on preparations for a trip.
(B) She wants to assess her colleagues' interest in attending an event.
(C) She is inquiring about her colleagues' weekend activities.
(D) She is checking staff readiness to host a conference.

174. What can be concluded about the writers?

(A) They will be traveling together.
(B) They are preparing a presentation.
(C) They have new mobile phone service.
(D) They are each attending a conference for the first time.

175. Why does Mr. Kim suggest SIM cards?

(A) They are less expensive than international plans.
(B) They can be used on any device.
(C) They are in stock at a nearby electronics store.
(D) They do not require a Wi-Fi connection.

GO ON TO THE NEXT PAGE

BLISSFUL HORSE STABLES

Part-time worker needed to feed, wash, and groom horses. Must be able to work a minimum of eight hours a week, including occasional weekend hours. Although training is available, applicants who have experience working with horses are preferred. To apply, send an e-mail to Dorothy Lu, dlu@blissfulhorsestables.com.au, and attach your résumé.

Blissful Horse Stables is the region's largest horse-boarding facility. It has been owned and operated by one family since 1988. Our business offers both long- and short-term boarding contracts. We have state-of-the-art indoor and outdoor exercise rings and a five-acre grazing pasture for our equine friends. A veterinarian is always on call.

E-mail	
From:	ota.kyle@opalmail.com.au
To:	dlu@blissfulhorsestables.com.au
Subject:	Part-time position
Date:	1 August
Attachment:	📎 ota.rfg

Dear Ms. Lu,

This e-mail is in response to the advertisement that appeared in yesterday's edition of the *Colby Today*. At this time, I work for Ness Large Animal Clinic as a technician's assistant, but only three days a week. The part-time position you are advertising would enable me to do something I enjoy while increasing my working hours. I am happy to provide references upon request.

All the best,

Kyle Ota

176. What is NOT indicated about Blissful Horse Stables?

(A) It provides grooming services.
(B) It requires a minimum stay of three days.
(C) It has a large, grassy field for grazing.
(D) It is a family-run business.

177. In the job advertisement, the word "facility" in paragraph 2, line 1, is closest in meaning to

(A) simplicity
(B) chance
(C) openness
(D) center

178. What most likely is *Colby Today* ?

(A) A regional newspaper
(B) A newsletter for horse owners
(C) A television program
(D) A tourism brochure

179. What is implied about Mr. Ota?

(A) He has experience working with animals.
(B) He graduated from a local school.
(C) He would like to become a journalist.
(D) He is not able to work on weekends.

180. What has Mr. Ota most likely attached to his e-mail?

(A) A diploma
(B) A résumé
(C) A letter of reference
(D) An article about horse care

GO ON TO THE NEXT PAGE

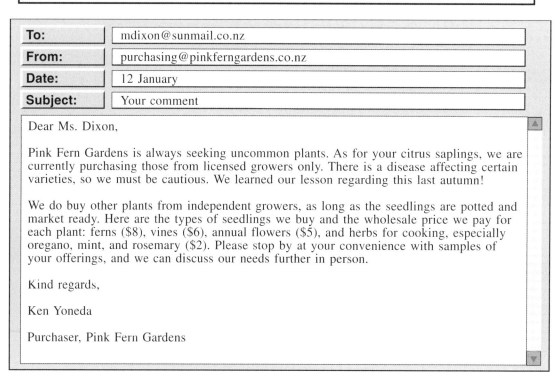

https://www.pinkferngardens.co.nz/contact

| About | Shop Online | Locations | **Contact Us** |

Located in Picton, New Zealand, Pink Fern Gardens sells a wide variety of plants, both edible and decorative. Please use the form below to submit your questions and comments.

Name: Mia Dixon

E-mail: mdixon@sunmail.co.nz

Comment:

I saw the callout to local growers on your social media feed. A few years ago, I started a large community food garden with my neighbours here in Helensville for us to tend in our free time. This year, we have more plants than we can consume ourselves. Specifically, we have dozens of potted mint and cardamom seedlings as well as other uncommon herbs, and I wonder if you are interested in expanding your offerings of herbs. We also have a half dozen two-year-old lemon tree saplings that are between two and three feet tall.

To:	mdixon@sunmail.co.nz
From:	purchasing@pinkferngardens.co.nz
Date:	12 January
Subject:	Your comment

Dear Ms. Dixon,

Pink Fern Gardens is always seeking uncommon plants. As for your citrus saplings, we are currently purchasing those from licensed growers only. There is a disease affecting certain varieties, so we must be cautious. We learned our lesson regarding this last autumn!

We do buy other plants from independent growers, as long as the seedlings are potted and market ready. Here are the types of seedlings we buy and the wholesale price we pay for each plant: ferns ($8), vines ($6), annual flowers ($5), and herbs for cooking, especially oregano, mint, and rosemary ($2). Please stop by at your convenience with samples of your offerings, and we can discuss our needs further in person.

Kind regards,

Ken Yoneda

Purchaser, Pink Fern Gardens

181. What motivated Ms. Dixon to contact Pink Fern Gardens?

(A) A positive review from a customer
(B) An online post from Pink Fern Gardens
(C) An article about Pink Fern Gardens
(D) A phone message from Mr. Yoneda

182. What is indicated about Ms. Dixon?

(A) She wants to turn her hobby into a full-time business.
(B) She would like a part-time job at Pink Fern Gardens.
(C) She founded a community garden with her neighbors.
(D) She is president of a gardening club in Helensville.

183. According to Mr. Yoneda, what happened last year?

(A) Some of his employees resigned.
(B) Some trees his company purchased were unhealthy.
(C) His company obtained a license to export citrus trees.
(D) His company ran out of fruit trees to sell.

184. What does Mr. Yoneda ask Ms. Dixon to do?

(A) Send him a list of supplies
(B) Contact an independent grower
(C) Buy seeds from Pink Fern Gardens
(D) Bring some plants to Pink Fern Gardens

185. How much would Mr. Yoneda pay Ms. Dixon for one of her potted seedlings?

(A) $8.00
(B) $6.00
(C) $5.00
(D) $2.00

GO ON TO THE NEXT PAGE

TEST 6

https://www.elektroproofrepair.com/about

Trust Elektroproof Repair to get your computer running right again!

Elektroproof Repair's no-surprises policy offers flat fees for labor at three price points: $145, $200, and $350. These fees do not include the cost of software or replacement parts. The majority of our repairs incur the $200 fee.

NOTE: Because of a dramatic increase in demand, we now require appointments for all services. For an initial consultation with one of our highly qualified technicians, simply select from the available time slots on our schedule page. When you schedule your appointment, we require a $60 nonrefundable deposit which will be credited toward the cost of services rendered.

If you have any questions, please e-mail us at inquiries@elektroproofrepair.com. Whenever possible, we will contact you the same day or on the following business day. Most repairs are completed within three to five business days.

E-Mail Message

To:	Jessica Nelson <jnelson17@saffronmail.com>
From:	Arthur Jacquet <ajacquet@elektroproofrepair.com>
Date:	January 14
Subject:	Re: Tea spill, please help!

Dear Ms. Nelson,

Thank you for contacting Elektroproof Repair. You asked if you could bring in your laptop for inspection tomorrow, January 15. Unfortunately, we are currently booked solid through January 18. The earliest available time slot is 8:00 A.M. on January 19. Please let me know if you would like to book that slot or if you have any questions.

Sincerely,

Arthur Jacquet, Elektroproof Repair

★ ★ ★ ★ ★

Elektroproof Repair

I spilled tea on the keyboard of my faithful old laptop, and while I dried the exterior rather quickly, I was afraid the internal components might have been ruined. Luckily for me, Elektroproof Repair came to the rescue! After booking my consultation on the Web site, I waited anxiously for a reply. Within an hour, I got an e-mail directly from the owner. Although the time slot I had requested was not available, when I responded to his e-mail to express how urgently I needed my laptop, the owner said they had an unexpected cancellation and asked if I could bring it in that very morning, which I did. Since my computer was not turned on at the time of the accident, an Elektroproof Repair technician was able to dry the computer's insides and prevent damage to the hard drive or internal circuits. Other than a new battery, no other part was needed, and Elektroproof Repair had my laptop fully functional and back in my hands within 24 hours.

—Jessica Nelson

186. According to the Web page, what is true about Elektroproof Repair?

(A) It recently raised its prices.
(B) It is hiring more repair technicians.
(C) It has experienced a sudden increase in business.
(D) It requires full payment before work can begin.

187. According to the e-mail, what is the earliest date when Ms. Nelson could bring in her laptop for service?

(A) On January 14
(B) On January 15
(C) On January 18
(D) On January 19

188. What is most likely true about Mr. Jacquet?

(A) He owns the business.
(B) He is a technician.
(C) He is a receptionist.
(D) He delivers repaired equipment.

189. According to the review, what was Ms. Nelson's main concern about her laptop?

(A) That the parts inside it might be damaged
(B) That it was too old to be repaired
(C) That it was responding too slowly
(D) That its operating system had a virus

190. What is suggested about the repair of Ms. Nelson's computer?

(A) It included installing new operating software.
(B) It was completed more quickly than advertised.
(C) It involved the replacement of internal circuits.
(D) It required an upgrade to the hard drive.

TEST 6

GO ON TO THE NEXT PAGE

Learn to play guitar at Alexis Instruments!

Alexis Instruments will offer group and individual guitar instruction beginning April 2. Each of our locations has been updated with newly constructed classrooms and practice rooms. Our instructors have years of experience teaching and playing as professional musicians. Call an Alexis Instruments store today for availability and pricing.

To:	Lucia Rivera <luciarivera@rapidonet.com>
From:	Krista Towers <ktowers@alexisinstruments.com>
Date:	April 26, 8:30 A.M.
Subject:	Order TS1058293

Dear Ms. Rivera,

I am following up on the order you placed with us on April 23. We have only one guitar of the model you want in stock. It was used as a display sample on the floor of our salesroom here in Santa Barbara. This means it is out of the box and has been played by customers browsing the store. Our in-house luthier has thoroughly inspected the guitar, and it is still in excellent condition. There are no scratches, scuffs, or dents on it whatsoever. Because you purchased the instrument on the understanding that it was brand new, we want to offer you two options:

1. If you do not want the floor model, you may cancel the order and receive an immediate full refund.
2. If you would like the floor model, we will ship it immediately and offer you a 10 percent discount off the original retail price.

If you choose the latter, we will make sure the guitar is delivered to your local store in time for your first lesson there tomorrow. We apologize for the inconvenience.

Sincerely,
Krista Towers
Alexis Instruments

Alexis Instruments
Order number: TS1058293
Date: April 26

Description	Price
Domingo 313 full-body acoustic guitar	$450.00
10% discount on guitar	-$45.00
Three-year repair and maintenance plan, good at any Alexis Instruments location	$75.00
Sales tax	$34.80
Total	$514.80

Ship To	Bill To
Alexis Instruments, store #23 3914 Joseph Drive Chico, CA 95926	Lucia Rivera 11437 Shady Grove Lane Chico, CA 95926

191. What is the purpose of the advertisement?

(A) To sell guitars
(B) To promote lessons
(C) To attract music teachers
(D) To announce a new location

192. What is most likely true about the store where Ms. Towers works?

(A) It has been renovated.
(B) It is hiring new employees.
(C) It has more inventory than other locations.
(D) It has extended its hours of operation.

193. What does the e-mail indicate about the guitar?

(A) It is in need of repairs.
(B) It has been on a shelf at the store in Chico.
(C) It was previously owned by an Alexis Instruments customer.
(D) It is the only one of its model currently available.

194. What can be inferred about Ms. Rivera?

(A) She damaged her guitar.
(B) She requested a refund.
(C) She was previously enrolled in an online class.
(D) She purchased the floor model.

195. According to the receipt, what is true about Alexis Instruments?

(A) It repairs instruments in its stores.
(B) It has two stores in Santa Barbara.
(C) It is holding an annual sale.
(D) It was founded by a professional musician.

GO ON TO THE NEXT PAGE

To:	All Instructors
From:	Jee-Young Choi
Subject:	New fee schedule
Date:	August 15

Dear Teachers,

Thank you for lending your skills as artists and educators to the Mirabel Museum of Art. Please use the updated fee schedule below when creating your monthly invoices.

Category	Description	Duration	Fee
Tour	Lead group tour	60 minutes	$50
Tour	Lead group tour	90 minutes	$75
Class	Teach art class	75 minutes	$65
Class	Teach art class	120 minutes	$110
Development	Plan new course content	Varies	$200
Training	Instruct museum staff on a specialized topic	Varies	$25/hour

Electronic payments should be available ten business days after invoice submission.

Jee-Young Choi, Education Coordinator

Devonte Merriweather
d.merriweather@camail.ca

Invoice #00278
For: Services at the Mirabel Museum of Art
Sent: September 30

Date	Description	Fee
September 22	Tour: Special exhibit	$50
September 22	Class: Drawing for Beginners	$65
September 25	Class: Sculpting with Clay	$110
	Total	$225

To:	Devonte Merriweather <d.merriweather@camail.ca>
From:	Jee-Young Choi <jy.choi@mirabelmuseumofart.ca>
Subject:	Payment
Date:	October 6

Dear Mr. Merriweather,

Thank you for submitting your September invoice. I noticed that you neglected to charge us for developing the curriculum for your sculpting class, which you taught for the first time on September 25. I checked with Carol Swann, and she said that because invoice #00278 has already been paid, it would be best if you submitted a second invoice for the development. I will ask her to process it quickly when I receive it.

You will be happy to know that the feedback from your students was very positive. I will e-mail scans of their feedback forms later today.

Best,

Jee-Young Choi, Education Coordinator

196. What is suggested in the first e-mail about the Mirabel Museum of Art?

(A) It hires art teachers to lead tours.
(B) It offers private tours to museum members.
(C) Its art classes are free to the public.
(D) Its next staff training will take place in ten days.

197. What does the invoice suggest about Mr. Merriweather?

(A) He worked at the museum on September 30.
(B) He has expertise in more than one art form.
(C) One of his art classes was canceled.
(D) Some of his artwork was exhibited in September.

198. How long was the sculpting class that Mr. Merriweather taught?

(A) 60 minutes
(B) 75 minutes
(C) 90 minutes
(D) 120 minutes

199. According to the second e-mail, who most likely is Ms. Swann?

(A) A bookkeeper
(B) An art teacher
(C) Mr. Merriweather's assistant
(D) Director of the Mirabel Museum of Art

200. What can be concluded about Ms. Choi?

(A) She forgot to read some student feedback forms.
(B) She believes that Mr. Merriweather is owed $200.
(C) She meets once a month with teachers.
(D) She rejected Mr. Merriweather's October invoice.

Stop! This is the end of the test. If you finish before time is called, you may go back to Parts 5, 6, and 7 and check your work.

토익®정기시험
기출문제집 4
1000

TEST 07
무료 동영상 강의

RC

기출 TEST
07

READING TEST

In the Reading test, you will read a variety of texts and answer several different types of reading comprehension questions. The entire Reading test will last 75 minutes. There are three parts, and directions are given for each part. You are encouraged to answer as many questions as possible within the time allowed.

You must mark your answers on the separate answer sheet. Do not write your answers in your test book.

PART 5

Directions: A word or phrase is missing in each of the sentences below. Four answer choices are given below each sentence. Select the best answer to complete the sentence. Then mark the letter (A), (B), (C), or (D) on your answer sheet.

101. Passengers must keep ------- boarding passes and luggage with them at all times.

(A) their
(B) his
(C) my
(D) our

102. The company's policy allows business travel by ------- train and airplane.

(A) both
(B) either
(C) further
(D) hardly

103. The production technicians are ------- for maintaining our factory equipment.

(A) responsibly
(B) responsible
(C) responsibility
(D) responsibilities

104. The team found Ms. Dietrich's advice on managing office staff to be especially -------.

(A) helpful
(B) thankful
(C) regular
(D) extra

105. The film crew ------- in Namibia earlier this week to prepare for the promotional tourism campaign.

(A) to arrive
(B) having arrived
(C) arrived
(D) arriving

106. The committee expects to be finished with the negotiations ------- 4:00 P.M.

(A) over
(B) until
(C) on
(D) by

107. United Medical Board is an ------- panel of physicians that makes recommendations for hospital improvements.

(A) expertise
(B) expert
(C) expertness
(D) expertly

108. Digital payments are ------- accepted at all Southern Coach bus stations.

(A) tightly
(B) far
(C) after
(D) now

109. The fund-raising event for the library was successful, ------- the author's reading was canceled.

(A) seldom
(B) though
(C) rarely
(D) secondly

110. To ------- the status of your delivery, select the Track Order option in the drop-down menu.

(A) place
(B) want
(C) check
(D) look

111. Our project-based mentoring approach enables executives with limited time ------- junior staff.

(A) to counsel
(B) should counsel
(C) counseling
(D) counseled

112. Mr. Yerkes is updating our quarterly sales ------- after receiving the final report from the Boston office.

(A) measures
(B) grounds
(C) instructions
(D) figures

113. ------- up your desk with beautiful paper products from Norimi Stationery.

(A) Brightens
(B) Brighten
(C) Brightened
(D) Brightening

114. Ultitemp, an application that allows users to ------- room temperature remotely, is currently available only in Asia.

(A) control
(B) impose
(C) announce
(D) encourage

115. ------- the cost of travel, the cost of attending the conference is reasonable.

(A) Along
(B) Even if
(C) Aside from
(D) Because

116. Customers are ------- anticipating the latest model pickup truck from Askio Automobiles.

(A) eagerly
(B) sharply
(C) voluntarily
(D) rapidly

117. Once you have Mr. Garcia's -------, please post the job listing to the usual Web sites.

(A) approve
(B) approves
(C) approval
(D) approving

118. Dabby's Restaurant broadened its customer base by making ------- changes to its menu.

(A) extensive
(B) precious
(C) commercial
(D) accurate

119. The redesigned intersection ------- shortens the street-crossing distance for pedestrians, making it safer.

(A) effectively
(B) effects
(C) effective
(D) effected

120. Workshop attendees are asked to ------- from asking questions until the end of the formal presentation.

(A) refrain
(B) forbid
(C) retreat
(D) hesitate

GO ON TO THE NEXT PAGE

121. The Tamano Foundation accepts grant ------- related to a wide range of scientific research.

(A) proposes
(B) proposed
(C) proposals
(D) proposing

122. Gateway Electronics will cancel any orders that have not been picked up ------- five days.

(A) about
(B) during
(C) within
(D) from

123. ------- who arrives at the company parking garage after 10:00 A.M. must contact security for an access code.

(A) Each
(B) Those
(C) Everything
(D) Anyone

124. To get to the conference room, turn left ------- after passing the employee cafeteria.

(A) immediately
(B) recently
(C) originally
(D) lately

125. The wellness ------- at Trayer Media Group directly led to greater employee satisfaction with the company.

(A) initiate
(B) initiator
(C) initiated
(D) initiative

126. We will keep producing our signature shoe designs ------- there is demand for them.

(A) or else
(B) as long as
(C) as well as
(D) in between

127. Regular applications of fertilizer improve seedling health and ------- enhance the growth of leafy vegetables.

(A) drama
(B) dramatic
(C) dramatically
(D) dramatize

128. Wantner Manufacturing received this year's Top Employer Award in ------- of its people-centered workplace environment.

(A) service
(B) accordance
(C) recognition
(D) dedication

129. The editor noted some ------- content and marked the text to be deleted.

(A) repetition
(B) repetitious
(C) repetitiously
(D) repetitiousness

130. Bay City Zoo members get ------- access to members-only activities, such as after-hours guided tours.

(A) exclusive
(B) unknown
(C) creative
(D) previous

PART 6

Directions: Read the texts that follow. A word, phrase, or sentence is missing in parts of each text. Four answer choices for each question are given below the text. Select the best answer to complete the text. Then mark the letter (A), (B), (C), or (D) on your answer sheet.

Questions 131-134 refer to the following e-mail.

To: Naomi Richter <naomirichter@mailcurrent.com>
From: Watanu Sakamoto <wsakamoto@RHNimports.com>
Date: 23 November
Subject: Follow-up
Attachment: Logistics coordinator description

Dear Ms. Richter,

Thank you for coming to our office to interview for the assistant import manager position last week. We were impressed with your credentials and enthusiasm. ------- we are moving ahead
131.
with another candidate, we would like to offer you a different position that just became available: logistics coordinator.

------- . The attached document contains the detailed job description and pay rate. This -------
132. **133.**
has not yet been posted publicly. If you are -------, please let me know by the end of this week.
134.

Sincerely,

Watanu Sakamoto
Human Resource Manager, RHN Imports

131. (A) Rather
(B) Although
(C) Similarly
(D) Consequently

132. (A) There are several other internal applicants.
(B) Unfortunately, the position is no longer available.
(C) My assistant will schedule your second interview.
(D) Your experience and skill set make you a great fit.

133. (A) opportunity
(B) authorization
(C) application
(D) capacity

134. (A) interest
(B) interests
(C) interested
(D) interesting

GO ON TO THE NEXT PAGE

Questions 135-138 refer to the following notice.

The Oakville Horticulture Club ------- a plant sale on Saturday, 9 September. The sale will be held
 135.

from 9:00 A.M. to 4:00 P.M. at the Oakville Community Centre at 478 Hill Avenue. There will be

great deals on hanging baskets, grasses, and herbs. ------- . We ------- have a delicious selection
 136.   **137.**

of fruits and vegetables available for purchase. Enjoy live talks and demonstrations

------- the day. For more information, visit the Oakville Horticulture Web site:
 138.

www.oakvillehorticultureclub.co.uk/events.

135. (A) host
(B) hosted
(C) is hosting
(D) has hosted

136. (A) Come early to get the best selection.
(B) Plants help make your home beautiful.
(C) Join the club for a discount on local
garden tours.
(D) The community center was just
renovated.

137. (A) later
(B) also
(C) nearly
(D) merely

138. (A) within
(B) forward
(C) following
(D) throughout

July 2

Dear Mr. Arakaki:

I am writing to inform you of scheduled road maintenance on Briggs Avenue. Beginning on

July 15, Briggs Avenue ------- reduced to one lane from Elm Street to Bay Road. ------- . Although
139.   140.

your ------- is not located in this section of Briggs Avenue, traffic on most of the street will move
141.

more slowly than usual while work is being performed. You may ------- consider advising your
142.

employees to take alternate routes to work during this time. The project is expected to be

completed on or before October 22. Thank you for your cooperation and assistance.

Sincerely,

Amalia Villalobos
Director of Transportation
Enclosure

---

139. (A) was
(B) will be
(C) can be
(D) has been

140. (A) Briggs Avenue is only two miles away.
(B) The event will take place on Elm Street.
(C) Please refer to the enclosed map of the affected area.
(D) However, all city services will close during this time.

141. (A) mailbox
(B) school
(C) signage
(D) business

142. (A) fortunately
(B) instead
(C) likewise
(D) therefore

GO ON TO THE NEXT PAGE

Franklin Planetarium to Move Downtown

(June 3)—After 48 years in its present location on Mayfield's south side, the Franklin Planetarium is moving to a new home. Construction is underway on the downtown facility, part of a complex that includes the new Natural History Museum. Both ------- are expected to open to the public next
143.
September.

The current planetarium's main attraction is a 300-seat theater, where visitors can view projections of stars and planets on the dome above. ------- a larger theater, the new planetarium
144.
will feature an upgraded digital projection system. ------- . Visitors will be able ------- the night sky
145. **146.**
more clearly and explore other planets and galaxies through new, interactive displays.

143. (A) trails
(B) buildings
(C) campuses
(D) performances

144. (A) In addition to
(B) In particular
(C) In agreement with
(D) For instance

145. (A) There are currently three other
museums in the Mayfield area.
(B) Attendance at the planetarium has
been up in recent years.
(C) Planning for the new planetarium
began five years ago.
(D) There will be room for three short-term
exhibits as well.

146. (A) to see
(B) will see
(C) who saw
(D) by seeing

PART 7

Directions: In this part you will read a selection of texts, such as magazine and newspaper articles, e-mails, and instant messages. Each text or set of texts is followed by several questions. Select the best answer for each question and mark the letter (A), (B), (C), or (D) on your answer sheet.

Questions 147-148 refer to the following notice.

NOTICE

As part of our routine maintenance of Selino Apartments, all public areas of our building will be painted according to the following schedule:

- Stairwells, first and second floors: 12 April

- Hallways, first and second floors: 13 April

- Stairwells, third and fourth floors: 14 April

- Hallways, third and fourth floors: 15 April

The elevators will be available during this time. Please use caution, and do not touch any wet paint.

Management, Selino Apartments

---

147. For whom is the notice most likely intended?

(A) Painting contractors
(B) Elevator repair workers
(C) Graphic artists
(D) Apartment residents

148. When will work on the stairwells of all floors most likely be completed?

(A) On April 12
(B) On April 13
(C) On April 14
(D) On April 15

GO ON TO THE NEXT PAGE

Questions 149-150 refer to the following coupon.

Jin-Hwa Grill
Serving the finest Korean cuisine in northern California for over 30 years

Come celebrate the reopening of our newly remodeled restaurant on Lakeside Drive! Purchase any two dinners and enjoy a complimentary appetizer platter during the entire month of May.

Valid only at Jin-Hwa Grill, 4104 Lakeside Drive, Oakland, CA. Coupon does not apply to takeout orders. Visit www.jin-hwagrill.com for a list of all our locations, hours of operation, and menus.

149. How can people receive the benefit from the coupon?

(A) By placing a takeout order
(B) By spending a minimum amount of money
(C) By ordering two meals
(D) By attending the opening day celebration

150. What is mentioned about Jin-Hwa Grill?

(A) It is celebrating an anniversary.
(B) It has more than one location.
(C) It recently began serving Korean food.
(D) It has expanded its hours of operation.

Questions 151-152 refer to the following e-mail.

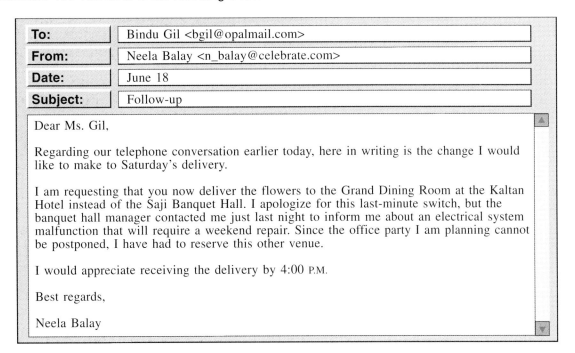

To: Bindu Gil <bgil@opalmail.com>

From: Neela Balay <n_balay@celebrate.com>

Date: June 18

Subject: Follow-up

Dear Ms. Gil,

Regarding our telephone conversation earlier today, here in writing is the change I would like to make to Saturday's delivery.

I am requesting that you now deliver the flowers to the Grand Dining Room at the Kaltan Hotel instead of the Saji Banquet Hall. I apologize for this last-minute switch, but the banquet hall manager contacted me just last night to inform me about an electrical system malfunction that will require a weekend repair. Since the office party I am planning cannot be postponed, I have had to reserve this other venue.

I would appreciate receiving the delivery by 4:00 P.M.

Best regards,

Neela Balay

151. Why did Ms. Balay send an e-mail to Ms. Gil?

(A) To reschedule a weekend business trip
(B) To invite her to an office party
(C) To request the services of an electrician
(D) To confirm some spoken instructions

152. What does Ms. Balay expect to receive on Saturday afternoon?

(A) Flowers
(B) Tickets
(C) A signed contract
(D) An updated cost estimate

GO ON TO THE NEXT PAGE

TEST 7

Questions 153-154 refer to the following online chat discussion.

Ae-Cha Kim (9:16 A.M.)
Good morning. I have an issue with an order I placed on the Winter Wear Web site.

Kelvin Long (9:18 A.M.)
Good morning. How can I help you?

Ae-Cha Kim (9:20 A.M.)
Well, I ordered some gloves two weeks ago, and they still haven't arrived.

Kelvin Long (9:21 A.M.)
I'm sorry to hear that. Did you get an order number?

Ae-Cha Kim (9:22 A.M.)
It's ADF193.

Kelvin Long (9:23 A.M.)
Thanks.

Kelvin Long (9:26 A.M.)
This is very unusual. The system is showing that the order was fulfilled. I'm not sure why it hasn't left the warehouse yet. I can have another pair of gloves sent to you with rush shipping, at no extra charge.

Ae-Cha Kim (9:27 A.M.)
That would be great! Thanks!

---

153. What problem does Ms. Kim have?

   (A) She received the wrong order.
   (B) Her order has not arrived.
   (C) An item was damaged in transport.
   (D) An item is missing from her order.

154. At 9:26 A.M., what does Mr. Long most likely mean when he writes, "This is very unusual"?

   (A) He is frustrated by the slow computer system.
   (B) He is sorry about taking so long to answer Ms. Kim's question.
   (C) He is surprised about the warehouse issue.
   (D) He is confused about which style of gloves was ordered.

Questions 155-157 refer to the following e-mail.

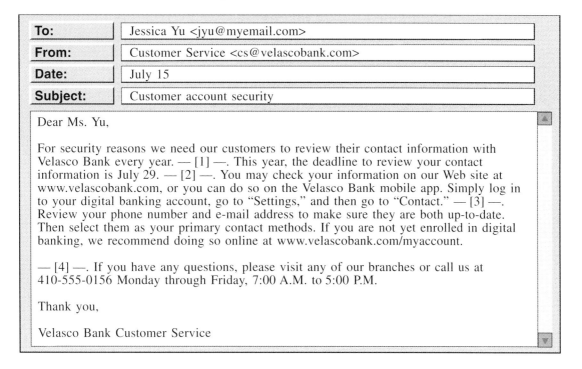

To: Jessica Yu <jyu@myemail.com>

From: Customer Service <cs@velascobank.com>

Date: July 15

Subject: Customer account security

Dear Ms. Yu,

For security reasons we need our customers to review their contact information with Velasco Bank every year. — [1] —. This year, the deadline to review your contact information is July 29. — [2] —. You may check your information on our Web site at www.velascobank.com, or you can do so on the Velasco Bank mobile app. Simply log in to your digital banking account, go to "Settings," and then go to "Contact." — [3] —. Review your phone number and e-mail address to make sure they are both up-to-date. Then select them as your primary contact methods. If you are not yet enrolled in digital banking, we recommend doing so online at www.velascobank.com/myaccount.

— [4] —. If you have any questions, please visit any of our branches or call us at 410-555-0156 Monday through Friday, 7:00 A.M. to 5:00 P.M.

Thank you,

Velasco Bank Customer Service

155. What is the purpose of the e-mail?

(A) To inquire about an account closure
(B) To inform customers of a change in banking hours
(C) To ask a customer to confirm personal data
(D) To provide information about a bank deposit

156. According to the e-mail, what should a customer do to register for digital banking?

(A) Go to the bank's Web site
(B) Contact a customer service representative
(C) Visit a local bank branch
(D) Install a mobile app

157. In which of the positions marked [1], [2], [3], and [4] does the following sentence best belong?

"This can be done in one of two ways."

(A) [1]
(B) [2]
(C) [3]
(D) [4]

TEST 7

GO ON TO THE NEXT PAGE

Sumner Woodcrafting

Sumner Woodcrafting of Memphis, Tennessee, was established nearly 45 years ago by Kiran Sumner, with the goal of providing personalized service to customers seeking high-quality, handmade furniture. Now semiretired, Mr. Sumner still takes orders and responds to questions himself through the company's customer-service telephone line at 901-555-0185 on Thursdays and Fridays. Sumner Woodcrafting offers a wide selection of custom-made bedroom sets, tables, desks, cabinetry, and more—all made from high-quality solid woods.

Prices for handcrafted furniture are naturally higher than for furniture that is mass-produced in a factory. Because our master crafters do exceptionally fine work, our customers never regret spending a bit more for pieces built to last for generations.

Note that it can take up to two months to create a piece of furniture once it is ordered. Delivery fees are based on distance from our workshop. Unpacking and placing the item is available for an additional $50.

For photos of our workshop, artisan biographies, customer reviews, and ordering information, please visit us online at www.sumnerwoodcrafting.com.

158. What is mentioned about Sumner Woodcrafting?

(A) Its prices are highly competitive.
(B) It offers free delivery in Memphis.
(C) Its founder handles telephone inquiries.
(D) It allows customers to tour its workshop.

159. The word "fine" in paragraph 2, line 2, is closest in meaning to

(A) small
(B) sharp
(C) skillful
(D) agreeable

160. What is suggested about Sumner Woodcrafting's products?

(A) They are extremely long-lasting.
(B) They contain both natural and human-made materials.
(C) They often require assembly after delivery.
(D) They are usually ordered for offices.

Questions 161-163 refer to the following article.

COLLINSVALE (28 March)—Over the last decade, instability in the pricing of raw materials has become the biggest concern for manufacturers. The issue now surpasses recruitment and technology, which had previously been ranked by businesses as the top two concerns respectively.

The reasons are not difficult to understand. For electronics manufacturers, materials typically represent 20 percent of all expenses, while makers of processed food can spend anywhere between 40 and 60 percent on materials. Thus, even a 10 percent rise in the cost of sugar can dramatically affect a factory's bottom line. Companies that can predict rising costs may be able to temper the effects of market volatility, but even the best forecasting cannot anticipate every change in the marketplace.

161. What is the article mainly about?

(A) An improvement in manufacturing methods
(B) A recent shift in consumer preferences
(C) The introduction of environmental regulations
(D) The changes in costs faced by producers

162. Why does the writer mention electronics manufacturers?

(A) To illustrate innovation over ten years
(B) To show the impact of global trade
(C) To explain recent staffing difficulties
(D) To make a comparison between industries

163. The word "temper" in paragraph 2, line 9, is closest in meaning to

(A) set
(B) toughen
(C) moderate
(D) combine

GO ON TO THE NEXT PAGE

Questions 164-167 refer to the following announcement.

The Lowenstein Bookstore in Mission Bay invites you to this month's book discussion featuring author Hilda Flores. The event will be held on Thursday, April 10, from 7:00 P.M. to 8:30 P.M. Ms. Flores will talk about her new novel, *Grinding the Gears*. — [1] —. The latest adventure in the popular Inspector Svensson series, *Grinding the Gears* finds the beloved inspector investigating strange equipment malfunctions at a national physics research laboratory. — [2] —.

Ms. Flores will discuss the background research she performed while writing the book. — [3] —. A question and answer session will follow the presentation. The event is free for all to attend. — [4] —. The bookstore requires that attendees register at least one day in advance.

164. What is being announced?

(A) The opening of a new bookstore
(B) A presentation by a book author
(C) A book describing a research project
(D) An upcoming movie based on a book

165. What type of book is *Grinding the Gears* ?

(A) A nonfiction story
(B) A biography of a scientist
(C) A collection of short stories
(D) A mystery novel

166. What is indicated about registration?

(A) It closes on April 9.
(B) It requires payment of a fee.
(C) It is optional but encouraged.
(D) It cannot be completed online.

167. In which of the positions marked [1], [2], [3], and [4] does the following sentence best belong?

"Part of her fact-finding involved interviewing government scientists."

(A) [1]
(B) [2]
(C) [3]
(D) [4]

Questions 168-171 refer to the following e-mail.

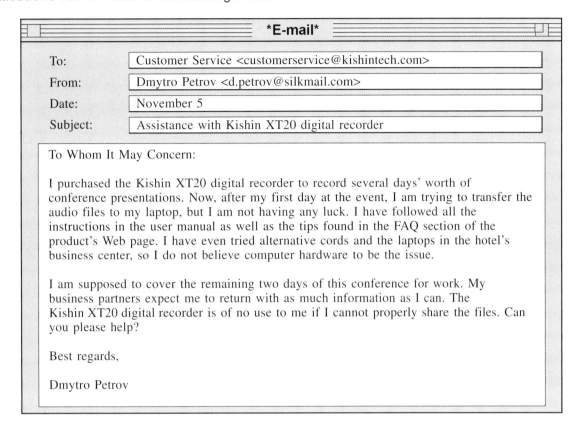

---

168. What problem does Mr. Petrov have with his device?

(A) He cannot move audio files to his computer.
(B) He dislikes its appearance.
(C) He is unable to rename the files.
(D) He is unsatisfied with the sound quality.

169. Why does Mr. Petrov mention a Web page?

(A) To suggest that an image is misleading
(B) To explain that he obtained additional information
(C) To recommend changing a product description
(D) To inquire about compatible accessories

170. The word "cover" in paragraph 2, line 1, is closest in meaning to

(A) protect
(B) contain
(C) extend over
(D) report on

171. What is true about Mr. Petrov?

(A) He volunteered to try some equipment.
(B) He is currently traveling with his business partners.
(C) He will share conference material with his colleagues.
(D) He will soon receive a new laptop from his company.

GO ON TO THE NEXT PAGE

Questions 172-175 refer to the following online chat discussion.

Kristin Burton (8:16 A.M.)

This is my first time posting on this small-business forum. Has anyone here experienced problems when ordering one of Atlara's credit card readers?

Marcos Menke (9:04 A.M.)

Are you referring to the little unit that attaches to your mobile phone or the larger, stand-alone tablet model?

Kristin Burton (9:30 A.M.)

The phone unit. I started an online shop using the Atlara Web hosting service and added pictures of the necklaces and rings I create. But most of my sales are still in person. So I just need a way to accept in-person payments when I'm out at fairs or markets.

Marcos Menke (10:19 A.M.)

Just go to www.atlara.com/pos/hardware and add what you want to your cart.

Kristin Burton (11:21 A.M.)

That's the problem. The system won't let me order it. I get the error message "Your account cannot be verified."

Suzanne Shroer (11:42 A.M.)

I think I know. You have to upload scans of your business registration, a government photo ID, and a statement from your business bank account.

Kristin Burton (12:23 P.M.)

I already did all that, and I still got the error message.

Suzanne Shroer (12:33 P.M.)

If that is the case, try logging back in and following the process again.

Cindy Acosta (1:05 P.M.)

You probably need to call the support line. I found them to be very helpful with my issues a few months ago.

Kristin Burton (1:10 P.M.)

I've spoken with three people already.

172. What does Mr. Menke ask Ms. Burton to clarify?

(A) The type of device she is trying to buy
(B) The experience she had with a Web site
(C) The way she charges her mobile phone
(D) The amount she was charged for a service

173. What does Ms. Burton sell?

(A) Art supplies
(B) Board games
(C) Jewelry
(D) Furniture

174. What does Ms. Shroer suggest?

(A) Filling out a service request
(B) Adjusting a card reader's settings
(C) Submitting some documentation
(D) Creating a separate business account

175. At 1:10 P.M., what does Ms. Burton most likely mean when she writes, "I've spoken with three people already"?

(A) She is impressed with a company's response.
(B) She has previously called the support line.
(C) She has thoroughly researched some specifications.
(D) She has confirmed that the product was shipped.

GO ON TO THE NEXT PAGE

Questions 176-180 refer to the following Web page and e-mail.

https://www.sunnywelcomehotel.co.in

At the Sunny Welcome Hotel in Kolkata, we work hard to ensure that you enjoy your stay.

Please note:

- Each room has a coffeemaker and complimentary coffee and tea. Guests may purchase snacks and other beverages in the vending areas located on each floor.
- Guests with small children may request a rollaway bed or crib for their rooms for no additional charge.
- The business center is open from 9:00 A.M. to 5:00 P.M. each day.
- The swimming pool and children's playground are open during daylight hours. Children must always be supervised by an adult.
- A deposit is necessary to guarantee a room reservation. The deposit will only be refunded if the reservation is cancelled or changed more than 24 hours prior to arrival.
- Guests may check in as early as 2:00 P.M. Checkout after noon on the day of departure is subject to an additional charge.
- Guests are required to present a passport or driver's license at the time of check-in.
- We offer free shuttle service to the airport. Guests can make arrangements at the front desk.
- Our reception desk is staffed 24 hours a day.

To:	generalmanager@sunnywelcomehotel.co.in
From:	samuelramon@myemail.co.uk
Date:	13 May
Subject:	Reservation number EX52417

Hello,

My family and I were very comfortable in the family suite at the Sunny Welcome Hotel in Kolkata last year, and we were looking forward to returning this year for a week starting on 17 April. Unfortunately, we suddenly had to postpone our trip until June, so I called the hotel on the morning of 17 April to change our reservation dates. I thought everything was in order, but when I opened my credit card statement this month, I discovered an additional charge from the Sunny Welcome Hotel.

Could you please look into the matter? I believe that an error has been made and that I should be reimbursed. I would appreciate having the money credited to my account. We still plan to return to Kolkata later this year and anticipate an enjoyable stay at your hotel.

Yours sincerely,

Samuel Ramon

176. According to the Web page, what are hotel guests asked to provide at check-in?

(A) A home address
(B) Payment in advance
(C) Proof of identification
(D) A confirmation number

177. What is NOT included with a stay at the Sunny Welcome Hotel?

(A) Hot beverages
(B) A light breakfast
(C) Airport shuttle service
(D) Use of a swimming pool

178. What does Mr. Ramon indicate in his e-mail?

(A) He usually travels alone.
(B) He has family living in Kolkata.
(C) He is planning to move to Kolkata.
(D) He has stayed at the Sunny Welcome Hotel before.

179. Why most likely was Mr. Ramon charged a fee by the Sunny Welcome Hotel?

(A) He canceled a reservation less than a day before arrival.
(B) He requested a rollaway bed for his room.
(C) He checked out of his room after midday.
(D) He reserved a work space in the business center.

180. What does Mr. Ramon request?

(A) A credit to his account
(B) A discount on a future hotel stay
(C) A room upgrade to a family suite
(D) An extension of a hotel stay

GO ON TO THE NEXT PAGE

Questions 181-185 refer to the following e-mail and Web page.

E-Mail Message

From: Dexter Abbott
To: Nina Sosa
Date: 20 August
Subject: Next steps

Dear Ms. Sosa,

I have good news. The plans for the layout of the new Fountain Road office building have just been approved by Lanfei Chan at our corporate office. We now need to start thinking about the artwork for the main open-plan office area on the third floor of the building. This is one of our last tasks before the office opens in October.

I have heard that Red Starling Art has a good reputation for helping with office interiors. Could you look at the company's Web site today and find out if any of its services might be suitable for us? I am wondering whether photography or paintings would look best in the space. What do you think? I am still waiting to hear back from Maxwell Willis in Finance about the budget for art, so please do not agree to anything with Red Starling Art until we know more.

Thank you,

Dexter Abbott, Facilities Manager
KLX Accountancy

---

https://www.redstarlingart.co.uk/offices/

| Home | About Us | **Services** | Contact Us |

Red Starling Art offers a range of consultancy services for office buildings:

- **Remake:** For clients who want a complete redesign of the interior of their office, we work with you to create a layout and decoration scheme that meets your needs.

- **Align:** For clients looking to incorporate artwork into a new office, we help you find the right pieces (paintings, photographs, prints, or sculptures) for your space.

- **Connect:** For clients who want to add a local touch to their offices, we collaborate with area artists and photographers to bring their unique perspective to you.

- **Reframe:** For clients who want to update but keep their existing artwork, we suggest new framing, new lighting, or new arrangements for a fresh look.

Our work is always tailored to the specific needs of our clients, so we cannot provide fixed prices. Please e-mail Birgit Lowenbruck at blowenbruck@redstarlingart.co.uk to book a free consultation. After the consultation, she will provide you with an estimate for the agreed-upon services.

181. What is suggested about the Fountain Road office building?

(A) It opened last October.
(B) It is the corporate headquarters of KLX Accountancy.
(C) It has more than one floor.
(D) It has a conference center.

182. In the e-mail, what does Mr. Abbott ask Ms. Sosa to do?

(A) Finish a task she started last week
(B) Approve plans for the layout of an office
(C) Agree to a price for purchasing artwork
(D) Research interior design options online

183. Who is responsible for the budget for artwork?

(A) Mr. Abbott
(B) Ms. Chan
(C) Mr. Willis
(D) Ms. Sosa

184. What Red Starling Art service would be most suitable for the Fountain Road office building?

(A) Remake
(B) Align
(C) Connect
(D) Reframe

185. According to the Web page, how can someone learn the cost of Red Starling Art's services?

(A) By submitting information through the Contact Us page
(B) By going to a Web page with cost information
(C) By submitting a document to Ms. Lowenbruck
(D) By attending a consultation with Ms. Lowenbruck

GO ON TO THE NEXT PAGE

To:	jdixon@milkalenterprises.com
From:	humanresources@milkalenterprises.com
Date:	April 28
Subject:	Employee survey responses

Dear Ms. Dixon,

I read through all the responses to the semiannual employee survey, and I want to highlight a few points that were repeatedly raised. We can use this list of suggestions to help determine our priorities.

Suggestion 1. A more flexible policy for working from home
Suggestion 2. An expanded in-office recycling strategy
Suggestion 3. More financial rewards for excellent work
Suggestion 4. More opportunities for technical training

Also, if you approve, I would like to simplify the survey form before we administer it again. The open-ended questions make the data difficult to analyze. I propose incorporating more yes-no questions or rating scales to determine how much a colleague agrees or disagrees with a statement.

Kind regards,

Judith Hathaway, Human Resources

MEMO

To: All Staff
From: Jenna Dixon, General Manager
Date: May 8
Subject: Volunteers needed

I am seeking volunteers to form a committee that will launch an office recycling program. Having such a program was one of the most frequently identified needs mentioned on the recent employee survey. This program will prevent recyclables, including plastics, glass, metal, paper, and cardboard, from ending up in landfills.

Also, we need a volunteer to be the coordinator of this committee. I will be happy to meet with this coordinator to discuss first steps. Note that time spent on coordination tasks would be in addition to your regular work duties. A small amount of funds will be made available to be spent on program setup costs.

To: All Staff
From: Mohammad Asghari
Date: June 13
Subject: Bins are here

As chairperson of the In-office Recycling Committee, I am happy to report that we now have recycling bins in the kitchen for glass bottles, soda cans, and cardboard and paper. It took us some time to get this program started because finding containers narrow enough to squeeze three between the door and the refrigerator proved challenging. But I was finally able to purchase some.

Please note that the recycling facility we are working with has stringent guidelines on what they accept, so I am creating illustrated instructions to hang above each bin. Those will be up tomorrow, and committee members will be monitoring our collection system to make sure the program is going smoothly. Please contact me with any questions, concerns, or feedback.

186. In the e-mail, how does Ms. Hathaway suggest improving future surveys?

(A) By changing the format of some questions
(B) By collecting the responses anonymously
(C) By conducting them more frequently
(D) By using specialized software

187. What suggestion from the survey results is Ms. Dixon acting on?

(A) Suggestion 1
(B) Suggestion 2
(C) Suggestion 3
(D) Suggestion 4

188. According to Mr. Asghari, why was a new program delayed?

(A) Some orders took a long time to be processed.
(B) Some equipment needed to be moved.
(C) A coordinator needed to approve it.
(D) A room had space limitations.

189. What is suggested about Mr. Asghari?

(A) He has led a training series on recycling.
(B) He paid for some items using the company's money.
(C) He meets with Ms. Dixon on a weekly basis.
(D) He was acknowledged in a company newsletter.

190. What is Mr. Asghari planning to do?

(A) Recruit volunteers
(B) Contact suppliers
(C) Display signs
(D) Take inventory

GO ON TO THE NEXT PAGE

Kooper's Vision is seeking an optician for its eyewear department. Must have a valid Massachusetts optician license and at least three years of relevant experience. The position requires excellent customer service skills and a strong awareness of current fashion trends in the industry. Responsibilities include helping clients choose frames, ordering eyeglasses, and filing insurance claims.

This full-time position is available at Kooper's Vision at Danvers Mall. Contact store manager Tanisha Mosley at 978-555-0101. Must be available to start during the last week of August.

---

https://www.koopersvision.com

Kooper's Vision at Danvers Mall
Hours:

Monday	10 A.M.–7 P.M.
Tuesday	10 A.M.–7 P.M.
Wednesday	10 A.M.–7 P.M.
Thursday	10 A.M.–7 P.M.
Friday	10 A.M.–7 P.M.
Saturday	10 A.M.–6 P.M.
Sunday	10 A.M.–4 P.M.

During the month of August, enjoy 50% off the second pair of eyeglasses.

Kooper's Vision is your local optical center for all your eye-care needs in Danvers, Massachusetts. We are located on the upper level of the Danvers Mall next to Eight Days Sporting Goods. Call 978-555-0101 today to schedule your annual eye exam. Exams by appointment only.

Optical Centers Reviews

Rating: 5 stars ★★★★★

I have been wearing eyeglasses since I was ten years old. I now have five children, and four of them wear glasses, so I have visited many opticians over the years. My recent visit to Kooper's Vision on August 31 was, by far, the best.

Ms. Palmer offered her help when she saw that I was overwhelmed by the eyeglass selection at Kooper's Vision. She looked at the shape of my face and steered me toward a few pairs of glasses that were perfect for me! She knew exactly what looked best on me and advised me about the size, color, quality, and cost of the frames I considered. Ms. Palmer also explained the different types of lenses and lens coatings available. I could not decide which was my favorite pair of eyeglasses, so I bought two pairs! I was incredulous when she told me it was her first day working at the store—she was the best optician I have ever had!

Melvin Drake

191. According to the job advertisement, what is true about the open position?

(A) It comes with health insurance.
(B) It starts at the end of August.
(C) It includes a fashionable company uniform.
(D) It requires that candidates work on a team.

192. What is indicated about Kooper's Vision on the Web page?

(A) It stays open later on Saturday.
(B) It is located on the lower level of a mall.
(C) It offers a selection of sports eyeglasses.
(D) It requires an appointment for an eye exam.

193. What is most likely true about Ms. Palmer?

(A) She works with Ms. Mosley.
(B) She previously worked at a fashion shop.
(C) She earned an optician license two years ago.
(D) She is the new owner of Kooper's Vision.

194. According to the review, how did Ms. Palmer help Mr. Drake?

(A) By recommending frames that fit his face
(B) By extending the length of his appointment
(C) By choosing glasses for his children
(D) By upgrading the coating on his eyeglass lenses

195. What is suggested about Mr. Drake?

(A) He thinks his prescription has changed.
(B) He started wearing eyeglasses recently.
(C) He frequently shops at Danvers Mall.
(D) He received a discount on his purchase.

TEST 7

GO ON TO THE NEXT PAGE

---

https://www.hellosnackvending.com/services

Our Services

Hello Snack Vending offers a variety of vending and coffee services for company break rooms and vending machines.

Service 1 (Micromarket)—We set up a small market in your break room, with customized products available on open shelves. Micromarkets are self-service and feature electronic payments. Shelving and fixtures are provided.

Service 2 (Pantry)—We stock your break room cabinets with a variety of products that you select. Pantry service is paid for in advance, freeing users from paying per item.

Service 3 (Coffee)—We keep your break room stocked with coffee, tea, and all related essentials. We supply you with group-sized coffee makers, coffee, and individually sized creamer and sugar varieties.

Service 4 (Traditional Vending)—We regularly stock your vending machine with a customized selection of carbonated beverages, juice, and water.

Service 5 (Healthy Vending)—We regularly stock your vending machine with a wide selection of healthy snacks.

E-Mail Message

To: customercare@hellosnackvending.com
From: dlewis@kivowitzcompany.com
Date: November 14
Subject: Vending service

Hello,

My company recently bought a gently used nonrefrigerated vending machine, which has been placed in our employee break room. I am looking for a stocking service to fill it so that the staff can start using it.

Does your company only stock vending machines that you own, or do you also offer a stocking service for other machines? If you can service ours, I would like to know more about the snacks you have available to fill the machine. Could you please send me a list of the products you offer?

Thank you for your assistance.

Best regards,

Denikia Lewis
Kivowitz Company

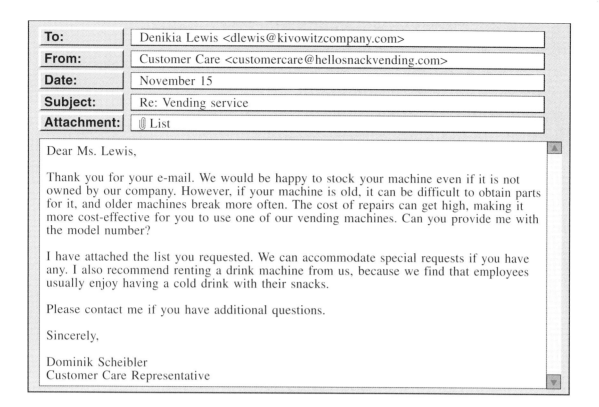

To:	Denikia Lewis <dlewis@kivowitzcompany.com>
From:	Customer Care <customercare@hellosnackvending.com>
Date:	November 15
Subject:	Re: Vending service
Attachment:	📎 List

Dear Ms. Lewis,

Thank you for your e-mail. We would be happy to stock your machine even if it is not owned by our company. However, if your machine is old, it can be difficult to obtain parts for it, and older machines break more often. The cost of repairs can get high, making it more cost-effective for you to use one of our vending machines. Can you provide me with the model number?

I have attached the list you requested. We can accommodate special requests if you have any. I also recommend renting a drink machine from us, because we find that employees usually enjoy having a cold drink with their snacks.

Please contact me if you have additional questions.

Sincerely,

Dominik Scheibler
Customer Care Representative

196. What is mentioned about Service 1 ?

(A) It comes with a fixed product selection.
(B) It allows users to pay electronically.
(C) It requires an annual contract.
(D) It includes shelving for an extra fee.

197. What does Ms. Lewis suggest about her company's vending machine?

(A) It is in poor condition.
(B) It was recently serviced.
(C) It was overpriced.
(D) It is currently empty.

198. What does Mr. Scheibler ask Ms. Lewis to send him?

(A) A signed contract for the service
(B) A picture of her vending machine
(C) A list of needed parts
(D) A model number

199. What is included in the list Mr. Scheibler attached to his e-mail?

(A) The snacks that his company offers
(B) The dates that his company can make deliveries
(C) The brand of vending machines that his company uses
(D) The costs involved with vending services

200. What additional service does Mr. Scheibler suggest?

(A) Service 2
(B) Service 3
(C) Service 4
(D) Service 5

Stop! This is the end of the test. If you finish before time is called, you may go back to Parts 5, 6, and 7 and check your work.

토익® 정기시험
기출문제집 4
1000

TEST 08
무료 동영상 강의

기출 TEST

08

In the Reading test, you will read a variety of texts and answer several different types of reading comprehension questions. The entire Reading test will last 75 minutes. There are three parts, and directions are given for each part. You are encouraged to answer as many questions as possible within the time allowed.

You must mark your answers on the separate answer sheet. Do not write your answers in your test book.

PART 5

Directions: A word or phrase is missing in each of the sentences below. Four answer choices are given below each sentence. Select the best answer to complete the sentence. Then mark the letter (A), (B), (C), or (D) on your answer sheet.

101. The order is estimated to arrive ------- November 15.

(A) by
(B) until
(C) at
(D) down

102. Please make sure that ------- personal belongings are safely stored out of sight.

(A) you
(B) yourself
(C) yours
(D) your

103. Be sure to fold all the clothes ------- before placing them in bags for customers.

(A) neatly
(B) deeply
(C) highly
(D) surely

104. Visitors should not take ------- while touring the restricted areas of the facility.

(A) photographic
(B) photographing
(C) photographs
(D) photographed

105. The new novel by mystery writer Meredith Delgado will be ------- in bookstores nationwide on July 9.

(A) regular
(B) available
(C) convenient
(D) completed

106. Cashiers should call for an ------- cashier when more than three customers are in line.

(A) addition
(B) additions
(C) additional
(D) additionally

107. Nga Ho, currently the sales manager for the southern division, will take on a new ------- within the Trang Media Group in February.

(A) view
(B) access
(C) role
(D) session

108. To prevent the sauce from scorching while being heated, stir it ------- with a wooden spoon.

(A) continues
(B) continue
(C) continuously
(D) continuous

109. Naito Travel Agency is ------- experienced guides to lead tours in Japan.

(A) seeking
(B) spreading
(C) working
(D) focusing

110. ------- a mineral-rich spring was discovered nearby, Hotel Denzali became a popular tourist destination.

(A) That
(B) After
(C) How
(D) Every

111. To save time, download your tickets to your mobile phone ------- arriving at the venue.

(A) since
(B) before
(C) although
(D) without

112. Several companies have already ------- bids to paint logos on our delivery trucks.

(A) submit
(B) submission
(C) submitted
(D) submitting

113. The jewel-toned fabrics featured in Norfolk Fashion's spring collection gave the ------- a luxurious look.

(A) marks
(B) portions
(C) types
(D) garments

114. Please do not share your resident access code with ------- living in communities other than Arbor Hill Apartments.

(A) anyone
(B) either
(C) most
(D) each

115. The social media specialist should always be looking for ways to make people more ------- of the Zintaman brand.

(A) concise
(B) aware
(C) precious
(D) defined

116. All Tayton residents ------- their unwanted appliances at the public works facility for a small fee.

(A) can discard
(B) have been discarded
(C) to be discarding
(D) discarding

117. Following numerous requests from customers, Manilla Lunchbox has ------- added vegetarian options to its menu.

(A) extremely
(B) typically
(C) finally
(D) closely

118. Crutchfield Heating and Cooling installs gas, oil, and electric furnaces from the industry's ------- manufacturers.

(A) leading
(B) leader
(C) leads
(D) leadership

119. To reduce stress and ------- productivity, Sciallo Corp. offers free lunchtime fitness classes to its employees.

(A) distribute
(B) boost
(C) sweat
(D) tone

120. Yoshimi Fashion customers ------- a secure online shopping experience.

(A) are guaranteed
(B) to guarantee
(C) guaranteeing
(D) having guaranteed

GO ON TO THE NEXT PAGE

TEST 8

121. Using last year's record profits, Mr. Shakar was able to invest ------- a new grocery delivery service.

(A) about
(B) near
(C) in
(D) of

122. Central Oregon Power must renew the ------- at least 30 days before the current one expires.

(A) contractor
(B) contract
(C) contracting
(D) contracted

123. Please park on the west side of the building ------- parking spaces closer to the entrance can be used by customers.

(A) instead of
(B) so that
(C) resulting from
(D) as if

124. The report was authored ------- by Chae-Won Sohn in the research department and by Ray Hahn, the head of marketing.

(A) joint
(B) joints
(C) jointed
(D) jointly

125. The Teason Resort offers ------- activities for children and adults throughout the day.

(A) capable
(B) dense
(C) absent
(D) numerous

126. Because the museum receives generous donations, it ------- raises the price of admission tickets.

(A) nearly
(B) likely
(C) generally
(D) rarely

127. Global Data LLC will promote Hae-In Ahn to Chief Financial Officer ------- June 1.

(A) effective
(B) effecting
(C) effected
(D) effect

128. The upcoming focus group will be an online meeting during ------- each participant can join via a videoconferencing program.

(A) through
(B) there
(C) which
(D) who

129. Patricia Park developed a proprietary ------- for Sprayeze, an all-organic cleaning compound.

(A) menu
(B) formula
(C) article
(D) decision

130. Rayel Pharmaceutical provides a list of its ------- and their affiliations on its Web site.

(A) research
(B) researching
(C) researched
(D) researchers

PART 6

Directions: Read the texts that follow. A word, phrase, or sentence is missing in parts of each text. Four answer choices for each question are given below the text. Select the best answer to complete the text. Then mark the letter (A), (B), (C), or (D) on your answer sheet.

Questions 131-134 refer to the following e-mail.

To: mnandy@gmantcs.com
From: jblaire@blaireaccounting.ca
Re: AUTOMATIC REPLY
Date: 9 January, 10:34 AM

Hello, and thank you for contacting Blaire Accounting. I will be out of the office until 31 January.

I will respond to your message when I ------- . If you need ------- assistance, please contact Susan
                                    131.   **132.**

Lewis, my administrative assistant, at slewis@blaireaccounting.ca. You can ------- call her directly
                                                      133.

at 416-555-0193. ------- .
                134.

Jean Blaire, President

---

131. (A) recover
(B) return
(C) begin
(D) finish

132. (A) immediate
(B) immediately
(C) immediacy
(D) immediacies

133. (A) also
(B) lightly
(C) similarly
(D) again

134. (A) Ms. Blaire will be back in the office earlier than expected.
(B) Please come and see us if you ever find yourself in Toronto.
(C) It is essential to hire a competent payroll and tax accountant.
(D) Ms. Lewis is in the office on weekdays from 9 A.M. to 5 P.M.

GO ON TO THE NEXT PAGE

Attention customers of Metro Coffee:

We are excited to announce that we ------- a second Metro Coffee store! As you know, we recently
135.

expanded our offerings to include baked goods as well as coffee. As a result, our ------- has
136.

increased significantly. To keep up with demand, we decided that a second store was necessary.

------- . Our new space is substantially ------- but offers the same wide selection of items. Make
137.   138.

sure to stop by and check out our new location today!

---

135. (A) will open
(B) can open
(C) are opening
(D) have opened

136. (A) debt
(B) payroll
(C) business
(D) investment

137. (A) Metro Coffee has been a part of the
community for nine years.
(B) We roast our coffee beans right here
on-site.
(C) Many people enjoy eating a pastry
while drinking a cup of coffee.
(D) It is located two miles away in the
historic district.

138. (A) large
(B) larger
(C) largely
(D) largest

Questions 139-142 refer to the following memo.

To: All Ferrese Hotel Employees
From: Sergio Prieto, Hotel Manager
Date: Monday, July 4
Subject: Global Shipping Partners Conference

The Ferrese Hotel will be hosting the Global Shipping Partners Conference next week, from Tuesday to Sunday. ------- , management expects to see many more customers in the hotel's
                                    139.

restaurants and gift shops. ------- . I will be hiring temporary staff to ensure that ------- can meet
                            140.   **141.**

these increased demands. Please take the time to help them learn our ------- when they are
                                                                        142.

here. Doing so will ensure that all operations run smoothly while the conference is taking place.

139. (A) If not
     (B) After all
     (C) Therefore
     (D) In the meantime

140. (A) Restaurant renovations are almost completed.
     (B) Conference registration forms have been posted online.
     (C) Applications will be reviewed later this week.
     (D) The business center will also be busier than usual.

141. (A) it
     (B) we
     (C) both
     (D) something

142. (A) lines
     (B) steps
     (C) names
     (D) routines

GO ON TO THE NEXT PAGE

Questions 143-146 refer to the following article.

DALLAS (July 28)—Zura Technology Solutions (ZTS) announced today that it has completed the

------- of an office building located at 425 Van Kirk Street here in Dallas. The building, most
143.

recently the headquarters of Brickhall Insurance, will serve as ZTS's ------- base of operations.
144.

The company's relocation from Fort Worth is expected to be complete by the end of the calendar

year. ------- . "Our decision to acquire the building reflects ZTS's ongoing commitment to the
145.

Dallas area and will enable us to better serve our customers, business partners, and

stakeholders," said Gloria Rubirosa, ZTS's CEO. "From our new home in Dallas, we

------- to work hard to meet the needs of each and every one of our customers around the world."
146.

143. (A) construction
     (B) cleaning
     (C) inspection
     (D) purchase

144. (A) voluntary
     (B) primary
     (C) short-term
     (D) occasional

145. (A) ZTS's leadership team sees the
         move as strategic.
     (B) For example, it provides a range of
         services to small businesses.
     (C) There are only a few available sites in
         the Main Street District.
     (D) Over 15,000 people are employed by
         ZTS worldwide.

146. (A) continued
     (B) continuing
     (C) would have continued
     (D) will continue

Directions: In this part you will read a selection of texts, such as magazine and newspaper articles, e-mails, and instant messages. Each text or set of texts is followed by several questions. Select the best answer for each question and mark the letter (A), (B), (C), or (D) on your answer sheet.

Questions 147-148 refer to the following advertisement.

Zoya's Basket
12 Tilton Street, Tenafly, NJ 07670
www.zoyasbasket.com

Do you love all the products at Zoya's Basket? Here's a reason to love them even more! Sign up for our reward program and get up to 5% back on everything Zoya's offers! Use your cash rewards in the store or online.

- Vitamins and supplements
- Nut and seed butters
- Jams, jellies, and fruit spreads
- Whole grains and cereals
- Health and wellness products

We ship throughout New Jersey. Shipping is free with a minimum $35 purchase. Please allow up to three days for delivery.

147. What is one purpose of the advertisement?

(A) To announce a sale on discontinued products
(B) To ask consumers for feedback on their favorite items
(C) To encourage consumers to join a reward program
(D) To advertise a special offer on fresh fruits and vegetables

148. What is indicated about deliveries?

(A) They require a signature.
(B) They arrive within three days.
(C) They are free with a coupon code.
(D) They must be scheduled at the time the order is placed.

GO ON TO THE NEXT PAGE

Grecian Terrace Hotel

Host your next business conference at our five-star hotel on the beautiful Messenian Gulf. Our facility has spacious meeting rooms overlooking the sea and the picturesque beach. The hotel is the perfect setting for a corporate retreat for your staff. Enjoy a team bonding experience while taking advantage of gourmet meals, great views, and first-rate entertainment.

Contact: Helena Samaras, Hospitality Manager
hsamaras@grecianterrace.com.gr
+30 2721 093365

---

149. For whom is the advertisement most likely intended?

(A) Residents of Kalamata
(B) Overseas visitors on holiday
(C) Corporate travel planners
(D) Local catering companies

150. What is indicated about the Grecian Terrace Hotel?

(A) It just renovated its dining room.
(B) It is under new management.
(C) It has several locations.
(D) It is near the seaside.

Questions 151-152 refer to the following report.

Cozilete Slippers
Social Media Report for December

Metric	Results
Number of posts this month	8
For each post, average number of times the post was viewed	223,648
Average number of individuals who viewed each post	87,122
Average number of advertisements for Cozilete Slippers per post	1
Average number of times a link to an advertisement in a post was clicked	24,015
Average total interactions per post (number of likes, shares, and comments)	674

Data for corporate internal use only

151. For whom is the report most likely intended?

(A) Cozilete Slippers' suppliers
(B) Cozilete Slippers' marketing team
(C) Cozilete Slippers' shipping department
(D) Cozilete Slippers' most loyal customers

152. What is indicated in the report?

(A) Every post contained more than one
    advertisement for Cozilete Slippers.
(B) Most individuals commented on each
    post they viewed.
(C) Each post was viewed by an average
    of about 87,000 individuals.
(D) Few individuals viewed a post more
    than one time.

TEST 8

GO ON TO THE NEXT PAGE

Questions 153-154 refer to the following text-message chain.

Keri Mohan (12:40 P.M.)
I'm nearly done readying the jewelry orders for shipment. I've inserted a packing slip and business card in each box. Should anything else be included before I seal them up and drop them off at the post office?

Sujay Rishi (12:42 P.M.)
Can you put a Rishi Gemstones magnet in each box?

Keri Mohan (12:43 P.M.)
Certainly! I'll do that right away.

Keri Mohan (12:50 P.M.)
Also, we're running low on shipping labels. I can order some more.

Sujay Rishi (12:54 P.M.)
Actually, we have an entire bin of them. Check the supply closet. Let me know if you can't find them.

153. What does Ms. Mohan ask about?

(A) What to include in some boxes
(B) When an order will be shipped
(C) How to safely package the jewelry
(D) Where the business cards are stored

154. At 12:54 P.M., what does Mr. Rishi most likely mean when he writes, "Actually, we have an entire bin of them"?

(A) Ms. Mohan can give away the magnets.
(B) Ms. Mohan can reorganize the supply closet.
(C) Ms. Mohan should not order more labels.
(D) Ms. Mohan should not go to the post office.

Twin Lakes
The best place to live in Tielersburg!

Please join the staff of Twin Lakes for our monthly resident information meeting.

Date and time: Tuesday, March 21, 7:00 P.M.–8:30 P.M.
Location: Community Center conference room (across the hall from the rental office)

Agenda items and presenters:

1. Property enhancements: overview of plans for fence repair and new landscaping in the pool area—Mr. Abgarian, groundskeeping and maintenance supervisor

2. Community garden: details for garden plot sign-up and annual biggest tomato contest—Ms. Kantor, events and activities coordinator

3. Water main work on Huron Street: progress update—Mr. Carter, Department of Public Works, City of Tielersburg

4. Utility rates: discussion about the rise in quarterly utility fees charged to Twin Lakes property management by the city—Mr. Underwood, general manager

5. New business: creation of Resident Advisory Board—Ms. Davis, leasing and resident relations manager

6. Questions and comments

7. Adjournment

---

155. What most likely is Twin Lakes?

(A) A group of shops
(B) A gardening center
(C) An amusement park
(D) A housing complex

156. What is Mr. Abgarian's role in the meeting?

(A) To provide information about scheduled improvements
(B) To explain details of an annual contest
(C) To plan the repair of a broken water pipe
(D) To set the fees people will pay

157. Who has job responsibilities outside of Twin Lakes?

(A) Ms. Kantor
(B) Mr. Carter
(C) Mr. Underwood
(D) Ms. Davis

TEST 8

GO ON TO THE NEXT PAGE

Questions 158-160 refer to the following notice.

Lingate Chemical Corporation
Laboratory Safety Rules

The following is a partial list of rules you must follow while in the laboratory. Before beginning work in the lab, all workers are also required to read our most recent safety manual and complete our basic safety course. Please contact Mr. Kang if you need to complete these prerequisites.

- Wear mandatory lab coat, goggles, and footwear.
- Follow directions on posted signs in case of an accident.
- Know how to properly operate all safety equipment (fire extinguishers, eye wash stations, etc.).
- Know the location of all emergency exits.
- Refrain from eating or drinking in the laboratory.
- Report any unsafe conditions, accidents, or spills immediately to your supervisor.
- In an emergency, exit immediately, call emergency services, and then contact your supervisor.

158. Who is the notice most likely intended for?

(A) Students
(B) Employees
(C) Cleaning crews
(D) Emergency personnel

159. Why would Mr. Kang be contacted?

(A) To obtain safety equipment
(B) To report unsafe conditions
(C) To arrange to complete a course
(D) To submit revisions to the safety manual

160. What is NOT a stated rule for working in the laboratory?

(A) Goggles must be worn.
(B) Exits must remain open.
(C) Food must not be eaten.
(D) Accidents must be reported.

Questions 161-163 refer to the following e-mail.

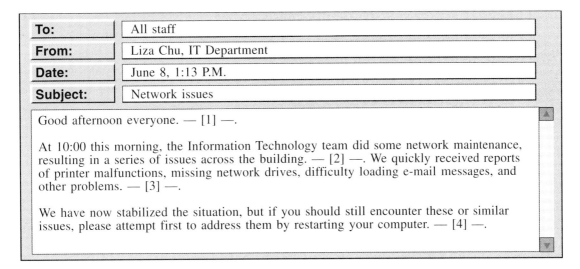

To:	All staff
From:	Liza Chu, IT Department
Date:	June 8, 1:13 P.M.
Subject:	Network issues

Good afternoon everyone. — [1] —.

At 10:00 this morning, the Information Technology team did some network maintenance, resulting in a series of issues across the building. — [2] —. We quickly received reports of printer malfunctions, missing network drives, difficulty loading e-mail messages, and other problems. — [3] —.

We have now stabilized the situation, but if you should still encounter these or similar issues, please attempt first to address them by restarting your computer. — [4] —.

161. What is the e-mail about?

(A) Scheduling a team meeting
(B) Setting up a new e-mail account
(C) Concerns about Web browsing security
(D) Problems with a computer network

162. What probably happened before Ms. Chu sent the e-mail?

(A) Employees requested assistance from the IT department.
(B) Log-on procedures for company accounts were changed.
(C) Computer equipment was removed from the building.
(D) Some staff members received new printers.

163. In which of the positions marked [1], [2], [3], and [4] does the following sentence best belong?

"If you continue to have problems after doing so, then give us a call."

(A) [1]
(B) [2]
(C) [3]
(D) [4]

GO ON TO THE NEXT PAGE

TEST 8

Questions 164-167 refer to the following text-message chain.

Sunisa Sommer (1:30 P.M.)
Hi Raphael and Hamed. Can either of you tell me where I can find the laptop that's usually in Conference Room B? It isn't on the cart with the projector.

Raphael Luongo (1:32 P.M.)
I used it for my presentation on Monday, but I left it in the conference room.

Hamed Gabr (1:32 P.M.)
I believe Martin Dabliz was going to ask someone in the IT department to look at it because it wasn't working properly.

Sunisa Sommer (1:34 P.M.)
Got it. Do you know if a repair ticket was submitted?

Hamed Gabr (1:35 P.M.)
I don't think Martin knows all the IT procedures. He's only in his first week.

Sunisa Sommer (1:37 P.M.)
Right. We should make sure that information is included in the employee orientation materials.

Raphael Luongo (1:41 P.M.)
I don't see a ticket on the IT site. I'll reach out to IT and take care of that now.

164. Why does Ms. Sommer message her colleagues?

(A) To alert them that a projector is broken
(B) To ask where a computer has been put
(C) To request help creating a presentation
(D) To find out whether a conference room is available

165. At 1:34 P.M., what does Ms. Sommer most likely mean when she writes, "Got it"?

(A) She found the repair ticket.
(B) She now has access to a Web site.
(C) She knows the correct procedure to follow.
(D) She understands what happened.

166. What is suggested about Mr. Dabliz?

(A) He was recently hired.
(B) He is Mr. Gabr's supervisor.
(C) He is the chief technology officer.
(D) He was interviewed on Monday.

167. What will Mr. Luongo probably do next?

(A) Revise a company policy
(B) Repair the laptop himself
(C) Contact the IT department
(D) Update the training materials

Questions 168-171 refer to the following e-mail.

```
╔══════════════════════════════════*E-mail*══════════════════════════════════╗
║                                                                              ║
║   To:             Lindsey Galloway <lgalloway@sportsupplies.com>             ║
║   From:           Samuel Bains <samuelbains@exertreks.com>                   ║
║   Date:           August 16                                                  ║
║   Subject:        Exertreks boots for winter activities                      ║
║                                                                              ║
║   Hello Ms. Galloway,                                                        ║
║                                                                              ║
║   I am sorry I missed your call this morning. The answers to your questions  ║
║   are given below.                                                           ║
║                                                                              ║
║   We here at Exertreks have recently completed the development of our Winter ║
║   Hikers. Like our other models, they are waterproof, but the Winter Hikers  ║
║   are most appropriate for use in extreme cold. The boots are lined with a   ║
║   proprietary material that is highly effective at retaining body heat. They ║
║   are also durable, light, and comfortable. For orders of 50 pairs or more   ║
║   of the Winter Hikers, the wholesale price per pair is $65. The recommended ║
║   retail price is $89. We can deliver your order in two weeks.               ║
║                                                                              ║
║   Presale reviews of the boots by experts in outdoor sports have been        ║
║   enthusiastic. You can expect the Winter Hikers to be a big hit with your   ║
║   customers this year. I look forward to hearing from you soon to answer     ║
║   any other questions and to help you with your first order.                 ║
║                                                                              ║
║   Sincerely,                                                                 ║
║                                                                              ║
║   Samuel Bains                                                               ║
║                                                                              ║
╚══════════════════════════════════════════════════════════════════════════════╝
```

168. What is implied in Mr. Bains's e-mail?

(A) Ms. Galloway asked him to check on an order she recently placed.
(B) Ms. Galloway left a message for him asking for information.
(C) He asked Ms. Galloway to return a call he had made the day before.
(D) He and Ms. Galloway met earlier in the day.

169. What is NOT mentioned about the boots?

(A) Their color
(B) Their weight
(C) Their durability
(D) Their warmth

170. The word "hit" in paragraph 3, line 2, is closest in meaning to

(A) match
(B) arrival
(C) success
(D) request

171. What does Mr. Bains want Ms. Galloway to do?

(A) Give the boots a good review online
(B) Contact him to arrange delivery of some boots
(C) Charge customers $65 for each pair of boots
(D) Sell him insulation material to be used in the boots

GO ON TO THE NEXT PAGE

TEST 8

https://www.hurnhamhistoricalsociety.org/news

Tuesday Evening Lecture Series

We are pleased to announce that our third annual lecture series will be hosted by the Hurnham Heritage Museum on Tuesday evenings over the next six weeks. — [1] —. Each guest speaker will focus on objects from the museum's permanent collection. — [2] —. The first lecture, on June 15 at 7:00 P.M., features Georgia Hinds, head curator of the Knowles Art Gallery. — [3] —. Ms. Hinds will use a writing desk, a chest, and a household table to discuss what furniture can reveal to us about the lives of the first Hurnham residents over 200 years ago.

The lecture series is open to the public and includes free admission to the Hurnham Heritage Museum. — [4] —. The Fasseller Café, next door to the museum, will stay open late on Tuesdays to accommodate lecture attendees and the general public.

Posted on June 8

172. What is true about the lecture series?

(A) It highlights modern arts and crafts.
(B) It schedules events on a monthly basis.
(C) It is sponsored by local art galleries.
(D) It is being offered for the third year.

173. Who owns the objects that Ms. Hinds will speak about?

(A) The Hurnham Historical Society
(B) The Knowles Art Gallery
(C) The Hurnham Heritage Museum
(D) The Fasseller Café

174. What is suggested about the town of Hurnham?

(A) It was founded more than a hundred years ago.
(B) It has an aging population.
(C) It attracts many artists.
(D) It was a center for furniture production.

175. In which of the positions marked [1], [2], [3], and [4] does the following sentence best belong?

"These include items such as furniture, needlework, diaries, musical instruments, and clothing."

(A) [1]
(B) [2]
(C) [3]
(D) [4]

TEST 8

Leadership: Essays on Being a Great Leader
Skymill Publishing
Joan Cristophe, Senior Editor

Table of Contents

Book Review: *Leadership: Essays on Being a Great Leader*

As a businessperson, I am glad there is a publisher whose sole focus is on business. Skymill Publishing's latest book is a great one for leaders in all industries. Joan Cristophe has sought out some of the world's best minds to write essays for this book that will provide readers with some unique perspectives. In her own introduction, she argues that there is a greater need than ever before for more effective leaders in business.

Cristophe expertly arranges the essays in this collection so that the voices of each author complement one another. The essay by Xiaofeng Li is the perfect example of this. It is strategically sandwiched between Francisca Conde's essay on leadership in action and Ron Blake's essay on focusing on the details. Roderick Muller's essay is the sole disappointment. Surprisingly little new information or insight is offered on its pages, and the writing style is rather flat. Besides that, the collection is excellent, and readers with an interest in leadership in many different situations will find useful nuggets of wisdom and vision within.

176. According to the table of contents, who is Ms. Cristophe?

(A) The owner of Skymill Publishing
(B) A book editor
(C) A local business person
(D) An industry leader

177. What is indicated about Skymill Publishing?

(A) It recently won an award.
(B) It specializes in business books.
(C) It is currently hiring.
(D) It is releasing its first book.

178. According to the book review, what is the topic of the book introduction?

(A) The current need for strong business leadership
(B) Learning from famous business leaders
(C) Popular training programs in corporations
(D) Process improvements that work

179. In the book review, the word "sole" in paragraph 2, line 5, is closest in meaning to

(A) underlying
(B) entire
(C) only
(D) usual

180. On what page does the essay with notably minimal new information begin?

(A) Page 34
(B) Page 51
(C) Page 83
(D) Page 119

GO ON TO THE NEXT PAGE

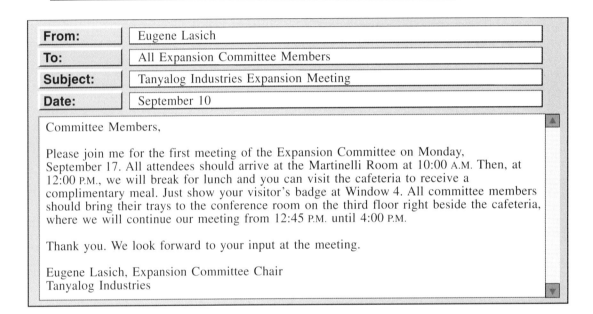

Tanyalog Industries Policy 4-02

The cafeteria (3rd floor) is open to all employees and guests from 8:00 A.M. to 2:30 P.M. Food from the cafeteria may be eaten there or brought on trays to the following conference rooms: Chestnut Room (1st floor), Burnside Room (2nd floor), Smith Room (3rd floor), and Danville Room (4th floor).

Using the rooms at lunchtime does not require a reservation. However, please do not enter the room if it is already occupied by staff members for a business meeting. The room schedule is displayed on a digital panel by the door of each conference room.

All food items and trash must be removed from the conference room after use. Bins are located directly outside each of the conference rooms.

No food or drink is allowed in the Essex Room (3rd floor) or the Martinelli Room (4th floor).

From:	Eugene Lasich
To:	All Expansion Committee Members
Subject:	Tanyalog Industries Expansion Meeting
Date:	September 10

Committee Members,

Please join me for the first meeting of the Expansion Committee on Monday, September 17. All attendees should arrive at the Martinelli Room at 10:00 A.M. Then, at 12:00 P.M., we will break for lunch and you can visit the cafeteria to receive a complimentary meal. Just show your visitor's badge at Window 4. All committee members should bring their trays to the conference room on the third floor right beside the cafeteria, where we will continue our meeting from 12:45 P.M. until 4:00 P.M.

Thank you. We look forward to your input at the meeting.

Eugene Lasich, Expansion Committee Chair
Tanyalog Industries

181. According to the policy, what is shown on a digital panel?

(A) The agenda for an upcoming meeting
(B) Rules for meeting room use
(C) Details about a room's availability
(D) Instructions for room devices

182. What are conference room users asked to do before leaving a room?

(A) Sign the attendance sheet
(B) Close the door
(C) Turn off the lights
(D) Clean up the space

183. In the e-mail, the word "complimentary" in paragraph 1, line 4, is closest in meaning to

(A) free
(B) healthy
(C) favorable
(D) balanced

184. What should committee members do at Window 4 ?

(A) Collect meeting materials
(B) Show proof of identification
(C) Submit their food orders
(D) Return their used trays

185. Where will committee members most likely be at 1:00 P.M.?

(A) In the cafeteria
(B) In the Smith Room
(C) In the Essex Room
(D) In the Martinelli Room

GO ON TO THE NEXT PAGE

Questions 186-190 refer to the following article and e-mails.

Hiking Permits to Be Required for Upton Parks

UPTON (January 8)—Starting on May 25, hikers will be required to obtain a permit for each day they hike on certain trails in Upton parks. The designated trails include some of the most popular hiking spots in the area. The permits are free of charge and require only that hikers register online at www.uptonparks.org or at any Upton Parks Department office. Upon registering, hikers will receive a permit that they can print out or display on a mobile device.

The move is part of an effort to reduce foot traffic on the most used trails, but some hikers are concerned. "I might not be able to get a permit for my favorite trails if none are left when I want to go," says Regina Faroni, an Upton parks hiker. "In addition, I often check the weather in the morning and then decide if it's a good day to hike," she says. Having to apply for a permit could prevent her from taking spontaneous hikes. "On the other hand, it would reduce the number of hikers on certain trails," Faroni admits.
—EJ Harjo, Upton Digest

E-mail

From:	Arlo Gomes <arlog@uptonhikingclub.org>
To:	Upton Parks Department <info@uptonparks.org>
Subject:	Hiking permits
Date:	January 22

To Whom It May Concern,

I read in the *Upton Digest* that hikers soon will be required to register for permits to hike on certain trails. As the organizer of the Upton Hiking Club, I would like more details on how this will affect our club. For example, is there a list of hiking trails that will require permits? I checked your Web site and could not find one.

Is it also the case that the number of permits issued will vary from trail to trail? About seventeen to twenty club members participate in our group hikes. I'm concerned that we may not get enough permits to hike together. Are there special considerations for large groups?

Finally, I am concerned that the permit requirement will not allow our club members to get together for a hike on the spur of the moment. We often will take an unplanned hike if we find that several members have a free day.

I hope you are able to respond soon, as we are already planning our spring and summer hikes.

Regards,

Arlo Gomes
Organizer, Upton Hiking Club

```
┌─────────────────────────────────────────────────────────────────────┐
│ ┊═══════════════════════════ *E-mail* ═══════════════════════════┊ │
│ ┌───────────────────────────────────────────────────────────────────┐│
│ │ From:        Upton Parks Department <info@uptonparks.org>          ││
│ │ To:          Arlo Gomes <arlog@uptonhikingclub.org>               ││
│ │ Subject:     RE: Hiking permits                                    ││
│ │ Date:        January 23                                            ││
│ │ Attachment:  🖉 Permit_Information_DRAFT                           ││
│ └───────────────────────────────────────────────────────────────────┘│
│ ┌───────────────────────────────────────────────────────────────────┐│
│ │ Hello, Mr. Gomes,                                                  ││
│ │                                                                    ││
│ │ Thank you for your e-mail. I apologize that our Web site has not   ││
│ │ yet been updated with the information you were searching for and   ││
│ │ that the article in the Upton Digest was not clear. I have         ││
│ │ attached a proposed list of the twelve trails that will require    ││
│ │ permits and the number of permits that will be issued per day for  ││
│ │ each trail. The list will be finalized next month.                 ││
│ │                                                                    ││
│ │ Permits can be reserved up to two weeks in advance, and the        ││
│ │ number of permits available for most trails is substantially       ││
│ │ higher than the number of Upton Hiking Club members who join       ││
│ │ your group hikes. Same-day permits can be obtained.                ││
│ │                                                                    ││
│ │ If you have not already done so, you can sign up on our Web site   ││
│ │ for our weekly newsletter. Doing so will ensure that you get       ││
│ │ advance notice of any updates to our policies.                     ││
│ │                                                                    ││
│ │ Jenny Grieb, Public Relations, Upton Parks Department              ││
│ └───────────────────────────────────────────────────────────────────┘│
└─────────────────────────────────────────────────────────────────────┘
```

186. According to the article, why will permits be required for some trails?

(A) To raise money to maintain the parks
(B) To encourage visitors to explore park activities other than hiking
(C) To ensure the trails are not too crowded
(D) To determine which trails are most frequently used

187. Why did Mr. Gomes contact the Upton Parks Department?

(A) To request information
(B) To obtain trail maps
(C) To apply for a group permit
(D) To discuss membership options

188. What concern does Mr. Gomes share with the *Upton Digest* reader?

(A) Too many trails will require permits.
(B) Last-minute permits may not be available.
(C) It is expensive to get a hiking permit.
(D) Overnight permits will be for groups only.

189. How many permits will likely be offered for most trails?

(A) Fewer than twelve
(B) Twelve to seventeen
(C) Eighteen to twenty
(D) More than twenty

190. According to the second e-mail, what does the newsletter provide?

(A) Articles written by the Upton Hiking Club
(B) Details about trail conditions
(C) Information about policy changes
(D) Access to additional permits

GO ON TO THE NEXT PAGE

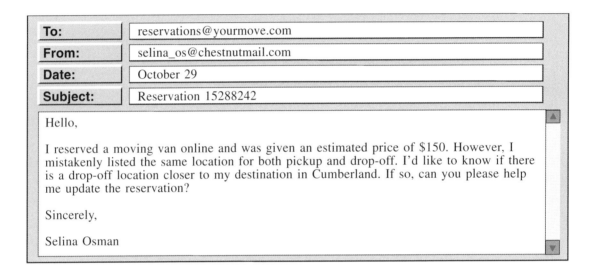

Your Move Vehicle Rental Company

Reservation Number: 15288242

Pickup Location: 2833 Centennial Rd., Muncie, IN 47303

Date and Time: October 31, 10:00 A.M.

Drop-off Location: Same as pickup

Date and Time: October 31, 6:30 P.M.

Vehicle Description: 5-meter moving van

If you need to change your reservation, you can do so via your online account until three days before your scheduled pickup. After that point, contact customer support at reservations@yourmove.com. Please include your reservation number in the e-mail subject.

To:	reservations@yourmove.com
From:	selina_os@chestnutmail.com
Date:	October 29
Subject:	Reservation 15288242

Hello,

I reserved a moving van online and was given an estimated price of $150. However, I mistakenly listed the same location for both pickup and drop-off. I'd like to know if there is a drop-off location closer to my destination in Cumberland. If so, can you please help me update the reservation?

Sincerely,

Selina Osman

To: selina_os@chestnutmail.com
From: reservations@yourmove.com
Date: October 30
Subject: RE: Reservation 15288242

Dear Ms. Osman,

We have a rental office just outside Indianapolis, about a ten-minute drive from Cumberland. If that is the drop-off location, you would have about 90 kilometers of driving from the starting point in Muncie. Based on this, we have updated your price estimate as follows.

Rental: 5-meter moving van for 1 day = $39.99

Rental: wheeled furniture cart = $6.99

Rental: furniture pads (set of 12) = $9.99

Distance: $1.05 per kilometer = $94.50 (90 kilometers estimated)

Vehicle damage insurance = $19.99

Total = $171.46

Please note that this total does not include taxes. The final price may vary based on the actual distance driven and will be calculated once the vehicle is returned to the drop-off location. Until that time, your credit card on file will be charged for the rental equipment only.

Sincerely,

Alistair Muhn
Your Move Vehicle Rental Company

---

191. When will a vehicle be rented?

(A) On October 28
(B) On October 29
(C) On October 30
(D) On October 31

192. What can be concluded about Ms. Osman?

(A) She has used the same rental company previously.
(B) She has been planning a move for a long time.
(C) She did not read the rental agreement carefully.
(D) She was unable to change her reservation online.

193. Who is Mr. Muhn?

(A) A furniture mover
(B) A vehicle insurance agent
(C) A reservation agent
(D) A storage facility manager

194. What is indicated about a furniture cart?

(A) It costs $6.99 per day to rent.
(B) It does not have to be returned.
(C) It folds up for easy transport.
(D) It is part of a set.

195. What is true about the new cost estimate?

(A) It is higher than the original estimate.
(B) It must be paid in full immediately.
(C) It includes the cost of fuel.
(D) It expires in three days.

GO ON TO THE NEXT PAGE

Questions 196-200 refer to the following e-mails and Web page.

E-mail

To: Soon-Yee Kim

From: Frank Zubiri

Date: February 12

Subject: Welcome

Dear Ms. Kim,

Welcome to Jacobi Technologies' sales team! Your first day is Monday, February 28. Please arrive at the Green Building, 1 Jacobi Circle, Naperville, at 9 A.M. Your team supervisor, Sophia Holland, will lead you through your first day. Here is an outline of what to expect.

1. Sign your employment contract and receive an ID badge.

2. Visit your assigned cubicle on the fourth floor of the Yellow Building.

3. Attend a luncheon with members of your team in the Yellow Building conference room.

4. Join other new hires for a guided tour of the campus. Look for an e-mail about this within a few days.

Best regards,

Frank Zubiri
Senior Director, Human Resources

E-mail

To: New Hires Distribution List

From: Toru Hada

Date: February 15

Subject: Campus Tour Dates

The next tour dates are February 21 and 28 and March 7 and 14. To sign up, simply reply to this e-mail with your full name and the date corresponding to your start day. Tours begin at 3:00 P.M. and last about an hour. Please meet me in the Blue Building lobby a few minutes before 3:00 P.M. Note that the Blue Building is on Jacobi Circle between the Green and Yellow Buildings. The tour will include stops at the labs, our sustainable power plant, and all employee amenities.

Should you have any questions about your start day, the tour, or any of the employee onboarding materials, please do not hesitate to contact me.

Jacobi Technologies develops, manufactures, and sells advanced microprocessors that power smart TVs, laptop computers, and other electronic devices. The company has more than 8,000 employees in Naperville, Illinois, and another 4,000 in Providence, Rhode Island.

Jacobi Technologies acquired its 900-acre Naperville property in 1950. Since then, the company has invested more than $3 billion in constructing ten Earth-friendly buildings and a sustainable infrastructure, including a waste-to-energy power plant. In addition to state-of-the-art research labs and production facilities, the campus boasts special amenities for workers, including two cafés, a gym, outdoor basketball and tennis courts, and a childcare center.

196. According to the first e-mail, what is one thing that Ms. Kim will do on her first day at work?

(A) Learn to use some company software
(B) Watch a video for new hires
(C) Eat a meal with her team
(D) Receive a laptop computer

197. Who most likely is Mr. Hada?

(A) A human resources staff member
(B) A sales team leader
(C) A technology expert
(D) A café worker

198. Where will Ms. Kim most likely be at 3 P.M. on February 28 ?

(A) In her cubicle in the Yellow Building
(B) In the lobby of the Blue Building
(C) In the Yellow Building conference room
(D) In Ms. Holland's office

199. What is suggested about guided tours at Jacobi Technologies?

(A) They are open to both employees and nonemployees.
(B) They stop at both indoor sites and outdoor sites.
(C) They last approximately two hours.
(D) They include a brief talk by a researcher.

200. According to the Web page, what is true about Jacobi Technologies?

(A) It will soon open a childcare facility.
(B) It acquired the Naperville property ten years ago.
(C) It charges employees a fee to use the company gym.
(D) It operates more than one campus.

TEST 8

Stop! This is the end of the test. If you finish before time is called, you may go back to Parts 5, 6, and 7 and check your work.

토익®정기시험
기출문제집4
1000

TEST 09
무료 동영상 강의

RC

기출 TEST
09

READING TEST

In the Reading test, you will read a variety of texts and answer several different types of reading comprehension questions. The entire Reading test will last 75 minutes. There are three parts, and directions are given for each part. You are encouraged to answer as many questions as possible within the time allowed.

You must mark your answers on the separate answer sheet. Do not write your answers in your test book.

PART 5

Directions: A word or phrase is missing in each of the sentences below. Four answer choices are given below each sentence. Select the best answer to complete the sentence. Then mark the letter (A), (B), (C), or (D) on your answer sheet.

101. Mr. Liu is known for negotiating employee disputes -------.

(A) calm
(B) calmly
(C) calmest
(D) calmness

102. The city is accepting proposals for the redesign of Oshida Public Park ------- January 25.

(A) when
(B) until
(C) a few
(D) whether

103. Sales ------- maintain client files and provide logistical support.

(A) assists
(B) assisted
(C) assisting
(D) assistants

104. Tonight at Harbor Falls Library, writer Delroy Greene will be ------- stories from his childhood in Jamaica.

(A) dividing
(B) sharing
(C) using
(D) awarding

105. Mr. Kam has invited all staff members to attend ------- retirement party.

(A) he
(B) his
(C) him
(D) himself

106. Stanley Point Theater in downtown Detroit will produce four plays and three ------- next season.

(A) actors
(B) audiences
(C) tickets
(D) musicals

107. There is enough money ------- in the budget to cover travel expenses.

(A) remains
(B) remainder
(C) remained
(D) remaining

108. Romm Industries staff trained nine new associates who were hired ------- the same day.

(A) as
(B) into
(C) on
(D) once

109. Taylor Kanagawa wrote several books on effective team management ------- his 40-year career at Sapp Publishers Ltd.

(A) between
(B) while
(C) beside
(D) during

110. The community clinic project is designed to improve health ------- in isolated areas.

(A) outcomes
(B) reasons
(C) corrections
(D) grades

111. Jingshen Airlines announced that it will be hiring 200 ------- employees next year.

(A) add
(B) adding
(C) additional
(D) additionally

112. The customer was impressed by how ------- Mr. Schmid operated the complicated machinery.

(A) skillfully
(B) primarily
(C) obviously
(D) richly

113. Staff are invited to participate in a ------- of social events during the first week of May.

(A) series
(B) status
(C) theory
(D) guest

114. The contract states that Solcus Corporation will be ------- for any costs resulting from work delays.

(A) accountable
(B) manageable
(C) knowledgeable
(D) flexible

115. Author Minh Phan's latest novel was ------- influenced by Vietnamese folk stories.

(A) heavy
(B) heavily
(C) heaviest
(D) heavier

116. Tourists are expected to flock to the Sorachi Discovery Museum when it opens ------- in Mikasa, Hokkaido.

(A) soon
(B) as
(C) almost
(D) initial

117. The factory floor is divided into four ------- sections: one for each stage of product assembly.

(A) previous
(B) eligible
(C) distinct
(D) installed

118. Handouts for the afternoon seminar must be prepared ------- the lunch break.

(A) down
(B) beside
(C) before
(D) off

119. Chat Mobile will determine, based on end-of-the-year sales numbers, ------- the company will open any additional stores.

(A) whether
(B) who
(C) since
(D) that

120. The red line will ------- only express stops from Finn Street to Boone Street on weekends.

(A) made
(B) makes
(C) make
(D) making

GO ON TO THE NEXT PAGE

121. The company's latest video game, *Hunting for Treasure*, has been praised ------- by reviewers.

(A) enthusiastically
(B) enthusiastic
(C) enthusiasm
(D) enthusiast

122. During the off-season, the Great Mountain Amusement Park operates on ------- hours.

(A) reduced
(B) employed
(C) slow
(D) busy

123. The construction project will ------- 30 residential units and 10 commercial spaces.

(A) overall
(B) first
(C) about
(D) include

124. Ms. Pham's employment contract cannot be finalized ------- her starting salary is still being negotiated.

(A) once
(B) because
(C) after
(D) until

125. Office supplies are available in our resources cabinet for ------- who needs them.

(A) anyone
(B) whichever
(C) such
(D) more

126. Through its network of local agents, new housing start-up Philocenia intends to ------- the rental sector.

(A) exercise
(B) indicate
(C) participate
(D) revolutionize

127. Rapid Books has the payroll solutions every company needs, allowing users ------- invoices in three easy steps.

(A) sent
(B) have sent
(C) sending
(D) to send

128. Epky Electronics will open eight additional retail stores ------- the next two years.

(A) above
(B) behind
(C) about
(D) within

129. The three-day workshop focuses on the public speaking ------- that are central to delivering memorable presentations.

(A) strategies
(B) strategized
(C) strategically
(D) strategic

130. Critics agree that the movie *An Unusual Introduction* ------- combines computer-generated images and live action.

(A) seamlessly
(B) collectively
(C) factually
(D) distantly

PART 6

Directions: Read the texts that follow. A word, phrase, or sentence is missing in parts of each text. Four answer choices for each question are given below the text. Select the best answer to complete the text. Then mark the letter (A), (B), (C), or (D) on your answer sheet.

Questions 131-134 refer to the following notice.

Sky Air First Pass

Thank you for flying Sky Air First with ------- . We hope you enjoy your flight.
131.

You can take advantage of our best prices on future flights ------- purchasing a Sky Air First Pass.
132.

For a ------- annual fee, you will get special discounts, seat upgrades, and the use of our exclusive
133.

travelers' lounge. ------- . Ask your flight attendant for more information and an application.
134.

131. (A) them
(B) theirs
(C) us
(D) ours

132. (A) at
(B) on
(C) by
(D) to

133. (A) lowers
(B) low
(C) lowly
(D) lowest

134. (A) We hope you will fly Sky Air First again.
(B) You will also get priority boarding.
(C) Please find your seat immediately.
(D) The flight delay will be minimal.

GO ON TO THE NEXT PAGE

CJOK Radio Show Welcomes New Staff

QUEENSVILLE (7 July)—Local radio station CJOK announced Katherine Dees as the new

producer of the popular show *Out and About in Queensville*. Ms. Dees is now ------- for
                                                                                135.

coordinating schedules, booking guests for the show, and managing media relations.

------- , the station hired sound editor Virginia Thacker and production assistant Reggie Dietrich
136.

to support Ms. Dees in her new role. ------- .
                                       137.

Out and About in Queensville, which has been airing for 30 years, is performed live weekly

from September to May in the Orpheum Theater in downtown Queensville. The show

------- musical guests, writers, and storytellers for an hour of weekly programming.
138.

135. (A) responsive
    (B) responsibly
    (C) responding
    (D) responsible

136. (A) Even so
    (B) In fact
    (C) For example
    (D) In addition

137. (A) CJOK was founded 60 years ago.
    (B) These recent hires follow the retirement
        of producer Ed Evans.
    (C) Ms. Dees was born and raised in
        Cedarburg.
    (D) CJOK has more than one popular show
        in its lineup.

138. (A) gives
    (B) marks
    (C) features
    (D) holds

To: Sandra Barga <sbarga97@hjmail.ca>
From: Artie Romanche <service@northwestbags.ca>
Date: 12 July
Subject: Order number 71280

Dear Ms. Barga:

We received your recent order asking for your name to be stitched on a Klamath Kool handbag.

We are, ------- , eager to complete your order. Unfortunately, our seamstress who fulfills
    139.

personalisation requirements will be on leave for the next three days. We wanted to let you know

that her ------- will cause a delay in shipping your bag.
    140.

------- for the wait, we would like to offer you a 10 percent discount on your current order. Or, if
141.

you prefer, you can opt for free personalisation on your next order. ------- . At Northwest Bags,
                                                142.

we strive for 100 percent customer satisfaction!

Sincerely,
Artie Romanche
Customer Service Representative, Northwest Bags

139. (A) still
(B) besides
(C) of course
(D) nevertheless

140. (A) absence
(B) arrival
(C) request
(D) investigation

141. (A) Compensated
(B) To compensate
(C) For compensating
(D) It is compensation

142. (A) The choice is yours.
(B) We appreciate your review.
(C) The bag will look great with your initials
on it.
(D) We are the only local retailer offering
custom services.

Questions 143-146 refer to the following article.

Sehelec Announces Wind-Solar Hybrid Project

MUMBAI (15 March)—Sehelec Ltd. announced it will begin construction on a 500-megawatt

wind-solar hybrid power ------- outside of Bangalore, India. ------- . Sehelec expects to begin
                        143.   **144.**

operations within 24 months, and it will sell the power to Indian energy giant Novaseon Industries.

"Our contract with Novaseon to provide ------- power moves us closer to our long-term corporate
                                        145.

goal," said Sumit Varma, CEO of Sehelec. "Our objective is to achieve a capacity of 20 gigawatts

within five years. Doing so will make us one of India's largest green power companies. And that,

in turn, will help the country ------- its carbon-reduction target."
                               146.

---

143. (A) plant
(B) planter
(C) planting
(D) planted

144. (A) Windy conditions can cause damage to
tall buildings.
(B) The facility will consist of a mix of solar
panels and wind turbines.
(C) Electric vehicles have fewer emissions
than other vehicles have.
(D) The pace of upgrades to India's power
grid slowed slightly this year.

145. (A) renew
(B) renewers
(C) renewable
(D) to renew

146. (A) understand
(B) explain
(C) block
(D) reach

Directions: In this part you will read a selection of texts, such as magazine and newspaper articles, e-mails, and instant messages. Each text or set of texts is followed by several questions. Select the best answer for each question and mark the letter (A), (B), (C), or (D) on your answer sheet.

Questions 147-148 refer to the following menu.

Carina's Café Lunch Specials

Monday through Friday from 11:00 A.M. to 3:00 P.M.

For only $8, combine the soup of the day with one of the following items:

Turkey Sandwich – Turkey, avocado, tomato, lettuce, and mayonnaise on wheat bread

Vegetable Panini – Sourdough bread filled with tomato, cucumber, spinach, and mayonnaise, then grilled

Mushroom Chicken Cavatappi – Chicken in a mushroom, celery, and onion sauce, served over S-shaped pasta

Vegetable Wrap – Fresh tomato, cucumber, and carrots with hummus (made with our secret recipe) on flatbread

147. What does each lunch special include?
   (A) A soup
   (B) Carrots
   (C) Tomatoes
   (D) A beverage

148. What item contains an ingredient that is only available from Carina's Café?
   (A) Turkey sandwich
   (B) Vegetable panini
   (C) Mushroom chicken cavatappi
   (D) Vegetable wrap

TEST 9

GO ON TO THE NEXT PAGE

Questions 149-150 refer to the following advertisement.

Certified Aqua Instructor Workshop

This workshop helps fitness professionals become certified aqua instructors by demonstrating how to design challenging and effective aquatic classes. Join instructor Deshonte Smith for a full-day course to learn a sequence of pool-based workouts that will motivate your students. Mr. Smith started his journey to instructor certification by taking classes at Valley Floor Fitness. He is also a professor at Wilkinson University.

The workshop costs $99 and will be held at Valley Floor Fitness in Missoula on August 27 from 9 a.m. to 5 p.m. For more information and to register, e-mail Maya Cramer at certification@valleyfloorfitness.com.

---

149. The word "design" in paragraph 1, line 2, is closest in meaning to

    (A) find
    (B) create
    (C) draw
    (D) name

150. What is indicated about the workshop?

    (A) It will be held at a pool at Wilkinson University.
    (B) It is being offered on two different dates.
    (C) It is available at a discounted rate in August.
    (D) It will be taught by a former student of Valley Floor Fitness.

Questions 151-152 refer to the following text-message chain.

Hyun-Jun Cho (3:27 P.M.)
I'm scheduled to work the front desk on Saturday from 7 A.M. to 3 P.M. A friend of mine is coming to town then, and he's only going to be here for one day. I was wondering if I could switch shifts with you. I can work on Sunday.

Stephanie Duchemin (3:29 P.M.)
Saturday is good for me. I hope you don't have a Sunday like last week. It was so busy. All the doctors attending the medical conference were checking in at the front desk.

Hyun-Jun Cho (3:31 P.M.)
And I heard that all the accountants from the other conference were also at the front desk reviewing their room charges at the same time!

Stephanie Duchemin (3:32 P.M.)
The lobby was certainly bustling.

Hyun-Jun Cho (3:34 P.M.)
Thank you for helping me out. I haven't seen my friend Kai since we graduated from university.

---

151. At 3:29 P.M., what does Ms. Duchemin most likely mean when she writes, "Saturday is good for me"?

(A) She prefers to work morning shifts.
(B) She is able to do a favor for Mr. Cho.
(C) She will attend a conference.
(D) She would like to meet Mr. Cho's friend.

152. Where most likely do Mr. Cho and Ms. Duchemin work?

(A) At a hotel
(B) At a university
(C) At a medical center
(D) At an accounting firm

GO ON TO THE NEXT PAGE

Questions 153-154 refer to the following e-mail.

To:	Madalena Navas <mnavas@cordovacreations.com>
From:	Hugo Jones <hkjones@sunmail.com>
Date:	April 2
Subject:	Thank you

Dear Ms. Navas,

I enjoyed speaking with you about the associate manager position last week, and as I mentioned, I am very excited about the possibility of working with you at Cordova Creations. I wanted to let you know that I have received a job offer from another company, and I have to respond to that hiring manager soon. I realize it has only been a few days since my interview, but if it is at all possible for you to update me on the status of my application before the end of the week, that would be very helpful. I have long admired Cordova Creations and would really like to be a part of it. I am hoping to hear positive news from you.

Thank you,

Hugo Jones

153. What does Mr. Jones indicate in his e-mail?

(A) He used to work with Ms. Navas.
(B) He is an associate manager.
(C) Another company wishes to hire him.
(D) His interview has been scheduled for next week.

154. What does Mr. Jones want to know by the end of the week?

(A) Whether an important decision has been made yet
(B) Whether Ms. Navas is available for a meeting
(C) Whether Ms. Navas would like to apply for a new position
(D) Whether the company will expand its product offerings

Questions 155-157 refer to the following article.

Hibiscus Supply to Run Its Own Container Ship

BUSAN (15 October)—As international shipping continues to increase, companies that transport goods between continents have found themselves competing for expensive space on container ships. — [1] —. Delays in getting goods to factories and into stores have become more common. — [2] —.

As one of the biggest exporters of home building supplies in the country, Hibiscus Supply is particularly vulnerable to these issues. — [3] —. To avoid potential shipping problems, Hibiscus Supply has decided to operate its own container ship to export products overseas. — [4] —.

According to Hibiscus Supply president James Koh, operating the company's own ship should improve efficiency at ports and decrease overall shipping costs. Says Mr. Koh, "The cost to ship with freight companies has doubled in the past year. By shipping our products ourselves, we'll be able to avoid passing shipping-related price increases on to our customers."

155. What products does Hibiscus Supply most likely sell?

(A) Construction materials
(B) Pillows and sheets
(C) Wholesale food items
(D) Spare automobile parts

156. Why does Hibiscus Supply want to operate its own container ship?

(A) To provide shipping services to other companies
(B) To ship its products quickly and cheaply
(C) To deliver its products to unusual locations
(D) To ship more goods than most freight companies can handle

157. In which of the positions marked [1], [2], [3], and [4] does the following sentence best belong?

"The newly acquired ship is scheduled to begin running later this month."

(A) [1]
(B) [2]
(C) [3]
(D) [4]

GO ON TO THE NEXT PAGE

Questions 158-160 refer to the following memo.

MEMO

To: All Accounting Staff
From: Jennifer Snow, Senior Manager
Date: January 8
Subject: Pedro Allende

Please join me in congratulating Pedro Allende as he prepares to enter his new role as a full-time administrative assistant in our accounting department. Mr. Allende, a part-time clerk in our mail room, completed a certificate program in computer support at Lander Vocational Institute last month. He was first hired by our company as a delivery driver, a role he held for two years before transferring to the mail room.

Mr. Allende's first day in the accounting department will be Monday, January 11. We all wish him well!

158. Why did Ms. Snow send the memo?

(A) To invite employees to an office party
(B) To announce a change to an employee's job
(C) To inform employees about a reduction in work hours
(D) To request employee feedback on a departmental policy

159. The word "prepares" in paragraph 1, line 1, is closest in meaning to

(A) assembles
(B) returns
(C) reaches out
(D) gets ready

160. What is indicated about Mr. Allende?

(A) He currently works as a delivery driver.
(B) He recently completed a training program.
(C) He previously assisted Ms. Snow in a different department.
(D) He will begin working part-time next week.

Help Wanted: Machinist

Camerley Corp. of Napier, New Zealand, has an opening for an experienced machinist to work in our 15,000-square-metre fabrication plant, which produces custom tools and machine parts for a variety of industries. Requirements for the position include:

• Ability to collaborate with engineers to fabricate tools and machine parts

• Familiarity with specialised equipment

• Skill with doing precision work based on technical drawings

• Comfort working with metal and various other materials, such as wood and plastics

• Ability to work both independently and as part of a team

To apply, please send CV and two references to jobs@camerleycorp.co.nz.

---

161. What type of business placed the advertisement?

(A) A land developer
(B) A car-repair shop
(C) A factory
(D) A hardware store

162. What material is NOT specified in the advertisement?

(A) Metal
(B) Glass
(C) Wood
(D) Plastic

163. What is listed as a requirement for the job?

(A) Training in business-to-business sales
(B) A university degree in engineering
(C) Experience creating technical drawings
(D) The ability to work alone and with others

TEST 9

GO ON TO THE NEXT PAGE

Questions 164-167 refer to the following text-message chain.

Lanie McGinnis (7:16 A.M.)
Good morning, Kelly and Matthieu. I removed the Funfair preregistration signs from the park entrances, but I think I forgot one at the north gate. Could one of you check to see if it is still there?

Kelly Sen (7:18 A.M.)
Hi, Lanie. I rode my bike to the park earlier this morning to help put pamphlets and other materials on the welcome table in the main tent. But I could head over to that entrance now since there are other volunteers here who can finish up.

Lanie McGinnis (7:19 A.M.)
That would be great, since I'm going to be on the other side of the park at the south entrance for a while. I'm meeting some representatives from the city parks department.

Matthieu Herman (7:21 A.M.)
I've got it, Kelly. I just arrived at the north entrance and will take down the sign we hung here. Lanie, what would you like me to do with it?

Lanie McGinnis (7:22 A.M.)
Perfect! Can you put it with the others behind the welcome table in the main tent? I will pick them up later today. We can change the dates and use them again next year.

Matthieu Herman (7:23 A.M.)
Will do. Here's to a successful fair!

164. What is probably true about the writers?

(A) They are registering people for a bike-to-work program.
(B) They are coordinating a public event.
(C) They work for a city parks department.
(D) They are members of a club that walks in a park.

165. What was Ms. Sen doing?

(A) Erecting a tent
(B) Designing pamphlets
(C) Placing items on the welcome table
(D) Attaching signs to the park entrance

166. At 7:21 A.M., what does Mr. Herman mean when he writes, "I've got it, Kelly"?

(A) He has already taken down a sign.
(B) He will perform a task requested by Ms. McGinnis.
(C) He will return unused materials to the office.
(D) He realizes that Ms. Sen does not need help.

167. What does Ms. McGinnis instruct Mr. Herman to do?

(A) Help her locate the main tent
(B) Meet her at the south entrance
(C) Write down participants' information
(D) Leave an object behind the welcome table

GO ON TO THE NEXT PAGE

TEST

Questions 168-171 refer to the following fact sheet.

Zealandia Airlines Fact Sheet for Fiscal Year Ending 30 June

Service Levels and Capacity: Zealandia Airlines provides regional service among four cities. In each case, average flight capacity exceeded the company goal of 85 percent.

On-Time Performance (OTP): For the purpose of measuring OTP, flights are considered "on time" when they reach their destination within fifteen minutes of the scheduled arrival time. Regional airlines are subject to fines when OTP drops below 50 percent. The following chart shows Zealandia's commendable OTP rates for the recent fiscal year.

City	OTP
Kelton Falls	52%
Grangerton	68%
Satcherville	79%
Barbour City	64%

Proposed Expansion: Zealandia Airlines provides regional passenger air service and is seeking to expand its fleet to begin providing commercial airfreight delivery. Establishing this service is a component of the airline's growth plan and corporate vision. The airline is currently in negotiations with aviation authorities to explore options.

Terminal and Service Improvements: Zealandia Airlines is participating in discussions with airport management about comprehensive renovations to its passenger lounge and café and has offered to commit $5 million from its budget to the project. Company executives have also finalized a plan and committed funds to overhaul its rewards program. The initiative supports the aim to be a leading service provider among similar airlines and capture an increasing percentage of the market share.

---

168. The word "exceeded" in paragraph 1, line 2, is closest in meaning to

(A) surpassed
(B) excelled
(C) perfected
(D) decided

169. According to the fact sheet, what is true about Zealandia Airlines?

(A) Executives aim to improve its flight capacity.
(B) Most of its flights arrive at their destinations on time.
(C) It is larger than 85 percent of regional airlines.
(D) It has received a fine from aviation authorities.

170. What does Zealandia Airlines want to provide in the future?

(A) Private charter flights
(B) Luxury travel tours
(C) Commercial shipping
(D) Aircraft leasing

171. How does Zealandia Airlines hope to improve service for passengers?

(A) By remodeling the passenger waiting area
(B) By moving to a new location within the terminal
(C) By upgrading the seating inside the aircraft
(D) By offering improved meal service on all flights

New Fleet for Northeast Railways

Northeast Railways expects to spend $5.6 billion to replace its fleet of 65 passenger trains, many of which are more than 40 years old. — [1] —.

The company has entered into a contract with Logiens Transport for a new fleet of trains that will operate on electrified tracks when those track systems are available and on diesel fuel at all other times. — [2] —. The trains will be capable of traveling at speeds of up to 130 kilometers per hour and will produce far less pollution than the current fleet does.

Logiens also promises an enhanced passenger experience. The train cars will have panoramic windows, improved ventilation, and wider aisles. — [3] —.

Northeast's contract with Logiens also includes equipment and replacement parts and provides a long-term service agreement. — [4] —.

172. What is Logiens Transport's role?

(A) To recommend ways to reduce pollution
(B) To acquire financing for a purchase
(C) To familiarize train engineers with new technology
(D) To manufacture and service the replacement fleet

173. What information is included in the press release?

(A) The date on which the trains will be delivered
(B) The budget for replacing the current trains
(C) The annual cost for parts and service
(D) The number of passenger seats in each train car

174. What is suggested about the tracks that Northeast Railways uses?

(A) They are owned by the government.
(B) They are not shared with freight trains.
(C) Most are in urgent need of repair.
(D) Some are not electrified.

175. In which of the positions marked [1], [2], [3], and [4] does the following sentence best belong?

"Each reclinable seat will have an individual power supply and USB port."

(A) [1]
(B) [2]
(C) [3]
(D) [4]

TEST 9

GO ON TO THE NEXT PAGE

To:	headquartersstaff@seonwulawfirm.com
From:	iqalandar@seonwulawfirm.com
Date:	October 1, 9:39 A.M.
Subject:	Remote work setup
Attachment:	📎 Equipment request form

Dear Associates,

On December 3, our headquarters will close for a month for renovation. As all of you normally work out of these offices in San Francisco, please plan to work off-site and collect everything you may need (your laptop, files, etc.) before December 1. Entry to the building will be restricted after that date.

If you would like a temporary space at our San Jose offices, please e-mail me, and I will reserve one for you. If you plan to work from home and need additional equipment (such as a printer), fill out the attached form from our technology department and return it to me. A representative of that department will mail the equipment to your home address.

We realize this work on the building is a disruption, but timing it with our slow season should make the situation easier. We think you will be happy with the changes when the building reopens on January 5. If you have any questions, please reach out to me.

Best,

Ian Qalandar, Manager
Seonwu Law Firm
(415) 555-0177

Seonwu Law Firm—Equipment Request Form

Employee name: Jason Kang

Employee ID: 102899

E-mail: jkang@seonwulawfirm.com

Date to receive: November 30

Equipment: desktop monitor, printer

_____

(This section is to be completed by the technology department.)

Request completed: ✓ Yes   No

Request filled by: Aubrey Smith

Equipment serial numbers: VN3902556, MXE96400

Date sent: November 27 via overnight mail

176. What is indicated about Seonwu Law Firm?

(A) It focuses on real estate law.
(B) It has a large advertising budget.
(C) It serves clients across the country.
(D) It is headquartered in San Francisco.

177. According to the e-mail, what will the technology department do?

(A) Install updates on employee laptops
(B) Send office equipment to employees
(C) Train employees to use new software
(D) Place equipment in renovated offices

178. What is suggested in the e-mail about Seonwu Law Firm?

(A) It plans to expand its operations.
(B) It mostly employs remote workers.
(C) It is usually not busy in December.
(D) It handles many high-profile cases.

179. What can be concluded about Mr. Kang?

(A) He chose not to work in the San Jose office.
(B) He is a senior partner at the Seonwu Law Firm.
(C) He will be on vacation after November.
(D) He has requested a larger office.

180. What most likely is Ms. Smith's occupation?

(A) Lawyer
(B) Office manager
(C) Technical support staff
(D) Administrative assistant

GO ON TO THE NEXT PAGE

TEST 9

Planning a Tour of Your Facility
by Didiane Lessard

Plant tours are commonplace in many factories, but not all tours are as effective as they could be. Too many companies make the mistake of adopting a one-size-fits-all approach rather than tailoring tours to maximize their usefulness. A potential investor and a casual tourist will probably not be impressed by the same things, so it is best to be clear about the tour's purpose early on. Here are some guidelines to make each tour as effective as possible.

Be selective. Unless your tour is for a safety inspection, your guests do not need (or want) to see every part of your factory. Choose a few sections that will interest your guests and give them a better sense of your product. For example, journalists will want to create a story about your plant, so show them the parts of the plant that have historical significance, such as a room with the company's original production equipment.

Timing is everything. Always be mindful of the physical demands of the tour. Even the hardiest guest will tire of standing or walking for long periods. It is a good idea to schedule breaks in tours lasting longer than an hour. The time spent in a single section matters also. If you allow guests only five minutes in an area, they will soon forget it. On the other hand, even the most impressive room gets boring after half an hour.

Personality is NOT everything. While having a personable and friendly tour guide is essential, your guests are coming to see what goes into making your product. Tour guides get asked a variety of questions, some unexpected, so a comprehensive knowledge of the production processes is important (and absolutely vital during inspections). You also want someone who will keep the tour moving—visitors will appreciate a tour that begins and ends on time.

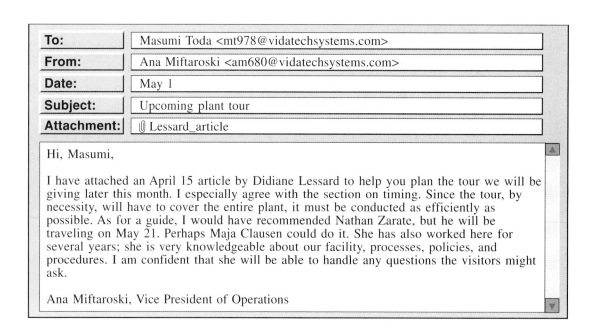

To:	Masumi Toda <mt978@vidatechsystems.com>
From:	Ana Miftaroski <am680@vidatechsystems.com>
Date:	May 1
Subject:	Upcoming plant tour
Attachment:	🖉 Lessard_article

Hi, Masumi,

I have attached an April 15 article by Didiane Lessard to help you plan the tour we will be giving later this month. I especially agree with the section on timing. Since the tour, by necessity, will have to cover the entire plant, it must be conducted as efficiently as possible. As for a guide, I would have recommended Nathan Zarate, but he will be traveling on May 21. Perhaps Maja Clausen could do it. She has also worked here for several years; she is very knowledgeable about our facility, processes, policies, and procedures. I am confident that she will be able to handle any questions the visitors might ask.

Ana Miftaroski, Vice President of Operations

181. What is one problem mentioned about factory tours in the article?

(A) They are often rescheduled at the last minute.
(B) They give the same information to all types of visitors.
(C) They fail to supply protective gear that fits everyone.
(D) They allow groups that are too large.

182. According to the article, what is the maximum amount of time that a tour should stay in one area?

(A) 10 minutes
(B) 20 minutes
(C) 30 minutes
(D) 60 minutes

183. What is NOT indicated in the article as a characteristic of a good tour guide?

(A) A friendly personality
(B) The ability to stand for long periods
(C) A deep knowledge of processes
(D) The ability to pay close attention to time

184. For whom is Mr. Toda most likely planning a tour?

(A) Casual tourists
(B) New employees
(C) Potential investors
(D) Safety inspectors

185. When is the tour scheduled to take place?

(A) On April 15
(B) On April 21
(C) On May 1
(D) On May 21

TEST 9

GO ON TO THE NEXT PAGE

https://www.zonecatering.com/home

Home	Menus	Testimonials	Contact Us

Zone Catering provides food trucks at film and television production sites throughout California. Just let us know where you need a food truck and how many people you need to feed. We can serve your entire cast and crew. Our trucks also move with you and your team if you are shooting scenes in various locations.

At Zone Catering, we offer a wide variety of cuisines. All the fruits and vegetables we use in our menus are grown here in California. Our menus are easily adapted to accommodate dietary restrictions. For convenience, our food trucks offer both full meals and individual items. We can serve meals buffet-style, or people can order directly from the truck.

Let us take care of the catering for your production. You will find our food delicious, and you will find our service friendly and convenient. We even offer 24-hour support in case any issues arise while we are at your location. We hope to serve you soon!

Zone Catering Food Trucks

Schedule Date: June 10

Film	Shooting Location	Contact Person
Trappings	Harpin Lot	Erin Begg
Make the Meeting	192 Laredo Street	Mark Lillo
Tutors and Tuxedos	Tandor Fields	Jun-Seo Kil
Jatem and the Storm	Spectrum Hall	Donna Gawason

| Home | Menus | **Testimonials** | Contact Us |

June 10—I have been in the acting business for over 25 years and am sometimes disappointed by the food trucks on film production sites. That was not the case today when we were filming *Make the Meeting*. The food truck had excellent coffee, and the strawberries in the large fruit salad were so fresh and tasty! Even though there was a long line of customers on an extremely hot and uncomfortable day, the server was able to get everyone's food ready quickly. She was friendly and easygoing, too! Even the food truck was pleasant-looking—the mural painted on the side of the truck was beautiful! I hope to see Zone Catering food trucks at future film shooting locations.

—Robert Chiodo

186. What does the Web page indicate about Zone Catering?

(A) It specializes in providing food at music concerts.
(B) It has lower prices than its competitors.
(C) It recently moved its corporate office to California.
(D) It provides customer support 24 hours a day.

187. According to the schedule, who was the contact person for the filming of *Trappings* on June 10 ?

(A) Erin Begg
(B) Mark Lillo
(C) Jun-Seo Kil
(D) Donna Gawason

188. Where was the food truck that Mr. Chiodo visited?

(A) At Harpin Lot
(B) At 192 Laredo Street
(C) At Tandor Fields
(D) At Spectrum Hall

189. What is probably true about the salad Mr. Chiodo ordered?

(A) It had an unusual taste.
(B) It was too big for him to finish.
(C) It included several types of berries.
(D) It contained fruit grown in California.

190. What is indicated about the food truck server in the testimonial?

(A) She had difficulty working in the heat.
(B) She paints murals in her spare time.
(C) She prepares orders quickly.
(D) She has worked in her industry for 25 years.

TEST 9

GO ON TO THE NEXT PAGE

To:	Hae-won Jeong
From:	Julia Laurent
Date:	July 28
Subject:	Dallas hotels
Attachment:	📎 List of downtown accommodations

Dear Hae-won,

I plan to attend the National Digital Marketing Conference in October. I know you have traveled to this conference in Dallas many times. This will be my first time attending, and I'm not sure which hotel to book. I have attached a list of accommodations that are near the convention center. Right now, I am leaning toward the Bonita Suites Hotel, but I would like to know which property you would recommend.

I hope you have settled into your new position with the digital marketing department. I am looking forward to the conference and hope to see you again there.

Kind regards,

Julia Laurent
E-mail Marketing Specialist
The 3R Marketing Firm

List of Downtown Accommodations (from www.topbusinesshotels.com/search/Dallashotels)

Hotel	Rate	Description
The Oaktree Hotel	$204/night	Luxury hotel in the heart of downtown Close to the convention center Outdoor pool, three on-site restaurants Close to shopping
Alessi Dallas Hotel	$155/night	Quaint boutique hotel in downtown Dallas Lobby restaurant for breakfast and dinner Near convention center and history museum
Bonita Suites Hotel	$125/night	New hotel in downtown convention center area Office and kitchen in each suite Computer center with printers located in lobby Meeting space available for groups Free on-site parking available

To:	Julia Laurent
From:	Hae-won Jeong
Date:	July 29
Subject:	RE: Dallas hotels

Dear Julia,

I will be attending the National Digital Marketing Conference this year as well! I love traveling to Dallas every year for this conference because it is a great networking opportunity. Since this is your first time attending, I recommend you go to the newcomers' reception on the first night. The conference executive planning committee is putting it on, and it could be an excellent occasion to socialize with other conference goers.

I will be staying at the Alessi Dallas Hotel. It is the closest to the convention center, and the rooms are comfortable. For you, I would suggest the one you already seem to prefer. It so happens that the newcomers' reception will be held in one of the event rooms there. It is a little farther away but still convenient. As a friendly reminder, we are advised not to book hotels with rates that exceed our company's limit of $175/night.

I look forward to seeing you in October. It will be lovely to catch up.

Best,

Hae-won Jeong
Digital Marketing Director
The 3R Marketing Firm

191. What is the purpose of the first e-mail?

(A) To schedule a meeting with a client
(B) To ask for assistance with a project
(C) To seek a suggestion from a colleague
(D) To congratulate a colleague who was promoted

192. According to the list, what is suggested about the Bonita Suites Hotel?

(A) It is located in a historic building.
(B) It features resources for business travelers.
(C) It is near many downtown tourist attractions.
(D) It charges a daily fee for parking.

193. What is true about Ms. Jeong?

(A) She has not attended a marketing conference before.
(B) She prefers the Alessi Dallas Hotel for its restaurant.
(C) She thinks Ms. Laurent should stay at the Bonita Suites Hotel.
(D) She works for a different company than Ms. Laurent.

194. Why would Ms. Jeong most likely suggest that Ms. Laurent avoid the Oaktree Hotel?

(A) It does not have an on-site restaurant.
(B) Its room rate exceeds the company's limit.
(C) Its clients are mostly noisy tourists.
(D) It is too far from the conference location.

195. What does the second e-mail indicate about the National Digital Marketing Conference?

(A) Its location changes to a different city each year.
(B) Last year it was held at the Alessi Dallas Hotel.
(C) Ms. Jeong is on its executive planning committee.
(D) It includes an event for first-time attendees.

GO ON TO THE NEXT PAGE

TEST 9

Dover Water Supply
7400 Rodney Boulevard, Dover, DE 19904

March 12

Ms. Na-Ri Cam
361 Farming Avenue
Dover, DE 19902

Dear Ms. Cam,

This letter is to confirm that Dover Water Supply will begin service at your address on Wednesday, April 6. Your customer account number, which is the same as your water meter number, is DWS4289.

Billing is monthly, and payment is due on the fifteenth of each month. Bills can be paid by mailing a check to our main address or by entering your account number and payment information on our secure page at www.doverwatersupply.com/billing.

We will be performing a system flush of the pipes in your area on Monday, April 4. Customers may temporarily see discoloration or sediment in their water around that time. Please visit our Web site for more information. You can also contact Customer Support at questions@doverwatersupply.com or call us at (302) 555-0135.

Sincerely,

Matthew Ensign

Matthew Ensign
Account Representative, Dover Water Supply

	E-mail
To:	questions@doverwatersupply.com
From:	Na-Ri Cam <n.cam@mailcurrent.com>
Date:	March 17
Subject:	Account number DWS4289

Hello,

I am in the process of moving to my new home in Dover. I received a letter stating that my water service will start on April 6. It also said something about pipes being flushed on April 4. Should I expect to see discoloration when I start using my water? Are there any steps I should take?

Also, I tried to use your secure page, but it gave me an error message saying that my account number was not valid. I will need your help in getting online access by the May 15 due date.

Thank you for any information you can provide.

Na-Ri Cam

```
To:        Na-Ri Cam <n.cam@mailcurrent.com>
From:      Customer Support <questions@doverwatersupply.com>
Date:      March 18
Subject:   RE: Account number DWS4289
```

Dear Ms. Cam,

Thank you for your message. Your water might look cloudy on April 6 when you first turn on your faucets. We recommend that you keep the water running until it is clear before you use it. I assure you that the water is not harmful in any way. The minerals that cause the discoloration occur naturally, and our latest water analysis showed very high quality.

I apologize for the problem you described. I have fixed it, so you should not have any further trouble.

If you have any other questions, please don't hesitate to reach out to us again.

Best regards,

Ramona Hizon
Customer Support, Dover Water Supply

196. What is one purpose of the letter?

(A) To list customer benefits
(B) To alert customers to a price change
(C) To confirm the start of a service
(D) To describe changes to a Web site

197. What most likely does Ms. Cam want to do online on May 15 ?

(A) Request a new water meter
(B) Complete a customer survey
(C) Report a leaking pipe
(D) Pay a water bill

198. According to the second e-mail, what should Ms. Cam do on April 6 ?

(A) Boil her drinking water for five minutes
(B) Allow her water to run for some time
(C) Contact her neighbors
(D) Request a service visit

199. In the second e-mail, what is indicated about the water from Dover Water Supply?

(A) It is safe to use.
(B) It is measured every month.
(C) It is distributed to many cities.
(D) It is naturally free of minerals.

200. What can be concluded about Ms. Hizon?

(A) She resolved the issue with Ms. Cam's account.
(B) She sent a copy of the water analysis to Ms. Cam.
(C) She will offer Ms. Cam a discount for new customers.
(D) She lives in Ms. Cam's area.

Stop! This is the end of the test. If you finish before time is called, you may go back to Parts 5, 6, and 7 and check your work.

TEST 9

토익®정기시험
기출문제집 4
1000

TEST 10
무료 동영상 강의

RC

기출 TEST

10

READING TEST

In the Reading test, you will read a variety of texts and answer several different types of reading comprehension questions. The entire Reading test will last 75 minutes. There are three parts, and directions are given for each part. You are encouraged to answer as many questions as possible within the time allowed.

You must mark your answers on the separate answer sheet. Do not write your answers in your test book.

PART 5

Directions: A word or phrase is missing in each of the sentences below. Four answer choices are given below each sentence. Select the best answer to complete the sentence. Then mark the letter (A), (B), (C), or (D) on your answer sheet.

101. According to the department head, ------- are ready to begin work on the Arborney Bridge project.

(A) us
(B) we
(C) our
(D) ours

102. The policy prohibiting visitor access to the laboratory must be ------- followed.

(A) strictly
(B) bitterly
(C) sizably
(D) colorfully

103. Yoon-Hee Kim is the ------- graduate of Serrica University to lead a Fortune 500 company.

(A) most
(B) for
(C) first
(D) nearly

104. Contact Frank Marilli in the IT department ------- you have any problems with the new database software.

(A) and
(B) then
(C) but
(D) if

105. A ------- efficiency expert will be visiting our work site in early November.

(A) led
(B) leader
(C) leading
(D) leads

106. At Gallant's Pet Store, customer ------- are accepted between 9:00 A.M. and 6:00 P.M.

(A) behaviors
(B) relations
(C) orders
(D) types

107. The management at Carette Industries ------- values the work of the research team.

(A) high
(B) highly
(C) highest
(D) higher

108. Pentrexa Pharmacy is able to ------- most prescriptions within one business day.

(A) care
(B) earn
(C) fill
(D) lift

109. The ------- of a parking structure for Huron General Hospital will begin on June 1.

(A) construct
(B) constructed
(C) construction
(D) constructs

110. Some of the flower beds surrounding Dale Valley Lodge had to be replanted ------- the recent rainstorm.

(A) after
(B) among
(C) opposite
(D) beside

111. Several water stations ------- along the route of next week's marathon.

(A) being installed
(B) will be installed
(C) to install
(D) installed

112. The Crown Lagoon Hotel has 150 rooms, each with a ------- view of the city.

(A) valid
(B) recent
(C) modern
(D) scenic

113. Overall, charitable donations rose last year, ------- specific dollar amounts are not yet available.

(A) although
(B) neither
(C) whenever
(D) so

114. We strongly advise you to back up the data stored on your electronic device ------- turning it in for repairs.

(A) once
(B) both
(C) then
(D) before

115. Because Ms. Garcia enjoys creating charts and graphs, her supervisor ------- asks her to make materials for presentations.

(A) frequent
(B) frequents
(C) frequenting
(D) frequently

116. Manufacturers of high-end products are dealing with excess ------- because consumers are buying fewer luxury items.

(A) confidence
(B) inventory
(C) capacity
(D) energy

117. The Hayle Group, ------- consists of business consultants and lawyers, advocates for tax policy reforms.

(A) themselves
(B) someone
(C) whoever
(D) which

118. Daishi Asayama is one of three applicants being ------- to oversee the Kingston franchises.

(A) decided
(B) corrected
(C) considered
(D) practiced

119. The reviewer of Ms. Chen's book noted that her research was -------.

(A) impressed
(B) impressive
(C) impress
(D) impression

120. Mr. Pereira has worked in our legal department ------- his transfer to the Atlanta office ten years ago.

(A) since
(B) between
(C) without
(D) like

GO ON TO THE NEXT PAGE

121. Pennypack Markets soon plans to break ground on its largest ------- center in the area.

(A) distributive
(B) distribute
(C) distributable
(D) distribution

122. Ms. Miller ------- welcomed the speakers who will be leading the workshops.

(A) accessibly
(B) abundantly
(C) briefly
(D) momentarily

123. Mr. Nayar ------- the need for enhanced safety protocols long before the government issued a report on the topic.

(A) stresses
(B) stressing
(C) will stress
(D) had stressed

124. Angelia Financial recently announced ------- changes to its benefits package that were greeted enthusiastically by its staff.

(A) judgmental
(B) substantial
(C) magnetic
(D) chaotic

125. ------- poems written by Mike Hanover are included in the new edition of *Merwyn's Anthology*.

(A) Whichever
(B) Several
(C) Something
(D) None

126. For a list of local farms that supply food to restaurants, please ------- to the Hueland Farm Association Web site.

(A) elect
(B) adapt
(C) present
(D) refer

127. Samidu Communications is soliciting suggestions from its staff about ways of improving employee -------.

(A) produced
(B) productive
(C) productivity
(D) productively

128. Mr. Ben-Moshe always reserves the banquet room at Saitomi's Kitchen ------- the sales team has a holiday event.

(A) whenever
(B) regarding
(C) whether
(D) besides

129. Annika Dulin ------- the marketing department at Tollason Industries' planning meeting tomorrow.

(A) will represent
(B) had represented
(C) to represent
(D) be representing

130. Do not post any statements about the company on social media without prior -------.

(A) authorization
(B) supplement
(C) consequence
(D) responsibility

PART 6

Directions: Read the texts that follow. A word, phrase, or sentence is missing in parts of each text. Four answer choices for each question are given below the text. Select the best answer to complete the text. Then mark the letter (A), (B), (C), or (D) on your answer sheet.

Questions 131-134 refer to the following article.

Kray Villa Museum To Celebrate Grand Opening

DEERFIELD (May 2)—The official opening of the Kray Villa Museum will take place on May 29 at 10 A.M. To mark the occasion, various festivities will be held throughout the day. ------- . Visit
131.
www.krayvillamuseum.org for details.

The museum is housed in the imposing structure ------- was home to the once-influential Kray
132.
family beginning in the late 1800s. Having laid abandoned for the last 30 years, the property was purchased 2 years ago by the Deerfield Historical Society. Subsequently, the gardens were restored to appear as they did when the first generation of Krays moved into the villa.

------- , furnishings of the kind most likely used by the family are on display.
133.

During the museum's opening festivities, a live band ------- music that was popular in the late
134.
nineteenth century.

131. (A) This year's celebrations are part of a weeklong national campaign.
(B) Results of the survey will be presented at 6:00 P.M.
(C) Programs will be distributed at the next meeting.
(D) Admission is free, but a donation is suggested.

132. (A) such
(B) that
(C) what
(D) all

133. (A) Conversely
(B) Additionally
(C) In the meantime
(D) To this end

134. (A) will perform
(B) had to perform
(C) was performing
(D) could have performed

GO ON TO THE NEXT PAGE

Questions 135-138 refer to the following e-mail.

To: All employees

From: Cecil Radu, Information Technology Manager

Date: April 8

Re: Network alert

We are experiencing some problems with our local network. Some of the affected services

include the ------- company Web site and the payroll database. We have also received
　　　　　　135.

information ------- network data becoming corrupted and files not saving properly. Therefore, to
　　　　　　136.

ensure that you do not lose any work, please avoid using the network this morning while my

team addresses these ------- . We anticipate that the systems will be fully functional by this
　　　　　　137.

afternoon. ------- .
　　　　138.

135. (A) internalizing
     (B) internalize
     (C) internally
     (D) internal

136. (A) as
     (B) in
     (C) about
     (D) with

137. (A) issues
     (B) clients
     (C) articles
     (D) proposals

138. (A) The network server will be expensive.
     (B) Your computer may be corrupted.
     (C) Thank you for your patience.
     (D) Contact the IT help desk.

April 2

Dear TP&G Customer,

Takoradi Power & Gas (TP&G) is committed to providing every customer with dependable electricity service. To this end, we need to make some improvements to our ------- . A maintenance
139.
crew will be upgrading transformers in your neighbourhood on or about 22 April, beginning at

10 A.M. ------- , we will need to shut off the electricity to residences in your area from approximately
140.
10 A.M. to 1 P.M. on that day. ------- . We hope that by ------- this notice, any disruptions caused by
141. **142.**
the planned outage will be minimized.

---

139. (A) office
(B) system
(C) vehicles
(D) records

140. (A) If not
(B) Nonetheless
(C) Unfortunately
(D) On the other hand

141. (A) We apologize for the temporary
inconvenience.
(B) We respond to most service requests
within 24 hours.
(C) Other companies specialize in lighting
installations.
(D) Here are some tips for reducing your
energy bill.

142. (A) sent
(B) to send
(C) will send
(D) sending

GO ON TO THE NEXT PAGE

Questions 143-146 refer to the following e-mail.

To: hanna.kalita@netmail.co.uk
From: patientoutreach@ebmp.co.uk
Date: 12 June
Subject: Invitation to patient portal

Dear Ms. Kalita,

East Burberry Medical Practice has recently rolled out its patient portal, Burmed Connect. This service ------- to help you manage your healthcare at your convenience. You are invited to create
143.

an account to access the portal. Once enrolled, you will be able to book appointments with our doctors as well as view your medical records and request prescriptions. ------- , you can use
144.

Burmed Connect to send messages to your doctor. Only you and your doctor will be able to see any messages exchanged between the two of you. ------- .
145.

To create an account, start by going to www.eastburberrymedicalpractice/patient-portal.co.uk. If you experience any difficulties with the ------- process, please call 20 5550 0169.
146.

Sincerely,

Emma Richardson, Patient Outreach Coordinator

---

143. (A) has been intended
     (B) will be intended
     (C) was intended
     (D) is intended

144. (A) Furthermore
     (B) Instead
     (C) However
     (D) Otherwise

145. (A) Our previous portal will no longer be
         updated.
     (B) The health app can be downloaded from
         our Web site.
     (C) Protecting your privacy is a responsibility
         we take seriously.
     (D) You will be locked out of your account
         after a third failed attempt.

146. (A) selection
     (B) registration
     (C) invention
     (D) deletion

Directions: In this part you will read a selection of texts, such as magazine and newspaper articles, e-mails, and instant messages. Each text or set of texts is followed by several questions. Select the best answer for each question and mark the letter (A), (B), (C), or (D) on your answer sheet.

Questions 147-148 refer to the following sign.

Galloway Office Park

Building 1
Harris Toddman, MD
Lansin Diagnostic Labs
Smiley Dental Offices

Building 2
Freel Primary Care Physicians
Rally Star Physical Therapy Associates

Building 3
Lee and Associates, Internists
Kare Medical Services

Building 4
Lurie Pharmaceuticals

No Truck Access
No Soliciting
No Trespassing

147. Where would the sign most likely be found?

(A) On an office desk
(B) In a hospital waiting room
(C) In the lobby of a real estate agency
(D) Near the entrance of an office complex

148. What type of businesses are listed on the sign?

(A) Health care
(B) Legal services
(C) Manufacturing
(D) Finance

GO ON TO THE NEXT PAGE

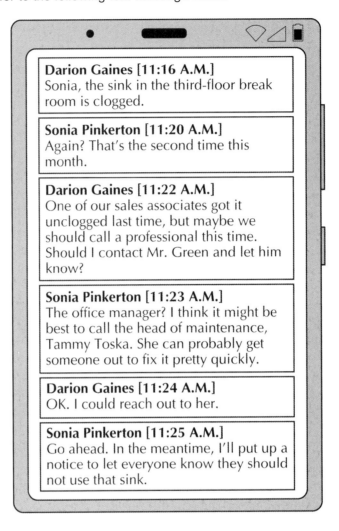

Darion Gaines [11:16 A.M.]
Sonia, the sink in the third-floor break room is clogged.

Sonia Pinkerton [11:20 A.M.]
Again? That's the second time this month.

Darion Gaines [11:22 A.M.]
One of our sales associates got it unclogged last time, but maybe we should call a professional this time. Should I contact Mr. Green and let him know?

Sonia Pinkerton [11:23 A.M.]
The office manager? I think it might be best to call the head of maintenance, Tammy Toska. She can probably get someone out to fix it pretty quickly.

Darion Gaines [11:24 A.M.]
OK. I could reach out to her.

Sonia Pinkerton [11:25 A.M.]
Go ahead. In the meantime, I'll put up a notice to let everyone know they should not use that sink.

149. Who most likely is Mr. Green?

(A) A custodian
(B) A plumber
(C) A manager
(D) A sales associate

150. At 11:25 A.M., what does Ms. Pinkerton most likely mean when she writes, "Go ahead"?

(A) Mr. Gaines may enter the break room.
(B) Mr. Gaines should contact Ms. Toska.
(C) Mr. Gaines should post a notice.
(D) Mr. Gaines can try to repair the sink.

Questions 151-152 refer to the following e-mail.

```
═══════════════════════ E-Mail Message ═══════════════════════

To:          Ramdeo Khemradj <rkhemradj@topofthehill.jm>
From:        Kerensa Mayne <kmayne@topofthehill.jm>
Date:        17 August
Subject:     Information
Attachment:  📎 Latest draft
─────────────────────────────────────────────────────────────

Hi, Ramdeo.

Please take a look at the latest draft and let me know what you think. I changed the
layout—desserts are now on the inside back cover—and provided descriptions of the
additional dinner dishes that you and your kitchen staff will be introducing next month.

I haven't updated the prices yet though, as I haven't decided whether we will need to
increase some of them.

I'm sure you agree with me that the design firm did a great job upgrading the kitchen
and making the dining room brighter and more inviting.

Kerensa
```

151. Who most likely is Mr. Khemradj?

(A) An interior decorator
(B) A restaurant owner
(C) An architect
(D) A head chef

152. What most likely is attached to the e-mail?

(A) A price list
(B) A revised menu
(C) A photograph of food
(D) A lighting plan for a dining room

GO ON TO THE NEXT PAGE ➤

TEST 10

Questions 153-154 refer to the following application form.

Page Turner Booksellers
Employment Application Form

Date of Application: 1 September

PERSONAL DATA

Name: Arturo Rami	Address: 10 Beamish Street, Werribee, VIC 3030
E-mail: arturo.rami@amail.com.au	Telephone: 03 9555 3744

EMPLOYMENT DESIRED

Desired position	Assistant Store Manager		
Available start date	20 September		
Preferred location	☐ Seaholme	☒ Werribee	☐ Port Melbourne
Preferred status	☒ Full-time	☐ Part-time	☐ Temporary

EDUCATION

Educational Institution	Diploma/Certificate/Degree Earned
South Bank High School	High school diploma
Dymocks University	Bachelor's degree

EMPLOYMENT HISTORY

Employer	Position	Duration
The Garment Barn	Sales associate	2 years
Altona Marketing	Assistant manager	3 years

EXPLANATION OF INTEREST IN THE POSITION

I flourish in a fast-paced and demanding work environment, which my most recent employers are known for. I expect the same is true of Page Turner Booksellers, which tends to be quite busy. Moreover, with my bachelor's degree in retail management, I believe I am well suited for the position.

153. What is suggested about Page Turner Booksellers?

(A) It has multiple locations.
(B) It is near South Bank High School.
(C) It will open a new store on September 20.
(D) It currently has only full-time positions available.

154. What is NOT indicated about Mr. Rami?

(A) He studied retail management.
(B) He recently moved to Werribee.
(C) He has experience working in sales.
(D) He prefers working in a busy setting.

Questions 155-157 refer to the following advertisement.

Donovan Auto Lube

Donavan Auto Lube (DAL) is the first choice for residents of Knebworth who want to keep their cars running smoothly. We provide oil changes, tyre rotations, and routine inspections. Our team of certified auto technicians can service all vehicle makes and models. Customers may schedule an appointment or simply drive up to any DAL location during our business hours of 8:00 A.M. to 8:00 P.M., Monday to Saturday, and 11:00 A.M. to 5:00 P.M. on Sunday.

This summer, DAL offers a special promotion: a 5-quart oil change, oil filter replacement, and comprehensive maintenance check for just £15. This offer is available at all DAL locations throughout Herfordshire but may not be combined with any other promotional offer. The quoted price does not include value-added tax and does not cover any additional maintenance, repairs, and parts that a vehicle inspection may call for.

Visit DAL for all your automotive needs.

---

155. The word "running" in paragraph 1, line 2, is closest in meaning to

(A) flowing
(B) speeding
(C) controlling
(D) functioning

156. When can a customer NOT be served at Donovan Auto Lube?

(A) On Monday at 8:00 A.M.
(B) On Wednesday at 6:00 P.M.
(C) On Saturday at 4:00 P.M.
(D) On Sunday at 6:00 P.M.

157. What is true about the promotional offer?

(A) It is not valid outside of Knebworth.
(B) It includes replacement of a filter.
(C) It does not apply to a maintenance check.
(D) It includes all taxes.

GO ON TO THE NEXT PAGE

Questions 158-160 refer to the following biography.

Kasem Ngam is a renowned speaker and author from Nonthaburi province in Thailand. — [1] —. Immediately upon graduating from Sangsuwan University in Bangkok, he joined Chanthara Gas & Electric (CG&E). Over a period of 25 years, he made a name for himself as one of CG&E's most dedicated and respected employees, even gaining national and international recognition. — [2] —.

Mr. Ngam currently runs a consulting firm that he started four years ago to help businesses develop innovative new technologies to power the modern world. — [3] —. He is the author of numerous articles on a variety of topics, including solar panels and hydrogen-powered vehicles. — [4] —. His honors include a Pax Innovation Award for *The Future's Fuel*, his book on biofuels, which has been translated into several languages. His forthcoming book, *Pricing Our Power: Funding the New Green Energy*, will be published in May.

158. What industry does Mr. Ngam most likely work in?

(A) Energy
(B) Travel
(C) Finance
(D) Journalism

159. What is indicated about Mr. Ngam?

(A) He is writing his first book.
(B) He knows several languages.
(C) He operates his own business.
(D) He is a recent university graduate.

160. In which of the positions marked [1], [2], [3], and [4] does the following sentence best belong?

"The last position he held at the company was director of research and development."

(A) [1]
(B) [2]
(C) [3]
(D) [4]

Questions 161-163 refer to the following article.

Jobs Coming to Willettville

WILLETTVILLE (March 8)—Tanney's Discount Mart (TDM) announced today that it will hold a job fair in Willettville later this month. The company, headquartered in nearby Lyter City, is looking to fill 300 positions at its new distribution center, set to open here next month. In addition to seeking technicians and supervisors, the company wants to fill positions in the processing, stock inspection, and maintenance departments.

"TDM's distribution centers use modern automated systems, which creates a big need for qualified technical staff in particular," Kent Siler, TDM's president, said in a press release announcing the job fair.

The event will be held from 9:30 A.M. to 6:30 P.M. on Thursday, March 20, in the ballroom of the Twin Ridges Hotel. Details can be found by visiting tdm.com/careers.

"This recruiting event will help us find the staff we need to meet the anticipated growth in demand for our products," said Mr. Siler. "TDM continues to expand its position in discount retail. So far this year, we have opened three stores, and we have five more slated to open by the end of next year." Mr. Siler noted, moreover, that TDM offers competitive wages for full-time and part-time employment.

---

161. What is stated about TDM's new distribution center?

(A) It is the company's first distribution center to use automated systems.
(B) It is the largest facility the company has built.
(C) It is scheduled to open in April.
(D) It was designed by an architectural firm in Willettville.

162. What is NOT mentioned about the job fair?

(A) The kinds of jobs offered
(B) The day and date it will be held
(C) The types of refreshments served
(D) The source for detailed information

163. What does Mr. Siler indicate about TDM?

(A) It is a growing business.
(B) It sponsors an annual job fair.
(C) It is staffed mostly by part-time workers.
(D) It relies heavily on online sales.

GO ON TO THE NEXT PAGE

Questions 164-167 refer to the following online chat discussion.

Rashaan Little (5:40 P.M.)
Hi, Amanda and Desmond. Earlier today I learned that the town has hired our company to demolish the lighthouse.

Amanda Richards (5:43 P.M.)
So did I. I have mixed feelings about taking down that structure, though.

Desmond Williams (5:43 P.M.)
This is the first time that I'm learning about that. I was out of the office all day today.

Rashaan Little (5:44 P.M.)
How so, Amanda?

Amanda Richards (5:46 P.M.)
Well, given that business has been quite slow lately, our company needs the work. Then again, the lighthouse has historic value: it has been a major landmark of Burlingate for 100 years.

Rashaan Little (5:48 P.M.)
I realize that. But the company can't afford to pass up this opportunity for the reason you mentioned. Besides, lighthouses have largely become outdated.

Desmond Williams (5:49 P.M.)
Not really. There's always a need for ships to get warnings about dangerous locations. Lighthouses have served that function for years.

Rashaan Little (5:51 P.M.)
True, but modern technological equipment exists now that simplifies navigation and increasingly makes lighthouses a thing of the past. Anyway, let's meet tomorrow at 10:00 A.M. to discuss how we'll carry out this job.

164. In what type of business do the writers most likely work?

(A) Building demolition
(B) Shipping technology
(C) Corporate accounting
(D) Historical preservation

165. What is indicated about the company the writers work for?

(A) It recently purchased ultramodern equipment.
(B) It has experienced a decline in business.
(C) It is regularly hired by the town council.
(D) It has been in business for 100 years.

166. At 5:48 P.M., what does Mr. Little most likely mean when he writes, "I realize that"?

(A) He knows why Mr. Williams had been absent.
(B) He recognizes the significance of the lighthouse for the town.
(C) He understands how important the company is for the town.
(D) He is aware that Ms. Richards knows much about the town's history.

167. What will the writers most likely do tomorrow morning?

(A) Advertise new job openings
(B) Attend a town council meeting
(C) Go on a tour of the lighthouse
(D) Start planning for an upcoming project

Contempo Spaces
Window Treatment Package

If you are considering redecorating the windows of your living room, dining room, or bedroom, Contempo Spaces has the perfect treatment design package for you. — [1] —. We will help you put together the right combination of shades, panels, drapes, and valances—all perfectly tailored to fit your windows.

Here's how it works:

• First, one of our style representatives will come to your home and measure and photograph the windows in each room.

• During that visit, our representative will show you samples of the many styles of fabrics and hardware available in our product line. — [2] —. Or, you can opt to visit our showroom after the home visit and make your selections there.

• One or two days after you've made your window treatment decisions, we will send you an invoice, listing the cost for materials, installation, and labor. The quoted price is valid for thirty days. Upon receipt of payment, materials will be ordered. It usually takes from seven to fourteen days for them to reach our store. — [3] —.

• Finally, we will contact you to schedule the date and time of installation. — [4] —. Depending on the size of the project, installation can take two to eight hours.

168. What is the purpose of the brochure?

(A) To explain a new policy
(B) To describe a popular product
(C) To advertise a special discount
(D) To present a standard process

169. After how many days might the total cost listed in an invoice change?

(A) Two
(B) Seven
(C) Fourteen
(D) Thirty

170. What is indicated in the brochure about installation?

(A) It is not available for all window treatments.
(B) It is the responsibility of the customer.
(C) It takes no more than eight hours to complete.
(D) It is subcontracted to an outside vendor.

171. In which of the positions marked [1], [2], [3], and [4] does the following sentence best belong?

"Our entire style collection can be viewed on our Web site."

(A) [1]
(B) [2]
(C) [3]
(D) [4]

Questions 172-175 refer to the following e-mail.

To:	Morgan Tebele <mtebele@newsom.com.na>
From:	Esme Mukaya <emukaya@skyleopard.com.na>
Date:	21 August
Subject:	Offer

Dear Mr. Tebele,

Whether you are refinancing a loan, training personnel, or marketing your financial services online, having fast, reliable Internet access is essential for bank managers like you. Sky Leopard Communications delivers just that, thanks to its highly advanced network and dedicated workforce.

In fact, a recent survey conducted by the Namibian Association of Small-Business Owners (NASO) revealed that 75 percent of its members prefer our services over those of our competitors.

The reason: in addition to our state-of-the-art Internet infrastructure and our outstanding pool of technicians, we offer premium Internet connectivity through our High-Velocity Internet Access (HIVIA) service plan. HIVIA provides download and upload speeds that are three times faster than those of our closest competitor.

Sky Leopard Communications offers new customers and those using one of our other service plans the opportunity to try HIVIA for free for 30 days. To subscribe, visit us at www.skyleopard.com.na or call us at 061-987-555. If at any time during the one-month trial period you are not satisfied with this plan, you can unsubscribe from the service at no cost to you.

Sincerely,

Esme Mukaya, Sales

172. What business is Mr. Tebele most likely in?

(A) Web design
(B) Hospitality
(C) Marketing
(D) Banking

173. What is indicated about Sky Leopard Communications?

(A) It offers a discount to NASO members.
(B) It is popular with small-business owners.
(C) It recently launched a new service plan.
(D) It is looking to increase its workforce.

174. The word "outstanding" in paragraph 3, line 1, is closest in meaning to

(A) diverse
(B) available
(C) excellent
(D) remaining

175. What can be concluded about the HIVIA service plan?

(A) It is more expensive than other plans.
(B) It was created following a customer survey.
(C) It requires the purchase of special equipment.
(D) It can be canceled within the first month at no charge.

GO ON TO THE NEXT PAGE

Introduction to Project Management
Online Webinar
18 January, 9 A.M.–2 P.M.
Presenter: Shrijana Patel
Cost: €45
(Register by 10 January and receive a 10% discount!)

This live webinar offers attendees a better understanding of how to improve the role that project management plays in their organizations. The presentation will provide the basics of managing projects and workers. Participants will learn strategies and best practices to effectively oversee their projects and foster buy-in from key players.

Participants will explore a simple step-by-step process for managing projects and learn how to use tools and documents such as scope statements and communication plans. The presenter will also cover topics such as developing a project's business case and facilitating productive team meetings.

To:	Maya Liu
From:	Leonard Chung
Subject:	Webinar
Date:	2 January

Dear Ms. Liu:

Thank you for sending me the webinar announcement. As a novice supervisor, I need to get all the training I can, but I'm not sure whether I will be able to take advantage of this particular offering. I am scheduled to present a detailed project update at my company's quarterly division meeting on the same day, and I don't think anyone else on the team would be able to take my place.

Do you know whether the webinar will be recorded or whether there will be a similar webinar at a later date? I have no schedule conflicts after 29 January.

Leonard Chung

176. What is indicated about the webinar?

(A) It includes a session on preparing for job interviews.
(B) It will show participants how to use specific tools.
(C) There is no charge for participants.
(D) Registration closes on January 10.

177. In the webinar description, the word "cover" in paragraph 2, line 3, is closest in meaning to

(A) protect
(B) spread
(C) ask for
(D) talk about

178. What is one purpose of the e-mail?

(A) To explain a scheduling conflict
(B) To request a deadline extension
(C) To apologize for arriving late to an event
(D) To ask for help in preparing a presentation

179. What is suggested about Mr. Chung?

(A) He plans to record his presentation.
(B) He often trains new project managers.
(C) He attends webinars on a regular basis.
(D) He has relatively little experience as a supervisor.

180. On what date is Mr. Chung scheduled to give a presentation?

(A) January 2
(B) January 10
(C) January 18
(D) January 29

GO ON TO THE NEXT PAGE

GALWAY (4 March)—Adelle Rosier, a third-generation soap maker, opened her shop in Galway eight years ago. Nestled behind Eglinton Gourmet Market on Raven Terrace, her business, Rosier and Finch, is booming.

Ms. Rosier credits the success to her commitment to lifelong learning. "Yes, my handcrafted soaps, shampoos, and lotions are luxurious," she said. "But there are a lot of high-quality skin-care products out there. So after learning the trade from my family, I have increased my sales knowledge by taking online courses in business-to-business (B2B) marketing."

Ms. Rosier adds that those courses built her confidence in selling her products directly to hotels. "Thanks to what I learned in my B2B strategies courses, I managed to persuade a number of boutique hotels in Europe to try my products." And so Rosier and Finch skin-care products are available in guest rooms at, for instance, the Bruadair Hotel in Galway, the Florinda Grand in Lisbon, Portugal, and the Zerra Inn in Reykjavik, Iceland.

Ms. Rosier further points out that many of her customers first learn of her products during a hotel stay. Afterward, they visit the shop in person or go online to purchase the items for themselves.

Rosier and Finch is located at 12 Raven Terrace and can be found online at www.rosierandfinch.co.ie.

---

https://www.florindagrand.pt/en/guest_reviews

I had to arrange a last-minute business trip to my company's Portugal office, and the usual hotel I book was completely full. Based on some online recommendations, I decided to stay at Florinda Grand. While this charming hotel is much smaller than the usual places I stay, it has every comfort one would want during a business trip. In addition to a tastefully decorated and comfortable room, there were gourmet treats on my pillowcase and the finest soap, shampoo, and other toiletries available for me to enjoy. My only regret is that I was in Lisbon for just three days. Next time I visit the Lisbon office, I will stay longer and book a room at the Florinda Grand.

—posted by Ashton Wu, 7 June

181. What is the purpose of the article?

  (A) To provide annual hotel ratings
  (B) To announce the opening of a store
  (C) To profile a small-business owner
  (D) To discuss online shopping trends

182. How did Ms. Rosier improve her marketing skills?

  (A) By visiting family members overseas
  (B) By joining a professional association
  (C) By working in the hotel industry
  (D) By participating in online classes

183. What is stated about Rosier and Finch?

  (A) It sells its products to other businesses.
  (B) It has shops in cities around the world.
  (C) It is redesigning its e-commerce site.
  (D) It offers courses on soapmaking.

184. What is suggested about Mr. Wu?

  (A) He manages Eglinton Gourmet Market.
  (B) He purchased Rosier and Finch products online.
  (C) He met Ms. Rosier on a business trip.
  (D) He likes Rosier and Finch products.

185. According to the review, what was Mr. Wu not pleased about?

  (A) The length of his trip
  (B) The decorations in the room
  (C) The comfort of the pillows
  (D) The size of the hotel

GO ON TO THE NEXT PAGE

Questions 186-190 refer to the following sales report, memo, and article.

Margot's House of Ice Cream
Flavor Purchases by Percentage of Sales
July

Flavor	Percent
Chocolate	22
Vanilla	18
Strawberry	11
Cookies and cream	8
Butter pecan	8
Mint chocolate chip	7
All others	26

MEMO

To: All Store Managers

From: June Willcox, CEO, Margot's House of Ice Cream

Subject: New Stores

Date: October 5

Margot's House of Ice Cream is proud to welcome the following new stores.

Store Number	Location	Opening Date	Manager
66	Framingham, Massachusetts, United States	September 1	Inga Slavin
67	Appleton, Wisconsin, United States	September 7	Zheng Tong
68	Wollongong, New South Wales, Australia	September 14	Geoffrey Pratt
69	Rotorua, New Zealand	September 15	Kehinde Ilogu
70	Greater Sudbury, Ontario, Canada	September 29	Hallie Strafford

For the next six months, we will be supporting these stores with advertisements in their local media markets.

In December, we plan to open stores in Italy and Switzerland. Demand for our quality product is higher than ever, our market share is increasing, and we are not finished expanding! Stay tuned for more information!

Popular Ice Cream Purveyor Comes to New Zealand

By Ysai Mendez

ROTORUA (2 November)—Residents of Rotorua have been flocking to Cargill Street, where Margot's House of Ice Cream has opened its first store in New Zealand.

"I don't know what their secret is, but their ice cream really is something special," said Jeremy Frank, a schoolteacher who was enjoying ice cream cones with his family on a recent afternoon. "We've been here several times already since they opened. I think we'll be regulars."

"I love strawberry, and their strawberry is the best I ever had," added his daughter, Olivia Frank, age 10.

Margot's House of Ice Cream was founded five years ago in San Francisco by Margot Summers, a former chemistry major. Its ice cream contains at least 11 percent milk fat. Milk used in production, according to company CEO June Willcox, is sourced locally or regionally whenever possible.

Kehinde Ilogu, the manager of the Rotorua store, says that the number of visitors has been rising steadily.

"We plan to keep the momentum going by having special events once a month," he said. "Next up is the strawberry festival. New Zealand's strawberry season will be getting started. In addition to our superb ice cream, we'll offer strawberries dipped in chocolate, strawberry cupcakes, and strawberry milkshakes. We look forward to a great future in Rotorua."

186. According to the sales report, what flavor of ice cream is purchased at the same rate as Butter pecan?

(A) Chocolate
(B) Vanilla
(C) Cookies and cream
(D) Mint chocolate chip

187. What is true about the products listed in the sales report?

(A) They contain at least 11 percent milk fat.
(B) They are made with artificial flavors.
(C) They will increase in price soon.
(D) They are sold mainly in San Francisco.

188. What is indicated in the memo about the company's new managers?

(A) They were trained in Italy and Switzerland.
(B) They will receive advertising support for six months.
(C) They expect their stores to become profitable in December.
(D) They offered special promotions on opening day.

189. What will soon happen at store 69 ?

(A) More ice cream flavors will be added to the menu.
(B) A child's birthday will be celebrated.
(C) An assistant manager will be hired.
(D) A range of special treats will be sold.

190. Who is most likely to enjoy the strawberry festival?

(A) Mr. Mendez
(B) Ms. Willcox
(C) Ms. Frank
(D) Ms. Summers

TEST 10

GO ON TO THE NEXT PAGE

Questions 191-195 refer to the following e-mails and memo.

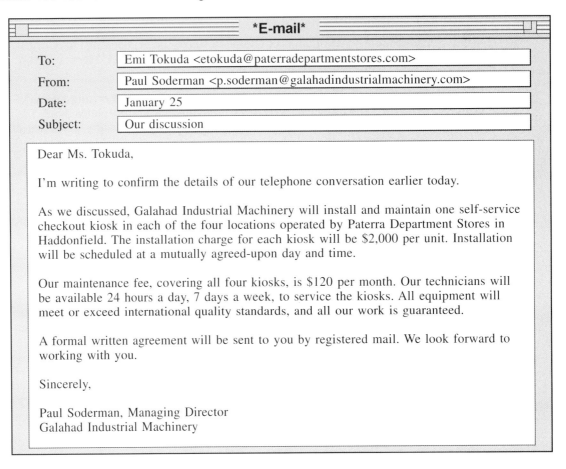

E-mail

To:	Emi Tokuda \<etokuda@paterradepartmentstores.com\>
From:	Paul Soderman \<p.soderman@galahadindustrialmachinery.com\>
Date:	January 25
Subject:	Our discussion

Dear Ms. Tokuda,

I'm writing to confirm the details of our telephone conversation earlier today.

As we discussed, Galahad Industrial Machinery will install and maintain one self-service checkout kiosk in each of the four locations operated by Paterra Department Stores in Haddonfield. The installation charge for each kiosk will be $2,000 per unit. Installation will be scheduled at a mutually agreed-upon day and time.

Our maintenance fee, covering all four kiosks, is $120 per month. Our technicians will be available 24 hours a day, 7 days a week, to service the kiosks. All equipment will meet or exceed international quality standards, and all our work is guaranteed.

A formal written agreement will be sent to you by registered mail. We look forward to working with you.

Sincerely,

Paul Soderman, Managing Director
Galahad Industrial Machinery

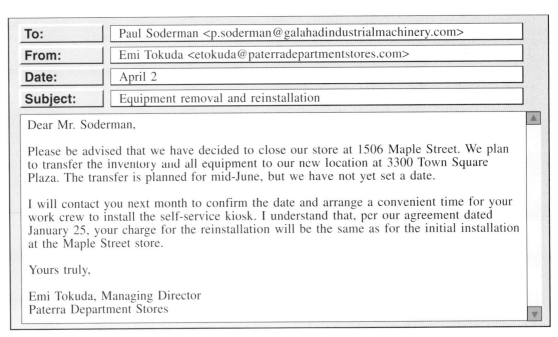

To:	Paul Soderman \<p.soderman@galahadindustrialmachinery.com\>
From:	Emi Tokuda \<etokuda@paterradepartmentstores.com\>
Date:	April 2
Subject:	Equipment removal and reinstallation

Dear Mr. Soderman,

Please be advised that we have decided to close our store at 1506 Maple Street. We plan to transfer the inventory and all equipment to our new location at 3300 Town Square Plaza. The transfer is planned for mid-June, but we have not yet set a date.

I will contact you next month to confirm the date and arrange a convenient time for your work crew to install the self-service kiosk. I understand that, per our agreement dated January 25, your charge for the reinstallation will be the same as for the initial installation at the Maple Street store.

Yours truly,

Emi Tokuda, Managing Director
Paterra Department Stores

MEMO

To: All Paterra Staff
From: Eleanor Bianchi, Branch Manager
Date: June 5
Re: Move update

Thanks to your hard work, our new store in the Town Square Plaza is on track to open on June 15. One of the problems with the store we are currently working out of is that it is not on a bus line. By contrast, the location we will be moving to is served by bus number 689, so we expect to have a larger number of customers at that location. We are only waiting for the last of our display shelves to be delivered from our warehouse so that we can finish the display in the gardening department.

In appreciation of your efforts, I've brought pastries from Aniqa's Bakery. I've put these treats on the break-room counter. Enjoy!

191. In the first e-mail, what is stated about Galahad Industrial Machinery?

(A) It completes repairs within one day.
(B) It is available to do maintenance service at all times.
(C) It has technicians with international work experience.
(D) It has an office in Haddonfield.

192. What is true about the reinstallation of the self-service kiosk?

(A) It will be done personally by Mr. Soderman.
(B) It will cost Paterra Department Stores $2,000.
(C) It will cause a change in the monthly maintenance fee.
(D) It will require a new agreement to be signed.

193. When will Ms. Tokuda discuss her moving plans with Mr. Soderman?

(A) In March
(B) In April
(C) In May
(D) In June

194. What is suggested about the Paterra store at 1506 Maple Street?

(A) It is not accessible by bus.
(B) It will be renovated and reopened.
(C) It is far from the warehouse.
(D) It contains a bakery section.

195. According to the memo, what must still be done at the new Paterra store location?

(A) Some products must be priced.
(B) Some areas must be painted.
(C) Some doors must be replaced.
(D) Some shelves must be delivered.

GO ON TO THE NEXT PAGE

Survey: Consumers Prefer Physical Stores

A recent consumer survey has shown that 33% of respondents prefer to touch the products they intend to purchase. Moreover, 61% of those surveyed said they are likely to spend more when shopping at a brick-and-mortar store rather than at an online store.

These data, backed up by other consumer preference studies, are causing many merchants who generate all their revenue from online sales to open physical stores as a supplement to their online presence.

The advantage of a physical space is that it helps retail owners build brand loyalty. "In terms of convenience, nothing beats online," says Marlene Fitzroy, who owns Toddles, a children's store in Shelburn, and an online site, toddles.com. "But a physical space fosters a sense of community that keeps local customers coming back and attracts new ones."

Ms. Fitzroy, a frequent speaker at local business events, is not only a strong supporter and promoter of customer engagement; she also practices what she preaches.

"Four times a year, we host a special sales event during which children can enjoy themselves with a variety of activities," she said. "These events are a hit with both the children and their parents. And even if the parents don't buy anything on such occasions, the next time they need a children's toy, game, book, or puzzle, they'll probably think of us."

Shelburn Business Coalition (SBC)

Businesspeople from Shelburn and the surrounding area are invited to join us at the Shelburn Convention Center on October 8 for our annual Business Summit.

Our keynote speaker this year will be Mr. Hansraj Deshpande, founder and CEO of Wintereden Hoteliers. Other speakers, all local business owners, are Ms. Omodele Akindjo, Ms. Marlene Fitzroy, Mr. Jasper Klinkhamer, and Mr. Alvin Liu. Topics to be covered include building a strong workforce, establishing a line of credit, engaging with customers, and attracting venture capital.

By registering for this event, you will automatically be added to our e-mail list. Please visit our Web site, www.shelburnbusinesscoalition.org, for the full schedule.

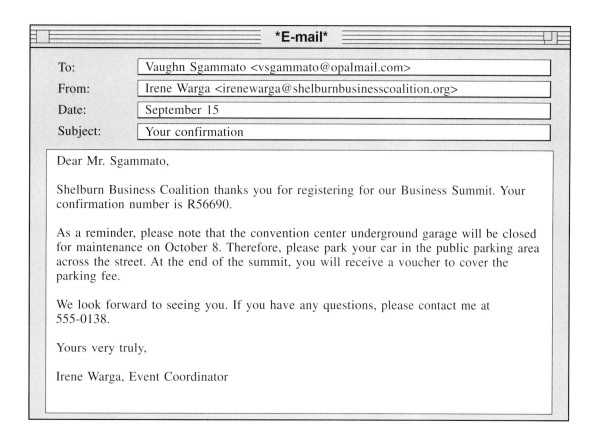

E-mail

To:	Vaughn Sgammato <vsgammato@opalmail.com>
From:	Irene Warga <irenewarga@shelburnbusinesscoalition.org>
Date:	September 15
Subject:	Your confirmation

Dear Mr. Sgammato,

Shelburn Business Coalition thanks you for registering for our Business Summit. Your confirmation number is R56690.

As a reminder, please note that the convention center underground garage will be closed for maintenance on October 8. Therefore, please park your car in the public parking area across the street. At the end of the summit, you will receive a voucher to cover the parking fee.

We look forward to seeing you. If you have any questions, please contact me at 555-0138.

Yours very truly,

Irene Warga, Event Coordinator

---

196. According to the article, what action is being considered by many online sellers?

(A) Redesigning their Web sites
(B) Increasing their advertising budgets
(C) Opening physical store locations
(D) Developing new lines of products

197. What does Ms. Fitzroy say she offers her customers?

(A) A convenient place to shop
(B) Discounts on children's clothing
(C) An enjoyable shopping experience
(D) Special deals on toys

198. Who most likely will speak on the topic of engaging with customers?

(A) Ms. Akindjo
(B) Ms. Fitzroy
(C) Mr. Deshpande
(D) Mr. Liu

199. What is most likely true about Mr. Sgammato?

(A) He was added to a mailing list.
(B) He will be starting a business.
(C) He received a discount on his registration fee.
(D) He has never attended an SBC event before.

200. What is Mr. Sgammato expected to do upon arrival at a convention center?

(A) Ask to see to Ms. Warga
(B) Park his car across the street
(C) Obtain a confirmation number
(D) Pick up some conference material

TEST 10

Stop! This is the end of the test. If you finish before time is called, you may go back to Parts 5, 6, and 7 and check your work.

토익 정기시험 기출문제집 4 1000

RC

ANSWERS

101 (B)	102 (D)	103 (C)	104 (B)	105 (D)
106 (D)	107 (A)	108 (D)	109 (A)	110 (B)
111 (A)	112 (B)	113 (A)	114 (C)	115 (D)
116 (C)	117 (D)	118 (B)	119 (A)	120 (A)
121 (D)	122 (A)	123 (B)	124 (A)	125 (D)
126 (D)	127 (C)	128 (C)	129 (C)	130 (B)
131 (D)	132 (D)	133 (A)	134 (B)	135 (C)
136 (A)	137 (B)	138 (B)	139 (A)	140 (C)
141 (B)	142 (C)	143 (A)	144 (B)	145 (C)
146 (A)	147 (C)	148 (B)	149 (B)	150 (C)
151 (B)	152 (D)	153 (A)	154 (B)	155 (A)
156 (D)	157 (B)	158 (B)	159 (A)	160 (B)
161 (A)	162 (C)	163 (D)	164 (C)	165 (C)
166 (D)	167 (A)	168 (D)	169 (B)	170 (C)
171 (A)	172 (D)	173 (B)	174 (C)	175 (C)
176 (B)	177 (C)	178 (C)	179 (A)	180 (B)
181 (A)	182 (D)	183 (B)	184 (C)	185 (C)
186 (C)	187 (D)	188 (B)	189 (A)	190 (B)
191 (D)	192 (C)	193 (A)	194 (B)	195 (C)
196 (A)	197 (C)	198 (C)	199 (D)	200 (B)

101 (C)	102 (C)	103 (A)	104 (B)	105 (D)
106 (A)	107 (C)	108 (D)	109 (C)	110 (D)
111 (A)	112 (D)	113 (C)	114 (A)	115 (C)
116 (A)	117 (A)	118 (B)	119 (B)	120 (D)
121 (C)	122 (A)	123 (A)	124 (C)	125 (B)
126 (B)	127 (C)	128 (D)	129 (B)	130 (B)
131 (C)	132 (A)	133 (D)	134 (A)	135 (D)
136 (C)	137 (C)	138 (A)	139 (B)	140 (C)
141 (A)	142 (C)	143 (C)	144 (D)	145 (C)
146 (A)	147 (A)	148 (B)	149 (A)	150 (D)
151 (A)	152 (C)	153 (A)	154 (B)	155 (D)
156 (C)	157 (B)	158 (D)	159 (D)	160 (B)
161 (C)	162 (D)	163 (B)	164 (C)	165 (C)
166 (A)	167 (C)	168 (B)	169 (D)	170 (B)
171 (D)	172 (A)	173 (C)	174 (A)	175 (D)
176 (B)	177 (B)	178 (C)	179 (D)	180 (B)
181 (A)	182 (D)	183 (C)	184 (C)	185 (B)
186 (C)	187 (D)	188 (A)	189 (B)	190 (D)
191 (B)	192 (C)	193 (A)	194 (D)	195 (B)
196 (D)	197 (A)	198 (B)	199 (C)	200 (B)

101 (C)	102 (B)	103 (A)	104 (B)	105 (D)
106 (C)	107 (C)	108 (B)	109 (A)	110 (D)
111 (D)	112 (C)	113 (C)	114 (D)	115 (A)
116 (A)	117 (B)	118 (A)	119 (C)	120 (D)
121 (D)	122 (D)	123 (C)	124 (B)	125 (D)
126 (A)	127 (D)	128 (A)	129 (B)	130 (D)
131 (C)	132 (D)	133 (A)	134 (B)	135 (C)
136 (B)	137 (B)	138 (A)	139 (C)	140 (B)
141 (C)	142 (A)	143 (C)	144 (D)	145 (A)
146 (A)	147 (A)	148 (D)	149 (D)	150 (B)
151 (C)	152 (A)	153 (B)	154 (C)	155 (D)
156 (B)	157 (C)	158 (C)	159 (C)	160 (A)
161 (C)	162 (B)	163 (D)	164 (B)	165 (B)
166 (D)	167 (C)	168 (A)	169 (A)	170 (C)
171 (C)	172 (B)	173 (B)	174 (A)	175 (D)
176 (B)	177 (B)	178 (A)	179 (A)	180 (B)
181 (D)	182 (B)	183 (D)	184 (B)	185 (D)
186 (C)	187 (B)	188 (D)	189 (A)	190 (D)
191 (D)	192 (B)	193 (C)	194 (C)	195 (D)
196 (D)	197 (A)	198 (B)	199 (C)	200 (D)

101 (A)	102 (C)	103 (A)	104 (B)	105 (D)
106 (D)	107 (B)	108 (D)	109 (C)	110 (B)
111 (A)	112 (A)	113 (B)	114 (D)	115 (D)
116 (C)	117 (A)	118 (D)	119 (B)	120 (C)
121 (C)	122 (C)	123 (A)	124 (A)	125 (D)
126 (B)	127 (A)	128 (D)	129 (C)	130 (A)
131 (C)	132 (D)	133 (B)	134 (A)	135 (B)
136 (D)	137 (C)	138 (C)	139 (A)	140 (A)
141 (C)	142 (B)	143 (A)	144 (B)	145 (D)
146 (A)	147 (B)	148 (C)	149 (C)	150 (D)
151 (D)	152 (C)	153 (A)	154 (C)	155 (B)
156 (C)	157 (A)	158 (A)	159 (B)	160 (D)
161 (B)	162 (C)	163 (D)	164 (C)	165 (B)
166 (D)	167 (C)	168 (B)	169 (C)	170 (D)
171 (A)	172 (B)	173 (C)	174 (D)	175 (B)
176 (B)	177 (D)	178 (A)	179 (C)	180 (B)
181 (D)	182 (A)	183 (C)	184 (B)	185 (A)
186 (B)	187 (A)	188 (D)	189 (A)	190 (C)
191 (D)	192 (B)	193 (C)	194 (D)	195 (A)
196 (C)	197 (B)	198 (A)	199 (B)	200 (D)

기출 TEST 5

동영상 강의

101 (D)	102 (A)	103 (C)	104 (B)	105 (C)
106 (B)	107 (B)	108 (C)	109 (C)	110 (A)
111 (B)	112 (C)	113 (D)	114 (B)	115 (A)
116 (A)	117 (D)	118 (A)	119 (D)	120 (D)
121 (D)	122 (A)	123 (A)	124 (B)	125 (C)
126 (C)	127 (B)	128 (D)	129 (C)	130 (D)
131 (B)	132 (C)	133 (A)	134 (D)	135 (B)
136 (C)	137 (C)	138 (A)	139 (A)	140 (D)
141 (C)	142 (B)	143 (B)	144 (D)	145 (A)
146 (C)	147 (B)	148 (B)	149 (C)	150 (D)
151 (D)	152 (A)	153 (A)	154 (D)	155 (C)
156 (B)	157 (D)	158 (A)	159 (C)	160 (C)
161 (B)	162 (D)	163 (A)	164 (B)	165 (C)
166 (A)	167 (D)	168 (C)	169 (B)	170 (D)
171 (C)	172 (D)	173 (B)	174 (C)	175 (D)
176 (D)	177 (C)	178 (A)	179 (D)	180 (B)
181 (C)	182 (C)	183 (A)	184 (C)	185 (D)
186 (A)	187 (A)	188 (D)	189 (B)	190 (B)
191 (C)	192 (A)	193 (A)	194 (D)	195 (C)
196 (A)	197 (C)	198 (B)	199 (D)	200 (A)

기출 TEST 6

동영상 강의

101 (B)	102 (B)	103 (C)	104 (C)	105 (B)
106 (C)	107 (C)	108 (D)	109 (A)	110 (A)
111 (A)	112 (A)	113 (C)	114 (C)	115 (A)
116 (B)	117 (D)	118 (C)	119 (C)	120 (A)
121 (A)	122 (D)	123 (D)	124 (D)	125 (B)
126 (A)	127 (D)	128 (A)	129 (C)	130 (A)
131 (B)	132 (A)	133 (C)	134 (B)	135 (C)
136 (A)	137 (C)	138 (D)	139 (B)	140 (D)
141 (C)	142 (B)	143 (A)	144 (D)	145 (B)
146 (B)	147 (C)	148 (C)	149 (C)	150 (C)
151 (C)	152 (C)	153 (A)	154 (D)	155 (B)
156 (A)	157 (C)	158 (C)	159 (B)	160 (B)
161 (A)	162 (C)	163 (C)	164 (D)	165 (A)
166 (B)	167 (A)	168 (B)	169 (D)	170 (C)
171 (C)	172 (B)	173 (A)	174 (A)	175 (D)
176 (B)	177 (D)	178 (A)	179 (A)	180 (B)
181 (B)	182 (C)	183 (B)	184 (D)	185 (D)
186 (C)	187 (B)	188 (A)	189 (A)	190 (B)
191 (B)	192 (A)	193 (D)	194 (D)	195 (A)
196 (A)	197 (B)	198 (D)	199 (A)	200 (B)

기출 TEST 7

동영상 강의

101 (A)	102 (A)	103 (B)	104 (A)	105 (C)
106 (D)	107 (B)	108 (D)	109 (B)	110 (C)
111 (A)	112 (D)	113 (B)	114 (A)	115 (C)
116 (A)	117 (C)	118 (A)	119 (A)	120 (A)
121 (C)	122 (C)	123 (D)	124 (A)	125 (D)
126 (B)	127 (C)	128 (C)	129 (B)	130 (A)
131 (B)	132 (D)	133 (A)	134 (C)	135 (C)
136 (A)	137 (B)	138 (D)	139 (B)	140 (C)
141 (D)	142 (D)	143 (B)	144 (A)	145 (D)
146 (A)	147 (D)	148 (C)	149 (C)	150 (B)
151 (D)	152 (A)	153 (B)	154 (C)	155 (C)
156 (A)	157 (B)	158 (C)	159 (C)	160 (A)
161 (D)	162 (D)	163 (C)	164 (B)	165 (D)
166 (A)	167 (C)	168 (A)	169 (B)	170 (D)
171 (C)	172 (A)	173 (C)	174 (C)	175 (B)
176 (C)	177 (B)	178 (D)	179 (A)	180 (A)
181 (C)	182 (D)	183 (B)	184 (B)	185 (D)
186 (A)	187 (B)	188 (D)	189 (B)	190 (C)
191 (B)	192 (D)	193 (A)	194 (A)	195 (D)
196 (B)	197 (D)	198 (D)	199 (A)	200 (C)

기출 TEST 8

동영상 강의

101 (A)	102 (D)	103 (A)	104 (C)	105 (B)
106 (C)	107 (C)	108 (C)	109 (A)	110 (B)
111 (B)	112 (C)	113 (D)	114 (A)	115 (B)
116 (A)	117 (C)	118 (A)	119 (B)	120 (A)
121 (C)	122 (B)	123 (B)	124 (D)	125 (D)
126 (D)	127 (A)	128 (C)	129 (B)	130 (D)
131 (B)	132 (A)	133 (A)	134 (D)	135 (D)
136 (C)	137 (D)	138 (B)	139 (C)	140 (D)
141 (B)	142 (D)	143 (D)	144 (B)	145 (A)
146 (D)	147 (C)	148 (B)	149 (C)	150 (D)
151 (B)	152 (C)	153 (A)	154 (C)	155 (D)
156 (A)	157 (B)	158 (B)	159 (C)	160 (B)
161 (D)	162 (A)	163 (D)	164 (B)	165 (D)
166 (A)	167 (C)	168 (B)	169 (A)	170 (C)
171 (B)	172 (D)	173 (C)	174 (A)	175 (B)
176 (B)	177 (B)	178 (A)	179 (C)	180 (D)
181 (C)	182 (D)	183 (A)	184 (B)	185 (B)
186 (C)	187 (A)	188 (B)	189 (D)	190 (C)
191 (D)	192 (C)	193 (C)	194 (A)	195 (A)
196 (C)	197 (A)	198 (B)	199 (B)	200 (D)

101 (B)	102 (B)	103 (D)	104 (B)	105 (B)
106 (D)	107 (D)	108 (C)	109 (D)	110 (A)
111 (C)	112 (A)	113 (A)	114 (A)	115 (B)
116 (A)	117 (C)	118 (C)	119 (A)	120 (C)
121 (A)	122 (A)	123 (D)	124 (B)	125 (A)
126 (D)	127 (D)	128 (D)	129 (A)	130 (A)
131 (C)	132 (C)	133 (B)	134 (B)	135 (D)
136 (D)	137 (B)	138 (C)	139 (C)	140 (A)
141 (B)	142 (A)	143 (A)	144 (B)	145 (C)
146 (D)	147 (A)	148 (D)	149 (B)	150 (D)
151 (B)	152 (A)	153 (C)	154 (A)	155 (A)
156 (B)	157 (D)	158 (B)	159 (D)	160 (B)
161 (C)	162 (B)	163 (D)	164 (B)	165 (C)
166 (B)	167 (D)	168 (A)	169 (B)	170 (C)
171 (A)	172 (D)	173 (B)	174 (D)	175 (C)
176 (D)	177 (B)	178 (C)	179 (A)	180 (C)
181 (B)	182 (C)	183 (B)	184 (D)	185 (D)
186 (D)	187 (A)	188 (B)	189 (D)	190 (C)
191 (C)	192 (B)	193 (C)	194 (B)	195 (D)
196 (C)	197 (D)	198 (B)	199 (A)	200 (A)

101 (B)	102 (A)	103 (C)	104 (D)	105 (C)
106 (C)	107 (B)	108 (C)	109 (C)	110 (A)
111 (B)	112 (D)	113 (A)	114 (D)	115 (D)
116 (B)	117 (D)	118 (C)	119 (B)	120 (A)
121 (D)	122 (C)	123 (D)	124 (B)	125 (B)
126 (D)	127 (C)	128 (A)	129 (A)	130 (A)
131 (D)	132 (B)	133 (B)	134 (A)	135 (D)
136 (C)	137 (A)	138 (C)	139 (B)	140 (C)
141 (A)	142 (D)	143 (D)	144 (D)	145 (C)
146 (B)	147 (D)	148 (A)	149 (C)	150 (B)
151 (D)	152 (B)	153 (A)	154 (B)	155 (D)
156 (D)	157 (B)	158 (A)	159 (C)	160 (B)
161 (C)	162 (C)	163 (A)	164 (A)	165 (B)
166 (B)	167 (D)	168 (D)	169 (D)	170 (C)
171 (B)	172 (D)	173 (B)	174 (C)	175 (D)
176 (B)	177 (D)	178 (A)	179 (D)	180 (C)
181 (C)	182 (D)	183 (A)	184 (D)	185 (A)
186 (C)	187 (A)	188 (B)	189 (D)	190 (C)
191 (B)	192 (B)	193 (C)	194 (A)	195 (D)
196 (C)	197 (C)	198 (B)	199 (A)	200 (B)

ANSWER SHEET

토익® 정기시험 기출문제집

수험번호

응시일자 : 20   년   월   일

Test 01 (Part 5~7)

101	ⓐⓑⓒⓓ	121	ⓐⓑⓒⓓ	141	ⓐⓑⓒⓓ	161	ⓐⓑⓒⓓ	181	ⓐⓑⓒⓓ
102	ⓐⓑⓒⓓ	122	ⓐⓑⓒⓓ	142	ⓐⓑⓒⓓ	162	ⓐⓑⓒⓓ	182	ⓐⓑⓒⓓ
103	ⓐⓑⓒⓓ	123	ⓐⓑⓒⓓ	143	ⓐⓑⓒⓓ	163	ⓐⓑⓒⓓ	183	ⓐⓑⓒⓓ
104	ⓐⓑⓒⓓ	124	ⓐⓑⓒⓓ	144	ⓐⓑⓒⓓ	164	ⓐⓑⓒⓓ	184	ⓐⓑⓒⓓ
105	ⓐⓑⓒⓓ	125	ⓐⓑⓒⓓ	145	ⓐⓑⓒⓓ	165	ⓐⓑⓒⓓ	185	ⓐⓑⓒⓓ
106	ⓐⓑⓒⓓ	126	ⓐⓑⓒⓓ	146	ⓐⓑⓒⓓ	166	ⓐⓑⓒⓓ	186	ⓐⓑⓒⓓ
107	ⓐⓑⓒⓓ	127	ⓐⓑⓒⓓ	147	ⓐⓑⓒⓓ	167	ⓐⓑⓒⓓ	187	ⓐⓑⓒⓓ
108	ⓐⓑⓒⓓ	128	ⓐⓑⓒⓓ	148	ⓐⓑⓒⓓ	168	ⓐⓑⓒⓓ	188	ⓐⓑⓒⓓ
109	ⓐⓑⓒⓓ	129	ⓐⓑⓒⓓ	149	ⓐⓑⓒⓓ	169	ⓐⓑⓒⓓ	189	ⓐⓑⓒⓓ
110	ⓐⓑⓒⓓ	130	ⓐⓑⓒⓓ	150	ⓐⓑⓒⓓ	170	ⓐⓑⓒⓓ	190	ⓐⓑⓒⓓ
111	ⓐⓑⓒⓓ	131	ⓐⓑⓒⓓ	151	ⓐⓑⓒⓓ	171	ⓐⓑⓒⓓ	191	ⓐⓑⓒⓓ
112	ⓐⓑⓒⓓ	132	ⓐⓑⓒⓓ	152	ⓐⓑⓒⓓ	172	ⓐⓑⓒⓓ	192	ⓐⓑⓒⓓ
113	ⓐⓑⓒⓓ	133	ⓐⓑⓒⓓ	153	ⓐⓑⓒⓓ	173	ⓐⓑⓒⓓ	193	ⓐⓑⓒⓓ
114	ⓐⓑⓒⓓ	134	ⓐⓑⓒⓓ	154	ⓐⓑⓒⓓ	174	ⓐⓑⓒⓓ	194	ⓐⓑⓒⓓ
115	ⓐⓑⓒⓓ	135	ⓐⓑⓒⓓ	155	ⓐⓑⓒⓓ	175	ⓐⓑⓒⓓ	195	ⓐⓑⓒⓓ
116	ⓐⓑⓒⓓ	136	ⓐⓑⓒⓓ	156	ⓐⓑⓒⓓ	176	ⓐⓑⓒⓓ	196	ⓐⓑⓒⓓ
117	ⓐⓑⓒⓓ	137	ⓐⓑⓒⓓ	157	ⓐⓑⓒⓓ	177	ⓐⓑⓒⓓ	197	ⓐⓑⓒⓓ
118	ⓐⓑⓒⓓ	138	ⓐⓑⓒⓓ	158	ⓐⓑⓒⓓ	178	ⓐⓑⓒⓓ	198	ⓐⓑⓒⓓ
119	ⓐⓑⓒⓓ	139	ⓐⓑⓒⓓ	159	ⓐⓑⓒⓓ	179	ⓐⓑⓒⓓ	199	ⓐⓑⓒⓓ
120	ⓐⓑⓒⓓ	140	ⓐⓑⓒⓓ	160	ⓐⓑⓒⓓ	180	ⓐⓑⓒⓓ	200	ⓐⓑⓒⓓ

Test 02 (Part 5~7)

101	ⓐⓑⓒⓓ	121	ⓐⓑⓒⓓ	141	ⓐⓑⓒⓓ	161	ⓐⓑⓒⓓ	181	ⓐⓑⓒⓓ
102	ⓐⓑⓒⓓ	122	ⓐⓑⓒⓓ	142	ⓐⓑⓒⓓ	162	ⓐⓑⓒⓓ	182	ⓐⓑⓒⓓ
103	ⓐⓑⓒⓓ	123	ⓐⓑⓒⓓ	143	ⓐⓑⓒⓓ	163	ⓐⓑⓒⓓ	183	ⓐⓑⓒⓓ
104	ⓐⓑⓒⓓ	124	ⓐⓑⓒⓓ	144	ⓐⓑⓒⓓ	164	ⓐⓑⓒⓓ	184	ⓐⓑⓒⓓ
105	ⓐⓑⓒⓓ	125	ⓐⓑⓒⓓ	145	ⓐⓑⓒⓓ	165	ⓐⓑⓒⓓ	185	ⓐⓑⓒⓓ
106	ⓐⓑⓒⓓ	126	ⓐⓑⓒⓓ	146	ⓐⓑⓒⓓ	166	ⓐⓑⓒⓓ	186	ⓐⓑⓒⓓ
107	ⓐⓑⓒⓓ	127	ⓐⓑⓒⓓ	147	ⓐⓑⓒⓓ	167	ⓐⓑⓒⓓ	187	ⓐⓑⓒⓓ
108	ⓐⓑⓒⓓ	128	ⓐⓑⓒⓓ	148	ⓐⓑⓒⓓ	168	ⓐⓑⓒⓓ	188	ⓐⓑⓒⓓ
109	ⓐⓑⓒⓓ	129	ⓐⓑⓒⓓ	149	ⓐⓑⓒⓓ	169	ⓐⓑⓒⓓ	189	ⓐⓑⓒⓓ
110	ⓐⓑⓒⓓ	130	ⓐⓑⓒⓓ	150	ⓐⓑⓒⓓ	170	ⓐⓑⓒⓓ	190	ⓐⓑⓒⓓ
111	ⓐⓑⓒⓓ	131	ⓐⓑⓒⓓ	151	ⓐⓑⓒⓓ	171	ⓐⓑⓒⓓ	191	ⓐⓑⓒⓓ
112	ⓐⓑⓒⓓ	132	ⓐⓑⓒⓓ	152	ⓐⓑⓒⓓ	172	ⓐⓑⓒⓓ	192	ⓐⓑⓒⓓ
113	ⓐⓑⓒⓓ	133	ⓐⓑⓒⓓ	153	ⓐⓑⓒⓓ	173	ⓐⓑⓒⓓ	193	ⓐⓑⓒⓓ
114	ⓐⓑⓒⓓ	134	ⓐⓑⓒⓓ	154	ⓐⓑⓒⓓ	174	ⓐⓑⓒⓓ	194	ⓐⓑⓒⓓ
115	ⓐⓑⓒⓓ	135	ⓐⓑⓒⓓ	155	ⓐⓑⓒⓓ	175	ⓐⓑⓒⓓ	195	ⓐⓑⓒⓓ
116	ⓐⓑⓒⓓ	136	ⓐⓑⓒⓓ	156	ⓐⓑⓒⓓ	176	ⓐⓑⓒⓓ	196	ⓐⓑⓒⓓ
117	ⓐⓑⓒⓓ	137	ⓐⓑⓒⓓ	157	ⓐⓑⓒⓓ	177	ⓐⓑⓒⓓ	197	ⓐⓑⓒⓓ
118	ⓐⓑⓒⓓ	138	ⓐⓑⓒⓓ	158	ⓐⓑⓒⓓ	178	ⓐⓑⓒⓓ	198	ⓐⓑⓒⓓ
119	ⓐⓑⓒⓓ	139	ⓐⓑⓒⓓ	159	ⓐⓑⓒⓓ	179	ⓐⓑⓒⓓ	199	ⓐⓑⓒⓓ
120	ⓐⓑⓒⓓ	140	ⓐⓑⓒⓓ	160	ⓐⓑⓒⓓ	180	ⓐⓑⓒⓓ	200	ⓐⓑⓒⓓ

ANSWER SHEET

수험번호

응시일자 : 20　　　년　　　월　　　일

성명

성명	한글
	한자
	영자

Test 03 (Part 5~7)

101 ~ 120, 121 ~ 140, 141 ~ 160, 161 ~ 180, 181 ~ 200

Test 04 (Part 5~7)

101 ~ 120, 121 ~ 140, 141 ~ 160, 161 ~ 180, 181 ~ 200

ANSWER SHEET

토익® 정기시험 기출문제집

응시일자 : 20   년   월   일

수험번호

Test 05 (Part 5~7)

101	ⓐⓑⓒⓓ	121	ⓐⓑⓒⓓ	141	ⓐⓑⓒⓓ	161	ⓐⓑⓒⓓ	181	ⓐⓑⓒⓓ
102	ⓐⓑⓒⓓ	122	ⓐⓑⓒⓓ	142	ⓐⓑⓒⓓ	162	ⓐⓑⓒⓓ	182	ⓐⓑⓒⓓ
103	ⓐⓑⓒⓓ	123	ⓐⓑⓒⓓ	143	ⓐⓑⓒⓓ	163	ⓐⓑⓒⓓ	183	ⓐⓑⓒⓓ
104	ⓐⓑⓒⓓ	124	ⓐⓑⓒⓓ	144	ⓐⓑⓒⓓ	164	ⓐⓑⓒⓓ	184	ⓐⓑⓒⓓ
105	ⓐⓑⓒⓓ	125	ⓐⓑⓒⓓ	145	ⓐⓑⓒⓓ	165	ⓐⓑⓒⓓ	185	ⓐⓑⓒⓓ
106	ⓐⓑⓒⓓ	126	ⓐⓑⓒⓓ	146	ⓐⓑⓒⓓ	166	ⓐⓑⓒⓓ	186	ⓐⓑⓒⓓ
107	ⓐⓑⓒⓓ	127	ⓐⓑⓒⓓ	147	ⓐⓑⓒⓓ	167	ⓐⓑⓒⓓ	187	ⓐⓑⓒⓓ
108	ⓐⓑⓒⓓ	128	ⓐⓑⓒⓓ	148	ⓐⓑⓒⓓ	168	ⓐⓑⓒⓓ	188	ⓐⓑⓒⓓ
109	ⓐⓑⓒⓓ	129	ⓐⓑⓒⓓ	149	ⓐⓑⓒⓓ	169	ⓐⓑⓒⓓ	189	ⓐⓑⓒⓓ
110	ⓐⓑⓒⓓ	130	ⓐⓑⓒⓓ	150	ⓐⓑⓒⓓ	170	ⓐⓑⓒⓓ	190	ⓐⓑⓒⓓ
111	ⓐⓑⓒⓓ	131	ⓐⓑⓒⓓ	151	ⓐⓑⓒⓓ	171	ⓐⓑⓒⓓ	191	ⓐⓑⓒⓓ
112	ⓐⓑⓒⓓ	132	ⓐⓑⓒⓓ	152	ⓐⓑⓒⓓ	172	ⓐⓑⓒⓓ	192	ⓐⓑⓒⓓ
113	ⓐⓑⓒⓓ	133	ⓐⓑⓒⓓ	153	ⓐⓑⓒⓓ	173	ⓐⓑⓒⓓ	193	ⓐⓑⓒⓓ
114	ⓐⓑⓒⓓ	134	ⓐⓑⓒⓓ	154	ⓐⓑⓒⓓ	174	ⓐⓑⓒⓓ	194	ⓐⓑⓒⓓ
115	ⓐⓑⓒⓓ	135	ⓐⓑⓒⓓ	155	ⓐⓑⓒⓓ	175	ⓐⓑⓒⓓ	195	ⓐⓑⓒⓓ
116	ⓐⓑⓒⓓ	136	ⓐⓑⓒⓓ	156	ⓐⓑⓒⓓ	176	ⓐⓑⓒⓓ	196	ⓐⓑⓒⓓ
117	ⓐⓑⓒⓓ	137	ⓐⓑⓒⓓ	157	ⓐⓑⓒⓓ	177	ⓐⓑⓒⓓ	197	ⓐⓑⓒⓓ
118	ⓐⓑⓒⓓ	138	ⓐⓑⓒⓓ	158	ⓐⓑⓒⓓ	178	ⓐⓑⓒⓓ	198	ⓐⓑⓒⓓ
119	ⓐⓑⓒⓓ	139	ⓐⓑⓒⓓ	159	ⓐⓑⓒⓓ	179	ⓐⓑⓒⓓ	199	ⓐⓑⓒⓓ
120	ⓐⓑⓒⓓ	140	ⓐⓑⓒⓓ	160	ⓐⓑⓒⓓ	180	ⓐⓑⓒⓓ	200	ⓐⓑⓒⓓ

성명 한글 한자 영자

Test 06 (Part 5~7)

101	ⓐⓑⓒⓓ	121	ⓐⓑⓒⓓ	141	ⓐⓑⓒⓓ	161	ⓐⓑⓒⓓ	181	ⓐⓑⓒⓓ
102	ⓐⓑⓒⓓ	122	ⓐⓑⓒⓓ	142	ⓐⓑⓒⓓ	162	ⓐⓑⓒⓓ	182	ⓐⓑⓒⓓ
103	ⓐⓑⓒⓓ	123	ⓐⓑⓒⓓ	143	ⓐⓑⓒⓓ	163	ⓐⓑⓒⓓ	183	ⓐⓑⓒⓓ
104	ⓐⓑⓒⓓ	124	ⓐⓑⓒⓓ	144	ⓐⓑⓒⓓ	164	ⓐⓑⓒⓓ	184	ⓐⓑⓒⓓ
105	ⓐⓑⓒⓓ	125	ⓐⓑⓒⓓ	145	ⓐⓑⓒⓓ	165	ⓐⓑⓒⓓ	185	ⓐⓑⓒⓓ
106	ⓐⓑⓒⓓ	126	ⓐⓑⓒⓓ	146	ⓐⓑⓒⓓ	166	ⓐⓑⓒⓓ	186	ⓐⓑⓒⓓ
107	ⓐⓑⓒⓓ	127	ⓐⓑⓒⓓ	147	ⓐⓑⓒⓓ	167	ⓐⓑⓒⓓ	187	ⓐⓑⓒⓓ
108	ⓐⓑⓒⓓ	128	ⓐⓑⓒⓓ	148	ⓐⓑⓒⓓ	168	ⓐⓑⓒⓓ	188	ⓐⓑⓒⓓ
109	ⓐⓑⓒⓓ	129	ⓐⓑⓒⓓ	149	ⓐⓑⓒⓓ	169	ⓐⓑⓒⓓ	189	ⓐⓑⓒⓓ
110	ⓐⓑⓒⓓ	130	ⓐⓑⓒⓓ	150	ⓐⓑⓒⓓ	170	ⓐⓑⓒⓓ	190	ⓐⓑⓒⓓ
111	ⓐⓑⓒⓓ	131	ⓐⓑⓒⓓ	151	ⓐⓑⓒⓓ	171	ⓐⓑⓒⓓ	191	ⓐⓑⓒⓓ
112	ⓐⓑⓒⓓ	132	ⓐⓑⓒⓓ	152	ⓐⓑⓒⓓ	172	ⓐⓑⓒⓓ	192	ⓐⓑⓒⓓ
113	ⓐⓑⓒⓓ	133	ⓐⓑⓒⓓ	153	ⓐⓑⓒⓓ	173	ⓐⓑⓒⓓ	193	ⓐⓑⓒⓓ
114	ⓐⓑⓒⓓ	134	ⓐⓑⓒⓓ	154	ⓐⓑⓒⓓ	174	ⓐⓑⓒⓓ	194	ⓐⓑⓒⓓ
115	ⓐⓑⓒⓓ	135	ⓐⓑⓒⓓ	155	ⓐⓑⓒⓓ	175	ⓐⓑⓒⓓ	195	ⓐⓑⓒⓓ
116	ⓐⓑⓒⓓ	136	ⓐⓑⓒⓓ	156	ⓐⓑⓒⓓ	176	ⓐⓑⓒⓓ	196	ⓐⓑⓒⓓ
117	ⓐⓑⓒⓓ	137	ⓐⓑⓒⓓ	157	ⓐⓑⓒⓓ	177	ⓐⓑⓒⓓ	197	ⓐⓑⓒⓓ
118	ⓐⓑⓒⓓ	138	ⓐⓑⓒⓓ	158	ⓐⓑⓒⓓ	178	ⓐⓑⓒⓓ	198	ⓐⓑⓒⓓ
119	ⓐⓑⓒⓓ	139	ⓐⓑⓒⓓ	159	ⓐⓑⓒⓓ	179	ⓐⓑⓒⓓ	199	ⓐⓑⓒⓓ
120	ⓐⓑⓒⓓ	140	ⓐⓑⓒⓓ	160	ⓐⓑⓒⓓ	180	ⓐⓑⓒⓓ	200	ⓐⓑⓒⓓ

ANSWER SHEET

토익® 정기시험 기출문제집

수험번호

응시일자 : 20 ___ 년 ___ 월 ___ 일

성명 한글
한자
영자

Test 07 (Part 5~7)

101 @ⓑⓒⓓ 121 @ⓑⓒⓓ 141 @ⓑⓒⓓ 161 @ⓑⓒⓓ 181 @ⓑⓒⓓ
102 @ⓑⓒⓓ 122 @ⓑⓒⓓ 142 @ⓑⓒⓓ 162 @ⓑⓒⓓ 182 @ⓑⓒⓓ
103 @ⓑⓒⓓ 123 @ⓑⓒⓓ 143 @ⓑⓒⓓ 163 @ⓑⓒⓓ 183 @ⓑⓒⓓ
104 @ⓑⓒⓓ 124 @ⓑⓒⓓ 144 @ⓑⓒⓓ 164 @ⓑⓒⓓ 184 @ⓑⓒⓓ
105 @ⓑⓒⓓ 125 @ⓑⓒⓓ 145 @ⓑⓒⓓ 165 @ⓑⓒⓓ 185 @ⓑⓒⓓ
106 @ⓑⓒⓓ 126 @ⓑⓒⓓ 146 @ⓑⓒⓓ 166 @ⓑⓒⓓ 186 @ⓑⓒⓓ
107 @ⓑⓒⓓ 127 @ⓑⓒⓓ 147 @ⓑⓒⓓ 167 @ⓑⓒⓓ 187 @ⓑⓒⓓ
108 @ⓑⓒⓓ 128 @ⓑⓒⓓ 148 @ⓑⓒⓓ 168 @ⓑⓒⓓ 188 @ⓑⓒⓓ
109 @ⓑⓒⓓ 129 @ⓑⓒⓓ 149 @ⓑⓒⓓ 169 @ⓑⓒⓓ 189 @ⓑⓒⓓ
110 @ⓑⓒⓓ 130 @ⓑⓒⓓ 150 @ⓑⓒⓓ 170 @ⓑⓒⓓ 190 @ⓑⓒⓓ
111 @ⓑⓒⓓ 131 @ⓑⓒⓓ 151 @ⓑⓒⓓ 171 @ⓑⓒⓓ 191 @ⓑⓒⓓ
112 @ⓑⓒⓓ 132 @ⓑⓒⓓ 152 @ⓑⓒⓓ 172 @ⓑⓒⓓ 192 @ⓑⓒⓓ
113 @ⓑⓒⓓ 133 @ⓑⓒⓓ 153 @ⓑⓒⓓ 173 @ⓑⓒⓓ 193 @ⓑⓒⓓ
114 @ⓑⓒⓓ 134 @ⓑⓒⓓ 154 @ⓑⓒⓓ 174 @ⓑⓒⓓ 194 @ⓑⓒⓓ
115 @ⓑⓒⓓ 135 @ⓑⓒⓓ 155 @ⓑⓒⓓ 175 @ⓑⓒⓓ 195 @ⓑⓒⓓ
116 @ⓑⓒⓓ 136 @ⓑⓒⓓ 156 @ⓑⓒⓓ 176 @ⓑⓒⓓ 196 @ⓑⓒⓓ
117 @ⓑⓒⓓ 137 @ⓑⓒⓓ 157 @ⓑⓒⓓ 177 @ⓑⓒⓓ 197 @ⓑⓒⓓ
118 @ⓑⓒⓓ 138 @ⓑⓒⓓ 158 @ⓑⓒⓓ 178 @ⓑⓒⓓ 198 @ⓑⓒⓓ
119 @ⓑⓒⓓ 139 @ⓑⓒⓓ 159 @ⓑⓒⓓ 179 @ⓑⓒⓓ 199 @ⓑⓒⓓ
120 @ⓑⓒⓓ 140 @ⓑⓒⓓ 160 @ⓑⓒⓓ 180 @ⓑⓒⓓ 200 @ⓑⓒⓓ

Test 08 (Part 5~7)

101 @ⓑⓒⓓ 121 @ⓑⓒⓓ 141 @ⓑⓒⓓ 161 @ⓑⓒⓓ 181 @ⓑⓒⓓ
102 @ⓑⓒⓓ 122 @ⓑⓒⓓ 142 @ⓑⓒⓓ 162 @ⓑⓒⓓ 182 @ⓑⓒⓓ
103 @ⓑⓒⓓ 123 @ⓑⓒⓓ 143 @ⓑⓒⓓ 163 @ⓑⓒⓓ 183 @ⓑⓒⓓ
104 @ⓑⓒⓓ 124 @ⓑⓒⓓ 144 @ⓑⓒⓓ 164 @ⓑⓒⓓ 184 @ⓑⓒⓓ
105 @ⓑⓒⓓ 125 @ⓑⓒⓓ 145 @ⓑⓒⓓ 165 @ⓑⓒⓓ 185 @ⓑⓒⓓ
106 @ⓑⓒⓓ 126 @ⓑⓒⓓ 146 @ⓑⓒⓓ 166 @ⓑⓒⓓ 186 @ⓑⓒⓓ
107 @ⓑⓒⓓ 127 @ⓑⓒⓓ 147 @ⓑⓒⓓ 167 @ⓑⓒⓓ 187 @ⓑⓒⓓ
108 @ⓑⓒⓓ 128 @ⓑⓒⓓ 148 @ⓑⓒⓓ 168 @ⓑⓒⓓ 188 @ⓑⓒⓓ
109 @ⓑⓒⓓ 129 @ⓑⓒⓓ 149 @ⓑⓒⓓ 169 @ⓑⓒⓓ 189 @ⓑⓒⓓ
110 @ⓑⓒⓓ 130 @ⓑⓒⓓ 150 @ⓑⓒⓓ 170 @ⓑⓒⓓ 190 @ⓑⓒⓓ
111 @ⓑⓒⓓ 131 @ⓑⓒⓓ 151 @ⓑⓒⓓ 171 @ⓑⓒⓓ 191 @ⓑⓒⓓ
112 @ⓑⓒⓓ 132 @ⓑⓒⓓ 152 @ⓑⓒⓓ 172 @ⓑⓒⓓ 192 @ⓑⓒⓓ
113 @ⓑⓒⓓ 133 @ⓑⓒⓓ 153 @ⓑⓒⓓ 173 @ⓑⓒⓓ 193 @ⓑⓒⓓ
114 @ⓑⓒⓓ 134 @ⓑⓒⓓ 154 @ⓑⓒⓓ 174 @ⓑⓒⓓ 194 @ⓑⓒⓓ
115 @ⓑⓒⓓ 135 @ⓑⓒⓓ 155 @ⓑⓒⓓ 175 @ⓑⓒⓓ 195 @ⓑⓒⓓ
116 @ⓑⓒⓓ 136 @ⓑⓒⓓ 156 @ⓑⓒⓓ 176 @ⓑⓒⓓ 196 @ⓑⓒⓓ
117 @ⓑⓒⓓ 137 @ⓑⓒⓓ 157 @ⓑⓒⓓ 177 @ⓑⓒⓓ 197 @ⓑⓒⓓ
118 @ⓑⓒⓓ 138 @ⓑⓒⓓ 158 @ⓑⓒⓓ 178 @ⓑⓒⓓ 198 @ⓑⓒⓓ
119 @ⓑⓒⓓ 139 @ⓑⓒⓓ 159 @ⓑⓒⓓ 179 @ⓑⓒⓓ 199 @ⓑⓒⓓ
120 @ⓑⓒⓓ 140 @ⓑⓒⓓ 160 @ⓑⓒⓓ 180 @ⓑⓒⓓ 200 @ⓑⓒⓓ

ANSWER SHEET

토익® 정기시험 기출문제집

응시일자 : 20   년   월   일

수험번호

성명

| 한글 |
| 한자 |
| 영자 |

Test 09 (Part 5~7)

101 102 103 104 105 106 107 108 109 110 111 112 113 114 115 116 117 118 119 120
121 122 123 124 125 126 127 128 129 130 131 132 133 134 135 136 137 138 139 140
141 142 143 144 145 146 147 148 149 150 151 152 153 154 155 156 157 158 159 160
161 162 163 164 165 166 167 168 169 170 171 172 173 174 175 176 177 178 179 180
181 182 183 184 185 186 187 188 189 190 191 192 193 194 195 196 197 198 199 200

Test 10 (Part 5~7)

101 102 103 104 105 106 107 108 109 110 111 112 113 114 115 116 117 118 119 120
121 122 123 124 125 126 127 128 129 130 131 132 133 134 135 136 137 138 139 140
141 142 143 144 145 146 147 148 149 150 151 152 153 154 155 156 157 158 159 160
161 162 163 164 165 166 167 168 169 170 171 172 173 174 175 176 177 178 179 180
181 182 183 184 185 186 187 188 189 190 191 192 193 194 195 196 197 198 199 200

*toeic®

토익® 정기시험
기출문제집 4
1000 RC

정답 및 해설

101 (B)	**102** (D)	**103** (C)	**104** (B)	**105** (D)
106 (D)	**107** (A)	**108** (D)	**109** (A)	**110** (B)
111 (A)	**112** (B)	**113** (A)	**114** (C)	**115** (D)
116 (C)	**117** (D)	**118** (B)	**119** (A)	**120** (A)
121 (D)	**122** (A)	**123** (B)	**124** (A)	**125** (D)
126 (D)	**127** (C)	**128** (C)	**129** (C)	**130** (B)
131 (D)	**132** (D)	**133** (A)	**134** (B)	**135** (C)
136 (A)	**137** (B)	**138** (B)	**139** (A)	**140** (C)
141 (B)	**142** (C)	**143** (A)	**144** (B)	**145** (D)
146 (A)	**147** (C)	**148** (B)	**149** (B)	**150** (C)
151 (B)	**152** (D)	**153** (A)	**154** (C)	**155** (A)
156 (D)	**157** (B)	**158** (B)	**159** (A)	**160** (B)
161 (A)	**162** (C)	**163** (D)	**164** (C)	**165** (C)
166 (D)	**167** (A)	**168** (D)	**169** (B)	**170** (C)
171 (A)	**172** (D)	**173** (B)	**174** (C)	**175** (C)
176 (B)	**177** (C)	**178** (C)	**179** (A)	**180** (B)
181 (A)	**182** (D)	**183** (B)	**184** (C)	**185** (C)
186 (C)	**187** (D)	**188** (B)	**189** (A)	**190** (B)
191 (D)	**192** (C)	**193** (A)	**194** (B)	**195** (C)
196 (A)	**197** (C)	**198** (C)	**199** (D)	**200** (B)

PART 5

101 인칭대명사의 격 _ 소유격

해설 빈칸에는 뒤에 온 복합명사 career experiences를 수식하는 인칭대명사가 들어가야 한다. 따라서 명사 앞에 쓰여 한정사 역할을 할 수 있는 소유격 인칭대명사 (B) his가 정답이다.

번역 센다이 회사의 전 최고 경영자인 켄 나카타가 자신의 경력에 대해 말했다.

어휘 former 이전의

102 형용사 자리 _ 명사 수식 / 현재분사

해설 빈칸 앞에는 부정관사, 뒤에는 「형용사+명사」로 이루어져 '국내선 항공편'을 뜻하는 명사구 domestic flight가 있으므로, 빈칸에는 명사 flight를 수식하는 형용사가 들어가 '연결하는 국내선 항공편'이라는 의미가 되어야 적절하다. 따라서 '연결하는'이라는 의미를 나타내며 형용사 역할을 하는 현재분사 (D) connecting이 정답이다. (A) connectivity는 명사, (B) connects와 (C) connect는 동사이므로 빈칸에 들어갈 수 없다.

번역 국내선 연결편을 이용하실 승객께서는 A 터미널로 가시기 바랍니다.

어휘 passenger 승객 domestic 국내의 connectivity 연결

103 형용사 어휘

해설 복합명사 apple-cider donuts를 수식하여 '신선하고 맛있는 사과 사이다 도넛'이라는 의미가 되어야 적절하므로 '맛있는'을 뜻하는 (C) tasty가 정답이다. (A) eaten은 '먹은', (B) open은 '열린', (D) free는 '무료의; 자유로운'이라는 의미이다.

번역 오크레스트 과수원의 소매점에서 신선하고 맛있는 사과 사이다 도넛을 12개당 6파운드에 구입할 수 있다.

어휘 orchard 과수원 retail 소매(의) per ~당 dozen 12개짜리 한 묶음

104 명사 어휘

해설 Zahn Flooring에서 보유하고 있는 품목으로 적절한 명사를 골라야 한다. 상호에 '바닥재'를 뜻하는 Flooring이 들어가 있는 것으로 보아 바닥재 제품을 판매하는 곳임을 알 수 있으므로 바닥재에 속하는 '타일'이 들어가야 가장 적절하다. 따라서 (B) tiles가 정답이다. (A)의 paint(페인트), (C) furniture(가구), (D)의 curtain(커튼)은 flooring 매장이 가장 다양한 종류를 보유할 품목으로 어울리지 않는다.

번역 잔 플로어링은 영국에서 가장 다양한 종류의 타일을 보유하고 있다.

어휘 a selection of 다양한, 엄선된

105 형용사 자리 _ 명사 수식 / 현재분사 vs. 과거분사

해설 빈칸에는 명사 software를 수식하는 형용사 또는 software와 복합명사를 이루는 명사가 들어갈 수 있다. 문맥상 '업데이트된 소프트웨어'라는 내용이 되어야 자연스러우므로, '업데이트된'이라는 수동의 의미를 나타내어 형용사 역할을 하는 과거분사 (D) updated가 정답이다. update가 명사로 쓰인 경우, (A) update와 (C) updates는 software와 복합명사를 이루기에 적절하지 않고, software는 update의 주체가 아닌 대상이므로 능동의 의미를 나타내는 현재분사 (B) updating은 답이 될 수 없다.

번역 IT 부서의 한 가지 책임은 회사가 업데이트된 소프트웨어를 사용하도록 보장하는 것이다.

어휘 responsibility 책임 ensure 보장하다

106 전치사 자리 / 어휘

해설 빈칸은 기주어 It, 진주어 to check ~ its head office인 문장에서 동사 check와 목적어 a company's dress code 뒤에 visiting its head office를 연결해 주는 자리이다. visiting과 함께 쓰여 '방문하기 전에'라는 내용이 되어야 자연스러우므로 (D) before가 정답이다. before -ing(~하기 전에)와 after -ing(~한 후에)는 빈출 표현이니 암기해 두자.

번역 본사를 방문하기 전에 회사의 복장 규정을 확인하는 것이 현명하다.

어휘 wise 현명한 head office 본사

107 부사 자리 _ 동사 수식

해설 빈칸이 조동사 will과 동사원형 support 사이에 있으므로 동사를 수

식하는 부사 자리이다. 따라서 '매우 열심히, 열광적으로'를 뜻하는 부사 (A) enthusiastically가 정답이다. (B) enthusiasm은 명사, (C) enthusiastic은 형용사, (D) enthused는 동사/과거분사이므로 빈칸에 들어갈 수 없다.

번역 웩슬러 스토어의 경영진은 직원들이 모든 신입 사원을 열심히 지원할 것으로 기대한다.

어휘 new hire 신입 사원   enthusiasm 열광

108 명사 자리 _ 복합명사

해설 빈칸은 동사 are의 주어 자리로, and 앞의 복합명사 Wheel alignments와 대등하게 연결되면서 빈칸 앞의 brake system과 함께 복합명사를 만들 수 있는 명사가 들어가야 한다. '휠 얼라인먼트와 브레이크 시스템 검사는 서비스의 일부'라는 내용이 되어야 자연스러우므로 '검사'를 뜻하는 (D) inspections가 정답이다. '조사관'을 뜻하는 (B) inspector는 가산 단수명사로, 한정사 an, the 등이 필요하므로 오답이다.

번역 휠 얼라인먼트와 브레이크 시스템 검사는 당사 차량 서비스 제도의 일부입니다.

어휘 wheel alignment 휠 얼라인먼트(차륜 정렬)   plan (보험금 등을 위한) 제도   inspect 검사하다

109 전치사 자리 / 어휘

해설 빈칸 앞에 Registration ~ Conference가 주어, is가 동사, open이 보여진 완전한 절이 있고 뒤에 명사구 September 30가 있으므로 빈칸은 전치사 자리이다. 빈칸 뒤에 시점을 나타내는 명사구가 왔고, '9월 30일까지 등록이 가능하다'라는 의미가 되어야 자연스러우므로 '~까지'를 뜻하는 전치사 (A) until이 정답이다. (B) into는 전치사이지만 '~ 안으로'라는 의미이고, (C) yet은 부사/접속사, (D) while은 접속사이므로 빈칸에 들어갈 수 없다.

번역 마케팅 연합 콘퍼런스의 등록은 현재 9월 30일까지 가능합니다.

어휘 registration 등록   coalition 연합(체)

110 형용사 어휘

해설 be동사 has been 뒤에 들어가 주어 Growth를 보충 설명하기에 적절한 형용사가 필요하다. 문맥상 '성장이 제한적이었다'라는 내용이 되어야 적절하므로 '제한된'을 뜻하는 (B) limited가 정답이다. (A) separate는 '분리된', (C) willing은 '자발적인', (D) assorted는 '여러 가지의'라는 의미이다.

번역 이번 분기에는 홈 엔터테인먼트 산업의 성장이 제한적이었다.

어휘 quarter 분기(1년의 4분의 1)

111 명사 자리 _ 동사의 목적어

해설 빈칸은 동사 will be making의 목적어 역할을 하는 명사 자리로, make와 함께 '배달하다'라는 의미를 완성하는 명사 (A) deliveries가 정답이다. (B) delivered는 동사/과거분사, (C) deliver는 동사이고, 형용사나 명사로 쓰이는 (D) deliverable은 명사인 경우 가산 단수명

사로 앞에 한정사 없이 쓸 수 없으므로 빈칸에 들어갈 수 없다.

번역 호손 가구는 목요일에 시내 동쪽에서 배달을 할 예정이다.

어휘 deliverable 배달할 수 있는; 상품, 배송품

112 동사 어휘

해설 명사 authority를 수식하는 to부정사 자리에 들어갈 동사 어휘를 고르는 문제이다. parking을 목적어로 취해 '주차를 금지할 권한'이라는 의미가 되어야 자연스러우므로 '금지하다'를 뜻하는 (B) prohibit이 정답이다. (A) drive는 '운전하다', (C) bother는 '귀찮게 하다', (D) travel은 '여행하다'라는 의미이다.

번역 말튼 시 의회는 시내 도로에 주차하는 것을 금지할 권한이 없다.

어휘 authority 권한

113 동사 어휘

해설 빈칸 뒤에 목적어가 없고, 전치사 for가 있으므로 for와 자연스럽게 연결될 수 있는 자동사가 들어가야 한다. 문맥상 '방법을 찾고 있다'라는 의미가 되어야 자연스러우므로 for와 함께 쓰여 '~을 찾다'라는 의미를 나타내는 동사 look의 현재분사형 (A) looking이 정답이다.

번역 프로젝트 어스 그룹은 운송 관련 온실가스 배출을 줄일 방법을 찾고 있다.

어휘 reduce 줄이다   transport 운송   related 관련된   greenhouse gas 온실가스   emission 배출

114 부사 자리 _ 동사 수식

해설 빈칸은 명사구 a custom-made suit를 수식하는 관계사절에 속해 있고, 앞에 온 동사 fits를 수식하는 부사 자리이므로 (C) perfectly가 정답이다. (A) perfect는 형용사/동사, (B) perfects는 동사, (D) perfection은 명사이므로 빈칸에 들어갈 수 없다.

번역 당사의 숙련된 재단사들이 귀하의 스타일과 예산에 완벽하게 맞는 맞춤 정장을 디자인할 수 있어서 기쁩니다.

어휘 skilled 숙련된   tailor 재단사   custom-made 맞춤의   suit 정장   fit 맞다   budget 예산

115 형용사 자리

해설 빈칸에는 동사 has proved의 보어 역할을 하는 to부정사 to be 뒤에 오기에 적절한 품사를 골라야 한다. to부정사의 동사가 2형식 동사 be이고 앞에 부사 very가 있으므로, 빈칸은 be동사의 보어 역할을 하면서 부사의 수식을 받을 수 있는 형용사 자리이다. 따라서 '도움이 되는'을 뜻하는 형용사 (D) helpful이 정답이다. (A) helpfulness는 명사, (B) help는 동사/명사, (C) helpfully는 부사이므로 빈칸에 들어갈 수 없다.

번역 프로젝트 매니저 한나 정이 회사 프로젝트를 완수하는 데 매우 도움이 된 것으로 드러났다.

어휘 prove (~임이) 드러나다, 밝혀지다

116 전치사 어휘

해설 빈칸 뒤에 기간을 나타내는 명사구 the month of August가 있고, 문맥상 '8월 한 달 동안'이라는 의미가 되어야 자연스러우므로 '~ 동안'을 뜻하는 (C) during이 정답이다. (A) onto는 '~ 위로', (B) above는 '~보다 위에', (D) between은 between A and B 형태로 쓰여 '(특정 시점) 사이에'라는 의미를 나타낸다.

번역 레후아 베케이션 클럽 회원들은 제휴 호텔에서 8월 한 달 동안 두 배의 포인트를 받게 될 것입니다.

117 부사 어휘

해설 빈칸에는 동사구 were not received를 수식하면서, 뒤에 나온 '~할 만큼 (충분히)'를 뜻하는 「enough+to부정사」 구문의 수식을 받는 적절한 부사가 들어가야 한다. 문맥상 '첫 리허설에 사용될 만큼 빨리 받지 못했다'라는 내용이 되어야 적절하므로 '곧, 빨리'를 뜻하는 부사 (D) soon이 정답이다. (A) far는 '멀리', (B) very는 '매우', (C) almost는 '거의'라는 의미이다.

번역 첫 드레스 리허설에 사용될 만큼 빨리 의상을 받지 못했다.

어휘 costume 의상 dress rehearsal 드레스 리허설(정식 무대와 같은 연습)

118 명사 자리 _ 복합명사

해설 빈칸은 앞의 명사 event와 함께 쓰여 전치사 of의 목적어 역할을 하는 명사 자리로, '행사 주최자'라는 의미의 복합명사를 만들 수 있는 '주최자, 조직자'라는 뜻의 (B) organizer가 정답이다. (A) organized는 동사/과거분사, (C) organizes는 동사, (D) organizational은 형용사이므로 빈칸에 들어갈 수 없다.

번역 몇몇 유명 오케스트라의 홍보 담당자였던 우 씨는 행사 주최자 역할에 뛰어날 것이다.

어휘 former 이전의 publicist 홍보 담당자 renowned 유명한 excel 뛰어나다

119 부사 어휘

해설 동사구 will be closed를 수식하여 적절한 문맥을 완성하는 부사를 고르는 문제이다. '공사로 인해 차선이 일시적으로 폐쇄된다'라는 내용이 되어야 자연스러우므로 '일시적으로'를 뜻하는 (A) temporarily가 정답이다. (B) competitively는 '경쟁적으로', (D) collectively는 '집합적으로'라는 의미로 문맥상 적절하지 않고, (C) recently(최근에)는 주로 과거나 현재완료 시제와 쓰이며 미래 시제와 어울리지 않는다.

번역 데이비스 가의 북행 차선은 시의 교량 보강 프로젝트로 인해 일시적으로 폐쇄될 예정이다.

어휘 northbound 북행의 lane 차선 reinforcement 보강, 강화

120 전치사 어휘

해설 빈칸 뒤 전치사구 to lost luggage와 함께 from A to B 구문을 이루어 '놓친 연결편부터 분실 수하물에 이르기까지'라는 의미가 되어야 자연스러우므로 (A) from이 정답이다.

번역 항공사 직원은 놓친 연결편부터 분실 수하물에 이르기까지 다양한 승객 문제를 처리해야 한다.

어휘 representative 직원 handle 처리하다 a range of 다양한 passenger 승객 issue 문제 connection (교통) 연결편 luggage 수하물

121 부사 자리 _ 동사 수식

해설 동사구 were deleted를 수식하는 부사 자리이므로 (D) accidentally(실수로, 우연히)가 정답이다. (A) accident와 (C) accidents는 명사, (B) accidental은 형용사이므로 빈칸에 들어갈 수 없다.

번역 회의록이 실수로 삭제되었지만, 함 씨는 기억을 더듬어 그것들을 되살릴 수 있었다.

어휘 delete 삭제하다 recreate 되살리다 memory 기억

122 형용사 자리 _ 명사 수식

해설 빈칸 앞에 정관사 the가 있고, 뒤에 명사 year가 있으므로 빈칸은 명사를 수식하는 형용사 자리이다. 따라서 '다음의'를 뜻하는 형용사 (A) next가 정답이다. (B) with는 전치사, (C) which는 관계대명사/의문사, (D) now는 부사이므로 빈칸에 들어갈 수 없다.

번역 〈파밍 씬〉 잡지의 이번 호에서는 옥수수 가격이 내년에 5퍼센트 오를 것으로 예측한다.

어휘 issue (정기 간행물의) 호 predict 예측하다 rise 오르다

123 동사 자리 _ 수 일치 + 시제

해설 빈칸은 선행사 Anyone을 수식하는 관계사절(who still ~ safety training)의 동사 자리이다. 관계사절의 동사는 선행사에 수를 일치시키는데, 선행사가 Anyone이므로 단수동사가 들어가야 한다. 또한 의무사항에 해당되는 사람의 조건을 설명하는 내용이므로 현재 시제를 써야 한다. 따라서 (B) needs가 정답이다. (A) needing은 현재분사/동명사이므로 품사상 답이 될 수 없고, (C) has needed는 시제가 맞지 않으며, (D) were needing은 Anyone과 수가 일치하지 않으므로 빈칸에 들어갈 수 없다.

번역 아직 소방 안전 교육을 받아야 하는 사람은 이달 말까지 받아야 한다.

124 부사 어휘

해설 동사구 have begun을 수식하여 적절한 문맥을 완성하는 부사를 고르는 문제이다. '신생 기술이 업계를 이미 탈바꿈하기 시작했다'라는 내용이 되어야 자연스러우므로 '이미, 벌써'라는 뜻의 (A) already가 정답이다. (B) exactly는 '정확히', (C) hardly는 '거의 ~않다', (D) closely는 '면밀히'라는 의미이다.

번역 신생 기술은 한때는 상상조차 할 수 없던 방식으로 해운 산업을 이미 탈바꿈하기 시작했다.

어휘 emerging 최근 생겨난, 신흥의 transform 탈바꿈하다 unimaginable 상상도 할 수 없는

125 명사 어휘

▶ 동영상 강의

해설 형용사 high와 관계사절(that employees ~ to meet every day)의 수식을 받기에 어울리는 명사를 고르면 된다. '직원들이 매일 충족해야 하는 높은 기준'이라는 내용이 되어야 자연스러우므로 '기준'을 뜻하는 (D) standards가 정답이다. (A)의 expert는 '전문가', (B)의 account는 '계좌', (-s) 회계', (C)의 recommendation은 '추천'이라는 의미이다.

번역 회사 안내서에는 직원들이 매일 충족해야 하는 높은 기준들이 설명되어 있다.

어휘 outline 개요를 서술하다   expect 기대하다   meet 충족시키다

126 부정대명사

해설 빈칸은 부사절 접속사 because가 이끄는 절에서 복수동사 have의 주어 자리로 복수대명사가 필요하고, 문맥상 '이사진 중 일부가 중복되는 일정이 있다'라는 내용이 되어야 자연스러우므로 '일부, 몇몇'을 뜻하는 (D) some이 정답이다. (A) any는 긍정문에서 '누구든지'를 뜻하므로 문맥에 어울리지 않고, (B) everybody는 단수동사와 쓰이므로 답이 될 수 없다. 지시대명사 (C) those는 앞서 언급된 복수명사를 반복해서 사용하는 것을 피하기 위해 쓰이므로 적절하지 않다.

번역 이사진 중 일부가 중복되는 일정이 있어서 이사회 회의는 전원 참석 가능한 날짜로 변경될 것입니다.

어휘 board 이사회   scheduling conflict 일정 충돌, 겹치는 일정

127 동사 어휘

▶ 동영상 강의

해설 주어 The project의 동사 자리로, '프로젝트는 협업을 필요로 했다'라는 의미가 되어야 적절하므로 '필요로 하다, 요구하다'라는 의미의 동사 require의 과거형 (C) required가 정답이다. (A)의 pass는 '통과하다', (B)의 decide는 '결정하다', (D)의 perform은 '수행하다'라는 의미이다.

번역 그 프로젝트는 회사 전체에 걸쳐 여러 팀의 협업을 필요로 했다.

어휘 collaboration 협업

128 동사 어형 _ 태 + 시제

▶ 동영상 강의

해설 부사절 접속사 until이 이끄는 절의 동사 자리로, 뒤에 목적어가 아닌 전치사 by가 이끄는 전치사구가 왔으므로 수동태가 들어가야 한다. 따라서 능동태인 (A) is approving과 (B) approves는 빈칸에 들어갈 수 없다. 또한 until(~까지)은 시간 부사절을 이끄는 접속사로, 시간 부사절에서는 현재 시제 또는 현재완료 시제가 미래 시제 또는 미래완료 시제를 대신하므로 미래 시제 (D) will be approved는 답이 될 수 없다. 따라서 (C) has been approved가 정답이다.

번역 전 씨의 승인을 받기 전까지는 매장 쿠폰 책자를 인쇄소에 보낼 수 없다.

어휘 booklet 소책자

129 구전치사 어휘

▶ 동영상 강의

해설 '기존 운송 회사의 폐업을 고려해 새 회사를 찾고 있다'라는 내용이 되어야 적절하므로 '~을 고려하여'라는 뜻의 (C) In light of가 정답이다. (A) In spite of는 '~에도 불구하고', (B) Just as는 '마치 ~처럼', (D) According to는 '~에 따르면'이라는 의미이다.

번역 버디골드 운송 서비스의 폐업을 고려하여, 우리는 새로운 운송 회사를 찾고 있다.

어휘 closure 폐업   transport 운송

130 형용사 어휘

해설 안내 책자에 제공되는 정보의 특성을 나타내는 형용사가 들어가야 한다. 신청자가 대출 조건을 이해하는 데 도움이 되는(helps applicants understand the terms of their loans) 정보여야 하므로 '추가의, 보충의'라는 뜻의 (B) supplemental이 정답이다. (A) arbitrary는 '임의적인', (C) superfluous는 '불필요한', (D) potential은 '잠재적인'이라는 의미이다.

번역 유니스 은행의 안내 책자에 제공되는 추가 정보는 신청자가 대출 조건을 이해하는 데 도움이 된다.

어휘 applicant 신청자, 지원자   terms 조건   loan 대출

PART 6

131-134 공지

맥슬리 하이츠 원예 센터에 오셔서 여러분의 가정이나 사업체를 위해 아름답고 친환경적인 정원을 만드는 방법을 배우세요. **131 다음 주 토요일 오후 4시에 일반인을 위한 무료 워크숍을 개최합니다.** 빗물 정원을 조성하는 방법을 가르쳐 드릴 예정이며, 빗물 정원은 인근 도로와 지붕에서 흘러오는 빗물로부터 오염 물질을 걸러내기 위해 특별한 토양 혼합물을 **132 사용하는** 얕은 침상원입니다. 이 정원들은 토종 식물과 꽃으로 조경을 할 수 있습니다. **133 무엇보다도,** 빗물 정원은 항상 지역 환경에 이롭습니다. 특히, **134 그것들은** 배수를 개선하고 강과 하천을 보호합니다.

등록하시려면, www.maxley-horticulture.org를 방문하세요.

어휘 horticulture 원예학   eco-friendly 친환경적인   shallow 얕은   sunken garden 침상원(지면보다 한 층 낮은 정원)   soil 토양   filter 거르다   pollutant 오염 물질   landscape 조경하다   native 토종의   beneficial 이로운   drainage 배수   stream 하천   register 등록하다

131 문맥에 맞는 문장 고르기

번역 (A) 모든 연령의 아이들이 새로운 전시를 좋아할 것입니다.
(B) 이 지역의 강우 패턴에 대해 알아보세요.
(C) 구하기 쉬운 재료로 간단한 옥외 테라스 가구 세트를 만드세요.
(D) 다음 주 토요일 오후 4시에 일반인을 위한 무료 워크숍을 개최합니다.

해설 앞 문장에서 원예 센터에 오셔서 정원 만드는 방법을 배워보라(learn how to create a ~ garden)고 권유하고 있고, 뒤 문장에서 빗물

정원 조성법을 가르쳐 드릴 예정(We will teach you how to plant a rain garden)이라고 한 것으로 보아 두 문장 사이에는 정원 조성법을 가르쳐 주는 강좌나 행사에 대한 내용이 들어가야 연결이 자연스럽다. 따라서 무료 워크숍을 안내하는 (D)가 정답이다.

어휘   exhibit 전시(회)   rainfall 강우   patio 옥외 테라스
easy-to-acquire 얻기 쉬운   material 재료   host 주최하다

132   주격 관계대명사 + 동사   ▶ 동영상 강의

해설   빈칸에는 빈칸 앞의 a shallow sunken garden과 빈칸 뒤의 명사구 a special soil mix를 자연스럽게 연결해 줄 수 있는 말이 필요하다. 문맥상 '특별한 토양 혼합물을 사용하는 얕은 침상원'이라는 내용이 되어야 적절하므로 a special soil mix를 목적어로 취해 관계사절의 형태로 빈칸 앞의 a shallow sunken garden을 수식할 수 있는 (D) that uses가 정답이다. 참고로, to부정사도 형용사적 역할을 하여 명사를 수식할 수 있지만 미래의 의미를 가지므로 (A) to use는 답이 될 수 없다.

133   접속부사   ▶ 동영상 강의

해설   빈칸 앞부분에 빗물 정원을 단순히 설명하는 내용이 이어지다가, 빈칸 뒤에 특별히 빗물 정원의 장점을 소개하는 문장이 왔다. 따라서 빈칸에는 빗물 정원의 장점이 돋보이도록 강조하는 말이 들어가야 적합하므로, '무엇보다도, 특히'라는 뜻의 (A) Best of all이 정답이다. (B) For example은 '예를 들어', (C) In any event는 '아무튼', (D) As a matter of fact는 '사실은'이라는 의미이다.

134   대명사 어휘

해설   빈칸은 동사 improve의 주어 자리로, 해당 문장은 앞 문장에서 언급된 빗물 정원(rain gardens)의 장점을 추가적으로 설명하는 내용이다. 따라서 빈칸에는 rain gardens를 지칭하는 대명사가 들어가야 하므로 (B) they가 정답이다.

135-138   편지

7월 31일

아콰시 돔보
4번가
GA 105
아크라, 가나

돔보 씨께,

도쿄 패션 위크의 오프닝 갈라를 기획할 수 있도록 도와주신 135 **어마어마한 지원**에 감사드립니다. 행사는 대성공이었고, 함께 일할 수 있어서 영광이었습니다. 저희 참석자들이 귀하의 작품을 면밀히 주시하며, 이 행사를 위해 제작된 디자인을 매우 좋아했다는 것을 알고 있습니다. 귀하의 디자인은 소셜 미디어에서 많은 136 **관심**을 받았습니다. 이와 같은 쇼는 도쿄를 지도상에서 최고의 패션 중심지로 유지시켜 줄 것입니다. 137 **행사를 기획하는 데에 보여 주신 융통성에도 감사드립니다.** 여러 번의 지연으로 기획 작업이 쉽지 않았다는 점을 알고 있습니다. 젊은 디자이너 상

프로그램에 138 **도움이 될** 경매가 곧 다가오니, 귀하와 그 일도 함께 할 수 있기를 기대합니다.

아사히 이시오카
이사, 일본 패션 디자이너 협회

어휘   gala 경축 행사   be honored 영광으로 생각하다
attendee 참석자   closely 면밀히   contribute 기여하다
premier 최고의   realize 알다, 깨닫다   multiple 다수의
planning 기획   auction 경매   guild 협회

135   형용사 자리 _ 명사 수식 / 현재분사 vs. 과거분사

해설   빈칸은 소유격과 명사 사이에서 명사 support를 수식하는 형용사 또는 support와 복합명사를 이루는 명사가 들어갈 수 있다. 문맥상 '어마어마한 지원'이라는 내용이 되어야 자연스러우므로, '놀라운, 엄청난'이라는 뜻으로 감정을 유발하는 대상을 묘사하는 현재분사 (C) amazing이 정답이다. 과거분사 (A) amazed는 수식 받는 명사 support가 감정을 느끼는 주체가 될 수 없으므로 답이 될 수 없고, (B) amazement는 '놀람'이라는 의미로 support와 복합명사를 이루기에 적절하지 않다. (D) amazingly는 부사이므로 품사상 빈칸에 들어갈 수 없다.

136   명사 어휘

해설   빈칸 앞 문장에서 참석자들이 돔보 씨의 작품을 면밀히 주시하며 행사를 위해 제작된 디자인을 매우 좋아했다고 했으므로, 빈칸이 있는 문장에서도 디자인에 대한 사람들의 반응에 있어 유사한 내용이 연결되어야 자연스럽다. 따라서 '디자인이 많은 관심을 받았다'라는 내용이 되어야 적절하므로 '관심, 주목'을 뜻하는 (A) attention이 정답이다. (B)의 proposal은 '제안', (C) innovation은 '혁신', (D) criticism은 '비평'이라는 의미이다.

137   문맥에 맞는 문장 고르기

번역   (A) 몇몇 다른 행사들은 놀라울 정도로 잘 진행되었습니다.
(B) 행사를 기획하는 데에 보여 주신 융통성에도 감사드립니다.
(C) 다음에 이 도시에 오실 때는 저희 사무실에 들러 주십시오.
(D) 도쿄는 많은 이유로 최고의 관광지입니다.

해설   빈칸 뒤에서 여러 번의 지연으로 기획 작업이 쉽지 않았다(the multiple delays made the planning no easy task)는 점을 알고 있다며 행사 기획이 일정대로 순조롭게 진행되지 않았음을 암시하고 있으므로, 일정 차질에 유연하게 대처해 준 데 감사하는 내용이 들어가야 연결이 자연스럽다. 따라서 (B)가 정답이다.

어휘   flexibility 융통성   stop by ~에 들르다   destination 목적지

138   to부정사의 형용사적 용법

해설   The auction이 주어, is coming up이 동사인 완전한 문장에서, 주어이자 명사인 The auction을 수식하면서 빈칸 뒤의 명사구 our Young Designers Award program을 목적어로 취할 수 있는 to부정사 (B) to benefit이 정답이다.

139-142 이메일

발신: 고객 서비스 〈patronservices@menachinlibrary.org〉
수신: 에드거 휴즈 〈hughese98@villachesta.com〉
제목: 카드 만료 날짜가 다가옵니다
날짜: 12월 3일

휴즈 씨께,

귀하의 메나 친 도서관 카드가 오늘로부터 한 달 뒤 만료될 예정임을 알려드립니다. 다음 해에도 회원 자격을 유지하시려면 139 **그것은 갱신되어야 합니다.** 140 **카드가 만료되기 최소 일주일 전에 갱신이 완료되어야 합니다.** 이는 전 지점의 안내 데스크에서 처리하실 수 있습니다.

계정을 종료하기로 결정141 **하신다면** 아무런 조치도 필요하지 않습니다. 142 **명시된** 날짜까지 갱신을 완료하지 못하면 도서관 권한이 만료됩니다.

본 통지 또는 전반적인 도서관 서비스에 관해 문의사항이 있으시면 이 이메일에 바로 회신하시면 됩니다.

고객 서비스

어휘 patron 고객 expiration 만료 approach 다가오다
expire 만료되다 renew 갱신하다 intend to ~하려고 하다
branch 지점 account 계정 renewal 갱신, (기한) 연장
result in (결과적으로) ~이 되다 privilege 권한, 특권 general
전반적인 reply 답장을 보내다

139 대명사 어휘

해설 빈칸은 동사 must be renewed의 주어 자리이므로 주격 대명사가 들어가야 한다. 앞 문장에서 도서관 카드가 곧 만료될 예정임을 상기시켜주는 것으로 보아, 갱신되어야 하는 것은 도서관 카드이므로 Mena Chin Library card를 지칭하는 (A) It이 정답이다.

140 문맥에 맞는 문장 고르기

번역 (A) 카드를 신청하시려면 해당 지역 도서관 지점을 방문하십시오.
(B) 도서관 회원에 대한 질문은 저희 웹사이트를 방문해 주십시오.
(C) 카드가 만료되기 최소 일주일 전에 갱신이 완료되어야 합니다.
(D) 언제든지 이 프로그램에서 탈퇴하실 수 있습니다.

해설 빈칸 앞에서 도서관 카드가 곧 만료될 예정(your ~ card will expire)임을 상기시키며 회원 자격 유지를 위해서는 카드를 갱신해야 한다(it must be renewed if you intend to keep your membership)고 했다. 따라서 카드 갱신과 관련된 정보를 안내하는 내용이 연결되어야 자연스러우므로 카드 갱신 기한을 알려주고 있는 (C)가 정답이다.

어휘 sign up for ~을 신청하다 opt out of ~에서 탈퇴하다

141 가정법 도치

▶ 동영상 강의

해설 빈칸은 두 개의 완전한 절을 연결하는 자리이므로 부사절 접속사가 필요한데, 문맥상 '계정을 종료하기로 결정한다면, 조치는 필요 없다'라고 미래에 대해 가정하는 내용이 되어야 자연스러우므로 가정법 미래 구문이 되어야 한다. 가정법의 if절에서 if가 생략되면 주어와 조동사 should가 도치되므로 (B) Should가 정답이다.

142 형용사 자리 _ 명사 수식 / 과거분사

해설 빈칸은 정관사와 명사 사이에서 명사 date를 수식하는 형용사 또는 date와 복합명사를 이루는 명사가 들어갈 수 있다. 문맥상 '명시된 날짜'라는 내용이 되어야 자연스러우므로, '명시된'이라는 수동의 의미를 나타내어 형용사 역할을 하는 과거분사 (C) specified가 정답이다. (A) specifically는 부사이므로 품사상 빈칸에 들어갈 수 없고, (B) specifics는 '세부사항', (D) specificity는 '특이성'이라는 뜻의 명사로 date와 복합명사를 이루기에 적절하지 않다.

143-146 편지

4월 7일

나오미 버웰
웨이마이어 로 43
사우스 포틀랜드, ME 04109

버웰 씨께,

저는 드롭라이트 스튜디오의 매니저 오마르 리다입니다. 143 **귀하께 저희 업체를 소개해 드리고 싶습니다.** 저희는 귀하와 같은 부동산 전문가를 위해 모든 범위의 사진 서비스를 제공합니다. 건물을 최상의 상태로 보이게 해주는 실내외 사진을 구성하는 것에 자부심을 가지고 있습니다. 드롭라이트 스튜디오는 우수한 디지털 이미지를 144 **만들기** 위한 노력을 아끼지 않습니다. 145 **실제로,** 전문가급 장비, 조명 및 연출 기술을 통해 건물 최고의 특징들을 강조할 수 있습니다. 그리고 사진 촬영이 끝나면 모든 이미지는 전문가의 편집을 146 **받습니다.** 이 모든 서비스는 모든 패키지에 기본으로 제공됩니다.

저희 웹사이트를 방문하셔서 작업물과 가격 및 일정 정보를 확인해 보십시오. 귀하와 작업하며 기꺼이 주문에 맞춰 드리겠습니다.

오마르 리다, 드롭라이트 스튜디오

어휘 range 범위 real estate 부동산 professional 전문가
take pride in ~을 자랑하다 compose 구성하다 interior
내부의 exterior 외부의 shot 사진 property 건물, 부동산
spare no effort 노력을 아끼지 않다 superior 우수한 grade
등급 staging 연출 highlight 강조하다 feature 특징 expert
전문가의 customize 주문 제작하다

143 문맥에 맞는 문장 고르기

번역 (A) 귀하께 저희 업체를 소개해 드리고 싶습니다.
(B) 멋진 사진은 귀하의 건물을 돋보이게 만들 수 있습니다.
(C) 귀하의 방문을 기대하고 있습니다.
(D) 이 지역에 문을 연 동종 업계 최초의 스튜디오였습니다.

해설 빈칸 앞에서 자신을 드롭라이트 스튜디오의 매니저(the manager of ~ Studio)라고 소개하고, 빈칸 뒤에서 귀하와 같은 부동산 전문가를 위한 사진 서비스(photography services for real estate professionals)를 제공한다고 설명했다. 앞뒤 문맥상 스튜디오에서 새로운 고객을 유치하는 내용이므로 업체를 소개하고 싶다는 내용의 (A)가 정답이다.

어휘 stand out 돋보이다 of its kind 동종의

144 동사 어휘

해설 앞 문장에서 건물을 최상으로 보이도록 사진을 구성하는 것에 자부심을 가지고 있다고 했고, 뒤 문장에서 전문가급 장비, 조명, 연출 기술로 건물 특징을 강조할 수 있다며 드롭라이트 스튜디오의 사진 제작 방식을 설명하고 있다. 따라서 빈칸이 있는 문장은 '우수한 디지털 이미지를 만들기 위한 노력을 아끼지 않는다'라는 내용이 되어야 문맥이 자연스럽게 연결되므로 '만들다'를 뜻하는 동사 create의 동명사형 (B) creating이 정답이다. (A)의 research는 '조사하다, 연구하다', (C)의 purchase는 '구매하다', (D)의 display는 '진열하다'라는 의미이다.

145 접속부사

해설 앞 문장에서 드롭라이트 스튜디오는 우수한 디지털 이미지를 만들기 위한 노력을 아끼지 않는다고 했고, 뒤 문장에서는 전문가급 장비, 조명, 연출 기술을 통해 건물의 최고 특징을 강조할 수 있다며 우수한 이미지를 만들기 위해 행해지는 노력을 실례로 들어 강조하고 있다. 따라서 앞서 언급된 내용을 강조하며 설명을 덧붙일 때 사용하는 '실제로'라는 뜻의 (D) Indeed가 정답이다. (A) If not은 '그렇지 않다면', (B) By comparison은 '그에 비해', (C) Otherwise는 '그렇지 않으면'이라는 의미이다.

146 동사 어형 _ 시제

해설 앞뒤 문맥에서 스튜디오에서 제공하는 서비스에 대해 현재 시제로 설명하고 있으므로, 빈칸이 있는 문장도 현재 시제로 '모든 이미지는 전문가의 편집을 받는다'라는 내용이 되어야 자연스럽다. 따라서 (A) receives가 정답이다.

PART 7

147-148 정보

잠시만요! 먼저 읽어 주십시오.

147 이 제품을 구입해 주셔서 감사합니다.

147 포장을 풀 때, 모든 부품이 포함되어 있는지 확인하고 분실이나 손상을 피하기 위해 물건을 안전한 장소에 놓으십시오. 147 **부드러운 표면**이나 납작하게 펼친 빈 상자 위에서 제품을 조립하십시오.

148 그림을 따라 주요 부품을 옆에 두고 조립을 시작하십시오. 나사나 볼트를 너무 과하게 조이지 마십시오. 그렇지 않으면 목재나 완충재가 손상될 수 있습니다. 유지 관리 팁을 얻고 품질 보증을 위해 제품을 등록하려면 당사의 웹사이트 www.indoordelight.com을 방문하십시오.

어휘 unpack 포장을 풀다 verify 확인하다 component 부품 loss 분실 damage 손상; 손상을 주다 assemble 조립하다 surface 표면 flattened 납작해진 assembly 조립 overtighten 과하게 조이다 screw 나사 cushioning 완충재 obtain 얻다 maintenance 유지 (관리) register 등록하다 warranty 품질 보증(서) coverage 보장

147 추론 / 암시

번역 정보는 어디에서 찾을 수 있을 것 같은가?
(A) 문 위
(B) 영수증
(C) 상자 안
(D) 웹사이트

해설 첫 문장에서 이 제품을 구입해 주셔서 감사하다(Thank you for purchasing this item)고 했고, 두 번째 단락의 첫 문장에서 포장을 풀 때 모든 부품이 포함되어 있는지 확인하라(As you do the unpacking, ~ all components are included)면서 두 번째 문장에서 부드러운 표면이나 납작하게 펼친 빈 상자 위에서 제품을 조립하라(Assemble the item ~ on the flattened empty box)고 했으므로 정보는 주문이 담긴 상자에 들어 있는 설명서임을 짐작할 수 있다. 따라서 (C)가 정답이다.

148 추론 / 암시

번역 언급되는 제품의 종류는 무엇일 것 같은가?
(A) 데스크톱 컴퓨터
(B) 가구
(C) 가전제품
(D) 전동 공구

해설 세 번째 단락의 첫 문장에서 그림을 따라 주요 부품을 옆에 두고 조립을 시작하라(Follow the pictures and begin the assembly ~ on its side)면서 나사나 볼트를 너무 과하게 조이지 말라(Never overtighten any screws or bolts)고 했고, 그렇지 않으면 목재나 완충재가 손상될 수 있다(or you may damage the wood or cushioning)고 했다. 따라서 조립이 필요한 제품인 것을 알 수 있으므로 (B)가 정답이다.

149-150 회의 일정표

149 모든 위니펙 직원들에게 사무실 간 회의 일정을 잡기 위해 빠르게 참고할 수 있는 도구로서 이 일정표의 복사본을 책상에 보관할 것을 요청 드립니다. 150 가능하면 항상 이 밑줄 친 시간 중 하나, 즉 오전 7시 이후에서 오전 11시 이전에 회의 일정을 잡으십시오.

149 위니펙		툴루즈
오전 7시	—	오후 2시
오전 8시	—	오후 3시
오전 9시	—	오후 4시
오전 10시	—	오후 5시
150 오전 11시	—	오후 6시
오후 12시	—	오후 7시

어휘 reference 참고 tool 도구 interoffice 사무실 간의 underlined 밑줄 친

149 추론 / 암시

번역 일정표에 의해 암시된 것은?
(A) 콘퍼런스가 예약되었다.
(B) 회사는 두 가지 시간대에 사무실을 가지고 있다.
(C) 행정 지원 직원들이 출장 계획을 세운다.
(D) 일부 회의 시간이 변경되었다.

해설 첫 문장에서 모든 위니펙 직원들에게 사무실 간 회의 일정을 잡기 위해 빠르게 참고할 수 있는 도구로서 이 일정표의 복사본을 책상에 보관할 것을 요청한다(We are asking all ~ scheduling interoffice meetings)고 했고, 두 번째 단락의 시간표에 위니펙(Winnipeg)과 툴루즈(Toulouse)라는 두 곳의 사무실 지역이 표시되어 있는 것으로 보아 회사는 시간대가 다른 두 지역에 사무실을 두고 있음을 알 수 있다. 따라서 (B)가 정답이다.

어휘 time zone 시간대 administrative 행정상의

150 추론 / 암시

번역 위니펙 시간으로 오전 11시에 대해 암시된 것은?
(A) 위니펙 사무실이 점심시간으로 문을 닫을 때이다.
(B) 툴루즈 직원들이 근무를 시작할 때이다.
(C) 회의를 잡기에 선호되는 시간이 아니다.
(D) 방금 일정표에 추가되었다.

해설 두 번째 문장에서 가능하면 항상 이 밑줄 친 시간 중 하나, 즉 오전 7시 이후에서 오전 11시 이전에 회의 일정을 잡으라(Whenever possible, please schedule these meetings during one of the underlined hours, that is, after 7:00 A.M. but before 11:00 A.M.)고 했고, 위니펙 시간으로 오전 11시(11:00 A.M.)에 밑줄이 그어져 있지 않으므로 해당 시간은 회의를 잡기에 선호되는 시간이 아님을 알 수 있다. 따라서 (C)가 정답이다.

151-152 안내 책자

브라이언트 포이어는 우리 지역 최고의 행사 공간 중 하나입니다. 언덕 위에 위치하여 인접한 식물원과 강을 한눈에 볼 수 있는 탁 트인 창문을 가지고 있습니다. ¹⁵¹**1897년에 지어진 이곳은 1여 년 전에 개조되기 전까지 프랑코나 자선 신탁의 본거지였습니다.** 오늘날, 이 공간은 최대 200명의 하객을 수용할 수 있으며 결혼 피로연, 사무실 파티 및 패널 프레젠테이션에 이상적입니다. 대리석 바닥, 대성당 천장, 그리고 멋진 예술작품을 갖춘 브라이언트 포이어는 귀하의 다음 모임을 위한 이상적인 장소입니다.

현장에 있는 식당인 안디토스는 행사에 음식을 제공하고 자체 식당으로도 운영됩니다. 요리사 미카엘라 리몬드가 이끌며 농장에서 식탁까지 관리하는 이 식당은 모든 식단 요구를 충족시키며 지역 요식업계에 혁신을 일으켰습니다. ¹⁵²**지역 주민들은 자리를 잡으려면 훨씬 전에 계획을 세워야 한다는 것을 알고 있습니다.**

행사 공간 예약이나 식사 예약을 하시려면 216-555-0157로 전화 주십시오.

어휘 premier 최고의 expansive 탁 트인 sweeping 전면적인 adjacent 인접한 botanical garden 식물원 charitable 자선(단체)의 trust 신탁 renovation 개조 accommodate 수용하다 ideal 이상적인 marble 대리석 cathedral 대성당 ceiling 천장 stunning 굉장히 멋진 gathering 모임 on-site 현장의 cater 음식을 공급하다 operate 운영되다 dietary 음식의 revolutionize 혁신을 일으키다 scene 분야, ~계 resident 주민 in advance 미리 reserve 예약하다

151 Not / True

번역 브라이언트 포이어에 대해 명시된 것은?
(A) 호숫가에 위치해 있다.
(B) 최근에 개조되었다.
(C) 손님들을 위한 식물원을 지을 것이다.
(D) 오로지 기업 행사만 예약이 된다.

해설 세 번째 문장에서 브라이언트 포이어에 대해 1897년에 지어진 이곳은 1여 년 전에 개조되기 전까지 프랑코나 자선 신탁의 본거지였다(Built in 1897, it was ~ until its renovation just over a year ago)고 했으므로 (B)가 정답이다. 두 번째 문장에서 언덕 위에 위치하여 인접한 식물원과 강을 한눈에 볼 수 있는 탁 트인 창문을 가지고 있다(Set on a hill, it has expansive windows ~ botanical gardens and the river)고 했으므로 (A)와 (C), 네 번째 문장에서 이 공간은 결혼 피로연, 사무실 파티 및 패널 프레젠테이션에 이상적(the space ~ is ideal for wedding receptions, office parties, panel presentations)이라고 했으므로 (D)는 오답이다.

어휘 shore 물가, 기슭 solely 오로지

Paraphrasing 지문의 just over a year ago
→ 정답의 recently

152 추론 / 암시

번역 안디토스에 대해 암시된 것은?
(A) 세계적인 요리사에 의해 시작되었다.
(B) 제한된 메뉴 선택권을 제공한다.
(C) 현재 자선 단체에 의해 자금을 지원받고 있다.
(D) 지역 주민들에게 매우 인기 있다.

해설 안디토스를 소개하는 두 번째 단락의 마지막 문장에서 지역 주민들은 자리를 잡으려면 훨씬 전에 계획을 세워야 한다는 것을 알고 있다(Area residents know to plan far in advance to get a seat)고 했으므로 안디토스가 지역 주민들에게 매우 인기 있는 식당임을 알 수 있다. 따라서 (D)가 정답이다.

어휘 fund 자금을 대다 organization 단체

153-154 문자 메시지

조안 치 (오후 12시 39분)
안녕하세요 미나. 현장 측량은 거의 끝나가나요? 배가 고파오네요.

미나 에버스 (오후 12시 40분)
미안해요, 조안. ¹⁵³,¹⁵⁴**아쉽게도 당신과 림 씨는 오늘 저를 빼고 점심을 먹으러 가셔야 할 것 같아요.** 현장 좌표에 문제가 있어요. 시간이 좀 걸릴 것 같아요.

조안 치 (오후 12시 51분)
아, 이런. 153 올 때 뭐 좀 사다 드릴까요?

미나 에버스 (오후 12시 59분)
153 치킨 샌드위치 좀 부탁해요.

조안 치 (오후 1시)
물론이죠, 미나. 154 잠시 후에 봐요.

어휘 field 현장 measurement 측량 site 현장, 부지 coordinate 좌표

---

153 의도 파악

번역 오후 1시에 치 씨가 "물론이죠, 미나"라고 쓴 의도는?
(A) 에버스 씨를 위해 점심을 가져다 줄 것이다.
(B) 에버스 씨에게 필요한 도구를 제공할 수 있다.
(C) 일부 현장 좌표는 정확하다.
(D) 일부 측량은 이중으로 확인되어야 한다.

해설 12시 40분에 에버스 씨가 치 씨에게 아쉽게도 치 씨와 림 씨는 오늘 본인을 빼고 점심을 먹으러 가야 할 것 같다(I'm afraid you and Ms. Lim will have to go to lunch without me today)고 했고, 12시 51분에 치 씨가 올 때 뭘 좀 사다 줄지(Should we bring something back for you?)를 묻자 12시 59분에 에버스 씨가 치킨 샌드위치를 부탁한다(Get me a chicken sandwich)고 한 데 대해 1시에 치 씨가 물론이죠, 미나(Sure thing, Mina)라고 대답했다. 따라서 치 씨는 에버스 씨에게 점심 식사로 치킨 샌드위치를 사다 주겠다는 의도로 한 말임을 알 수 있으므로 (A)가 정답이다.

154 세부사항

번역 다음에 일어날 일은?
(A) 치 씨는 새로운 현장 좌표를 얻을 것이다.
(B) 치 씨와 림 씨는 잠시 나갈 것이다.
(C) 에버스 씨는 조리법을 공유할 것이다.
(D) 림 씨는 측량을 시작할 것이다.

해설 12시 40분에 에버스 씨가 치 씨에게 아쉽게도 치 씨와 림 씨는 오늘 본인을 빼고 점심을 먹으러 가야 할 것 같다(I'm afraid you and Ms. Lim will have to go to lunch without me today)고 했고, 1시에 치 씨가 에버스 씨에게 잠시 후에 보자(See you in a while)며 인사를 하고 있으므로 치 씨와 림 씨는 점심 식사를 하러 외출할 것임을 알 수 있다. 따라서 (B)가 정답이다.

Paraphrasing 지문의 go to lunch
→ 정답의 be out for a while

155-157 공지

155, 156 이번 계절의 좋은 날씨로 상당한 양의 과일과 채소가 수확되어, 대부분의 경우 재배자들이 구매자를 찾을 수 있는 것보다 수확량이 더 많은 상태입니다. 155 지역 단체에 잉여 농산물을 기부하고 싶으신 분들은 보시 팜 앤 가든의 웹사이트(www.vfgrdn.org)를 방문하시면, 물건을 가져다 놓을 장소의 목록을 찾으실 수 있습니다.

만약 저희가 대신 방문해야 하는 경우라면 연락 주십시오. 157 친절하게 운송을 지원해 준 여러 개인 트럭 운전자들 중 한 명에게 연락을 취해 귀하의 기부 식품이 필요하며 심사를 받은 단체에 신속하게 나눠줄 것입니다. 본 서비스에 대한 자세한 내용과 북부 대초원 지역의 농업 및 원예 관련 주제에 대한 이해를 원하시면 저희 웹사이트를 확인해 주십시오.

어휘 yield (농작물 등을) 생산하다 substantial 상당한 harvest 수확 donate 기부하다 surplus 잉여의 produce 농산물 organization 단체 drop-off 내려놓는 곳 reach out to ~에게 연락을 취하다 independent 독자적인, 자영의 transport 운반하다 distribute 나눠주다 donation 기부 vetted 심사[조사]를 받은 insight 이해 related to ~와 관련된 Great Plains 대초원 지대(로키산맥 동쪽의 대평원)

---

155 추론 / 암시

번역 공지의 대상은 누구일 것 같은가?
(A) 농부
(B) 전문 요리사
(C) 트럭 운전사
(D) 슈퍼마켓 관리자

해설 첫 문장에서 이번 계절의 좋은 날씨로 상당한 양의 과일과 채소가 수확되어 대부분의 경우 재배자들이 구매자를 찾을 수 있는 것보다 수확량이 더 많은 상태(This season's excellent weather has yielded ~ more than growers may find buyers for)라면서, 두 번째 문장에서 지역 단체에 잉여 농산물을 기부하고 싶은 사람들은 보시 팜 앤 가든의 웹사이트를 방문하면 물건을 가져다 놓을 장소의 목록을 찾을 수 있다(Those of you wishing to donate surplus produce ~ find our list of drop-off locations)고 한 것으로 보아 공지는 농산물을 직접 생산하는 사람들을 대상으로 한 것임을 짐작할 수 있다. 따라서 (A)가 정답이다.

156 Not / True

번역 공지에서 날씨에 대해 명시한 것은?
(A) 운송 지연을 야기했다.
(B) 평소보다 더 많은 비가 내렸다.
(C) 지역 뉴스에서 자주 화제가 되었다.
(D) 농작물에 유익했다.

해설 첫 문장에서 이번 계절의 좋은 날씨로 상당한 양의 과일과 채소가 수확되어 대부분의 경우 재배자들이 구매자를 찾을 수 있는 것보다 수확량이 더 많은 상태(This season's excellent weather has yielded a substantial harvest ~ growers may find buyers for)라고 했으므로, 날씨가 좋아 작물 경작이 수혜를 입었다는 것을 알 수 있으므로 (D)가 정답이다.

어휘 transportation 운송 heavy (양 등이) 많은[심한] frequently 자주 beneficial 유익한 crop 농작물

Paraphrasing 지문의 fruits and vegetables → 정답의 crops

157 Not / True

번역 공지에서 언급한 서비스는?
(A) 현지 기업을 위한 직원 채용
(B) 식품 수거 및 배분
(C) 농기계 수리
(D) 원예 워크숍

해설 두 번째 단락의 두 번째 문장에서 친절하게 운송을 지원해 준 여러 개인 트럭 운전사들 중 한 명에게 연락을 취해 기부 식품이 필요하며 심사를 받은 단체에 신속하게 나눠줄 것(We will reach out to one of the many ~ transport and quickly distribute your food donations to vetted groups that need it)이라고 했으므로 (B)가 정답이다.

어휘 staffing 직원 채용 distribution 배분 machinery 기계(류)

Paraphrasing 지문의 transport and distribute
→ 정답의 collection and distribution

158-160 공지

오늘 행사에 함께해 주셔서 정말 기쁩니다. 참석자 모두 즐거운 경험을 할 수 있도록 다음 지침을 준수해 주시기 바랍니다.

158 행사장에 입장하자마자 모든 전자기기를 무음 모드로 바꿔 주십시오. 158,160 벨소리와 밝은 화면은 연주자와 주변 관객 모두에게 매우 방해됩니다. 전화 통화 또는 문자를 보내는 행위를 항상 자제해 주십시오. 160 또한, 관객들은 공연을 음성 녹음 또는 영상 녹화할 수 없습니다.

통로에 있는 가방 및 기타 물품은 안전 문제의 원인이 됩니다. 159 가방이 너무 커서 좌석 밑에 제대로 들어갈 수 없다면, 단돈 2달러로 보관함에 보관하는 것을 고려해 주십시오. 저희 안내원 중 한 명이 기꺼이 도와드릴 것입니다.

협조해 주셔서 감사합니다.

어휘 delighted 아주 기뻐하는 adhere to (약속 등을) 지키다 attendee 참석자 venue 행사장 device 장치 silent 무음의 ringtone 벨소리 lit 밝은(light의 과거분사) distracting 방해가 되는 fellow 같은 상황에 있는 aisle 통로 pose 제기하다 properly 제대로 store 보관하다 attendant 안내원 cooperation 협조

158 추론 / 암시

번역 공지가 게시되어 있을 것 같은 장소는?
(A) 기내
(B) 공연장
(C) 식당
(D) 우체국

해설 두 번째 단락의 첫 문장에서 행사장에 입장하자마자 모든 전자기기를 무음 모드로 바꿔 달라(Upon entering the venue ~ devices in silent mode)고 요청했고, 벨소리와 밝은 화면은 연주자와 주변 관객 모두에게 매우 방해된다(Ringtones ~ both the performers and your fellow audience members)고 했으므로 공연장에 게시되어 있을 가능성이 높다. 따라서 (B)가 정답이다.

159 Not / True

번역 큰 가방에 대해 언급된 것은?
(A) 유료로 보관함에 둘 수 있다.
(B) 건물 밖에 두어야 한다.
(C) 안내원이 검사할 것이다.
(D) 반드시 좌석 아래 놓아야 한다.

해설 세 번째 단락의 두 번째 문장에서 가방이 너무 커서 좌석 밑에 제대로 들어갈 수 없다면 단돈 2달러로 보관함에 보관하는 것을 고려해 달라(If your bag is too big ~ storing it in a locker for just $2)고 했으므로 (A)가 정답이다.

어휘 inspect 검사하다

160 문장 삽입

번역 [1], [2], [3], [4]로 표시된 위치 중에서 다음 문장이 들어가기에 가장 적합한 곳은?

"전화 통화 또는 문자를 보내는 행위를 항상 자제해 주십시오."
(A) [1]
(B) [2]
(C) [3]
(D) [4]

해설 주어진 문장은 '전화 통화나 문자 보내기를 자제해 달라'며 삼가야 할 행동을 안내하고 있다. 따라서 벨소리와 밝은 화면은 공연에 방해가 되고(Ringtones and lit screens are very distracting ~ audience members), 관객은 공연을 음성 녹음 또는 녹화할 수 없다(audience members are not allowed ~ recording of the performance)며 관객들의 자제를 요청하는 문장들 사이에 들어가는 것이 글의 흐름상 자연스러우므로 (B)가 정답이다.

어휘 refrain from ~을 자제하다

161-164 이메일

수신: 카밀 아얄라 〈ayala@esplinelectronics.com〉
발신: 마사에 아다치 〈madachi@sweeterspecialties.com〉
날짜: 2월 12일
제목: 행사 순서
첨부: ⑩ 스위터 스페셜티스 요청서

아얄라 씨께,

3월 에스플린 전자 콘퍼런스에 제과류를 제공하는 데 저희 업체를 선택해 주셔서 감사합니다. 162 4년 연속 저희를 선택해 주셔서 영광입니다! 163 3월 29일에는 말씀하신 열 곳에 각각 큰 바닐라 케이크를 제공하고, 그 다음 날에는 주문 제작된 다층 케이크를 배달해 드릴 것입니다. 3월 28일에는 청구서가 발송됩니다. 161 첨부된 주문서를 검토하시고 7일 이내에 반송해 주시기 바랍니다.

163 3월 30일을 위해 주문하신 케이크에 관해서는, 저희 수석 파티시에가 귀하의 주문서에 따라 제작할 예정입니다. 사실, 오늘 아침 그가 완전한 조리법 샘플로 신선한 라즈베리 속을 채운 아몬드 크림 케이크를 만들었습니다. 저희는 그것이 정말 맛있는 간식이 될 것이라 164 판단하며 귀하께서도 만족하시리라 확신합니다.

문의사항이 있으시면 저에게 이메일을 보내 주십시오. 저희는 언제나 귀사를 소중히 생각합니다.

마사에 아다치, 사장
스위터 스페셜티스

> 어휘 honored 영광으로 생각하는 in a row 연이어 venue 장소 multilayer 다층의 bill 청구하다 head 수석, 책임자 pastry chef 파티시에 specification 주문서, 명세서 filling (케이크 등의) 속 judge 판단하다 delectable 아주 맛있는 value 소중히 여기다

161 주제 / 목적

번역 이메일의 주요 목적은?
(A) 주문 확인을 요청하려고
(B) 일부 배송 날짜를 조정하려고
(C) 사업 확장을 발표하려고
(D) 디저트 신제품을 홍보하려고

해설 첫 단락의 마지막 문장에서 첨부된 주문서를 검토하고 7일 이내에 반송해 달라(Please review the attached order form and return it to me within seven days)고 했으므로 주문사항을 확인해 달라고 요청하는 이메일임을 알 수 있다. 따라서 (A)가 정답이다.

어휘 confirmation 확인 adjust 조정하다 expansion 확장

162 추론 / 암시

번역 아얄라 씨에 대해 암시된 것은?
(A) 전문가상을 받을 것이다.
(B) 파티시에로 근무했다.
(C) 과거에 스위터 스페셜티스 고객이었다.
(D) 요리사에 대해 긍정적인 추천을 받았다.

해설 두 번째 문장에서 아얄라 씨에게 4년 연속 저희를 선택해 주셔서 영광이다(We are honored that you chose us for a fourth year in a row!)라고 한 것으로 보아 아얄라 씨는 스위터 스페셜티스의 기존 고객임을 알 수 있다. 따라서 (C)가 정답이다.

163 추론 / 암시

번역 다층 케이크에 대해 암시된 것은?
(A) 고객들에게 가장 잘 팔리는 제품이었다.
(B) 스위터 스페셜티스에서 가장 비싼 케이크이다.
(C) 매년 에스플린 전자를 위해 제작된다.
(D) 스위터 스페셜티스의 새로운 맛 조합이다.

해설 세 번째 문장에서 3월 29일에는 언급한 열 곳에 각각 큰 바닐라 케이크를 제공하고, 그다음 날에는 주문 제작된 다층 케이크를 배달할 것(On March 29, we will ~ multilayer cake on the following day)이라고 했고, 두 번째 단락의 첫 문장에서 3월 30일을 위해 주문한 케이크에 관해서는 수석 파티시에가 주문서에 따라 제작할 예정(Regarding the cake you ordered ~ our head pastry chef will produce it according to your specifications)이며 오늘 아침 그가 완전한 조리법 샘플로 신선한 라즈베리로 속을 채운 아몬드

크림 케이크를 만들었다(In fact, he created a sample ~ fresh raspberry filling)고 했다. 따라서 3월 30일에 제작할 다층 케이크는 스위터 스페셜티스에서 새롭게 시도하는 맛임을 짐작할 수 있으므로 (D)가 정답이다.

어휘 annually 매년 combination 조합

164 동의어 찾기

번역 두 번째 단락 3행의 "judged"와 의미가 가장 가까운 단어는?
(A) 비판했다
(B) 해결했다
(C) 단정했다
(D) 설명했다

해설 의미상 새로 만든 케이크가 맛있는 간식이 될 거라 '판단했다', 즉 '판단[결정]을 내렸다'라는 뜻으로 쓰였으므로 '결정했다, 단정했다'를 뜻하는 (C) determined가 정답이다.

165-167 제품 후기

> **훌륭한 식기세척기!**
>
> 저는 전에 식기세척기를 가져본 적이 없습니다. 부엌을 개조한 뒤, 마침내 소형 식기세척기를 놓을 공간이 생겼습니다. [165] **조사를 많이 했고, 디시 매직 300이 최고의 선택인 것 같습니다.** 다른 모델들보다 비쌌지만 후기가 모두 훌륭했습니다. 그래서 저는 돈을 좀 더 쓰기로 결심했습니다. 지금 식기세척기를 한 달째 사용하고 있는데, 제 결정에 더할 나위 없이 만족합니다. 가장 중요한 것은 접시들이 아무리 더러운 상태로 기계에 들어가더라도 반짝거리는 깨끗한 상태로 나온다는 것입니다. 또한 기계가 아주 조용해서 [166] **작동하고 있는지**조차 알지 못합니다. [167] **마지막으로, 기기는 물을 효율적으로 사용하도록 설계되었으며, 이는 저에게 매우 중요합니다.** 전반적으로 저는 이 식기세척기에 아주 만족합니다.
>
> — 안나 야코블레바

> 어휘 room 공간 compact 소형의 pricey 값비싼 sparkling 반짝거리는 no matter how 아무리 ~해도 efficiently 효율적으로 overall 전반적으로

165 세부사항

번역 야코블레바 씨가 디시 매직 300 식기세척기를 선택한 이유는?
(A) 대부분의 모델보다 덜 비쌌다.
(B) 구입 가능한 가장 큰 모델이었다.
(C) 매우 높은 평가를 받았다.
(D) 그녀의 다른 가전제품과 같은 브랜드였다.

해설 세 번째 문장에서 조사를 많이 했고, 디시 매직 300이 최고의 선택인 것 같았다(I did a lot of research ~ to be the best choice)면서, 다른 모델들보다 비쌌지만 후기가 모두 훌륭했다(It was pricier ~ all of the reviews were excellent)고 했으므로 (C)가 정답이다.

어휘 rate 평가하다 appliances 가전제품

Paraphrasing 지문의 all of the reviews were excellent
→ 정답의 It was rated very highly

166 동의어 찾기

번역 첫 번째 단락 7행의 "running"과 의미가 가장 가까운 단어는?
(A) 조정하고 있는
(B) 통제하고 있는
(C) 옮기고 있는
(D) 작동하고 있는

해설 의미상 기계가 조용해서 '작동하고 있는지'조차 모른다는 뜻으로 쓰인 것이므로 '작동하고 있는'을 뜻하는 (D) operating이 정답이다.

167 Not / True

번역 야코블레바 씨에 대해 명시된 것은?
(A) 물을 절약하는 것에 관해 신경을 쓴다.
(B) 최근에 새집으로 이사했다.
(C) 1년 전에 식기세척기를 샀다.
(D) 전문적으로 주방을 개조한다.

해설 아홉 번째 문장에서 야코블레바 씨가 마지막으로 기기는 물을 효율적으로 사용하도록 설계되었으며 이는 자신에게 매우 중요하다(Lastly, it is designed to use water efficiently, which is very important to me)고 언급했으므로 (A)가 정답이다.

Paraphrasing 지문의 use water efficiently
→ 정답의 saving water

168-171 정보

스카일러 항공은 전 세계에서 2만 명 이상을 고용하고 있습니다. 168, 171 우리는 빠르게 성장하고 있으며 많은 일자리가 있습니다. 당사의 일자리는 매우 다양한 능력을 아우릅니다. 168, 171 따라서 당신의 배경과 상관없이 우리 팀에는 당신을 위한 자리가 있을 것입니다. 스카일러 직원들은 많은 혜택을 누립니다. 예를 들어, 169 (B) 우리의 할인 프로그램은 직원들이 평균 항공권 가격의 일부만 내면 당사의 취항지 어느 곳으로든 비행할 수 있게 해 줍니다. 169 (A), 169 (C) 우리는 상향적이고 세계적인 이동성, 교육비 상환, 멘토링 프로그램, 그리고 후한 보상 패키지를 제공합니다. 169 (D) 연간 유급 휴가는 편안한 일과 삶의 균형을 가능하게 해 줍니다. 170 스카일러 항공이 3년 연속 〈트래블 비스타 저널〉에 의해 '가장 근무하기 좋은 항공사'로 선정된 것은 당연한 일입니다.

어휘 employ 고용하다 regardless of ~에 상관없이 background 배경 perk 혜택, 특전 enable 가능하게 하다 destination 목적지 fraction 부분, 분수 average 평균의 upward mobility 경제적[사회적] 지위의 향상 tuition 교육비 reimbursement 상환 generous 후한 compensation 보상 paid vacation 유급 휴가 in a row 연속으로, 연이어

168 추론 / 암시

번역 정보의 대상은?
(A) 스카일러 항공 직원
(B) 스카일러 항공 고객
(C) 잠재적 정기 간행물 구독자
(D) 현재 구직자

해설 두 번째 문장에서 스카일러 항공은 빠르게 성장하고 있으며 많은 일자리가 있다(We're growing fast and have many positions available)고 한 뒤, 당신의 배경과 상관없이 팀에는 당신을 위한 자리가 있을 것(So regardless of ~ there's probably a place for you on our team)이라고 했으므로 정보는 구직자를 대상으로 한 글임을 알 수 있다. 따라서 (D)가 정답이다.

어휘 potential 잠재적인 subscriber 구독자 job seeker 구직자

169 Not / True

번역 정보에서 직원에게 제공되는 것으로 언급되지 않은 것은?
(A) 교육비 지급
(B) 무료 항공권
(C) 멘토링 기회
(D) 유급 휴가

해설 일곱 번째 문장에서 상향적이고 세계적인 이동성, 교육비 상환, 멘토링 프로그램, 그리고 후한 보상 패키지를 제공한다(We offer ~ tuition reimbursement, a mentorship program, and a generous compensation package)고 했으므로 (A)와 (C), 연간 유급 휴가는 편안한 일과 삶의 균형을 가능하게 해 준다(Annual paid vacations ~ work-life balance)고 했으므로 (D)는 직원에게 제공되는 것이 맞고, 여섯 번째 문장에서 할인 프로그램은 직원들이 평균 항공권 가격의 일부만 내면 당사의 취항지 어느 곳으로든 비행할 수 있게 해 준다(our discount program ~ a fraction of the average ticket price)고 했으므로 직원들은 무료가 아닌 할인가로 항공권을 살 수 있음을 알 수 있다. 따라서 (B)가 정답이다.

어휘 educational 교육의 expense 비용 opportunity 기회

Paraphrasing 지문의 tuition reimbursement
→ 보기 (A)의 Payment for educational expenses
지문의 mentorship program
→ 보기 (C)의 Opportunities for mentoring
지문의 paid vacations
→ 보기 (D)의 Paid days off

170 Not / True

번역 스카일러 항공에 대해 언급된 것은?
(A) 전 세계에서 가장 많은 목적지로 운항한다.
(B) 다른 항공사와 합병할 계획이다.
(C) 업계 간행물에 의해 호평을 받았다.
(D) 좌석을 더 편안한 것으로 교체했다.

해설 마지막 문장에서 스카일러 항공이 3년 연속 〈트래블 비스타 저널〉에 의해 '가장 근무하기 좋은 항공사'로 선정된 것은 당연한 일(It's no wonder that Skyler Airlines was named "Best Airline to Work For" by Travel Vista Journal ~)이라고 했으므로 (C)가 정답이다.

어휘 merge 합병하다 praise 칭찬하다 trade 업계, 사업

171 문장 삽입

번역 [1], [2], [3], [4]로 표시된 위치 중에서 다음 문장이 들어가기에 가장 적합한 곳은?

"당사의 일자리는 매우 다양한 능력을 아우릅니다."
(A) [1]
(B) [2]
(C) [3]
(D) [4]

해설 주어진 문장은 '당사의 일자리는 다양한 능력을 아우른다'며 광범위한 일자리 기회를 언급하고 있다. 따라서 스카일러 항공이 빠르게 성장 중이고 많은 일자리가 있으며(We're growing fast and have many positions available), 당신의 배경과 상관없이 당신을 위한 자리가 있을 것(So regardless of your background, there's probably a place for you on our team)이라며 다양한 구직 기회를 강조하는 문장들 사이에 들어가는 것이 글의 흐름상 자연스러우므로 (A)가 정답이다.

어휘 opening 일자리　cover 포함하다　skill set 다양한 능력

172-175 온라인 채팅

수잔 고완 오전 9시 16분
좋은 아침입니다. ¹⁷²새로운 헤드폰 라인에 대한 프레젠테이션 슬라이드가 많은 파트너 매장에 배포될 준비가 거의 다 되었습니다. 다음 주 월요일에 그것들을 발송할 계획입니다.

매기 로렌츠 오전 9시 17분
슬라이드는 언제 보이나요?

수잔 고완 오전 9시 20분
아직 일부 누락된 요소들이 있습니다.

앨런 우드슨 오전 9시 21분
¹⁷³스포츠용 헤드폰을 검토한 사용자 연구의 정보가 주로 필요합니다. ^{173,174}수요일까지 연구 개발실에서 해당 보고서를 받아야 합니다.

매기 로렌츠 오전 9시 22분
네, 그 부분을 간과하지 않도록 합시다. 그리고 ¹⁷⁴만약 보고서가 수요일까지 오지 않을까 봐 걱정된다면 매트 하븐에게 연락해서 우리에게 요약본을 신속히 전달하도록 상기시켜 주세요.

수잔 고완 오전 9시 23분
요약본을 일찍 받아서 슬라이드에 연구 결과를 포함시킬 수 있다고 가정하면, ¹⁷⁵우리 셋이 목요일이나 금요일에 프레젠테이션 시연 일정을 잡아야 할까요?

매기 로렌츠 오전 9시 24분
¹⁷⁵목요일 오후로 합시다. 그러면 우리는 여전히 금요일에 필요한 변경을 할 수 있을 겁니다.

앨런 우드슨 오전 9시 25분
저는 좋습니다. 오후 2시 이후에는 시간이 있습니다.

어휘 distribution 배포　be on track 순조롭게 나아가다 missing 빠진　element 요소　overlook 간과하다　expedite 신속히 처리하다　summary 요약　assuming (that) 만약 ~이라면 incorporate 포함하다　findings 연구 결과　trial run 시연

172 Not / True

번역 프레젠테이션에 대해 명시된 것은?
(A) 제작하는 데 비용이 많이 들 것이다.
(B) 가장 질 팔리는 제품들을 강조할 것이다.
(C) 고완 씨의 첫 프로젝트가 될 것이다.
(D) 여러 장소로 보내질 것이다.

해설 9시 16분에 고완 씨가 새로운 헤드폰 라인에 대한 프레젠테이션 슬라이드가 많은 파트너 매장에 배포될 준비가 거의 다 되었다(The presentation slides about the new line of headphones are almost ready for distribution to our many partner stores)고 했으므로 프레젠테이션이 여러 매장으로 보내질 것임을 알 수 있다. 따라서 (D)가 정답이다.

어휘 highlight 강조하다　multiple 다수의

173 의도 파악

번역 오전 9시 22분에 로렌츠 씨가 "그 부분을 간과하지 않도록 합시다"라고 쓴 의도는?
(A) 더 많은 직원들이 회의에 참석해야 한다.
(B) 사용자 연구의 정보가 중요하다.
(C) 발표가 순조롭게 진행되어야 한다.
(D) 파트너 매장에 곧 받아 보게 될 보고서에 대해 알려야 한다.

해설 9시 21분에 우드슨 씨가 스포츠용 헤드폰을 검토한 사용자 연구의 정보가 주로 필요하다(We mainly need the information from the user studies ~ for sport use)면서 수요일까지 연구 개발실에서 해당 보고서를 받아야 한다(We should have ~ office by Wednesday)고 하자, 9시 22분에 로렌츠 씨가 그 부분을 간과하지 않도록 하자(let's not overlook that)고 했으므로 헤드폰에 대한 사용자 연구 정보의 중요성을 강조하려는 의도로 한 말임을 알 수 있다. 따라서 (B)가 정답이다.

어휘 smoothly 순조롭게　notify 알리다　upcoming 곧 있을

174 추론 / 암시

번역 하븐 씨는 누구일 것 같은가?
(A) 매장 관리자
(B) 아마추어 운동선수
(C) 제품 연구원
(D) 광고 부서 임원

해설 9시 21분에 우드슨 씨가 수요일까지 연구 개발실에서 해당 보고서를 받아야 한다(We should have that report from the research and development office by Wednesday)고 했고, 9시 22분에 로렌츠 씨가 만약 보고서가 수요일까지 오지 않을까 봐 걱정된다면 매트 하븐에게 연락해서 우리에게 요약본을 신속히 전달하도록 상기시켜 달라(if you're concerned ~ please contact Matt Harven and remind him to expedite a summary to us)고 했다. 따라서 하븐 씨가 연구 개발실에서 근무하는 직원임을 짐작할 수 있으므로 (C)가 정답이다.

어휘 athlete 운동선수　executive 임원

175 세부사항

번역 채팅 작성자들은 언제 슬라이드 프레젠테이션을 검토하기 위해 만날 계획인가?
(A) 월요일
(B) 수요일
(C) 목요일
(D) 금요일

해설 오전 9시 23분에 고완 씨가 우리 셋이 목요일이나 금요일에 프레젠테이션 시연 일정을 잡아야 할지(should the three of us schedule a trial run through the presentation on Thursday or Friday?) 묻자 9시 24분에 로렌츠 씨가 목요일 오후로 하자(Let's try for Thursday afternoon)고 했으므로 (C)가 정답이다.

176-180 보도 자료 + 후기

아파르나 코타리, 언론 연락 담당
키친 스위프츠
akothari@kitchenswifts.com.au

즉각 발표용

시드니 (6월 4일) — 176 **키친 스위프츠와 다리우스 코데로 셰프가 함께 힘을 합해 집에서 요리하는 사람들에게 새로운 요리 경험을 선사한다.** 179 **수상 경력이 있는 이 요리사는 최근 문을 연 엔리쿠아스를 포함해 필리핀과 호주 두 지역에 레스토랑을 소유하고 있다.** 그는 자신의 요리가 많은 문화가 혼합되어 있는 자신의 필리핀 전통을 177 **반영한다**고 말한다.

"저는 집에서 요리하시는 분들이 새롭고 흥미로운 맛을 쉽게 즐길 수 있도록 키친 스위프츠를 위해 이 간소화된 조리법들을 개발했습니다."라고 그는 말했다. "이 식사를 준비하고 먹는 동안 여러분은 저와 함께 세계 여행을 하고 있는 것처럼 느낄 수 있습니다."

키친 스위프츠의 부사장인 자흐라 챔버스는 코데로 셰프와 함께 작업하며 고객들에게 맛있는 새 조리법을 제공하게 되어 기쁘다고 말한다. 178 **키친 스위프츠는 다양한 채식 메뉴를 포함해 2인, 4인 또는 6인을 위한 메뉴와 조리법 그리고 재료를 제공한다.** 고객이 가장 적합한 식사 옵션을 선택하고 나면 매주 상자 하나가 배달된다. 현고객에게는 파트너십을 통해 가격이 인상되지 않을 것이다. 자세한 사항은 키친 스위프츠 웹사이트 www.kitchenswifts.com.au를 방문하면 된다.

어휘 immediate 즉각적인 release 발표 culinary 요리의 reflect 반영하다 Filipino 필리핀의 heritage 전통, 유산 blend 조합 simplified 간소화된 flavour 맛 with ease 쉽게 vice president 부사장 ingredient 재료 selection 선택 가능한 것들 appropriate 적절한

https://www.sydenyrestaurants.com.au

179 **제가 시드니에서 콘퍼런스에 참석하는 동안 동료가 엔리쿠아스에서 식사를 할 수 있도록 주선해 주었습니다.** 180 **그곳은 보통 저녁 식사 예약이 꽉 차서 테이블을 예약하려면 몇 달 전에 전화를 해야 할 수도 있습니다.** 대신 우리는 거기서 멋진 점심 식사를 했습니다. 모든 것이 맛있었고, 빵과 디저트는 현장에서 구워집니다! 비행기를 타고 홍콩으로 돌아오

기 전에 가치 있는 식사였습니다.

- 메일리 관

어휘 colleague 동료 arrange 주선하다, 마련하다 fully booked 예약이 꽉 찬 in advance 미리 on-site 현장에서 worthwhile 가치 있는 treat 대접, 한턱

176 주제 / 목적

번역 보도 자료의 목적은?
(A) 레스토랑 개점을 홍보하려고
(B) 사업 제휴를 발표하려고
(C) 여행 프로그램을 소개하려고
(D) 수상자를 축하하려고

해설 보도 자료의 첫 문장에서 키친 스위프츠와 다리우스 코데로 셰프가 함께 힘을 합해 집에서 요리하는 사람들에게 새로운 요리 경험을 선사한다(Kitchen Swifts and Chef Darius Cordero are joining together ~ a new culinary experience)고 했으므로 두 사업 주체가 협업 관계를 맺어 새로운 서비스를 출시하는 것을 알리려는 목적으로 보도 자료가 작성되었음을 알 수 있다. 따라서 (B)가 정답이다.

어휘 recipient 수령인

177 동의어 찾기

번역 보도 자료의 첫 번째 단락 4행의 "reflects"와 의미가 가장 가까운 단어는?
(A) ~을 야기하다
(B) 바꾸다
(C) 보여주다
(D) ~에 대해 생각하다

해설 의미상 요리가 필리핀 전통을 '반영한다'라는 뜻으로 쓰였으므로 '보여주다'를 뜻하는 (C) shows가 정답이다.

178 Not / True

번역 키친 스위프츠에 대해 명시된 것은?
(A) 모든 고객들에게 가격을 인상했다.
(B) 배송 일정을 변경했다.
(C) 여러 식사 옵션을 제공한다.
(D) 부사장이 새로 왔다.

해설 보도 자료의 세 번째 단락 두 번째 문장에서 키친 스위프츠는 다양한 채식 메뉴를 포함해 2인, 4인 또는 6인을 위한 메뉴와 조리법 그리고 재료를 제공한다(Kitchen Swifts supplies ~ a range of vegetarian selections)고 했으므로 (C)가 정답이다. 네 번째 문장에서 현고객에게는 파트너십을 통해 가격이 인상되지 않을 것(Current customers will see no price increase with the partnership)이라고 했으므로 (A)는 오답이고, (B)와 (D)는 언급되지 않았다.

어휘 raise 인상하다 revise 변경하다

179 연계

번역 관 씨에 대해 사실일 것 같은 것은?
(A) 고네로 씨의 레스토랑에 갔다.
(B) 최근에 시드니로 휴가를 갔다.
(C) 챔버스 씨의 동료이다.
(D) 정기적으로 키친 스위프츠에서 주문한다.

해설 후기의 첫 문장에서 관 씨는 시드니에서 콘퍼런스에 참석하는 동안 동료가 엔리쿠아스에서 식사를 할 수 있도록 추천해 주었다(A colleague arranged for us to eat at Enriqua's ∼ at a conference in Sydney)고 했고, 보도 자료의 두 번째 문장에서 수상 경력이 있는 이 요리사(Mr. Cordero)는 최근 문을 연 엔리쿠아스를 포함해 필리핀과 호주 두 지역에 레스토랑을 소유하고 있다(The award-winning chef is the owner of ∼ the recently opened Enriqua's)고 했다. 따라서 관 씨는 코데로 씨가 운영하고 있는 엔리쿠아스를 방문한 것을 알 수 있으므로 (A)가 정답이다.

180 추론 / 암시

번역 관 씨가 후기에서 엔리쿠아스에 대해 암시한 것은?
(A) 점심 메뉴가 한정되어 있다.
(B) 저녁 예약이 필요하다.
(C) 현지 제과점의 빵을 제공한다.
(D) 홍콩에 지점이 있다.

해설 후기의 두 번째 문장에서 관 씨가 엔리쿠아스에 대해 그곳은 보통 저녁 식사 예약이 꽉 차서 테이블을 예약하려면 몇 달 전에 전화를 해야 할 수도 있다(It is usually fully booked for dinner; you may need to call months in advance for a table)고 한 것으로 보아 엔리쿠아스는 저녁 식사 예약이 필요한 곳임을 알 수 있다. 따라서 (B)가 정답이다.

어휘 serve (음식을) 제공하다

Paraphrasing 지문의 call months in advance for a table
→ 정답의 takes dinner reservations

181-185 이메일 + 티켓

수신: laura.3avard@orbitmail.scot
발신: cboyle@ceoleire.co.uk
날짜: 5월 25일
제목: 회신: 제안

사바드 씨께,

181, 183, 184 온라인 주문품을 제 매장에서 찾아가시거나 항공 또는 열차 운송비를 추가로 지불하시겠다는 친절한 제안에 감사드립니다. 181, 182, 184 스트란래어에 계신 고객님께 제가 직접 물건을 배달하게 되어 기쁘게 생각하며, 따라서 그 어느 것도 준비하실 필요가 없습니다. 182 마침 저의 여동생과 그녀의 아이들이 근처 커크콤에 살고 있습니다. 그들을 보러 가기 전에 제가 고객님 댁으로 렌터카를 몰고 가서 제품을 손수 배달해 드리겠습니다.

아시다시피, 제 상품은 100퍼센트 수제작된 것입니다. 운송 중에 손상이 발생할 경우, 수리하는 데 비용이 많이 들고 시간이 걸립니다. 183 지난 몇 년간, 부주의한 수하물 취급자에 의해 손상되는 것을 너무 많이 보아

왔습니다. 저의 방침은 가능할 때마다 물건을 직접 배달하거나 제가 신뢰하는 육상 또는 해상 택배 서비스를 이용하는 것입니다.

6월 5일에 만나 뵙기를 기대합니다. 오후 5시까지는 고객님 댁에 도착할 것으로 예상합니다.

코너 보일
시올레 클래식스

어휘 transport 운송 arrangement 준비 merchandise 상품 handcrafted 수제작된 occur 발생하다 transit 운송 time-consuming 시간이 걸리는 ordeal (힘들거나 불쾌한) 일 inattentive 부주의한 baggage 수하물 feasible 실현 가능한 courier 택배 회사 no later than 늦어도 ∼까지

---

185 **북아일랜드 페리 서비스**

발행일: 5월 26일
184, 185 **승객 이름: 코너 보일**

벨파스트 출항: 6월 5일 금요일 오후 1시 5분
185 **케언리안 입항: 6월 5일 금요일 오후 3시 20분**

수하물: 여행 가방 1개(소형), 184 **악기 케이스 2개(만돌린 1개, 기타 1개)**
차량 운송: 없음

성인 일반석: 55파운드

출발 30분 전에 도착해 주십시오.

어휘 ferry 페리, 여객선 issuance 발행 passenger 승객 dock (배를) 부두에 대다 instrument 악기

181 주제 / 목적

번역 이메일의 목적은?
(A) 계획을 마무리하기 위해서
(B) 초대를 수락하기 위해서
(C) 새로운 서비스를 홍보하기 위해서
(D) 정책에 대한 의견을 요청하기 위해서

해설 이메일의 첫 문장에서 온라인 주문품을 매장에서 찾아가거나 항공 또는 열차 운송비를 추가로 지불하겠다는 친절한 제안에 감사하다(Thank you for your kind offer ∼ for air or train transport)고 했고, 스트란래어에 있는 고객에게 직접 물건을 배달하게 되어 기쁘게 생각하며, 따라서 그 어느 것도 준비할 필요가 없다(Neither arrangement is necessary ∼ in Stranraer myself)고 했다. 따라서 주문품의 배송 방식에 대한 계획을 마무리하려고 이메일을 쓴 것이므로 (A)가 정답이다.

어휘 finalize 마무리 짓다 accept 수락하다

182 세부사항 ▶ 동영상 강의

번역 보일 씨가 스트란래어에서 커크콤까지 여행하는 이유는?
(A) 배달을 하기 위해서
(B) 회의에 참석하기 위해서
(C) 렌터카를 반납하기 위해서
(D) 가족을 방문하기 위해서

해설 이메일의 두 번째 문장에서 보일 씨가 스트란래어에 있는 고객에게 직접 물건을 배달하게 되어 기쁘다(I am happy to deliver your items to you in Stranraer myself)고 했고, 세 번째 문장에서 마침 여동생과 그녀의 아이들이 근처 커크콤에 살고 있다(It so happens that my sister and her children live nearby in Kirkcolm)며, 그들을 보러 가기 전에 고객의 집으로 렌터카를 몰고 가서 제품을 손수 배달하겠다(Before seeing them ~ deliver the items to you)고 했다. 따라서 보일 씨는 커크콤에 여동생 가족을 만나러 가는 것이므로 (D)가 정답이다.

어휘 drop off ~을 가져다 놓다, 내려놓다

Paraphrasing 지문의 my sister and her children
→ 정답의 family members

183 추론 / 암시

번역 이메일에 암시된 것은?
(A) 보일 씨의 여동생은 시올레 클래식스의 공동 설립자이다.
(B) 보일 씨는 항공 및 열차 화물 회사에 실망했다.
(C) 사바드 씨는 과거에 보일 씨로부터 물건을 구매한 적이 있다.
(D) 사바드 씨는 특정 브랜드의 여행 가방을 선호한다.

해설 이메일의 첫 번째 단락 첫 문장에서 보일 씨가 사바드 씨에게 온라인 주문품을 매장에서 찾아가거나 항공 또는 열차 운송비를 추가로 지불하겠다는 친절한 제안에 감사하다(Thank you for your kind offer ~ for air or train transport)고 했고, 두 번째 단락 세 번째 문장에서 보일 씨가 지난 몇 년간 부주의한 수하물 취급자에 의해 손상되는 것을 너무 많이 보아 왔다(Over the years, I've seen too much damage done by inattentive baggage handlers)고 하며, 보일 씨의 방침은 가능할 때마다 물건을 직접 배달하거나 신뢰하는 육상 또는 해상 택배 서비스를 이용하는 것(My policy is to deliver items ~ hire a ground- or sea-based courier service I trust)이라고 한 것으로 보아 보일 씨는 항공 및 열차 화물 회사의 제품 운송 서비스에 실망했기 때문에 사바드 씨가 제안한 항공 또는 열차 운송을 거절하고 직접 배송하는 방법을 택했음을 알 수 있다. 따라서 (B)가 정답이다.

어휘 cofounder 공동 설립자 freight 화물 specific 특정한

184 연계

번역 사바드 씨에 대해 사실일 것 같은 것은?
(A) 일 때문에 자주 출장을 다닌다.
(B) 물건이 직접 배달되도록 추가 비용을 지불했다.
(C) 최근에 악기를 구입했다.
(D) 렌터카 사무실에서 보일 씨를 만날 예정이다.

해설 이메일의 첫 문장에서 보일 씨가 사바드 씨에게 온라인 주문품을 매장에서 찾아가거나 항공 또는 열차 운송비를 추가로 지불하겠다는 친절한 제안에 감사하다(Thank you for your kind offer ~ for air or train transport)며 스트란래어에 있는 고객에게 직접 물건을 배달하게 되어 기쁘다(I am happy to deliver your items to you in Stranraer myself)고 했고, 티켓의 승객 이름이 코너 보일(Passenger Name: Conor Boyle)이고 수하물 목록에 악기 케이스 2개(만돌린 1개, 기타 1개)(2 instrument cases (1 mandolin, 1 guitar))가 포함되어 있다. 따라서 사바드 씨가 보일 씨로부터 구입

해서 보일 씨가 직접 배송을 하게 된 물건은 악기 2개임을 알 수 있으므로 (C)가 정답이다.

185 세부사항

번역 보일 씨는 6월 5일에 케언리안으로 어떻게 갈 것인가?
(A) 차로
(B) 기차로
(C) 배로
(D) 비행기로

해설 티켓의 상단에 북아일랜드 페리 서비스(Northern Ireland Ferry Service)라고 적혀 있고, 두 번째 줄에 승객 이름이 코너 보일(Passenger Name: Conor Boyle)이며 네 번째 줄에 케언리안 입항 일정이 6월 5일 금요일 오후 3시 20분(Docking at Cairnryan: Friday, 5 June, 3:20 PM)이라고 나와 있다. 따라서 보일 씨는 6월 5일 케언리안에 배를 타고 갈 예정임을 알 수 있으므로 (C)가 정답이다.

186-190 광고 + 온라인 포럼 게시글 + 개요

트레인 투 어치브 (TTA) - 저희 수업으로 성공을 준비하세요!

〈비즈니스 디렉션스 나이지리아〉 소식지 최신호에 소개된 트레인 투 어치브 (TTA)는 서아프리카에서 가장 혁신적인 교육 제공 업체 중 하나입니다. 수업을 전적으로 온라인 형식으로 제공함으로써, 교실을 여러분의 가정으로 가져옵니다. 186 모든 수업에는 개별화된 지도가 포함되며 각자의 분야에서 인정받는 전문가들이 가르칩니다. 187 성공적으로 수업을 완료하면, 이력서에 가치 있는 추가 요소인 공인 교육 수료증을 받게 됩니다. 전체적인 수료비 및 시간표 목록을 보시려면, 저희 웹사이트 www.traintoachieve.org.ng를 방문하세요. 다음은 가장 인기 있는 수업 중 일부입니다.

189 소셜 미디어 마케팅 입문 (TTA1504): 마케팅 컨설턴트 마커스 아크판이 가르치는 이 수업은 사업을 온라인으로 홍보하는 노하우를 제공합니다.

성공적인 프리랜서 작가 되기 (TTA3283): 비즈니스 작가 브렌다 아칸데가 글쓰기 기술을 연마하고 작문 서비스를 판매하는 방법에 대한 전문적인 지도를 제공합니다.

인터넷 라디오 방송국 시작하기 (TTA7629): 온라인 라디오 진행자 나탈리 카비루가 목표 시장의 관심을 끄는 방법을 알려주고 방송 서비스를 시작하는 데 실용적인 팁을 드립니다.

그래픽 디자인 기초 (TTA7633): 베테랑 그래픽 디자이너 더그 우마루가 그래픽 디자인 사업을 시작하는 데 필요한 기본적인 기술을 습득할 수 있도록 도와줍니다.

어휘 profile 소개하다, 프로필을 알려주다 latest 최신의 innovative 혁신적인 entirely 전적으로 individualized 개별화된 instruction 지도, 교육 recognized 인정받는 respective 각자의 field 분야 completion 완료 official 공인된 certificate 수료증, 자격증 valuable 가치 있는 addition 추가 equip 갖추게 하다 promote 홍보하다 expert 전문적인 guidance 안내, 지도 hone 연마하다 host 진행자 appeal 관심을 끌다 practical 실용적인 broadcast 방송 veteran 베테랑 acquire 습득하다

¹⁸⁹**트레인 투 어치브 TTA1504 수업 등록 학생들을 위한 토론 포럼**

게시일: 5월 21일 오전 9시 41분   **게시자:** 조셉 에그베   **주제:** 프레젠테이션

¹⁸⁸이 수업에 등록된 학생들의 명단을 보면서 1월 포스터 디자인 수업을 위한 포럼에서 여러분 중 몇 명과 이야기했던 기억이 났습니다. 이번 수업에서도 우리가 배운 경험을 다시 공유할 수 있기를 기대합니다. ¹⁸⁹어제 저는 제 사업에 대한 개인 화상 회의를 위해 아크판 씨를 만난 두 번째 학생이었습니다. ¹⁹⁰저는 제과류를 판매하는 푸드 트럭을 가지고 있는데, 아크판 씨에게 저의 웹사이트 개요를 공유했을 때 그가 저의 모든 제과 제품의 생생한 이미지가 담긴 섹션을 추가할 것을 제안했습니다. 그 조언은 도움이 되었습니다.

어휘 enroll 등록하다 individual 개인의 outline 개요 vivid 생생한

에그베스 베이커리 - 먹을 때마다 느껴지는 특별한 구운 맛!

- **섹션 1:** 메뉴 및 가격표 탐색하기
- ¹⁹⁰**섹션 2:** 맛있는 간식 사진 둘러보기
- **섹션 3:** 출장 요리 서비스에 대해 알아보기
- **섹션 4:** 재료 목록 살펴보기

어휘 flavour 맛 bite 한 입 explore 탐색하다 browse 둘러보다 treat 간식 catering 출장 요리 ingredient 재료

186 Not / True

번역 TTA에 대해 명시된 것은?
(A) 그래픽 디자이너에 의해 설립되었다.
(B) 자체 온라인 소식지를 발행한다.
(C) 업계 전문가가 이끄는 수업을 제공한다.
(D) 서아프리카 전역의 도시에 교실 시설을 가지고 있다.

해설 광고의 첫 단락 세 번째 문장에서 모든 수업에는 개별화된 지도가 포함되며 각자의 분야에서 인정받는 전문가들이 가르친다(All classes ~ are taught by recognized professionals in their respective fields)고 했으므로 (C)가 정답이다.

어휘 found 설립하다 facility 시설

187 세부사항

번역 광고에 따르면, TTA가 수업을 마친 학생들에게 제공하는 것은?
(A) 이력서 작성 워크숍
(B) 후속 수업 할인
(C) 현재 채용 공고 목록
(D) 인증서

해설 광고의 첫 단락 네 번째 문장에서 성공적으로 수업을 완료하면 이력서에 가치 있는 추가 요소인 공인 교육 수료증을 받게 된다(Upon successful completion of a class, you will receive an official Certificate of Training, a valuable addition to any résumé)고 했으므로 (D)가 정답이다.

어휘 follow-up 후속편 job posting 채용 공고 certification 증명

Paraphrasing 지문의 an official Certificate of Training
→ 정답의 A certification document

188 추론 / 암시

번역 에그베 씨에 대해 사실일 것 같은 것은?
(A) 토론 포럼 설계를 도왔다.
(B) 이전에 TTA 수업을 들은 적이 있다.
(C) 화상 회의 소프트웨어를 개발한다.
(D) 최근에 베이커리 푸드 트럭을 팔았다.

해설 온라인 포럼 게시글의 첫 문장에서 에그베 씨가 이 수업에 등록된 학생들의 명단을 보면서 1월 포스터 디자인 수업을 위한 포럼에서 여러분 중 몇 명과 이야기했던 기억이 났다(Viewing the list of students ~ I remembered chatting with some of you on the forum for January's poster design class)며, 이번 수업에서도 우리가 배운 경험을 다시 공유할 수 있기를 기대한다(I look forward to sharing our learning experiences again for this class)고 한 것으로 보아 에그베 씨는 전에도 TTA 수업을 들은 경험이 있다는 것을 알 수 있다. 따라서 (B)가 정답이다.

어휘 previously 이전에

189 연계

번역 에그베 씨가 등록한 TTA 수업은?
(A) 소셜 미디어 마케팅 입문
(B) 성공적인 프리랜서 작가 되기
(C) 인터넷 라디오 방송국 시작하기
(D) 그래픽 디자인 기초

해설 온라인 포럼 게시글의 제목에서 트레인 투 어치브 TTA1504 수업에 등록된 학생들을 위한 토론 포럼(Discussion forum for students enrolled in Train to Achieve Class TTA1504)이라고 했고, 세 번째 문장에서 에그베 씨가 자신은 어제 사업에 대한 개인 화상 회의를 위해 아크판 씨를 만난 두 번째 학생이었다(Yesterday I was the second student to meet with Mr. Akpan ~ about my business)고 했다. 광고의 수업 목록을 보면 마케팅 컨설턴트 마커스 아크판이 가르치는 TTA1504 수업은 소셜 미디어 마케팅 입문(Introduction to Social Media Marketing(TTA1504): Taught by marketing consultant Marcus Akpan)이므로 (A)가 정답이다.

190 연계

번역 에그베 씨가 아크판 씨와 이야기한 후 개요에 추가했을 것 같은 섹션은?
(A) 섹션 1
(B) 섹션 2
(C) 섹션 3
(D) 섹션 4

해설 온라인 포럼 게시글의 네 번째 문장에서 에그베 씨가 제과류를 판매하는 푸드 트럭을 가지고 있는데 아크판 씨에게 웹사이트에 대한 개요를 공유했을 때 그가 모든 제과 제품의 생생한 이미지가 담긴 섹션을 추가하라고 제안했다(I own a food truck from which I sell ~

he suggested that I add a section with vivid images of all my baked goods)고 했고, 개요의 섹션 2에 맛있는 간식 사진 둘러보기(Section 2: Browse photos of our delicious treats)가 나와 있다. 따라서 에그베 씨는 제과 제품 이미지가 담긴 섹션을 추가하라는 아크판 씨의 제안을 듣고 섹션 2를 추가했음을 알 수 있으므로 (B)가 정답이다.

191-195 기사 + 후기 + 이메일

카리브해의 풍부한 맛
레베카 로츠 작성

노팅엄 (8월 1일) — ¹⁹¹ **오렌지 베이 키친은 현재 6개월째 느긋한 카리브해 분위기에서 자메이카의 맛을 불어넣고 있다.** 케론 데슬란데스가 운영하는 150석 규모의 이 레스토랑은 웨스터 스퀘어의 북적이는 상점과 음식점들 사이에 자리한 향기로운 보석이다. 종업원들은 식사 손님들이 염소 카레, 소꼬리 수프, 홍돔을 포함한 폭넓은 메뉴의 다양한 즐거움 속에서 선택할 수 있도록 항상 친절하게 도와준다. ¹⁹² **이 레스토랑은 저크 치킨으로 가장 유명하다.** 굽기 전에 24시간 동안 양념에 재우고 조린 양배추와 코코넛 라이스를 곁들인 이 요리는 12파운드라는 좋은 가격에 제공된다.

¹⁹³ **만약 금요일 밤 7시에서 11시 사이에 들른다면 라이브 레게 음악을 즐길 수 있다.**

어휘 flavour 맛 abound 풍부하다 infusion 주입
laid-back 느긋한 atmosphere 분위기 aromatic 향기로운
jewel 보석 amid ~ 사이에서 bustling 북적거리는 eatery
식당 diner 식사 손님 delight 즐거움 extensive 폭넓은
curried 카레를 넣은 oxtail 소꼬리 red snapper 홍돔 jerk
저크(양념에 절여 두었다 장작불에 구운 고기) marinate 양념장에
재우다 stewed 불에 오래 끓인 deal 거래

---

https://www.dinerreviews.co.uk/orangebaykitchen

8월 22일에 타미카 피터킨이 게시함, tpeterkin@sunmail.co.uk

오렌지 베이 키친: 별 2/5개

레베카 로츠가 작성한 오렌지 베이 키친에 대해 극찬하는 기사를 읽은 후, 저는 그곳을 꼭 가보고 싶었습니다. ¹⁹³ **남편과 저는 저녁 식사와 함께 라이브 음악을 즐기고 싶어서 어제저녁 7시에 그곳에 도착했습니다.** 안타깝게도 그날 밤 밴드 공연은 취소되었습니다. 단념하지 않고 우리는 남아서 둘 다 저크 치킨을 주문했습니다. 치킨의 훈제된 맛은 뛰어났지만 조린 양배추는 맛이 없었습니다. 또한 1인분 양이 예상했던 것보다 적어서 배고픈 채로 집에 가지 않기 위해 애피타이저를 하나 더 주문했습니다. ¹⁹⁵ **수석 주방장이 나와서 사과했고 매우 친절했지만 우리는 아마 당분간 다시 가지는 않을 것입니다.**

어휘 glowing 극찬하는 be eager[keen] to ~하고 싶어 하다
undeterred 단념하지 않은 smoky 훈제한 맛이 나는
outstanding 뛰어난 portion 1인분 anticipate 예상하다

수신: tpeterkin@sunmail.co.uk
발신: vsmith@orangebaykitchen.co.uk
날짜: 8월 24일
제목: 귀하의 후기
첨부: @0258

피터킨 씨께,

오렌지 베이 키친을 방문한 후기를 남겨 주셔서 감사합니다. ¹⁹⁴ **저희 매니저인 케론 데슬란데스가 귀하의 방문과 그날 저녁 귀하의 기대에 부응하지 못한 일에 대해 자세히 알려주었습니다.** 첨부된 20파운드 상품권을 받아주시고 다시 한번 저희를 찾아주시기 바랍니다.

귀하께서 방문한 동안 저희 밴드는 장비가 고장 나서 막판에 취소를 하게 되었습니다. 하지만 이 밴드는 9월부터 다시 매주 공연을 할 예정입니다. 또한, ¹⁹⁵ **아디오 브라운 수석 주방장이 조린 양배추에 사용하는 향신료를 바꿨다는 점도 알아주셨으면 합니다.** 귀하께서 그것들을 마음에 들어 하시리라 확신합니다.

비 스미스, 사장
오렌지 베이 키친

어휘 live up to (기대 등에) 부응하다 expectation 기대
accept 받아 주다 gift certificate 상품권 malfunction 고장
last-minute 마지막 순간의 cancellation 취소 spice 향신료
delightful 마음에 드는

---

191 Not / True

번역 기사에서 오렌지 베이 키친에 대해 언급하는 것은?
(A) 현재 웨이터를 채용 중이다.
(B) 조용한 거리에 위치해 있다.
(C) 자메이카에 지점이 하나 더 있다.
(D) 6개월 전에 문을 열었다.

해설 기사의 첫 문장에서 오렌지 베이 키친은 현재 6개월째 느긋한 카리브해 분위기 속에서 자메이카의 맛을 불어넣고 있다(Orange Bay Kitchen has been ~ for six months now)고 했으므로 식당이 6개월 전에 영업을 시작했다는 것을 알 수 있다. 따라서 (D)가 정답이다. 두 번째 문장에서 케론 데슬란데스가 운영하는 150석 규모의 이 레스토랑은 웨스터 스퀘어의 북적이는 상점과 음식점들 사이에 자리한 향기로운 보석(Managed by Keron ~ amid the bustling shops and eateries in Wester Square)이라고 했으므로 (B)는 오답이고, (A)와 (C)에 대한 언급은 없으므로 답이 될 수 없다.

192 세부사항

번역 기사에 따르면, 오렌지 베이 키친에서 가장 인기 있는 메뉴는?
(A) 홍돔
(B) 소꼬리 수프
(C) 저크 치킨
(D) 염소 카레

해설 기사의 네 번째 문장에서 이 레스토랑은 저크 치킨으로 가장 유명하다 (The restaurant is most famous for its jerk chicken)고 했으므로 (C)가 정답이다.

193 연계

번역 피터킨 씨의 오렌지 베이 키친 방문에 대해 암시된 것은?
(A) 금요일에 그곳에 있었다.
(B) 혼자 식사를 했다.
(C) 밥을 추가로 요청했다.
(D) 디저트를 주문했다.

해설 후기의 두 번째 문장에서 남편과 피터킨 씨는 저녁 식사와 함께 라이브 음악을 즐기고 싶어서 어제저녁 7시에 그곳에 도착했다(My husband and I arrived there at 7 P.M. yesterday ~ live music with our dinner)고 했고, 기사의 마지막 문장에서 만약 금요일 밤 7시에서 11시 사이에 들른다면 라이브 레게 음악을 즐길 수 있다(If you stop in on any Friday night between 7 and 11 P.M., you will enjoy live reggae music)고 했다. 따라서 피터킨 씨는 공연이 있는 금요일 저녁에 오렌지 베이 키친을 방문했다는 것을 알 수 있으므로 (A)가 정답이다.

194 주제 / 목적

번역 이메일의 목적은?
(A) 질문에 답변하기 위해서
(B) 사과하기 위해서
(C) 의견을 요청하기 위해서
(D) 예약을 확인하기 위해서

해설 이메일의 두 번째 문장에서 매니저 케론 데슬란데스가 귀하의 방문과 그날 저녁 귀하의 기대에 부응하지 못한 일에 대해 자세히 알려주었다(Our manager ~ our failure to live up to your expectations that evening)면서, 첨부된 20파운드 상품권을 받고 다시 한번 찾아 주기 바란다(Please accept ~ give us another try)고 했으므로 실망한 손님에게 사과하기 위해 이메일을 쓴 것임을 알 수 있다. 따라서 (B)가 정답이다.

어휘 apology 사과

195 연계

번역 피터킨 씨가 오렌지 베이 키친에서 만난 사람은?
(A) 로츠 씨
(B) 데슬란데스 씨
(C) 브라운 씨
(D) 스미스 씨

해설 후기의 마지막 문장에서 피터킨 씨가 수석 주방장이 나와서 사과를 했고 매우 친절했다(The head chef came out ~ was extremely nice)고 했고, 이메일의 두 번째 단락 세 번째 문장에서 아디오 브라운 수석 주방장(Head Chef Adio Brown)이라고 했다. 따라서 피터킨 씨는 오렌지 베이 키친에서 수석 주방장인 브라운 씨를 만난 것이므로 (C)가 정답이다.

196-200 청구서 + 공지 + 이메일

오비스 유통

고객: 그린 캐년   197 날짜: 6월 10일
계정: 4352-0

품목	가격
196 정원용 흙, 33세제곱미터	1,170달러
196 분쇄 자갈, 30미터톤	1,710달러
196 장식용 돌, 20미터톤	1,140달러
포장용 돌 70개, 0.6x0.6미터	630달러
197 소계	4,650달러
197 할인 (10퍼센트)	465달러
배송비	350달러
총계	4,535달러

귀하의 청구서 발행에 대한 중요한 변경사항을 요약한 공지를 동봉하오니 참고하십시오.

어휘 distributor 유통업체 cubic meter 세제곱미터 crushed 분쇄된 gravel 자갈 metric ton 미터톤 decorative 장식용의 paving 포장재 subtotal 소계 enclosed 동봉된 outline 요약 설명하다 billing 청구서 발행

오비스 유통

소중한 고객님께:
198, 199 당사의 현 청구서 발행 시스템은 오비스 유통이 20년 전 설립된 이래로 사용되어 왔습니다. 198 매우 필요한 업그레이드로서 저희는 전자 청구서 발행으로 전환할 예정입니다. 8월 1일부터 청구서는 매월 자동으로 생성되어 귀사의 계정과 연계된 이메일 주소로 전송됩니다.

당사의 장기 우대책은 그대로 유지되므로 안심하십시오:

- 197 4,000달러 이상 주문 시 10퍼센트 할인
- 자선단체 20퍼센트 할인
- 당사 공급 센터에서 5마일 이내의 장소로는 무료 배송
- 단골 구매자 클럽 회원을 위한 무료 샘플

전자 청구서 발행 전환에 대한 자세한 정보는 당사 웹사이트에서 확인하실 수 있습니다. 고객님의 지원에 감사드립니다. 오비스 유통은 귀사의 거래에 감사드립니다.

어휘 valued 소중한 invoicing 청구서 발행 found 설립하다 switch 전환하다, 바꾸다 invoice 청구서 generate 만들어 내다 automatically 자동으로 be associated with ~와 관련되다 rest assured that 안심하다 long-standing 오래 지속되는 incentive 우대책 in place 제자리에 charitable 자선의 organization 단체 supply 공급 frequent 빈번한 transition 전환

수신: 메리 피터슨, 청구 부서
발신: 탄비르 싱, 계정 관리자
날짜: 9월 12일
제목: 계정 1012-4

안녕하세요 메리,

오늘 테소리에로 리모델링의 윌리엄 테소리에로로부터 문의를 받았습니다. 그의 8월 월간 청구서가 도착하지 않았습니다.

아시다시피, 199 테소리에로 씨는 우리의 첫 고객 중 한 명이었습니다. 우리가 처음 사업을 시작한 이래로, 그는 정기적으로 우리에게서 구매를 해왔습니다. 그는 또한 단골 구매자 클럽 회원이기도 합니다. 이 고객은 우리가 절대 잃고 싶지 않은 고객입니다. 저는 그에게 당사의 전자 청구서 발행 시스템 도입이 기대했던 것처럼 원활하게 진행되지 않았다고 설명했고, 다시는 이런 일이 일어나지 않을 것이라고 약속했습니다.

200 지체 없이 이 문제를 조사해서 8월 청구서를 테소리에로 씨에게 보내 주시면 감사하겠습니다.

탄비르

어휘 query 문의 on a regular basis 정기적으로 rollout 도입, 출시 smoothly 순조롭게 investigate 조사하다

196 추론 / 암시

번역 청구서에서 그린 캐년에 대해 암시하는 것은?
(A) 조경 프로젝트를 한다.
(B) 고속도로를 설계한다.
(C) 낡은 집을 수리한다.
(D) 농장을 운영한다.

해설 청구서의 품목에 정원용 흙(Garden soil), 분쇄 자갈(Crushed gravel), 장식용 돌(Decorative stone) 등이 나열된 것으로 보아 그린 캐년은 정원을 조성하는 데 필요한 물품을 구입했음을 알 수 있다. 따라서 (A)가 정답이다.

어휘 landscaping 조경 highway 고속도로

197 연계

번역 그린 캐년이 6월 10일 자 주문에서 할인받은 이유일 것 같은 것은?
(A) 자선 단체이다.
(B) 단골 구매자 클럽에 속해 있다.
(C) 상품에 4,000달러 이상을 썼다.
(D) 오비스 유통 공급 센터 근처에 있다.

해설 공지의 우대책 항목 중 첫 번째에 4,000달러 이상 주문 시 10퍼센트 할인(A 10% discount for orders of more than $4,000)이라고 나와 있고, 청구서의 날짜가 6월 10일(Date: June 10)이고, 소계는 4,650달러(Subtotal 4,650.00), 할인(10퍼센트) 금액이 465달러(Discount (10%) 465.00)라고 나와 있다. 따라서 그린 캐년이 6월 10일 자 주문에서 할인을 받은 이유는 주문 금액이 4,0000달러를 넘었기 때문임을 알 수 있으므로 (C)가 정답이다.

어휘 belong to ~에 속하다

198 세부사항

번역 공지에 따르면, 오비스 유통에 생긴 변화는?
(A) 이메일 주소
(B) 우대책 목록
(C) 청구서 발행 시스템
(D) 배송 일정

해설 공지의 첫 문장에서 당사의 현 청구서 발행 시스템은 오비스 유통이 20년 전 설립된 이래로 사용되어 왔다(Our current invoicing system~ founded over twenty years ago)며, 매우 필요한 업그레이드로서 전자 청구서 발행으로 전환할 예정(As a much-needed upgrade, we are switching to electronic invoicing)이라고 했다. 따라서 청구서 발행 시스템에 변화가 생기는 것임을 알 수 있으므로 (C)가 정답이다.

199 연계

번역 테소리에로 씨에 대해 암시된 것은?
(A) 싱 씨를 만나자고 요청했다.
(B) 오비스 유통의 고용에 관심이 있다.
(C) 최근에 몇몇 건설 기계를 주문했다.
(D) 약 20년간 오비스 유통의 고객이었다.

해설 이메일의 두 번째 단락 첫 문장에서 테소리에로 씨는 우리의 첫 고객 중 한 명이었다(Mr. Tesoriero was one of our very first customers)며 처음 사업을 시작한 이래로 그는 정기적으로 우리에게서 구매를 해왔다(Since we first opened ~ from us on a regular basis)고 했고, 공지의 첫 문장에서 당사의 현 청구서 발행 시스템은 오비스 유통이 20년 전 설립된 이래로 사용되어 왔다(Our current invoicing ~ founded over twenty years ago)고 했다. 따라서 테소리에로 씨는 오비스 유통이 사업을 시작한 20년 전부터 고객이었던 것이므로 (D)가 정답이다.

어휘 employment 고용 construction 건설 machinery 기계(류)

200 세부사항

번역 싱 씨가 피터슨 씨에게 요청하는 것은?
(A) 청구서 지불
(B) 문제 해결
(C) 주문 확인
(D) 계정 번호 업데이트

해설 이메일의 마지막 문장에서 싱 씨는 피터슨 씨에게 지체 없이 이 문제를 조사해서 8월 청구서를 테소리에로 씨에게 보내 주면 감사하겠다(I would appreciate it if you could please investigate the problem without delay and send the invoice for August to Mr. Tesoriero)고 했으므로 청구서 관련 문제를 즉시 해결할 것을 요청하고 있음을 알 수 있다. 따라서 (B)가 정답이다.

기출 TEST 2 동영상 강의

101 (C)	**102** (C)	**103** (A)	**104** (B)	**105** (D)
106 (A)	**107** (C)	**108** (D)	**109** (C)	**110** (D)
111 (A)	**112** (D)	**113** (C)	**114** (A)	**115** (C)
116 (A)	**117** (A)	**118** (B)	**119** (B)	**120** (D)
121 (C)	**122** (A)	**123** (A)	**124** (C)	**125** (B)
126 (B)	**127** (D)	**128** (D)	**129** (B)	**130** (B)
131 (C)	**132** (A)	**133** (D)	**134** (A)	**135** (D)
136 (C)	**137** (C)	**138** (A)	**139** (B)	**140** (C)
141 (A)	**142** (C)	**143** (C)	**144** (D)	**145** (B)
146 (A)	**147** (A)	**148** (B)	**149** (A)	**150** (D)
151 (A)	**152** (C)	**153** (A)	**154** (D)	**155** (D)
156 (C)	**157** (B)	**158** (D)	**159** (D)	**160** (B)
161 (C)	**162** (D)	**163** (D)	**164** (D)	**165** (B)
166 (A)	**167** (C)	**168** (B)	**169** (D)	**170** (B)
171 (D)	**172** (A)	**173** (C)	**174** (A)	**175** (D)
176 (B)	**177** (B)	**178** (D)	**179** (D)	**180** (B)
181 (A)	**182** (D)	**183** (C)	**184** (B)	**185** (B)
186 (C)	**187** (D)	**188** (A)	**189** (B)	**190** (D)
191 (B)	**192** (C)	**193** (A)	**194** (D)	**195** (B)
196 (D)	**197** (A)	**198** (B)	**199** (C)	**200** (B)

PART 5

101 동사 어휘

해설 빈칸은 주어가 없는 명령문에서 the enclosed cable을 목적어로 취하는 타동사 자리로, 그것(=your handheld device)을 충전하기 위해 '동봉된 케이블을 사용하라'는 내용이 되어야 하므로 '사용하다'라는 의미의 동사 (C) use가 정답이다. (A) plan은 '계획하다', (D) finish는 '끝내다'라는 의미로 문맥상 어울리지 않고, (B) remain은 '~인 채로 있다'라는 의미의 자동사로 목적어를 취하지 않는다.

번역 휴대용 장치를 작동하기 전에 동봉된 케이블을 사용하여 충전하십시오.

어휘 handheld 손에 들고 쓰는 enclosed 동봉된 charge 충전하다

102 부사 자리 _ 동사 수식 ▶ 동영상 강의

해설 조동사 can과 동사원형 store 사이에서 동사를 수식하는 부사 자리이므로, '안전하게'라는 의미의 부사 (C) securely가 정답이다. (A) secure는 형용사/동사, (B) security는 명사, (D) secured는 과거분사이므로 품사상 빈칸에 들어갈 수 없다.

번역 사파일의 새로운 외장 하드 드라이브는 최대 1테라바이트의 데이터를 안전하게 저장할 수 있다.

어휘 external 외부의 store 저장하다

103 전치사 어휘

해설 빈칸 앞에 이동을 의미하는 동사 travel이, 뒤에 장소를 나타내는 명사 the Tokyo office가 있다. '도쿄 사무소로 출장을 간다'는 내용이 되어야 적절하므로, 이동 방향을 나타내어 '~로[에]를 뜻하는 전치사 (A) to가 정답이다.

번역 피터슨 씨는 연례 회의를 위해 도쿄 사무소로 출장을 갈 예정이다.

어휘 annual 연례의

104 인칭대명사의 격 _ 주격

해설 빈칸은 접속사 until이 이끄는 부사절에서 동사 have left의 주어 역할을 하는 자리이므로, 주격 대명사인 (B) they가 정답이다. (A) them과 (C) themselves는 목적어 역할을 하고, (D) their는 소유격으로 뒤에 명사가 있어야 하므로 답이 되지 않는다.

번역 용수 화장품은 이월 주문품에 대해 상품이 창고에서 출고될 때까지 대금을 청구하지 않을 것입니다.

어휘 cosmetics 화장품 charge 청구하다 back order 이월 주문, (재고가 없어) 처리 못한 주문 warehouse 창고

105 전치사 어휘

해설 빈칸 뒤 명사구 the Aprico River와 함께 historic sites를 수식하는 적절한 전치사를 고르는 문제다. '아프리코 강변을 따라 있는 유적지'라는 문맥이므로 '~을 따라'라는 의미의 전치사 (D) along이 정답이다. (A) onto는 '~ (위)로', (B) since는 '~ 이후로', (C) inside는 '~ 안에'라는 의미로 문맥상 부적절하다.

번역 자사의 프리미엄 데이 투어는 방문객들을 아프리코 강변을 따라 있는 유적지로 안내합니다.

어휘 historic site 유적지

106 명사 자리 _ 전치사의 목적어

해설 빈칸은 수단을 나타내는 전치사 on의 목적어 자리이므로 명사가 들어가야 한다. 명사 보기인 (A) electricity(전기)와 (C) electricians(전기 기사) 중에서 자동차를 움직이게 하는 동력이 될 수 있는 단어가 필요하므로 (A) electricity가 정답이다. (B) electrically는 부사, (D) electrify는 동사로 빈칸에 들어갈 수 없다.

번역 설문에 응한 운전자의 80퍼센트가 전기로 움직이는 차량 구입을 고려하겠다고 말했다.

어휘 electrify 전기를 공급하다

107 동사 어휘 ▶ 동영상 강의

해설 Petrin Engineering을 목적어로 취하는 타동사 자리로, 빈칸 앞 조동사 has와 함께 '부사장으로 회사에 입사했다'는 내용이 되어야 자연스러우므로 동사 join(입사[가입]하다)의 과거분사형 (C) joined가 정답이다. (A)의 attach는 '첨부하다', (B)의 resign은 '(직·지위를) 사직하다', (D)의 combine은 '결합하다'라는 의미이다.

번역 신저 주는 페트린 엔지니어링에 운영 부사장으로 입사했다.

어휘 vice president 부사장   operation 운영, 사업

108 인칭대명사의 격 _ 소유격

해설 명사구 third author's hour를 한정 수식하는 자리이다. 앞에서
명사구를 수식할 수 있는 인칭대명사는 소유격이고, 문맥상 '그것
(=Barder House Books)의 세 번째 작가의 시간'이 적절하므로
(D) its가 정답이다. (C) its own에서 own은 소유격 뒤에서 소유 관
계를 강조하는 형용사이므로 문맥상 답이 되기에 부적절하다.

번역 다음 달에 바더 하우스 북스는 클리블랜드에서 세 번째 작가의 시간
을 주최할 예정이다.

어휘 author 작가

109 부사 어휘

해설 동사 expanded를 수식하여 '최근 두 번째 지점으로 확장했다'는 내
용이 되어야 자연스러우므로 '최근에'를 뜻하는 (C) recently가 정답
이다. (A) severely는 '혹독하게', (B) usually는 '보통', (D) exactly
는 '정확하게'의 의미이다.

번역 체스터스 타일스는 최근 터닝턴에 두 번째 지점으로 확장했다.

어휘 expand 확장하다

110 부사 자리 _ 동사 수식

해설 빈칸은 동사구 has increased를 수식하는 부사 자리이므로 '크게,
상당히'를 의미하는 (D) significantly가 정답이다. (A) significant는
형용사, (B) significance는 명사, (C) signifies는 동사이므로 품사
상 빈칸에 들어갈 수 없다.

번역 타브리노스는 넛 메들리 스낵팩의 아몬드 수를 크게 늘렸다.

111 접속사 자리 _ 부사절 접속사

해설 빈칸 뒤에 주어 she와 동사 travels를 갖춘 완전한 절이 왔으므로 부
사절 접속사가 들어가야 한다. 따라서 '어디에서나, 어디든지'를 뜻하
는 부사절 접속사 (A) Wherever가 정답이다. (B) In addition to
와 (D) In contrast to는 전치사로 뒤에 명사(구)가 나와야 하고, (C)
Either는 or와 함께 쓰이는 상관접속사로 답이 되지 않는다.

번역 저신다 플로레스는 여행하는 곳 어디에서나 현지 직물과 패턴 견본을
수집한다.

어휘 fabric 직물   in addition to ~에 더하여   in contrast to ~와는
대조적으로

112 명사 자리 _ 동사의 주어 / 수 일치   동영상 강의

해설 문장의 동사가 복수동사 go이므로, 빈칸에는 picture와 복합명사를
이루어 주어 역할을 하는 복수명사가 들어가야 한다. 따라서 정답은
'액자, 틀'을 뜻하는 복수명사인 (D) frames이다. (A) framer(액자
세공사)와 (B) framing(구성)은 단수명사, (C) framed는 동사/과거
분사이므로 답이 될 수 없다.

번역 글로잉 포토 랩의 사진 액자 대부분이 오늘 오후 3시에 할인 판매
된다.

113 형용사 어휘

해설 경영학 수업 학생들의 학위(college degrees) 수준을 나타내는 형용
사가 필요하다. 따라서 일반 학사보다 높은 석사 등의 고급 학위를
나타내도록 '고급의, 상급의'라는 뜻의 형용사 (C) advanced가 정답
이다. (A) late는 '늦은', (B) developed는 '발달한', (D) elated는 '의
기양양한'이라는 의미로 문맥상 어울리지 않는다.

번역 경영학 수업의 학생들은 모두 고급 대학 학위를 소지하고 있다.

어휘 advanced degree (학사 위의) 고급 학위, 석박사 학위

114 to부정사 / 능동태 vs. 수동태

해설 빈칸 앞에 완전한 절(We hired Noah Wan of Shengyao
Accounting Ltd.)이 있고 뒤에 명사구가 있으므로, 빈칸에는 뒤에 나
온 명사구 our company's financial assets를 목적어로 취하면서
앞에 나온 완전한 절을 수식할 수 있는 준동사가 들어가야 한다. 따라
서 능동형 to부정사 (A) to evaluate가 정답이다. 수동형 (B) to be
evaluated는 목적어를 취할 수 없고, (C) will be evaluated와 (D)
evaluate는 동사이므로 빈칸에 들어갈 수 없다.

번역 우리는 우리 회사의 금융 자산을 평가하기 위해 성야오 회계법인의
노아 완을 고용했다.

어휘 asset 자산   evaluate 평가하다

115 접속사 자리 _ 부사절 접속사

해설 빈칸은 두 개의 완전한 절을 이어주는 접속사 자리이다. 따라서 보기
중에 유일한 접속사로 '~한 뒤에'라는 의미를 나타내는 (C) after가
정답이다. (A) with와 (D) between은 전치사, (B) going은 현재분
사이므로 절을 연결할 수 없다.

번역 차리스 씨는 모리슨 프로젝트를 마무리한 뒤 새로운 고객을 맡을 예
정이다.

어휘 take on (일 등을) 맡다   account 고객, 거래처

116 형용사 자리 _ 주격 보어 / 비교급

해설 빈칸은 주어 Cormet Motors' profits를 보충 설명하는 주격 보어
자리이고, 뒤에 than과 함께 this year와 last year가 비교되고 있
으므로 비교급 형용사 (A) higher가 정답이다. (B) high는 원급 형용
사, (C) highly는 부사, (D) highest는 최상급 형용사이므로 빈칸에
들어갈 수 없다.

번역 올해 코멧 모터스의 수익은 작년보다 높다.

어휘 profit 수익, 이윤

117 형용사 어휘

해설 빈칸 뒤의 명사구 advertising campaign을 수식하기에 적절한 형용사를 고르는 문제이다. 빈칸 뒤 절에서 현재 시제로 광고 내용을 설명하고 있으므로 '현재 (진행 중인) 광고 캠페인에서'라는 의미가 되어야 가장 적절하므로, '현재의'라는 뜻의 형용사 (A) current가 정답이다. (B) relative는 '상대적인', (C) spacious는 '널찍한', (D) collected는 '수집된'이라는 의미이다.

번역 현재 광고 캠페인에서 제이머 툴스는 자사 제품이 얼마나 믿을 만한지를 보여 준다.

어휘 demonstrate 보여 주다, 시연하다 reliable 믿을 수 있는

118 접속사 자리 _ 부사절 접속사

해설 빈칸 앞에 동사 Remember와 목적어 to submit receipts for reimbursement를 갖춘 명령문 형태의 완전한 절이 있으므로, returning from a business trip은 분사구문 또는 동명사구로 볼 수 있다. 문맥상 '출장에서 돌아오면 영수증을 제출하라'는 내용이 적절하므로 분사구문을 이끄는 부사절 접속사 (B) when(~하면, ~할 때)이 정답이다. returning을 동명사로 볼 경우, 전치사도 빈칸에 들어갈 수 있지만 (A) such as(~와 같은)와 (D) within(~ 이내에)은 문맥상 적절하지 않다. 부사 (C) then(그리고 나서) 또한 분사 returning을 수식하기에 적절하지 않다.

번역 출장에서 돌아오면 환급을 위해 잊지 말고 영수증을 제출하십시오.

어휘 submit 제출하다 receipt 영수증 reimbursement 환급, 상환

119 부사 어휘

해설 빈칸 뒤 형용사 acquired를 수식하기에 적절한 부사를 고르는 문제이다. 앞으로 이용할 수 있게 될 도서관 장서에 관한 내용이므로 '새로 입수된 도서'라는 의미가 되어야 적절하다. 따라서 '새로, 최근에'라는 뜻의 (B) newly가 정답이다. (A) instantly는 '즉시', (C) early는 '일찍', (D) naturally는 '자연스럽게'라는 의미로 문맥상 적절하지 않다.

번역 이용객들은 화요일에 웨스트사이드 도서관에 새로 입수된 장서를 이용할 수 있을 것입니다.

어휘 patron 고객, 이용객 access 이용하다, 접근하다 acquired 입수된

120 동사 자리 _ 명령문의 동사원형

해설 주어가 생략된 채 Please로 시작하는 명령문에서 동사가 보이지 않으므로 빈칸은 동사 자리이다. 따라서 동사원형 (D) direct(보내다)가 정답이다. 과거형 (C) directed는 명령문의 동사로 쓰일 수 없다.

번역 근무 시간 기록표에 관한 모든 질문은 급여 지급 부서의 타비사 존스에게 보내 주십시오.

어휘 time sheet 근무 시간 기록표 payroll department 급여 지급 부서 directive 지시하는

121 명사 어휘

해설 동명사 signing의 목적어 역할을 하는 명사 자리로, 서명할(sign) 수 있는 대상인 동시에 빈칸 앞의 명사 delivery와 함께 자연스러운 복합명사를 만들 수 있어야 한다. '배송 영수증에 서명하기 전에 배송품을 다시 확인하라'는 내용이 적절하므로 '영수증'을 뜻하는 (C) receipt가 정답이다. (A) decision은 '결정', (B) announcement는 '발표, 고지', (D) limit는 '제한'의 의미이다.

번역 배송 영수증에 서명하기 전에, 주문한 모든 상품이 배송품에 포함되어 있는지 다시 확인해 주십시오.

어휘 shipment 수송(품)

122 과거분사   동영상 강의

해설 빈칸 앞에 완전한 절(Funds have been added ~ for expenses)이 있으므로 빈칸에는 전치사구 with the new building과 함께 명사 expenses를 수식하는 말이 들어가야 한다. 비용은 신축 건물과 관련된 것이므로, 전치사 with와 함께 쓰여 '~와 관련된'이라는 수동의 의미를 나타내는 과거분사 (A) associated가 정답이다. '협회, 제휴'를 뜻하는 명사 (B) association은 빈칸 앞의 expenses와 복합명사를 이루기에 적절하지 않고, 문장에 이미 동사 have been added가 있으므로 동사 (C) associate와 (D) associates도 답이 되지 않는다. 참고로, associate는 형용사(제휴한)와 명사(동료)로도 쓰인다.

번역 신축 건물과 관련된 비용을 위해 자금이 예산에 추가되었다.

어휘 fund 자금 budget 예산 expense 비용

123 동사 어휘

해설 빈칸 뒤 that절을 목적어로 취하는 동사 자리로, '마감일이 다가오고 있다는 것을 알았다'는 의미가 되어야 뒤에 이어지는 '그래서 도움을 요청했다'는 내용과 자연스럽게 연결된다. 따라서 동사 notice(알아차리다, 인지하다)의 과거형 (A) noticed가 정답이다. (B)의 obscure는 '모호하게 하다', (C)의 withdraw는 '철회하다', (D)의 appear는 '나타나다'라는 의미이다.

번역 버나드 씨는 마감일이 다가오고 있다는 것을 알고서 지원을 요청했다.

어휘 approach 다가오다 assistance 지원, 도움

124 형용사 자리 _ 주격 보어

해설 빈칸은 be동사의 보어 자리로, 빈칸 뒤에 온 that절과 함께 쓸 수 있는 형용사가 와야 한다. 따라서 'that절의 내용을 기대한다'는 의미를 나타내는 형용사 (C) hopeful(기대하는)이 정답이다. (A) hopes는 동사, (D) hopefully는 부사이므로 품사상 빈칸에 들어갈 수 없다. 과거분사 (B) hoped는 be동사 뒤에 들어가면 수동태가 되므로 that절을 연결할 수 없고, 의미상으로도 적절하지 않다.

번역 모스코비츠 씨는 타나카 박사가 올해 콘퍼런스에서 기조연설을 하는 데에 동의할 것으로 기대하고 있다.

어휘 present 발표하다 keynote speech 기조연설

125 명사절 접속사 _ 의문형용사 동영상 강의

해설 빈칸에는 가주어 it의 진주어 역할을 하는 명사절을 이끌 수 있는 단어가 들어가야 한다. 빈칸 뒤의 명사 phone을 수식하면서 명사절을 이끌어 '어느 스마트폰이 먼저 출시될지'라는 의미를 나타내는 의문형용사 (B) which가 정답이다. (A) if도 명사절 접속사로서 진주어 자리에 쓰일 수 있지만 명사 phone을 수식할 수 없으며, (C) before와 (D) because는 부사절 접속사이므로 답이 될 수 없다.

번역 오스트레일리아의 두 회사가 새로운 스마트폰을 개발하고 있지만, 어느 스마트폰이 먼저 출시될지는 불확실하다.

어휘 develop 개발하다 unclear 불확실한 available 이용할 수 있는

126 명사 자리 _ to부정사의 목적어 동영상 강의

해설 전치사 in의 목적어 역할을 하는 「how+to부정사구」 구문으로, 빈칸은 to부정사 to use의 목적어 역할을 하는 명사 자리이다. 따라서 '웨이트, 역기'를 뜻하는 명사 (B) weights가 정답이다. (A) weighs는 동사, (C) weighty는 형용사, (D) weighed는 동사/과거분사이므로 품사상 빈칸에 들어갈 수 없다.

번역 코너스 짐은 회원들에게 웨이트를 제대로 사용하는 법에 대한 무료 수업을 제공한다.

어휘 properly 제대로, 올바르게 weighty 무거운; 중대한

127 전치사 어휘

해설 뒤의 명사 the rules를 목적어로 취해 '규정에 따라 야간 주차가 허용되지 않는다'는 의미가 되어야 자연스러우므로 '~에 따라'를 뜻하는 (D) According to가 정답이다. (A) Prior to는 '~에 앞서', (B) Except for는 '~을 제외하고', (C) Instead of는 '~ 대신에'라는 의미이다.

번역 규정에 따라 클럽하우스 시설에서는 야간 주차가 허용되지 않습니다.

어휘 overnight 야간의 permit 허용[허락]하다 clubhouse (스포츠 클럽 등의) 클럽 회관 facility 시설

128 동사 어형 _ 시제 동영상 강의

해설 Once가 이끄는 부사절의 주어 everyone 뒤에 동사가 없으므로 빈칸은 동사 자리이다. 주절에서 전화 회의를 시작할 수 있다(can begin)는 것으로 보아 미래의 일이고, 회의를 시작하는 미래의 특정 시점까지 완료될 일을 나타내야 하므로 미래완료 시제 will have arrived가 들어가야 하지만, Once가 '~하자마자, 일단 ~하면'이라는 뜻으로 시간 부사절을 이끌고 있으므로 미래완료 대신 현재완료 시제를 쓴다. 따라서 (D) has arrived가 정답이다. (B) is arriving도 시간 부사절에서 미래를 나타낼 수 있지만 완료의 의미가 아니므로 오답이다.

번역 모두 도착하면 전화 회의를 시작할 수 있습니다.

129 명사 어휘

해설 빈칸은 주어 a motivational video와 동사 is shown 사이에서 주어를 수식하는 관계사절의 동사 highlights의 목적어 자리이다. 동

기부여 영상을 수식하는 내용이 되어야 하므로 '지난해의 성과를 강조한다'는 의미가 되어야 적절하다. 따라서 '성과, 업적'을 뜻하는 (B) accomplishments가 정답이다. (A)의 preference는 '선호(도)', (C)의 communication은 '의사소통', (D)의 uncertainty는 '불확실성'이라는 의미이다.

번역 매년 여름 지난 한 해의 성과를 강조하는 동기부여 영상이 회사의 전 직원에게 공개된다.

어휘 motivational 동기부여의 highlight 강조하다

130 to부정사 _ 형용사적 용법 동영상 강의

해설 주어 Employees와 동사 should contact 사이에서 주어를 수식하는 관계사절에 빈칸이 있다. 빈칸 앞에 완전한 절(who wish to attend the retirement dinner)이 있고 뒤에 명사구(Ms. Howell's 30 years of service)가 있으므로 빈칸에는 또 다른 동사가 들어갈 수 없다. 따라서 Ms. Howell's 30 years of service를 목적어로 취하면서 the retirement dinner를 수식하는 형용사적 역할의 to부정사 (B) to honor가 정답이다.

번역 하월 씨의 30년 근무를 기념하는 퇴직 만찬에 참석을 희망하는 직원은 이 씨에게 연락해 주시기 바랍니다.

어휘 attend 참석하다 retirement 퇴직, 은퇴 honor 기리다

PART 6

131-134 이메일

수신: 한명희
발신: 델윈 홈 스토어
날짜: 1월 15일
제목: 주문 업데이트

한 씨께,

귀하가 **131특별 주문**하신 레드 오크 식탁과 여섯 개 의자 세트가 오늘 오전 저희 매장에 도착했습니다. 이제 **132가구** 배송을 준비하고자 합니다. 517-555-0188로 전화하셔서 저희 배송 관리자인 콜먼 콥에게 **133통화**를 요청해 주십시오. **134그가 편리한 시간을 잡아드릴 수 있습니다.**

고객 서비스, 델윈 홈 스토어

어휘 oak 오크 (나무) dining table 식탁 matching 짝이 맞는, 어울리는 arrange 준비[주선]하다

131 형용사 자리 _ 명사 수식

해설 빈칸 앞에 소유격 Your, 뒤에 명사 order가 있으므로 명사를 수식하는 형용사 자리이다. '당신의 특별한 주문'이라는 의미가 되어야 적합하므로 '특별한'을 뜻하는 형용사 (C) special이 정답이다. (A) specially는 부사, (B) specialize는 동사이므로 품사상 답이 될 수 없다. 현재분사 (D) specializing은 전치사 in과 함께 쓰여 '~을 전문으로 하는'이라는 의미를 나타내므로 명사를 앞에서 수식하는 자리에 어울리지 않는다.

132 명사 어휘

해설 앞 문장에서 레드 오크 식탁과 의자 세트가 매장에 도착했다(a red oak dining table and six matching chairs arrived)고 하고 빈칸이 있는 문장에서 배송을 준비하고자 한다(arrange for the delivery)고 했으므로, 배송할 제품이 식탁과 의자 세트임을 알 수 있다. 따라서 식탁과 의자를 대신할 수 있는 단어로 '가구'를 뜻하는 (A) furniture가 정답이다. (B)의 appliance는 '가전제품', (C) refund는 '환불', (D)의 tool은 '도구'를 의미한다.

133 to부정사 _ 동사의 목적어

해설 등위접속사 and로 연결된 절에서 빈칸 앞에 있는 동사 ask의 목적어 자리이다. ask는 to부정사를 목적어로 취해 '~할 것을 요청[부탁]하다'라는 의미를 나타내므로 to부정사 (D) to speak가 정답이다. (A) speak과 (C) is speaking은 동사, (B) spoken은 과거분사로 동사의 목적어 자리에 들어갈 수 없다.

134 문맥에 맞는 문장 고르기

번역 (A) 그가 편리한 시간을 잡아드릴 수 있습니다.
(B) 그는 어제부터 여기서 일하기 시작했습니다.
(C) 그는 오전 11시에 귀하를 만날 수 있습니다.
(D) 그는 최근에 델윈으로 이사했습니다.

해설 앞에서 가구 배송을 준비하고자 한다면서 배달 관리자 콜먼 콥과 통화하라(Please call us ~ and ask to speak to Coleman Cobb)고 했다. 문맥상 통화로 처리할 내용이 들어가야 적절하므로, 콜먼 콥을 He로 받으며 그가 편리한 시간을 잡아줄 것이라고 언급하는 (A)가 정답이다.

어휘 convenient 편리한

135-138 광고

킵 쿨 서비스 컨트랙터스:
메인 로 67, 에든버러 빌리지
차구아나스, 트리니다드토바고

킵 쿨 서비스 컨트랙터스는 고객님께 마음의 평화를 가져다드릴 수 있습니다. 연간 계약의 일환으로 에어컨 시스템을 점검하여 고객님의 ¹³⁵**안전**과 편안함을 보장해 드립니다. 여기에는 시스템 점검, 필요시 수리, 전문적인 송풍구 청소가 포함됩니다. ¹³⁶**게다가**, 필요한 경우 고객님의 노후한 에어컨 시스템을 비용 효율적인 새것으로 교체해 드릴 수도 있습니다.

저희 직원들은 고도의 자격을 갖춘 공인 기술자들로 지속적인 교육을 통해 최신 기술을 보유하고 있습니다. ¹³⁷**또한, 그들은 친절하고 청결하며 박식합니다.** 킵 쿨 품질 보증으로 ¹³⁸**보장되는** 공정한 가격과 전문적인 작업을 약속드립니다. 오늘 무료 견적을 받으려면 1-868-555-0129로 전화 주십시오.

어휘 contractor 도급[하청]업자; 계약자 ensure 보장하다
comfort 편안함 inspect 점검하다 repair 수리하다
professionally 전문적으로 air duct 송풍구 replace 교체하다

---

cost-efficient 비용 효율적인 qualified 자격을 갖춘 licensed 자격증[면허증]을 소지한 up-to-date 최신의 ongoing 지속적인 fair 공정한 guarantee 품질 보증(서) quote 견적(서)

135 명사 자리 _ 동사의 목적어

해설 빈칸은 분사구문에서 ensuring의 목적어 역할을 하며 소유격 대명사 your의 수식을 받는 자리이다. 또한 등위접속사 and 뒤의 명사 comfort와 대등하게 연결될 수 있는 품사가 들어가야 하므로 '안전'을 뜻하는 명사 (D) safety가 정답이다. (A) safe는 형용사(안전한) 외에 명사로도 쓰이지만 명사일 때 '금고'를 뜻하므로 문맥상 어울리지 않는다.

136 접속부사

해설 앞에서 에어컨 시스템 서비스에 대해 설명하며 시스템 점검, 수리 및 송풍구 청소가 포함된다고 했고, 빈칸 뒤에 에어컨 시스템을 새것으로 교체할 수도 있다며 추가 서비스 내용을 언급하고 있다. 따라서 '게다가, 뿐만 아니라'라는 뜻으로 추가적인 내용을 덧붙일 때 사용하는 (C) Furthermore가 정답이다. (A) On one hand는 '한편으로는', (B) Nonetheless는 '그럼에도 불구하고', (D) And yet은 '그렇다 하더라도'라는 의미이다.

137 문맥에 맞는 문장 고르기

번역 (A) 수십 가지 유용한 온라인 도구를 활용하십시오.
(B) 게다가, 고객님께서 선택하신 에어컨은 매우 인기 있습니다.
(C) 또한, 그들은 친절하고 청결하며 박식합니다.
(D) 저희 계약자 전시장을 방문해 주셔서 감사합니다.

해설 빈칸 앞에서 직원들이 고도의 자격을 갖춘 공인 기술자들(highly qualified licensed technicians)이라며 직원들의 뛰어난 자격을 홍보하고 있으므로, 직원들을 they로 받으며 그들의 우수한 자질에 대해 추가적으로 강조하는 내용이 들어가는 것이 자연스럽다. 따라서 Plus(또한, 게다가)로 시작해 직원들이 친절하고 청결하며 박식하다고 언급하는 (C)가 정답이다.

어휘 take advantage of ~을 활용하다 dozens of 수십의 knowledgeable 많이 아는 showroom (상품) 전시장

138 분사구문

해설 앞에 완전한 절(We promise ~ professional work)과 콤마가 있으므로, 빈칸은 전치사구 by our Keep Cool guarantee와 함께 앞 절을 수식하는 분사 자리이다. 빈칸 뒤에 목적어 없이 전치사구가 왔고 '킵 쿨 품질 보증에 의해 보장되는'이라는 의미가 되어야 적절하므로 수동의 의미를 나타내는 과거분사 (A) backed가 정답이다. (B) backs와 (D) back은 완전한 절 뒤에서 전치사구를 자연스럽게 연결할 수 없고, 현재분사 (C) backing은 능동의 의미를 나타내어 뒤에 목적어가 와야 하므로 답이 되지 않는다.

어휘 back 지지하다, 뒷받침하다

139-142 이메일

수신: 전 고객
발신: asquires@lightidea.com
날짜: 3월 6일
제목: 정보

라이트 아이디어 고객분께,

라이트 아이디어는 4월 17일부터 일부 에너지 효율 제품에 가격 인상을 시행합니다. 구체적인 제품 가격은 139 **다양할** 것입니다. 자세한 내용과 질문은 영업 담당자에게 문의해 주십시오.

현재 가격으로 주문할 수 있는 마지막 날짜는 4월 16일입니다. 이 날짜 이후에 140 **접수되는** 모든 주문은 새로운 가격표를 따를 예정입니다. 141 **업데이트된 가격표는 3월 20일에 확인하실 수 있습니다.** 고객분들은 저희 웹사이트에서 이 표를 확인하실 수 있습니다.

저희는 계속해서 소중한 고객분들께 양질의 제품과 142 **탁월한** 서비스를 제공할 것입니다. 거래해 주셔서 감사합니다.

아빈 스콰이어스
영업 책임자, 라이트 아이디어

어휘 enact 행하다 select 선택된 energy-efficient 에너지 효율적인 effective 시행되는 specific 구체적인 pricing 가격 책정 sales representative 영업 담당자 details 세부 사항 current 현재의 quality 양질의 valued 소중한

139 동사 어휘 ▶ 동영상 강의

해설 빈칸 뒤 문장에서 자세한 내용은 영업 담당자에게 문의하라(contact your sales representative for details)고 했으므로 인상되는 '제품의 가격이 다양하다'는 내용이 되어야 적절하다. 따라서 '다양하다'라는 의미의 (B) vary가 정답이다. (A) agree는 '동의하다', (C) wait는 '기다리다'라는 뜻으로 pricing의 동사로 적절하지 않고, (D) decline은 '감소하다'라는 뜻으로 가격 인상을 언급하는 지문 내용과 어울리지 않는다.

140 과거분사 ▶ 동영상 강의

해설 빈칸은 주어 All orders와 동사 will follow 사이에서 주어를 수식하는 자리이다. 빈칸 뒤에 목적어가 없고 전치사구 after this date와 함께 '이 날짜 이후에 접수되는 주문'이라는 의미가 되어야 하므로 과거분사 (C) received가 정답이다. 현재분사 (A) receiving과 (B) having received는 뒤에 목적어가 필요하고, (D) will be received는 동사이므로 빈칸에 들어갈 수 없다.

141 문맥에 맞는 문장 고르기

번역 (A) 업데이트된 가격표는 3월 20일에 확인하실 수 있습니다.
(B) 불편을 드려 죄송합니다.
(C) 귀하의 주문은 4월 17일 이후에 발송될 예정입니다.
(D) 저희는 비용 상승으로 인해 가격을 인상합니다.

해설 빈칸 앞에서 4월 16일 이후에는 새롭게 인상된 가격표(the new price list)가 적용된다고 안내하고 있고, 빈칸 뒤에서 이 표(this)를

웹사이트에서 확인할 수 있다고 했으므로, 빈칸에는 this가 가리키는 것, 즉 새 가격표에 대한 내용이 들어가야 자연스럽다. 따라서 업데이트된 가격표를 확인할 수 있는 날짜를 언급하는 (A)가 정답이다.

어휘 apologize 사과하다 inconvenience 불편 rising 상승하는

142 형용사 자리 _ 명사 수식

해설 빈칸 앞 quality products와 등위접속사 and로 대등하게 연결되는 구문으로, 문맥상 '양질의 제품과 어떤 서비스를 제공한다'는 의미가 되어야 적절하므로 빈칸에는 명사 service를 수식하는 형용사가 들어가야 한다. 따라서 '탁월한'이라는 뜻의 형용사 (C) exceptional이 정답이다. 부사 (A) exceptionally는 명사를 수식할 수 없고, 명사 (B) exception과 (D) exceptionalism은 service와 복합명사를 이루기에 부적절하므로 답이 되지 않는다.

어휘 exceptionalism 예외론

143-146 이메일

수신: 권장호 〈jkwon@newart.nz〉
발신: 케네스 오킴 〈k.okim@okimjewelry.nz〉
제목: 좋은 소식
날짜: 8월 30일

장호 씨께,

지난달에 보석 제품 80개를 보내 주셔서 감사합니다. 제 매장에서 그 제품들이 매우 잘 팔리고 있다는 말씀을 전하게 되어 기쁩니다. 저의 143 **고객들**은 당신의 우수한 세공 품질뿐 아니라 다채로운 디자인을 정말 좋아합니다. 144 **합리적인 가격 또한 당신의 작품에 큰 가치를 부여합니다.**

당신으로부터 주문하는 상품의 수를 늘리고 싶습니다. 9월 배송에 제 주문을 145 **두 배로 늘릴** 수 있을까요?

마지막으로, 당신의 작품을 제 매장에서 독점 취급할 수 있는 가능성에 대해 논의하고 싶습니다. 저는 제가 당신의 목표 고객층에 가장 잘 다가갈 수 있으며 이 협약이 146 **우리** 두 사람 모두에게 아주 도움이 될 것이라고 믿습니다. 연락 기다리겠습니다.

케네스 오킴
오킴 주얼리

어휘 shipment 수송(품) unit (상품의) 한 개 jewelry 보석류 workmanship 세공, 솜씨 feature 특징으로 하다 exclusively 독점적으로 target audience 목표 고객[대상] agreement 협약, 계약 serve 도움이 되다

143 명사 어휘

해설 앞 문장에서 매장에서 제품들이 잘 팔리고 있다(they have been selling very well)고 했으므로 우수한 세공 품질뿐 아니라 다채로운 디자인을 좋아하는 주체는 매장에서 물건을 구매하는 사람들임을 알 수 있다. 따라서 '고객'을 의미하는 (C) customers가 정답이다.

144 문맥에 맞는 문장 고르기

번역 (A) 시간이 더 필요하면 알려 주십시오.
(B) 안타깝게도, 이번에는 충분한 진열 공간이 없습니다.
(C) 제가 직접 디자인한 몇 가지 작품을 보여 드리고 싶습니다.
(D) 합리적인 가격 또한 당신의 작품에 큰 가치를 부여합니다.

해설 빈칸 앞에서 제품들이 잘 팔리고 있으며 고객들이 우수한 세공 품질과 다채로운 디자인을 좋아한다고 했고 빈칸 뒤 두 번째 단락에서 주문 수량을 늘리고 싶다(I would like to increase ~ units I order from you)고 했으므로, 빈칸에는 이메일 수신자가 제작하는 제품에 대한 호평이 이어져야 일관성 있는 문맥이 완성된다. 따라서 합리적인 가격 또한 작품에 큰 가치를 부여한다며 제품의 장점을 추가로 언급하고 있는 (D)가 정답이다.

어휘 adequate 충분한 shelf space (매장에서 상품이 점하는) 진열대 공간 reasonable 합리적인

145 동사 어휘

해설 앞 문장에서 주문하는 상품의 수를 늘리고(increase the number of units) 싶다고 했으므로, 빈칸에는 주문을 늘리는 것을 의미하는 동사가 들어가야 한다. 따라서 '두 배로 늘리다'라는 의미의 (B) double이 정답이다. (A) include는 '포함하다', (C) repeat는 '반복하다', (D) insure는 '보험에 들다'의 의미이다.

146 인칭대명사의 격 _ 목적격

해설 빈칸은 동사 serve의 목적어 자리이므로 목적격 대명사가 들어가야 한다. 또한 문맥상 이 협약이 이메일 수신자(you)와 발신자(I) 모두에게 도움이 된다는 내용이 되어야 하므로, you와 I를 포함하는 인칭대명사 we의 목적격 (A) us가 정답이다.

PART 7

147-148 초대장

소셜 미디어 입지에 주력하라

¹⁴⁷소규모 사업주에게 있어 경쟁적인 소셜 미디어 환경에서 두각을 나타내는 것은 도전이 될 수 있습니다. 목표 시장에 성공적으로 도달하는 데에는 효과적이고 기억에 남는 방식으로 제품을 홍보하는 방법과 장소를 아는 것이 필요합니다. ¹⁴⁷사반 비즈니스 센터는 바로 그 일을 하는 데 부양책이 필요한 사업주들을 지원합니다. 50년이 넘는 기간 동안 저희는 현재 업계 동향에 대한 통찰력과 고객의 고유한 요구에 대한 이해를 통해 사업주들이 매출을 신장할 수 있도록 도움을 드리고 있습니다.

¹⁴⁸효과적이고 영향력이 큰 소셜 미디어 콘텐츠를 만드는 데 있어 귀사가 보다 체계적일 수 있도록 도와드리겠습니다. 저희의 최신 웨비나인 '소셜 미디어 입지에 주력하라'에서는 귀사의 비즈니스를 돋보이게 만드는 것과 관련된 주제들을 다룹니다. 저희의 이벤트 웹페이지에서 등록하실 수 있습니다.

날짜: 2월 5일
시간: 오전 10시부터 오전 11시
이벤트 웹페이지: https://www.savanbusinesscenter.com/socialmedia

어휘 presence 존재(함) challenge 도전 stand out 눈에 띄다, 돋보이다 competitive 경쟁적인 involve 수반[포함]하다 promote 홍보하다 effective 효과적인 memorable 기억할 만한 boost 부양책 entrepreneur 사업가 insight 통찰력 unique 고유의, 특유의 organized 체계적인 far-reaching (영향이) 멀리까지 미치는 webinar 웨비나, 웹 세미나 cover 다루다 related to ~와 관련 있는

147 Not / True

번역 사반 비즈니스 센터에 대해 사실인 것은?
(A) 소규모 업체들을 대상으로 한다.
(B) 주간 소식지를 발행한다.
(C) 최근에 새로운 웹사이트를 개설했다.
(D) 웨비나 주제에 대한 제안을 구하고 있다.

해설 첫 문장에서 소규모 사업주에게 있어 경쟁적인 소셜 미디어 환경에서 두각을 나타내는 것은 도전이 될 수 있다(For small-business owners ~ in a competitive social media environment)고 언급한 데 이어 세 번째 문장에서 사반 비즈니스 센터는 바로 그 일을 하는 데 부양책이 필요한 사업주들을 지원한다(The Savan Business Center offers support for business owners who need a boost ~)고 했다. 따라서 사반 비즈니스 센터가 소규모 사업체를 대상으로 운영하는 곳임을 알 수 있으므로 (A)가 정답이다.

어휘 work with ~을 작업 대상으로 하다, ~와 함께 일하다 newsletter (조직의) 소식지 launch 시작[개시]하다

148 Not / True

번역 웨비나에 대해 명시된 것은?
(A) 오전 11시에 시작한다.
(B) 홍보 콘텐츠 제작에 대한 조언이 포함된다.
(C) 매월 제공되고 있다.
(D) 참석하는 데 소정의 수수료가 필요하다.

해설 두 번째 단락의 첫 문장에서 효과적이고 영향력이 큰 소셜 미디어 콘텐츠를 만드는 데 있어 보다 체계적일 수 있도록 도와주겠다(Let us help you get more organized in creating ~ social media content)고 한 뒤, 자사의 최신 웨비나에서 비즈니스를 돋보이게 만드는 것과 관련된 주제들을 다룬다(Our latest webinar ~ topics related to making your business stand out)고 덧붙였다. 따라서 웨비나에서 업체를 홍보하기 위한 소셜 미디어 콘텐츠 제작을 다룬다는 것을 알 수 있으므로 (B)가 정답이다.

어휘 feature 특별히 포함하다 promotional 홍보의

Paraphrasing 지문의 creating ~ social media content
→ 정답의 creating promotional content

다인 아웃 다빌이 돌아왔습니다!

¹⁴⁹ 올해 6월 22일부터 28일까지 운영하는 **다인 아웃 다빌**은 다빌에 있는 레스토랑을 처음 시도하거나 이 도시에서 가장 좋아하는 레스토랑 중 하나를 재방문할 수 있는 완벽한 기회입니다. ¹⁴⁹ **일주일 간의 행사 동안** 여러 레스토랑을 방문할 수도 있습니다! ¹⁵⁰ 인기 있는 레스토랑 열두 곳에서 수프, 샐러드, 메인 코스, 디저트를 포함한 4코스 특별 정식을 할인된 가격 30달러에 제공합니다. 예약이 적극 권장됩니다. 다인 아웃 다빌은 매년 수백 명의 현지인과 관광객을 맞이하고 있으며, 여러분은 훌륭한 가격에 훌륭한 식사를 할 수 있는 기회를 결코 놓치고 싶지 않을 것입니다.

참여 레스토랑 목록을 확인하려면 www.darvillebusinesscouncil.org/dineout을 방문하세요.

어휘 multiple 다수의 weeklong 일주일 간의 reduced 할인된 local 현지인, 주민 miss 놓치다 opportunity 기회 participating 참여하는

149 Not / True

번역 다인 아웃 다빌에 대해 언급된 것은?
(A) 일주일 동안 지속된다.
(B) 매년 다른 장소에서 개최된다.
(C) 처음으로 열린다.
(D) 점심과 저녁 둘 다 포함된다.

해설 첫 문장에서 올해 6월 22일부터 28일까지 운영되는 다인 아웃 다빌(Dine Out Darville, which runs this year from June 22 to 28)이라고 하고, 그 다음 문장에서도 일주일 간의 행사 동안(during the weeklong event) 여러 레스토랑을 방문할 수 있다고 했으므로 (A)가 정답이다.

어휘 last 지속되다

150 Not / True

번역 할인된 식사에 포함되지 않는 것은?
(A) 수프
(B) 샐러드
(C) 디저트
(D) 음료

해설 세 번째 문장에서 인기 있는 레스토랑 열두 곳에서 수프 한 컵, 샐러드, 메인 코스, 디저트를 포함한 4코스 특별 정식을 할인된 가격 30달러에 제공한다(Twelve popular restaurants will offer ~ including a cup of soup, a salad, a main course, and a dessert—all for a reduced price of $30)고 했으므로, (A), (B), (C)는 할인된 식사에 포함됨을 알 수 있다. 따라서 포함되지 않는 것은 '음료'이므로 (D)가 정답이다.

레인시의 본사 이전

데이드 (7월 11일) — 레인시 LLC는 어제 본사를 데이드로 이전한다고 발표했다.

¹⁵¹ 현재 솔트크리크에 본사를 둔 데이터 저장 및 분석 회사인 레인시는 국내 최대의 신용카드사, 온라인 소매업체 및 소프트웨어 공급업체를 포함한 고객들을 보유하고 있다. 레인시는 이러한 기업들이 고객 데이터를 관리하고 이해할 수 있도록 돕고 있다.

레인시가 솔트크리크에 있는 현재 사무실을 닫을 계획은 없다. 하지만 일부 경영진이 데이드 지사에서 근무할 예정임에 따라 그곳이 새로운 운영 기반이 될 것이다. ¹⁵² 회사의 최고 경영 책임자와 최고 재무 책임자는 약 50퍼센트의 회사 직원과 함께 데이드로 이전할 것이다.

레인시의 최고 기술 책임자 사무실은 솔트크리크에 남을 예정이며, 회계관리팀도 마찬가지이다. 회사의 새로운 데이드 사무실은 글레이셔 파크웨이 12번지에 위치해 있다.

어휘 headquarters 본사 storage 저장 analytics 분석 firm 회사 based in ~에 기반을 둔 retailer 소매업체 operation 운영, 사업 executive team 경영진, 임원진 relocate 이전하다 approximately 거의 workforce (기업의) 전 직원 remain 남다

151 세부사항

번역 레인시 LLC가 하는 일은?
(A) 소비자 정보를 저장하고 분석한다.
(B) 온라인에서 기술 제품을 판매한다.
(C) 소매업체를 위한 신용카드 결제를 처리한다.
(D) 컴퓨터 소프트웨어 프로그램을 개발한다.

해설 두 번째 단락에서 솔트크리크에 본사를 둔 데이터 저장 및 분석 회사인 레인시는 국내 최대의 신용카드사, 온라인 소매업체 및 소프트웨어 공급업체를 포함한 고객들을 보유하고 있으며(A data storage and analytics firm ~ Rainsy has clients that include some of the country's largest credit card companies, online retailers, and software providers) 이러한 기업들이 고객 데이터를 관리하고 이해할 수 있도록 돕고 있다(Rainsy helps ~ manage and understand their customer data)고 했다. 따라서 레인시가 기업 고객의 소비자 데이터를 저장 및 분석하는 회사임을 알 수 있으므로 (A)가 정답이다.

어휘 consumer 소비자 process 처리하다

152 세부사항

번역 데이드에 기반을 둘 사람은?
(A) 레인시 최고 기술 책임자
(B) 레인시 경영진 전체
(C) 레인시 직원의 약 절반
(D) 레인시 회계관리팀

해설 세 번째 단락의 마지막 문장에서 최고 경영 책임자와 최고 재무 책임자는 약 50퍼센트의 회사 직원과 함께 데이드로 이전할 것(The company's chief executive officer and chief financial officer will relocate to Dade along with approximately 50 percent of the company's workforce)이라고 했으므로 (C)가 정답이다.

TEST

153-154 문자 메시지

마이클 리우 (오전 9시 43분) 안녕하세요, 제나. 지금 비즈 플러스에 있는데요. 당신이 필요한 종이가 다음 주까지 재고가 없어요. 다른 색도 될까요?
제나 바트 (오전 9시 45분) 어떤 선택지가 있나요?
마이클 리우 (오전 9시 46분) 당신이 선호하는 브랜드에 노란색, 초록색, 분홍색이 있어요.
제나 바트 (오전 9시 47분) 153, 154 저는 파란색이 꼭 필요해요. 다른 브랜드의 파란색 프린터 용지가 있나요?
마이클 리우 (오전 9시 48분) 153, 154 네, 하지만 모두 진한 파란색이에요. 가격도 더 비싸고요.
제나 바트 (오전 9시 49분) 알겠어요, 신경 쓰지 마세요. 154 제가 온라인으로 주문할게요.
어휘 　out of stock 재고가 떨어진, 품절된　cost (비용이) 들다 place an order 주문하다

153 추론 / 암시

 동영상 강의

번역　리우 씨가 사려고 하는 종이에 대해 암시된 것은?
(A) 연한 파란색이다.
(B) 비싸다.
(C) 비즈 플러스에서만 판매된다.
(D) 단종되었다.

해설　9시 47분에 바트 씨가 파란색이 꼭 필요하다(I really need blue)며 다른 브랜드의 파란색 프린터 용지가 있는지(Are there other brands of blue printer paper?) 묻자, 9시 48분에 리우 씨가 있지만 모두 진한 파란색(Yes, but they're all a darker blue)이라고 했다. 따라서 리우 씨가 사려는 종이는 파란색이지만 진하지 않은, 즉 연한 파란색임을 짐작할 수 있으므로 (A)가 정답이다.

어휘　exclusively 오로지, 독점적으로　discontinue (생산을) 중단하다

154 의도 파악

 동영상 강의

번역　오전 9시 49분에 바트 씨가 "알겠어요, 신경 쓰지 마세요"라고 쓴 의도는?
(A) 예산을 확인하고 싶어 한다.
(B) 리우 씨가 비즈 플러스에서 종이를 구매하지 않아야 한다고 생각한다.
(C) 리우 씨가 이번 주에 주문을 해서는 안 된다고 믿는다.
(D) 주문을 취소할 계획이다.

해설　9시 47분에 바트 씨가 다른 브랜드의 파란색 프린터 용지가 있는지(Are there other brands of blue printer paper?)를 물었고, 9시 48분에 리우 씨가 있지만 모두 진한 파란색(Yes, but they're all a darker blue)이고 가격도 더 비싸다(They also cost more)고 하자, 9시 49분에 바트 씨가 알겠으니 신경 쓰지 말라(OK, forget it)면서 본인이 온라인으로 주문하겠다(I'll place an order online)고 덧붙였다. 따라서 바트 씨는 리우 씨에게 종이를 구입하지 말라는 의도로 한 말임을 알 수 있으므로 (B)가 정답이다.

155-157 편지

5월 20일 닐 크로프트, 관장 퀸즐랜드 도서관 허모키 로 13 브리즈번 QLD 4003 크로프트 씨께, 155 퀸즐랜드 전역의 도서관에 재무관리 과정을 개설하는 것에 관한 귀하의 문의를 읽었습니다. 재무관리 자문가 협회(SFMA)는 기초 재무관리 정보에 보다 널리 접근할 수 있도록 도서관과 협력할 수 있는 기회를 환영합니다. 157 귀하는 SFMA 회원들이 몇몇 도서관 분관에서 입문 과정을 지도해 줄 것을 제안했습니다. 이는 제가 기꺼이 추천할 수 있는 것입니다. 157 과거에 SFMA 회원들은 최근 졸업생들, 직업을 바꾸려는 사람들, 처음 투자하는 사람들에게 비슷한 과정을 제공했었습니다. 156 첫 행사 시리즈를 진행할 도서관 분관 목록이 있으시다면 해당 도서관 근처에서 근무하거나 그 도서관으로 갈 의향이 있는 진행자들을 제안해 드릴 수 있습니다. 예상 참가자들의 일반적인 프로필이 있으십니까? 그 정보는 수강생의 요구와 관심에 맞게 과정을 조정하는 데 도움이 될 것입니다. 귀하와 만나 뵙고 계획을 세우기를 기대합니다. 과정에 대해 논의할 시간을 잡기 위해 07 5550 1344로 전화 주시기 바랍니다. 로버타 오트니 협회장, 재무관리 자문가 협회
어휘　inquiry 문의　financial management 재무관리 society 협회　partner 협력[제휴]하다　widely 널리 introductory 입문의　branch 지사, 분점　graduate 졸업생 investor 투자자　host 주최하다　facilitator (교육 과정 등의) 진행자　general 일반적인　attendee 참석자　tailor 맞추다, 조정하다　chairperson 회장, 의장

155 주제 / 목적

번역　오트니 씨가 편지를 쓴 이유는?
(A) 새로운 도서관장을 환영하려고
(B) SFMA 재무 과정에 등록하려고
(C) 교육 자격증을 확인하려고
(D) 크로프트 씨의 질문에 답하려고

해설　첫 문장에서 오트니 씨가 크로프트 씨에게 퀸즐랜드 전역의 도서관에 재무관리 과정을 개설하는 것에 관한 귀하의 문의를 읽었다

(I have read your inquiry ~ courses at libraries across Queensland)며 재무관리 자문가 협회(SFMA)는 기초 재무관리 정보에 보다 널리 접근할 수 있도록 도서관과 협력할 수 있는 기회를 환영한다(The Society for Financial Management Advisors (SFMA) welcomes the opportunity ~ more widely available)고 했으므로, 도서관에 재무관리 과정을 개설하는 일에 대한 크로프트 씨의 문의에 응답하기 위해 편지를 썼음을 알 수 있다. 따라서 (D)가 정답이다.

어휘　register 등록하다　educational 교육의　credentials 자격증

156 세부사항

번역　오트니 씨가 요청한 한 가지는?
(A) 도서관 회원 자격
(B) 과정 강사 명단
(C) 도서관들의 위치
(D) 크로프트 씨의 전화번호

해설　세 번째 단락의 첫 문장에서 오트니 씨가 첫 행사 시리즈를 진행할 도서관 분관 목록이 있다면 해당 도서관 근처에서 근무하거나 그 도서관으로 갈 의향이 있는 진행자들을 제안해 줄 수 있다(If you have a list of library branches ~ suggest facilitators who work near those libraries or would be willing to travel to them)고 했다. 따라서 도서관들의 위치를 알기 위해 분관 목록을 요청하고 있음을 알 수 있으므로 (C)가 정답이다.

어휘　instructor 강사

157 문장 삽입

번역　[1], [2], [3], [4]로 표시된 위치 중에서 다음 문장이 들어가기에 가장 적합한 곳은?

"이는 제가 기꺼이 주선할 수 있는 것입니다."
(A) [1]
(B) [2]
(C) [3]
(D) [4]

해설　주어진 문장에서 이는 제가 주선할 수 있는 것이라고 했으므로 편지 작성자(Ms. Oteny)가 주선할(arrange) 수 있는 이것(This)에 대한 내용이 앞에 있어야 한다. [2] 앞에서 SFMA 회원들이 도서관에서 입문 과정을 지도해 줄 것을 제안받은 일(You proposed that SFMA members could lead introductory courses ~)을 언급했고, 뒤에서 SFMA 회원들이 과거에 비슷한 과정을 진행한 경험이 있다(SFMA members have offered similar courses ~ in the past)며 오트니 씨가 어렵지 않게 이 일을 할 수 있다는 점을 뒷받침하고 있으므로, 이 사이에 주어진 문장이 들어가야 자연스럽다. 따라서 (B)가 정답이다.

158-160 광고

クラロ 비전
차이가 분명합니다.

158 기간 한정 할인을 이용하세요:
9월 30일까지 모든 안경테 50% 할인

오늘 그리고 매일 이용 가능한 기타 혜택:
• 159 무료 안경 피팅 및 조정
• 완전히 만족하지 못할 경우 환불 보증
• 캐나다 전역의 쇼핑몰에 있는 500개 이상의 지점
• 160 공인 안경사의 저렴한 시력 검사

가까운 매장을 찾으시려면 www.clarovision.ca/locations를 방문하시거나 오늘 416-555-0122로 전화 주세요!

어휘　limited-time offer 기간 한정 할인　eyeglass frame 안경테　advantage 이점　adjustment 조정　guarantee 보증　completely 완전히　satisfied 만족하는　vision 시력　optician 안경사

158 주제 / 목적

번역　광고는 왜 제작되었을 것 같은가?
(A) 잘 이용되지 않는 전문 서비스에 관심을 끌기 위해서
(B) 보증 정책의 혜택을 홍보하기 위해서
(C) 새로운 매장 지점의 개점을 알리기 위해서
(D) 일시적인 가격 할인을 홍보하기 위해서

해설　광고 상단에 기간 한정 할인을 이용하라며 9월 30일까지 모든 안경테 50% 할인(Take advantage of our limited-time offer: 50% off all eyeglass frames through 30 September)이라고 홍보하고 있으므로 (D)가 정답이다.

어휘　draw attention 관심을 끌다　underused 충분히 이용되지 않는　publicize 알리다, 광고하다　warranty 품질 보증　temporary 일시적인

Paraphrasing　지문의 limited-time offer: 50% off
→ 정답의 a temporary price discount

159 Not / True

번역　클라로 비전 매장에 대해 언급된 것은?
(A) 경쟁업체 매장보다 크다.
(B) 모든 주요 신용카드를 받는다.
(C) 쇼핑몰 옆에 위치해 있다.
(D) 무료로 안경 피팅을 제공한다.

해설　광고 중반부에 나열된 클라로 비전의 기타 혜택 중 첫 번째 항목에 무료 안경 피팅 및 조정(Free eyeglass fittings and adjustments)이 있으므로 (D)가 정답이다.

어휘　competitor 경쟁업체　accept 수락하다　major 주요한　at no cost 무료로

Paraphrasing　지문의 free → 정답의 at no cost

160 Not / True

번역　시력 검사에 대해 언급된 것은?
(A) 제휴사에 의해 이루어진다.
(B) 공인 전문가에 의해 수행된다.
(C) 10개월마다 행해져야 한다.
(D) 제한된 일수 동안 제공된다.

해설 광고 중반부에 나열된 클라로 비전의 기타 혜택 중 마지막 항목에 공인 안경사의 저렴한 시력 검사(Low-cost vision checkups by licensed opticians)가 언급되어 있으므로 (B)가 정답이다.

어휘 perform 수행하다 certified 공인의, 면허증을 소지한 professional 전문가

Paraphrasing 지문의 licensed opticians
→ 정답의 a certified professional

161-163 편지

로제리 빌딩 코퍼레이션
사우스 엑스머스 드라이브 2710
싱가포르 188509

4월 1일

엘리자베스 발라크리쉬난
발라 홈 퍼니싱스
홀리턴 드라이브 C2 416
싱가포르 793801

발라크리쉬난 씨께,

161 귀하의 공간에 대한 1년 임대차 계약이 4월 30일에 종료됨을 알려 드립니다. 163 임대차 계약 갱신을 위한 약속을 잡으시려면 제 사무실 1555 0124로 연락 주십시오. 운영비 상승으로 인해 임대료 및 수수료가 소폭 인상될 예정입니다.

임대차 계약 갱신 시 변경된 요금:

월세	1,800싱가포르달러
162 주차 공간 요금	50싱가포르달러
청소 서비스	10싱가포르달러
보안 수수료	35싱가포르달러
월 총액	1,895싱가포르달러

만약 임대차 계약을 갱신하지 않을 경우, 4월 15일까지 당사로 통지 부탁드립니다. 4월 30일 오후 5시까지 건물을 비워 주시기 바랍니다. 건물 점검이 있을 예정이며, 정상적인 사용을 넘어선 수리 또는 손상에 대한 비용이 발생할 수 있습니다.

163 알렉시스 탄

어휘 reminder 상기시켜 주는 편지, 독촉장 lease 임대차 계약 renew 갱신하다 operating cost 운영비 charge 요금 renewal 갱신 security 보안 notify 알리다 vacate 비우다 property 건물, 부동산 inspection 점검 repair 수리, 보수 damage 손상 normal 정상적인 usage 사용

161 주제 / 목적

번역 편지의 목적은?
(A) 장비 설치 수수료를 설명하려고
(B) 서비스에 대한 할인을 제공하려고
(C) 임대차 계약에 대한 정보를 제공하려고
(D) 건물 편의시설에 대한 변경을 요청하려고

해설 첫 문장에서 귀하의 공간에 대한 1년 임대차 계약이 4월 30일에 종

료됨을 알린다(This is a reminder that the one-year lease for your space will end on 30 April)고 한 것으로 보아 임대차 계약의 만기일과 관련 정보를 제공하기 위해 편지를 썼음을 알 수 있다. 따라서 (C)가 정답이다.

어휘 equipment 장비 installation 설치 amenity 편의시설

162 세부사항

번역 편지에 따르면, 발라크리쉬난 씨는 매달 무엇에 대해 지불해야 하는가?
(A) 가구 대여
(B) 사무용품
(C) 점검 비용
(D) 주차 공간

해설 두 번째 단락에 제시된 요금 목록에 주차 공간 요금(Parking space fee)이 있는 것으로 보아 발라크리쉬난 씨가 매달 지불해야 하는 비용에 주차 요금이 포함되어 있음을 알 수 있다. 따라서 (D)가 정답이다.

163 추론 / 암시

번역 탄 씨는 누구일 것 같은가?
(A) 수리 기사
(B) 부동산 관리인
(C) 환경미화원
(D) 보안회사 직원

해설 편지 하단에 보내는 사람 이름이 알렉시스 탄(Alexis Tan)이고 편지의 두 번째 문장에서 임대차 계약 갱신을 위한 약속을 잡으려면 자신의 사무실로 연락 달라(Please contact my office ~ to make an appointment to renew your lease)고 한 것으로 보아 탄 씨는 부동산 관리 회사의 직원임을 알 수 있다. 따라서 (B)가 정답이다.

164-167 이메일

수신: lkhoury@britelyauto.co.uk
발신: khagel@qualiview.co.uk
날짜: 4월 14일
제목: 귀사의 변경사항 제안

쿠우리 씨께,

164, 165 퀄리뷰 사가 귀사의 자동차 창유리 도매 공급업체가 되는 계약에 수정 사항 제안을 보내 주셔서 감사합니다.

먼저, 계약 기간을 1년에서 3년으로 연장하는 데 기꺼이 동의합니다. 두 번째로, 포장재에 대한 귀사의 우려를 166 해소하기 위해 저희가 무엇을 더 할 수 있을지 잘 모르겠습니다. 저희는 배송 중 파손 위험을 줄이기 위해 주문 제작한 상자와 혁신적인 포장재를 사용합니다. 운송 중에 손상될 수도 있는 물품은 모두 교체해 드릴 것이지만, 이러한 손상이 발생할 경우 추가 위약금을 지불하는 데에는 동의하지 않습니다.

164 다음 주에 귀하와 이에 대해 추가적으로 논의하고 싶습니다만, 제가 화요일 오후까지 사무실을 비울 예정입니다. 167 수요일이나 목요일 오전 11시 전에 만나 뵐 수 있을까요? 금요일도 가능합니다. 편한 날짜와 시간을 알려 주십시오.

칼 헤이글
퀄리뷰 사

어휘 **forward** 보내다, 전달하다 **revision** 수정 (사항)
wholesale 도매의 **supplier** 공급업체 **automotive** 자동차의
gladly 기꺼이 **extension** 연장 **term** 기간 **address** (문제를)
해결하다, 처리하다 **concern** 우려, 걱정 **packaging** 포장(재)
custom-built 주문 제작한 **crate** (운송용) 나무 상자 **innovative**
혁신적인 **reduce** 줄이다 **breakage** 파손 **damage** 손상을
입히다; 손상 **in transit** 운송 중에 **additional** 추가의 **penalty
fee** 위약금 **in the event of** ~의 경우에는 **further** 더 나아가

164 주제 / 목적

번역 헤이글 씨가 이메일을 쓴 이유는?
(A) 물품에 대한 손상을 보고하려고
(B) 구매를 마무리 지으려고
(C) 제품 샘플을 요청하려고
(D) 계약을 협상하려고

해설 첫 단락에서 헤이글 씨가 퀄리뷰 사가 귀사의 자동차 창유리 도매
공급업체가 되는 계약에 수정 사항 제안을 보내 주셔서 감사하다
(Thank you for forwarding your proposed revisions to the
contract ~ of automotive window glass)고 한 뒤, 두 번째 단
락에서 동의하는 사항과 동의하지 않는 사항을 언급하고 세 번째 단락
에서 다음 주에 귀하와 이에 대해 추가적으로 논의하고 싶다(I would
like to discuss this further with you next week)고 했다. 따라
서 헤이글 씨가 거래처와 계약 사항을 협상하기 위해 이메일을 보낸
것임을 알 수 있으므로 (D)가 정답이다.

어휘 **finalize** 마무리 짓다 **negotiate** 협상하다

Paraphrasing 지문의 discuss this further
→ 정답의 negotiate a contract

165 Not / True

번역 퀄리뷰 사에 대해 명시된 것은?
(A) 온라인으로 제품을 판매한다.
(B) 차량용 창을 제작한다.
(C) 과거에 위약금을 지불한 적이 있다.
(D) 최근에 배송 상자를 다시 디자인했다.

해설 첫 문장에서 퀄리뷰 사가 귀사의 자동차 창유리 도매 공급업체가 되
는 계약에 수정 사항 제안을 보내 주셔서 감사하다(Thank you for
~ the contract for Qualiview Ltd. to be your wholesale
supplier of automotive window glass)고 한 것으로 보아 퀄리뷰
사는 차량용 창 제조업체임을 알 수 있다. 따라서 (B)가 정답이다.

166 동의어 찾기

번역 두 번째 단락 2행의 "address"와 의미가 가장 가까운 단어는?
(A) ~에 대응하다
(B) ~에 대해 생각하다
(C) 인사하다
(D) 배달하다

해설 의미상 포장재에 대한 우려를 '해소하다'라는 뜻으로 쓰였으므로 '~에
대응하다'를 뜻하는 (A) respond to가 정답이다.

167 세부사항

번역 헤이글 씨는 다음 주 언제 시간이 되는가?
(A) 월요일 오전
(B) 화요일 오후
(C) 수요일 오전
(D) 목요일 오후

해설 세 번째 단락의 두 번째 문장에서 헤이글 씨가 수요일이나 목요일 오
전 11시 전에 만나 뵐 수 있을지(Would you be available to meet
before 11:00 A.M. on either Wednesday or Thursday?)를 묻
고 있는 것으로 보아 헤이글 씨는 수요일과 목요일 오전에 시간이
된다는 것을 알 수 있다. 따라서 (C)가 정답이다.

Paraphrasing 지문의 before 11:00 A.M. → 정답의 morning

168-171 기사

배송 중단 사태

싱가포르 (6월 6일) — **168 최근 국제 화물 적재 공간에 대한 수요가 운
송 컨테이너의 가용성을 앞지르고 있다.** 이러한 컨테이너 부족은 아시아
항구에서 선적되는 상품의 비용 증가로 이어졌다. 컨테이너의 제작 원료
인 강철 롤의 생산 감소는 상황을 더욱 복잡하게 만들었다.

일부 수출업체들은 항공 화물이라는 더 비싼 옵션을 감안하였으나,
기업들은 여전히 어려운 선택에 직면해 있다. 고객에게 배송 지연을 감수
할 것을 요청하거나 급송 비용을 감당하기 위해 고객 가격을 대폭 인상
해야 한다. 어느 쪽이든 공급업체는 고객 불만을 촉발시킬 위험을 떠안게
된다.

**169 "저희는 이 문제의 해결책을 논의하기 위해 사업 파트너, 투자
자, 그리고 정부 관계자들과 함께 일하고 있습니다."라고 가정용품 생산
업체인 QET 그룹의 대변인 헨리 램이 말했다. "해결책을 찾기 위해서는
모든 이해 당사자들의 총체적인 협력이 필요할 것입니다."**

그렇다고 모든 기업들이 고통받고 있는 것은 아니다. 예를 들어,
170 운동복 및 신발 생산업체인 페즈커는 이 상황을 보다 잘 극복하기
위한 전략을 시행했다. **171 페즈커는 서양 국가 대상의 수출에서 벗어
나 국내 및 지역 시장을 확장하는 방향으로 노력을 다시 집중하는 데 성
공했다.** 이 시장들은 보다 쉽게 이용 가능한 트럭 및 열차 운송을 이용해
공급된다.

"저희는 신속하게 움직여서 운송 컨테이너 부족이 수익에 큰 영향을
미치지 않았습니다."라고 페즈커의 CEO 누와 리는 말했다.

어휘 **disruption** 중단; 붕괴 **demand** 수요 **freight** 화물
outpace 앞지르다 **availability** 이용 가능성 **shortage** 부족
port 항구 **production** 생산 **roll** 롤, 두루마리 **raw material**
원료, 원자재 **complicate** 복잡하게 하다 **exporter** 수출업체[자]
delay 지연 **substantially** 상당히 **expedited shipping**
급송 **trigger** 촉발시키다 **dissatisfaction** 불만 **government
official** 정부 관리 **spokesperson** 대변인 **household
goods** 가정용품 **stakeholder** 이해 당사자 **suffer** 고통받다
athletic apparel 운동복 **implement** 시행하다 **strategy** 전략
overcome 극복하다 **expand** 확장하다 **domestic** 국내의

regional 지방의   significant 상당한   impact 영향
profits 수익, 이익

168 Not / True

번역   운송 컨테이너에 대해 언급된 것은?
(A) 다양한 크기로 나온다.
(B) 공급이 부족한 상태이다.
(C) 다양한 재료로 만들어진다.
(D) 장기 보관에 사용될 수 있다.

해설   첫 문장에서 최근 국제 화물 적재 공간에 대한 수요가 운송 컨
테이너의 가용성을 앞지르고 있다(Recently, the demand
for international freight space has been outpacing the
availability of shipping containers)면서 이러한 컨테이너 부족
이 아시아 항구에서 선적되는 상품의 비용 증가로 이어졌다(This
container shortage has led to higher costs for goods ~)고
했으므로, 최근 운송 컨테이너의 공급이 수요에 비해 부족하다는 것을
알 수 있다. 따라서 정답은 (B)이다.

어휘   long-term 장기적인   storage 보관, 저장

169 세부사항

번역   램 씨는 상황을 해결하기 위해 무엇이 필요하다고 말하는가?
(A) 고객 수의 급격한 증가
(B) 정부 규제의 완화
(C) 새로운 기술의 개발
(D) 영향을 받는 그룹 간의 소통

해설   세 번째 단락에서 QET 그룹의 대변인 헨리 램은 이 문제의 해결책을
논의하기 위해 사업 파트너, 투자자, 그리고 정부 관계자들과 함께 일
하고 있다(We are working with business partners, investors,
and government officials ~ to this problem)면서 해결책을 찾
기 위해서는 모든 이해 당사자들의 총체적인 협력이 필요할 것(It's
going to take total cooperation of all stakeholders to find a
solution)이라고 했다. 따라서 램 씨가 필요하다고 한 것은 이해 당사
자들 간의 논의와 협력이므로 (D)가 정답이다.

어휘   relaxation 완화   restriction 규제   development 개발
communication 의사소통   affected 영향을 받는

Paraphrasing   지문의 stakeholders
→ 정답의 affected groups

170 세부사항

번역   페즈커가 생산하는 의복의 종류는?
(A) 비옷
(B) 운동복
(C) 정장
(D) 작업복

해설   네 번째 단락의 두 번째 문장에서 운동복 및 신발 생산업체인 페즈커
(Fezker, the producer of athletic apparel and footwear)라고
했으므로 (B)가 정답이다.

Paraphrasing   지문의 athletic apparel
→ 정답의 Sportswear

171 문장 삽입

번역   [1], [2], [3], [4]로 표시된 위치 중에서 다음 문장이 들어가기에 가
장 적합한 곳은?

"이 시장들은 보다 쉽게 이용 가능한 트럭 및 열차 운송을 이용해 공급
된다."
(A) [1]
(B) [2]
(C) [3]
(D) [4]

해설   주어진 문장에서 이 시장들(These markets)은 보다 쉽게 이용 가
능한 트럭 및 열차 운송을 이용해 공급된다고 했으므로, 주어진 문장
앞에는 이 시장들에 대한 내용이 있어야 한다. 따라서 페즈커의 국내
및 지역 시장들(domestic and regional markets)을 향한 전략에
대해 언급하는 [4] 뒤에 들어가는 것이 글의 흐름상 자연스러우므로
(D)가 정답이다.

172-175 온라인 채팅

게리 웬델 (오전 7시 40분)
좋은 아침입니다, 팀 여러분. 173 **여러분의 프로젝트 현황을 공유해 주시
겠습니까?**

징 유 (오전 7시 42분)
저는 팰리세이드 프로젝트 B단계의 시작일을 확인하기 위해 지난주에
고객과 만났습니다.

로비 주니가 (오전 7시 43분)
172, 174 저는 지금 리버뷰 프로젝트 현장으로 가고 있습니다. 지난주에
내린 비로 보도에 콘크리트 타설 작업이 지연되었습니다. 상황이 나아졌
는지 보기 위해 오늘 아침에 상태 점검을 할 예정입니다.

게리 웬델 (오전 7시 44분)
팰리세이드 프로젝트 B단계는 언제 시작되나요?

징 유 (오전 7시 46분)
172 3월에 착공해서 11월까지 건물을 완공할 계획입니다.

게리 웬델 (오전 7시 47분)
3월 시작일에 관한 좋은 소식이군요. 고객이 좋아할 거라고 확신해요.

게리 웬델 (오전 7시 50분)
로비, 현장 상황에 대해 파악한 사항을 알려 주세요. 아마 네이선 버리가
현장에서 도움을 줄 수 있을 겁니다. 그는 우리 회사에서 가장 박식한 콘
크리트 마감 작업자예요.

로비 주니가 (오전 7시 55분)
175 사실 오늘 아침 현장에서 네이선을 만날 예정이라서 언제 콘크리트
를 타설할 수 있을지 그의 의견을 구하겠습니다. 나머지 프로젝트는 이
작업을 할 수 있을 때까지 보류됩니다.

게리 웬델 (오전 7시 57분)

175 계속해서 소식을 알려 주세요. 아직 너무 습하다면 서두르고 싶지 않습니다. 174 동시에 리버뷰 프로젝트는 장비 문제와 건축 자재 배송 지연으로 이미 일정보다 늦어지고 있습니다.

로비 주니가 (오전 7시 58분)

그렇게 하겠습니다.

어휘 status 상황 phase 단계 delay 지연시키다: 지연 pour 붓다 sidewalk 보도, 인도 break ground 착공하다 finisher 마무리하는 직공 on hold 보류된 rush 서두르다 behind schedule 예정보다 늦은

---

172 추론 / 암시

번역 채팅 작성자들은 어떤 업계에서 일할 것 같은가?
(A) 건설
(B) 에너지
(C) 제조
(D) 여행

해설 7시 43분에 주니가 씨가 지금 리버뷰 프로젝트 현장으로 가고 있다(I am headed ~ for the Riverview project)면서 지난주에 내린 비로 보도에 콘크리트 타설 작업이 지연되었다(The rain last week delayed pouring the concrete for the sidewalks)고 했고, 7시 46분에 유 씨가 3월에 착공해서 11월까지 건물을 완공할 계획(We will break ground in March and plan to have the building completed by November)이라고 한 것으로 보아 채팅 작성자들은 건설업계에서 근무하는 사람들임을 알 수 있다. 따라서 (A)가 정답이다.

173 주제 / 목적

번역 웬델 씨가 논의를 시작한 이유는?
(A) 고객 미팅을 계획하려고
(B) 일기 예보에 대해 논의하려고
(C) 일부 작업에 대한 최신 정보를 구하려고
(D) 행사의 시작일을 변경하려고

해설 7시 40분에 웬델 씨가 팀원들에게 프로젝트 현황을 공유해 줄 것(Can you share the current status of your projects, please?)을 요청하며 채팅을 시작한 것으로 보아 프로젝트의 최신 진행 상황을 보고받으려는 것임을 알 수 있으므로 (C)가 정답이다.

어휘 weather forecast 일기 예보 obtain 얻다, 구하다

Paraphrasing 지문의 share the current status of your projects → 정답의 obtain an update on some work

---

174 Not / True

번역 리버뷰 프로젝트에 대해 명시된 것은?
(A) 여러 차례 지연되었다.
(B) 유 씨가 관리하고 있다.
(C) 11월에 완료될 예정이다.
(D) 고객들이 진행 상황에 만족한다.

해설 7시 43분에 주니가 씨가 리버뷰 프로젝트 현장으로 가면서 지난주에 내린 비로 보도에 콘크리트 타설 작업이 지연되었다(The rain last week delayed pouring the concrete for the sidewalks)고 했고, 7시 57분에 웬델 씨가 동시에 리버뷰 프로젝트는 장비 문제와 건축 자재 배송 지연으로 이미 일정보다 늦어지고 있다(At the same time, the Riverview project is already behind schedule ~ late delivery of building materials)고 했다. 따라서 리버뷰 프로젝트는 비, 장비 문제, 건축 자재 배송 지연으로 여러 번 지연되었음을 확인할 수 있으므로 (A)가 정답이다.

175 의도 파악

번역 오전 7시 58분에 주니가 씨가 "그렇게 하겠습니다"라고 쓴 의도는?
(A) 배송 일정을 변경할 것이다.
(B) 추가 장비를 구입할 것이다.
(C) 현장에서 도와줄 작업자들을 고용할 것이다.
(D) 회의 결과를 공유할 것이다.

해설 7시 55분에 주니가 씨가 사실 오늘 아침 현장에서 네이선을 만날 예정이라서 언제 콘크리트를 타설할 수 있을지 그의 의견을 구하겠다(Actually, I'm meeting Nathan ~ so I'll get his opinion on when we can pour the concrete)고 했고, 7시 57분에 웬델 씨가 계속해서 소식을 알려 달라(Keep me posted)고 하자 7시 58분에 주니가 씨가 그렇게 하겠다(Will do)고 대답한 것이므로, 주니가 씨는 네이선과의 회의 결과를 웬델 씨에게 알려 주겠다는 의도로 한 말임을 알 수 있다. 따라서 정답은 (D)이다.

어휘 revise 변경[수정]하다 outcome 결과

176-180 이메일 + 설문지

발신: 매덜린 케를루크 〈mkerluke@karabel.ca〉
수신: 오마르 니클라우스 〈oniklaus@karabel.ca〉,
        제이 톤킥 〈jtoncic@karabel.ca〉
날짜: 2월 3일 금요일 오후 2시 16분
제목: 맛 테스트 결과
첨부: ⓤ 파티오르 연구소 설문 조사 결과

안녕하세요, 팀 여러분.

방금 파티오르 연구소로부터 새 아이스크림 맛 테스트에 대한 1월 24일 ~26일 설문 조사 결과를 받았습니다. 첨부된 문서에서 볼 수 있다시피, 결과는 매우 실망스럽습니다. 우리가 최고라고 생각했던 네 가지 맛을 보냈지만, 그 중 어느 것도 다음 개발 단계로 진행시킬 만큼 충분히 높은 평가를 받지 못했습니다. 180 우리의 목표 시장인 25세부터 40세까지의 소비자에 해당하는 맛 테스트 참가자 92명 사이에서 대부분의 평가는 일치했습니다. 176 테스트 단계에서 제품 색상이 낮은 점수를 받더라도 연구실에서 쉽게 조정할 수 있기 때문에 크게 문제되지 않습니다. 하지만 결코 맛 부문에서 3점 이하의 점수를 받는 샘플을 내보내서는 안 됩니다.

177 어떻게 진행할지 방법을 찾기 위해 월요일(2월 6일) 오전 9시에 모이고 싶습니다. 대다수 테스트 참가자들이 제안했듯이 몇 가지를 조정하면 개발이 가능한 맛이 한 가지 있습니다. 또한 **178** 6월 초까지 프레스턴 그로서스의 냉동 선반에 새 아이스크림을 입고시키려면 늦어도 3월 1일까지는 파티오르 연구소에 새로운 맛을 보내야 할 것입니다.

매덜린 케롤루크

어휘 survey (설문) 조사 attached 첨부된 rating 평가, 등급 advance 진행시키다 consistent 일치하는 participant 참가자 consumer 소비자 score 점수 adjust 조정하다 laboratory 연구실 category 범주, 부문 figure out 생각해 내다 proceed 나아가다, 진행하다 adjustment 조정 grocer 식료품점 freezer 냉동고

---

180 파티오르 연구소 소비자 맛 테스트 설문 조사

날짜: 1월 24일
회사: 카라벨 인더스트리스
180 참가자 번호: 54번

방법: 네 가지 다른 아이스크림의 45그램 샘플을 받게 됩니다. 각 아이스크림의 맛, 식감, 단맛, 색상을 1(매우 불만족)에서 5(매우 만족)까지의 등급으로 평가해 주십시오. 추가 의견은 아래에 적어 주십시오.

향미	맛	식감	단맛	색상
레몬	2	3	2	4
망고	3	3	2	1
솔티드 캐러멜	2	1	1	5
피넛 브리틀	3	4	2	2

의견: 과일 맛이 나는 아이스크림은 놀랄 정도로 시큼했습니다. 전혀 마음에 들지 않았습니다. **179** 피넛 브리틀이 가장 잠재력 있다고 생각하지만, 무언가 부족합니다. 초콜릿 스월이나 브라우니 조각을 추가하면 성공작이 될 것이 분명합니다.

어휘 directions 지시, 사용법 rate 평가하다, 등급을 매기다 texture 식감 scale 등급, 척도 unpleasant 불쾌한 sour 신 care for ~을 좋아하다 brittle 견과류를 섞은 납작한 과자 potential 잠재력 bet (~이) 분명하다 swirl 소용돌이 (모양) bit 조각

---

176 Not / True

번역 이메일에서 카라벨 인더스트리스 아이스크림에 대해 명시한 것은?
(A) 현재 네 가지 맛이 판매되고 있다.
(B) 색상은 쉽게 바꿀 수 있다.
(C) 최근 인기가 감소했다.
(D) 카라벨 인더스트리스 매장에서 판매된다.

해설 이메일의 첫 단락 다섯 번째 문장에서 테스트 단계에서 제품의 색상이 낮은 점수를 받더라도 연구실에서 쉽게 조정할 수 있기 때문에 크게 문제되지 않는다(It's not a big problem ~ since we can easily adjust that in the laboratory)고 했으므로 (B)가 정답이다.

어휘 currently 현재 popularity 인기

Paraphrasing 지문의 easily adjust
→ 정답의 be changed easily

---

177 세부사항

번역 케롤루크 씨가 하고 싶다고 언급한 것은?
(A) 연구소 방문
(B) 팀 회의 개최
(C) 식료품 매장에 연락
(D) 새로운 설문 조사 질문 작성

해설 이메일의 두 번째 단락 첫 문장에서 케롤루크 씨가 어떻게 진행할지 방법을 찾기 위해 월요일(2월 6일) 오전 9시에 모이고 싶다(I would like to meet ~ to figure out how to proceed)고 했으므로 정답은 (B)이다.

Paraphrasing 지문의 meet → 정답의 Hold a team meeting

---

178 추론 / 암시

번역 파티오르 연구소에 대해 암시된 것은?
(A) 직원이 92명 있다.
(B) 식용 색소를 제조한다.
(C) 카라벨 인더스트리스를 위해 추가로 맛 테스트를 수행할 것이다.
(D) 프레스턴 그로서스에 아이스크림을 공급한다.

해설 이메일의 마지막 문장에서 6월 초까지 프레스턴 그로서스의 냉동 선반에 새 아이스크림을 입고시키려면 늦어도 3월 1일까지는 파티오르 연구소에 새로운 맛을 보내야 할 것(We will also need to get some new flavours to Fatior Labs ~ to get a new ice cream on the Preston Grocers freezer shelves by the beginning of June)이라고 한 것으로 보아 파티오르 연구소에서 카라벨 인더스트리스의 새 아이스크림 맛 테스트를 추가 진행할 것임을 추론할 수 있다. 따라서 (C)가 정답이다.

어휘 manufacture 제조하다 food coloring 식용 색소 supply 공급하다

---

179 추론 / 암시

번역 설문지에 의하면, 카라벨 인더스트리스는 어떤 맛을 조정할 것 같은가?
(A) 레몬
(B) 망고
(C) 솔티드 캐러멜
(D) 피넛 브리틀

해설 설문지 하단 의견란의 세 번째 문장에서 작성자는 피넛 브리틀이 가장 잠재력 있다고 생각하지만 무언가 부족하다(I think the Peanut Brittle has the most potential, but it's missing something)며, 초콜릿 스월이나 브라우니 조각을 추가하면 성공작이 될 것이 분명하다(I bet that adding chocolate swirls or brownie bits would make it a winner)고 평가했다. 따라서 (D)가 정답이다.

180 연계

번역 번역 54번 참가자에 대해 결론지을 수 있는 것은?
(A) 아이스크림을 여러 통 구입했다.
(B) 25세에서 40세 사이이다.
(C) 정기적으로 소비자 설문 조사에 응한다.
(D) 과일 맛 아이스크림을 선호한다.

해설 이메일의 네 번째 문장에서 목표 시장인 25세부터 40세까지의 소비자에 해당하는 맛 테스트 참가자 92명(the 92 taste-test participants ~ ages 25 through 40)이라며 테스트 참가자들에 대해 언급했고, 설문지 상단에 파티오르 연구소 소비자 맛 테스트 설문 조사(Fatior Labs Consumer Taste-Testing Survey)의 참가자 번호가 54번(Participant number: 54)이라고 나와 있다. 따라서 54번 참가자의 나이가 25세에서 40세 사이임을 알 수 있으므로 (B)가 정답이다.

어휘 container 용기, 그릇 regularly 정기적으로

181-185 웹페이지 + 편지

https://www.creategreat.ca/openings

패션업계에서 다양한 글로벌 고객을 보유한 온타리오 소재 크리에이티브 에이전시인 크리에이트 그레이트가 패션에 열정적이고 시장 동향을 이해하며 디지털 도구를 쉽게 다룰 수 있는 카피라이터를 찾고 있습니다.

이상적인 지원자는 국제적인 배경을 가진 팀원들과 함께 빠른 작업 환경에서 일을 잘하는 사람입니다. 카피라이터는 크리에이티브팀과 협력하여 고객 요구에 182 **적합한** 브랜드 전략을 개발하고, 마케팅팀과 협력하여 현재 및 잠재 고객을 위한 브랜드 기반의 홍보 캠페인을 성공시킬 것입니다. 181 **카피라이터에게는 원격 근무가 허용되므로** 캐나다 거주가 요구되지 않습니다.

지원하시려면 자기소개서와 이력서를 크리에이트 그레이트, 콜버트 로 838, 런던, ON N6B 3P5, 크리에이티브팀 책임자 프랜 벤저민 앞으로 보내 주세요. 183 **지원 마감일: 8월 5일**

어휘 based 본사[근거지]를 둔 diverse 다양한 passionate 열정적인 with ease 쉽게 ideal 이상적인 candidate 지원자 fast-paced 속도가 빠른 background (개인의) 배경 collaborate 협력하다 strategy 전략 suit 적합하다 ensure 반드시 ~하게 하다 publicity 홍보 prospective 장래의 remote 원격의 residence 거주 apply 지원하다 cover letter 자기소개서 application 지원(서)

애니 스미스
사우스 브라이언트 로 4810
포틀랜드, OR 97206

183 **8월 6일**

프랜 벤저민
크리에이트 그레이트
콜버트 로 838
런던, ON N6B 3P5

벤저민 씨께,

크리에이트 그레이트의 카피라이터 자리에 지원하고자 편지를 씁니다. 글을 쓴 경험이 있는 전문 패션 디자이너로서, 저는 귀하의 팀에 가치 있는 추가 인력이 될 것이라고 믿습니다. 제 이력서를 동봉해 드립니다.

저는 포틀랜드의 의류 브랜드인 모다에서 여성복 컬렉션의 수석 디자이너로서 10년간의 경력이 있습니다. 184 **저는 초기 시장 조사부터 완제품에 이르기까지 디자인 생산 과정을 감독합니다.** 제 역할에서 저는 마케팅팀 및 생산팀과 긴밀히 협력하며 작업합니다.

또한 185 지난 5년 동안 제 개인 블로그를 유지해 오고 있습니다. 제 게시물은 여성 패션 트렌드와 의류 및 화장품을 보다 지속 가능하게 하는 방법에 초점을 맞추고 있습니다. 취미로 시작한 것이 지금은 유료 광고주와 15,000명 이상의 팔로워를 유치했습니다. 185 **제 글을 살펴보시려면 www.medesheen.com을 방문하십시오.**

제 지원을 고려해 주셔서 감사합니다.

애니 스미스

서류 동봉

어휘 expert 전문적인 valuable 가치 있는 addition 추가(된 것) enclosed 동봉된 decade 10년 oversee 감독하다 production 생산 initial 초기의 finished product 완제품 maintain 유지하다 cosmetics 화장품 sustainable 지속 가능한 attract 끌어들이다 advertiser 광고주 enclosure 동봉된 것

181 세부사항

번역 웹페이지에 따르면, 구직자가 할 수 있는 것은?
(A) 원격 근무
(B) 팀 관리
(C) 해외 출장
(D) 캐나다로 이주

해설 웹페이지의 두 번째 단락 마지막 문장에서 카피라이터에게는 원격 근무가 허용된다(remote work is permitted for copywriters)고 했으므로 (A)가 정답이다.

어휘 remotely 원격으로 relocate 이동하다

182 동의어 찾기

번역 웹페이지의 두 번째 단락 4행의 "suit"와 의미가 가장 가까운 단어는?
(A) 조정하다
(B) 결정하다
(C) 투자하다
(D) 만족시키다

해설 의미상 고객 요구에 적합한 전략, 즉 '~에 적합하게 하다'라는 뜻으로 쓰였으므로 '만족시키다'라는 의미의 (D) satisfy가 정답이다.

183 연계

번역 스미스 씨에 대해 암시된 것은?
(A) 이미 벤저민 씨를 만났다.
(B) 카피라이터로 근무한 적이 있다.
(C) 지원 마감일을 놓쳤다.
(D) 필요한 서류 제출을 잊었다.

해설 웹페이지 마지막 줄에 지원 마감일이 8월 5일(Application deadline: August 5)이라고 나와 있고, 편지 상단에 스미스 씨가 편지를 보낸 날짜가 8월 6일(August 6)이라고 나와 있다. 따라서 스미스 씨는 지원 마감일이 지난 뒤에 편지를 보낸 것이므로 (C)가 정답이다.

어휘 miss 놓치다 submit 제출하다

184 세부사항

번역 편지에 따르면, 모다에서 스미스 씨의 업무 중 하나는?
(A) 패션 디자이너 채용
(B) 광고 초안 작성
(C) 생산 과정 관리
(D) 지속 가능한 의류 옵션 조사

해설 편지의 두 번째 단락에서 스미스 씨는 포틀랜드의 의류 브랜드인 모다에서의 경력을 언급하면서 초기 시장 조사부터 완제품에 이르기까지 디자인 생산 과정을 감독한다(I oversee the design production process from initial market research to finished product)고 했으므로 (C)가 정답이다.

어휘 draft 초안

Paraphrasing 지문의 oversee → 정답의 Managing

185 추론 / 암시

번역 메드신은 무엇일 것 같은가?
(A) 화장품 브랜드
(B) 패션 블로그
(C) 온라인 잡지
(D) 광고대행사

해설 편지의 세 번째 단락 첫 문장에서 스미스 씨가 지난 5년 동안 개인 블로그를 운영하고 있다(for the last five years, I have been maintaining my own blog)며 게시물은 여성 패션 트렌드와 의류 및 화장품을 보다 지속 가능하게 만드는 방법에 초점을 두고 있다(My posts focus on trends in women's fashion ~ more sustainable)고 소개한 뒤, 마지막 문장에서 자신의 글을 살펴보려면 www.medesheen.com을 방문하라(Visit www.medesheen.com for examples of my writing)고 했다. 따라서 메드신은 스미스 씨의 개인 블로그로 패션 트렌드와 의류, 화장품을 주제로 다루고 있음을 알 수 있으므로 (B)가 정답이다.

186-190 이메일 + 이메일 + 영수증

발신: 아키히토 나카시마 〈a.nakashima@gilchristshipping.com〉
수신: 파울러 사무용품 〈support@fowlerofficesupplies.com〉
제목: 주문 B19849
날짜: 8월 19일

관계자분께,

어제 귀사의 웹사이트에서 사무용품을 몇 개 구입했습니다. **186 이메일 영수증을 받았는데, 비용이 품목별로 기재되어 있지 않습니다. 새로운 회사 정책을 충족시키려면, 저는 상관에게 각 품목에 대한 요금이 별도로 기재된 영수증을 제출해야 합니다. 그런 영수증을 이메일로 보내 주실 수 있을까요?** 만약 안 될 경우, 제가 귀사의 웹사이트에서 직접 해당 정보를 구할 수 있을까요? **189 마지막으로, 향후 주문에 대한 확인서를 두 개 이상의 이메일 주소로 보내 주실 수 있을까요?** 제 상관이 확인서를 자동으로 받는 것이 가장 좋을 것 같습니다.

아키히토 나카시마, 비서
길크리스트 해운

어휘 office supplies 사무용품 itemize 항목별로 적다 satisfy 충족시키다 policy 정책 supervisor 감독관, 관리자 charge 요금 separately 별도로 confirmation 확인(서) ideal 이상적인, 가장 알맞은 automatically 자동적으로

발신: 파울러 사무용품 〈support@fowlerofficesupplies.com〉
수신: 아키히토 나카시마 〈a.nakashima@gilchristshipping.com〉
제목: 회신: 주문 B19849
날짜: 8월 19일
첨부: ⬙ B19849

나카시마 씨께,

요청하신 영수증을 첨부했습니다. **187 불편을 끼쳐드린 데 대한 사과의 뜻으로, 다음 주문 시 총 가격에서 10퍼센트 할인을 제공해 드리겠습니다.** 이전 주문의 전체 내역을 보시려면 먼저 저희 웹사이트의 계정에 로그인하시고, '나의 주문' 탭으로 이동하신 다음 주문번호를 클릭하십시오.

188 고객님의 지난 몇 건의 주문마다 특정 품목 10개에 대한 동일 주문이 포함된 것을 알게 되었습니다. 이것을 반복 주문으로 표시하면 그 품목의 가격을 5퍼센트 할인해 드린다는 점을 알아주시기 바랍니다. 이렇게 하시려면, 온라인 주문서에서 '반복 주문' 칸에 체크만 하시면 됩니다.

189 고객님의 마지막 문의에 관해서는 현재로서는 불가능합니다. 하지만 해당 의견을 기술팀과 공유하도록 하겠습니다.

캐머런 히긴스, 고객 상담실
파울러 사무용품

어휘 in apology for ~을 사과하여 inconvenience 불편 description 기술, 서술 previous 이전의 account 계정 identical 동일한 particular 특정한 reduce 낮추다, 할인하다 mark 표시하다 recurring 반복되어 발생하는 query 문의

파울러 사무용품

주문 영수증: B19849

주문 날짜: 8월 18일

품목	가격	수량	총계
188 **프린터 용지**	8달러/500장	10	80달러
토너 (검정)	50달러/카트리지	1	50달러
젤 펜 (파랑)	5달러/8팩	3	15달러
스테이플	3.5달러/상자	2	7달러
총액			152달러

반품 정책: 미개봉 상품은 구매일로부터 60일 이내에 우편으로 또는 저희 매장 중 한 곳에서 반품할 수 있습니다. 우편으로 반품하시려면, www.fowlerofficesupplies.com 계정에 로그인하셔서 배송 라벨을 인쇄하십시오. 190 **매장 내 반품의 경우, 물품과 주문번호를 파울러 사무용품 지점으로 가져오십시오.**

어휘 quantity 수량 merchandise 상품 return 반품하다; 반품 in-store 매장 내의

186 주제 / 목적

번역 나카시마 씨가 이메일을 보낸 이유는?
(A) 주문한 물품을 받지 못했다.
(B) 실수로 한 품목에 대해 두 번 청구되었다.
(C) 충분히 상세하지 않은 영수증을 받았다.
(D) 구매 내역에 대한 확인 이메일을 받지 못했다.

해설 첫 이메일의 두 번째 문장에서 나카시마 씨가 이메일 영수증을 받았는데 비용이 품목별로 기재되어 있지 않다(I received an e-mail receipt, but the costs are not itemized on it)고 했고, 새로운 회사 정책을 충족시키려면 상관에게 각 품목에 대한 요금이 별도로 기재된 영수증을 제출해야 한다(To satisfy a new company policy ~ a receipt with the charges for each item listed separately)면서 그런 영수증을 이메일로 보내 줄 수 있는지(Could you e-mail me such a receipt?)를 문의하고 있으므로 (C)가 정답이다.

어휘 mistakenly 실수로 charge 청구하다 detailed 상세한

187 세부사항

번역 두 번째 이메일에 따르면, 나카시마 씨가 다음 주문에 받게 될 것은?
(A) 카탈로그
(B) 무료 펜
(C) 인쇄된 영수증
(D) 가격 할인

해설 두 번째 이메일의 두 번째 문장에서 나카시마 씨에게 불편을 끼친 데 대한 사과의 뜻으로 다음 주문 시 총 가격에서 10퍼센트 할인을 제공하겠다(In apology for the inconvenience, we will provide you with 10 percent off the total price of your next order)고 했으므로 (D)가 정답이다.

Paraphrasing 지문의 **10 percent off the total price** → 정답의 **A price discount**

188 연계

번역 히긴스 씨가 나카시마 씨에게 '반복 주문'을 선택하라고 제안한 품목은?
(A) 프린터 용지
(B) 토너
(C) 젤 펜
(D) 스테이플

해설 두 번째 이메일의 두 번째 단락 첫 문장에서 히긴스 씨가 나카시마 씨에게 지난 몇 번의 주문마다 특정 품목 10개에 대한 동일 주문이 포함된 것을 알게 되었다(I noticed that included ~ an identical order for ten of a particular item)면서 이것을 반복 주문으로 표시하면 그 품목의 가격을 5퍼센트 할인해 드린다는 점을 알아달라(You should know ~ if you mark this as a recurring order)고 했고, 영수증을 보면 첫 항목에 프린터 용지(Printer paper)의 수량이 10개로 나와 있다. 따라서 히긴스 씨가 나카시마 씨에게 매번 10개씩 주문하는 프린터 용지를 반복 주문으로 표시해 할인받으라고 제안한 것임을 알 수 있으므로 (A)가 정답이다.

189 연계

번역 히긴스 씨가 기술팀에 검토해 달라고 요청할 것은?
(A) 웹사이트의 응답률 개선
(B) 복수의 이메일 주소로 영수증을 발송하는 옵션 제공
(C) 홈페이지에 고객의 주문 내역에 대한 링크 배치
(D) 모든 기기에서 인쇄 가능한 반품 라벨 제작

해설 첫 이메일의 여섯 번째 문장에서 나카시마 씨가 마지막으로 향후 주문에 대한 확인서를 두 개 이상의 이메일 주소로 보내 줄 수 있는지(Finally, can confirmations ~ be sent to more than one e-mail address?)를 문의했고, 두 번째 이메일의 세 번째 단락 첫 문장에서 히긴스 씨가 고객님의 마지막 문의에 관해서는 현재로서는 불가능하지만(As for your final query, this is not possible right now) 해당 의견을 기술팀과 공유하겠다(However, I will share the idea with our technical team)고 했다. 따라서 히긴스 씨는 복수의 이메일 주소로 주문 확인서를 보내 달라는 나카시마 씨의 요청 사항에 대해 기술팀에 검토를 의뢰할 것임을 알 수 있으므로 (B)가 정답이다.

어휘 response rate 응답률 multiple 다수[복수]의 printable 인쇄 가능한

Paraphrasing 지문의 **more than one** → 정답의 **multiple**

190 세부사항

번역 파울러 사무용품 매장에서 상품을 반품하기 위해 필요한 것은?
(A) 원본 영수증
(B) 신용카드 번호
(C) 확인 이메일
(D) 주문번호

해설 영수증의 마지막 문장에서 매장 내 반품의 경우 물품과 주문번호를 파울러 사무용품 지점으로 가져오라(For in-store returns, bring the item and the order number to any Fowler Office Supplies location)고 했으므로 (D)가 정답이다.

크로포드 앤 듀발
오프라인 매장 오픈

홍콩 (2월 18일) — 191 **수공예 담요, 장식용 베개, 기타 가정용품으로 유명한 온라인 소매업체인 크로포드 앤 듀발이 홍콩에 네 개의 오프라인 매장을 설립했다.** 지난 월요일, 회사는 194 **센트럴 디스트릭트에 대형 백화점뿐** 아니라 코즈웨이 베이, 디스커버리 베이, 성완에 부티크 매장의 그랜드 오픈을 축하했다. 부티크 매장들이 크로포드 앤 듀발의 유명한 소형 가정용품 중 가장 인기 있는 물건들을 취급하는 한편, 194 **센트럴 디스트릭트 지점은 실내 식물 코너와 스페셜티 커피와 티, 가벼운 스낵을 갖춘 매장 내 카페를 자랑한다.** 게다가 이곳은 회사의 웹사이트를 통해 구입할 수 있는 것보다 훨씬 더 광범위한 종류의 상품을 갖추고 있다.

어휘 brick-and-mortar 오프라인 거래의 retailer 소매업체 handcrafted 수공예품인 blanket 담요 decorative 장식용의 pillow 베개 household goods 가정용품 establish 설립하다 department store 백화점, 여러 상품을 부문별로 나누어 진열해 판매하는 대형소매점 district 지구, 구역 carry 취급하다 boast 자랑하다 on-site 현장의 extensive 광범위한

---

https://www.crawfordandduval.com.hk

| 홈 | 베스트셀러 | 전체 카탈로그 | 장바구니 |

크로포드 앤 듀발이 홍콩의 충성 고객들에게 다가갑니다!

크로포드 앤 듀발은 다음 장소에 첫 오프라인 매장 개점 소식을 알리게 되어 기쁘게 생각합니다: 코즈웨이 베이, 디스커버리 베이, 성완, 센트럴 디스트릭트.

5년 전 온라인 매장을 시작한 이래로, 저희는 여러분이 꿈에 그리는 주거 공간을 만들 수 있도록 도왔습니다. 이제 여러분의 집을 꾸미는 일이 훨씬 더 쉬워집니다. 192 **각 지점에는 인테리어 디자이너가 직원으로 상주하고 있어서 인기 상품을 둘러보면서 전문가와 직접 상담하실 수 있습니다.**

모든 지점이 대중교통을 이용하기에 편리합니다. 센트럴 디스트릭트 지점은 부설 주차장에서 무료 주차를 제공합니다.

개점 기념의 일환으로 3월 1일 이전에 매장 중 한 곳을 방문하는 고객은 방문 중에 사용할 수 있는 70홍콩달러 상당의 산품권을 받게 됩니다.

195 **당사의 온라인 단골 구매 클럽 회원들은 500홍콩달러 이상 구매 시 10퍼센트 할인을 포함해 매장에서도 동일한 혜택을 받게 됩니다.**

어휘 loyal (브랜드에) 충성스러운 launch 시작, 출시 decorate 장식하다 expert 전문가 in person 직접 browse (가게 안을) 둘러보다 public transportation 대중교통 attached 부속된, 소속된 frequent 빈번한 benefit 혜택

크로포드 앤 듀발

고객 영수증
날짜: 2월 23일

품목	가격
대나무 테이블 램프	1,450홍콩달러
장식용 쿠션 두 개 세트	750홍콩달러
7.5리터 알로에 화분	300홍콩달러
193 세탁기 세탁 가능한 울 담요	2,000홍콩달러
소계	4,500홍콩달러
195 10% 할인	450홍콩달러
총계	4,050홍콩달러

☐ 현금
☐ 상품권 번호:
☑ 신용카드 번호: ***********5598
신용카드 명의: 메이린 퐁

194 **매장 카페에 들러 즐거운 시간을 보내세요!**

어휘 bamboo 대나무 planter 화분 machine-washable 세탁기로 세탁할 수 있는 treat 대접, 한턱

---

191 주제 / 목적

번역 기사의 목적은?
(A) 현지 생산 제품을 비교하려고
(B) 매장 개점을 알리려고
(C) 웹사이트의 변경사항을 나열하려고
(D) 카페를 평가하려고

해설 기사의 첫 문장에서 수공예 담요, 장식용 베개, 기타 가정용품으로 유명한 온라인 소매업체인 크로포드 앤 듀발이 홍콩에 네 개의 오프라인 매장을 설립했다(Crawford and Duval ~ has established four brick-and-mortar stores in Hong Kong)고 한 것으로 보아 소매업체의 오프라인 매장 개점 소식을 전하는 기사이므로 (B)가 정답이다.

어휘 compare 비교하다 locally 현지에서

Paraphrasing 지문의 established ~ stores
→ 정답의 store openings

192 Not / True

번역 웹사이트에서 크로포드 앤 듀발에 대해 명시한 것은?
(A) 전 세계에 매장을 보유하고 있다.
(B) 사업한 지 10년이 되었다.
(C) 인테리어 디자이너를 고용한다.
(D) 모든 매장에서 무료 주차를 제공한다.

해설 웹페이지의 두 번째 단락 세 번째 문장에서 각 지점에는 인테리어 디자이너가 직원으로 상주하고 있어서 인기 상품을 둘러보면서 전문가와 직접 상담할 수 있다(Each location has an interior designer on staff ~ browse our popular items)고 언급했으므로 (C)가 정답이다. 첫 오프라인 매장을 연다(the opening of its first brick-

and-mortar stores)고 했으므로 (A), 5년 전 온라인 매장을 시작했다(the launch of our online store five years ago)고 했으므로 (B), 센트럴 디스트릭트 지점 부설 주차장에서 무료 주차를 제공한다(Our Central District location offers free parking)며 특정 지점 한 곳만 언급했으므로 (D)는 모두 오답이다.

Paraphrasing　지문의 has an interior designer on staff
　　　　　　→ 정답의 employs interior designers

193 Not / True

번역　영수증에 따르면, 담요에 대해 명시된 것은?
(A) 기계로 세탁할 수 있다.
(B) 면으로 만들어졌다.
(C) 퀸 사이즈이다.
(D) 베개가 딸린 세트로 제공된다.

해설　영수증의 네 번째 품목에 세탁기 세탁 가능한 울 담요(Machine-washable wool blanket)라고 나와 있으므로 (A)가 정답이다.

어휘　cotton 면직물

194 연계

번역　퐁 씨가 구입한 곳은 어디일 것 같은가?
(A) 웹사이트
(B) 부티크숍
(C) 카페
(D) 백화점

해설　퐁 씨의 영수증 하단에 매장 카페에 들러 즐거운 시간을 보내라(Stop at our in-store café for a treat!)고 권유하는 문장이 있는데, 기사에 따르면 스페셜티 커피와 티, 가벼운 스낵을 제공하는 매장 내 카페가 있는 곳은 센트럴 디스트릭트 지점(the Central District location also boasts ~ an on-site café that features specialty coffees, teas, and light snacks), 즉 센트럴 디스트릭트에 오픈한 대형 백화점(a large department store in Central District)이므로 (D)가 정답이다.

195 연계

번역　퐁 씨에 대해 암시된 것은?
(A) 크로포드 앤 듀발에서 종종 식품을 산다.
(B) 단골 구매 클럽의 회원이다.
(C) 구매 시 상품권을 썼다.
(D) 개점 기념 행사 동안 쇼핑을 했다.

해설　웹사이트의 마지막 문장에서 당사의 온라인 단골 구매 클럽 회원들은 500홍콩달러 이상 구매 시 10퍼센트 할인을 포함해 매장에서도 동일한 혜택을 받게 된다(Members of our online Frequent Purchase Club will receive ~ a 10 percent discount on purchases of HK$500 or more)고 했고, 영수증의 총계 위에 10% 할인(Less 10%)이 있는 것으로 보아 퐁 씨는 온라인 단골 구매 클럽 회원임을 알 수 있다. 따라서 (B)가 정답이다.

어휘　apply 적용하다

196-200 웹페이지 + 웹페이지 + 웹페이지

https://www.osawacorporateteambuilding.com/home

| 홈 | 신청 | 후기 | 연락 |

오사와 코퍼레이트 팀 빌딩

팀이 함께 모여 즐기면서 협력을 증진시키세요! 저희 활동은 직업 만족도와 참여도를 높여 줍니다. 여러분이 편히 쉴 수 있도록 저희가 모든 것을 계획합니다. 여러분의 팀에 알맞은 행사를 고르기만 하세요.

196 물건 찾기 - 팀에게 물건 목록을 주면 찾아서 휴대폰이나 카메라로 사진을 찍는 야외 게임입니다. 단체 규모: 10~50명. 시간: 3시간.

197 게임 데이 - 즐거운 팀 활동과 함께 하는 고활력 게임의 날입니다. 이 행사는 팀의 체력, 의사소통, 문제해결 능력을 키워 줍니다. 단체 규모: 20~500명. 시간: 2시간.

팀 페인팅 - 각 팀원은 미리 정해진 주제에 따라 야외에서 그림을 그립니다. 이 그림들은 마지막에 서로 연결됩니다. 단체 규모: 6~30명. 시간: 1~2시간.

로봇 만들기 - 여러분의 단체는 팀으로 나뉩니다. 각 팀은 다른 팀과 대결할 때 사용할 로봇을 만듭니다. 단체 규모: 10~30명. 시간 2~3시간.

올 초콜릿 - 여러분의 단체는 공학 기술을 사용하여 초콜릿 타워를 세울 수 있는 기회를 갖게 됩니다. 그런 다음 지역 쇼콜라티에로부터 초콜릿 만드는 법을 배웁니다. 단체 규모: 8~150명. 시간: 2시간.

198 10월에 행사를 예약하고 15퍼센트 할인을 받으세요.

어휘　team building 팀워크 육성　promote 증진시키다 cooperation 협력　engagement 참여　scavenger hunt 물건 찾기 게임　object 물건　problem-solving 문제해결 predetermined 미리 정해진　theme 주제　challenge 도전 engineering 공학　chocolatier 초콜릿 제조 판매업(자)

https://www.osawacorporateteambuilding.com/requests

| 홈 | 신청 | 후기 | 연락 |

이름　198 알렉산드라 피터슨
회사명　199 휘튼 테크
이메일 주소　apeterson@whittentech.com
전화번호　617-555-0123

행사 장소 및 날짜　보스턴 시내, 198 10월 15일

199 관심 있는 행사는 무엇입니까? 상위 3개를 선택하십시오.
1 게임 데이　2 물건 찾기　3 팀 페인팅

참가 인원　28명

추가 정보

바쁜 판매 시기가 시작되기 전에 영업팀을 위한 즐거운 활동에 관심이 있습니다. 사무실에서 많은 시간을 보내기 때문에 야외 행사를 원합니다.

영업일 기준 3일 이내에 견적서 및 확인서를 가지고 연락 드리겠습니다.

https://www.osawacorporateteambuilding.com/reviews

| 홈 | 신청 | **후기** | 연락 |

고객의 의견

10월 20일 휘튼 테크 작성

우리 팀은 휘튼 테크의 영업 직원을 위한 활동을 진행하는 데 오사와 코퍼레이트 팀 빌딩을 고용했습니다. ¹⁹⁹**물건 찾기의 진행자 로렌조 벤포드는 훌륭했습니다.** 우리 영업팀의 28명 모두가 긍정적인 평가를 했습니다. 그들은 춥고 흐린 날이었음에도 도시를 탐험하고, 도시의 역사를 배우고, 새로운 지역 명소를 찾는 것이 좋았다고 했습니다. 이 활동을 적극 추천합니다. ²⁰⁰**유일한 단점은 우리가 얼마나 멀리 걷게 될지 알지 못했다는 점입니다.** 충분히 준비할 수 있도록 도보 거리에 대한 정보가 있었다면 도움이 되었을 것입니다.

어휘   facilitator 진행자   positive 긍정적인   explore 탐험하다   attraction 명소   highly 매우, 대단히   downside 단점   realize 인식하다   walking distance 도보 거리

196   Not / True

번역   첫 번째 웹페이지에서 물건 찾기에 대해 명시한 것은?
(A) 참가자들이 카메라를 대여해야 한다.
(B) 참가자들에게 상을 주며 끝난다.
(C) 실내에 적합한 활동이다.
(D) 끝마치는 데 3시간이 소요된다.

해설   첫 번째 웹페이지에서 물건 찾기(Scavenger Hunt)에 소요 시간이 3시간(Time: 3 hours)이라고 설명되어 있으므로 (D)가 정답이다. 팀에게 목록을 주면 물건을 찾아 자신의 휴대폰이나 카메라로 사진을 찍는 야외 게임(An outdoor game ~ with their phone or camera)이라고 했으므로 (A)와 (C)는 오답이고, (B)에 대한 언급은 없다.

어휘   conclude 끝나다   suitable 적합한

197   세부사항

번역   200명 이상의 단체에 가장 좋은 행사는?
(A) 게임 데이
(B) 팀 페인팅
(C) 로봇 만들기
(D) 올 초콜릿

해설   첫 번째 웹페이지에 나열된 활동 중 200명 이상이 참여할 수 있는 유일한 활동은 단체 규모가 20~500명(Group size: 20-500 people)인 게임 데이(Game Day)이므로 (A)가 정답이다.

198   연계

번역   피터슨 씨에 대해 암시된 것은?
(A) 과거에 로봇 만들기 행사에 참여한 적이 있다.
(B) 행사에 할인을 받을 것이다.
(C) 최근에 휘튼 테크에서 일을 시작했다.
(D) 행사 기획자였다.

해설   첫 번째 웹페이지의 마지막 문장에서 10월에 행사를 예약하고 15퍼센트 할인을 받으라(Book an event in October and receive 15 percent off)고 했고, 두 번째 웹페이지의 상단에 행사 신청자의 이름이 알렉산드라 피터슨(Name: Alexandra Peterson), 행사 장소 및 날짜가 보스턴 시내, 10월 15일(Location and date of event: Downtown Boston, October 15)로 나와 있다. 따라서 피터슨 씨는 10월에 행사를 예약해 할인받을 것이라는 사실을 알 수 있으므로 (B)가 정답이다.

199   연계

번역   휘튼 테크에 대해 결론지을 수 있는 것은?
(A) 행사 참가자 수를 변경했다.
(B) 직원들에게 박물관 무료 입장권을 제공했다.
(C) 1순위 선택 활동을 예약할 수 없었다.
(D) 외부에서 행사를 개최할 수 없었다.

해설   신청 화면인 두 번째 웹사이트에 회사명이 휘튼 테크(Whitten Tech)이고, 관심 있는 활동에 1순위 게임 데이(Game Day), 2순위 물건 찾기(Scavenger Hunt), 3순위 팀 페인팅(Team painting)이라고 답했는데, 후기 화면인 세 번째 웹사이트 두 번째 문장에서 물건 찾기의 진행자 로렌조 벤포드가 훌륭했다(The facilitator of the Scavenger Hunt, Lorenzo Benford, was excellent)고 평가했다. 따라서 휘튼 테크가 1순위로 선택한 게임 데이가 아닌 2순위의 물건 찾기 활동이 진행된 것을 알 수 있으므로 (C)가 정답이다.

200   세부사항

번역   후기에 따르면, 행사에 대해 실망스러웠던 점은?
(A) 지역 역사에 대한 초점
(B) 도보 거리에 대한 정보 부족
(C) 단체를 유지하는 것의 어려움
(D) 재미없는 진행자

해설   세 번째 웹사이트의 여섯 번째 문장에서 유일한 단점은 우리가 얼마나 멀리 걷게 될지 알지 못했다는 점(The only downside was that we did not realize how far we would be walking)이라고 했으므로 (B)가 정답이다.

어휘   lack 부족

Paraphrasing   지문의 how far we would be walking
→ 정답의 walking distances

기출 TEST 3
동영상 강의

101 (C)	102 (B)	103 (A)	104 (B)	105 (D)
106 (C)	107 (C)	108 (B)	109 (A)	110 (D)
111 (D)	112 (C)	113 (C)	114 (D)	115 (A)
116 (A)	117 (B)	118 (A)	119 (C)	120 (D)
121 (D)	122 (D)	123 (C)	124 (D)	125 (D)
126 (A)	127 (D)	128 (A)	129 (B)	130 (D)
131 (C)	132 (B)	133 (A)	134 (B)	135 (C)
136 (B)	137 (B)	138 (A)	139 (C)	140 (B)
141 (C)	142 (A)	143 (C)	144 (D)	145 (A)
146 (A)	147 (B)	148 (D)	149 (C)	150 (B)
151 (C)	152 (A)	153 (B)	154 (D)	155 (D)
156 (B)	157 (C)	158 (C)	159 (C)	160 (A)
161 (C)	162 (B)	163 (D)	164 (C)	165 (A)
166 (D)	167 (C)	168 (B)	169 (A)	170 (C)
171 (C)	172 (B)	173 (B)	174 (A)	175 (D)
176 (B)	177 (B)	178 (A)	179 (A)	180 (B)
181 (D)	182 (D)	183 (D)	184 (B)	185 (D)
186 (C)	187 (B)	188 (D)	189 (A)	190 (D)
191 (D)	192 (B)	193 (C)	194 (C)	195 (D)
196 (D)	197 (A)	198 (B)	199 (C)	200 (D)

PART 5

101 접속사 자리 _ 부사절 접속사

해설 주어(your order)와 동사(is being processed)를 갖춘 완전한 절을 콤마 뒤 주절에 연결하는 자리이므로, 빈칸에는 부사절 접속사가 들어가야 한다. 따라서 '~하는 동안'이라는 의미의 접속사 (C) While이 정답이다. (A) Still, (D) Also는 부사, (B) Either는 or와 함께 쓰이는 상관접속사로 빈칸에 들어갈 수 없다.

번역 주문이 처리되는 동안, 문의사항이 있으면 고객 서비스로 전화 주십시오.

어휘 process 처리하다

102 형용사 어휘

해설 '다양한, 엄선된'이라는 의미의 a selection of는 형용사 wide와 함께 '매우 다양한'의 뜻으로 자주 쓰인다. 따라서 빈칸 앞 정관사 the와 함께 wide의 최상급으로 '가장 다양한 소음기'라는 의미가 자연스러운 (B) widest가 정답이다. (A) natural은 '자연의', (C) overall은 '전반적인', (D) positive는 '긍정적인'이라는 의미로 문맥상 적절하지 않다.

번역 ABC 트럭 서플라이즈는 주 전역에서 가장 다양한 소음기를 보유하고 있다.

어휘 muffler (내연 기관의) 소음기, 머플러

103 명사 자리 _ 전치사의 목적어

해설 전치사 of의 목적어 자리로 형용사 five-star(별 다섯 개짜리의)의 수식을 받아 '별 다섯 개짜리 평가'라는 의미가 되어야 하므로 '후기, 평가'라는 뜻의 명사 (A) reviews가 정답이다. 참고로, 빈칸 앞 dozens of는 '수십 개의'라는 의미로 뒤에 복수명사를 수식하기 때문에 명사 (B) reviewer(비평가, 검열자)는 문맥상 어울리지 않을 뿐 아니라 dozens of와 수 일치도 되지 않는다. (C) reviewed는 동사/과거분사, (D) reviewing은 동명사/현재분사로 구조상 빈칸에 적절하지 않다.

번역 샤스우드 조경은 작업에 대해 별 다섯 개짜리 평가 수십 개를 받았다.

어휘 landscaping 조경

104 인칭대명사의 격 _ 주격

해설 빈칸은 접속사 since가 이끄는 부사절의 주어 자리이므로 주격 인칭대명사 (B) she가 정답이다. 소유대명사인 (A) hers도 주어 자리에 들어갈 수 있지만, '그녀의 것'이라는 뜻으로 문맥상 적절하지 않고, (C) her는 목적격/소유격, (D) herself는 재귀대명사로 주어 자리에 들어갈 수 없으므로 오답이다.

번역 조 박사는 텔레데어 연구소를 볼 기회가 다시없을 수도 있기 때문에 일 년에 한번 있는 공개일 동안 연구소를 방문할 예정이다.

어휘 open house (시설, 학교 등의) 공개일, 참관일

105 동사 어휘

해설 동사 decided의 목적어 역할을 하는 to부정사에 들어갈 적절한 동사 어휘를 고르는 문제이다. 문맥상 '이미 다양한 제품군을 확대하기로 결정했다'라는 내용이 되어야 적절하므로 '확대하다, 확장하다'라는 뜻의 (D) expand가 정답이다. (A) create는 '만들다', (B) enforce는 '시행하다', (C) apply는 '적용하다'라는 의미이다.

번역 돈 백화점은 이미 다양한 가정용품을 확대하기로 결정했다.

어휘 a selection of 다양한   housewares 가정용품

106 동사 어형 _ 수 일치

해설 We가 주어, 빈칸 뒤 that절이 목적어인 문장에 동사가 필요하므로 빈칸은 동사 자리이다. 복수주어 We와 수 일치하는 복수동사가 와야 하므로 (C) ask가 정답이다. (A) was asking과 (D) asks는 3인칭 단수동사로 We와 수 일치되지 않고, (B) having asked는 동명사/현재분사로 문장의 동사 역할을 할 수 없다.

번역 면접에 작업 샘플 포트폴리오를 지참해 주시기 바랍니다.

107 형용사 자리 _ 명사 수식
▶ 동영상 강의

해설 빈칸은 동사 receive의 목적어 역할을 하는 명사 discounts를 수식하는 형용사 자리이다. 따라서 '깊은'이라는 의미의 형용사 (C) deep이 정답이다. (A) depth는 명사, (B) deepen은 동사, (D) deeply는 부사이므로 답이 될 수 없다.

번역 볼드스톤팜 스토어 회원은 모든 구매에 대해 큰 할인을 받는다.

어휘 depth 깊이   deepen 깊어지다   deeply 깊이, 크게

108 명사 자리 _ 전치사의 목적어

해설 전치사 of의 목적어 자리로, 소유격 뒤에는 명사가 와야 하고 '예약 시간 24시간 전에'라는 의미가 되어야 자연스럽다. 따라서 '예약'이라는 뜻의 명사 (B) reservation이 정답이다. (A) reserved는 동사/과거분사, (C) reservable은 형용사, (D) reserve는 동사이므로 빈칸에 들어갈 수 없다. 참고로 reserve는 명사로도 쓰이지만, '비축; 보호 구역'이라는 의미이므로 문맥에 어울리지 않는다.

번역 계획이 변경될 경우, 적어도 예약 시간 24시간 전에 연락 주십시오.

어휘 reserve 예약하다, 비축하다   reservable 비축할 수 있는

109 한정사 자리 _ 수 일치

해설 빈칸은 동명사 harming의 목적어 역할을 하는 명사 roots를 수식하는 자리이다. 명사 앞에 쓰여 한정사 역할을 하고 문맥상으로도 '그것(the tomato seedling)의 뿌리'라는 내용이 적절하므로 소유격 인칭대명사 (A) its가 정답이다. (B) at과 (D) in은 전치사로 빈칸에 들어갈 수 없고, 지시형용사 (C) that은 복수명사와 쓸 수 없으므로 답이 되지 않는다.

번역 뿌리가 다치지 않게 토마토 묘목을 줄기 쪽으로 살며시 잡으세요.

어휘 seedling 묘목   gently 살며시   stem 줄기   harm 손상시키다

110 전치사 자리

해설 빈칸은 뒤에 오는 entering the conference와 함께 앞에 있는 완전한 절(be sure to collect your name tag)을 수식하는 자리이다. entering과 함께 쓰여 '들어가기 전에'라는 의미를 나타내는 것이 적절하므로 (D) before가 정답이다. 부사인 (A) very, (B) often, (C) always 또한 구조상으로 가능해 보일 수 있으나, (A) very는 동사를 수식하지 않고, (B) often과 (C) always는 의미상 어색하므로 정답이 될 수 없다.

번역 회의에 입장하기 전에 등록 테이블에서 반드시 이름표를 수령하세요.

어휘 registration 등록   collect 수령하다

111 명사 어휘

해설 문맥상 빈칸에 들어갈 명사는 마이하마 차량(Maihama vehicles)에 포함된 것으로, to부정사구 to cover engine repairs의 수식을 받아 '엔진 수리를 보장하는 보증'이라는 내용이 되어야 자연스럽다. 따라서 '보증'이라는 의미의 (D) warranty가 정답이다. (A) record는 '기록', (B) operation은 '작동; 운영', (C) budget은 '예산'이라는 의미로 문맥상 빈칸에 적절하지 않다.

번역 마이하마 차량에는 엔진 수리를 보장하는 연장된 보증이 포함되어 있다.

112 형용사 어휘

해설 명사 collection을 수식하기에 적절한 형용사를 고르는 문제

이다. collection이 고품질 이미지들로 구성되었다는 수식어구(of high-quality images)로 보아 문맥상 '고품질 이미지를 인상적으로 모아놓은 것'이라는 내용이 되어야 적절하므로 '인상적인'이라는 뜻의 (C) impressive가 정답이다. (A) absolute는 '절대적인', (B) efficient는 '효율적인', (D) undefeated는 '무패의'라는 의미이다.

번역 호텔의 새로운 웹사이트는 인상적인 고품질 이미지 컬렉션이 특징이다.

어휘 feature 특징으로 삼다   high-quality 고품질의, 고급의

113 부사 어휘   동영상 강의

해설 동사 thank를 수식하여 적절한 문맥을 완성하는 부사를 고르는 문제이다. '지속적인 이용에 진심으로 감사드린다'는 내용이 되어야 자연스러우므로 '진심으로'라는 뜻의 (C) sincerely가 정답이다. (A) deservedly는 '마땅히', (B) commonly는 '흔히', (D) perfectly는 '완벽하게'라는 의미로 문맥상 어울리지 않는다.

번역 유니언타운 은행의 모든 임직원을 대표하여, 귀하의 지속적인 이용에 진심으로 감사드립니다.

어휘 on behalf of ~을 대표하여   continued 지속적인   patronage (고객의) 애용, 후원

114 부사 자리 _ 동사 수식

해설 빈칸은 be동사 is와 과거분사 damaged 사이에서 동사를 수식하는 부사 자리이다. 따라서 '우연히, 실수로'라는 뜻의 부사 (D) accidentally가 정답이다. (A) accident와 (B) accidents는 명사, (C) accidental은 형용사이므로 품사상 오답이다.

번역 깨지기 쉬운 장비는 실수로 손상되지 않도록 안전한 장소에 보관되어야 한다.

어휘 fragile 깨지기 쉬운   store 보관하다   secure 안전한   location 장소   damage 손상시키다, 훼손하다

115 전치사 어휘   동영상 강의

해설 문맥상 '우리 팀의 발표 이후에야 도착할 것이다', 즉 '우리 팀의 발표가 끝난 이후까지 도착하지 않을 것이다'라는 의미가 되어야 자연스럽다. 따라서 빈칸 뒤 after와 함께 '~ 이후까지'라는 의미를 나타내는 (A) until이 정답이다. until after(~ 이후끼지), until before(~ 이전까지), from within(~ 안에서부터), from behind(~ 뒤에서부터) 등의 관용 표현을 알아 두자.

번역 샘슨 씨는 우리 팀의 발표가 끝난 이후에야 컨벤션에 도착할 것이다.

116 전치사 자리 / 어휘

해설 명사구 the park를 목적어로 취하는 전치사 자리로, 보기에서 (A) in과 (C) for 중 하나를 선택해야 한다. the park가 장소를 나타내는 명사이고, 문맥상 '공원에서 열릴 것이다'라는 내용이 되어야 자연스러우므로 장소 명사와 함께 쓰여 '~에서'를 뜻하는 전치사 (A) in이 정답이다. (C) for(~을 위한)는 문맥상 어색하고, (B) all은 한정사/부사, (D) here는 부사이므로 빈칸에 적절하지 않다.

번역 지역 사회 피크닉은 셸처 공공 도서관 뒤에 있는 공원에서 열릴 예정이다.

어휘 community 지역 공동체

117 동사 자리

해설 빈칸은 주어 The new hires의 동사 자리이다. 따라서 문장에서 본동사 역할을 할 수 있는 (B) will gather가 정답이다. (A) to be gathering과 (D) to gather는 to부정사, (C) gathering은 명사/동명사/현재분사이므로 품사상 답이 될 수 없다.

번역 신입 사원들은 5월 10일 오전 9시에 오리엔테이션을 위해 모일 예정이다.

어휘 hire 신입 사원 gather 모이다

118 부사 자리 _ 동사 수식

해설 빈칸은 주어 the receptionist와 동사 offered 사이에서 동사를 수식하는 부사 자리이다. 따라서 '정중하게'를 뜻하는 부사 (A) politely가 정답이다. (B) polite는 형용사, (C) politeness는 명사, (D) politest는 형용사의 최상급이므로 품사상 빈칸에 들어갈 수 없다.

번역 영 씨가 데스크로 다가가자 접수 담당자는 정중하게 대기실 자리를 권했다.

어휘 approach 접근하다 waiting room 대기실 polite 정중한, 예의 바른 politeness 예의 바름

119 인칭대명사 _ 소유대명사 / 수 일치

해설 빈칸은 주절의 동사 claimed의 목적어 역할을 하는 that절의 주어 자리이다. was는 단수동사이므로 복수주어인 (A) they는 답이 될 수 없고, 문맥상 '그들(Members of the Marvale marketing team)의 것'이라는 의미를 나타내는 소유대명사 (C) theirs가 정답이다.

번역 마베일의 마케팅 팀원들은 그들의 것이 새로운 회사 로고를 위한 최고의 디자인이라고 주장했다.

어휘 claim 주장하다 corporate 회사[기업]의

120 전치사 어휘

해설 문맥상 '세금을 포함하지 않고'라는 의미가 되어야 하는데 앞에 not이 있으므로 '~을 포함하여'라는 뜻의 전치사 (D) including이 정답이다. '~을 제외하고'라는 뜻의 (A) excepting은 not과 함께 '~도 예외 없이'를 의미하므로 문맥에 맞지 않다. (B) alongside는 '~와 나란히', (C) within은 '~ 이내에'라는 의미이다.

번역 신형 키츠나 비디오카메라는 현재 세금을 포함하지 않고 375달러에 판매되고 있다.

어휘 currently 현재 on sale 판매되는

121 동사 어휘

해설 be동사 are와 to부정사 to follow 사이에서 과거분사 형태로 적절한 문맥을 완성하는 동사를 골라야 한다. '절차를 따라야 한다', 즉 '절차를 따를 것으로 기대된다'라는 의미가 되어야 하므로 'be expected to'의 형태로 쓰여 '~할 것으로 기대[예상]되다'를 의미하는 (D) expected가 정답이다. (A) concerned는 '우려하는'이라는 의미로 뒤에 주로 전치사 about이나 that절을 취하므로 빈칸에 적절하지 않고, (B)의 tend는 '경향이 있다'라는 뜻의 자동사로 수동태로 쓰이지 않으며, (C)의 maintain은 '유지하다'라는 뜻으로 문맥상 오답이다.

번역 모든 직원들은 안내서에 기술된 표준 운영 절차를 따라야 한다.

어휘 associate 동료, 직원 operating 운영상의 procedure 절차 outline 개요를 서술하다 handbook 안내서

122 형용사 자리 _ 명사 수식

해설 빈칸 앞에 소유격, 뒤에 명사 expansion이 있으므로 빈칸에는 명사를 수식하는 형용사나 복합명사를 이루는 명사가 들어갈 수 있다. 문맥상으로 '가장 야심 찬 확장 사업'이라는 의미가 되어야 자연스러우므로 '야심 찬'이라는 뜻의 형용사 ambitious의 최상급 (D) most ambitious가 정답이다. 명사인 (C) ambition은 '야심'이라는 뜻으로 expansion과 복합명사를 이루지 않고, (A) ambitiously와 (B) most ambitiously는 부사이므로 품사상 빈칸에 들어갈 수 없다.

번역 이번 달 프램리 출판사는 지금까지 했던 것 중 가장 야심 찬 확장 사업을 착수할 것이다.

어휘 embark on ~을 착수하다 expansion 확장 so far 지금까지 ambitiously 야심 차게

123 부사 어휘

해설 빈칸 뒤의 동사 released를 수식하여 '마침내 출시했다'는 의미가 되어야 적절하므로 '마침내'라는 뜻의 (C) finally가 정답이다. (A) profoundly는 '깊이', (B) overly는 '지나치게', (D) intensely '몹시'라는 의미이다.

번역 몇 달간의 협업 끝에 매트릭스 테크놀로지의 소프트웨어 개발자들은 마침내 최고 품질의 제품을 출시했다.

어휘 collaboration 협업 release 출시하다

124 명사 어휘

해설 빈칸 뒤 장소를 나타내는 전치사구 into the venue가 있고 앞에서 티켓은 1회 입장에만 유효하다(Tickets are valid for one-time access)고 했으므로, '행사장에 재입장할 수 없다'라는 내용으로 연결되어야 자연스럽다. 따라서 '재입장'을 뜻하는 (B) reentry가 정답이다. (A) duplication은 '이중, 중복', (C) permission은 '허락', (D) turnover는 '(상품의) 회전율'이라는 의미로 문맥에 어울리지 않는다.

번역 티켓으로는 1회 입장만 유효하며 행사장에 재입장할 수 없습니다.

어휘 valid 유효한 access 입장, 접근 venue 행사장

125 접속사 자리 _ 부사절 접속사 / 어휘

해설 빈칸 뒤 완전한 절(it was not the lowest bidder on the project)을 이끄는 부사절 접속사 자리로 (A) if only, (C) whereas, (D) even though가 가능하다. 문맥상 '최저 입찰자가 아님에도 불구하고'라는 의미가 되어야 자연스러우므로 '~에도 불구하고, ~일지라도'를 뜻하는 (D) even though가 정답이다. (A) if only는 '~하면 (좋을 텐데)'의 의미로 주로 가정법 시제와 쓰이고, (C) whereas는 '반면에'라는 뜻으로 의미상 적절하지 않으며, (B) alternatively는 부사이므로 품사상 오답이다.

번역 우리는 오카포 건설이 프로젝트의 최저 입찰자가 아님에도 불구하고 보수 공사 담당 업체로 고용했다.

어휘 renovation 보수 공사 bidder 입찰자 alternatively 그 대신에

126 명사 자리 _ 동사의 주어

해설 빈칸은 동사 will introduce의 주어 자리로, 빈칸 앞에 관사 The와 형용사 first가 있으므로 명사가 와야 한다. 따라서 명사인 (A) part가 정답이다. (B) parted는 동사/과거분사, (D) partial은 형용사이므로 품사상 빈칸에 들어갈 수 없다. (C) parting은 동명사로 쓰일 경우 주어 자리에 들어갈 수 있지만 '갈라짐'을 의미하므로 답이 될 수 없다.

번역 교육의 첫 부분은 특정한 직장에서의 책무를 직원들에게 소개할 것이다.

어휘 certain 특정한 workplace 직장, 업무 현장 responsibility 책무, 의무 part 부분; 갈라지다 partial 부분적으로

127 명사 자리 _ 복합명사

▶ 동영상 강의

해설 전치사 According to의 목적어 역할을 하는 명사 자리로, 빈칸 앞의 industry와 함께 '업계 보도'라는 의미의 복합명사를 이루는 (D) reports가 정답이다. (A) reported는 동사/과거분사, (B) reportedly는 부사이므로 품사상 답이 될 수 없고, (C) reporter는 가산 단수명사이므로 앞에 한정사가 있어야 목적어 역할을 할 수 있으므로 빈칸에 들어갈 수 없다.

번역 업계 보도에 따르면, 기라 컴퍼니는 호주로 본사를 이전할 계획이다.

어휘 relocate 이전하다 headquarters 본사 reportedly 전하는 바에 따르면 reporter 기자

128 형용사 자리 _ 명사 수식

해설 빈칸은 전치사 of의 목적어 역할을 하는 명사 furniture and clothing을 수식하는 형용사 자리이다. 문맥상 '진품인 가구와 의복'이라는 의미가 되어야 하므로 형용사 (A) authentic이 정답이다. (D) authenticity는 명사, (B) authentically는 부사, (C) authenticate는 동사로 품사상 빈칸에 들어갈 수 없다.

번역 다음 달, 크니스 하우스는 18세기의 진품 가구 및 의복 전시회를 개최할 예정이다.

어휘 host 개최[주최]하다 authenticate 진짜임을 증명하다 authenticity 진품[진짜]임

129 전치사 어휘

해설 빈칸 뒤의 명사구 the direction과 함께 '지휘[감독]하에'라는 의미를 나타내는 (B) under가 정답이다. (A) among은 '(셋 이상의) ~ 사이에'라는 의미로 복수명사가 뒤따라야 하므로 적절하지 않고, (C) behind는 '~ 뒤에', (D) opposite는 '~ 맞은편에'를 뜻하므로 문맥에 어울리지 않는다.

번역 PKTM의 지역 관리자들은 부사장의 지휘하에 근무한다.

어휘 regional 지역의 serve 근무하다 direction 지휘, 감독 vice president 부사장

130 전치사 자리

해설 빈칸은 명사구 a recent surge in demand와 함께 콤마 뒤 완전한 절(Vanita's Catering is hiring ~ servers)을 수식하는 자리이므로 전치사가 들어가야 한다. 따라서 '~ 때문에'라는 의미의 전치사 (D) Owing to가 정답이다. (A) Everywhere는 대명사/부사, (B) Possibly와 (C) In total은 부사이므로 품사상 빈칸에 들어갈 수 없다.

번역 최근 수요 급증으로 인해 바니타 케이터링은 네 명의 서빙 종업원을 추가로 채용 중이다.

어휘 surge 급증 demand 수요 server 서빙하는 사람 everywhere 도처에, 어디든지 possibly 가능하게 in total 통틀어

PART 6

131-134 이메일

수신: 전 직원
발신: 요렐리 코스타
날짜: 2월 15일
제목: 플로렌스 숀

안녕하세요, 여러분.

인사부의 **131 변화**에 대해 공유할 소식이 있습니다. 코메티 크리에이티브에서 거의 20년을 근무한 끝에 플로렌스 숀이 인사부 이사직에서 은퇴하기로 결정했습니다.

숀 씨가 은퇴하면 현재 인사부의 선임 관리자인 마코토 이치세가 그녀의 후임이 될 예정입니다. 숀 씨는 이치세 씨가 5년 전 입사한 이래로 그를 **132 지도해 왔습니다**.

숀 씨의 **133 마지막** 날은 2월 22일입니다. 그날 오후 4시에 테리 로비에서 그녀를 위한 은퇴 파티가 열릴 것입니다. **134 여러분 모두 참석해 그녀의 안녕을 기원할 수 있기를 바랍니다.**

요렐리 코스타
코메티 크리에이티브 운영 이사

어휘 human resources department 인사부 senior 선임의, 상급의 replace ~의 후임으로 임명되다 retirement 은퇴

131 명사 어휘

해설 빈칸이 있는 문장의 다음 문장에서 회사에서 거의 20년을 근무한 플로렌스 숀이 인사부 이사직에서 은퇴하기로 했다고 했으므로, 인사부에 관해 공유할 소식은 바로 인사부 구성원에 있어서의 변화라는 것을 알 수 있다. 따라서 '변화'라는 뜻의 (C) change가 정답이다. (A) difference는 '차이점', (B) strategy는 '전략', (D) practice는 '관행'이라는 의미이다.

132 동사의 시제

해설 빈칸 뒤의 since와 과거동사 joined가 문제 해결의 단서로, 과거 시제 동사가 있는 since 절은 '~한 이래로'라는 뜻으로 쓰일 수 있고, 이때 주절에는 현재완료나 현재완료진행 시제가 온다. 문맥상, '이치세 씨가 5년 전 입사한 이래로 현재까지 숀 씨가 그를 지도해 왔다'는 의미가 되어야 하므로, 과거부터 현재까지 계속된 행위를 나타내는 시제인 현재완료진행 (D) has been mentoring이 정답이다.

133 형용사 어휘

해설 뒤 문장에서 그날(on that day) 오후 4시에 그녀를 위한 은퇴 파티가 열린다고 한 것으로 보아 2월 22일은 숀 씨가 은퇴하는 날, 즉 회사에서 근무하는 마지막 날임을 알 수 있다. 따라서 '마지막의'라는 의미의 (A) last가 정답이다. (B) original은 '원래의; 독창적인', (C) flexible은 '유연한', (D) alternate는 '번갈아 하는'이라는 의미이므로 빈칸에 적절하지 않다.

134 문맥에 맞는 문장 고르기

번역 (A) 코메티 크리에이티브는 곧 후임자를 고용할 것입니다.
(B) 여러분 모두 참석해 그녀의 안녕을 기원할 수 있기를 바랍니다.
(C) 숀 씨는 코메티 크리에이티브 첫 인사 담당 이사였습니다.
(D) 첫 번째 프로젝트는 재능 개발 프로그램을 만드는 것입니다.

해설 앞 문장에서 2월 22일 오후 4시에 로비에서 그녀(Ms. Shawn)를 위한 은퇴 파티가 열린다고 했으므로, 파티 참석을 권하는 내용이 이어져야 자연스럽다. 따라서 모두 참석해 그녀의 안녕을 기원하자고 언급하는 (B)가 정답이다.

어휘 replacement 후임자   wish ~ well ~의 안녕[성공]을 기원하다   creation 제작   talent development 재능 개발

135-138 광고

러빗 부동산

매니토바 가족들이 꿈꾸는 집을 찾도록 도와드립니다.

러빗 부동산의 135 **소유주**인 마누엘 러빗은 17년 넘게 부동산을 매매해 왔습니다. 러빗 씨와 수상 경력이 있는 그의 팀은 위니펙, 브랜든, 도핀 지역에서 가족을 위한 집을 136 **전문으로 합니다.** 그들은 고객이 거주하기를 원하는 지역의 학교, 공원, 서비스, 교통, 그리고 가족의 삶을 향상시켜 주는 활동에 대해 잘 알고 있습니다. 137 **그것은 그들이 서비스를 제공하는 지역에 살고 있기 때문입니다.**

지금 러빗 부동산에 연락하시면 저희 팀이 고객님을 꿈의 집138 **으로** 안내해 드리겠습니다. 저희 팀은 고객님의 요구에 귀를 기울이고 고객님을 대신해 협상하고 고객님이 애써서 번 돈에 맞춰 최고의 집을 구해 드릴 것입니다.

자세한 정보는 431-555-0168로 전화해 직원에게 말씀하시거나 www.lovittrealestate.ca를 방문하세요.

어휘 real estate 부동산   award-winning 상을 받은   transportation 교통 수단   enhance 향상시키다   reside 거주하다   needs 요구   negotiate 협상하다   on one's behalf ~을 대신[대리]하여   hard-earned 애써서 번   agent 대리인

135 명사 자리

해설 빈칸 앞에 문장의 주어인 Manuel Lovitt과 콤마가 있고, 뒤에 동사 has been selling이 있는 것으로 보아 빈칸은 Manuel Lovitt의 동격 자리임을 알 수 있다. 따라서 '소유자'라는 뜻의 명사 (C) owner가 정답이다. (A) own은 동사/형용사, (B) owned는 동사/과거분사, (D) owning은 동명사/현재분사이므로 구조상 빈칸에 들어갈 수 없다.

136 동사 어휘

해설 빈칸 뒤에 목적어가 없고 전치사 in이 있으므로 전치사 in과 어울릴 수 있는 자동사가 들어가야 한다. 문맥상으로도 '가족을 위한 집을 전문으로 다룬다'는 의미가 되어야 자연스러우므로 전치사 in과 함께 '~을 전문적으로 다루다'라는 의미를 만드는 (B) specialize가 정답이다. (A) practice는 '연습하다', (C) report는 '보고하다'라는 의미로 문맥에 맞지 않고, (D) purchase(구매하다)는 타동사이므로 뒤에 전치사가 올 수 없다.

137 문맥에 맞는 문장 고르기

번역 (A) 그들은 고객의 지역 초등학교를 위한 교통편을 마련할 수 있습니다.
(B) 그것은 그들이 서비스를 제공하는 지역에 살고 있기 때문입니다.
(C) 여름 동안 문을 닫지만 그들은 곧 다시 오픈할 것입니다.
(D) 그러므로 그들은 고객의 은행 업무에 필요한 모든 것을 도울 수 있습니다.

해설 앞 문장에서 그들(Mr. Lovitt and his award-winning team)이 고객의 거주 희망 지역의 학교, 공원, 서비스, 교통 및 활동 등을 파악하고 있다며 지역 관련 정보를 잘 안다는 점을 강조하고 있으므로, 이를 뒷받침할 수 있는 근거가 이어져야 자연스럽다. 따라서 그들이 서비스를 제공하는 지역에 살고 있기 때문이라고 언급하는 (B)가 정답이다.

어휘 arrange 마련하다   serve (서비스를) 제공하다, 근무하다   community 지역 사회   banking 은행 업무

138 전치사 자리 / 어휘

해설 빈칸 앞 완전한 절과 뒤의 명사구 the home (of your dreams)를 연결하는 구조로, 전치사 (A) toward(~쪽으로, ~을 향하여)와 (D) along(~을 따라), 현재분사 (B) fixing(고치는)이 가능하다. 문맥상 '꿈의 집으로 안내하겠다'가 되어야 자연스러우므로 '~쪽으로, ~을 향하여'를 뜻하는 (A) toward가 정답이다. (C) because는 부사절 접속사이므로 구조상 빈칸에 들어갈 수 없다.

139-142 소개문

> '저축 분산하기'에 오신 것을 환영합니다. 이 슬라이드 **139 발표**는 '은퇴 준비'라는 열두 개의 부분으로 구성된 교육 시리즈 중 세 번째입니다. **140 본 시리즈는 정보에 근거한 재무 의사 결정을 내리는 데 도움이 되도록 고안되었습니다.**
>
> 본 시리즈는 **141 보충적인** 조언만 제공합니다. 이것이 여러분의 투자 설계사가 제공하는 안내를 대체해서는 안 됩니다. 이 시리즈는 여러분이 투자 설계사와 **142 상담할** 때 중요한 질문을 할 수 있도록 돕기 위한 배경 자료로 개발되었습니다. 이 정보가 도움이 되기를 바랍니다.
>
> 스웨인슨-그레이 인베스트먼츠
>
> ---
>
> 어휘 distribute 분산[분배]하다 savings 저축 segment 부분 educational 교육의 guidance 지도, 안내 investment 투자 background 배경 material 자료 key 중요한, 핵심적인

139 명사 자리 _ 복합명사

해설 동사 is의 주어 역할을 하는 명사 자리로, 빈칸 앞의 명사 slide와 함께 쓰여 '슬라이드 발표'라는 의미의 복합명사를 만들 수 있는 (C) presentation이 정답이다. (B) presents는 명사로 쓰인 경우 '선물'이라는 의미로 slide와 복합명사를 이루기에 적절하지 않고 동사 is와 수 일치도 되지 않아 오답이다.

140 문맥에 맞는 문장 고르기

번역 (A) 무료 포트폴리오 검토를 위해 저희 사무실을 방문해 주시기 바랍니다.
(B) 본 시리즈는 정보에 근거한 재무 의사 결정을 내리는 데 도움이 되도록 고안되었습니다.
(C) 예약 시간 전에 서류를 작성해 주십시오.
(D) 여러분의 답변은 향후 더 나은 서비스를 제공하는 데 도움이 됩니다.

해설 빈칸 앞에서 이 슬라이드 발표는 '은퇴 준비'라는 열두 개의 부분으로 구성된 교육 시리즈 중 세 번째 발표(This slide presentation is ~ educational series called "Preparing for Retirement")라고 했고, 뒤에 이어지는 단락에서 본 시리즈는 보충적인 조언만 제공한다 (This series provides only supplemental advice)고 했으므로, 빈칸에는 교육 시리즈에 대한 내용이 언급되어야 자연스럽다. 따라서 본 시리즈는 정보에 근거한 재무 의사 결정을 내리는 데 도움이 되는 것이라고 설명한 (B)가 정답이다.

어휘 encourage 권장하다 informed 정보에 근거한 fill out ~을 작성하다 paperwork 서류 serve (서비스를) 제공하다

141 형용사 어휘

해설 뒤 문장에서 이것이 투자 설계사가 제공하는 안내를 대체해서는 안 된다고 한 것으로 보아 재무 계획에 대해 보완이 될 수 있는, 즉 '보충적인 조언만을 제공한다'는 내용이 되어야 하므로 '보충의'라는 뜻의 (C) supplemental이 정답이다. (A) regional은 '지역의', (B) expensive는 '비싼', (D) playful는 '장난스러운'이라는 의미로 문맥상 적절하지 않다.

142 동사 어휘

해설 부사절 접속사 when 뒤의 분사 자리에 들어갈 동사 어휘를 고르는 문제로 빈칸 뒤에 목적어가 없고 전치사 with가 있으므로 전치사 with와 어울릴 수 있는 자동사가 들어가야 한다. '투자 설계사와 상담할 때'라는 의미가 되어야 자연스러우므로 전치사 with와 함께 '~와 상담하다'를 뜻하는 동사 consult의 현재분사형 (A) consulting이 정답이다. (B)의 prescribe는 '처방하다', (C)의 list는 '목록을 작성하다', (D)의 follow는 '뒤를 잇다'라는 의미이다.

143-146 이메일

> 수신: 데이나 폴웰
> 발신: 사일러스 라보
> 날짜: 8월 22일
> 제목: 저의 의견
> 첨부: 기사글
>
> 폴웰 박사님께,
>
> 이 메시지는 어제 있었던 직원 회의, 특히 병원의 특정 측면이 우리의 업무 및 사명에 어떤 영향을 미칠 수 있는지에 대한 논의에 관한 것입니다. **143 저는 이 주제에 대해 제안을 하고 싶습니다.**
>
> 현재, 대기실 밖 복도에 있는 자판기에는 청량음료와 감자칩 같은 달고 짠 제품들이 구비되어 있습니다. 의료 서비스 제공자로서, 우리는 건강을 위해 헌신하고 있음을 보여 주는 음료와 간식을 **144 제공해야 합니다.** **145 결국,** 우리의 사명은 건강에 초점을 맞추고 있습니다.
>
> 우리와 같은 의료 기관들이 접대 구역 개선을 위해 취하고 있는 조치들에 대한 기사를 첨부했습니다. 기사가 **146 도움이 되기를** 바랍니다. 여기에는 우리가 고려해 볼 수 있는 쉽고 비용 효율적인 변화 몇 가지가 자세히 나와 있습니다.
>
> 사일러스 라보
>
> ---
>
> 어휘 input 조언[의견](의 제공) in response to ~에 응답하여, ~의 회신으로 particularly 특히 aspect 측면 affect 영향을 미치다 mission 사명, 임명 vending machine 자판기 be stocked with ~이 구비되다, ~으로 채워지다 sugary 단, 설탕이 든 commitment 헌신, 의무 wellness 건강 hospitality 접대 station (특정 서비스가 제공되는) 장소 detail 상술하다 cost-effective 비용 효율적인

143 문맥에 맞는 문장 고르기　　동영상 강의

번역 (A) 저는 그것이 필요 이상으로 오래 지속되었다고 생각했습니다.
(B) 그 일에 대해 좀 더 일찍 알게 되었다면 좋았을 것입니다.
(C) 저는 이 주제에 대해 제안을 하고 싶습니다.
(D) 제가 후속 세션을 진행하게 되어 영광입니다.

해설 앞 문장에서 이 메시지는 어제 직원 회의에서 있었던 논의에 관한 것이라고 한 뒤, 뒤 문단에서 의료 서비스 제공자로서 건강을 위해 헌신하고 있음을 보여 주는 음료 및 간식을 제공해야 한다고 제안하고 있다. 따라서 회의 내용과 관련된 제안사항을 건의하고 싶다는 내용이 이어져야 자연스러우므로 (C)가 정답이다.

어휘 go on 지속[계속]되다 inform 알리다 honored 영광으로 생각하는 follow-up 후속

144 동사의 시제

해설 앞 문장에서 현재 자판기에 달고 짠 제품들이 구비되어 있다고 상황을 설명했고, 뒤 문장에서는 우리의 사명은 건강에 초점을 맞추고 있다 (our mission is focused on good health)고 했다. 따라서 빈칸이 있는 문장은 건강을 염두에 둔 음료와 간식을 '제공해야 한다'라는 사명에 근거한 의무 및 당위성을 나타내는 내용이 되어야 적합하므로 (D) should be offering이 정답이다.

145 접속부사

해설 앞 문장에는 의료 서비스 제공자로서 건강을 위해 헌신하고 있음을 보여 주는 음료와 간식을 제공해야 한다고 했고, 뒤 문장에는 우리의 사명은 건강에 초점을 맞추고 있다고 했다. 뒤 문장의 내용이 앞 문장에서 펼친 주장에 대한 이유를 설명한 것이므로 '결국, 어쨌든'이라는 뜻으로 설명이나 이유를 덧붙일 때 사용하는 (A) After all이 정답이다. (B) By the way는 '그런데', (C) In the meantime은 '그동안에', (D) On the other hand는 '다른 한편으로는, 반면에'라는 의미로 문맥에 어울리지 않는다.

146 형용사 어휘

해설 앞 문장에서 관련 기사를 첨부했다고 했고, 뒤 문장에서 우리가 고려할 수 있는 쉽고 비용 효율적인 변화가 설명되어 있다(It details some easy ~ changes we could consider)며 기사가 어떤 식으로 도움이 될 수 있는지에 대해 언급하고 있다. 따라서 빈칸이 있는 문장은 '기사가 도움이 되길 바란다'는 내용이 되어야 자연스러우므로 '도움이 되는, 유용한'이라는 뜻의 (A) useful이 정답이다. (B) eventful는 '다사다난한', (C) profitable은 '수익성이 있는', (D) comfortable은 '편안한'의 의미로 문맥상 적절하지 않다.

PART 7

147-148 광고

> **메딜로 슈즈가 케이프타운에서 20주년을 맞이합니다!**
> 246 브레다 플레이스, 윈버그, 케이프타운 7800
> 021 555 0149 | www.medilloshoes.co.za
>
> 하루 종일 서 있어야 하는 직업을 갖고 계십니까? 필요한 도움을 받으세요! 메딜로 슈즈에서는 스타일리시하면서도 어떠한 비즈니스나 의료 환경에도 적합한 편안하고 지지력 좋은 신발을 전문으로 합니다.
>
> ¹⁴⁷**5월 10일에 매장을 방문해 기념일 행사 동안 한 켤레 이상의 신발을 구입하고 20퍼센트 할인을 받으세요.** 직업상 필요하신 최고의 신발을 찾는 데 도움을 원하시면 저희 신발 전문가가 도움을 드리기 위해 대기하고 있을 것입니다. ¹⁴⁸**오래 기다리는 것을 피하시려면 www.medilloshoes.co.za에서 무료 상담 일정을 잡으세요.**
>
> 어휘 support 도움; 지지력 specialise in ~을 전문으로 하다 supportive 지지력이 좋은, 지지하는 suitable 적합한 setting 환경 anniversary 기념일 specialist 전문가 on hand 대기하여, 준비된 consultation 상담

147 세부사항

번역 5월 10일에 메딜로 슈즈에서 일어날 일은?
(A) 모든 신발이 할인될 것이다.
(B) 매장 직원이 채용될 것이다.
(C) 신발 스타일 한 가지가 단종될 것이다.
(D) 운영 시간이 연장될 것이다.

해설 두 번째 단락의 첫 문장에서 5월 10일에 매장을 방문해 기념일 행사 동안 한 켤레 이상의 신발을 구입하고 20퍼센트 할인을 받으라(Visit us on 10 May to receive 20 percent off your purchase ~ during this anniversary event)고 했으므로 (A)가 정답이다.

어휘 shop assistant 매장 직원 discontinued 단종된 operational 운영의 extend 연장하다

> **Paraphrasing** 지문의 20 percent off
> → 정답의 discounted

148 Not / True

번역 메딜로 슈즈에 대해 명시된 것은?
(A) 사업한 지 10년이 되었다.
(B) 운동화를 전문으로 취급한다.
(C) 병원 옆에 위치하고 있다.
(D) 고객들이 예약할 수 있게 해 준다.

해설 마지막 문장에서 오래 기다리는 것을 피하려면 www.medilloshoes.co.za에서 무료 상담 일정을 잡으라(Schedule a free consultation ~ to avoid a long wait)고 한 것으로 보아 고객들이 상담 예약을 잡을 수 있다는 것을 알 수 있으므로 (D)가 정답이다. 광고 제목에 메딜로 슈즈가 20주년을 맞이한다(Medillo Shoes Celebrates Twenty Years)고 했고, 메딜로 슈즈는 모든 비즈니스와 의료 환경에 적합한(suitable for any business or medical setting) 신발을 전문으로 한다고 했으므로 (A)와 (B)는 명백한 오답이다.

어휘 athletic footwear 운동화

> **Paraphrasing** 지문의 schedule a ~ consultation
> → 정답의 make appointments

149-150 이메일

> 수신: 영업팀
> 발신: 닐 컬런
> 날짜: 4월 10일
> ¹⁴⁹**제목: 저의 다음 주 일정**
>
> 팀원 여러분,
>
> ¹⁴⁹**저는 다음 주 4월 15일부터 19일까지 글래스고에서 열리는 국립 기술 연맹 콘퍼런스에 참석하느라 사무실을 비울 예정입니다.** 출장 중에는 이메일과 음성 메일을 자주 확인하지 못할 것입니다. 급한 일이 생기면 제 조수인 크리스티나 추에게 연락하십시오. ¹⁵⁰**에젠엑스 인더스트리스 고객사에 대한 특정 문의사항이 있을 경우 마이아 소로카에게 이메일을 보내십시오.** 저는 4월 22일에 사무실로 돌아올 예정이며 여러분 모두 그때 뵙겠습니다.

닐 컬런, 영업 및 마케팅 담당 이사
샬록 테크놀로지

어휘 alliance 연맹, 연합 infrequently 거의 ~ 않다, 드물게
urgent 긴급한 specific 특정한 account 고객, 거래처

어휘 permit 허가(증) resident 주민, 거주자 contractor
시공사, 설비업체 application 신청 average 평균의
processing 처리 remain 그대로 (~의 상태)이다 business
day 영업일, 평일 lower 낮추다 maintain 유지하다 standard
수준, 기준

149 주제 / 목적

번역 이메일의 목적은?
(A) 콘퍼런스에 등록하려고
(B) 새로운 거래처를 발표하려고
(C) 회의 일정을 잡으려고
(D) 동료들에게 부재를 알리려고

해설 이메일의 제목이 저의 다음 주 일정(Subject: My schedule next
week)이고, 첫 문장에서 다음 주 4월 15일부터 19일까지 글래스고
에서 열리는 국립 기술 연맹 콘퍼런스에 참석하느라 사무실을 비울 예
정(I will be out of the office next week ~ in Glasgow)이라며
자신이 사무실에 없을 예정임을 알리고 있으므로 (D)가 정답이다.

어휘 register for ~에 등록하다 absence 부재, 결근

Paraphrasing 지문의 out of the office → 정답의 absence

150 추론 / 암시

번역 소로카 씨에 대해 사실일 것 같은 것은?
(A) 컬런 씨와 함께 출장을 갈 것이다.
(B) 에젠엑스 인더스트리스 고객사 업무를 맡고 있다.
(C) 추 씨의 상사이다.
(D) 4월 22일까지 사무실에 없을 예정이다.

해설 네 번째 문장에서 컬런 씨가 에젠엑스 인더스트리스 고객사에 대
한 특정 문의사항이 있을 경우 마이아 소로카에게 이메일을 보내라
(If you have a specific question about the Ezenx Industries
account, please e-mail Mya Soroka)고 한 것으로 보아 소로카
씨는 컬런 씨와 함께 에젠엑스 인더스트리스 고객사 업무를 맡고 있다
는 것을 짐작할 수 있다. 따라서 (B)가 정답이다.

어휘 supervisor 상사

151-152 공지

브라이언튼 시
건축 허가 사무소

브라이언튼에서 일하는 주민 및 시공사를 위한 공지

7월 1일 월요일부터 퍼 가 912에 위치한 브라이언튼 시 건축 허가 사
무소는 월요일부터 목요일 오전 9시부터 오후 5시까지 문을 열 예정입
니다. 151 금요일이나 토요일에는 더 이상 허가 신청을 받지 않습니다.
허가 신청에 걸리는 평균 처리 시간은 그대로 영업일 기준 3일입니다.
152 이 변경으로 시는 주민들을 위한 높은 수준의 서비스를 유지하면서
운영 비용을 낮출 것입니다.

151 세부사항

번역 건축 허가 사무소에서 변경하려는 것은?
(A) 새로운 장소로 이전한다.
(B) 허가 신청 절차를 간소화한다.
(C) 허가 신청 접수 일수를 줄인다.
(D) 허가 신청에 걸리는 처리 시간을 늘린다.

해설 두 번째 문장에서 금요일이나 토요일에는 더 이상 허가 신청을 받지
않는다(Applications for permits will no longer be accepted
on Fridays or Saturdays)고 했다. 따라서 허가 신청을 할 수 있는
날이 줄어드는 변화가 생기는 것이므로 (C)가 정답이다.

어휘 simplify 간소화하다 process 절차; 처리하다 reduce 줄이다

152 세부사항

번역 공지에 따르면, 변경이 이루어지는 이유는?
(A) 시 자금을 아끼려고
(B) 더 많은 주민을 유치하려고
(C) 서비스 품질을 개선하려고
(D) 신규 허가 신청 건수를 줄이려고

해설 마지막 문장에서 이 변경으로 시는 주민들을 위한 높은 수준의 서비
스를 유지하면서 운영 비용을 낮출 것(With this change, the city
will lower its operating costs ~ for residents)이라고 했으므
로 (A)가 정답이다.

어휘 attract 유치하다, 끌어들이다 decrease 줄이다

Paraphrasing 지문의 lower its operating costs
→ 정답의 save the city money

153-155 영수증

https://www.riverthamestours.uk/order/confirmation

템스강 투어
저희 템스강 투어를 예약해 주셔서 감사합니다. 귀하의 승선을 열렬히 환
영합니다. 각 투어는 3시간 동안 진행됩니다. 153 귀하의 투어에는 오후
1시에 제공되는 오찬이 포함되어 있습니다. 메뉴는 당사 웹사이트를 참
고해 주십시오. 식이 제한이 있어 특별식을 요청하시려면 적어도 투어
48시간 전에 고객 경험 관리자인 마틴 토르마에게 연락 주십시오.

155 또한 이번 예약으로 에저튼 워킹 투어의 도보 관광을 10퍼센트 할인
된 가격으로 이용할 수 있는 자격이 주어지며, 예약 시 확인 코드만 제공
하시면 됩니다.

154 성명:	루이스 칼리프
구매일:	4월 18일
확인 코드:	H102057
투어 시작:	5월 1일 오전 11시 30분
154 수량:	4
합계:	180파운드
결제:	1037로 끝나는 신용카드

주의사항: 승선은 출발 시간 10분 전에 종료됩니다.
투어 일정은 변경될 수 없습니다.

어휘 eager 열렬한 aboard 승선[탑승]하여 last 지속되다
luncheon 오찬 consult 참고하다, 찾아보다 dietary 식이 요법의
restriction 제한, 제약 prior to ~ 전에 entitle 자격을 주다
confirmation 확인 quantity 수량 boarding 승선, 탑승

153 Not / True

번역 강 투어에 대해 명시된 것은?
(A) 한 시간이 걸린다.
(B) 식사가 나온다.
(C) 일정이 변경될 수 있다.
(D) 빨리 매진된다.

해설 첫 번째 단락의 네 번째 문장에서 템스강 투어에는 오후 1시에 제공되는 오찬이 포함되어 있다(Your tour includes a luncheon served at 1:00 p.m.)고 했으므로 (B)가 정답이다. 각 투어는 3시간 동안 진행된다(Each tour lasts 3 hours)고 했으므로 (A), 마지막 문장에서 투어 일정은 변경될 수 없다(Tours cannot be rescheduled)고 했으므로 (C)는 오답이고, (D)는 매진에 대한 언급이 없으므로 답이 될 수 없다.

Paraphrasing 지문의 includes a luncheon
→ 정답의 comes with a meal

154 세부사항

번역 칼리프 씨는 티켓을 몇 장 구매했는가?
(A) 1
(B) 3
(C) 4
(D) 7

해설 세 번째 단락에 성명이 루이스 칼리프(Name: Lewis Califf)이고, 티켓 수량은 4장(Quantity: 4)이라고 나와 있으므로 칼리프 씨는 티켓을 4장 구입했음을 알 수 있다. 따라서 (C)가 정답이다.

155 세부사항

번역 고객은 어떻게 도보 관광에 할인을 받을 수 있는가?
(A) 온라인으로 예약함으로써
(B) 신용카드로 지불함으로써
(C) 선장에게 쿠폰을 요청함으로써
(D) 확인 코드를 언급함으로써

해설 두 번째 단락 첫 문장에서 이번 예약으로 에저튼 워킹 투어의 도보 관광을 10퍼센트 할인된 가격으로 이용할 수 있는 자격이 주어지며 예약 시 확인 코드만 제공하면 된다(This reservation also entitles you to a 10 percent discount ~ just provide your confirmation code when booking)고 했으므로 (D)가 정답이다.

Paraphrasing 지문의 provide → 정답의 mentioning

156-157 문자 메시지

미치코 손더스 [오전 8시 6분]
안녕하세요, 제이콥. 사무실로 오시는 중인가요?

제이콥 권 [오전 8시 8분]
네. 25분 정도 뒤에 도착할 겁니다.

미치코 손더스 [오전 8시 10분]
네. 댄스비 그룹을 위한 디자인 제안서를 막 인쇄하기 시작했는데, 156 종이가 다 떨어졌어요. 수요일이나 되어야 배송이 더 될 거예요.

제이콥 권 [오전 8시 12분]
길 건너편에 사무용품점이 보입니다. 막 문을 열었네요.

미치코 손더스 [오전 8시 13분]
정말 잘됐네요. 용지 세 팩이면 충분할 거예요.

제이콥 권 [오전 8시 15분]
알겠습니다. 그런데 157 댄스비 그룹 직원들은 우리 사무실에 언제 오나요? 제가 회의를 위해 커피와 간식을 사 가도 될 것 같아요.

어휘 on one's way to ~으로 오는[가는] 중에 run out of (공급품이) 다 떨어지다 office supply 사무용품 representative 직원, 대리인 pick up ~을 (간단히) 사가다[오다]

156 의도 파악

번역 오전 8시 12분에 권 씨가 "길 건너편에 사무용품점이 보입니다"라고 쓴 의도는?
(A) 건물을 찾는 데 도움이 필요하다.
(B) 용지를 구입할 수 있다.
(C) 새로운 프린터를 찾아볼 것이다.
(D) 배송 일정을 협의할 것이다.

해설 8시 10분에 손더스 씨가 종이가 다 떨어졌다(we've run out of paper)며 수요일이나 되어야 배송이 더 될 것(we don't have another delivery of it coming until Wednesday)이라고 하자 8시 12분에 권 씨가 길 건너편에 사무용품점이 보인다고 했다. 따라서 권 씨는 사무용품점에서 종이를 사 갈 수 있다는 의도로 한 말임을 알 수 있으므로 (B)가 정답이다.

어휘 negotiate 협의[협상]하다

157 추론 / 암시

번역 손더스 씨는 다음에 무엇을 할 것 같은가?
(A) 회의 일정 변경
(B) 다과 준비
(C) 도착 시간 확인
(D) 디자인 제안서 수정

해설 8시 15분에 권 씨가 손더스 씨에게 댄스비 그룹 직원들은 언제 사무실에 오는지(when will the representatives from the Dansby Group be coming to our office?)를 묻고 있으므로, 손더스 씨는 댄스비 직원들이 사무실에 도착하는 시간을 확인해서 알려 줄 것임을 짐작할 수 있다. 따라서 (C)가 정답이다.

어휘 refreshments 다과

Paraphrasing 지문의 when will ~ be coming to our office
→ 정답의 an arrival time

158-160 편지

킵뱅크 비즈니스 서비스
시카모어 레이크 로 548
그린베이, WI 54301

4월 2일

매들린 오마르
패션플라워 인테리어 디자인
디어 런 로 1556
그린베이, WI 54301

오마르 씨께,

¹⁶⁰ **사업주의 하루는 고객, 직원 및 납품업체가 원하는 것, 필요로 하는 것, 요구하는 것들을 조율하는 일로 가득 차 있습니다.** 일상적인 재무사항은 집중을 방해하는 요소를 더할 뿐입니다.

귀하께서 귀사의 제품과 사람에 집중하실 수 있도록 ¹⁵⁸ **킵뱅크가 귀하의 소규모 사업에 적합한 해법을 찾아 드리겠습니다.** 킵뱅크는 입출금 계좌, 법인 신용카드, 사업 대출, 급여 및 부기 서비스를 제공합니다. 올가을에는 귀하와 귀하의 직원들이 귀사의 미래를 계획할 수 있도록 돕기 위해 재무 설계사들도 저희 팀에 충원될 예정입니다.

¹⁵⁹ **킵뱅크 고객은 당사의 법인 신용카드로 엄선된 호텔, 사무용품 및 항공 여행 제휴사로부터 비용 절감 혜택을 누릴 수 있습니다. 이러한 혜택은 적격한 구매에 자동으로 적용됩니다.** 그리고 사업주는 각 카드에 지출 제한을 설정할 수 있습니다.

920-555-0122로 전화하셔서 예약을 하시거나 편하실 때 방문해 주시기 바랍니다. 저희는 귀하를 만나 뵙고 귀사에 우수한 서비스를 제공할 수 있기를 기대합니다.

토마스 피스코르크시, 킵뱅크 고객 컨시어지

어휘 be filled with ~으로 가득 차다 juggle 잘 조절[처리]하다 demand 요구 supplier 납품[공급]업체 solution 해법 checking account 입출금 계좌 corporate 법인의 loan 대출 payroll 급여 bookkeeping 부기 take advantage of ~을 이용하다 selected 엄선된 automatically 자동적으로

---

apply 적용하다 qualified 적격한, 자격을 갖춘 place a limit on ~에 제한을 두다 enterprise 기업 superior 우수한 concierge 관리인, 고객 담당자

158 추론 / 암시

번역 오마르 씨에 대해 암시된 것은?
(A) 회계사이다.
(B) 피스코르크시 씨를 위해 일한다.
(C) 작은 회사를 운영한다.
(D) 킵뱅크 고객이다.

해설 두 번째 단락의 첫 문장에서 오마르 씨에게 킵뱅크가 소규모 사업에 적합한 해법을 찾아 주겠다(Let Kipbank find the right solutions for your small business)고 한 것으로 보아 오마르 씨는 작은 사업체를 운영하는 사업주임을 짐작할 수 있다. 따라서 (C)가 정답이다.

어휘 accountant 회계사 operate 운영하다

159 Not / True

번역 신용카드에 대해 언급된 것은?
(A) 다양한 색상으로 나온다.
(B) 연회비를 내야 한다.
(C) 특정 구매에 대한 할인이 포함되어 있다.
(D) 개인 물품을 사는 데 사용될 수 있다.

해설 세 번째 단락의 첫 번째 문장에서 킵뱅크 고객은 킵뱅크의 법인 신용카드로 엄선된 호텔, 사무용품 및 항공 여행 제휴사로부터 비용 절감 혜택을 누릴 수 있다(With our corporate credit cards, Kipbank customers can take advantage of money-saving offers from ~ and air travel partners)고 했고, 이러한 혜택은 적격한 구매에 자동으로 적용된다(These deals are automatically applied to qualified purchases)고 했다. 따라서 킵뱅크의 신용카드를 이용할 경우 자격이 되는 구매에 할인 혜택을 받을 수 있다는 것이므로 (C)가 정답이다.

어휘 a variety of 다양한 annual fee 연회비

Paraphrasing 지문의 money-saving offers
→ 정답의 discounts

160 문장 삽입

번역 [1], [2], [3], [4]로 표시된 위치 중에서 다음 문장이 들어가기에 가장 적합한 곳은?

"일상적인 재무사항은 집중을 방해하는 요소를 더할 뿐입니다."
(A) [1]
(B) [2]
(C) [3]
(D) [4]

해설 주어진 문장은 일상적인 재무사항이 업무에 방해 요소를 더한다는 의미이므로, 앞에 업무에 방해가 될 수 있는 것들이 제시되어 있어야 적절하다. [1] 앞에서 업무에 집중하는 데 방해가 될 수 있는 것들로 고객, 직원 및 납품업체가 원하는 것, 필요로 하는 것, 요구하는 것들을

예로 들어 사업주의 하루가 이러한 것들로 가득 차 있다(A business owner's days are filled with juggling the wants, needs, and demands of customers, staff, and suppliers)고 언급했으므로, 이 문장 뒤에 주어진 문장이 들어가는 것이 자연스럽다. 따라서 (A)가 정답이다.

어휘 distraction 집중을 방해하는 것, 주의를 산만하게 하는 것

161-163 기사

오타와 (5월 22일) — 〈월든스톤 비즈니스 리뷰〉는 올해 명망 높은 국제 비즈니스 상에 새로운 부문을 추가했다. ¹⁶¹**월든스톤 기업상은 회사의 장기적인 성공 가능성을 보장하는 데 도움이 되는 전략을 개발하는 선견지명이 있는 기업에 수여된다.**

¹⁶¹**올해의 상은 전자 제품 분야의 주요 업체인 카릴라 코퍼레이션에게 수여되었다.** 최고 경영자인 앗삭 카카르의 지휘 아래, ¹⁶²**카릴라 코퍼레이션은 불과 3년 만에 파산 직전에서 수익성이 매우 높은 수준으로 전환했다.**

"이 상을 수상하는 것은 저뿐만 아니라 회사 전체에 매우 기쁜 일이었습니다."라고 카카르 씨가 상을 수상하면서 말했다. "모두가 이 회사를 탄탄한 재정 기반으로 되돌리기 위해 무척 열심히 일했습니다. 장기적인 ¹⁶³**해결책**은 우리 주주들에게 탁월한 가치를 가져다주었습니다."

어휘 esteemed 높이 평가받는, 존중받는 award 상; 수여하다 corporate 기업의 foresight 선견지명, 통찰력 strategy 전략 ensure 보장하다 long-term 장기적인 viability 성공[실행] 가능성 present 수여하다, 주다 sector 분야, 부문 under the direction of ~의 지휘[감독]하에 bankruptcy 파산 profitability 수익성 gratifying 기쁜 entire 전체의 solid 탄탄한, 견고한 ground 기반 exceptional 탁월한 shareholder 주주

161 주제 / 목적

번역 기사의 목적은?
(A) 새로 창업한 사업체를 소개하려고
(B) 전자 산업의 동향을 분석하려고
(C) 기업의 성과를 강조하려고
(D) 고용 계약의 변경사항을 논의하려고

해설 첫 단락의 두 번째 문장에서 월든스톤 기업상은 회사의 장기적인 성공 가능성을 보장하는 데 도움이 되는 전략을 개발하는 선견지명이 있는 기업에 수여된다(The Waldenstone Corporate Prize is awarded ~ the company's long-term viability)고 했고, 두 번째 단락의 첫 문장에서 올해의 상은 전자 제품 분야의 주요 업체인 카릴라 코퍼레이션에게 수여되었다(This year's award was presented to Carila Corporation, a major player in the electronics sector)면서 뒤이어 카릴라 코퍼레이션의 성과에 대해 논하고 있으므로 (C)가 정답이다.

어휘 profile (인물, 단체 등을) 소개하다, 프로필[개요]를 작성하다 analyze 분석하다 trend 동향, 추세 highlight 강조하다 achievement 성과 employment 고용

162 추론 / 암시

번역 카릴라 코퍼레이션에 대해 암시된 것은?
(A) 더 이상 전자 제품을 개발하지 않는다.
(B) 한때 어려움을 겪은 업체였다.
(C) 더 많은 고객을 유치할 수 없었다.
(D) 최고 경영자 교체를 모색하고 있다.

해설 두 번째 단락의 두 번째 문장에서 카릴라 코퍼레이션은 불과 3년 만에 파산 직전에서 수익성이 매우 높은 수준으로 전환했다(Carila Corporation went from near bankruptcy to a high level of profitability in just three years)고 한 것으로 보아 카릴라 코퍼레이션이 3년 전에 파산할 정도로 어려움을 겪었다는 것을 알 수 있다. 따라서 (B)가 정답이다.

어휘 once 한때 struggling 어려움을 겪는, 고군분투하는 seek 모색하다

Paraphrasing 지문의 near bankruptcy → 정답의 struggling

163 동의어 찾기

번역 세 번째 단락 6행의 "solution"과 의미가 가장 가까운 단어는?
(A) 혼합물
(B) 증명
(C) 진술
(D) 해답

해설 의미상 장기적인 '해결책'으로 가치를 얻게 되었다(The long-term solution has brought exceptional value)는 뜻으로 쓰였으므로 '해답, 답'을 뜻하는 (D) answer이 정답이다.

164-167 광고

모두를 위한 콤볼트!

¹⁶⁴**콤볼트 고객으로서 고객님은 안정적인 초고속 인터넷, 명확한 가격 옵션 그리고 모든 요구에 즉각 대응하는 친절한 전문가의 우수한 고객 서비스에 있어 최고를 기대하고 계실 것입니다.** 경쟁사와 달리 저희는 고객님을 절대 융통성 없는 약정에 가두거나 예고 없이 갑자기 월간 청구 요금을 올리지 않을 것을 약속합니다.

콤볼트에서는 인터넷 서비스 공급업체를 고르는 데에 관한 한 선택권이 고객님에게 있다는 것을 알고 있습니다. 고객님의 애용에 감사를 표하고자 저희는 특별 한정 기간 추천 보너스를 제공하고 있습니다.

¹⁶⁷**진행 방식은 간단합니다. 고객님의 고유 추천 코드를 친구 및 가족들과 공유하세요.** 이메일, 소셜 미디어 또는 문자 메시지를 이용하여 모두에게 콤볼트에 대해 알리면 됩니다. ¹⁶⁶**새로운 사용자가 고객님의 코드를 사용하여 가입하면 고객님과 신규 가입자는 각각 금전적인 크레디트를 받게 됩니다.** ¹⁶⁵**새로 추천받은 사람이 월 45달러 요금제에 가입하면 10달러를 받고, 월 60달러 요금제 가입 시에는 20달러를 받으세요.** 가장 좋은 소식은요? 크레디트에 제한이 없어 더 많은 사람을 가입시킬수록 더 많은 금액을 받게 됩니다.

고객님의 고유 코드는 XA4R177입니다.

어휘 reliable 안정적인, 믿을 수 있는 straightforward 명확한, 간단한 pricing 가격 책정 top-notch 아주 뛰어난, 최고의 professional 전문가 responsive 즉각 대응하는 competition 경쟁 상대 lock ~ into ~을 가두다 inflexible 융통성[유연성]이 없는 raise 올리다 bill 청구서 when it comes to ~에 관한 한 gratitude 감사 loyalty 충성(심) referral 추천[소개]; 추천된 사람 sign up 가입하다, 등록하다 plan 요금제 monetary 금전의, 화폐의 credit 크레디트(현금처럼 사용 가능한 적립금)

164 세부사항

번역 광고에서 언급하는 콤볼트의 이점은?
(A) 저렴한 가격
(B) 우수한 고객 서비스
(C) 평생 약정
(D) 편리한 설치 일정

해설 첫 번째 단락의 첫 문장에서 콤볼트 고객으로서 안정적인 초고속 인터넷, 명확한 가격 옵션 그리고 모든 요구에 즉각 대응하는 친절한 전문가의 우수한 고객 서비스에 있어 최고를 기대할 것(As a Commbolt customer, you've come to expect the best in ~ top-notch customer service from friendly professionals who are responsive to your every need)이라고 했으므로 고객에 대한 우수한 서비스를 장점으로 내세우고 있음을 알 수 있다. 따라서 (B)가 정답이다.

어휘 benefit 이점, 혜택 convenient 편리한 installation 설치

Paraphrasing 지문의 top-notch → 정답의 excellent

165 세부사항

번역 추천받은 사람 한 명이 서비스에 가입할 경우 고객이 받을 수 있는 최대 금액은?
(A) 10달러
(B) 20달러
(C) 45달러
(D) 60달러

해설 세 번째 단락의 네 번째 문장에서 추천받은 사람이 월 45달러 요금제에 가입하면 10달러를 받고, 월 60달러 요금제 가입 시에는 20달러를 받는다(Receive $10 when new referrals sign up ~ and receive $20 for a plan costing $60 per month)고 했으므로 추천 등록인 한 명에 대해 고객이 받을 수 있는 최대 금액은 20달러임을 알 수 있다. 따라서 (B)가 정답이다.

166 Not / True

번역 콤볼트 판촉 행사에 대해 사실인 것은?
(A) 소셜 미디어에 게시되지 않을 수도 있다.
(B) 세 건 이상의 추천에 대해서는 크레디트를 제공하지 않는다.
(D) 일년 내내 진행될 것으로 예상된다.
(D) 신규 및 기존 고객 모두에게 보상한다.

해설 세 번째 단락의 세 번째 문장에서 새로운 사용자가 고객의 코드를 사용하여 가입하면 고객과 신규 가입자는 각각 금전적인 크레디트를 받게 된다(When a new user signs up using your code, each of you will receive a monetary credit)고 했다. 따라서 새로운 사용자가 추천인의 코드를 이용해 가입할 경우, 신규 가입자 및 기존 고객 모두 크레디트를 얻게 되는 것이므로 (D)가 정답이다.

어휘 promotion 판촉 행사 post 게시하다 reward 보상하다 existing 기존의

Paraphrasing 지문의 receive a monetary credit → 정답의 rewards

167 문장 삽입

번역 [1], [2], [3], [4]로 표시된 위치 중에서 다음 문장이 들어가기에 가장 적합한 곳은?

"고객님의 고유 추천 코드를 친구 및 가족들과 공유하세요."
(A) [1]
(B) [2]
(C) [3]
(D) [4]

해설 주어진 문장에서 고유 추천 코드를 친구와 가족들에게 공유하라며 일종의 지침사항을 안내하고 있으므로, 앞에 이 지침사항이 무엇에 관한 것인지를 알려 주는 내용이 제시되어야 자연스럽다. [3] 앞의 진행 방식이 간단하다(The way it works is simple)는 문장 뒤에 들어가면, 진행 방식을 설명하는 주어진 문장으로 자연스럽게 연결되므로 (C)가 정답이다.

168-171 웹페이지

https://www.sarahscatering.com

사라스 케이터링 — 어떤 음식을 제공하는지가 중요합니다

사라스 케이터링은 가족이 소유하고 운영하는 회사입니다. 회사는 10년 전 우리 지역에 최고 품질의 출장 요리 서비스를 제공한다는 사명하에 설립되었습니다. 168우리는 지역 재배자들과 긴밀히 협력하여 가장 신선한 재료만을 사용합니다. 메뉴 항목은 고객의 169취향이나 식이 요구에 맞게 조정될 수 있습니다. 예를 들어, 채식주의자와 비건, 글루텐 프리 옵션을 준비할 수 있습니다.

우리는 생일 파티, 결혼 피로연, 기업 회의, 회사 연말 파티 그리고 기타 다양한 행사를 위한 출장 요리를 제공합니다. 170메뉴 계획과 음식 준비에서부터 행사를 위한 서빙 종업원과 청소 직원 동원에 이르기까지, 사라스 케이터링이 모두 처리해 드립니다.

사라스 케이터링은 고객 근무처에서 최소 인원 20명부터 점심 식사 제공이 가능합니다. 우리는 단체 고객의 식사가 만족스러운 경험이 되도록 맛있는 옵션을 제공합니다.

귀하께 음식을 제공하기 위해 우리가 여기 있습니다! 주문은 빠르고 간편합니다. 다음 행사에 대한 비용 견적을 요청하려면 www.sarahscatering.com/quote를 방문하세요.

사람들의 평가

171 "사라스 케이터링은 함께 일을 진행하기에 매우 수월했고 음식도 맛있었습니다! 사무실에 있는 이들 모두가 음식이 얼마나 좋았는지에 대해 한마디씩 했습니다. ." — 글렌 리우, 퍼킨스 부동산

"모든 음식이 완벽했고 직원들도 최고였어요." — 애니 피어스, 카니아 마케팅 주식회사

어휘 catering 출장 요리 matter 중요하다 found 설립하다 mission 사명 closely 긴밀하게 grower 재배자 ingredient 재료 adapt 조정하다 taste 취향 dietary 식이 요법의 vegetarian 채식주의자 vegan (우유, 달걀도 먹지 않는) 엄격한 채식주의자 gluten-free 글루텐을 함유하지 않은 reception (결혼) 피로연, 축하 연회 engage 고용하다, 참여시키다 cover 다루다 cater 음식을 공급하다 satisfying 만족스러운 estimate 견적 comment 언급하다, 의견을 말하다

168 Not / True

번역 사라스 케이터링에 대해 명시된 것은?
(A) 현지에서 조달한 제품을 사용한다.
(B) 20년이 되었다.
(C) 주로 결혼식을 전문으로 한다.
(D) 현장 식당이 있다.

해설 첫 번째 단락의 세 번째 문장에서 사라스 케이터링은 지역 재배자들과 긴밀히 협력하여 가장 신선한 재료만을 사용한다(We work closely with local growers and use only the freshest ingredients)고 언급하고 있으므로 (A)가 정답이다. 회사는 10년 전 설립되었다(The company was founded ten years ago)고 했으므로 (B), 생일 파티, 결혼 피로연, 기업 회의 등 다양한 행사를 위한 출장 요리를 제공한다(We provide catering for ~ many other types of events)고 했으므로 (C)는 답이 될 수 없고, 식당에 대한 언급이 없으므로 (D) 또한 오답이다.

어휘 sourced (특정한 곳에서) 공급받는 specialize in ~을 전문으로 하다 on-site 현장의 dining room 식당

Paraphrasing 지문의 work closely with local growers and use only the freshest ingredients
→ 정답의 uses locally sourced products

169 동의어 찾기

번역 첫 번째 단락 4행의 "taste"와 의미가 가장 가까운 단어는?
(A) 선호
(B) 견본
(C) 경험
(D) 맛

해설 의미상 고객의 '취향', 즉 고객이 선호하는 것이라는 뜻으로 쓰인 것이므로 (A) preference가 정답이다.

170 Not / True

번역 사라스 케이터링에 의해 제공되는 서비스로 언급된 것은?
(A) 엔터테인먼트 기획
(B) 요리 시연
(C) 식후 청소
(D) 식탁 및 의자 대여

해설 두 번째 단락의 두 번째 문장에서 메뉴 계획과 음식 준비에서부터 행사를 위한 서빙 종업원과 청소 직원 동원에 이르기까지 사라스 케이터링이 모두 처리한다(From planning the menu ~ to engaging servers and cleanup staff for the event, Sarah's Catering has it covered)고 했으므로 (C)가 정답이다.

어휘 demonstration 시연 rental 대여[임대]

171 추론 / 암시

번역 리우 씨는 누구일 것 같은가?
(A) 사라스 케이터링의 직원
(B) 전문 행사 기획자
(C) 사라스 케이터링의 고객
(D) 마케팅 회사의 조수

해설 '사람들의 평가(What people are saying)'란의 첫 번째 평가 작성자 이름이 글렌 리우(Glen Liu)이고, 사라스 케이터링은 함께 일을 진행하기에 매우 수월했고 음식도 맛있었으며 사무실에 있는 이들 모두가 음식이 얼마나 좋았는지에 대해 한마디씩 했다((Sarah's Catering was ~ how good the food was)는 내용으로 보아 리우 씨는 사라스 케이터링을 이용했던 고객임을 알 수 있다. 따라서 (C)가 정답이다.

172-175 온라인 채팅

마커스 스튜버 [오전 10시 41분] 172오늘 작가 화상 회의를 여전히 할 계획인가요? 제가 아직 회의 초대를 받지 못했어요.

브린다 라잔 [오전 10시 42분] 제 일정표에는 회의가 있어요. 전달해 드릴게요. 우리 편집 보조가 당신을 빠뜨린 것 같네요.

마커스 스튜버 [오전 10시 43분] 감사합니다. 방금 받았어요. 그런데 저는 시간대가 안 맞는데요. 173헤이즐 루엉과 싱가포르 공장의 인쇄 문제를 논의하기로 약속이 되어 있어요.

브린다 라잔 [오전 10시 44분] 173, 174그걸 연기하실 수 있을까요? 174우리와 함께 일할 새 작가는 최종 책 디자인과 서식 설정에 관해 당신의 도움이 절실해요. 당신이 우리 중 가장 박식한 제작 편집자이시잖아요.

마커스 스튜버 [오전 10시 45분] 제 상관에게 확인해 볼게요. 보그 씨를 우리 채팅에 추가하겠습니다.

조슈아 보그 [오전 10시 47분] 안녕하세요, 팀 여러분. 마커스, 174헤이즐과의 일정을 우선적으로 처리해야 합니다. 제가 다음 주에 공장을 방문할 예정이라 그 전에 실행 가능한 해결책이 필요합니다.

브린다 라잔 [오전 10시 48분] 알겠습니다. 174, 175그럼 제가 베노이트 씨에게 연락해서 그날 늦게 만날 수 있는지 알아보겠습니다.

마커스 스튜버 [오전 10시 48분] 그러면 될 것 같아요. 저는 오후 4시에서 6시 사이에 시간이 있습니다.

172 주제 / 목적

번역 스튜버 씨가 라잔 씨에게 메시지를 쓴 이유는?
(A) 전문적인 행사에 초대하려고
(B) 회의 진행 상태를 확인하려고
(C) 출장을 위한 여행 계획을 세우려고
(D) 조수의 업무 성과를 물으려고

해설 10시 41분에 스튜버 씨가 오늘 작가 화상 회의를 여전히 할 계획인지(Are we still planning to have the author video conference today?)를 물었고, 아직 회의 초대를 받지 못했다(I haven't yet received a meeting invitation)며 회의 진행 여부를 확인하고 있으므로 (B)가 정답이다.

어휘 status (진행) 상태 performance 업무 성과

173 의도 파악

번역 오전 10시 45분에 스튜버 씨가 "제 상관에게 확인해 볼게요"라고 쓴 의도는?
(A) 책 디자인에 대한 최종 승인이 필요하다.
(B) 약속을 변경하는 것에 대한 조언을 원한다.
(C) 회사 일정에 대한 접근 권한을 필요로 한다.
(D) 채팅에 팀원을 추가하는 방법을 모른다.

해설 10시 43분에 스튜버 씨가 헤이즐 루엉과 싱가포르 공장의 인쇄 문제를 논의하기로 약속이 되어 있다(I have an appointment ~ at our Singapore plant)고 하자 10시 44분에 라잔 씨가 그 일정을 연기할 수 있는지(Could you postpone that?)를 물었고, 10시 45분에 스튜버 씨가 상관에게 확인해 보겠다(Let me check with my supervisor)고 했다. 따라서 스튜버 씨는 상관에게 기존의 약속을 변경해도 되는지에 대해 문의해 보겠다는 의도로 한 말이므로 (B)가 정답이다.

어휘 approval 승인 access 접근 corporate 회사[기업]의 uncertain 잘 모르는

174 추론 / 암시

번역 베노이트 씨는 누구일 것 같은가?
(A) 작가
(B) 디자이너
(C) 제작 편집자
(D) 인쇄 공장 감독관

해설 10시 44분에 라잔 씨가 스튜버 씨에게 그것, 즉 헤이즐 루엉과의 약속을 연기할 수 있는지(Could you postpone that?)를 물으며 우리와 함께 일할 새 작가는 최종 책 디자인과 서식 설정에 관해 스튜버 씨의 도움이 절실하다(The new author ~ really needs your guidance on the final book design and formatting)고 했고, 10시 47분에 스튜버 씨의 상관인 보그 씨가 스튜버 씨에게 헤이즐과의 일정을 우선적으로 처리해야 한다(you should prioritize your appointment with Hazel)며 연기가 불가하다고 하자 10시 48분에 라잔 씨가 그럼 베노이트 씨에게 연락해서 그날 늦게 만날 수 있는지 알아보겠다(I'll contact Ms. Benoit ~ can meet later in the day, then)고 했다. 따라서 베노이트 씨가 함께 일할 작가임을 알 수 있으므로 (A)가 정답이다.

175 추론 / 암시

번역 라잔 씨는 다음에 무엇을 할 것 같은가?
(A) 인쇄 문제에 대한 해결책 제시
(B) 싱가포르 공장 방문 준비
(C) 루엉 씨와의 회의 참석
(D) 화상 회의 일정 변경

해설 10시 48분에 라잔 씨가 베노이트 씨에게 연락해서 그날 늦게 만날 수 있는지 알아보겠다(I'll contact Ms. Benoit to find out if she can meet later in the day, then)고 했으므로 (D)가 정답이다.

176-180 일정표 + 문자 메시지

램블링 리버 페스티벌
음악 행사 일정

9월 8일 금요일
• 오후 3시 30분　　조해나 그린블랫
• 176, 180 **오후 8시**　　블라스 브라더스 밴드가 출연하는 베데스다 라디오 쇼 176 (브램리 극장에서 녹음 예정)

9월 9일 토요일
• 오후 6시 30분　　롤링 더즌
• 오후 7시 45분　　제퍼슨 케이지

177 모든 행사는 별도의 언급이 없는 한 베데스다 공원 야외무대에서 진행됩니다. 소풍용 담요를 가져오셔도 됩니다.

발신: 램블링 리버 페스티벌, 180 **9월 8일 오전 9시 14분**

178 오늘 오후 공연은 악천후가 예상되어 콜 홀에서 열릴 예정입니다. 부피가 큰 물품은 허용되지 않지만, 코트 보관 서비스는 이용 가능합니다.

180 오늘 저녁 공연은 내일 오후 2시 30분으로 179 연기되며, 대신 지역 밴드인 키르샤우가 원래 시간대에 공연할 예정입니다.

토요일 전체 프로그램은 베데스다 공원 야외무대에서 진행될 것으로 예상됩니다.

어휘   in anticipation of ~을 예상하여   inclement weather
굿은 날씨   bulky 부피가 큰   coat-check 코트 보관, 휴대품 일시
보관   be pushed to ~으로 연기되다[미뤄지다]   time slot 시간대

176 세부사항

번역   원래 브램리 극장에서 공연할 예정이었던 사람은?
(A) 조해나 그린블랫
(B) 블라스 브라더스 밴드
(C) 롤링 더즌
(D) 제퍼슨 케이지

해설   일정표에 따르면, 9월 8일 금요일 오후 8시에 블라스 브라더스 밴
드가 출연하는 베데스다 라디오 쇼(Bethesda Radio Show
featuring the Blass Brothers Band)가 브램리 극장에서 녹음 예
정(to be recorded at the Bramley Theater)이라고 나와 있으므
로 (B)가 정답이다.

177 추론 / 암시

번역   일정에서 램블링 리버 페스티벌에 대해 암시하는 것은?
(A) 매년 열린다.
(B) 입장권이 필요하다.
(C) 지역 음식 노점상들이 참여한다.
(D) 주로 야외 행사이다.

해설   일정표의 마지막 단락에서 모든 행사는 별도의 언급이 없는 한 베데
스다 공원 야외무대에서 진행된다(All events take place at the
Bethesda Park Open-Air Stage unless otherwise noted)
고 한 뒤 소풍용 담요를 가져와도 된다(Feel free to bring picnic
blankets)고 덧붙이고 있으므로 페스티벌이 기본적으로 야외에서 진
행되는 행사임을 알 수 있다. 따라서 (D)가 정답이다.

어휘   entry 입장, 출입   vendor 노점상

Paraphrasing   지문의 Open-Air → 정답의 outdoor

178 세부사항

번역   문자 메시지에 따르면, 관객들이 콜 홀에서 할 수 있는 것은?
(A) 코트 보관하기
(B) 부피가 큰 물품 보관하기
(C) 콘서트 티켓 구매하기
(D) 행사 일정표 가져가기

해설   문자 메시지의 첫 문장에서 오늘 오후 공연은 악천후가 예상되어
콜 홀에서 열릴 예정(This afternoon's performance will take
place in Cole Hall in anticipation of inclement weather)이
라고 했고, 부피가 큰 물품은 허용되지 않지만 코트 보관 서비스는
이용 가능하다(Bulky items are not allowed, but coat-check
service will be available)고 했으므로 (A)가 정답이다.

179 동의어 찾기

번역   문자 메시지의 두 번째 단락 1행의 "pushed"와 의미가 가장 가까
운 단어는?
(A) 옮겨진
(B) 연장된
(C) 관리된
(D) 압력이 가해진

해설   의미상 공연이 '연기되었다', 즉 공연 시간이 옮겨졌다는 뜻으로 쓰였
으므로 '옮겨진'을 뜻하는 (A) moved가 정답이다.

180 연계   ▶ 동영상 강의

번역   키르샤우는 언제 공연하는가?
(A) 금요일 오후 3시 30분
(B) 금요일 오후 8시
(C) 토요일 오후 2시 30분
(D) 토요일 오후 6시 30분

해설   9월 8일에 발송된 문자 메시지의 두 번째 단락에 오늘 저녁 공연은
내일 오후 2시 30분으로 연기되며 대신 지역 밴드인 키르샤우가 원
래 시간대에 공연할 예정(This evening's performance is being
pushed to 2:30 P.M. tomorrow; local band Kirschau will
perform during the original time slot instead)이라고 했는데,
일정표에는 9월 8일 금요일 오후 8시에 블라스 브라더스 밴드가 출연
하는 베데스다 라디오 쇼(Bethesda Radio Show featuring the
Blass Brothers Band)를 한다고 나와 있다. 따라서 키르샤우는 원
래 블라스 브라더스 밴드가 공연하기로 되어 있던 9월 8일 금요일 오
후 8시에 공연하는 것이므로 (B)가 정답이다.

181-185 이메일 + 기사

181 수신: 지점장 전원
발신: 프랜 콜리스
181 제목: 모바일 뱅킹에 대한 설문 조사 결과
날짜: 4월 7일

안녕하세요, 여러분.

181 오그덴 은행은 자사 고객을 대상으로 최근 모바일 뱅킹에 관한 설문
조사를 실시했습니다. 여기 몇 가지 주요 핵심사항이 있습니다.

우리 고객 중 95퍼센트 이상이 모바일 기기를 소유하고 있습니다. 하지
만 182 모바일 뱅킹에 관한 관심이 높은데도 불구하고, 우리 고객 중 39
퍼센트만이 자사 애플리케이션을 사용합니다. 일부 고객은 보안 문제(23
퍼센트)를 언급하지만, 대다수(78퍼센트)는 앱이 제대로 작동하지 않는
것 같다고 이야기합니다.

이 문제에 대응하기 위한 전략을 브레인스토밍하기 위해 184 4월 12일
오후 4시에 본사에서 지점장 전원을 위한 의무 회의가 열릴 것입니다.

프랜 콜리스
오그덴 은행 모바일 뱅킹 담당 이사

모바일 뱅킹 활성화

작성: 에드워드 판지우스

플레밍턴 (5월 25일) — 오그덴 은행이 모바일 뱅킹 애플리케이션에 대한 주요 개선책들을 내놓았다. 앱으로 할 수 있는 업무의 다양성을 확대하고 훨씬 더 사용하기 쉽게 만들었다.

"과거에는 우리 계좌 소유자 중 다수가 투박하고 제한적인 앱 때문에 불편을 많이 느껴 왔습니다."라고 184**오그덴 은행 플레밍턴 지점의 지점장인 알리스 드프리스는 말했다.** 185**"전화를 하거나 지점을 직접 방문해야 할 수 있었던 거의 모든 업무를 이제는 앱으로 할 수 있습니다. 이것은 우리가 가능한 모든 방식으로 어떻게 고객을 지원하는지를 보여 주는 또 하나의 예시일 뿐입니다."**

드프리스 씨에 따르면, 업그레이드 이후 몇 주 만에 계좌 소유자 중 20퍼센트가 온라인으로 수표를 예치하고 고지서를 지불하는 방식으로 전환했다고 한다. 그녀는 더 많은 고객들이 이 사용하기 쉬운 앱에 대해 알게됨에 따라 그 수가 증가할 것으로 183**예상한다.**

"편리함이 저에게 큰 차이를 만들었습니다."라고 계좌 소유자인 야이르바움은 말했다. 또 다른 고객인 마리아 리드는 "원한다면 언제 어디서나 은행 업무를 할 수 있다는 유연성이 마음에 듭니다."라고 덧붙였다.

181 주제 / 목적

번역 이메일의 목적은?
(A) 새로운 개인 정보 정책에 대한 세부 정보를 제공하려고
(B) 은행 업무 습관에 대한 설문 조사를 제안하려고
(C) 은행 직원에게 모바일 앱 테스트를 요청하려고
(D) 관리자들에게 회사의 문제를 공지하려고

해설 이메일의 수신자가 지점장 전원(To: All Branch Managers), 제목이 모바일 뱅킹에 대한 설문 조사 결과(Subject: Survey results on mobile banking)이고, 첫 문장에서 오그덴 은행은 자사 고객을 대상으로 최근 모바일 뱅킹에 관한 설문 조사를 실시했다(Ogden Bank recently conducted a survey of its customers concerning mobile banking)며 여기 몇 가지 주요 핵심사항이 있다(Here are some key takeaways)고 했다. 따라서 이메일은 은행의 지점장들에게 고객 설문 조사 결과에 따른 주요 안건을 알리기 위한 것이므로 (D)가 정답이다.

어휘 privacy 개인 정보

182 세부사항

번역 이메일에 따르면, 은행 고객 중 모바일 앱 사용자의 비율은?
(A) 23퍼센트
(B) 39퍼센트
(C) 78퍼센트
(D) 95퍼센트

해설 이메일의 두 번째 단락 두 번째 문장에서 모바일 뱅킹에 관한 관심이 높은데도 불구하고 은행 고객 중 39퍼센트만이 자사 애플리케이션을 사용한다(although interest in mobile banking is high, only 39 percent of our customers use our application)고 했으므로 (B)가 정답이다.

183 동의어 찾기

번역 기사의 세 번째 단락 5행의 "anticipates"와 의미가 가장 가까운 단어는?
(A) 고려하다
(B) 기다리다
(C) 준비하다
(D) 기대하다

해설 의미상 수가 증가할 것으로 '예상한다'는 뜻으로 쓰였으므로 '기대하다, 예상하다'를 뜻하는 (D) expects가 정답이다.

184 연계

번역 4월 12일에 오그덴 은행 본사 회의에 참석했을 것 같은 사람은?
(A) 판지우스 씨
(B) 드프리스 씨
(C) 바움 씨
(D) 리드 씨

해설 이메일의 마지막 문장에서 4월 12일 오후 4시에 본사에서 지점장 전원을 위한 의무 회의가 열릴 것(A mandatory meeting for all branch managers will be held at our headquarters on April 12 at 4:00 P.M.)이라고 했고, 기사의 두 번째 단락 첫 문장에서 알리스 드프리스 씨가 오그덴 은행 플레밍턴 지점의 지점장(Alys DeFreese, manager of the Flemington branch of Ogden Bank)이라고 했다. 따라서 오그덴 은행의 지점장인 드프리스 씨가 4월 12일 지점장 회의에 참석했음을 알 수 있으므로 (B)가 정답이다.

185 추론 / 암시

번역 오그덴 은행의 경영진에 대해 암시된 것은?
(A) 계좌 소유자들이 대면으로 은행 업무를 보는 것을 선호한다.
(B) 신규 계좌 소유자들에게 무료 당좌 예금 계좌 제공을 고려 중이다.
(C) 더 많은 직원을 고용하는 과정에 있다.
(D) 고객 경험의 개선을 우선시한다.

해설 기사의 두 번째 단락 두 번째 문장에서 드프리스 씨가 전화를 하거나 지점을 직접 방문해야 할 수 있었던 거의 모든 업무를 이제는 앱으로 할 수 있다(They can now do ~ with the app that they could over the phone or by visiting a branch in person)며, 이것은

자신들이 가능한 모든 방식으로 어떻게 고객을 지원하는지 보여 주는 또 하나의 예시일 뿐(This is ~ how we support our customers in any way we can)이라고 언급한 내용으로 보아 오그덴 은행이 고객 서비스 향상을 위해 최선을 다 하고 있다는 것을 알 수 있다. 따라서 (D)가 정답이다.

어휘 checking 당좌 예금[입출금] (계좌) in the process of ~의 과정에 있는, ~하는 중인 prioritize 우선시하다

Paraphrasing 지문의 support our customers in any way we can
→ 정답의 prioritizes improvements in customer experience

186-190 공지 + 웹페이지 + 이메일

도서관 회원 여러분께 알립니다.

186 웨스트우드 도서관은 모든 도서관 회원들에게 개방되는 북클럽의 시작을 알리게 되어 기쁩니다. 189 클럽은 매월 마지막 목요일 오후 7시부터 9시까지 해리슨 미팅룸에 모여 우리의 전문 직원이 선택한 책에 관해 토론할 예정입니다. 187 1월부터 6월까지는 최근에 출판된 비소설 작품들을 읽을 것이고, 7월부터 12월까지는 현대 소설 출판물에 초점을 둘 것입니다. 더 자세한 정보를 원하시면 www.westwoodlibrary.org를 방문하시거나 도서 대출 데스크에 있는 직원에게 문의하세요.

어휘 attention (안내문에서) 알립니다 published 출판된 nonfiction 비소설 work 작품 contemporary 현대의 fiction 소설 title 출판물, 서적 circulation desk (도서관) 대출 데스크

https://www.westwoodlibrary.org/bookclub

매월 마지막 주 목요일 저녁 7시에 열리는 북클럽에 함께해 주시기 바랍니다! 아래는 상반기에 선정된 서적들입니다.

187 1월: 잭슨 맥도널드의 〈와일드 오픈 레인지〉

2월: 루시 시의 〈노래의 여정〉

3월: 이사벨 벡의 〈듀 노스: 알래스카 북쪽 지역에서의 모험〉

4월: 피터 랜더스의 〈마음을 다하는 목공술〉

188 5월: 카이 노블의 〈메리 스완: 시대를 앞선 전설〉

6월: 공지 예정

어휘 journey 여정 territory 지역, 영토 art 기술, 예술 mindful 마음을 다하는, 명상의 carpentry 목공 before one's time 시기에 앞서서

수신: 리사 콜 〈lcalle@worldmail.com〉
발신: 게일 프레이 〈gfrey@myemail.com〉
날짜: 3월 27일
제목: 북클럽

콜 씨께,

189 어제저녁에 당신이 북클럽을 이끄는 것을 보니 정말 좋았습니다. 190 벡 씨의 〈듀 노스〉는 너무 길어서 모임 전에 다 읽기가 어려웠어요. 하지만, 그 책으로 알래스카 여행에 대한 제 어린 시절의 관심이 되살아났으니 그 책을 선택해 주신 데 감사해야 할 것 같습니다. 사실, 벌써 몇몇 여행 상품을 찾아봤습니다!

클럽 미팅에 사람이 너무 많아서 당신과 대화를 거의 나누지 못했습니다. 조만간 뵙고 이야기를 나누면 좋겠어요. 아마 루퍼 가에 새로 생긴 프랑스 식당을 가보는 것도 괜찮을 것 같습니다. 훌륭하고 가격도 합리적이라고 들었습니다.

게일 프레이

어휘 delightful 기분 좋은 lengthy 너무 긴, 장황한 challenge 어려움, 난제 .revive 되찾게 하다 childhood 어린 시절 packed (특히 사람들이) 많은, 꽉 들어찬 catch up ~을 만나다, 따라잡다 reasonably 합리적으로 priced 가격이 매겨진

186 주제 / 목적

번역 공지의 목적은?
(A) 도서관에 있는 일부 도서를 부각시키려고
(B) 도서관 이용 시간 변경을 공지하려고
(C) 도서관에서의 활동을 홍보하려고
(D) 새로운 사서를 소개하려고

해설 공지의 첫 문장에서 웨스트우드 도서관은 모든 도서관 회원들에게 개방되는 북클럽의 시작을 알리게 되어 기쁘다(The Westwood Library is excited to announce the start of a book club, which is open to all library members)고 했으므로 (C)가 정답이다.

어휘 highlight 부각시키다, 강조하다 librarian (도서관의) 사서

Paraphrasing 지문의 a book club
→ 정답의 an activity at the library

187 연계

번역 〈와일드 오픈 레인지〉라는 책에 대해 암시된 것은?
(A) 베스트셀러 도서이다.
(B) 비소설 작품이다.
(C) 10년 전에 출간되었다.
(D) 도서관 회원에게는 할인이 적용된다.

해설 공지의 세 번째 문장에서 1월부터 6월까지는 최근에 출판된 비소설 작품들을 읽을 것(From January to June, we will read recently published nonfiction works)이라고 했고, 웹페이지의 월별 선정 도서 목록의 첫 번째 항목에서 1월에 잭슨 맥도널드의 〈와일드 오픈 레인지〉(Wild Open Range by Jaxon McDonald)를 읽는다고 나와 있다. 〈와일드 오픈 레인지〉는 비소설 작품을 읽는 1월의 선정 도서이므로 (B)가 정답이다.

188 추론 / 암시

번역 어느 작가가 유명 인사에 대한 글을 썼을 것 같은가?
(A) 잭슨 맥도널드
(B) 루시 시
(C) 피터 랜더스
(D) 카이 노블

해설 웹페이지에 제시된 도서 중 5월에 있는 도서가 카이 노블의 〈메리 스완: 시대를 앞선 전설〉(*Mary Swan: A Legend Before Her Time* by Kai Noble)이고, 제목으로 미루어 봤을 때 메리 스완이라는 유명 인사에 대한 도서임을 알 수 있다. 따라서 (D)가 정답이다.

189 연계

번역 콜 씨에 대해 결론지을 수 있는 것은?
(A) 도서관 직원이다.
(B) 서평을 썼다.
(C) 프레이 씨의 상사이다.
(D) 역사 소설을 좋아한다.

해설 공지의 두 번째 문장에서 클럽은 매월 마지막 목요일 오후 7시부터 9시까지 해리슨 미팅룸에 모여 도서관의 전문 직원이 선택한 책에 관해 토론할 예정(The club will meet ~ to discuss a book chosen by one of our professional staff)이라고 했고, 이메일의 첫 문장에서 프레이 씨가 콜 씨에게 어제저녁에 콜 씨가 북클럽을 이끄는 것을 보니 정말 좋았다(It was delightful to see you leading the book club yesterday evening)고 했다. 따라서 콜 씨가 도서관 소속의 전문 직원임을 알 수 있으므로 (A)가 정답이다.

어휘 supervisor 상사 favor 선호하다, 편애하다

190 Not / True

번역 프레이 씨가 자신이 읽은 책에 대해 명시한 것은?
(A) 그녀에게 생소한 주제에 대해 논했다.
(B) 부정확하다고 생각했던 부분들이 있었다.
(C) 주어진 시간 안에 읽기 쉬웠다.
(D) 오래된 관심사를 탐구하도록 영감을 주었다.

해설 이메일 첫 번째 단락의 두 번째 문장에서 프레이 씨가 벡 씨의 〈듀 노스〉는 너무 길어서 모임 전에 다 읽기가 어려웠지만(Ms. Beck's Due North is lengthy, and it was a challenge to finish it before the meeting), 그 책으로 알래스카 여행에 대한 자신의 어린 시절의 관심이 되살아났으니 그 책을 선택해 준 데 감사해야 할 것 같다(However, I have to thank you ~ because it revived my childhood interest in traveling to Alaska)고 했으므로 (D)가 정답이다.

어휘 unfamiliar 생소한 inaccurate 부정확한 inspire 영감을 주다 explore 탐구하다

Paraphrasing 지문의 revived my childhood interest
→ 정답의 inspired her to explore an old interest

191-195 이메일 + 영수증 + 이메일

발신: 타티아나 슈워츠 〈orders@georgestreetsweets.co.uk〉
수신: 알레한드로 오르다즈 〈aordaz@brooksidestationery.co.uk〉
날짜: 4월 28일
제목: 주문 번호 47892 확인
첨부: ⬚주문 영수증

오르다즈 씨께,

조지 스트리트 스위츠에 주문해 주셔서 감사합니다. 이 이메일은 고객님의 요청을 받았음을 확인하기 위한 것입니다. 고객님의 영수증은 이메일에 첨부되었습니다.

문의사항이 있거나 주문을 변경해야 할 경우, 이 메시지에 회신하거나 (091) 498 0172로 전화 주십시오. 예약된 픽업 시간으로부터 48시간 이내에 제출된 주문 변경사항은 수용할 수 없다는 점에 유념하십시오.

주문품을 픽업하실 경우, 저희는 조지 가 29에 위치해 있습니다. 주차는 옆 건물 스파이크스 사이클 숍 바로 뒤에 하실 수 있습니다. ¹⁹²저희 매장에서 10킬로미터 이내의 고객들에게는 2.50파운드의 수수료로 배달을 제공합니다. ¹⁹¹픽업 또는 배달 시간으로부터 24시간 이내에 취소한 경우에는 환불되지 않는 점을 유의하시기 바랍니다.

타티아나 슈워츠

어휘 place an order 주문하다 attach 첨부하다 make a change 변경하다 reply 회신하다 note 유의[유념]하다 accommodate 수용하다 submit 제출하다 scheduled 예정된 directly 바로 cancellation 취소 refund 환불하다

조지 스트리트 스위츠

주문: 47892
주문일: 4월 28일
픽업 날짜 및 시간: 해당 없음
배달 날짜 및 시간: 5월 2일 오전 11시 30분
¹⁹²배달 위치: 스펜 로 2, 비즈니스 스위트 202
결제 방법: 신용카드 – 알레한드로 오르다즈

주문 제작 지시사항: 없음

품목	가격
¹⁹³18인치 원형 케이크 (비닐라 아이싱 초콜릿)	32파운드
초 1세트	5파운드
¹⁹²배달	2.50파운드
합계	39.50파운드

어휘 N/A 해당 없음(not applicable의 줄임말) payment method 결제 방법 customisation 주문 제작 instructions 지시

발신: 알레한드로 오르다즈 〈aordaz@brooksidestationery.co.uk〉
수신: 타티아나 슈워츠 〈orders@georgestreetsweets.co.uk〉
날짜: 4월 29일
제목: 회신: 주문 번호 47892 확인

슈워츠 씨께,

저의 주문 확인 이메일과 영수증을 받고 오류를 하나 발견했습니다. **193 주문 시 저와 통화한 분이 제가 요청한 메시지를 받아 적지 않은 것 같습니다.** 제가 지정한 주문 제작 내용은 '행복한 은퇴'라고 케이크 위에 작성하는 것이었습니다.

시기에 상관없이 이 메시지를 넣는 것이 아직 가능하기를 바랍니다. **194 확인을 위해 이 이메일에 회신해 주세요.** 또한 **195 당초 예상했던 것보다 더 많은 분들이 오실 것**이라서 다시 업체에 전화드려 추가 주문을 할 수 있습니다.

알레한드로 오르다즈

어휘 notice 인지하다 copy down ~을 (그대로) 옮겨 적다
specify 명시하다 timing 시기 originally 당초, 원래
additional 추가의

191 세부사항

번역 조지 스트리트 스위츠의 정책은?
(A) 주문을 변경할 수 없다.
(B) 픽업 전 48시간 이내에 주문한 경우 추가 요금이 발생한다.
(C) 주문에 대한 지불은 주문 시 해야 한다.
(D) 주문은 픽업으로부터 24시간 이내에 환불될 수 없다.

해설 첫 이메일의 세 번째 단락 마지막 문장에서 픽업 또는 배달 시간으로부터 24시간 이내에 취소한 경우에는 환불되지 않는 점을 유의하기 바란다(Please note that cancellations within 24 hours of your pickup ~ will not be refunded)고 했으므로 (D)가 정답이다.

어휘 incur 발생시키다

192 연계

번역 스펜 로 2의 건물에 대해 암시된 것은?
(A) 자전거 매장 뒤에 주차 공간이 있다.
(B) 조지 스트리트 스위츠에서 10킬로미터 이내에 위치해 있다.
(C) 주거용 아파트 건물이다.
(D) 슈워츠 씨가 소유하고 있다.

해설 첫 이메일의 세 번째 단락 세 번째 문장에서 매장(조지 스트리트 스위츠)에서 10킬로미터 이내의 고객들에게는 2.50파운드의 수수료로 배달을 제공한다(We offer delivery to customers within 10 kilometres of our shop for a fee of £2.50)고 했고, 조지 스트리트 스위츠에서 발행한 영수증의 배달 위치가 스펜 로 2, 비즈니스 스위트 202(Delivery Location: 2 Spen Lane, Business Suite 202)이고 품목 중 배달료가 2.50파운드(Delivery: £2.50)로 나와 있다. 따라서 스펜 로 2의 건물이 조지 스트리트 스위츠에서 10킬로미터 이내에 위치하고 있음을 알 수 있으므로 (B)가 정답이다.

어휘 residential 주거용의

193 연계

번역 케이크에 대해 결론지을 수 있는 것은?
(A) 아직 지불되지 않았다.
(B) 초콜릿 아이싱만 있을 것이다.
(C) 전화로 주문되었다.
(D) 아이스크림이 들어 있다.

해설 영수증의 품목 첫 번째 항목에 18인치 원형 케이크(18-inch round cake)를 주문했다고 나와 있고, 두 번째 이메일의 첫 단락 두 번째 문장에서 주문 시 통화한 직원이 요청한 메시지를 받아 적지 않은 것 같다(It seems that the person to whom I spoke on the phone while placing my order ~ requested)고 했다. 따라서 케이크 주문은 전화상으로 이루어진 것임을 알 수 있으므로 (C)가 정답이다.

어휘 contain ~이 들어 있다

194 세부사항

번역 두 번째 이메일에서 오르다즈 씨가 요청한 것은?
(A) 전액 환불
(B) 다른 맛
(C) 이메일에 대한 회신
(D) 추가 양초

해설 두 번째 이메일의 두 번째 단락 두 번째 문장에서 오르다즈 씨가 확인을 위해 이 이메일에 회신해 달라(Please respond to this e-mail to confirm)고 했으므로 (C)가 정답이다.

어휘 response 회신, 응답

195 Not / True

번역 오르다즈 씨가 이메일에서 행사에 대해 언급한 것은?
(A) 4월 29일에 열릴 것이다.
(B) 기념일 파티이다.
(C) 시작 시간이 변경되었다.
(D) 예상보다 규모가 클 것이다.

해설 두 번째 이메일의 마지막 문장에서 오르다즈 씨가 당초 예상했던 것보다 더 많은 사람들이 올 것(there will be more guests than I originally expected)이라고 했으므로 (D)가 정답이다.

어휘 anniversary 기념일

Paraphrasing 지문의 there will be more guests
→ 정답의 It will be larger

196-200 이메일 + 설문 조사 + 보고서

수신: 비공개 수신인
발신: iqbal_grewal@woolfflooring.com.au
날짜: 6월 12일
제목: 비용 절감 설문 조사

동료 직원 여러분께,

울프 플로어링에서는 제품 품질, 고객 서비스 또는 직원의 사기를 희생하지 않고 일상적인 비용을 절감할 수 있는 방법을 찾고 있습니다. 이를 위해 www.surveyquest.com.au/109820에서 확인할 수 있는 온라인 설문 조사를 통해 다양한 부서에서 선정된 직원들로부터 의견을 구하고 있습니다. **198 설문 조사에 참여하도록 선택된 모든 직원들은 최소 10년 동안 이 회사에 근무해 왔기 때문에 당사의 절차에 매우 익숙한 분들입니다.**

설문 조사 완료 기한은 6월 19일입니다. **196 이 설문 조사는 본 이메일의 수신자만 대상으로 한다는 점에 유념하십시오. 이 이메일을 다른 사람에게 전달하거나 설문 조사 링크를 다른 곳에 게시하지 마십시오.**

197 또한 외부 컨설턴트를 고용하여 당사의 운영을 검토하고 결과 보고서를 작성하게 할 계획입니다. 일부 동료들은 비용 절감에 대한 이러한 접근 방식에 동의하지 않는다는 점을 알고 있습니다. 그렇지만 외부의 관점을 얻는 것이 장기적으로 비용을 아낄 수 있는 가치 있는 투자라고 결정했습니다.

이크발 그레왈, 비즈니스 혁신 이사
울프 플로어링

---

https://www.surveyquest.com.au/109820

울프 플로어링 비용 절감 설문 조사
울프 플로어링의 직원으로서 귀하의 경험을 바탕으로 생산성 향상과 비용 절감을 위해 시행될 수 있는 변화에 대한 아이디어 한 가지를 제공해 주십시오. 감사합니다.

날짜: 6월 18일
198 이름 및 직함: 영업 관리자 베스 메이어

일부 직원들이 휴식을 취하고 돌아올 때마다 일회용 장갑을 새것으로 사용한다는 것을 알게 되었습니다. **200 같은 장갑을 하루 종일 사용해도 괜찮습니다. 장갑 사용을 하루에 한 켤레로 제한함으로써 울프 플로어링은 연간 수천 달러를 절약할 수 있을 것입니다.** 그렇게 하면 쓰레기도 줄일 수 있습니다. **199 개인 보호 용품의 사용에 관한 새로운 정책은 즉시 시행하기 쉬우며 이를 설명하기 위해 회사 전체에 이메일을 보내기만 하면 됩니다.**

미요코 컨설팅
울프 플로어링 보고서 요약

지난 몇 주 동안 귀사의 운영 실태를 검토할 수 있도록 허락해 주셔서 감사합니다. 다음 페이지에서 예상 절감액이 포함된 상세한 경비 절감 보고서를 확인하실 수 있습니다. 다음은 주요 권장사항 목록입니다.

1. 직원들이 목재 착색제 및 기타 자재를 항상 최대한 효율적으로 사용하는 것은 아닙니다. 이와 관련해 더 많은 교육 시간을 할애할 수 있습니다.

2. 사용하지 않을 때 모든 전등과 기계 전원을 끄는 등 전기 비용에 더 주의를 기울일 수 있습니다.

3. 현재 여러 인터넷 서비스 공급업체가 특별 요금을 제공하고 있습니다. 해당 공급업체 중 한 곳으로 전환하면 장기적으로 상당한 금액을 절약할 수 있습니다.

200 4. 용품을 재사용하는 데 더 많은 노력을 기울일 수 있는데, 예를 들어 일부 기본적인 개인 보호 장비는 여러 번 사용될 수 있습니다.

196 Not / True

번역 이메일에서 그레왈 씨가 설문 조사에 대해 명시한 것은?
(A) 종료일이 없다.
(B) 암호를 사용해야 한다.
(C) 지면으로 작성될 수 있다.
(D) 다른 사람과 공유되어서는 안 된다.

해설 이메일의 두 번째 단락 두 번째 문장에서 그레왈 씨가 이 설문 조사는 본 이메일의 수신자만 대상으로 한다는 점에 유념하라(Note that this survey is for recipients of this e-mail only)면서 이 이메일을 다른 사람에게 전달하거나 설문 조사 링크를 다른 곳에 게시하지 말라(Please do not forward this e-mail to others or post the link to the survey elsewhere)고 당부하고 있으므로 (D)가 정답이다.

Paraphrasing 시문의 not forward ~ to others or post the link
→ 정답의 not be shared with others

197 세부사항

번역 이메일에 따르면, 일부 울프 플로어링 직원들이 동의하지 않는 것은?
(A) 컨설턴트 채용 계획
(B) 설문 조사 구성 방법
(C) 예산 보고서 제시 방법
(D) 의견 제공을 위해 선정된 부서

해설　이메일의 세 번째 단락 첫 번째 문장에서 외부 컨설턴트를 고용하여 당사의 운영을 검토하고 결과 보고서를 작성하게 할 계획(We also plan to hire outside consultants ~ their findings)이라면서, 일부 동료들은 비용 절감에 대한 이러한 접근 방식에 동의하지 않는다는 점을 알고 있다(We understand that some colleagues disagree with this approach to cutting costs)고 했다. 따라서 일부 직원들은 외부 컨설턴트를 고용하는 것에 찬성하지 않는다는 것을 알 수 있으므로 (A)가 정답이다.

어휘　structure 구성하다　present 제시하다, 보여 주다

198　연계

번역　메이어 씨에 대해 결론지을 수 있는 것은?
(A) 변화에 대한 아이디어를 정기적으로 제공한다.
(B) 울프 플로어링에서 수년간 근무했다.
(C) 의견 수집하는 것을 도울 것이다.
(D) 생산 부서에서 일한다.

해설　이메일의 첫 단락 마지막 문장에서 설문 조사에 참여하도록 선택된 모든 직원들은 최소 10년 동안 이 회사(울프 플로어링)에 근무해 왔다(Everyone who has been chosen ~ has been with the company for at least ten years)고 했고, 설문 조사에서 참여자의 이름 및 직함이 영업 관리자 베스 메이어(Name and role: Beth Mair, sales manager)라고 나와 있다. 즉, 메이어 씨가 울프 플로어링 비용 절감 설문 조사에 참여한 것으로 보아 해당 회사에서 10년 이상 근무했음을 알 수 있으므로 (B)가 정답이다.

어휘　regularly 정기적으로　production 생산

Paraphrasing　지문의 for at least ten years
→ 정답의 for many years

199　Not / True

번역　설문 조사에서 메이어 씨가 자신의 제안에 대해 언급한 것은?
(A) 새 장비가 필요할 수 있다.
(B) 다른 회사에서 효과가 있었다.
(C) 즉시 시행될 수 있다.
(D) 이전에 경영진에 제안된 적이 있다.

해설　설문 조사의 마지막 문장에서 메이어 씨가 개인 보호 용품의 사용에 관한 새로운 정책은 즉시 시행하기 쉽다(A new policy ~ easy to implement immediately)고 했으므로 (C)가 정답이다.

어휘　work 효과가 있다　right away 즉시, 곧바로　management 경영진

Paraphrasing　지문의 immediately → 정답의 right away

200　연계

번역　미요코 컨설팅의 권장사항 중 메이어 씨의 제안과 일치하는 것은?
(A) 권장사항 1
(B) 권장사항 2
(C) 권장사항 3
(D) 권장사항 4

해설　설문 조사 의견란의 두 번째 문장에서 메이어 씨가 같은 장갑을 하루 종일 사용해도 괜찮다(They could be using the same ones throughout the whole day)며 장갑 사용을 하루에 한 켤레로 제한함으로써 울프 플로어링은 연간 수천 달러를 절약할 수 있을 것(By limiting the use of gloves ~ save thousands of dollars per year)이라고 했고, 보고서의 권장사항 4번에서 용품을 재사용하는 데 더 많은 노력을 기울일 수 있는데, 예를 들어 일부 기본적인 개인 보호 장비는 여러 번 사용될 수 있다(More effort ~ some basic personal protective equipment could be used more than once)고 했다. 따라서 (D)가 정답이다.

어휘　correspond with ~와 일치[부합]하다

101 (A)	**102** (C)	**103** (A)	**104** (B)	**105** (D)
106 (D)	**107** (B)	**108** (D)	**109** (C)	**110** (B)
111 (A)	**112** (A)	**113** (B)	**114** (D)	**115** (D)
116 (C)	**117** (A)	**118** (D)	**119** (B)	**120** (C)
121 (C)	**122** (C)	**123** (A)	**124** (A)	**125** (D)
126 (B)	**127** (A)	**128** (D)	**129** (C)	**130** (A)
131 (C)	**132** (D)	**133** (B)	**134** (B)	**135** (B)
136 (D)	**137** (C)	**138** (C)	**139** (A)	**140** (A)
141 (C)	**142** (B)	**143** (A)	**144** (B)	**145** (D)
146 (A)	**147** (B)	**148** (C)	**149** (C)	**150** (D)
151 (D)	**152** (C)	**153** (A)	**154** (C)	**155** (B)
156 (C)	**157** (D)	**158** (A)	**159** (B)	**160** (D)
161 (B)	**162** (C)	**163** (D)	**164** (C)	**165** (B)
166 (D)	**167** (C)	**168** (B)	**169** (C)	**170** (D)
171 (A)	**172** (B)	**173** (C)	**174** (B)	**175** (B)
176 (B)	**177** (D)	**178** (A)	**179** (C)	**180** (B)
181 (D)	**182** (A)	**183** (C)	**184** (B)	**185** (A)
186 (B)	**187** (A)	**188** (D)	**189** (A)	**190** (C)
191 (D)	**192** (B)	**193** (C)	**194** (D)	**195** (A)
196 (C)	**197** (B)	**198** (A)	**199** (B)	**200** (D)

PART 5

101 전치사 자리 / 어휘

해설 빈칸 앞에 Mr. Barrientos가 주어, has worked가 동사인 완전한 절이 있고 뒤에 명사구 six years가 있으므로 빈칸은 전치사 자리이다. six years가 기간을 나타내는 말이고, 문맥상 '6년 동안 일했다'라는 의미가 되어야 자연스러우므로 '~ 동안'을 뜻하는 (A) for가 정답이다. (B) since는 '~ 이후로'라는 뜻으로 과거 특정 시점을 나타내는 명사구를 목적어로 취하고, (C) with는 '~와 함께, ~을 가지고'라는 의미이다. (D) lately는 부사이므로 빈칸에 들어갈 수 없다.

번역 배리엔토스 씨는 회사에서 6년 동안 근무했다.

102 동사 어휘

해설 동사 stops의 목적어 자리에 들어갈 동명사 형태의 동사 어휘를 고르는 문제이다. lunch를 목적어로 취해 '점심 식사 제공을 멈추다'라는 내용이 되어야 자연스러우므로 '(식당 등에서 음식을) 제공하다'라는 뜻의 (C) serving이 정답이다. (A)의 take는 '가지고 가다', (B)의 buy는 '사다', (D)의 work는 '일하다; 효과가 있다'라는 의미이다.

번역 직원 식당은 오후 2시에 점심 식사 제공을 마친다.

103 인칭대명사의 격 _ 주격

해설 빈칸은 after로 시작하는 부사절의 동사 make의 주어 자리이므로 인

칭대명사 주격인 (A) I가 정답이다. 참고로, 재귀대명사 (C) myself는 주어 역할을 하지 않는다.

번역 연례 보고서는 제가 필요한 수정을 한 뒤 준비될 것입니다.

어휘 revision 수정

104 전치사 어휘

해설 빈칸 뒤의 명사구 a division manager를 목적어로 취해 '부서 관리자로'라는 내용이 되어야 자연스러우므로 '~로(서)'를 뜻하는 (B) as가 정답이다.

번역 루덴 씨는 포르텔리오 사에서 부서 관리자로 정규직을 제안받았다.

어휘 full-time position 정규직 division 부서

105 동사 어형 _ 조동사 + 동사원형

해설 조동사 will 뒤에는 동사원형이 와야 하므로 '계속하다'라는 뜻의 동사원형 (D) continue가 정답이다.

번역 케네디 스포츠는 1월 한 달 내내 시즌 말 세일을 계속할 것이다.

106 전치사 어휘   동영상 강의

해설 빈칸 뒤의 명사구 workplace regulations를 목적어로 취해 '직장 규정에 대한 발표'라는 내용이 되어야 자연스러우므로 '~에 관하여'를 뜻하는 (D) on이 정답이다. (A) near(~ 가까이에), (B) to(~으로), (C) past(~을 지나서)는 장소나 위치를 나타내는 명사를 목적어로 취한다.

번역 나자르 씨는 정오에 직장 규정에 대해 발표할 예정이다.

어휘 regulation 규정

107 형용사 자리 _ 명사 수식 / 과거분사

해설 빈칸은 정관사 the와 명사 surveys 사이에서 명사를 수식하는 형용사 자리이므로 분사가 들어갈 수 있다. surveys는 완료를 하는 주체가 아닌 완료가 되는 대상이고, '완료된 설문 조사를 제출했다'라는 내용이 되어야 자연스러우므로 수동의 의미를 나타내어 형용사 역할을 하는 과거분사 (B) completed가 정답이다. (A) completely는 부사, (C) completing은 현재분사/동명사, (D) completes는 동사로 빈칸에 들어갈 수 없다.

번역 텔걸드 씨는 월례 이사회 전에 완료된 설문 조사를 제출했다.

어휘 submit 제출하다 board meeting 이사회

108 명사 어휘   동영상 강의

해설 '~에서'를 의미하는 전치사 from의 목적어 자리로, 문맥상 위치나 장소를 나타내는 명사가 들어가야 한다. 정도를 강조하는 형용사 significant(상당한; 중요한)의 수식을 받아 '상당히 먼 곳에서'라는 내용이 되어야 적절하므로 '먼 곳, 거리'를 뜻하는 (D) distance가 정답이다. (A) location은 '장소, 위치'라는 뜻으로 significant의 수식을 받으면 '중요한 장소'를 의미해 문맥상 적절하지 않다. (B) amount는 '양', (C) reason은 '이유'라는 의미이다.

번역 상당히 먼 곳에서 콘퍼런스에 참석하는 학생 발표자에게는 이동 경비가 제공된다.

어휘 fund 자금   presenter 발표자

109 동사 어형 _ 태

해설 be동사 뒤에 빈칸이 있고, 빈칸 뒤에 a new social media campaign이라는 목적어가 있으므로 능동태를 만들 수 있는 현재분사 (C) organizing이 정답이다. 빈칸 앞에 is가 있으므로 동사원형 (A) organize는 들어갈 수 없고, be동사와 함께 수동태를 만드는 과거분사 (B) organized는 빈칸 뒤에 목적어를 취할 수 없다. 명사 (D) organization은 보어로 쓰이는 경우 be동사 뒤에 위치할 수 있지만 주어 Ms. Okada와 동격도 아니고, 빈칸 뒤의 명사구를 연결할 수도 없으므로 답이 될 수 없다.

번역 오카다 씨는 우리 사무실 관리자의 요청으로 새로운 소셜 미디어 캠페인을 기획하고 있습니다.

110 명사 어휘   동영상 강의

해설 빈칸 앞의 purchasing과 함께 복합명사를 이루는 동시에 형용사 wise(현명한)의 수식을 받기에 적절한 명사를 골라야 한다. '현명한 구매 결정'이라는 의미가 되어야 자연스러우므로 '결정'을 뜻하는 (B) decisions가 정답이다. (A)의 item은 '품목', (C)의 value는 '가치'라는 뜻으로 형용사 wise와 의미상 수식 관계가 어울리지 않고, (D)의 remedy는 '치료법'을 뜻하므로 purchasing과 복합명사를 이루기에 어색하다.

번역 강연자는 현명한 구매 결정을 내리기 위한 5가지 조언을 제공할 것이다.

111 전치사 자리

해설 빈칸 앞에 완전한 절(Please log on to your online checking account)이 있고 뒤에 명사구 the next 30 days가 있으므로 빈칸은 전치사 자리이다. 따라서 '~ 이내에'를 뜻하는 전치사 (A) within이 정답이다. (B) how는 의문사/관계부사, (C) whether는 명사절/부사절 접속사이므로 구조상 들어갈 수 없고, 등위접속사 (D) and는 명사구를 연결할 수는 있으나 의미상 적합하지 않다.

번역 활성화 상태를 유지하시려면 30일 이내에 온라인 예금 계좌에 로그인하십시오.

어휘 checking account 당좌 예금 (계좌)   active (계좌 등이) 사용 중인

112 동사 어휘   동영상 강의

해설 빈칸 뒤의 명사구 live jazz music을 목적어로 취하여 '라이브 재즈 음악을 제공한다'라는 의미가 되어야 자연스러우므로 '~을 특징으로 삼다, 특별히 포함하다'라는 뜻의 동사 feature의 3인칭 단수형 (A) features가 정답이다. (B)의 mark는 '표시하다', (C)의 sound는 '소리가 나다, 울리다', (D)의 collect는 '모으다'라는 의미이다.

번역 브래디빌 호텔은 금요일 저녁에 식사 공간에서 라이브 재즈 음악을 제공합니다.

어휘 dining 식사

113 부사 자리 _ 동사 수식

해설 빈칸이 없어도 완전한 절(Leeann's Organic Fruit Spreads can be purchased)과 전치사구(from ~ Web site)로 이루어진 문장으로 빈칸은 문장 구조에 영향을 주지 않는 부사 자리이다. 동사구 can be purchased를 수식하여 '직접 구매할 수 있다'라는 내용이 되어야 자연스러우므로 '직접, 곧장'을 뜻하는 부사 (B) directly가 정답이다. (A) direction과 (C) directness는 명사, (D) directed는 동사/과거분사로 빈칸에 들어갈 수 없다.

번역 리안스 유기농 과일 스프레드는 회사 웹페이지에서 직접 구매할 수 있다.

어휘 direction 방향   directness 솔직함

114 전치사 어휘

해설 빈칸 뒤의 명사구 the event organizers' best efforts를 목적어로 취하는 전치사 자리로, 행사 주최 측이 최선의 노력을 한 것(the event organizers' best efforts)과 충분한 자원봉사자들을 모을 수 없었던 것(unable to attract enough volunteers)은 상충되는 상황이므로 '~에도 불구하고'를 뜻하는 (D) Despite가 정답이다.

번역 행사 주최 측의 최선의 노력에도 불구하고, 그들은 올봄에 충분한 자원봉사자들을 모을 수 없었다.

어휘 organizer 주최자   effort 노력   volunteer 자원봉사자

115 동사 자리 _ 태

해설 주어 Mr. Perez의 동사 자리로, 타동사인 employ(고용하다) 뒤에 목적어가 보이지 않으므로 수동태가 와야 한다. 따라서 (D) has been employed가 정답이다. to부정사구인 (B) to be employed는 품사상 빈칸에 들어갈 수 없고, (A) employs와 (C) is employing은 능동태이므로 뒤에 목적어가 필요하다.

번역 페레즈 씨는 개벌리 로지스틱스에서 산업 엔지니어로 거의 20년간 근무해 오고 있다.

어휘 industrial 산업의   logistics 물류

116 부사 어휘   동영상 강의

해설 동사 began의 목적어로 쓰인 to increase를 수식하여 '생산성이 눈에 띄게 증가하기 시작했다'는 의미가 되어야 적절하므로 '눈에 띄게'라는 뜻의 (C) noticeably가 정답이다. (A) mainly는 '주로', (B) respectively는 '각각', (D) closely는 '면밀히'라는 의미이다. 참고로, increase, rise, decrease 등의 증감 동사를 수식하는 부사로는 noticeably, significantly, dramatically 등이 자주 쓰인다.

번역 마닐라 씨가 채용된 직후, 영업부의 생산성이 눈에 띄게 증가하기 시작했다.

어휘 productivity 생산성

117 관계대명사 _ 주격

해설 빈칸 이하(participate in the Get Ahead program)는 주어 Small businesses와 동사 will receive 사이에서 주어를 수식하는 관계사절로, 빈칸 뒤에 동사가 나오므로 주격 관계대명사인 (A) that이 정답이다. 앞에 선행사가 있으므로 명사절 접속사 역할을 하는 (C) what과 (D) whoever는 빈칸에 들어갈 수 없다.

번역 겟 어헤드 프로그램에 참여하는 중소기업은 고객을 유치하는 데 도움이 되는 마케팅 툴을 제공받을 것이다.

어휘 participate in ~에 참여하다   get ahead 성공[출세]하다   tool (컴퓨터) 툴, 도구   attract 유치하다, 끌어들이다

118 접속사 자리 _ 등위접속사 / 어휘

해설 빈칸에는 앞의 동사구 will review the manuscript와 뒤의 동사구 will not return it을 연결해 줄 등위접속사가 필요하다. '원고를 검토하겠지만 돌려주지 않을 것이다'는 내용이 되어야 자연스러우므로 대조를 나타내는 등위접속사 (D) but이 정답이다. 등위접속사 (A) or는 '또는'이라는 의미이고, (B) once는 부사/부사절 접속사이며, (C) either는 or와 함께 상관접속사 구문을 이끄므로 빈칸에 들어갈 수 없다.

번역 우리 교열 담당자들이 원고를 검토하겠지만 다음 주 말까지는 원고를 돌려주지 않을 것이다.

어휘 copy editor 교열 담당자   manuscript 원고

119 형용사 자리 _ 주격 보어 / 최상급

해설 정관사 the와 함께 최상급을 이루어 주어인 Mira Kumar를 보충 설명하는 주격 보어 자리이다. 따라서 최상급 형용사가 들어가야 하므로 (B) most ambitious(가장 의욕적인)가 정답이다. (A) ambitious는 원급 형용사, (C) ambitiously와 (D) more ambitiously는 부사로 품사상 빈칸에 들어갈 수 없다.

번역 미라 쿠마르는 아마 지난여름 콜브리 미디어의 모든 인턴들 중 가장 의욕적이었을 것이다.

120 전치사 자리 / 어휘

 동영상 강의

해설 빈칸 앞에 완전한 절(Orbin's Fish Company expanded ~ 26 stores)이 있고 뒤에 명사구 its takeover of a rival chain이 있으므로 빈칸은 전치사 자리이다. '경쟁 체인을 인수한 후 26개 매장으로 확장했다'는 의미가 되어야 자연스러우므로 (C) following(~ 후에)이 정답이다. 전치사 (B) toward는 '~을 향해서'라는 의미이므로 문맥상 어울리지 않고, (A) whenever는 복합관계부사, (D) usually는 부사이므로 빈칸에 들어갈 수 없다.

번역 오빈스 피시 사는 경쟁 체인점을 인수한 후 총 26개 매장으로 확장했다.

어휘 expand 확장하다   takeover 인수   rival 경쟁하는; 경쟁자

121 인칭대명사의 격 _ 목적격

해설 빈칸은 타동사 wanted의 목적어 자리로, her team members를 받는 대명사가 필요하므로 목적격 인칭대명사 (C) them이 정답이다. 소유대명사 (A) theirs(그들의 것)는 앞에 가리키는 대상이 있어야 하고, 재귀대명사 (D) themselves는 동사 wanted의 주어인 she와 동일 인물이 아니므로 답이 될 수 없다.

번역 카트라이트 씨는 그녀의 팀원들에게 회사의 조립 공정을 간소화하길 원한다고 말했다.

어휘 streamline 간소화하다   assembly 조립   process 공정

122 형용사 어휘

해설 빈칸에는 모든 배송을 추적하는 기술을 수식하기에 적절한 형용사가 들어가야 하므로 '고급의'라는 뜻의 (C) advanced가 정답이다. (A) strict는 '엄격한', (D) crowded는 '붐비는'이라는 뜻으로 technology를 수식하는 말로 어울리지 않고, (B) numerous는 '수많은'이라는 뜻으로 뒤에 복수명사가 와야 하므로 답이 될 수 없다.

번역 루퍼트 푸드 서비스는 고급 기술을 사용하여 모든 배송을 추적합니다.

어휘 track 추적하다   shipment 배송

123 명사 자리 _ 동사의 목적어

해설 빈칸은 타동사 includes의 목적어 자리로, 앞에 부정관사 a가 있으므로 단수명사가 들어가야 한다. 따라서 '계산기'라는 뜻의 단수명사 (A) calculator가 정답이다. (B) calculated는 동사/과거분사, (C) calculating은 현재분사/동명사이므로 품사상 답이 될 수 없고, (D) calculations(계산)는 복수명사이므로 부정관사와 함께 쓸 수 없다.

번역 저희 앱에는 사용자가 예산 목표 내에 있는지 여부를 파악할 수 있도록 계산기가 포함되어 있습니다.

어휘 include 포함하다   determine 알아내다   budget 예산

124 동사 어휘

해설 완전한 절(the Selboa Company has hired more janitors)을 수식하는 부사적 역할의 to부정사에 들어갈 동사 어휘를 고르는 문제이다. that절을 목적어로 취해 '반드시 시설이 매일 청소될 수 있도록 하기 위해'라는 내용이 되어야 자연스러우므로 '반드시 ~하게 하다'를 뜻하는 (A) ensure가 정답이다. (B) affect는 '영향을 미치다', (C) provide는 '제공하다', (D) secure는 '확보하다'라는 의미이다.

번역 시설이 반드시 매일 청소될 수 있도록 셀보아 사는 더 많은 청소부들을 고용했다.

어휘 facility 시설   janitor 청소부, (건물 등의) 관리인

125 부사 자리 _ 동사 수식

해설 주어 Jeremy Moran과 동사 promoted 사이에서 동사를 수식하는 부사 자리이므로 '적극적으로'라는 뜻의 부사 (D) actively가 정답이다. (A) act는 동사/명사, (B) action은 명사, (C) active는 형용사로 품사상 빈칸에 들어갈 수 없다.

번역 제레미 모란은 국회의원 임기 동안 사회 기반 시설 개선의 필요성에 대한 대중의 인식을 적극적으로 고취시켰다.

어휘   term 임기   legislator 국회의원   promote 고취[촉진]하다
awareness 의식   infrastructure 사회 기반 시설
improvement 개선   act 행동하다; 행동, 법률

126 형용사 어휘

해설   명사 clients를 수식하여 '잠재 고객들'이라는 의미가 되어야 적합하
므로 '잠재적인'을 뜻하는 (B) potential이 정답이다. (A) trained는
'훈련된', (C) elected는 '선출된', (D) paid는 '유급의'라는 의미이다.

번역   픽시 프린트의 사업은 매우 새로운 것이라서 잠재 고객들에게 서비스
의 전 영역을 설명해야 한다.

어휘   range 범위

127 동사 어형 _ 태

해설   주어인 Phone orders를 수식하는 관계사절에서 be동사 뒤에 들
어갈 알맞은 형태를 고르는 문제이다. 빈칸 뒤에 목적어가 없고 전
화 주문은 '접수되는' 대상이므로 수동의 의미를 나타내는 과거분사
(A) submitted가 정답이다. 명사 (B) submission은 주격 보어로
서 be동사 뒤에 위치할 수 있지만 의미상 주어가 되는 선행사 Phone
orders와 동격 관계가 아니므로 답이 될 수 없고, 능동/진행의 의미
를 나타내는 현재분사 (C) submitting은 뒤에 목적어가 필요하며, 관
계사절에 이미 동사 are가 있으므로 동사 (D) submits는 들어갈 수
없다.

번역   오전 11시까지 지역 상점으로 접수된 전화 주문은 당일 픽업이 가능
합니다.

어휘   eligible 가능한, 자격이 있는

128 부사 어휘   ▶ 동영상 강의

해설   동사구 place an order를 수식하여 '기꺼이 주문을 할 것이다'는 의
미가 되어야 자연스러우므로 '기꺼이'를 뜻하는 (D) gladly가 정답
이다. (A) slightly는 '약간', (B) wholly는 '전적으로', (C) busily는
'바쁘게'라는 의미이다.

번역   오스왈드 하드웨어 직원은 재고에 있는 것보다 더 많은 수량이 필요
한 고객을 위해 기꺼이 주문을 할 것입니다.

어휘   associate 직원, 동료   place an order 주문하다   quantity
수량   in stock 재고의; 재고로

129 분사구문

해설   콤마 앞에 완전한 절(Mia Daushvili performed ~ evening)이 있
고, 빈칸 뒤에 목적어 역할을 하는 명사구 her virtuosic skills가
왔으므로 빈칸 이하는 분사구문이 되어야 한다. 문맥상 '오케스트라
와 연주하며, 거장다운 기술을 펼쳤다'라는 의미가 되어야 자연스러
우므로 능동의 의미를 나타내는 현재분사 (C) displaying이 정답
이다. (A) displays는 명사/동사, (B) had displayed와 (D) was
displayed는 동사로 빈칸에 들어갈 수 없다.

번역   미아 다우슈빌리는 월요일 저녁에 베이헤드 오케스트라와 함께 연주
하며 피콜로의 거장다운 그녀의 기술을 펼쳤다.

어휘   perform 연주[공연]하다   virtuosic 거장의   piccolo
피콜로(고음의 작은 플루트)   display 보여주다, 발휘하다

130 형용사 어휘

해설   명사 experience를 수식하여 '이전 경력'이라는 의미가 되어야 적합
하므로 '이전의'라는 뜻의 (A) prior가 정답이다. (B) quick은 '빠른',
(C) lean은 '부족한, 마른', (D) calm은 '침착한'이라는 의미이다.

번역   서기직 지원자를 검토할 때, 응 씨는 학력과 이전 경력 두 가지를 모
두 고려할 것이다.

어휘   applicant 지원자   clerk 사무원   education 학력, 교육

PART 6

131-134 공지

디-자인 팝

디-자인 팝은 패션계의 최신 **131 트렌드**에 대한 정보를 제공하는 원천입
니다. 소셜 미디어 실험으로 시작했던 것이 전 세계 17개국에 구독자를
보유한 콘텐츠 플랫폼으로 **132 발전했습니다.** 우리는 사용자 경험을 개
선하고 현재 인기 있는 의류 및 액세서리를 공유하기 위해 끊임없이 게
시물을 추가하고 있습니다. 또한 서비스 약관을 주기적으로 업데이트합
니다. 구독자의 **133 지속적인** 콘텐츠 이용은 이들 약관의 동의 여부에 달
려 있으므로 dzinepop.com/privacy에서 이를 검토하고 동의할 것
을 권장합니다. 문의사항이 있으시면 support@dzinepop.com에서
고객 서비스팀에 연락하십시오. **134 담당자들이 하루 24시간 여러분을
도와드립니다.**

어휘   source 원천, 정보원   latest 최신의   experiment 실험
subscriber 구독자   constantly 끊임없이   feature 연재물
apparel 의류   periodic 주기적인   term 조건   access 이용,
접근   contingent (~의) 여부에 따른   consent 동의하다   accept
수락하다

131 명사 어휘

해설   뒤에서 현재 인기 있는 의류 및 액세서리를 공유(share what
apparel ~ are popular right now)하기 위해 게시물을 추가하고
있다고 했으므로 디-자인 팝은 패션계의 '최신(latest) 트렌드'에 대
한 정보를 제공한다는 내용이 되어야 한다. 따라서 '동향, 유행'을 뜻
하는 (C) trends가 정답이다. (A)의 controversy는 '논란', (B)의
consumer는 '소비자', (D)의 version은 '~ 버전, ~판'이라는 의미
이다.

132 동사 자리 _ 시제

해설   빈칸은 주어 역할을 하는 명사절 What started as a social media
experiment의 동사 자리이므로 동사인 (C) will be evolving과 (D)
has evolved 중에서 선택해야 한다. 앞뒤 문장에서 디-자인 팝의 현
재 상황에 대해 설명하고 있으므로, 빈칸이 있는 문장은 '소셜 미디어
실험으로 시작했던(started) 것이 세계적인 콘텐츠 플랫폼으로 발전
해 왔다'며 과거부터 현재까지의 변천 과정을 언급하는 내용이 되어야
자연스럽다. 따라서 현재완료 시제인 (D) has evolved가 정답이다.
(A) evolving은 동명사/현재분사, (B) evolution은 명사이므로 동사
자리에 들어갈 수 없다.

어휘   evolve 발전하다, 진화하다

133 형용사 자리 _ 명사 수식

▶ 동영상 강의

해설 빈칸에는 소유격 Subscribers'와 명사 access 사이에서 명사 access를 수식하는 형용사 또는 access와 복합명사를 이루는 명사가 들어갈 수 있다. 문맥상 '구독자의 지속적인 이용'이라는 내용이 되어야 하므로 '지속적인'이라는 뜻의 형용사 (B) continued가 정답이다. (A) continue와 (D) continues는 동사이므로 빈칸에 들어갈 수 없고, (C) continuation은 '연속(되는 것)'이라는 뜻의 명사로 access와 복합명사를 이루기에 의미상 어색하므로 오답이다.

134 문맥에 맞는 문장 고르기

번역 (A) 담당자들이 하루 24시간 여러분을 도와드립니다.
(B) 사용자 개인 정보 보호 정책에 대한 변경사항은 더 이상 유효하지 않습니다.
(C) 휴대폰 및 컴퓨터 앱을 통해 새로운 콘텐츠를 이용하실 수 있습니다.
(D) 구독을 갱신하실 경우 더 이상 할인 요금을 제공하지 않습니다.

해설 빈칸 앞에서 문의사항이 있으면 서비스팀에 연락하라(Contact our customer service team ~ if you have any questions)고 했으므로, 빈칸에는 고객 서비스팀의 지원 방식을 설명하는 내용이 들어가야 연결이 자연스럽다. 따라서 담당자들이 고객 지원을 위해 하루 24시간 대기 중임을 설명하고 있는 (A)가 정답이다.

어휘 policy 정책 effective 유효한 accessible 이용 가능한 rate 요금 renew 갱신하다 subscription 구독

135-138 광고

폰 튠-업으로 단말기를 복구하세요.

스마트폰 화면에 흠집이나 금이 갔나요? **135 배터리를 충전하는 데 하루 종일 걸리나요?** 앱이 멈추거나 작동이 안 되나요? 폰 튠-업의 전문가들이 도울 수 있습니다! 저희는 여러분의 휴대폰을 **136 수리하기** 위해 최고 품질의 부품만을 사용합니다. 저희 공인 기술자가 휴대폰을 새것으로 교체하는 데 드는 시간과 비용을 절약해 드립니다. 작업이 **137 완료되면** 오래된 휴대폰이 새것처럼 느껴질 것입니다. 예약하시려면 604-555-0198로 전화하시거나 www.phonetuneup.com을 방문하세요. 필요한 부품이 재고가 **138 있다면** 종종 당일 서비스가 가능합니다.

어휘 rescue 구하다 cracked 금이 간 freeze 멈추다 crash 고장 나다 expert 전문가 nothing but 단지 ~일 뿐인 part 부품 certified 공인된, 증명된 expense 비용 involved in ~와 관련된 brand new 완전 새것인

135 문맥에 맞는 문장 고르기

번역 (A) 프린터에 잉크를 자주 리필해야 하나요?
(B) 배터리를 충전하는 데 하루 종일 걸리나요?
(C) 간단한 설문 조사를 완료해 주시겠어요?
(D) 데이터 요금제에 너무 많은 비용을 내고 계시나요?

해설 빈칸 앞에는 스마트폰 화면에 흠집이나 금이 갔는지(Is your smartphone screen scratched or cracked?)를 묻고 있고, 빈칸 뒤에는 앱이 멈추거나 작동이 안 되는지(Do your apps freeze or crash?)를 묻고 있으므로 빈칸에는 휴대폰의 오작동이나 사용하는 데 있어 불편한 점에 대한 내용이 들어가야 일관성 있는 문맥을 완성

할 수 있다. 따라서 배터리 충전이 오래 걸리는지를 묻고 있는 (B)가 정답이다.

어휘 frequent 잦은 refill 리필 제품 recharge 충전하다 plan (자금 등의) 제도

136 동사 어휘

해설 앞에서 질문 형식으로 언급한 휴대폰의 기능상 문제점들을 폰 튠-업의 전문가들이 도울 수 있다고 한 것으로 보아, 문맥상 '휴대폰을 수리하기 위해 최고 품질의 부품만 사용한다'는 내용이 되어야 자연스럽다. 따라서 '수리하다'를 의미하는 (D) repair가 정답이다. (A) remove는 '제거하다', (B) borrow는 '빌리다', (C) examine은 '검사하다'라는 의미이다.

137 형용사 어휘

해설 빈칸은 be동사 뒤 자리로 보기의 과거분사나 형용사 모두 답이 될 수 있으므로 문맥상 적합한 단어를 골라야 한다. 앞 문장에서 휴대폰 수리 서비스를 언급하며 우리 기술자들이 휴대폰 교체에 드는 시간과 비용을 절약해 드린다고 했으므로, '기술자들이 (작업을) 완료하면 오래된 휴대폰이 새것처럼 느껴질 것'이라는 내용이 되어야 자연스럽다. 따라서 '다 끝난, 완료된'을 뜻하는 (C) done이 정답이다. (A) trained는 '훈련받은', (B) available은 '이용할 수 있는', (D) dismissed는 '해고된'이라는 의미이다.

138 접속사 자리 _ 부사절 접속사

해설 빈칸 뒤 주어 needed parts와 동사 are를 갖춘 완전한 절을 빈칸 앞의 절에 연결하여 '필요한 부품이 재고로 있다면 당일 서비스도 가능하다'는 내용이 되어야 하므로 '~이라면'을 뜻하는 부사절 접속사 (C) if가 정답이다. 절을 연결하는 자리이므로 조동사 (B) must와 전치사 (D) of는 품사상 빈칸에 들어갈 수 없고, (A) whose는 관계대명사로 쓰일 경우 앞에 선행사가 필요하다.

139-142 보도 자료

즉시 배포용

새크라멘토 (7월 28일) — 새크라멘토에 본사를 둔 슈퍼마켓 체인 싱 마켓이 10월에 산 호세에 **139 지점을** 연다고 오늘 발표했다. 지점은 작년에 폐업한 왓슨 오피스 슈퍼스토어가 있던 웨스트 오크 가 1539의 건물에 입주할 예정이다.

싱 마켓의 최고 경영자 앨리스 트란은 "**140 마침내** 산 호세에 매장을 열게 되어 매우 기쁩니다. **141 우리는 꽤 오랜 시간 그 도시를 주시하고 있었습니다.** 왓슨 건물이 이용 가능해졌을 때, 우리는 입주할 기회에 뛰어들었습니다."라고 말했다.

지역 식료품점으로서 싱 마켓은 지역 사회에서 지원자를 채용하는 것을 자랑스럽게 여긴다. 약 75퍼센트의 직원들이 **142 근무하는** 매장에서 2마일 이내에 거주한다.

어휘 immediate 즉각적인 release 공개, 배포 -based ~에 본사를 둔 chain 체인점 branch 지점 occupy (건물 등을)

139 명사 자리 _ 복합명사

해설 동사 is opening의 목적어 자리로 빈칸 앞 명사 branch와 함께 '지점'을 의미하여 복합명사를 만들 수 있는 명사가 들어가야 한다. 따라서 '장소, 부지'라는 의미의 (A) location이 정답이다. 문장에 이미 동사가 있으므로 동사 (B) locate는 들어갈 수 없고, to부정사 (C) to locate와 현재분사 (D) locating은 명사 branch를 뒤에서 수식하는 역할로 쓰이기 위해서는 뒤에 타동사 locate의 목적어가 와야 하므로 답이 될 수 없다.

140 부사 어휘

해설 빈칸 뒤 문장에서 꽤 오랜 시간 그 도시를 주시하고 있었고 건물이 이용 가능해졌을 때 입주할 기회에 뛰어들었다고 한 것으로 보아 '마침내 매장을 열게 되어 기쁘다'는 내용이 되어야 적절하다. 따라서 '마침내'라는 뜻의 (A) finally가 정답이다. (B) instead는 '대신에', (C) likewise는 '마찬가지로', (D) suddenly는 '갑자기'라는 의미이다.

141 문맥에 맞는 문장 고르기

번역 (A) 매장은 신선하고 준비된 다양한 식품을 특징으로 합니다.
(B) 우리는 여러분이 우리의 개점 축하 행사에 함께할 수 있기를 바랍니다.
(C) 우리는 꽤 오랜 시간 그 도시를 주시하고 있었습니다.
(D) 우리 회사 본사는 곧 개조될 예정입니다.

해설 빈칸 앞에서 마침내 산 호세에 매장을 열게 되어 기쁘다(We are very excited to finally open a store in San Jose)고 했고 빈칸 뒤에서 왓슨 건물이 이용 가능해졌을 때 입주 기회에 뛰어들었다(When the Watson building became available, we jumped on the opportunity to move in)고 했으므로, 빈칸에는 산 호세 지역에 매장을 열 장소를 물색하는 데 기울인 노력이나 시간을 강조하는 내용이 들어가야 앞뒤 연결이 자연스럽다. 따라서 상당 시간 해당 지역을 주시하고 있었다고 언급하는 (C)가 정답이다.

어휘 feature 특징으로 하다 have one's eyes on ~에 주의를 기울이다 corporate 회사의 renovate 개조하다

142 동사 어휘

해설 앞 문장에서 싱 마켓은 지역 사회에서 지원자를 채용한다고 했으므로, 직원들이 '근무하는 매장에서 2마일 이내에 거주하고 있다'는 내용이 되어야 한다. 따라서 '근무하다'는 뜻의 (B) work가 정답이다. (A) save는 '절약하다', (C) shop은 '쇼핑하다', (D) register는 '등록하다'라는 의미이다.

143-146 웹페이지 정보

리피 직물에 대하여

트로픽 텍스타일스는 최근 시장에서 구할 수 있는 직물의 ¹⁴³ **범위**를 확대했습니다. 면과 기타 전통 섬유들에 대한 친환경적인 대안을 도입하기

위한 노력으로 회사는 일반적으로 폐기되는 재료로 만들어진 새로운 섬유를 ¹⁴⁴ **개발했습니다**. 트로픽 텍스타일스는 바나나와 파인애플 잎을 가지고 대나무 섬유와 결합하여 리피 직물을 만듭니다. 과일이 수확되고 ¹⁴⁵ **나면** 이 식물의 잎들은 보통 버려집니다. 트로픽 텍스타일스의 공정은 많은 잎들이 쓰레기 매립지로 들어가는 것을 막고, 대신 그것들을 사용 가능한 재료로 바꿉니다. ¹⁴⁶ **그 결과로 만들어진 내구성 있는 직물은 면직물의 적절한 대용품입니다.**

어휘 cloth 직물 textile 섬유, 직물 expand 확대하다 fabric 직물 environmentally friendly 친환경적인 alternative 대안 traditional 전통적인 fiber 섬유 material 재료 typically 일반적으로 discard 폐기하다 combine 결합하다 ordinarily 보통 dispose of ~을 버리다, 처리하다 harvest 수확하다 process 과정 prevent 막다 landfill 쓰레기 매립지 convert 전환하다 usable 사용 가능한

143 명사 어휘

해설 빈칸 뒤 문장에서 회사에서 면과 기타 전통 섬유들에 대한 대안을 도입하고자 새로운 섬유를 개발했다고 했으므로 '직물의 범위를 확대했다'는 내용이 되어야 적합하다. 따라서 '범위'를 뜻하는 (A) range가 정답이다. (B) expense는 '비용', (C) strength는 '강도', (D) appearance는 '외모'라는 의미이다.

144 동사 자리 _ 수 일치 + 시제

해설 빈칸은 주어가 the company인 절의 동사 자리이므로 (D) to develop은 품사상 들어갈 수 없고, (A) are developed는 단수 주어와 수 일치가 되지 않는다. 앞 문장에서 트로픽 텍스타일스가 직물의 범위를 확대했다고 과거 시제(expanded)로 설명하고 있으므로, 직물의 범위를 확대시킨 일에 대한 부연 설명인 친환경적인 대안으로 새로운 섬유를 개발했다는 것 또한 이미 완료된 일임을 알 수 있다. 따라서 현재완료 시제인 (B) has developed가 정답이다.

145 접속사 자리 _ 부사절 접속사

해설 빈칸은 완전한 두 개의 절을 연결해 주는 접속사 자리이다. 따라서 '일단 ~하면'이라는 의미의 부사절 접속사인 (D) once가 정답이다. (A) now와 (B) thus는 부사, (C) even은 형용사/부사이므로 절을 이끌 수 없다.

146 문맥에 맞는 문장 고르기

번역 (A) 그 결과로 만들어진 내구성 있는 직물은 면직물의 적절한 대용품입니다.
(B) 리피 직물에 관한 문의는 영업부로 전달되었습니다.
(C) 트로픽 텍스타일스는 올해 100주년을 기념할 예정입니다.
(D) 최근 트로픽 텍스타일스의 제조 비용이 증가하고 있습니다.

해설 앞에서 면과 기타 전통 섬유에 대한 친환경적 대안으로 새로운 섬유를 개발했다고 한 뒤, 버려지는 바나나와 파인애플 잎을 사용 가능한 재료로 바꾼다고 언급하며 개발한 섬유의 공정을 설명하고 있다. 따라서 빈칸에는 이 공정으로 만들어진 직물에 관한 결론적인 언급, 즉 개발한 직물이 면직물의 적절한 대용품이라고 언급한 (A)가 정답이다.

어휘 resulting 결과로 초래된 durable 내구성 있는 suitable
적절한 substitute 대용품 inquiry 문의 direct ~에게 보내다
anniversary 기념일 manufacturing 제조

PART 7

147-148 영수증

<table>
<tr><td colspan="2" align="center">지피 페트롤 마트</td></tr>
<tr><td colspan="2" align="center">M64 고속도로</td></tr>
<tr><td colspan="2" align="center">레스터</td></tr>
<tr><td colspan="2" align="center">0113 4960423</td></tr>
<tr><td colspan="2" align="center">147 5월 23일</td></tr>
<tr><td>147 비스킷</td><td>2파운드</td></tr>
<tr><td>147 과일 컵</td><td>0.95파운드</td></tr>
<tr><td>147 감자칩</td><td>1.1파운드</td></tr>
<tr><td>부가 가치세
포함</td><td>0.81파운드</td></tr>
<tr><td>총</td><td>4.86파운드</td></tr>
</table>

148 지피 클럽 리워드 카드에 가입하세요.
이 거래에 대해 지피 클럽 포인트 4점을 받을 수 있습니다.
포인트는 할인 상품, 자동차 제품, 휴대폰 액세서리 등에
사용할 수 있습니다!

어휘 petrol 휘발유 motorway 고속도로 crisps 감자칩 VAT
부가 가치세 inclusive (가격에 ~이) 포함된 rewards card
리워드 카드(구매 금액에 따라 할인이나 포인트를 적립하는 보상 카드)
transaction 거래 merchandise 상품

147 세부사항

번역 5월 23일에 구입된 물건은?
(A) 연료
(B) 간식
(C) 자동차 부품
(D) 휴대폰 액세서리

해설 영수증 상단에 있는 발행일이 5월 23일(23 May)이고, 중반부에 나
열된 구입 품목이 비스킷(Biscuits), 과일 컵(Fruit cup), 감자칩
(Crisps)이므로 (B)가 정답이다.

어휘 fuel 연료

148 Not / True

번역 영수증에서 지피 페트롤 마트에 대해 명시하는 것은?
(A) 여러 지점이 있다.
(B) 대부분의 주요 신용카드를 받는다.
(C) 고객 보상 프로그램이 있다.
(D) 모든 상품의 가격을 낮췄다.

해설 영수증 하단에 지피 클럽 리워드 카드에 가입하라(Sign up for our
Zippy Club rewards card)고 하면서 이 거래에 대해 지피 클
럽 포인트 4점을 받을 수 있다(You could have earned 4 Zippy
Club points on this transaction)고 한 뒤, 포인트는 할인 상품,
자동차 제품, 휴대폰 액세서리 등에 사용할 수 있다(Points can be
used for discounted merchandise, car products, phone
accessories, and more!)고 했으므로 지피 페트롤 마트에서는 고
객이 구매 혜택을 받을 수 있는 프로그램을 운영하고 있다는 것을 알
수 있다. 따라서 (C)가 정답이다.

어휘 multiple 다수의 accept 받아 주다 reward 보상
reduce 낮추다

149-150 공지

곧 만나요: 최고의 PBQ 라디오

4월 21일부터 27일까지 일주일 동안 PBQ 라디오는 10년 중 최고의
프로그램을 진행할 예정입니다. 지난 10년간 리코딩 아티스트들의 가장
인기 있던 곡들이 하루 종일 흘러나올 것입니다. 잘 알려진 리코딩 아티
스트와 잘 알려지지 않은 리코딩 아티스트들이 모두 포함됩니다. 각 아티
스트의 최고 작품을 선보일 계획입니다.

10년 동안의 최고의 음악을 특집으로 다루는 것 외에도 149 우리는 우
리 지역 업체들도 집중 조명하고 싶습니다. 광고 시간을 구입하실 수 있
습니다. 우리 청취자들에게 귀하의 업체가 우리 지역에서 최고 중 하나라
는 것을 알리세요! 프로그램 진행자에게 귀사를 언급해 줄 것을 요청하
거나, 150 우리의 전문 마케팅팀이 30초짜리 광고를 작성하고 녹음할 수
있습니다.

세부사항 및 가격은 www.pbqradio.com/advertise를 참조하세요.

어휘 tune 곡 recording artist 리코딩 아티스트(음반을 녹음하고
출시한 음악가) lesser-known 덜 알려진 feature 특별히
포함하다 showcase 소개하다 highlight 강조하다 shout-out
샤라웃(공개적인 감사나 지지의 표시) pricing 가격 책정

149 추론 / 암시

번역 공지는 누구를 대상으로 작성되었을 것 같은가?
(A) 라디오 쇼 진행자
(B) 신인 리코딩 아티스트
(C) 사업주
(D) 음향 기술자

해설 두 번째 단락의 첫 문장에서 지역 업체들도 집중 조명하고 싶다(we
would like to highlight our region's businesses)고 했고, 광
고 시간을 구입할 수 있다(Advertising time is available for
purchase)며 청취자들에게 귀하의 업체가 지역에서 최고 중 하나라
는 것을 알리라(Let our listeners know that your business is
one of the best in the community!)고 한 것으로 보아 지역에서
업체를 운영하고 있는 사람들에게 광고를 판매하기 위한 글임을 알 수
있다. 따라서 (C)가 정답이다.

150 Not / True

번역 PBQ 라디오에 대해 사실인 것은?
(A) 사업한 지 10년이 되었다.
(B) 경험 많은 음악가들을 찾고 있다.
(C) 지역 최고의 방송국으로 뽑혔다.
(D) 자체 마케팅 부서를 가지고 있다.

해설 두 번째 단락의 마지막 문장에서 자신들의 전문 마케팅팀이 30초짜리 광고를 작성하고 녹음할 수 있다(our professional marketing team can write and record a 30-second advertisement)고 했으므로 PBQ 라디오 내부에 마케팅팀이 있다는 것을 알 수 있다. 따라서 (D)가 정답이다. 지문에 언급된 10년은 10년 동안 가장 인기 있었던 음악을 특집으로 다루는 프로그램에 대한 설명으로 사업 기간은 알 수 없으므로 (A)는 오답이며, (B)와 (C)에 대한 언급은 없다.

어휘 vote (투표로) 선출하다 station 방송국

151-152 문자 메시지

프랭크 자바티 [오전 11시 12분]
안녕하세요, 맥신. 151 오늘 이 배달 건이 늦어지고 있습니다. 디벨로 씨에게 연락해서 알려 주시겠습니까?

맥신 라르센 [오전 11시 13분]
물론이죠! 151 그녀가 그 새 제품들을 간절히 기다리고 있다고 알고 있어요. 오늘 밤 특별한 식사를 준비할 수 있도록 부엌을 제대로 갖춰 놓아야 한다고 합니다. 152 거기에 몇 시쯤 도착할 것 같습니까?

프랭크 자바티 [오전 11시 15분]
152 잘 모르겠습니다. 제가 가던 길이 정비 작업으로 폐쇄되었습니다. 우회로는 교통량이 많네요.

맥신 라르센 [오전 11시 17분]
유감이네요. 어느 정도로 예상하시나요?

프랭크 자바티 [오전 11시 19분]
아마 오후 1시경으로요.

맥신 라르센 [오전 11시 20분]
네, 좋습니다. 제가 디벨로 씨에게 연락해서 그 시간에 집에 있을 것인지 확인하겠습니다. 그런 다음 다시 연락드리겠습니다.

프랭크 자바티 [오전 11시 22분]
감사합니다!

어휘 be eager to 몹시 ~하고 싶어 하다 properly 제대로 detour road 우회로 estimate 추정(치) get in touch with ~와 연락하다 confirm 확인하다

151 추론 / 암시

번역 디벨로 씨가 구입했을 것 같은 물건은?
(A) 리넨 제품
(B) 책장
(C) 원예 도구
(D) 가전제품

해설 11시 12분에 자바티 씨가 오늘 이 배달 건이 늦어지고 있다(I'm running late with this delivery today)면서 디벨로 씨에게 연락해서 알려달라(Could you contact Ms. Dibello to let her know?)고 하자 11시 13분에 라르센 씨가 그녀가 그 새 제품들을 간절히 기다리고 있다고 알고 있다(I know that she is eager to get those new items)며 오늘 밤 특별한 식사를 준비할 수 있도록 부엌을 제대로 갖춰 놓아야 한다고 한다(She says she needs to set up her kitchen properly so that she can prepare a special meal tonight)고 했으므로, 디벨로 씨가 구입한 것은 부엌에서 식사

를 준비하는 데 사용하는 가전제품임을 짐작할 수 있으므로 (D)가 정답이다.

152 의도 파악

번역 오전 11시 17분에 라르센 씨가 "어느 정도로 예상하시나요?"라고 쓴 의도는?
(A) 경로의 거리를 확인해야 한다.
(B) 교통량이 얼마나 되는지 알고 싶다.
(C) 배송 시간을 알고 싶다.
(D) 배송료를 계산해야 한다.

해설 11시 13분에 라르센 씨가 거기에 몇 시쯤 도착할 것 같은지(What time do you think you will arrive there?) 물었고, 11시 15분에 자바티 씨가 잘 모르겠다(I'm not sure)며 가던 길이 정비 작업으로 폐쇄되었고(the road I was taking was closed for repairs), 우회로는 교통량이 많다(The detour road has heavy traffic)고 상황을 설명하자 11시 17분에 라르센 씨가 어느 정도로 예상하는지(What's your estimate?)를 다시 묻고 있다. 따라서 라르센 씨는 자바티 씨의 목적지 도착 예상 시간을 확인하려는 의도로 한 말임을 알 수 있으므로 (C)가 정답이다.

어휘 verify 확인하다 distance 거리 traffic 교통(량) calculate 계산하다 charge 요금

153-154 이메일

수신: 자넷 허쉬먼
발신: customerservice@readymadeofficesupplies.net
날짜: 9월 3일
제목: 감사합니다

허쉬먼 씨께,

레디메이드 사무용품의 커스터머스 카운트 보상 프로그램에 가입하신 것을 환영합니다. 고객님의 계정 번호 41120이 등록되었습니다.

153 저희 웹사이트에서 구매하는 모든 제품에 대해 포인트를 받으시려면 반드시 계정 번호를 입력해 주십시오. 조건이 충족되는 구매에 대해 지불하는 1달러당 1포인트를 받게 됩니다. 154 계정 페이지에 있는 포인트를 무료 2일 신속 배송, 특별 할인 등을 포함한 보상으로 교환하십시오. 153 귀하께서는 여전히 인쇄 카탈로그에서 우편으로 주문하시거나 저희 직원의 도움을 받아 전화로 주문하시거나 미국과 캐나다 전역의 소매점을 방문하셔서 주문하실 수 있습니다. 그러나 이러한 구매는 현재 보상 프로그램에 적용되지 않습니다.

질문이 있으십니까? https://www.readymadeofficesupplies. net/customerservice를 방문하십시오.

어휘 office supplies 사무용품 reward 보상 account 계정 register 등록하다 qualifying 자격을 주는 redeem (현금, 상품 등으로) 교환하다 expedited 신속한 retail 소매 qualify for ~의 자격이 되다

153 세부사항

번역 보상 포인트를 받을 수 있는 구매 종류는?
(A) 온라인 구매
(B) 우편 구매
(C) 전화 구매
(D) 매장 구매

해설 두 번째 단락의 첫 문장에서 웹사이트에서 구매하는 모든 제품에 대해 포인트를 받으려면 반드시 계정 번호를 입력해 달라(Be sure to enter your account number to earn points on all your purchases from our Web site)고 했고, 같은 단락의 네 번째 문장에서 여전히 인쇄 카탈로그에서 우편으로 주문하거나 직원의 도움을 받아 전화로 주문하거나 미국과 캐나다 전역의 소매점을 방문해 주문할 수 있지만(You can still order ~ or by visiting our retail locations across the United States and Canada) 다섯 번째 문장에서 그러나 이러한 구매는 현재 보상 프로그램에 적용되지 않는다(However, those purchases do not currently qualify for the rewards program)고 안내하고 있다. 따라서 웹사이트에서 구매한 제품에 대해서만 포인트를 받을 수 있다는 것을 알 수 있으므로 (A)가 정답이다.

154 세부사항

번역 이 프로그램의 이점은?
(A) 소매 행사 초대
(B) 무료 샘플
(C) 더 빠른 배송
(D) 제품 보증 연장

해설 두 번째 단락의 세 번째 문장에서 계정 페이지에 있는 포인트를 무료 2일 신속 배송, 특별 할인 등을 포함한 보상으로 교환하라(Redeem your points ~ free two-day expedited shipping, special discounts, and more)고 했다. 따라서 해당 프로그램을 이용하면 무료 신속 배송과 할인을 제공받을 수 있다는 것이므로 (C)가 정답이다.

어휘 extended 연장된 warranty 품질 보증

Paraphrasing 지문의 expedited → 정답의 Faster

155-157 편지

토착 식물 협회 본부
서섹스 가 161
시드니, NSW 2001

4월 15일

야스민 하라비
쿨작 로 247
퍼스, 웨스턴 오스트레일리아 6280

회원번호 4290

하라비 씨께,

협회 회원으로서 지속적인 지원에 감사드립니다. 155,156 귀하의 최근 이사로, 귀하의 회원권이 퍼스 시에 위치한 지부로 이전되었습니다. 155 며칠 내로 대체 회원 카드를 우편으로 보내 드리겠습니다.

156,157 캔버라 시 지부와는 달리 퍼스 지부는 매월 첫째 주 토요일에 모이므로 다음 회의는 3주 후가 될 것입니다. 질문이 있으시면 평일 오전 8시부터 오후 4시 사이에 (08) 5555 0145로 연락 주십시오.

레티샤 데이비스
회원 관리 부서

어휘 native 토착의 society 협회, 연구회 headquarters 본사 given ~을 고려해 볼 때 transfer 옮기다 chapter (협회 등의) 지부 replacement 대체 identification 신원 확인

155 주제 / 목적

번역 편지의 목적은?
(A) 특별 행사를 발표하려고
(B) 이사에 따른 변경사항을 설명하려고
(C) 새로운 회의 시간을 제안하려고
(D) 업데이트된 연락처 정보를 요청하려고

해설 두 번째 문장에서 귀하의 최근 이사로 회원권이 퍼스 시에 위치한 지부로 이전되었다(Given your recent move, your membership has been transferred ~ in the city of Perth)며 며칠 내로 대체 회원 카드를 우편으로 보내겠다(We will be mailing ~ card within a few days)고 한 것으로 보아 회원의 이사로 인한 회원권 관련 변경사항을 안내하기 위해 쓴 글임을 알 수 있다. 따라서 (B)가 정답이다.

어휘 relocation 이전

Paraphrasing 지문의 move → 정답의 relocation

156 추론 / 암시

번역 캔버라 시에 대해 암시된 것은?
(A) 많은 정원으로 유명하다.
(B) 데이비스 씨의 단체의 본부가 있다.
(C) 하라비 씨가 전에 살던 곳이다.
(D) 호주에서 가장 희귀한 식물들의 서식지이다.

해설 두 번째 문장에서 하라비 씨에게 귀하이 최근 이사로 회원권이 퍼스 시에 위치한 지부로 이전되었다(Given your recent move, your membership ~ in the city of Perth)고 했고, 두 번째 단락의 첫 문장에서 캔버라 시 지부와는 달리 퍼스 지부는 매월 첫째 주 토요일에 모이므로 다음 회의는 3주 후가 될 것(Unlike the chapter in the city of Canberra, the Perth branch meets ~ will be in three weeks)이라고 했다. 따라서 하라비 씨는 캔버라 시에 살다가 퍼스 시로 이사한 것임을 알 수 있으므로 (C)가 정답이다.

어휘 house 장소를 제공하다 organization 단체 previously 이전에 rare 희귀한

157 추론 / 암시

번역 토착 식물 협회에 대해 결론지을 수 있는 것은?
(A) 새로운 지도부 하에 있다.
(B) 회원 수가 늘고 있다.
(C) 회비를 인상할 예정이다.
(D) 지부는 매월 회의를 연다.

해설 두 번째 단락의 첫 문장에서 캔버라 시 지부와는 달리 퍼스 지부는 매월 첫째 주 토요일에 모이므로 다음 회의는 3주 후가 될 것(Unlike the chapter in the city of Canberra, the Perth branch meets the first Saturday of every month, so your next meeting will be in three weeks)이라고 했다. 따라서 지부마다 날짜는 다르지만 매월 회의가 열린다는 것을 알 수 있으므로 (D)가 정답이다.

어휘 leadership 지도부 raise 올리다 due 회비

Paraphrasing 지문의 meets ~ every month
→ 정답의 monthly meetings

158-160 웹페이지

https://www.greenroofplus.com

| 기본사항 | 사진 | 자료 | 뉴스 |

녹색 지붕이란 무엇인가요?

159 (D)녹색 지붕은 사무실 건물과 주택을 위한 에너지 절약 옵션입니다. 158 녹색 지붕은 잔디, 화초 또는 기타 식물들로 덮인 지붕입니다. 159 (A), (C)이것은 건축물의 미적 매력을 높이는 동시에 냉난방 비용을 낮춰 줍니다. 158 이 웹사이트는 녹색 지붕을 만들고 유지하기 위한 아이디어, 사진 그리고 자료를 공유하기 위해 고안되었습니다.

옥상 정원을 꾸미는 일은 자신이 직접 하는 보람 있는 프로젝트이지만, 특수 방수 처리 및 기타 준비 작업에는 숙련된 시공사의 서비스가 필요합니다. 비용은 지역, 지붕 크기, 조성하고자 하는 정원의 복잡성에 따라 크게 달라집니다. 최소 두 곳의 시공사로부터 견적을 받도록 하십시오.

시공사가 지붕이 흙, 식물 및 관개 시설의 추가 중량을 160 견딜 수 있다고 확정하면, 프로젝트의 일정에 대해 문의하십시오. 작고 단순한 옥상 정원은 완성되는 데 일주일밖에 걸리지 않을 수도 있습니다.

어휘 energy-saving 에너지를 절약하는 grass 잔디 lower 낮추다 structure 건축물 aesthetic 미적인 appeal 매력 maintain 유지하다 rewarding 보람 있는 do-it-oneself 자신이 하는 waterproofing 방수 처리 preparation 준비 experienced 숙련된 contractor 시공사 vary 다르다 complexity 복잡성 estimate 견적 determine 결정하다 handle 견디다, 감당하다 soil 흙 irrigation 관개

158 세부사항

번역 웹페이지에 따르면, 웹사이트의 방문객들이 할 수 있는 일은?
(A) 정원을 만드는 방법에 대해 논의한다.
(B) 채소 생산을 극대화하는 방법을 배운다.
(C) 조경 문제에 대한 조언을 구한다.
(D) 시공사가 비용을 계산하는 것을 돕는다.

해설 첫 단락의 두 번째 문장에서 녹색 지붕은 잔디, 화초 또는 기타 식물들로 덮인 지붕(A green roof is one that's covered with grasses, flowers, or other plants)이라고 한 뒤, 같은 단락의 마지막 문장에서 이 웹사이트는 녹색 지붕을 만들고 유지하기 위한 아이디어, 사진 그리고 자료를 공유하기 위해 고안되었다(This Web site is designed for sharing ideas, photos, and resources to create and maintain a green roof)며 개설 목적을 설명하고 있다. 따라서 녹색 지붕은 옥상 정원이고, 웹페이지에서 이 옥상 정원의 제작 및 유지에 대해 의견 및 정보를 나누고 토론할 수 있음을 알 수 있으므로 (A)가 정답이다.

어휘 maximize 극대화하다 seek 구하다 landscaping 조경 calculate 계산하다

Paraphrasing 지문의 sharing ideas → 정답의 Discuss

159 Not / True

번역 녹색 지붕에 대해 언급되지 않은 것은?
(A) 에너지 비용을 줄인다.
(B) 공기 중의 오염 물질을 제거한다.
(C) 건축물을 더 아름답게 만든다.
(D) 상업용 및 주거용 건물에 설치될 수 있다.

해설 첫 단락에서 건축물의 미적 매력을 높이는 동시에 냉난방 비용을 낮춰 준다(It lowers heating and cooling costs while increasing a structure's aesthetic appeal)고 했고, 녹색 지붕은 사무실 건물과 주택을 위한 에너지 절약 옵션(Green roofs are an energy-saving option for office buildings and homes)이라고 했으므로 (A), (C), (D)는 지문에 명확히 언급되어 있다. 공기 중의 오염 물질 제거에 대한 언급은 없으므로 (B)가 정답이다.

어휘 decrease 줄이다 bill 비용, 계산서 remove 제거하다 pollution 오염 물질 install 설치하다 commercial 상업의 residential 주거의

Paraphrasing 지문의 lowers heating and cooling costs
→ 보기 (A)의 decrease energy bills
지문의 increasing a structure's aesthetic appeal → 보기 (C)의 make a structure more beautiful
지문의 office buildings and homes
→ 보기 (D)의 commercial and residential buildings

160 동의어 찾기

번역 세 번째 단락 1행의 "handle"과 의미가 가장 가까운 단어는?
(A) 만지다
(B) 통제하다
(C) 배달하다
(D) 떠받치다

해설 의미상 지붕이 추가 중량을 '견디다'라는 뜻으로 쓰였으므로 '떠받치다'를 뜻하는 (D) support가 정답이다.

161-163 광고

> 어휘 majority 대다수 rehearse 리허설을 하다 blend 섞다, 혼합하다 balance 균형을 잡다 post 게시하다 promote 홍보하다 impressive 인상적인 track record 업적, 실적

161 Not / True

번역 마르티노 테크니컬에 대해 명시된 것은?
(A) 소셜 미디어를 통해 대부분의 고객을 확보한다.
(B) 30년도 더 전에 창립되었다.
(C) 많은 업계 상을 받았다.
(D) 전 세계에 사무실이 있다.

해설 첫 문장에서 마르티노 테크니컬은 30년 넘게 라이브 사운드 믹싱 서비스를 제공해 왔다(Martino Technical has been providing live sound-mixing services for more than 30 years)고 했으므로 (B)가 정답이다.

어휘 acquire 얻다 found 설립하다 industry 업계

162 동의어 찾기

번역 두 번째 단락 4행의 "promote"와 의미가 가장 가까운 단어는?
(A) 격려하다
(B) 일정을 잡다
(C) 홍보하다
(D) 촉진하다

해설 의미상 공연을 '홍보한다'는 뜻으로 썼으므로 '홍보하다, 알리다'를 뜻하는 (C) publicize가 정답이다.

163 Not / True

번역 라이브 사운드 믹싱 엔지니어들에 대해 언급되지 않은 것은?
(A) 홍보 자료를 만든다.
(B) 상당한 전문 지식을 가지고 있다.
(C) 해외 출장을 자주 간다.
(D) 음악 학위를 가지고 있다.

해설 두 번째 단락의 마지막 문장에서 우리는 그들이 공연을 홍보하기 위해 소셜 미디어에 올릴 수 있는 녹음 음원을 제작한다(we create recordings for them that they can post on social media to promote their shows)고 했으므로 (A), 세 번째 단락의 첫 문장에서 우리의 사운드 믹싱 엔지니어들은 경험과 전문성을 갖춘 것으로 유명하며 전 세계 투어 작업에 있어 화려한 실적을 가지고 있다(Our sound-mixing engineers are known for their experience and professionalism and have an impressive track record working on tours worldwide)고 했으므로 (B)와 (C)는 언급되었으나 학위에 대한 내용은 없으므로 (D)가 정답이다.

어휘 material 자료 considerable 상당한 expertise 전문 지식 abroad 해외로 frequently 자주 degree 학위

Paraphrasing 지문의 recordings ~ to promote → 보기 (A)의 promotional materials
지문의 professionalism → 보기 (B)의 expertise
지문의 worldwide → 보기 (C)의 abroad

164-167 이메일

> 어휘 formal 공식의 honor 기리다 founder 창립자 express 표현하다 appreciation 감사 banquet 연회 intend 의도하다 avoid 삼가다, 피하다 be involved with ~와 관련되다 setup 준비, 설치 attendee 참석자 no later than 늦어도 ~까지

in anticipation of ~을 예상하여 wrap up 끝내다 envelope
봉투 RSVP 회답 주시기 바랍니다

164 주제 / 목적

번역 이메일의 주요 목적은?
(A) 직원들에게 기념식에서의 연설을 신청하도록 요청하려고
(B) 만찬에 다양한 물품을 자발적으로 가져올 사람을 찾으려고
(C) 직원들을 깜짝 파티에 초대하려고
(D) 행사 계획을 도울 자원봉사자를 찾으려고

해설 첫 번째 단락의 첫 문장에서 11월 28일 저녁에 회사의 사장이자 창
립자인 보나훔 씨를 기리기 위한 공식 만찬이 있을 예정(On the
evening of November 28, there will be a formal dinner to
honor our company president and founder, Mr. Bonahoom)
이라고 했고, 두 번째 단락의 첫 문장에서 이 행사는 셰 비스트로의 전
용 연회실에서 열리며 깜짝 이벤트로 기획되었으므로 그에게 언급하
는 것을 삼가 달라(This event will be held in ~ intended to be
a surprise, so please avoid mentioning it to him)고 했다. 따
라서 보나훔 씨를 기리기 위한 깜짝 만찬에 직원들을 초대하기 위한
이메일임을 알 수 있으므로 (C)가 정답이다.

어휘 sign up 신청하다 willing 자발적인 various 다양한

165 세부사항

번역 이메일에 따르면, 대부분의 사람들이 도착할 것으로 예상되는 시간은?
(A) 오후 5시
(B) 오후 6시 15분
(C) 오후 6시 30분
(D) 오후 8시

해설 두 번째 단락의 세 번째 문장에서 보나훔 씨가 오후 6시 30분에 도착
할 것으로 예상되어 다른 모든 참석자들은 늦어도 오후 6시 15분까지
는 와야 한다(All other attendees should come no later than
6:15 P.M. in anticipation of Mr. Bonahoom's arrival at 6:30
P.M.)고 공지하고 있으므로 (B)가 정답이다.

166 세부사항

번역 카드에 서명하고 싶은 사람들이 해야 할 일은?
(A) 보나훔 씨에게 카드를 요청해야 한다.
(B) 노 씨에게 이메일을 보내야 한다.
(C) 카드가 사무실에 돌아서 전달되기를 기다려야 한다.
(D) 뮬러 씨의 책상으로 가야 한다.

해설 세 번째 단락의 세 번째 문장에서 이번 주 중 시간을 내어 그를 위
한 카드에 서명을 해 주기 바란다(We do ask, though, that you
find time this week to sign a card for him)고 했고, 카드는 뮬
러 씨의 책상에서 찾을 수 있으며 '11월 28일'이라고 표시된 봉투
안에 있다(It can be found at Ms. Mueller's desk, inside an
envelope marked "November 28.")고 했다. 따라서 카드에 서
명하려면 뮬러 씨의 책상으로 가서 카드를 찾아야 하므로 (D)가 정답
이다.

167 문장 삽입

번역 [1], [2], [3], [4]로 표시된 위치 중에서 다음 문장이 들어가기에 가
장 적합한 곳은?
"고위급 직원들이 사무실 전체를 대표하여 기념패를 수여할 예정입
니다."
(A) [1]
(B) [2]
(C) [3]
(D) [4]

해설 주어진 문장은 '고위급 직원들이 사무실을 대표해 기념패를 수여할
것'이라며 보나훔 씨에게 기념 만찬 때 증정할 선물에 대해 언급하고
있다. [3] 앞에서 선물을 준비할 필요가 없다(There is no need to
bring a gift)고 한 뒤, [3] 뒤에서 그 대신 시간을 내 그에게 줄 카드
에 서명해 줄 것을 요청하고 있으므로, 그 사이에 들어가는 것이 글의
흐름상 자연스럽다. 따라서 (C)가 정답이다.

어휘 senior 고위의 present 수여하다 commemorative 기념하는
plaque 명판 on behalf of ~을 대표하여

168-171 온라인 채팅

콜린 비칸데르 (오전 10시 23분) 168 새로운 고객 설문지 초안을 검토
했는데 전체적으로 훌륭해 보입니다. 168,169 그런데 저라면 회계 전략
에 대한 질문을 더 개방형으로 만들 것 같습니다. 작성된 대로라면 응답
자들이 간단히 예 또는 아니요로 대답하게 될 수 있습니다.

미도리 사카이 (오전 10시 24분) 좋은 지적입니다. 그 부분을 고칠 필
요가 있습니다. 168,170 또한 저는 과거에 재무 및 세금 보고서가 처리된
방식에 대한 질문을 몇 가지 추가하고 싶습니다.

엘라 하미다 (오전 10시 24분) 회계 질문을 살펴보고 제가 제안할 수 있
는 것이 있는지 확인해 보겠습니다.

콜린 비칸데르 (오전 10시 25분) 글쎄요, 이미 4페이지나 되는걸요.

미도리 사카이 (오전 10시 27분) 그러네요. 세 번째 질문에 대한 엘라의
수정만 기다리겠습니다. 그런 다음 잭 넬리건이 우리 웹사이트에 양식 초
안을 올릴 수 있습니다.

콜린 비칸데르 (오전 10시 28분) 종이 양식은 수집할 계획이 없다는 것
이 사실인가요?

미도리 사카이 (오전 10시 30분) 그렇게 할 수도 있지만 171 고객이 양
식을 출력하고, 작성하고, 스캔해서 반송하기를 기다리는 지체 시간을 피
하기 위해 디지털 수집이 더 좋습니다.

어휘 draft 초안 questionnaire 설문지 overall 전체적으로
bookkeeping 회계, 부기 strategy 전략 open-ended
개방형의, 제한 없는 respondent 응답자 fix 고치다 financial
재무의 handle 처리하다 come up with ~을 제안하다
revision 수정 form 양식 preferable 더 좋은 lag time 지체
시간 fill out ~을 작성하다

168 추론 / 암시 ▶ 동영상 강의

번역 채팅 작성자들은 어떤 종류의 회사에 근무할 것 같은가?
(A) 출판
(B) 회계
(C) 소매
(D) 디자인

해설 10시 23분에 비칸데르 씨가 새로운 고객 설문지 초안을 검토했는데 전체적으로 훌륭해 보인다(I have reviewed the draft of the new client questionnaire, and it look great overall)며 그런데 본인이라면 회계 전략에 대한 질문을 더 개방형으로 만들 것 같다(I would make the question about bookkeeping strategies more open-ended, though)고 했고, 10시 24분에 사카이 씨가 과거에 재무 및 세금 보고서가 처리된 방식에 대한 질문을 몇 가지 추가하고 싶다(I also want to add a couple of questions about how financial and tax reports have been handled in the past)고 했다. 채팅 작성자들이 논의하고 있는 고객 대상 설문지 내용이 회계 및 경리에 관한 것으로 보아 그들이 회계 법인에 근무하고 있음을 짐작할 수 있다. 따라서 (B)가 정답이다.

169 세부사항 ▶ 동영상 강의

번역 비칸데르 씨가 질문에 대해 제안하는 것은?
(A) 잘못 분류되었다.
(B) 읽기 어렵다.
(C) 말을 바꿔 써야 한다.
(D) 선택사항으로 만들어져야 한다.

해설 10시 23분에 비칸데르 씨가 본인이라면 회계 전략에 대한 질문을 더 개방형으로 만들 것 같다(I would make the question about bookkeeping strategies more open-ended, though)며 질문을 수정할 것을 제안하고 있으므로 (C)가 정답이다.

어휘 reword 바꿔 쓰다 optional 선택적인

Paraphrasing 지문의 make ~ more open-ended
→ 정답의 be reworded

170 의도 파악

번역 오전 10시 25분에 비칸데르 씨가 "글쎄요, 이미 4페이지나 되는걸요"라고 쓴 의도는?
(A) 고객들의 긴 답변에 놀랐다.
(B) 설문지가 얼마나 빨리 작성되는지에 대해 감탄한다.
(C) 첫 네 페이지의 정보를 삭제해야 한다고 생각한다.
(D) 설문지가 더 길어져서는 안 된다고 생각한다.

해설 10시 24분에 사카이 씨가 과거에 재무 및 세금 보고서가 처리된 방식에 대한 질문을 몇 가지 추가하고 싶다(I also want to add a couple ~ have been handled in the past)고 한 데 대해 10시 25분에 비칸데르 씨가 글쎄요(Well)라고 의구심을 표하면서 이미 4페이지나 된다(it's four pages already)고 대답한 것이므로, 비칸데르 씨는 설문지가 이미 충분히 길다는 의도로 한 말임을 알 수 있다. 따라서 (D)가 정답이다.

어휘 come along 되어 가다, 생기다 cut out ~을 삭제하다, 제거하다

171 세부사항

번역 사카이 씨가 종이를 쓰지 않는 양식이 더 좋을 것이라고 생각하는 이유는?
(A) 더 빠른 데이터 수집을 가능하게 한다.
(B) 오류의 수를 줄인다.
(C) 환경에 좋다.
(D) 사무실 공간을 차지하지 않는다.

해설 10시 30분에 사카이 씨가 고객이 양식을 출력하고, 작성하고, 스캔해서 반송하기를 기다리는 지체 시간을 피하기 위해 디지털 수집이 더 좋다(digital collection is preferable to avoid the lag time of waiting ~ back)고 언급한 것으로 보아 종이를 쓰지 않는 디지털 수집이 시간을 단축시킬 수 있어 좋다고 생각하고 있음을 알 수 있다. 따라서 (A)가 정답이다.

어휘 paperless 종이를 쓰지 않는 take up ~을 차지하다

Paraphrasing 지문의 avoid the lag time of waiting
→ 정답의 faster

172-175 웹사이트 게시물

https://www.trehospitalityassociation.com/discussion/tunisia

[173] 저는 수년 동안 TRE 접객 협회 회원이었지만 지금까지는 그리스와 이집트 포럼에만 글을 올렸었습니다. 이 글은 튀니지 포럼에 올리는 저의 첫 게시글입니다.

[172] 저는 제르바 섬에 있는 청소 서비스 추천을 구하고 있습니다. 저희 회사는 그곳에 호텔을 개장할 예정입니다. [175] 저희 호텔은 80개의 객실과 부지 내에 두 개의 레스토랑을 제공할 것입니다. 큰 회의실도 있을 것입니다. 네 명 정도의 정규직 관리 직원과 객실 청소 담당자에 더해 호텔 내 대형 행사가 있을 경우 필요 시마다 추가로 다섯 명의 근로자를 제공할 수 있는 회사와 계약을 맺기를 원합니다.

전에 접객 콘퍼런스 중 한 곳에서 여러분을 만났을지도 모르겠습니다. 그렇다면 저에게 알려 주십시오. [174] 사실, 저는 라바트에서 가장 최근에 열린 콘퍼런스에 참석했습니다. 다시 연락하고 싶습니다!

존 카리카스, 개발 책임자

시넥도키 호텔 그룹

어휘 hospitality 접객(업) association 협회 recommendation 추천 janitorial service 청소 용역 on-site 현장에 contract with ~와 계약을 맺다 custodial 관리인의 housekeeper 객실 청소 담당자 additional 추가적인 as-needed 필요에 따른 property 건물 (구내) previously 이전에 reconnect 다시 연락[연결]하다

172 주제 / 목적

번역 카리카스 씨가 게시물을 작성한 이유는?
(A) 채용박람회를 홍보하려고
(B) 서비스 제공업체 추천을 요청하려고
(C) 관광지를 추천하려고
(D) 개업식에 동료들을 초대하려고

해설 두 번째 단락의 첫 문장에서 카리카스 씨가 제르바 섬에 있는 청소 서비스 추천을 구하고 있다(I am looking for recommendations for a janitorial service on the island of Djerba)고 했으므로 (B)가 정답이다.

어휘 job fair 채용박람회 referral 추천 tourist destination 관광지 colleague 동료

Paraphrasing 지문의 recommendations → 정답의 referrals

173 추론 / 암시

번역 TRE 접객 협회에 대해 암시된 것은?
(A) 이집트에 본부가 있다.
(B) 최근 확장하여 호텔 소유주들까지 포함시켰다.
(C) 국제적인 조직이다.
(D) 청소 용역을 제공한다.

해설 첫 번째 단락의 첫 문장에서 카리카스 씨가 수년 동안 TRE 접객 협회 회원이었지만 지금까지는 그리스와 이집트 포럼에만 글을 올렸다(I have been a member of the TRE Hospitality Association ~ I have posted messages only on the Greece and Egypt forums)고 했고, 이 글은 튀니지 포럼에 올리는 자신의 첫 게시글(This is my first post on the Tunisia forum)이라고 했다. TRE 회원인 카리카스 씨가 여러 국가의 포럼에 글을 올렸다고 한 것으로 보아 TRE는 국제 조직임을 알 수 있으므로 (C)가 정답이다.

어휘 based in ~에 본부를 둔 expand (사업 등을) 확장하다 organization 조직

174 Not / True

번역 카리카스 씨에 대해 명시된 것은?
(A) 접객 강좌를 가르친다.
(B) 라바트에 산다.
(C) 전직 레스토랑 주인이다.
(D) 적어도 한 번은 접객 콘퍼런스에 참석했다.

해설 마지막 단락의 세 번째 문장에서 카리카스 씨가 사실 라바트에서 가장 최근에 열린 콘퍼런스에 참석했다(In fact, I attended the most recent one in Rabat)고 언급했으므로 카리카스 씨는 최소 한 번 콘퍼런스에 참석했다는 것을 알 수 있다. 따라서 (D)가 정답이다.

어휘 former 이전의

175 문장 삽입

번역 [1], [2], [3], [4]로 표시된 위치 중에서 다음 문장이 들어가기에 가장 적합한 a?
"큰 회의실도 있을 것입니다."
(A) [1]
(B) [2]
(C) [3]
(D) [4]

해설 주어진 문장은 그것(It)은 큰 회의실을 가지고 있을 것이라고 언급하면서 also(또한)를 사용했으므로 주어진 문장 앞에는 It이 가리키는 단

수 명사와 함께 회의실 외에 그것이 갖추고 있는 시설들에 대한 내용이 와야 한다. 따라서 호텔의 객실 및 레스토랑의 수에 대해 설명하는 문장 뒤, 즉 [2]에 들어가는 것이 글의 흐름상 자연스러우므로 (B)가 정답이다.

176-180 이메일 + 이메일

수신: 마누엘 토레스 〈m.torres@opalmail.co.uk〉
발신: 안야 파텔 〈a.patel@support.harlund.co.uk〉
날짜: 5월 3일
제목: 자동차 보험

토레스 씨께,

할룬드 유한회사에 오신 것을 환영합니다. 176 **귀하의 새 차량에 대한 종합 자동차 보험을 제공하게 되어 기쁩니다.** 귀하의 첫 납입금인 36파운드를 수령하였으며, 현재 177 **보장**은 효력이 발생 중입니다. 고객님의 보험 증서 번호는 M413927입니다.

귀하의 청구 일정은 연간 보험료 432파운드를 기준으로 합니다. 남은 납입금은 월 36파운드씩 6월부터 매월 15일에 지불하셔야 합니다.

179 **비용을 지불하고 보험 증서를 관리하기 위해 www.harlund. co.uk에서 온라인으로 당사를 방문하실 수 있습니다. 저희 웹사이트는 고객님의 계좌 정보를 관리하고 고객님의 은행에서 곧바로 예약 이체로 납입할 수 있는 쉬운 옵션을 제공합니다.**

질문이 있거나 보험을 변경하시려면 020 7946 0516으로 고객 지원 센터에 전화 주십시오. 178 **차량 사고가 발생할 경우, 020 7946 0520으로 가능한 한 빨리 담당자에게 연락하십시오.** 고객님의 보험 증서 번호를 준비해 주십시오. 할룬드 유한회사를 신뢰해 주셔서 감사합니다. 고객님께 우수한 서비스를 제공해 드리게 되기를 기대합니다.

안야 파텔, 할룬드 유한회사 고객 지원 담당자

어휘 insurance 보험 comprehensive 종합적인 coverage 보상 (범위) in effect 효력이 있는 policy 보험 증권 billing 청구 premium 보험료 remaining 남아 있는 due 지불 기일이 된 transfer 이체 directly 곧장 incident 사고 at hand 준비하여 superior 우수한

수신: 안야 파텔 〈a.patel@support.harlund.co.uk〉
발신: 마누엘 토레스 〈m.torres@opalmail.co.uk〉
날짜: 5월 4일
제목: 회신: 자동차 보험

파텔 씨께,

확인 감사합니다. 신뢰할 수 있는 회사에서 보험을 들게 되어 기쁩니다. 참고로 새 차는 현재 제 명의로 등록되어 있습니다.

179 **첫 결제는 신용카드로 했지만 향후 결제를 위해 귀하의 이메일에 명시된 절차를 따를 계획입니다.**

180 **또한 아직 제가 보험 증서를 받지 못했다는 점도 알려드리고 싶습니다. 귀사의 웹사이트에서 다운로드할 수 있는 것을 찾아봤지만 찾지 못했습니다.** 증서 사본을 제게 보내 주시겠습니까?

마누엘 토레스

176 추론 / 암시

번역 토레스 씨에 대해 추론할 수 있는 것은?
(A) 새집으로 이사를 간다.
(B) 최근에 차를 샀다.
(C) 곧 은퇴할 예정이다.
(D) 최근에 은행 계좌를 개설했다.

해설 첫 이메일의 두 번째 문장에서 토레스 씨에게 귀하의 새 차량에 대한 종합 자동차 보험을 제공하게 되어 기쁘다(We are pleased ~ for your new vehicle)고 한 것으로 보아 토레스 씨는 최근 차를 구입해 자동차 보험에 새로 들었다는 것을 짐작할 수 있다. 따라서 (B)가 정답이다.

Paraphrasing 지문의 new vehicle → 정답의 bought a car

177 동의어 찾기

번역 첫 번째 이메일에서 첫 번째 단락 3행의 "coverage"와 의미가 가장 가까운 단어는?
(A) 치수
(B) 정보
(C) 해설
(D) 보장

해설 의미상 보험의 '보장'이 발효되었다는 뜻으로 쓰였으므로 '(보험) 보장'을 뜻하는 (D) protection이 정답이다.

178 세부사항

번역 파텔 씨가 토레스 씨에게 권하는 것은?
(A) 필요한 경우 담당자에게 연락하기
(B) 지역 사무소에 등록하기
(C) 신속하게 주문하기
(D) 계약서 수정하기

해설 첫 이메일의 네 번째 단락 두 번째 문장에서 파텔 씨가 토레스 씨에게 차량 사고가 발생할 경우 020 7946 0520으로 가능한 한 빨리 담당자에게 연락하라(In the event of a vehicle incident, please contact an agent as soon as possible at 020 7946 0520)고 당부하고 있으므로 (A)가 정답이다.

어휘 promptly 신속하게 revise 수정하다 agreement 계약서

Paraphrasing 지문의 contact → 정답의 Call

179 연계

번역 토레스 씨는 앞으로 어떻게 지불할 생각인가?
(A) 현금으로
(B) 신용카드로
(C) 전자 이체로
(D) 개인 수표로

해설 두 번째 이메일의 두 번째 단락에서 토레스 씨가 첫 결제는 신용카드로 했지만 향후 결제를 위해 파텔 씨의 이메일에 명시된 절차를 따를 계획(Although I made ~ I plan to follow the process outlined in your e-mail for future payments)이라고 했고, 첫 이메일의 세 번째 단락 첫 문장에서 비용을 지불하고 보험 증서를 관리하기 위해 www.harlund.co.uk에서 온라인으로 당사를 방문할 수 있으며(You can visit us online ~ to pay bills and manage your policy), 웹사이트는 고객의 계좌 정보를 관리하고 고객의 은행에서 곧바로 예약 이체로 납입할 수 있는 쉬운 옵션을 제공한다(Our Web site offers easy options ~ for making payments with scheduled transfers directly from your bank)고 안내하고 있다. 따라서 토레스 씨는 첫 이메일에 안내된 내용에 따라 온라인으로 예약 이체를 이용해 납입할 계획임을 알 수 있으므로 (C)가 정답이다.

180 세부사항

번역 토레스 씨가 찾아보았다고 언급하는 것은?
(A) 사무실로 가는 길
(B) 다운로드할 문서
(C) 고객 후기
(D) 연락처 정보

해설 두 번째 이메일의 마지막 단락 첫 문장에서 토레스 씨가 아직 보험 증서를 받지 못했다는 점도 알려 주고 싶다(I also wanted to let you know that I have not yet received the insurance certificate)며 웹사이트에서 다운로드할 수 있는 것을 찾아봤지만 찾지 못했다(I looked for one that I could download from your Web site, but I could not find anything)고 했으므로 (B)가 정답이다.

어휘 directions 길

Paraphrasing 지문의 the insurance certificate
→ 정답의 A document

181-185 일정표 + 서평

앤드류 대어의 도서 출간을 위한 투어 일정

181 (A), (B) 출연할 때마다 대어 씨는 그의 신작 소설인 〈산 아래〉의 발췌본을 읽고 질의응답 시간을 가질 것입니다. 181 (C) 그 후에, 대어 씨는 자신의 책에 사인하는 시간을 가질 것입니다.

장소	도시	날짜	시간
182 네이버후드 북스	토론토, 온타리오	5월 18일	오후 6시
웨인스탁 도서 및 문구	오타와, 온타리오	5월 27일	오후 7시
포티지 애비뉴 북스	위니펙, 매니토바	6월 6일	오후 6시 30분
다운타운 북스 앤 카페	레지나, 서스캐처원	6월 15일	오후 7시

어휘 launch 출간 appearance 출연 excerpt 발췌본
afterward 그 후에 autograph 사인하다 venue 장소
stationery 문구류

서평: 〈산 아래〉

평론가: 카밀 린
[182] 날짜: 5월 15일

[182, 184] 탐정 찰스 마틴을 다룬 베스트셀러 시리즈의 작가인 앤드류 대어가 이번 주에 우리 도시를 방문해 그의 신작 소설 〈산 아래〉를 홍보하러 네이버후드 북스에 출연할 예정입니다. 이 새 작품에서 마틴은 프랑스 알프스의 스키 리조트에서 벌어진 기이한 사건들을 조사합니다.

[183] 대어의 이야기는 독자들이 〈초인종〉에서 찰스 마틴을 처음 만난 이후 많은 진전을 이루었고, 이번 연재물은 지금까지 나온 대어의 작품 중 가장 강력합니다. 이 이야기의 팬들은 3년의 기다림 끝에 대어의 재치가 귀환한 것을 환영할 것이고, 마틴 시리즈를 처음 접하는 이들은 이야기에 빠져드는 스스로를 발견하게 될 것입니다.

이 이야기는 긴장감과 유머가 적절한 균형을 이루고 있으며 대어의 가장 열성적인 독자들조차 예측할 수 없는 결말을 보여줍니다. [185] 저는 이 책을 모든 미스터리 팬들에게 적극 추천합니다. 실망하지 않을 겁니다.

어휘 reviewer 평론가 author 작가 detective 탐정
appear 출연하다 promote 홍보하다 investigate 조사하다
mysterious 기이한 come a long way 진전을 이루다, 발전하다
installment (연재물의) 1회분 to date 지금까지 wit 재치
newcomer 신입, 새로 온 사람 captivate 마음을 사로잡다
suspense 긴장감 unpredictable 예측할 수 없는 devoted
열성적인 disappointed 실망한

181 Not / True

번역 일정표에 따르면, 대어 씨의 활동으로 언급되지 않은 것은?
(A) 자신의 책 읽기
(B) 질문에 답변하기
(C) 사람들을 위해 책에 서명하기
(D) 참가자들과 사진 찍기

해설 일정표의 첫 단락에 출연할 때마다 대어 씨는 그의 신작 소설인 〈산 아래〉의 발췌본을 읽고 질의응답 시간을 가질 것(At each appearance, Mr. Darr will read an excerpt from his new novel, *Down the Mountainside*, followed by a question-and-answer session)이라고 했으므로 (A), (B), 그 후에 대어 씨는 자신의 책에 사인할 시간을 가질 것(Afterward, Mr. Darr will be available to autograph copies of his books)이라고 했으므로 (C)는 대어 씨의 활동으로 언급되었다. 사진 촬영에 대한 언급은 없으므로 (D)가 정답이다.

어휘 individual 사람, 개인 participant 참가자

Paraphrasing 지문의 his new novel → 보기 (A)의 his book
지문의 question-and-answer session
→ 보기 (B)의 Answering questions
지문의 autograph → 보기 (C)의 Signing

182 연계

번역 평론가가 있는 도시는?
(A) 토론토
(B) 오타와
(C) 위니펙
(D) 레지나

해설 서평의 작성 날짜가 5월 15일(Date: 15 May)이고 첫 문장에서 탐정 찰스 마틴을 다룬 베스트셀러 시리즈의 작가인 앤드류 대어가 이번 주에 우리 도시를 방문해 그의 신작 소설 〈산 아래〉를 홍보하러 네이버후드 북스에 출연할 예정(Andrew Darr ~ will be visiting our city this week, appearing at Neighbourhood Books to promote his new novel, *Down the Mountainside*)이라고 했는데, 일정표의 앤드류 대어의 첫 투어 일정에 장소는 네이버후드 북스(Neighbourhood Books), 도시는 토론토, 온타리오(Toronto, Ontario), 날짜는 5월 18일(18 May)이라고 나와 있다. 따라서 서평가는 온타리오주 토론토에 살고 있음을 알 수 있으므로 (A)가 정답이다.

183 추론 / 암시

번역 〈산 아래〉에 대해 사실일 것 같은 것은?
(A) 작가의 첫 책이다.
(B) 단편 소설 모음집이다.
(C) 시리즈의 일부이다.
(D) 프랑스어로 번역중이다.

해설 서평의 두 번째 단락 첫 문장에서 대어의 이야기는 독자들이 〈초인종〉에서 찰스 마틴을 처음 만난 이후 많은 진전을 이루었고 이번 연재물(〈산 아래〉)은 지금까지 나온 대어의 작품 중 가장 강력하다(Darr's storytelling has come a long way since readers first met Charles Martin in *The Doorbell*, and this installment is Darr's strongest work to date)고 했으므로 〈산 아래〉는 대어의 시리즈물 중 하나라는 것을 알 수 있다. 따라서 (C)가 정답이다.

어휘 collection 모음집 translate 번역하다

Paraphrasing 지문의 installment → 정답의 part of a series

184 세부사항

번역 마틴 씨는 누구인가?
(A) 작가의 팬
(B) 책 속의 등장인물
(C) 서평 작성자
(D) 서점 주인

해설 서평의 첫 문장에서 탐정 찰스 마틴을 다룬 베스트셀러 시리즈의 작가인 앤드류 대어(Andrew Darr, the author of the best-selling series about detective Charles Martin ~)라고 했으므로 찰스 마틴은 소설 주인공임을 알 수 있다. 따라서 (B)가 정답이다.

어휘 character (책 등의) 등장인물

185 추론 / 암시

번역 서평에 따르면, 〈산 아래〉를 읽을 것 같은 사람은?
(A) 미스터리 읽는 것을 좋아하는 사람들
(B) 실화를 바탕으로 한 소설을 즐기는 사람들
(C) 여행을 자주 다니는 사람들
(D) 공상과학 소설을 좋아하는 사람들

해설 서평의 세 번째 단락 두 번째 문장에서 이 책을 모든 미스터리 팬들에게 적극 추천한다(I highly recommend this book to all mystery fans)고 한 것으로 보아 미스터리 이야기를 좋아하는 독자들이 〈산 아래〉의 잠재 독자임을 알 수 있으므로 (A)가 정답이다.

어휘 frequently 자주   science fiction 공상과학 소설

Paraphrasing 지문의 mystery fans → 정답의 People who like to read mysteries

186-190 보고서 + 편지 + 기사

---

¹⁸⁶ **유마 카운티의 연간 감귤류 과일 생산**

- ¹⁸⁶ **감귤류 과일 82톤**
- ¹⁸⁶ **레몬 12만 상자 이상**
- ^{186,190} **오렌지 1만 5천 상자**
- ¹⁸⁶ **자몽 9천 상자**
- 1억 9천만 달러의 수익

3,000명에 가까운 직원을 고용하고 카운티의 공공 서비스에 자금을 제공할 수 있도록 세금으로 약 2백만 달러를 기여하고 있습니다.

- 애리조나 농업국

어휘 citrus 시트러스(감귤류 과일)   county 자치주   grapefruit 자몽   revenue 수익   contribute 기여하다   fund 자금을 대다   agriculture 농업   division (조직의) 국, 부

시티 웨스트 뱅크
캐니언 가 455
피닉스, 애리조나 85007

3월 21일

도밍고 라미레즈, 국장
애리조나 농업국
6번가 55
유마, 애리조나 85364

라미레즈 씨께,

^{187,189} **유마 카운티의 감귤류 산업 성공을 요약한 애리조나 농업국의 최근 보고서를 읽었습니다. 시티 웨스트 뱅크는 이 산업을 더욱 확대함으로써 귀하께서 이끌고 계신 애리조나 농업국을 돕고자 합니다.** 우리는 저금리 대출을 제공하고 지역 상공 회의소 및 애리조나 주립 대학의 농업 연구원들과의 연결을 통해 전문적인 조언을 제공합니다.

¹⁸⁸ 우리는 애리조나 남서부의 농촌 체험 관광이 농장 투어, 조류 관찰, 경치 좋은 시골 숙소에 대한 인기의 결과로 성장하고 있다는 것을 알고 있지만, 관광업이 이 지역의 농업 생산력을 넘어설 것 같지는 않습니다. 우리는 애리조나의 많은 카운티에 있는 농부들을 지원하고 유마 카운티의 감귤류 경작자들을 도울 준비가 되어 있습니다. ¹⁸⁷ **우리는 함께 위대한 일들을 이룩할 수 있습니다.**

비앙카 슈라이버
산업 투자 프로그램

어휘 summarize 요약하다   expand 확장하다   industry 산업   low-interest 저금리   loan 대출   expert 전문적인   connection 연결   chamber of commerce 상공 회의소   state 주립의   recognize 알다, 인식하다   agritourism 농촌 체험 관광   scenic 경치가 좋은   lodging 숙소   unlikely ~할 것 같지 않은   surpass 뛰어넘다   strength 능력, 강점   be poised to ~할 준비가 되다   accomplish 달성하다   cordially 진심으로   investment 투자

슈라이버, 국가 투자 전략 부사장으로 임명

피닉스 (1월 19일) — 시티 웨스트 뱅크는 오늘 비앙카 슈라이버 씨가 2월 1일부터 국가 투자 전략의 부사장으로 승진할 것이라고 발표했다. 슈라이버 씨는 현재 애리조나 전역의 기업에 서비스를 제공하는 시티 웨스트 뱅크의 산업 투자 프로그램을 감독하고 있다.

¹⁹⁰ 윌리엄 돌 은행장은 농업 부문에 있어 슈라이버 씨의 성공적인 투자 기록을 언급했다. "^{189,190} 애리조나 농업국과 함께 일하며 쏟은 슈라이버 씨의 노력으로 감귤류 생산이 크게 증가했습니다. ¹⁹⁰ 유마 카운티는 현재 오렌지만큼 많은 자몽을 생산합니다. 슈라이버 씨의 예리한 통찰력이 그녀의 새로운 역할에서 그녀를 훨씬 더 가치 있게 만들 것입니다."라고 돌 씨는 말했다.

어휘 vice president 부사장   strategy 전략   effective 시행되는   oversee 감독하다   serve (서비스를) 제공하다   cite 언급하다, 인용하다   sector 부문   effort 노력   significantly 상당히   boost 신장시키다   keen 예리한   insight 통찰력   valuable 가치 있는   remark 언급하다

186 Not / True

번역 보고서에서 유마 카운티 지역에 대해 명시하는 것은?
(A) 그곳에서 판매되는 과일에는 세금을 부과하지 않는다.
(B) 여러 종류의 과일이 재배된다.
(C) 농업 일자리에 더 많은 노동자가 필요하다.
(D) 새로운 종류의 과일이 생산되고 있다.

해설 보고서의 제목이 유마 카운티의 연간 감귤류 과일 생산(Annual Citrus Production in Yuma County)이고 그 아래 생산되는 과일 품목에 감귤류 과일(citrus fruit), 레몬(lemons), 오렌지(oranges), 자몽(grapefruit)이 나열되어 있으므로 여러 종류의 과일이 생산되고 있다는 것을 확인할 수 있다. 따라서 (B)가 정답이다.

어휘 tax 세금을 부과하다   cultivate 재배하다

187 주제 / 목적

번역 슈라이버 씨가 라미레즈 씨에게 편지를 쓴 이유는?
(A) 함께 사업을 하는 것의 이점을 설명하려고
(B) 보고서의 정보를 명확히 하려고
(C) 대출금 상환을 상기시키려고
(D) 대학 농업 연구원들의 조언을 제공하려고

해설 편지의 첫 문장에서 슈라이버 씨가 라미레즈 씨에게 유마 카운티의 감귤류 산업 성공을 요약한 애리조나 농업국의 최근 보고서를 읽었다(I read the recent report ~ Yuma County's success in the citrus industry)며, 시티 웨스트 뱅크는 이 산업을 더욱 확대함으로써 라미레즈 씨가 이끌고 있는 애리조나 농업국을 돕고자 한다(City West Bank wants to help the Arizona Agriculture Division you lead by expanding this industry further)면서 그 뒤로 지원 방법 및 이유를 설명하고 있고, 마지막 문장에서 우리는 함께 위대한 일들을 이룩할 수 있다(Together, we can accomplish great things)고 사업 협력에 따른 이점을 강조하며 마무리하고 있다. 따라서 (A)가 정답이다.

어휘 benefit 이점 clarify 명확히 하다

188 세부사항

번역 편지에 따르면, 관광객들이 유마 카운티를 방문하는 이유는?
(A) 농산물 시장에서 쇼핑하려고
(B) 사진을 찍으려고
(C) 테마파크를 즐기려고
(D) 야생동물을 관찰하려고

해설 편지의 두 번째 단락 첫 문장에서 애리조나 남서부의 농촌 체험 관광이 농장 투어, 조류 관찰, 경치 좋은 시골 숙소에 대한 인기의 결과로 성장하고 있다는 것을 알고 있다(We recognize that agritourism in southwest Arizona is growing as a result of the popularity of farm tours, bird-watching, and scenic country lodging)고 했다. 따라서 관광객들이 유마 카운티를 찾는 한 가지 이유는 조류 관찰이므로 (D)가 정답이다.

어휘 theme park 테마파크 observe 관찰하다 wildlife 야생동물

Paraphrasing 지문의 bird-watching
→ 정답의 observe wildlife

189 연계

번역 라미레즈 씨에 대해 암시된 것은?
(A) 슈라이버 씨의 제안을 받아들였다.
(B) 시티 웨스트 뱅크에 고용된 적이 있다.
(C) 유마 상공 회의소의 회원이다.
(D) 최근에 감귤 농장을 샀다.

해설 편지의 첫 문장에서 슈라이버 씨가 애리조나 농업국장인 라미레즈 씨에게 유마 카운티의 감귤류 산업 성공을 요약한 애리조나 농업국의 최근 보고서를 읽었다(I read the recent report ~ Yuma County's success in the citrus industry)고 했고, 시티 웨스트 뱅크는 이 산업을 더욱 확대함으로써 라미레즈 씨가 이끌고 있는 애리조나 농업국을 돕고자 한다(City West Bank wants to help the Arizona

Agriculture Division you lead by expanding this industry further)고 사업 제안을 했다. 그리고 기사의 두 번째 단락 두 번째 문장에서 애리조나 농업국장과 함께 일하며 쏟은 슈라이버 씨의 노력으로 감귤류 생산이 크게 증가했다(Ms. Schreiber's efforts in working with the director of the Arizona Agriculture Division have significantly boosted citrus production)고 했다. 따라서 라미레즈 씨는 슈라이버 씨의 협업 제안을 받아들였다는 것을 알 수 있으므로 (A)가 정답이다.

어휘 accept 받아들이다 employ 채용하다, 고용하다

190 연계

번역 돌 씨는 어떤 업적에 대해 슈라이버 씨를 칭찬하는가?
(A) 농산물 출하를 준비한 일
(B) 다수의 시티 웨스트 뱅크 지점을 개점한 일
(C) 자몽 생산을 1만 5천 상자로 늘리도록 지원한 일
(D) 유마 카운티를 휴양지로 홍보한 일

해설 기사의 두 번째 단락 첫 문장에서 윌리엄 돌 은행장은 농업 부문에 있어 슈라이버 씨의 성공적인 투자 기록을 언급했다(Bank President William Dolle cited Ms. Schreiber's record of successful investment in the agricultural sector)며 애리조나 농업국장과 함께 일하며 쏟은 슈라이버 씨의 노력으로 감귤류 생산이 크게 증가했다(Ms. Schreiber's efforts ~ have significantly boosted citrus production)고 했고, 유마 카운티는 현재 오렌지만큼 많은 자몽을 생산한다(Yuma County now produces as many grapefruit as it does oranges)고 했다. 보고서의 생산 과일 품목에 오렌지 생산량이 1만 5천 상자(15,000 boxes of oranges)라고 나와 있는 것으로 보아 돌 씨는 슈라이버 씨가 애리조나 농업국과 함께 유마 카운티를 지원해 자몽 생산을 1만 5천 상자로 늘린 일을 칭찬하는 것이므로 (C)가 정답이다.

어휘 arrange 준비하다 agricultural 농업의 vacation destination 휴양지, 휴가지

191-195 초대장 + 웹페이지 + 이메일

https://www.unetcon.org/messages_audreysmith80

191 유넷콘 - 메시지 센터

보류 중인 초대장

발신: 돈 피츠패트릭
지점장, 윌슨빌 금융

수신: 오드리 스미스

오드리 씨께,

191, 193 유넷콘에서 업무상으로 교류하려면 이 초대를 수락해 주십시오. 저는 스톤룩 대학 졸업 동기이며 항상 인맥을 넓히는 데 관심이 있습니다. 이번에 저는 우리 졸업생 동기들이 하는 모든 일에 대해 최신 정보 상태를 유지하기 위해 비공개 스톤룩 동문 그룹 페이지에 함께하는 데 귀하께서 관심이 있는지 알아보려고 연락드렸습니다. https://www.unetcon.org/private/stonerookugrads.

돈 피츠패트릭

초대 수락	초대 무시	돈에게 답장

어휘 pending 미정인 accept 수락하다 fellow 동료 graduate 졸업생 expand 확장하다 reach out 연락을 취하다 private 비공개의, 사적인 alumni 동문 ignore 무시하다

---

https://www.unetcon.org/private/stonerookugrads

스톤룩 대학 졸업생

스톤룩 졸업생 조나 힐리어드로부터 지속적인 성공과 최신 정보를 확인하세요.

192 현재	교육	194 경력
대학원장, 올브라이트 경영 대학원 설립자 겸 이사, 클리어 패스 연락처 전화: 843-555-0139 이메일: jhilliard@mccleese.edu 사무실: 코든홀 403 북켄싱턴 가 530 192 **찰스턴**, SC 29425	경영학 석사 - 턴불 대학교 교육학 학사 - 스톤룩 대학교	힐리어드 씨는 2017년 이후로 올브라이트 경영 대학원을 이끌고 있다. 194 **2007년과 2017년 사이에 그는 나이지리아 라고스에서 경영학을 가르치면서 서아프리카의 신흥 시장에 대한 광범위한 연구를 수행했다.** 2년 전, 그는 미국에서 공부하기를 원하는 전 세계 학생들에게 조언을 해주는 기업인 클리어 패스를 설립했다.

어휘 founder 설립자 education 교육 Master 석사 business administration 경영학 Bachelor of Arts 문과 학사 carry out ~을 수행하다 extensive 광범위한 emerging 신흥의 found 설립하다 pursue 추구하다

발신: 오드리 스미스 〈audrey_smith80@rapidonet.co.uk〉
수신: 조나 힐리어드 〈jhilliard@mccleese.edu〉
날짜: 9월 19일
제목: 추천

조나 씨께,

우리가 마지막으로 이야기한 지 오래되었습니다. 193 **저는 최근에 유넷콘에서 당신의 프로필을 우연히 발견했고** 당신이 현재 맥리스에서 경영 대학원을 이끌고 있다는 것을 보았습니다! 194 **라고스에서의 제 연구는 작년에 프라이어 앤 마텔의 수석 컨설턴트 자리를 수락하면서 끝났습니다.** 그 이후로 이곳 맨체스터에 기반을 두고 있습니다.

최근 벤처 사업에 대해 축하드립니다. 클리어 패스는 이미 상당히 인상 깊은 명성을 가지고 있습니다! 195 **저에게 미국에서 경영 정보 시스템 학위를 취득하는 데 관심 있는 조카가 있는데, 그가 이 분야에서 당신의 새 회사의 전문 지식을 활용할 수 있도록 두 사람을 연결해 드리고 싶습니다.**

오드리 스미스

어휘 come across ~을 우연히 발견하다 based in ~에 기반을 둔 business venture 벤처 사업 impressive 인상 깊은 reputation 명성 nephew 조카 degree 학위 put ~ in touch ~을 소개해 주다 take advantage of ~을 활용하다 expertise 전문 지식

191 Not / True

번역 초대장에서 유넷콘에 대해 명시하는 것은?
(A) 비즈니스 컨설팅 회사이다.
(B) 금융 서비스 회사이다.
(C) 직업 소개소이다.
(D) 업무상 인맥 형성 웹사이트이다.

해설 초대장의 상단에 유넷콘이 메시지 센터(Unetcon – Message Center)라고 나와 있고, 첫 문장에서 유넷콘에서 업무상으로 교류하려면 이 초대를 수락해 달라(Please accept this invitation to connect professionally on Unetcon)고 했으므로 유넷콘은 직업인들이 인맥을 쌓을 수 있는 온라인 회사임을 알 수 있다. 따라서 (D)가 정답이다.

어휘 firm 회사 employment 고용

> Paraphrasing 지문의 connect professionally
> → 정답의 professional networking

192 세부사항

번역 웹페이지에 따르면, 힐리어드 씨가 현재 근무하는 곳은?
(A) 라고스
(B) 찰스턴
(C) 윌슨빌
(D) 맨체스터

해설 웹페이지에서 힐리어드 씨의 정보를 알려주는 왼쪽 현재(Current) 상태 란에 사무실 주소가 찰스턴(Charleston)이라고 나와 있으므로 (B)가 정답이다.

193 연계 ▶ 동영상 강의

번역 스미스 씨에 대해 암시된 것은?
(A) 스톤룩 대학에서 가르쳤다.
(B) 윌슨빌 파이낸셜에서 일한다.
(C) 피츠패트릭 씨의 초대를 수락했다.
(D) 올해 라고스를 방문할 계획이다.

해설 초대장의 첫 문장에서 피츠패트릭 씨가 스미스 씨에게 유넷콘에서 업무상으로 교류하려면 이 초대를 수락해 달라(Please accept this invitation to connect professionally on Unetcon)고 했고, 이 메일의 첫 단락 두 번째 문장에서 스미스 씨가 힐리어드 씨에게 최근에 유넷콘에서 당신의 프로필을 우연히 발견했다(I recently came across your profile on Unetcon)고 했다. 따라서 스미스 씨가 유넷콘을 이용하고 있는 것으로 보아 유넷콘에서 피츠패트릭 씨가 보낸 초대에 응했다는 것을 알 수 있으므로 (C)가 정답이다.

194 연계

번역 스미스 씨와 힐리어드 씨의 공통점은?

(A) 클리어 패스를 공동 설립했다.

(B) 프라이어 앤 마텔의 동료들이다.

(C) 턴불 대학에서 동기였다.

(D) 둘 다 나이지리아에서 연구를 수행했다.

해설 웹페이지의 오른쪽 경력(Professional) 란의 두 번째 문장에서 힐리어드 씨가 2007년과 2017년 사이에 나이지리아 라고스에서 경영학을 가르치면서 서아프리카의 신흥 시장에 대한 광범위한 연구를 수행했다(Between 2007 and 2017, he carried out extensive research ~ in Lagos, Nigeria)고 했고, 이메일의 첫 단락 세 번째 문장에서 스미스 씨가 라고스에서의 자신의 연구는 작년에 프라이어 앤 마텔의 수석 컨설턴트 자리를 수락하면서 끝났다(My research in Lagos ended last year ~ at Pryor and Martell)고 했다. 따라서 두 사람 모두 나이지리아 라고스에서 연구를 수행했다는 것을 알 수 있으므로 (D)가 정답이다.

어휘 cofound 공동 설립하다   conduct (특정 활동을) 하다

Paraphrasing 지문의 carried out → 정답의 conducted

195 주제 / 목적

번역 힐리어드 씨에게 발송된 스미스 씨 이메일의 목적은?

(A) 전문적인 서비스를 요청하려고

(B) 전문적인 추천서를 제공하려고

(C) 정보 제공 인터뷰를 수행하려고

(D) 올브라이트 경영 대학원에 일자리를 지원하려고

해설 이메일의 마지막 문장에서 스미스 씨가 미국에서 경영 정보 시스템 학위를 취득하는 데 관심 있는 조카가 있는데, 그가 이 분야에서 힐리어드 씨의 새 회사의 전문 지식을 활용할 수 있도록 두 사람을 연결해 주고 싶다(I have a nephew who is interested in ~ I was hoping I could put you both in touch so that he can take advantage of your new company's expertise in this area)고 했으므로 (A)가 정답이다.

어휘 reference 추천서   informational 정보를 제공하는

Paraphrasing 지문의 expertise
→ 정답의 professional services

196-200 안내 책자 + 기사 + 이메일

모던 살롱 아카데미
www.modernsalonacademy.ca

20년도 더 이전에 설립된 모던 살롱 아카데미는 토론토에서 가장 인정받는 미용 학교입니다. 196 이 학교는 다음의 프로그램에서 업계 최고의 전문가들로부터 실습 교육, 소규모 학급, 개별화된 지도를 제공합니다.

- 미용학 I: 이발과 스타일링의 기초 지식을 습득합니다.

- 199 미용학 II: 이발과 스타일링, 염색 기술을 배웁니다.

- 피부 관리: 고급 피부 관리 시술을 제공하는 기술을 배웁니다.

- 리더십: 살롱 관리, 사업 운영 및 규정 준수를 공부합니다.

모던 살롱 아카데미는 국제 미용 협회의 명망 높은 우수상 수상 기관입니다. 그러니 우리 졸업생의 95퍼센트 이상이 미용과 패션 산업 모두에서 성공적인 경력을 쌓아가는 것이 놀라운 일이 아닙니다.

어휘 establish 설립하다   recognized 인정받는   hands-on 직접 해 보는   individualized 개별화된   instruction 지도   leading 최고의, 선두의   cosmetology 미용학   gain 얻다   foundational 기초적인   advanced 고급의   treatment 치료   compliance 규정 준수   prestigious 명망 높은   go on to ~으로 나아가다

온타리오로 확장하는 모던 살롱 아카데미

토론토 (8월 23일) — 198 이곳 토론토에서 높이 평가받는 미용 학교인 모던 살롱 아카데미가 오샤와에 지역 캠퍼스를 열 예정이다. 학교는 이미 10월 4일에 시작하기로 예정된 수업을 위해 학생들을 입학시키고 있다.

197 모던 살롱 아카데미는 지난 몇 년 동안 등록자 수가 상당히 증가했다. 198 모던 살롱 아카데미의 교육 책임자 프랑신느 뒤퓌는 "우리 학생들의 절반 이상이 시외에 거주하기 때문에 분교를 내는 것은 극히 합리적입니다."라고 말한다.

모던 살롱 아카데미는 헤어 관리, 피부 관리, 메이크업을 포함한 다양한 분야의 직업을 위한 전문 교육과 자격증을 제공한다. 입학 조건, 수업료 및 학사 일정을 포함해 모던 살롱 아카데미에 대한 자세한 정보를 원하면 www.modernsalonacademy.ca를 방문하면 된다.

- 〈온타리오 데일리 타임스〉의 크리시 젤렌

어휘 regarded 평가되는   regional 지역의   admit 입학을 허락하다   substantial 상당한   enrollment 등록, 등록자 수   educational 교육의   outside the city limits 시외에   certification 자격증   admission 입학

수신: 프랑신느 뒤퓌 〈francine.dupuis@modernsalonacademy.ca〉
발신: 아미트 펄사우드 〈amit@shorelinebarbers.ca〉
제목: 초보자 취업 기회
날짜: 11월 19일

뒤퓌 씨께,

198 제 이름은 아미트 펄사우드이고, 쇼어라인 바버스의 주인이자 운영자입니다. 귀하의 새로 설립된 지역 캠퍼스에서 모퉁이를 돌면 바로 위치한 저의 이발소에서 일할 졸업생들을 모집하는 데 관심이 있습니다. 199 저는 이발과 염색 서비스를 모두 제공할 수 있는 우수한 자격을 갖춘 신입 직원을 구하고 있습니다.

200 관심 있는 학생들에게 저와 이야기할 기회를 주기 위해 근처 캠퍼스를 방문할 수 있을까요? 이 방법은 제가 채용하고자 하는 일자리에 대해 그들을 평가하기에 편리할 것이고, 그들이 가지고 있는 질문에 제가 대답할 수도 있습니다. 주선이 이루어질 수 있는지 알려 주십시오.

아미트 펄사우드

어휘 entry-level job 신입직 opportunity 기회 barber 이발소 recruit 모집하다 regional 지역의 qualified 자격을 갖춘 convenient 편리한 evaluate 평가하다 fill 채우다 arrangement 주선

196 세부사항

번역 모던 살롱 아카데미에서 학생들을 가르치는 방식은?
(A) 온라인 과정을 통해
(B) 학술 강연을 통해
(C) 개별화된 교육을 통해
(D) 대규모 그룹 토론을 통해

해설 안내 책자의 두 번째 문장에서 이 학교는 업계 최고의 전문가들로부터 실습 교육, 소규모 학급, 개별화된 지도를 제공한다(The school offers ~ individualized instruction from leading industry professionals)고 했으므로 (C)가 정답이다.

어휘 lecture 강연

Paraphrasing 지문의 instruction → 정답의 training

197 세부사항

번역 기사에 따르면, 모던 살롱 아카데미에서 증가한 것은?
(A) 수업료
(B) 학생 수
(C) 입학 요건
(D) 자격증 취득에 필요한 시간

해설 기사의 두 번째 단락 첫 문장에서 모던 살롱 아카데미는 지난 몇 년 동안 등록자 수가 상당히 증가했다(Modern Salon Academy has had a substantial rise in enrollment over the past few years)고 했으므로 (B)가 정답이다.

어휘 tuition 수업(료) requirement 요건, 필요조건

198 연계

번역 쇼어라인 바버스에 대해 사실일 것 같은 것은?
(A) 오샤와에 위치해 있다.
(B) 토론토에 매장을 열 예정이다.
(C) 프랑신느 뒤퓌에게 팔렸다.
(D) 매우 저렴한 가격의 서비스를 제공한다.

해설 기사의 첫 문장에서 이곳 토론토에서 높이 평가받는 미용 학교인 모던 살롱 아카데미가 오샤와에 지역 캠퍼스를 열 예정(Modern Salon Academy ~ is opening a regional campus in Oshawa)이라고 했고, 두 번째 단락의 두 번째 문장에서 모던 살롱 아카데미의 교육 책임자 프랑신느 뒤퓌(Francine Dupuis, educational director of Modern Salon Academy)를 언급했다. 이메일의 첫 문장에서 펄사우드 씨가 뒤퓌 씨에게 자신의 이름은 아미트 펄사우드이고 쇼어라인 바버스의 주인이자 운영자(My name is Amit Persaud, and I am the owner and operator of Shoreline Barbers)이며 귀하의 새로 설립된 지역 캠퍼스에서 모퉁이를 돌면 바로 위치한 자신의 이발소에서 일할 졸업생들을 모집하는 데 관심이 있다(I am

interested ~ at my barbershop, which is just around the corner from your newly established regional campus)고 했다. 따라서 쇼어라인 바버스는 모던 살롱 아카데미의 오샤와 지역 캠퍼스 근처에 위치해 있다는 것을 알 수 있으므로 (A)가 정답이다.

어휘 affordable (가격이) 저렴한

199 연계

번역 펄사우드 씨의 요구에 가장 잘 맞을 사람은?
(A) 미용학 I 학생들
(B) 미용학 II 학생들
(C) 피부 관리 학생들
(D) 리더십 학생들

해설 이메일의 첫 단락 세 번째 문장에서 펄사우드 씨가 이발과 염색 서비스를 모두 제공할 수 있는 우수한 자격을 갖춘 신입 직원을 구하고 있다(I am seeking ~ employees who can provide both haircutting and hair-colouring services)고 했고, 안내 책자의 프로그램 항목에 미용학 II에서 이발과 스타일링, 염색 기술을 배운다(Cosmetology II: Learn techniques in haircutting, styling, and colouring)고 나와 있다. 따라서 펄사우드 씨의 요구에 가장 적합한 지원자는 이발과 염색 기술을 모두 습득한 미용학 II 학생들임을 알 수 있으므로 (B)가 정답이다.

200 세부사항

번역 이메일에 따르면, 펄사우드 씨가 하고 싶어 하는 것은?
(A) 추가 업체 설립
(B) 직원 재교육
(C) 수업 지도
(D) 학생 면접

해설 이메일의 두 번째 단락 첫 문장에서 펄사우드 씨가 관심 있는 학생들에게 자신과 이야기할 기회를 주기 위해 근처 캠퍼스를 방문할 수 있을지(Would it be possible for me to visit the nearby campus to give interested students an opportunity to talk with me?)를 물었고, 이 방법은 채용하고자 하는 일자리에 대해 그들을 평가하기에 편리할 것이고 그들이 가지고 있는 질문에 대답할 수도 있다(This would be a convenient way for me to evaluate them ~ I can also answer any questions they may have)라고 했다. 따라서 펄사우드 씨는 캠퍼스에서 직접 학생들을 채용하기 위한 면접을 진행하기를 원한다는 것을 알 수 있으므로 (D)가 정답이다.

101 (D)	**102** (A)	**103** (C)	**104** (B)	**105** (C)
106 (B)	**107** (B)	**108** (C)	**109** (C)	**110** (A)
111 (B)	**112** (C)	**113** (D)	**114** (B)	**115** (A)
116 (A)	**117** (D)	**118** (A)	**119** (D)	**120** (D)
121 (D)	**122** (A)	**123** (A)	**124** (B)	**125** (C)
126 (C)	**127** (B)	**128** (D)	**129** (C)	**130** (D)
131 (B)	**132** (C)	**133** (A)	**134** (D)	**135** (B)
136 (C)	**137** (C)	**138** (D)	**139** (A)	**140** (D)
141 (C)	**142** (D)	**143** (B)	**144** (D)	**145** (A)
146 (C)	**147** (D)	**148** (B)	**149** (C)	**150** (D)
151 (D)	**152** (A)	**153** (A)	**154** (D)	**155** (C)
156 (B)	**157** (D)	**158** (A)	**159** (D)	**160** (C)
161 (B)	**162** (D)	**163** (A)	**164** (B)	**165** (C)
166 (A)	**167** (D)	**168** (C)	**169** (B)	**170** (D)
171 (C)	**172** (D)	**173** (B)	**174** (C)	**175** (D)
176 (D)	**177** (C)	**178** (A)	**179** (D)	**180** (B)
181 (C)	**182** (C)	**183** (A)	**184** (C)	**185** (D)
186 (A)	**187** (A)	**188** (D)	**189** (B)	**190** (B)
191 (C)	**192** (A)	**193** (A)	**194** (D)	**195** (C)
196 (A)	**197** (C)	**198** (B)	**199** (D)	**200** (A)

PART 5

101 동명사 _ 동사의 목적어

해설 빈칸은 동사 began의 목적어 자리이므로 동명사인 (D) having이 정답이다. (A) has와 (C) have는 동사, (B) had는 동사/과거분사이므로 목적어 자리에 들어갈 수 없다.

번역 프로 데이터 위즈로 업그레이드한 뒤, 고객들은 스프레드시트에 문제를 겪기 시작했다.

102 동사 어휘
 동영상 강의

해설 be동사 are와 함께 수동태를 이루는 과거분사 자리로, 문맥상 '요청이 정 씨에 의해 승인된다'라는 의미가 되어야 자연스러우므로 '승인하다'라는 뜻의 (A) approved가 정답이다. (B)의 drop은 '떨어뜨리다', (C)의 reach는 '도달하다', (D)의 remind는 '상기시키다'라는 뜻으로 문맥상 적절하지 않다.

번역 추가적인 휴가 요청은 인사부의 정 씨에 의해 승인된다.

어휘 additional 추가의 day off 휴가

103 전치사 어휘

해설 문맥상 '다음 소프트웨어 업데이트를 위한 변경사항 목록'이라는 의미가 되어야 적절하므로 '~을 위한'이라는 뜻으로 목적을 나타내는

(C) for가 정답이다. 참고로, (A) between은 '~ 사이에'라는 뜻으로 뒤에 'A and B' 또는 둘을 나타내는 복수명사가 와야 한다.

번역 프로그래머들은 다음 소프트웨어 업데이트를 위한 변경사항 목록을 가지고 있다.

104 목적격 보어 _ 동사원형
 동영상 강의

해설 「let + 목적어(Farida Banquet Service) + 목적격 보어」 구조에서 목적격 보어에 해당하는 자리로, 사역동사 let은 동사원형이나 과거분사를 목적격 보어로 취한다. 따라서 동사원형인 (B) provide가 정답이다. (A) providing은 동명사/현재분사, (C) provides는 동사, (D) to provide는 to부정사로 빈칸에 들어갈 수 없다.

번역 파리다 연회 서비스가 귀사의 중요한 기업 행사에 전문적인 출장 요리를 제공하도록 해 주십시오.

어휘 banquet 연회 catering 출장 요리 corporate 기업의

105 명사 어휘

해설 동사 has improved의 목적어 자리로, 문맥상 '타일의 품질을 개선해 왔다'라는 내용이 되어야 적절하다. 따라서 '품질'을 뜻하는 (C) quality가 정답이다. (A) closure는 '종료; 폐쇄', (B) product는 제품, (D) method는 '방법'이라는 의미이다.

번역 다양한 혁신 기술을 이용하여 보이드 인더스트리스는 타일의 품질을 개선해 왔다.

어휘 various 다양한 innovative 혁신적인

106 명사 자리 _ 동사의 주어 / 수 일치

해설 빈칸은 복수동사 are의 주어 자리이므로 복수명사가 들어가야 한다. 따라서 '판매'라는 뜻의 (B) Sales가 정답이다. (A) Sale은 단수명사이므로 단수동사와 쓰이고, (C) Sells는 동사이므로 품사상 빈칸에 들어갈 수 없다. (D) Selling은 동명사일 경우 주어 자리에 들어갈 수는 있지만 단수 취급되므로 복수동사 are의 주어가 될 수 없다.

번역 모든 화장품의 판매는 최종 판매이며, 어떠한 경우에도 환불되지 않습니다.

어휘 cosmetics 화장품 final 최종적인, 변경할 수 없는 refund 환불 circumstance 경우, 상황

107 형용사 어휘

해설 부정을 나타내는 한정사 no와 명사 action 사이에서 action을 수식하는 형용사 자리이다. 앞에 '이미 답변을 제출한 경우'라는 내용이 온 것으로 보아 '추가적인 조치는 필요 없다'라는 의미가 되어야 적절하므로 '추가의, 더 이상의'를 뜻하는 (B) further가 정답이다. (A) bright는 '밝은', (C) previous는 '이전의', (D) average는 '평균의'라는 의미로 문맥상 어울리지 않는다.

번역 답변을 이미 제출한 경우 추가적인 조치는 필요하지 않습니다.

어휘 submit 제출하다 response 답변 required 필요한, 필수인

108 인칭대명사의 격 _ 소유격

해설 빈칸에는 뒤에 온 명사구 own research를 수식하는 말이 들어가야 한다. 따라서 명사 앞에 쓰여 한정사 역할을 하고, 형용사 own과 함께 소유 관계를 강조하는 소유격 인칭대명사인 (C) her가 정답이다.

번역 시글락 씨는 앱 설계가 자신의 연구를 토대로 한 것이라고 말했다.

어휘 state 말하다, 밝히다   based on ~에 근거하여

109 접속사 자리 _ 부사절 접속사 / 어휘

해설 뒤에 the organization이 주어, has doubled가 동사, its outreach efforts가 목적어인 완전한 절이 왔으므로, 빈칸에는 부사절 접속사가 들어가야 한다. 문맥상 '지원 활동을 두 배로 늘렸지만'이라는 내용이 되어야 자연스러우므로 '~이기는 하지만'이라는 뜻의 접속사 (C) Although가 정답이다. 부사절 접속사 (A) Until은 '~까지', (B) Because는 '~ 때문에'라는 뜻으로 문맥상 적절하지 않고, (D) Therefore는 '그러므로'라는 접속부사로 절을 연결할 수 없다.

번역 그 조직은 지원 활동을 두 배로 늘렸지만 아직 신규 고객의 증가는 보지 못했다.

어휘 organization 조직   double 두 배로 늘리다   outreach 지원 활동   effort 노력, 활동   have yet to 아직 ~하지 않았다

110 형용사 자리 _ 수량 형용사

해설 빈칸은 주어 역할을 하는 복합명사 board of education meetings를 수식하는 형용사 자리이다. meetings가 복수이므로 '모든'이라는 뜻으로 복수명사를 수식할 수 있는 (A) all이 정답이다. (B) so는 접속사/부사, (D) to는 전치사/to부정사이므로 품사상 답이 될 수 없고, (C) that은 형용사로 쓰일 경우 뒤에 단수명사가 와야 한다.

번역 10월 8일부터 모든 교육 위원회 회의는 학군 웹사이트에서 생중계될 예정이다.

어휘 board of education 교육 위원회   stream (방송이나 동영상을) 중계하다, 스트리밍하다   live 생방송으로   school district 학군

111 형용사 자리 _ 명사 수식 / 어휘

해설 빈칸은 명사 experience를 수식하는 형용사 자리이다. '다양한 헤어 제품을 가지고 일한 많은 경험'이라는 의미가 되어야 하므로 '많은, 상당한'이라는 뜻의 (B) considerable이 정답이다. (A) considers는 동사이므로 품사상 답이 될 수 없고, (C) considerate은 '사려 깊은'을 뜻하는 형용사로 명사 experience와 어울리지 않으며, (D) considering은 현재분사일 경우 '고려하는'을 뜻하므로 문맥상 적절하지 않다.

번역 어바나이트 살롱의 미용사들은 다양한 헤어 제품을 다루는 데 많은 경험을 가지고 있다.

어휘 a variety of 다양한   product 제품

112 부사 어휘

해설 형용사 suitable을 수식하여 적절한 문맥을 완성하는 부사를 고르는 문제이다. '후보자 둘 다 동등하게 적합하다'라는 내용이 되어야 자연스러우므로 '동등하게, 똑같이'를 뜻하는 (C) equally가 정답이다. (A) permanently는 '영구적으로', (B) promptly는 '즉시', (D) gradually는 '점차적으로'라는 의미이다.

번역 두 후보자 모두 대리 직책에 동등하게 적합하다.

어휘 candidate 후보자   suitable 적합한

113 부사 자리 _ 동사 수식

해설 빈칸은 동사구 has expanded를 수식하는 부사 자리로, 문맥상 '크게 확장했다'라는 의미가 되어야 하므로 '크게'를 뜻하는 부사 (D) greatly가 정답이다. (B) greatness는 명사로 품사상 빈칸에 들어갈 수 없고, 주로 형용사로 쓰이는 (A) greater와 (C) great는 부사로 쓰이기도 하지만 '아주 잘'이라는 뜻으로 보통 동사 뒤에 온다.

번역 블룸 서킷 인수를 통해 웰스트롬 하드웨어는 제품 및 서비스를 크게 확장했다.

어휘 acquisition 인수   expand 확장하다   offering 제품, 팔 것

114 동사 어휘

해설 빈칸 뒤의 명사구 capital letters or spaces를 목적어로 취해 적절한 문맥을 만드는 동사를 골라야 한다. '대문자나 공백이 들어 있으면 안 된다'라는 내용이 되어야 하므로 '~이 들어 있다'라는 뜻의 (B) contain이 정답이다. (A) differ는 '다르다'라는 뜻의 자동사로 목적어를 취할 수 없으므로 빈칸에 들어갈 수 없고, (C) match는 '맞추다', (D) pick은 '고르다'라는 의미로 문맥상 적합하지 않다.

번역 파일 이름에는 대문자나 공백이 들어 있으면 안 된다는 점에 유의하십시오.

어휘 note 유의하다   capital letter 대문자   space (글자 사이의) 공백, 띄어쓰기

115 형용사 어휘

해설 빈칸 뒤의 명사 customers를 수식하여 적절한 문맥을 완성하는 형용사를 골라야 한다. 별 5개 평가를 15,000개 이상 받았다고 했으므로 '만족한 고객'이라는 의미가 되어야 적절하다. 따라서 '만족한'을 뜻하는 (A) satisfied가 정답이다. (B) checked는 '확인된', (C) adjusted는 '조정된', (D) allowed는 '허용된'이라는 의미이다.

번역 선-테크 천장 선풍기는 만족한 고객으로부터 별 5개 평가를 15,000개 이상 받았다.

어휘 ceiling 천장   fan 팬, 선풍기

116 동사 어형 _ 명령문의 동사원형

해설 Please로 시작하는 명령문의 동사 자리로 동사원형이 들어가야 한다. 따라서 (A) visit가 정답이다. (B) visits는 3인칭 단수주어와 쓰이는 동사의 현재형, (C) visited는 동사의 과거형/과거분사, (D) visiting은 동명사/현재분사이므로 답이 될 수 없다.

번역 주문 제품에 조금이라도 불만이 있으시면 당사 웹사이트의 반품 섹션을 방문하십시오.

117 명사 어휘

해설 빈칸에 들어갈 명사는 자동차 회사에서 중고 차량에 대해 제공하는 것이어야 하므로 앞의 형용사 excellent와 함께 '훌륭한 할인 혜택, 특가'라는 의미가 되어야 적합하다. 따라서 '할인 혜택, 특가'라는 뜻을 지닌 (D) deals가 정답이다. (A)의 trip은 '여행', (B)의 reason은 '이유', (C) customs는 '세관'이라는 의미로 자동차 회사가 중고 차량과 관련해 제공하는 것이 되기에는 부적절하다.

번역 이토 자동차 그룹은 이번 달에 중고 차량에 대해 훌륭한 할인 혜택을 제공합니다.

어휘 pre-owned 중고의   vehicle 차량

118 전치사 자리 / 어휘

해설 빈칸은 수동태로 쓰인 완전한 절(Product prices are influenced) 뒤에 명사구 such factors를 연결하는 전치사 자리이다. 문맥상 '그러한 요소들에 의해 영향을 받는다'는 의미가 되어야 하므로 '~에 의하여'라는 의미인 (A) by가 정답이다. (B) under는 '~ 아래'를 뜻하는 전치사/부사로 문맥상 어울리지 않고, (C) those는 지시대명사/지시형용사, (D) nearly는 '거의'라는 뜻의 부사이므로 품사상 답이 될 수 없다.

번역 제품 가격은 소비자 수요와 소매 경쟁과 같은 요인에 의해 영향을 받는다.

어휘 influence 영향을 미치다   such A as B B와 같은 A   factor 요인   consumer 소비자   demand 수요   retail 소매   competition 경쟁

119 동사 어휘

해설 be동사 뒤에 현재분사 형태로 들어가 빈칸 뒤의 명사구 prefabricated houses를 목적어로 취해 적절한 문맥을 완성하는 동사를 고르는 문제이다. '조립식 주택을 상품으로 판촉할 것이다'라는 내용이 되어야 자연스러우므로 '(상품을) 판촉하다, 마케팅하다'라는 뜻의 (D) marketing이 정답이다. (A)의 predict는 '예측하다', (B)의 pass는 '지나가다', (C)의 retain은 '유지하다'라는 뜻으로 문맥상 어울리지 않는다.

번역 몬머스 엔터프라이시스는 4월 1일부터 온라인으로 조립식 주택을 상품으로 판촉할 예정이다.

어휘 prefabricated 조립식의

120 재귀대명사

해설 빈칸은 동사 should familiarize의 목적어 자리로, 목적어 자리에 들어갈 수 있는 목적격 인칭대명사 (B) them, 소유대명사 (C) theirs, 재귀대명사 (D) themselves 중 하나를 선택해야 한다. 모든 직원이 회사 정책 및 절차에 익숙하게 만들어야 하는 대상은 그들 자신이므로 주어 All employees를 가리키며 주어와 목적어가 동일할 경우 쓰이는 재귀대명사 (D) themselves가 정답이다.

번역 모든 직원은 회사의 정책 및 절차를 익혀야 한다.

어휘 familiarize oneself with ~을 익히다, 숙지하다   policy 정책   procedure 절차

121 전치사 어휘

해설 빈칸 뒤 시간을 나타내는 명사구 the time이 있고, 문맥상 '주문 시에'라는 의미가 되어야 하므로 '~에'를 뜻하는 시간의 전치사 (D) at이 정답이다. (A) as는 '~로서, ~같이', (B) off는 '~에서 떨어져서', (C) into는 '~ 속으로'를 뜻하므로 문맥상 적절하지 않다.

번역 맞춤 가구 주문에는 주문 시 50퍼센트의 보증금이 필요하다.

어휘 custom 맞춤의   deposit 보증금

122 명사 자리 _ 동사의 목적어

해설 부정관사 a와 함께 동사 are planning의 목적어 역할을 하는 명사 자리로, 문맥상 '20주년 기념행사'라는 의미가 되어야 하므로 '기념행사'를 뜻하는 (A) celebration이 정답이다. (B) celebrated는 동사/과거분사, (D) celebrate는 동사로 품사상 빈칸에 들어갈 수 없고, 명사 (C) celebrity는 '유명 인사'라는 뜻으로 문맥상 적절하지 않다.

번역 우리는 클렘너 사의 20주년 기념행사를 기획하고 있다.

어휘 anniversary 기념일

123 부사 어휘

해설 형용사 impressive를 수식하여 적절한 문맥을 만드는 부사를 고르는 문제이다. '꽤 강한 인상을 주었다'는 내용이 되어야 자연스러우므로 '꽤, 상당히'라는 의미의 (A) quite가 정답이다. (B) soon은 주로 미래 시제에서 사용되고, (C) ever는 '지금까지'라는 의미로 비교급, 최상급을 강조하는 데 쓰이며, (D) next는 '다음에'라는 의미이다.

번역 디아즈 씨는 비록 정치적 경험은 부족하지만 시장으로서의 첫 임기 중에는 꽤 강한 인상을 주었다.

어휘 lack ~이 부족하다   political 정치적인   impressive 강한 인상을 주는, 인상적인   term 임기   mayor 시장

124 형용사 자리 _ 명사 수식

해설 빈칸에는 동사 acquires의 목적어인 명사 copies를 수식하는 형용사 또는 복합명사를 이루는 명사가 들어갈 수 있다. '베스트셀러 책 여러 권'이라는 의미가 되어야 하므로 '여러, 다수의'를 뜻하는 형용사 (B) multiple이 정답이다. (A) multiply는 '곱하다'라는 뜻의 동사이므로 품사상 답이 될 수 없고, (C) multiples는 '배수', (D) multiplicity는 '다양성'이라는 뜻의 명사로 copies와 복합명사를 만들지 않으므로 오답이다.

번역 대학 도서관은 보통 학생들의 수요를 맞추기 위해 베스트셀러 책을 여러 권 구입한다.

어휘 acquire 획득하다   meet one's demand 수요를 맞추다

125 부사 자리 _ 동사 수식

해설 동사구 were donated를 수식하는 부사 자리이므로 '후하게'라는 뜻의 부사 (C) generously가 정답이다. (A) generous는 형용사, (B) generosity와 (D) generosities는 명사이므로 품사상 빈칸에 들어갈 수 없다.

번역 올해 학회의 토트백은 에타니 디자인스가 후하게 기부해 주었다.

어휘 conference 학회, 회의 donate 기부하다 generous 후한 generosity 관대함

126 명사 어휘

해설 콴 씨의 30년 경력을 기리기 위한 것이라는 내용으로 보아 '축하연을 연다'라는 의미가 되어야 적절하다. 따라서 '축하연'을 뜻하는 (C) reception이 정답이다. (A) record는 '기록', (B) share는 '몫', (D) place는 '장소'를 뜻하므로 문맥상 어울리지 않는다.

번역 콴 씨의 30년간의 엔지니어링 경력을 기리기 위해 금요일에 축하연을 열 예정입니다.

어휘 hold (행사 등을) 열다, 개최하다 honor 기리다

127 전치사 자리

해설 앞에 완전한 절(Groove Background creates ~ music)이 있으므로 빈칸 뒤 명사구 classical and jazz와 함께 수식어구를 이끄는 전치사 자리이다. 따라서 '~을 포함하여'라는 의미의 전치사 (B) including이 정답이다. (A) instead(대신에), (C) in addition (게다가), (D) indeed(사실)는 모두 부사로 품사상 답이 될 수 없다.

번역 그루브 백그라운드는 클래식과 재즈를 포함하는 편안한 기악곡 재생 목록을 만들어 준다.

어휘 soothing 마음을 달래는, 위로가 되는 playlist 재생 목록 instrumental 악기의

128 동사 자리 _ 태

해설 주어 Members of the finance department의 동사 자리로, 타동사인 invite(초대하다) 뒤에 목적어가 없고 전치사 to가 있으므로 수동태가 와야 한다. 따라서 (D) are invited가 정답이다. (A) to be invited는 to부정사, (B) inviting은 동명사/현재분사이므로 품사상 답이 될 수 없고, (C) invite는 능동형 동사이므로 뒤에 목적어가 필요하다.

번역 재무부서 직원들은 주아 씨의 리스크 방지에 대한 강의에 초대되었습니다.

어휘 lecture 강의 risk 위험 avoidance 방지, 회피

129 전치사 어휘

해설 빈칸 앞의 몇 시간 동안 논의했다는 내용으로 보아 빈칸 뒤의 the revised hiring policies는 토론의 주제로 연결되어야 자연스럽다. 따라서 '~에 대한, ~을 두고'라는 뜻의 전치사 (C) over가 정답이다. (A) during은 '~ 동안', (B) above는 '~보다 위에', (D) across는

'~을 가로질러'라는 의미로 문맥상 적절하지 않다.

번역 이사회는 개정된 고용 정책을 놓고 몇 시간 동안 논의했다.

어휘 board 위원회 trustee 이사 debate 논의하다 revised 수정된

130 현재분사

해설 The participants가 주어, tend가 동사인 문장이다. 따라서 빈칸에는 명사구 the fitness instructor's movements를 목적어로 취하면서 주어 The participants를 수식하는 준동사가 들어가야 하므로, '따라 하는, 모방하는'이라는 뜻의 현재분사 (D) imitating이 정답이다. (A) imitate는 동사, (B) imitations는 명사, (C) imitative는 형용사로 빈칸에 들어갈 수 없다.

번역 피트니스 강사의 동작을 유심히 따라 하는 참가자들은 적절한 기술을 더 빨리 익히는 경향이 있다.

어휘 participant 참가자 closely 유심히, 면밀히 instructor 강사 movement 동작, 움직임 tend to ~하는 경향이 있다 proper 적절한 imitation 모조품 imitative 모방하는

PART 6
131-134 기사

> **식료품 체인에서 행사를 주최하다**
>
> 레이튼 (10월 8일) — 이 지역에서 가장 큰 슈퍼마켓 체인 중 하나인 오헤일 푸즈에서 100여 개에 달하는 일자리를 채우고자 한다. 이러한 이유로, 이 회사는 10월 20일에 **131 채용** 행사를 열 예정이다. 현재 14개의 모든 오헤일 매장에 일자리 기회가 있다. **132 추가적으로,** 오헤일은 아직 공사 중인 웨스트사이드의 신규 매장을 위한 직원도 모집한다. **133 이곳의 개점은 11월 중순으로 예정되어 있다.**
>
> 행사에 **134 참석하려는** 사람들은 오전 10시에서 오후 7시 사이에 팰리스 스위치 호텔 그랜드 볼룸으로 이력서 사본을 가져와야 한다. 예약은 필요하지 않다.
>
> ---
>
> **어휘** grocery 식료 잡화 host 주최하다 seek to ~하려고 (시도)하다 fill 채우다 opportunity 기회 exist 존재하다 under construction 공사 중인 appointment 예약 required 필요한

131 명사 자리 / 어휘 _ 복합명사

해설 앞에 부정관사 a, 뒤에 명사 event가 있으므로 빈칸에는 event를 수식하는 형용사나 복합명사를 이루는 명사가 들어갈 수 있다. 앞 문장에서 슈퍼마켓 체인 오헤일 푸즈에서 100여 개에 달하는 일자리를 채우고자 한다는 것으로 보아 이 회사에서 '채용 행사'를 연다는 내용이 되어야 문맥상 자연스럽다. 따라서 빈칸 뒤의 명사 event와 함께 '채용 행사'라는 의미의 복합명사를 만들 수 있는 '채용'이라는 뜻의 명사 (B) hiring이 정답이다. (A) manufacturing은 명사로 '제조업', (C) political은 형용사로 '정치적인', (D) sporting은 형용사일 때 '스포츠의', 명사인 경우 '스포츠'라는 뜻이므로 문맥상 어울리지 않는다.

132 접속부사

해설 앞 문장에서 현재 14개의 모든 오헤일 매장에 일자리 기회가 있다 (Job opportunities exist at all ~ stores)고 했고, 뒤 문장에서 아직 공사 중인 웨스트사이드의 신규 매장을 위한 직원도 모집한다 (Ohale is seeking employees for its new Westside location) 며 기존 매장 이외에 새로 개점할 매장을 위해서도 직원을 추가적으로 모집할 예정이라고 언급하고 있다. 따라서 '추가적으로, 또한'이라는 의미의 (C) Additionally가 정답이다. (A) If not은 '그렇지 않다면', (B) After all은 '결국', (D) For example은 '예를 들어'라는 뜻이므로 문맥상 적절하지 않다.

133 문맥에 맞는 문장 고르기

번역 (A) 이곳의 개점은 11월 중순으로 예정되어 있다.
(B) 대부분의 지원자들은 이전 경력이 있다.
(C) 분석가들은 린다 오쿠무가 최고 경영자로 임명된 것에 놀랐다.
(D) 지역 경쟁업체들은 그곳과 가격을 맞출 수가 없다.

해설 빈칸 앞에서 아직 공사 중인 웨스트사이드의 신규 매장(its new Westside location)을 위한 직원도 모집한다고 했으므로 빈칸에는 이 새로운 매장에 대한 내용이 연결되어야 자연스럽다. 따라서 신규 매장의 개점 예정 시기를 언급하고 있는 (A)가 정답이다.

어휘 prior 이전의 appointment 임명 analyst 분석가 competitor 경쟁업체 match 대등하게 만들다

134 동사 자리 _ 시제

해설 빈칸은 선행사 Those를 수식하는 관계사절(who ~ the event)의 동사 자리이다. 기사가 발행된 날짜는 10월 8일(October 8)이고, 빈칸 뒤 the event는 앞에서 언급된 10월 20일에 열릴 채용 행사를 가리키는 것이므로 미래를 나타내는 시제가 들어가야 한다. 따라서 가까운 미래의 계획된 일정을 나타낼 때 쓰이는 현재진행형 (D) are attending이 정답이다. (A) attending은 동명사/현재분사, (B) to attend는 to부정사이므로 빈칸에 들어갈 수 없고, (C) attended는 과거형 동사/과거분사이므로 답이 될 수 없다.

135-138 설명

아자즈 물 필터 주전자를 구매해 주셔서 감사합니다. 이 제품은 맛있는 물을 위한 훌륭한 해결책입니다! 아자즈 물 필터 주전자의 효능을 높이기 위해 첫 사용 전에 필터를 활성화시켜 주시기를 ¹³⁵ **권장합니다.** ¹³⁶ **이를 위해 3분 동안 차가운 수돗물을 필터를 통해 흘려보내세요.** 그런 다음 필터를 물 주전자의 뚜껑 안에 ¹³⁷ **꽉** 맞을 때까지 시계 방향으로 조이세요. 물 주전자를 사용할 때 ¹³⁸ **약해진** 물의 흐름은 필터가 막히고 있으며 곧 교체되어야 한다는 신호임을 기억하세요.

어휘 purchase 구매 pitcher 물주전자 effectiveness 효능 prime 활성화시키다 screw 돌려서 조이다 clockwise 시계 방향으로 lid 뚜껑 fit 맞다 flow 흐름 clog (관, 배수구 등을) 막히게 하다 replace 교체하다

135 동사 어휘

해설 앞 문장에서 아자즈 물 필터 주전자 구매에 감사하다고 한 것으로 보아 이 글은 제품 구입 시 딸려 오는 사용 설명서임을 알 수 있다. 따라서 '첫 사용 전에 필터를 활성화시켜 줄 것을 권장한다'며 고객에게 제품 사용법을 설명하거나 권고사항을 안내하는 내용이 되어야 적절하므로 '권장[추천]하다'라는 뜻의 (B) recommend가 정답이다. (A)의 try는 목적어 자리에 동명사가 올 경우 '시도하다, 해보다'라는 뜻이고, (C) consider는 '고려하다', (D) start는 '시작하다'라는 의미이다.

136 문맥에 맞는 문장 고르기

번역 (A) 우리의 여과 시스템은 내년 안에 재설계될 것입니다.
(B) 식기세척기 사용 횟수를 줄임으로써 물 사용을 줄일 수 있습니다.
(C) 이를 위해 3분 동안 차가운 수돗물을 필터를 통해 흘려보내세요.
(D) 주 저장 탱크에는 항상 150리터의 물이 있습니다.

해설 빈칸 앞에는 필터 주전자의 효능을 높이기 위해 사용 전 필터 활성화 작업(priming the filter)을 권장한다고 했고, 빈칸 뒤에는 그런 다음 필터를 주전자 뚜껑에 맞게 조이라는 지침을 설명하고 있다. 따라서 빈칸에는 필터를 뚜껑에 끼우기 전 필터 준비 작업에 해당하는 지침이 들어가야 연결이 자연스러우므로, 3분간 수돗물을 필터를 통해 흘려보내라는 지침을 설명하고 있는 (C)가 정답이다.

어휘 filtration 여과 redesign 재설계하다 reduce 줄이다 run 작동하다; (액체를) 흐르게 하다 dishwasher 식기세척기 frequently 자주 tap water 수돗물 storage 저장

137 부사 어휘

해설 빈칸은 '(모양, 크기 등이 어떤 물건에) 맞다'를 뜻하는 동사 fits를 수식하는 부사 자리로, '필터(it)를 꽉 맞을 때까지'라는 의미가 되어야 하므로 '꽉, 단단하게'를 뜻하는 (C) tightly가 정답이다. (A) extremely는 '극히', (B) highly는 '매우'라는 뜻의 강조 부사로, 주로 형용사와 부사를 수식하므로 동사 fits와는 함께 쓰이지 않는다. (D) steadily는 '꾸준히'라는 뜻으로 문맥상 적절하지 않다.

138 형용사 자리 _ 명사 수식 / 과거분사

해설 빈칸은 that절의 주어인 복합명사 water flow를 수식하는 형용사 자리이므로 과거분사 (A) diminished나 형용사 (D) diminishable이 들어갈 수 있다. '약해진 물의 흐름'이라는 의미가 되어야 자연스러우므로 '약해진, 감소된'을 뜻하는 (A) diminished가 정답이다. (D) diminishable은 '줄일 수 있는'이라는 뜻으로 문맥상 적절하지 않으며, '약해지다, 줄어들다'를 뜻하는 동사 (B) diminishes와 (C) diminish는 품사상 빈칸에 들어갈 수 없다.

139-142 정책

제품 반품

애브니 홈 프로덕츠는 뛰어난 서비스를 제공하기 위해 전념하고 있으며 카탈로그에 있는 전 제품의 ¹³⁹ **상태**를 보증합니다. 구매 제품에 만족하

지 않으시면 339-555-0177로 고객 서비스 라인에 전화하셔서 반품 승인 코드를 요청하십시오. 서비스 담당자가 제품 안내서에 있는 청구서 번호를 140 **요청할 것입니다.** 141 **제품을 반송하실 때 반드시 승인 코드를 포함시켜 주십시오.** 애브니 홈 프로덕츠는 상품 반송 시 배송비를 142 **책임지지** 않는다는 점에 유념하십시오.

> 어휘 return 반품하다; 반품 merchandise 제품, 상품 be committed to ~에 전념하다 outstanding 뛰어난 guarantee 품질 보증을 하다 authorization 승인 agent 직원, 대리인 invoice 청구서 package insert (약이나 제품 포장 안에 있는) 제품 안내서 postage 우송료, 우편 요금

139 명사 어휘

해설 상품 반품 정책을 설명하는 글이므로 '카탈로그에 있는 전 제품의 상태를 보증한다'는 내용이 되어야 적합하다. 따라서 '상태'를 뜻하는 (A) condition이 정답이다. (B) object는 '물건', (C) explanation은 '설명', (D) preview는 '사전 검토'라는 의미이다.

140 동사의 시제

해설 빈칸은 주어 The service agent의 동사 자리이며 알맞은 시제를 골라야 한다. 앞 문장에서 구매 제품 불만족 시 취할 수 있는 절차에 대한 설명으로 고객 서비스 라인에 전화해 반품 승인 코드를 요청하라고 했고, 빈칸이 있는 문장은 전화를 받는 서비스 담당자가 하게 될 절차를 설명하고 있으므로 '서비스 담당자가 청구서 번호를 요청할 것'이라는 내용이 되어야 한다. 따라서 미래 시제인 (D) will ask가 정답이다. 참고로, 현재진행형인 (B) is asking도 미래 시제를 대신할 수 있지만, 가까운 미래의 정해진 일정을 나타내므로 해당 문맥에는 적절하지 않다.

141 문맥에 맞는 문장 고르기

번역 (A) 우리 직원들은 소프트웨어 교육을 받고 있으며 문제 해결에 능숙합니다.
(B) 가구 배송을 취소하시려면 주문 후 24시간 이내에 전화 주십시오.
(C) 제품을 반송하실 때 반드시 승인 코드를 포함시켜 주십시오.
(D) 카탈로그에는 주방용품, 조명, 가전제품 등에 대한 섹션이 있습니다.

해설 앞에서 제품 불만족 시 전화로 반품 승인 코드를 요청할 것과 이때 서비스 담당자가 청구서 번호를 요청할 것이라며 반품 절차를 안내하고 있다. 따라서 빈칸에는 제품 반품과 관련된 다음 절차를 안내하는 내용이 들어가야 자연스러우므로 제품 반송 시 승인 코드를 포함해 달라고 설명하고 있는 (C)가 정답이다.

어휘 be skilled at ~에 능숙하다 resolve 해결하다 section 구획 goods 제품 lighting 조명 appliance 가전제품

142 형용사 자리 _ 주격 보어

해설 빈칸은 be동사 is 뒤 주격 보어 자리이므로 형용사나 분사, 또는 명사가 들어갈 수 있다. '배송비를 책임지지 않는다'라는 내용이 되어야 하므로 '(~에 대해) 책임을 져야 할'을 뜻하는 형용사

(B) responsible이 정답이다. (A) responsibly는 부사이므로 빈칸에 들어갈 수 없고, 명사인 (C) responsibility(책임)와 (D) responsibleness(책임짐)는 주어인 Abney Home Products와 동격이 아니므로 오답이다.

143-146 회람

> 수신: 전 직원
> 발신: 마리나 파판토니오, 안전 연락 담당자
> 날짜: 11월 12일
> 제목: 안전 교육
>
> 다시 한번 연례 안전 교육 워크숍을 할 시기가 왔습니다. 올해 훈련은 사기 방지 및 사이버 공격에 대비하여 방어하는 것과 같은 디지털 안전 조치에 중점을 둘 것입니다. 우리의 기술 전문가들은 위험을 줄이기 위하여 이미 당사의 정보 시스템 전반에 새로운 프로그램을 설치하였습니다. 143 **하지만,** 우리 모두는 프로그램이 어떻게 작동하고 문제 발생 시 무엇을 해야 하는지 알아야 할 필요가 있습니다.
>
> 144 **모두를** 수용하기 위해 다음 주 내내 워크숍이 여럿 실시될 예정입니다. 당사의 내부 전산망 페이지에서 이 145 **세션들** 중 하나에 등록할 수 있습니다. '안전 교육' 링크를 클릭하십시오.
>
> 146 **등록에 최선을 다해 주십시오.** 어떤 사유로든 본 워크숍의 어떤 일정에도 참여할 수 없는 경우, 상관에게 반드시 알려야 합니다.

> 어휘 liaison 연락 담당자 focus on ~에 초점을 두다[집중하다] measure 조치 avoid 막다, 피하다 scam 사기 cyberattack 사이버 공격 install 설치하다 arise 발생하다 accommodate 수용하다 conduct (특정 활동을) 하다 upcoming 다가오는 register for ~에 등록하다 intranet 내부 전산망 take part in ~에 참여하다 supervisor 상관, 상사

143 접속부사 ▶ 동영상 강의

해설 앞 문장에서는 기술 전문가들이 위험을 줄이기 위해 이미 시스템 전반에 새로운 프로그램을 설치했다(Our technology experts already have installed new programs ~ to reduce risk)고 했는데, 빈칸 뒤에서는 우리 모두가 프로그램 작동법과 유사시 할 일을 알고 있어야 한다(we all need to understand how the programs work ~ when a problem arises)고 했다. 전문가가 아니더라도 우리 모두가 이와 관련해 처리 방안을 알고 있어야 한다는 서로 상반되는 내용이므로 '하지만, 그러나'라는 의미의 (B) However가 정답이다. (A) If so는 '그렇다면', (C) Otherwise는 '그렇지 않으면', (D) In that case는 '그런 경우에는'이라는 뜻으로 문맥에 적합하지 않다.

144 부정대명사

해설 빈칸은 to부정사구 To accommodate의 목적어 자리이고, '모두를 수용하기 위해 워크숍이 여럿 진행될 것'이라는 내용이 되어야 하므로 '모두, 모든 사람'을 뜻하는 부정대명사 (D) everyone이 정답이다. (A) itself는 재귀대명사로 주어와 목적어가 동일한 경우에 쓰이며, 소유대명사 (B) his는 목적어 자리에 들어갈 수는 있으나 '그의 것'을 나타내는 대상이 앞에 언급되어야 하고, (C) whose는 의문사/관계대명사이므로 품사상 빈칸에 들어갈 수 없다.

145 명사 어휘

▶ 동영상 강의

해설 앞 문장에서 다음 주 내내 워크숍이 여럿(several workshops) 진행될 예정이라고 했으므로 빈칸에는 워크숍을 대신할 수 있는 명사가 들어가야 한다. 따라서 '(특정 활동) 시간[기간]'을 뜻하는 (A) sessions가 정답이다. (B)의 position은 '위치', (C)의 conference는 '회의', (D)의 competition은 '대회, 경쟁'을 뜻한다.

146 문맥에 맞는 문장 고르기

번역 (A) 사이버 공격이 증가하고 있습니다.
(B) 교육은 매년 여름에 열립니다.
(C) 등록에 최선을 다해 주십시오.
(D) 작년 프로그램은 취소되었습니다.

해설 앞에서 모두를 수용하기 위해 다음 주 내내 여러 워크숍이 진행되며 내부 전산망 페이지에서 '안전 교육' 링크를 클릭하면 등록할 수 있다고 했고, 빈칸 뒤에는 참여할 수 없는 경우 상관에게 반드시 알려야 한다고 했다. 앞뒤 문장 모두 워크숍 등록 및 참여에 대한 내용이므로 빈칸에도 워크숍 등록과 관련된 내용이 들어가야 연결이 자연스럽다. 따라서 등록에 최선을 다해 달라며 워크숍 참석을 권장하고 있는 (C)가 정답이다.

어휘 on the rise 증가하고 있는   make every effort to ~하는 데 최선[전력]을 다하다   cancel 취소하다

PART 7

147-148 광고

부엉이와 달

147 매트리스 하나를 구매하시고 멋진 러그 하나를 무료로 선택하세요!

owlandmoon.co.uk에서 결제하실 때 다음 쿠폰 코드를 사용하세요: ESSZRS4T

우리 매트리스는 고객님 댁으로 바로 배송되며 보통 일주일 내에 도착합니다. 148 매트리스를 90일 동안 사용해 보고 만족스럽지 못하면 전액 환불을 위해 반송하세요. 또한 모든 가구에 대해 2년간 저금리 할부를 제공합니다.

어휘 owl 부엉이   check out 결제하다   directly 곧바로
low-interest 저금리의   financing 할부, 융자

---

147 주제 / 목적

번역 광고되고 있는 제품의 종류는?
(A) 캠핑 장비
(B) 가정용품
(C) 사무기기
(D) 자동차 부속품

해설 첫 문장에서 매트리스 하나를 구매하고 멋진 러그 하나를 무료로 선택하라(Buy one mattress, and choose one of our beautiful rugs for free!)며 가정용품에 속하는 매트리스를 광고하고 있다. 따

라서 (B)가 정답이다.

어휘 gear 장비   household 가정   accessories 부속품

148 Not / True

번역 회사에 대해 명시된 것은?
(A) 2년 동안 사업을 해왔다.
(B) 제품 반품을 허용한다.
(C) 당일 배송을 한다.
(D) 매년 세일을 한다.

해설 세 번째 단락의 두 번째 문장에서 매트리스를 90일 동안 사용해 보고 만족스럽지 못하면 전액 환불을 위해 반송하라(Try out a mattress for 90 days ~ send it back for a full refund)고 안내하고 있으므로 (B)가 정답이다. 보통 일주일 내에 도착한다(usually arrive within one week)고 했으므로 (C)는 오답이며, 지문에 언급된 2년은 저금리 할부 제공(offer low-interest financing for two years)에 관한 것으로 사업 기간과는 무관하므로 (A) 또한 정답이 될 수 없다.

어휘 in business 사업을 하는   accept 허용하다   yearly 매년 하는

Paraphrasing   지문의 send it back for a full refund
→ 정답의 product returns

149-150 이메일

수신: 데마코 하인즈 ⟨d.hines@worldmail.com⟩
발신: 박순이 ⟨customerservice@thebestbags.co.kr⟩
제목: 품목 F208 (캔버스 여행 가방)
날짜: 6월 19일

하인즈 씨께,

149 주문하신 베스트 백스 캔버스 여행 가방이 현재 요청하신 색상으로 구입이 불가능합니다. 고객님께 제공되는 옵션이 몇 가지 있습니다.

1. 주문을 취소하시면 흔쾌히 전액 환불해 드리겠습니다.

2. 150 다른 색상을 선택해 주세요. 해당 품목은 현재 하늘색, 진녹색, 진회색으로 구매 가능합니다.

3. 저희 웹사이트나 카탈로그에서 동일한 가격의 제품을 선택해 주십시오.

4. 150 주문하신 연회색 품목이 재입고될 때까지 기다려 주십시오. 3주에서 5주 정도 소요됩니다.

어떤 옵션이 마음에 드는지 알려 주십시오. 불편을 드려 죄송합니다.

감사합니다,

박순이, 고객 서비스 담당자

어휘   overnight bag 작은 여행 가방   available 구입할 수 있는, 제공되는   gladly 흔쾌히, 기꺼이   select 선택하다   equal 동일한   value 가격, 가치   in stock 재고가 있는   apologize 사과하다   inconvenience 불편

---

149 주제 / 목적

번역 이메일의 목적은?
(A) 주문품 배송을 확인하려고
(B) 반품 수령을 알리려고
(C) 주문품에 대한 대안을 제시하려고
(D) 주문에 대해 고객에게 감사의 뜻을 전하려고

해설 첫 문장에서 고객이 주문한 베스트 백스 캔버스 여행 가방이 현재 요청한 색상으로 구입이 불가능하다(The Best Bags canvas overnight bag you ordered is not currently available in the colour you requested)며 고객에게 제공되는 옵션이 몇 가지 있다(There are several options available to you)고 한 것으로 보아 주문한 제품 대신 선택할 수 있는 대안을 제안하기 위한 글임을 알 수 있다. 따라서 (C)가 정답이다.

어휘 acknowledge (우편 등을) 받았음을 알리다   alternative 대안

150 세부사항

번역 현재 구입이 불가능한 색상의 가방은?
(A) 하늘색 가방
(B) 진녹색 가방
(C) 진회색 가방
(D) 연회색 가방

해설 옵션 제안의 2번 항목에서 다른 색상을 선택해 달라(Select a different colour)며 해당 품목은 현재 하늘색, 진녹색, 진회색으로 구매 가능하다(That item is currently available in light blue, dark green, and dark gray)고 했고, 4번 항목에서 주문한 연회색 품목이 재입고될 때까지 기다려 달라(Wait until the item you ordered is back in stock in light gray)고 한 것으로 보아 현재 재고가 없어 구입이 불가능한 가방은 연회색임을 알 수 있다. 따라서 (D)가 정답이다.

151-152 문자 메시지

크리스티 모로프 (오전 9시 47분)
좋은 아침입니다, 렌. 방금 당신 사무실에 들렀어요.

렌 노무라 (오전 9시 48분)
그럼 오늘 제가 사무실에 없는 것을 벌써 알고 계시겠네요.

크리스티 모로프 (오전 9시 48분)
네, 151 이름은 기억나지 않지만 당신의 새로운 회사 동료가 당신이 화요일마다 원격 근무를 시작했다고 알려 줬어요. 152 저는 빈 바인더를 몇 개 찾고 있었어요.

렌 노무라 (오전 9시 49분)
그녀는 셰릴이에요. 이미 만나신 줄 알았어요. 물품 보관함에 바인더가 있나요?

크리스티 모로프 (오전 9시 50분)
아니요, 방금 확인했어요. 프랭크가 좀 더 주문했는데 다음 주나 되어서야 올 거예요. 152 저는 지금 두세 개 정도 필요해요.

렌 노무라 (오전 9시 51분)
셰릴에게 문의해 보세요. 그녀는 정말 도움이 돼요.

크리스티 모로프 (오전 9시 52분)
알겠습니다. 그럴게요.

어휘 stop by ~에 들르다   mate 동료   remotely 원격으로   binder (종이 등을 함께 묶는) 바인더   supply closet 물품 보관함

151 추론 / 암시

 동영상 강의

번역 노무라 씨에 대해 암시된 것은?
(A) 보통 화요일에는 근무하지 않는다.
(B) 모로프 씨와 사무실을 같이 쓴다.
(C) 최근에 사무용품을 구매했다.
(D) 일주일에 하루는 외부에서 근무한다.

해설 9시 48분에 모로프 씨가 노무라 씨에게 노무라 씨의 새로운 직장 동료가 노무라 씨는 화요일마다 원격 근무를 시작했다고 알려 주었다(your new office mate ~ told me that you just started working remotely on Tuesdays)고 했으므로 노무라 씨는 화요일마다 사무실에서 근무하지 않는다는 것을 알 수 있다. 따라서 (D)가 정답이다.

어휘 off-site 부지 밖에서

Paraphrasing 지문의 working remotely
→ 정답의 works off-site

152 의도 파악

번역 오전 9시 51분에 노무라 씨가 "셰릴에게 문의해 보세요"라고 쓴 의도는?
(A) 셰릴이 여분의 바인더를 가지고 있을 수 있다.
(B) 셰릴이 구매를 승인해야 한다.
(C) 셰릴이 프랭크를 찾을 수 있을 것이다.
(D) 셰릴이 언제 배송이 도착할지 알고 있다.

해설 9시 48분에 모로프 씨가 빈 바인더를 몇 개 찾고 있었다(I was looking for some empty binders)고 했고, 9시 50분에 지금 두세 개 정도가 필요하다(I need two or three of them now)고 하자 9시 51분에 노무라 씨가 셰릴에게 문의해 보라(Check with Cheryl)고 권했다. 따라서 노무라 씨는 셰릴에게 바인더가 몇 개 있을 수 있으니 물어보라는 의도로 한 말임을 알 수 있으므로 (A)가 정답이다.

어휘 locate ~의 위치를 찾아내다

153-154 양식

코르티카 은행

은행 신규 계좌를 개설하시려면 다음 양식을 작성하십시오.

153 코르티카 은행에 이번 계좌가 처음이십니까? ___ 예 153 X 아니요

기존 계좌번호(해당되는 경우): 190-37580

신규 계좌 유형: ___ 당좌 예금   X 보통 예금   ___ 투자

이름: 프랜시스 윌크스

우편 주소: 존스 로 17
노스 시드니 NSW 2060

전화번호: (02) 7010 8624

이메일 주소: fwilkes@myemail.com.au

초기 예치 금액(최소 500달러): 1,500달러

154 전자 통신을 신청하시겠습니까? __ 예　154 X 아니요

'예'를 선택하실 경우, 음성 메일, 이메일 또는 문자를 통해 연락드립니다.
154 '아니요'를 선택하실 경우, 매월 종이 명세서를 우편으로 받으시게 됩니다.

계좌는 개설하는 데 영업일 기준 최대 2일이 소요된다는 점을 유의해 주십시오. 이 기간 이후에 예금을 사용하실 수 있습니다. 영업일 기준 최대 5일 이내에 직불 카드를 우편으로 받으실 수 있습니다.

어휘　fill out ~을 작성하다　account 계좌　existing 기존의
applicable 해당[적용]되는　chequing 당좌 예금, 입출금 예금
savings 보통 예금　investment 투자　initial 초기의　deposit
예치금　sign up for ~에 등록[가입]하다　electronic 전자의
communication 통신　via ~을 통하여　statement 명세서
establish 개설하다　period 기간　debit card 직불 카드

---

153 Not / True

번역　월크스 씨에 대해 명시된 것은?
(A) 코르티카 은행에 다른 계좌를 가지고 있다.
(B) 투자 계좌를 개설할 계획이다.
(C) 직불 카드를 잃어버렸다.
(D) 수표를 주문했다.

해설　양식 첫 번째 항목에서 코르티카 은행에 이번 계좌가 처음인지(Is this your first account with Cortica Bank?)를 묻자 아니요(No)에 체크했으므로 월크스 씨는 코르티카 은행에 계좌를 이미 가지고 있는 고객임을 알 수 있다. 따라서 (A)가 정답이다. 세 번째 항목 신규 계좌 유형(New account type)에서 보통 예금(Savings)에 체크했으므로 (B)는 오답이고, (C)와 (D)는 언급하지 않았다.

어휘　place an order 주문하다　check 수표

---

154 세부사항

번역　은행은 월크스 씨에게 어떻게 연락할 것 같은가?
(A) 이메일로
(B) 문자로
(C) 전화로
(D) 서신으로

해설　양식 마지막 질문에서 전자 통신을 신청하겠는지(Would you like to sign up for electronic communications?)를 묻자 월크스 씨가 아니요(No)에 체크했고, 그 아래 '아니요'를 선택할 경우 매월 종이 명세서를 우편으로 받게 된다(If you select "No," you will receive monthly paper statements in the mail)고 했다. 따라서 (D)가 정답이다.

Paraphrasing　지문의 in the mail → 정답의 By letter

155-157 구인 광고

> 건설 현장 감독관
> 존스-리치먼드 건설(JRC)
>
> 155 25년 전에 설립된 JRC는 위니펙과 주변 지역의 고객에게 서비스를 제공하는 종합 서비스 시공사입니다.
>
> 업무:
> • 프로젝트 상급 관리자에 보고
> • 현장 공사 상황 관리
> • 156(D) 안전 규정 준수 보장
> • 156(C) 구매 및 계약 협상
> • 156(A) 공사 일정 수립
>
> 자격:
> • 최소 5년 이상의 상업 건물 건설 경력
> • 157 작업 현장을 매일 다닐 의향(보통 반경 50km 이내)
> • 뛰어난 서면 소통 능력
>
> 지원하려면 www.jrc.ca/apply를 통해 이력서와 자기소개서를 제출하십시오.

어휘　construction 건설　superintendent 감독관, 관리자
found 설립하다　general 종합적인　contractor 시공사, 설비업체
surrounding 주변의　responsibility 책무, 책임　senior
상급(고위)의　on-site 현장의　ensure 보장하다　compliance
준수　regulation 규정　negotiate 협상하다　establish 수립하다
qualification 자격　commercial 상업의　willingness 의향
radius 반경　written 서면의, 문서의　cover letter 자기소개서

---

155 추론 / 암시

번역　존스-리치먼드 건설에 대해 암시된 것은?
(A) 신생 회사이다.
(B) 작업으로 업계에서 상을 수상했다.
(C) 위니펙에 기반을 두고 있다.
(D) 주택 건설 프로젝트를 전문으로 한다.

해설　첫 문장에서 25년 전에 설립된 JRC는 위니펙과 주변 지역의 고객에게 서비스를 제공하는 종합 서비스 시공사(Founded 25 years ago, JRC is ~ serving clients throughout Winnipeg and the surrounding area)라고 소개하고 있으므로 존스-리치먼드 건설은 위니펙 지역을 기반으로 하는 회사임을 알 수 있다. 따라서 (C)가 정답이다.

어휘　industry 업계　based in ~에 기반을 둔　specialize in ~을 전문으로 하다

---

156 Not / True

번역　건설 현장 감독관의 업무로 열거되지 않은 것은?
(A) 일정 설정
(B) 경험이 부족한 작업자 교육
(C) 계약 논의 참여
(D) 작업자 안전 보장

TEST 5

해설 업무(Responsibilities) 항목에 열거된 안전 규정 준수 보장(Ensure compliance with safety regulations)은 (D), 구매 및 계약 협상(Negotiate purchases and contracts)은 (C), 공사 일정 수립(Establish construction schedules)은 (A)에 해당되지만, 작업자 교육에 관한 언급은 없으므로 (B)가 정답이다.

어휘 inexperienced 경험이 부족한, 미숙한 participate in ~에 참여하다

Paraphrasing 지문의 Establish → 보기 (A)의 Setting

157 세부사항

번역 광고에 따르면, 채용 합격자가 보유하고 있어야 하는 것은?
(A) 기술 자격증
(B) 이전 고용주로부터의 추천서
(C) 고위 경영진 경력
(D) 각 근무일에 공사 현장을 방문할 수 있는 능력

해설 구인 광고 하단의 자격(Qualifications) 항목에 작업 현장을 매일 다닐 의향(Willingness to travel to job sites daily)이 제시되어 있으므로 (D)가 정답이다.

어휘 successful job applicant 채용 합격자 certification 자격증 reference letter 추천서 former 이전의 employer 고용주 management 경영진

Paraphrasing 지문의 Willingness to travel
→ 정답의 The ability to visit
지문의 daily → 정답의 each workday

158-160 이메일

수신: 슬레지해머 체육관 전 직원
발신: 루카스 슬레지
날짜: 9월 15일
제목: 급여 지급 변경
첨부파일: ⬀양식

직원들께,

여러분의 헌신적인 근무 덕분에 우리 작은 체육관에 대한 소문이 퍼졌습니다. 지난 12개월 동안 등록 인원이 상당히 증가했고 강사진도 마찬가지로 늘었습니다. 158 **이러한 성장은 멋진 일이지만 저 혼자 급여를 처리해야 하는 것이 꽤 부담스러워졌습니다. 그래서 저는 트럼불 앤 컴퍼니와 계약하여 여러분의 은행 계좌로 급여를 바로 입금하기로 했습니다.** 따라서 여러분은 더 이상 직접 급여 지불 수표를 입금할 필요가 없습니다. 또한 급여 명세서 및 세금 정보를 이제 온라인으로 받으실 수 있습니다.

이러한 변경을 감안하여 159 **여러분 모두 필요한 은행 정보를 저에게 제공해 줄 것을 요청합니다.** 160 **첨부된 양식을 작성하여 9월 25일까지 보이드 체크와 함께 사무실로 가져오세요.** 제가 자리에 없을 경우 저의 비서에게 전달하세요. 새로운 절차는 10월에 시행될 것입니다. 문의사항이 있으면 알려 주세요.

루카스

어휘 payroll 급여 (지급) dedicated 헌신적인 word 소문, (떠도는) 말 spread 퍼지다 enrollment 등록자 수 significantly 상당히 growth 성장 process 처리하다; 절차 rather 꽤 burdensome 부담스러운 contract 계약하다 direct deposit (급여의) 계좌 입금 wage 급여 consequently 따라서 deposit 입금하다 paycheck 급여 (지불 수표) pay stub 급여 명세서 allow for ~을 감안하다 complete 작성하다 voided check 보이드 체크, 무효 수표(주로 계좌 정보 제공 시 사용) no later than 늦어도 ~까지는, 이전에 take effect 시행되다, 효력을 발휘하다

158 Not / True

번역 새로운 결제 시스템의 이점으로 언급된 것은?
(A) 슬레지 씨의 업무량을 줄일 것이다.
(B) 더 많은 직원 참여를 포함할 것이다.
(C) 세금 징수를 간소화할 것이다.
(D) 결제 오류가 줄어드는 결과를 낳을 것이다.

해설 첫 번째 단락의 세 번째 문장에서 슬레지 씨가 이러한 성장은 멋진 일이지만 혼자 급여를 처리해야 하는 것이 꽤 부담스러워졌다(Although this ~ to process the payroll by myself has become rather burdensome)고 했고, 그래서 트럼불 앤 컴퍼니와 계약하여 직원들의 은행 계좌로 급여를 바로 입금하기로 했다(Therefore, I have contracted Trumbull and Company to provide direct deposit of your wages into your bank accounts)고 했다. 슬레지 씨가 새로운 결제 시스템을 도입한 이유는 본인의 급여 처리 업무 부담을 줄이기 위한 것이므로 (A)가 정답이다.

어휘 workload 업무량 involvement 참여 simplify 간소화하다 collection 징수, 수거 result in (결과적으로) ~을 낳다[야기하다]

159 세부사항

번역 슬레지 씨가 직원들에게 요청하는 것은?
(A) 연락처 정보 업데이트
(B) 체육관 개선 방법에 관한 아이디어 제출
(C) 은행 계좌에 대한 정보 제공
(D) 전문 개발 강좌에 등록

해설 두 번째 단락의 첫 문장에서 슬레지 씨가 직원들 모두 필요한 은행 정보를 본인에게 제공해 줄 것을 요청한다(I am asking everyone to provide me with the necessary banking details)고 했으므로 (C)가 정답이다.

Paraphrasing 지문의 details → 정답의 information

160 문장 삽입

번역 [1], [2], [3], [4]로 표시된 위치 중에서 다음 문장이 들어가기에 가장 적합한 곳은?

"제가 자리에 없을 경우 저의 비서에게 전달하세요."
(A) [1]
(B) [2]
(C) [3]
(D) [4]

해설 주어진 문장에서 '자신이 자리에 없을 경우 비서에게 전달하라'며 자신을 만나지 못할 경우 할 수 있는 대안을 제시하고 있으므로 주어진 문장 앞에는 슬레지 씨를 만나야 할 이유에 대한 내용이 와야 한다. 따라서 양식을 작성해 9월 25일까지 보이드 체크와 함께 사무실로 가져오라(Please complete the attached form and bring it to the office with a voided check no later than September 25)고 지시하는 문장 뒤에 들어가는 것이 글의 흐름상 자연스러우므로 (C)가 정답이다.

161-163 기사

이번 주말 호주 커피 박람회

시드니 (6월 4일) — 이번 주말 국내 161 **최고의** 주방용품 제조업체인 홈웨어스가 주최하는 호주 커피 박람회에서 커피가 주요 관심사가 될 것이다. 이 행사는 하버 엑스포 센터에서 열릴 예정이다.

162 **이틀간의 행사는 커피 재배자와 로스터, 음식 전문 작가, 주방 장비 제조업체, 요리사가 커피를 중심으로 진행하는 다양한 프레젠테이션으로 구성될 것이다.** 센터 곳곳의 부스에서 음식과 음료가 보고 맛보고 구입할 수 있게 제공될 예정이다.

세션에는 커피를 이용한 요리 시연과 최고의 커피를 내리는 팁뿐만 아니라 커피의 식품 이외의 용도에 대한 정보도 포함될 것이다. 또한 가정에서 진정한 커피 하우스 경험을 할 수 있도록 돕기 위한 토론을 위해 요리 전문가들이 커피 애호가들과 만날 예정이다.

호주 커피 박람회 입장은 무료이다. 그러나 163 **공간이 한정되어 있어 등록은 필수이다.** 정보 및 온라인 등록을 원한다면 www.aussiecoffeefair.com을 방문하면 된다.

어휘 Aussie 오스트레일리아(의) fair 박람회 attraction 관심을 끄는 것, 인기물 host 주최하다 kitchen appliance 주방용품 manufacturer 제조업체 feature ~을 특징으로 하다 oriented ~을 중심으로 하는[지향하는] grower 재배자 roaster 로스터(커피 원두를 볶는 사람이나 기계) beverage 음료 throughout 곳곳에, 도처에 session (특정 활동) 시간 demonstration 시연 brew (커피 등을) 내리다 nonfood 식품(류) 이외의 culinary 요리의 on hand 자리에 있는, 대기하고 있는 enthusiast 열광적인 팬 entry 입장 registration 등록 required 필수인, 필요한 limited 한정된, 제한된

161 동의어 찾기

번역 첫 번째 단락 3행의 "top"과 의미가 가장 가까운 단어는?
(A) 유일한
(B) 선두의
(C) 가장 높은
(D) 현대의

해설 의미상 국내 '최고의' 주방용품 제조업체라는 뜻으로 쓰였으므로, '선두의, 일류의'를 뜻하는 (B) leading이 정답이다. 참고로, (C) highest는 '가장 높은 제조업체'라는 어색한 의미가 되어 답이 될 수 없다.

162 Not / True

번역 박람회에서 정보 제공 프레젠테이션을 하지 않을 사람은?
(A) 요리사
(B) 커피 재배자
(C) 장비 제조업자
(D) 커피 하우스 주인

해설 두 번째 단락의 첫 문장에서 이틀간의 행사는 커피 재배자와 로스터, 음식 전문 작가, 주방 장비 제조업체, 요리사가 커피를 중심으로 진행하는 다양한 프레젠테이션으로 구성될 것(The two-day event will feature ~ presentations by coffee growers and roasters, food writers, makers of kitchen equipment, and chefs)이라고 했지만, 커피 하우스 주인에 대한 언급은 없으므로 (D)가 정답이다.

163 세부사항

번역 박람회에 참석하기 위해 사람들이 해야 할 일은?
(A) 웹사이트에서 등록하기
(B) 예약 전화하기
(C) 행사 장소에서 티켓 구매하기
(D) 홈웨어스 제품 영수증 제시하기

해설 마지막 단락의 두 번째 문장에서 공간이 한정되어 있어 등록은 필수(registration is required ~ limited)라고 했고, 정보 및 온라인 등록을 원한다면 www.aussiecoffeefair.com을 방문하라(For information and to register online, go to www.aussiecoffeefair.com)고 안내하고 있다. 따라서 (A)가 정답이다.

어휘 reservation 예약 location 장소 present 제시하다

Paraphrasing 지문의 register online
→ 정답의 Sign up on a Web site

164-167 이메일

발신: melissa@grandgrainsbakery.com
수신: elinorotero@webmail.com
날짜: 10월 28일
회신: 디저트

오테로 씨께,

164 **11월 7일에 자택에서 주최하시는 파티를 위해 큰 케이크 한 개 대신 디저트 모음으로 하시겠다는 요청과 관련해 방금 저희 제빵사에게 연락을 취했습니다.** 디저트는 1인당 세 개씩 주문하실 것을 제안 드립니다. 디저트 세 개의 가격은 1인당 10달러에서 12달러 사이입니다. 164 **가장 인기 있는 디저트는 미니 치즈케이크, 베리 타틀렛 그리고 브라우니입니다.**

점심에는 별도의 음식 제공 업체를 이용할 것이며, 그들이 서빙과 파티가 끝난 뒤 청소를 도울 예정이라고 알고 있습니다. 고객님께서는 또한 디저트 테이블을 뒷마당에 둘지, 집 안에 둘지 고민 중이라고 하셨습니다. 165 **치즈케이크를 주문하실 경우 케이크를 두 시간 이상 밖에 두어서는 안 된다는 것을 유념해 주십시오.** 디저트를 어디에 놓을지에 대해 구체적인 지시를 주시면 저희 직원들이 파티에 166 **방해되지** 않게 적당한 장소에 놓아 둘 수 있습니다.

167 디저트를 선택하시고 나서 예상 손님이 몇 분인지 알려 주시면 나머지는 저희가 알아서 처리해 드리겠습니다.

멜리사 루히아
그랜드 그레인스 베이커리

> 어휘 follow up with 후속 조치를 위해 연락하다 baker 제빵사 an assortment of ~의 모음, 각종의 tartlet 타틀렛, 작은 파이 separate 별도의 caterer 음식 제공 업체 keep in mind ~을 유념[명심]하다 specific 구체적인 instruction 지시 appropriate 적절한 disturb 방해하다 take care of ~을 처리하다

164 주제 / 목적

번역 이메일의 목적은?
(A) 새 페이스트리를 광고하려고
(B) 행사를 위한 선택사항을 제시하려고
(C) 더 큰 케이크 제공을 권고하려고
(D) 주문에 대한 결제를 요청하려고

해설 첫 문장에서 11월 7일에 자택에서 주최하는 파티를 위해 큰 케이크 한 개 대신 디저트 모음으로 하겠다는 요청과 관련해 제빵사에게 연락을 취했다(I just followed up with our baker about your request to have an assortment of desserts instead of one large cake for the party ~ on November 7)며, 디저트를 1인당 세 개씩 주문할 것을 제안(We suggest ordering three dessert pieces per person)하고 가장 인기 있는 디저트는 미니 치즈케이크, 베리 타틀렛, 브라우니(Our most popular desserts ~ brownies)라고 했다. 따라서 이 글은 행사에 필요한 디저트 모음을 주문할 경우 선택할 수 있는 사항들을 제시하고 있으므로 (B)가 정답이다.

어휘 pastry 페이스트리 present 제시하다, 보여 주다

165 Not / True

번역 루히아 씨가 미니 치즈케이크에 대해 명시한 것은?
(A) 가장 비싼 디저트이다.
(B) 여러 가지 맛으로 주문 가능하다.
(C) 오랫동안 상온에 두면 안 된다.
(D) 더 큰 사이즈로 주문될 수 없다.

해설 두 번째 단락의 세 번째 문장에서 치즈케이크를 주문할 경우 케이크를 두 시간 이상 밖에 두어서는 안 된다는 것을 유념하라(Just keep in mind ~ cheesecakes, they should not be left out for more than two hours)고 했으므로 (C)가 정답이다.

어휘 flavor 맛, 풍미 unrefrigerated 상온의, 냉장되지 않은

> Paraphrasing 지문의 left out → 정답의 unrefrigerated

166 동의어 찾기

번역 두 번째 단락 6행의 "disturbing"과 의미가 가장 가까운 단어는?
(A) 방해하기
(B) 놀라게 하기
(C) 재배치하기
(D) 옮기기

해설 의미상 파티에 '방해되지' 않게 적당한 곳에 둔다는 뜻으로 쓰였으므로 '방해하기'를 뜻하는 (A) interrupting이 정답이다.

167 세부사항

번역 루히아 씨가 오테로 씨에게 요청하는 정보는?
(A) 주소
(B) 대략적인 예산
(C) 음식 제공 업체명
(D) 손님 인원수

해설 마지막 단락에서 루히아 씨가 디저트를 선택하고 나서 예상 손님이 몇 명인지 알려 주면 나머지는 알아서 처리하겠다(Once you make your dessert choices, simply let us know how many guests you expect, and we can take care of the rest)고 했으므로 정답은 (D)이다.

어휘 approximate 대략적인 budget 예산

> Paraphrasing 지문의 how many guests
> → 정답의 The number of guests

168-171 이메일

> 수신: 셰릴 푸트렐 〈cfutrel@zephyrmail.com〉
> 발신: 리디아 마츠다 〈service@candella.com〉
> 날짜: 6월 9일
> 제목: 집 꾸미기
>
> 푸트렐 씨께,
>
> 칸델라 인테리어 디자인에 관심을 주셔서 감사합니다. **168** 저희는 이 지역에서 가장 오래되고 가장 성공한 온라인 디자인 컨설팅 회사라고 자부합니다. 저희는 귀하를 새로운 고객으로 환영합니다. 소박한 시골집에서 도시의 아파트까지 저희는 모든 것을 다룹니다.
>
> **169** 고객님이 처음 보낸 문의를 통해 고객님께서 곧 아파트를 매도할 계획이며 어떻게 하면 잠재 구매자에게 아파트를 최상으로 보여 줄 수 있을지에 관심이 많으시다는 것을 알고 있습니다. **171** 저희의 디자인 서비스가 진행되는 방식은 다음과 같습니다. 첫 단계는 온라인 설문지를 작성하는 것입니다. 답변을 통해 저희는 고객님의 취향과 요구사항을 파악하게 됩니다. 다음으로, 페인트 색상, 창문 처리, 바닥재에 대한 모든 선택을 도와드릴 온라인 전문 인테리어 디자이너를 소개해 드립니다. 방 배치 계획과 가구 및 장식품에 대한 맞춤형 아이디어 목록을 받으시게 되며, 전 제품은 온라인으로 구매 가능합니다. **170** 특별 보너스로 지금부터 7월 1일까지 저희 온라인 소매 협력사들은 당사 링크를 통해 구매된 제품에 10퍼센트 할인을 제공하기로 합의했습니다.
>
> 마지막으로 저희가 디자인 아이디어에 대해 시간당이 아닌 방에 따라서 청구한다는 점을 아시면 기뻐하실 것이며 평균 가격은 방당 약 275달러입니다.
>
> 고객님의 답변을 기다리며 곧 함께 작업하게 되기를 고대합니다.
>
> 리디아 마츠다

168 Not / True

번역 칸델라 인테리어 디자인에 대해 명시된 것은?
(A) 본사가 대도시에 있다.
(B) 직원들이 고객의 집을 방문한다.
(C) 경쟁사들보다 더 오래 사업을 해왔다.
(D) 가족 경영 사업체이다.

해설 첫 단락의 두 번째 문장에서 자신들(=칸델라 인테리어 디자인)은 이 지역에서 가장 오래되고 가장 성공한 온라인 디자인 컨설팅 회사라고 자부한다(We are proud to claim that we are the oldest and most successful online design consulting company in the region)고 했으므로 지역에서 누구보다 이 사업을 오래 한 업체라는 점을 알 수 있다. 따라서 (C)가 정답이다.

어휘 major 주요한 competitor 경쟁사 family-run 가족 경영의

169 세부사항

번역 푸트렐 씨가 자신의 아파트를 다시 꾸미고 싶어 하는 이유는?
(A) 친척 방문을 준비하려고
(B) 잠재 구매자에게 매력적으로 보이게 하려고
(C) 싫어하는 가구를 교체하려고
(D) 자신의 고객들을 위한 본보기로 사용하려고

해설 두 번째 단락의 첫 문장에서 마츠다 씨가 고객인 푸트렐 씨에게 처음 보낸 문의를 통해 곧 아파트를 매도할 계획이며 어떻게 하면 잠재 구매자에게 아파트를 최상으로 보여 줄 수 있을지에 관심이 많다는 것을 알고 있다(We understand from your original inquiry that you intend to sell your apartment ~ interested in how best to present it to prospective buyers)고 했으므로 (B)가 정답이다.

어휘 relative 친척 attractive 매력적인 potential 잠재적인

Paraphrasing 지문의 prospective → 정답의 potential

170 세부사항

번역 7월 1일에 일어날 일은?
(A) 실내 장식품이 유통될 것이다.
(B) 새 프로젝트에 대한 작업이 시작될 것이다.
(C) 고객 명단이 확장될 것이다.
(D) 특가 행사가 종료될 것이다.

해설 두 번째 단락의 마지막 문장에서 특별 보너스로 지금부터 7월 1일까지 온라인 소매 협력사들이 당사 링크를 통해 구매된 제품에 10퍼센트 할인을 제공하기로 합의했다(As a special bonus, from now until July 1 our online retail partners have agreed to offer a 10 percent discount on products purchased through our links)고 했다. 따라서 7월 1일은 10퍼센트 할인을 받을 수 있는 마지막 날이므로 (D)가 정답이다.

어휘 distribute 유통하다 expand 확장하다

171 문장 삽입

번역 [1], [2], [3], [4]로 표시된 위치 중에서 다음 문장이 들어가기에 가장 적합한 곳은?

"답변을 통해 저희는 고객님의 취향과 요구사항을 파악하게 됩니다."
(A) [1]
(B) [2]
(C) [3]
(D) [4]

해설 주어진 문장에서 '답변을 통해 고객의 취향과 요구사항을 파악한다'고 했으므로, 주어진 문장 앞에는 고객이 취향 및 요구사항 등에 관한 질문에 답변을 하는 것과 관련된 내용이 있어야 한다. 따라서 업체의 디자인 서비스가 진행되는 방식을 설명하며 온라인 설문지를 작성하는 것(completing an online questionnaire), 즉 온라인으로 질문에 답변하는 것을 언급한 문장 뒤에 들어가는 것이 글의 흐름상 자연스러우므로 (C)가 정답이다.

어휘 sense 감각, 지각 taste 취향 requirement 요구사항

172-175 문자 메시지

다리우스 윌킨스 (오전 11시 9분)
안녕하세요, 클라크 씨. 로토 자전거의 다리우스입니다. 172 **자전거를 정비하기 전에 고객님과 상의하기로 약속드렸어요.**

로렌 클라크 (오전 11시 14분)
감사합니다. 어떻게 생각하세요?

다리우스 윌킨스 (오전 11시 15분)
정기 정비 서비스 외에 구동계 청소와 새 브레이크 장치를 제안 드립니다.

로렌 클라크 (오전 11시 16분)
알겠습니다. 그러면 어떻게 되죠?

다리우스 윌킨스 (오전 11시 18분)
정기 정비 서비스와 동일한 기어 및 브레이크 조정에 구동계 청소를 추가한 포괄 정비 서비스는 140달러입니다. 173 **두 개의 새 브레이크 장치와 패드에 70달러, 그리고 인건비로 30달러가 추가됩니다. 그러면** 174 **총 240달러 정도가 될 것입니다. 진행할까요?**

로렌 클라크 (오전 11시 21분)
와! 그렇게 많이요?

다리우스 윌킨스 (오전 11시 22분)
175 **특히 고객님은 중요한 자전거 경주를 앞두고 있으니까요.**

로렌 클라크 (오전 11시 24분)
맞아요. 해야 할 것 같네요. 준비되면 알려 주세요.

어휘 service 정비[점검]하다 maintenance 정비 drivetrain 구동계[동력 전달 장치] mechanism 기계 장치[기구] extensive 포괄적인, 광범위한 adjustment 조정 labor charge 인건비 altogether 총[전체] move forward 추진하다 major 중요한, 주요한 ahead of ~을 앞두고

172 주제 / 목적

번역 윌킨스 씨가 클라크 씨에게 연락한 이유는?
(A) 신제품을 추천하려고
(B) 일정 문제를 논의하려고
(C) 자전거 부품이 주문되었는지 확인하려고
(D) 일부 작업을 수행할 수 있도록 허락을 구하려고

해설 11시 9분에 윌킨스 씨가 클라크 씨에게 자전거를 정비하기 전에 고객인 클라크 씨와 상의하기로 약속했다(I promised to check with you before servicing your bicycle)고 한 것으로 보아 윌킨스 씨는 자전거 수리의 진행 여부에 대한 허락을 받기 위해 고객인 클라크 씨에게 연락했다는 것을 알 수 있다. 따라서 (D)가 정답이다.

어휘 scheduling 일정 관리 confirm 확인하다 permission 허락

173 세부사항

번역 비용이 약 30달러인 것은?
(A) 새 브레이크 장치
(B) 인건비
(C) 기본 정비 서비스
(D) 구동계 청소

해설 11시 18분에 윌킨스 씨가 두 개의 새 브레이크 장치와 패드에 70달러, 인건비로 30달러가 추가된다(Add $70 for ~ and another $30 for labor charges)고 했다. 따라서 30달러는 인건비에 해당하는 것이므로 (B)가 정답이다.

174 의도 파악

번역 오전 11시 21분에 클라크 씨가 "그렇게 많이요?"라고 쓴 의도는?
(A) 윌킨스 씨가 얼마나 바쁜지 알지 못했다.
(B) 그녀의 타이어 압력이 놀라울 정도로 낮았다.
(C) 수리비가 비싼 것 같다.
(D) 자전거 수리에 예상했던 것보다 더 많은 시간이 걸릴 것이다.

해설 11시 18분에 윌킨스 씨가 총비용이 240달러 정도 된다(it should come to around $240 altogether)면서 진행할지(Shall I move forward?) 여부를 묻자 11시 21분에 클라크 씨가 그렇게 많이요?(That much?)라고 되묻고 있다. 따라서 클라크 씨는 자전거 수리 비용 금액이 예상보다 비싼 데 대한 놀라움을 표하려는 의도로 한 말임을 알 수 있으므로 (C)가 정답이다.

어휘 realize 인식하다 pressure 압력 surprisingly 놀랍도록

175 추론 / 암시

번역 클라크 씨에 대해 암시된 것은?
(A) 현금으로 지불하는 것을 선호한다.
(B) 새 자전거를 살 예정이다.
(C) 수리의 질에 만족하지 못한다.
(D) 곧 자전거 경주에 참가할 예정이다.

해설 11시 22분에 윌킨스 씨가 고객인 클라크 씨에게 특히 고객님은 중요한 자전거 경주를 앞두고 있다(Especially with that major bicycle race you have ahead of you)고 한 것으로 보아 클라크 씨가 곧 자전거 경주에 참가할 예정이라는 것을 짐작할 수 있다. 따라서 (D)가 정답이다.

어휘 compete (시합 등에) 참가하다

176-180 이메일 + 웹페이지

수신: 캐시 라퍼티 〈cassie@mailcurrent.ie〉
발신: 유세프 짐리 〈zimri@zimrimechanical.ie〉
제목: 후속 조치
날짜: 9월 12일
첨부: ⬇ cmcclinic

라퍼티 씨께,

176 지금까지 당신의 작업에 매우 만족합니다. 우리 기록 보관소에 있는 사진을 추가하자는 당신의 제안으로 '회사 연혁' 페이지가 확실히 멋지게 꾸며졌습니다. 홈페이지의 구인 광고 팝업창도 보기 좋습니다. 잘하면, 기계 관련 경력을 가진 지원자들의 관심을 끌 것입니다.

'포트폴리오' 페이지에 프로젝트를 하나 더 추가해 주셨으면 합니다. 177 우리는 드디어 골웨이에 있는 클라리 메디컬 센터 부속 진료소의 배관 및 난방 시스템 교체 작업을 끝냈습니다. 쉽지 않은 작업이었지만 결과가 자랑스럽습니다. 첨부 파일에는 사진과 우리가 그곳에서 한 일에 대한 간단한 설명이 들어 있습니다.

유세프 짐리
대표, 짐리 머캐니컬

어휘 follow up 후속 조치를 하다 archive 기록 보관소 certainly 확실히 dress up ~을 (보기 좋게) 꾸미다 help-wanted 구인 광고 pop-up bubble 팝업창 hopefully 잘하면, 바라건대 applicant 지원자 mechanical 기계와 관련된 plumbing 배관 satellite 부속의, 위성 같은 challenging 어려운, 까다로운 description 설명

https://www.clarymedicalcentre.ie

| 소개 | 소식 | 직원 | 연락처 |

진료소가 곧 문을 엽니다

178 우리는 골웨이 하이 가 47을 부속 진료소로 용도를 변경하였으며, 10월 28일 금요일에 개원 파티로 축하할 예정입니다. 실리아 올리어리 진료소장 및 현지 선출직 공직자들의 축사가 오후 1시 정각에 시작되며, 오후 4시 30분까지 리본 커팅식과 시설 견학이 이어집니다.

177 클라리 메디컬 센터의 메인 캠퍼스에서 30마일 떨어진 클라리 진료소는 20여 년 전에 문을 닫은 역사적인 브랜드모어 신발 공장에 자리하고 있습니다. 개조 공사 동안 외부의 19세기 건축적 특색을 **179** 유지하기 위해 주의를 기울였습니다. **180** 진료소 내부는 18개의 검사실, 최첨단 X레이 시설, 환자 진찰을 위한 개별 진료실, 환자 샘플 처리를 위한 실험실을 자랑스럽게 갖추고 있습니다.

진료소 직원은 11월 1일 화요일부터 환자 진료를 시작할 예정입니다. 예약하시려면 020 915 1424로 전화하십시오.

어휘 repurpose 다른 용도에 맞게 고치다   remarks (연설 등의) 발언   elected 선출된   official 공직자   promptly 정각에   followed by ~이 뒤따르는   ceremony 기념식   decade 10년   renovation 개조   maintain 유지하다   exterior 외부   architectural 건축(학)의   feature 특징   boast 가지고 있다, 뽐내다   examination 검사   state-of-the-art 최첨단의   facility 시설   process 처리하다   make an appointment 예약하다

176 추론 / 암시

번역 라퍼티 씨는 누구일 것 같은가?
(A) 채용 담당자
(B) 배관 설비업자
(C) 골웨이 역사학자
(D) 웹사이트 디자이너

해설 이메일 첫 번째 단락의 첫 문장에서 짐리 씨가 라퍼티 씨에게 지금까지 라퍼티 씨의 작업에 매우 만족한다(I am very happy with your work so far)면서 자신들의 기록 보관소에 있는 사진을 추가하자는 라퍼티 씨의 제안으로 '회사 연혁' 페이지가 확실히 멋지게 꾸며졌다(Your suggestion to add photos from our archive certainly dressed up the "Company History" page)고 했고, 홈페이지의 구인 광고 팝업창도 보기 좋다(The help-wanted pop-up bubble on the home page also looks good)고 했다. 라퍼티 씨가 작업한 회사의 홈페이지에 만족한다는 내용으로 보아 라퍼티 씨는 웹사이트를 디자인하는 사람임을 알 수 있으므로 (D)가 정답이다.

어휘 recruiter 모집자   contractor 설비업자   historian 역사학자

177 연계

번역 짐리 씨에 대해 명시된 것은?
(A) 보조 건축가를 채용하려고 애쓰고 있다.
(B) 클라리 메디컬 센터의 이사회 구성원이다.
(C) 예전에 신발 공장이었던 곳에서 자신의 회사가 한 작업에 만족한다.
(D) 포트폴리오에 대한 올리어리 박사의 의견을 기다리고 있다.

해설 이메일의 두 번째 단락 두 번째 문장에서 짐리 씨가 드디어 골웨이에 있는 클라리 메디컬 센터 부속 진료소의 배관 및 난방 시스템 교체 작업을 끝냈다(We have finally finished replacing ~ at Clary Medical Centre's satellite clinic in Galway)며 쉽지 않은 작업이었지만 그 결과가 자랑스럽다(It was a challenging job, and I'm proud of our results)고 했고, 웹페이지의 두 번째 단락 첫 문장에서 클라리 메디컬 센터의 메인 캠퍼스에서 30마일 떨어진 클라리 진료소는 20여 년 전에 문을 닫은 역사적인 브랜드모어 신발 공장에

자리하고 있다(Thirty miles from the Clary Medical Centre's main campus, the Clary Clinic is housed in the historic Brandmore shoe factory, which closed more than two decades ago)고 했다. 따라서 짐리 씨는 20여 년 전 신발 공장이 있던 자리에 생긴 클라리 메디컬 센터의 부속 진료소에서 자신의 회사가 진행한 작업을 자랑스러워하는 것이므로 (C)가 정답이다.

어휘 recruit 채용하다   architect 건축가   board of directors 이사회   former 예전의, 이전의

178 세부사항

번역 웹페이지에 따르면, 개원 행사에서 일어날 일은?
(A) 정부 공직자들이 참석할 것이다.
(B) 샌드위치가 제공될 것이다.
(C) 새로운 건축 계획이 공개될 것이다.
(D) 이전 환자들을 인터뷰할 것이다.

해설 웹페이지의 첫 번째 단락 첫 문장에서 골웨이 하이 가 47을 부속 진료소로 용도를 변경하였으며, 10월 28일 금요일에 개원 파티로 축하할 예정(We have repurposed ~ will celebrate with a grand opening party on Friday, 28 October)이라고 했고, 실리아 올리어리 진료소장 및 현지 선출직 공직자들의 축사가 오후 1시 정각에 시작된다(Remarks by ~ local elected officials will begin promptly at 1:00 P.M.)고 했으므로 개원 행사에 정부 공직자들이 참석해 발언할 것임을 알 수 있다. 따라서 (A)가 정답이다.

어휘 in attendance 참석한   reveal 공개하다

179 동의어 찾기

번역 웹페이지에서 두 번째 단락 3행의 "maintain"과 의미가 가장 가까운 단어는?
(A) 주장하다
(B) 치유하다
(C) 지지하다
(D) 보존하다

해설 의미상 특색을 '유지하기' 위해 주의를 기울였다는 뜻으로 쓰였으므로 '보존하다'를 뜻하는 (D) preserve가 정답이다.

180 Not / True

번역 웹페이지에 따르면, 클라리 진료소의 일부가 아닌 것은?
(A) 의료 실험실
(B) 약국
(C) 의료 영상 장비
(D) 의사를 위한 사무실

해설 웹페이지의 두 번째 단락 마지막 문장에서 진료소 내부는 18개의 검사실, 최첨단 X레이 시설, 환자 진찰을 위한 개별 진료실, 환자 샘플 처리를 위한 실험실을 갖추고 있다(The clinic's interior boasts eighteen examination rooms, a state-of-the-art x-ray facility, private offices for patient consultations, and a lab for processing patient samples)고 했다. 최첨단 X레이 시설이 있다고 했으므로 (C), 환자 진찰을 위한 개별 진료실이 있다고 했으므로 (D), 환자 샘플 처리를 위한 실험실이 있다고 했으므로 (A)는 진료

소의 일부 시설로 거론되었으나 약국에 대한 언급은 없으므로 (B)가 정답이다.

어휘 laboratory 실험실 pharmacy 약국 clinician 의사

Paraphrasing 지문의 x-ray
→ 보기 (C)의 Medical imaging equipment

181-185 양식 + 이메일

구매 주문서

파이럿츠 바운티 씨푸드   10월 2일
하버 로 11   구매 주문: 5338
샬럿타운, 프린스에드워드아일랜드, C1A 0A5

판매업체	배송지
로셰츠 상업 냉장 라이온스 가 2175 구엘프, 온타리오, N1C 0A1 519-555-0112	파이럿츠 바운티 씨푸드 하버 로 11 샬럿타운, 프린스에드워드아일랜드, C1A 0A5 레노어 오키야 귀하 782-555-0145

품목 번호	183 설명	수량	가격	합계
BF550	블리자드 워크인 냉동고	1	6,400달러	6,400달러
	특징: 1.5mx2mx2.5m, 183 **조절 가능 선반,** **알루미늄 바닥,** **아연 도금 강판**			

181 비고 또는 특별 지시사항	소계	6,400달러
181 **레스토랑 확장.** 11월 17일까지 물건이 필요함.	세금	960달러
	총계	7,360달러

어휘 pirate 해적 vendor 판매업체[자] commercial 상업의 refrigeration 냉장 attn ~귀하(Attention) quantity 수량 walk-in (크기가 커서) 사람이 걸어서 드나들 수 있는 freezer 냉동고 feature 특징 adjustable 조절 가능한 flooring 바닥 galvanized 아연을 씌운 instruction 지시 expand 확장하다 unit (상품의) 한 개[단위] grand total 총계

수신: 레노어 오키야 ⟨l.okiya@piratesbounty.ca⟩
발신: 샬리야 우무마 ⟨customerservice@rochettesrefrigeration.ca⟩
날짜: 10월 3일
제목: 구매 주문 5338

오키야 씨께,

182 **블리자드 워크인 냉동고에 대한 주문서를 받았습니다. 안타깝게도 요청하신 모델은 주문이 밀린 상태라 3개월 동안 구매가 불가능합니다.** 불편을 드려 죄송하며 몇 가지 옵션을 제공해 드리고자 합니다.

---

183 **치수가 2m x 2.5m x 3m인 블리자드 BF600을 세금이 별도인 6,900달러의 할인된 가격으로 제공해 드릴 수 있습니다. 이 제품은 주문하신 상품과 동일한 특징을 갖추고 있습니다.** 또는 BF400의 리퍼 제품이 재고에 있습니다. 이 제품은 BF550과 크기는 같지만 BF550에는 온도 설정을 위한 리모컨이 포함된 반면 BF400에는 같은 용도의 벽걸이형 장치가 있습니다. 184 **BF400 제품에는 2년 품질 보증이 제공됩니다.** 가격은 5,600달러에 세금이 추가됩니다.

어떻게 진행하기를 원하시는지 알려 주십시오. 이 이메일에 185 **그저** 답장해 주시면 됩니다.

샬리야 우무마, 고객 서비스 관리자

어휘 back order (재고가 없어) 처리 못한 주문, 이월 주문 regret 유감스럽게 생각하다 inconvenience 불편 measure (치수가) ~이다 plus tax 세금 별도 feature 특징, 기능 alternately 또는, 그렇지 않으면 refurbished 재정비된, 재단장된 in stock 재고가 있는 remote control 리모컨 set 설정하다 temperature 온도 wall-mounted 벽걸이형의, 벽에 고정된 device 장치 purpose 목적 warranty 품질 보증 proceed 진행하다

181 세부사항

번역 파이럿츠 바운티 씨푸드에서 새 장비를 구매해야 하는 이유는?
(A) 현재 사용 중인 냉장고가 작동을 멈췄다.
(B) 현재 사용 중인 냉장고의 보증 기간이 만료되었다.
(C) 레스토랑이 규모를 키운다.
(D) 레스토랑이 새로운 장소로 이전한다.

해설 주문서 하단 왼쪽에 있는 비고 또는 특별 지시사항(COMMENTS OR SPECIAL INSTRUCTIONS)에 레스토랑 확장(Restaurant expanding)이라고 나와 있는 것으로 보아 파이럿츠 바운티 씨푸드는 레스토랑 규모 확장을 위해 장비를 구입한 것임을 알 수 있다. 따라서 (C)가 정답이다.

어휘 refrigerator 냉장고 expire 만료되다

Paraphrasing 지문의 expanding
→ 정답의 increasing in size

182 세부사항

번역 오키야 씨가 주문한 제품의 문제는?
(A) 배송 중 분실되었다.
(B) 단종되었다.
(C) 일시적으로 품절되었다.
(D) 제어판이 손상되었다.

해설 이메일의 첫 단락 첫 번째 문장에서 오키야 씨에게 블리자드 워크인 냉동고에 대한 주문서를 받았다(We received your purchase order for the Blizzard walk-in freezer)고 했고, 안타깝게도 요청한 모델은 주문이 밀린 상태라 3개월 동안 구매가 불가능하다(Unfortunately, the model you requested is on back order and will not be available for three months)고 했다. 따라서 오키야 씨가 주문한 제품은 현재 품절된 상태이므로 (C)가 정답이다.

discontinued 단종된   temporarily 일시적으로   out of stock 품절된   damaged 손상된   control panel 제어판

Paraphrasing   지문의 on back order → 정답의 out of stock

183 연계

번역 블리자드 BF600의 특징이 아닌 것은?
(A) 급랭 스위치가 있다.
(B) 조절 가능한 선반이 있다.
(C) 알루미늄 바닥으로 되어 있다.
(D) 아연 도금된 강판으로 되어 있다.

해설 양식 중간에 있는 오키야 씨가 주문한 제품의 설명(DESCRIPTION)에 조절 가능 선반, 알루미늄 바닥, 아연 도금 강판(adjustable shelves, aluminum flooring, galvanized steel panels)이라고 나와 있고, 이메일의 두 번째 단락 첫 문장에서 치수가 2m X 2.5m X 3m인 블리자드 BF600을 세금이 별도인 6,900달러의 할인된 가격으로 제공해 줄 수 있다(I can offer you the Blizzard BF600, ~ $6,900 plus tax)며 이 제품은 주문한 상품과 동일한 특징을 갖추고 있다(It comes with the same features as the item you ordered)고 했다. 따라서 블리자드 BF600은 오키야 씨가 원래 주문한 제품과 동일한 조절 가능 선반, 알루미늄 바닥, 아연 도금 강판의 특징을 갖추고 있는 것을 알 수 있으므로 (A)가 정답이다.

어휘 fast-freeze 급랭

184 세부사항

번역 이메일에 따르면, BF400 모델에 제공되는 것은?
(A) 사용 설명서
(B) 리모컨
(C) 품질 보증
(D) 세금 면제

해설 이메일의 두 번째 단락 마지막 문장에서 BF400 제품에는 2년 품질 보증이 제공된다(The BF400 unit comes with a two-year warranty)고 했으므로 (C)가 정답이다.

어휘 manual 설명서   waiver 면제

185 동의어 찾기

번역 이메일에서 세 번째 단락 1행의 "just"와 의미가 가장 가까운 단어는?
(A) 즉시
(B) 친절히
(C) 곧
(D) 간단히

해설 의미상 이메일에 '그저' 답장만 해주면 된다는 뜻으로 쓰였으므로 '간단히, 그저'를 뜻하는 (D) simply가 정답이다.

186-190 일정표 + 이메일 + 기사

제5회 국제 마케팅 협회 연례 학회
10월 23일-25일, 런던 그랜트 호텔 콘퍼런스 센터

1일 차:

시간	설명	장소
오전 7시 - 오전 8시	[186]**오전 친목회: 무료 오믈렛, 페이스트리, 커피, 차**	메자닌
오전 8시 30분 - 오전 10시	[188]**마르코스 세카다, 그라인드스톤 마케팅 그룹 창립자 겸 최고 경영자**	2호실
[187]**오전 10시 30분 - 정오**	[187]**클레어 송, 비즈니스 칼럼니스트 겸 베스트셀러 작가**	10호실
오후 12시 30분 - 오후 2시	점심 식사 (입장권 구매 필수)	알렉산더 볼룸

어휘 society 협회   description 설명   venue 장소   social 친목회   complimentary 무료의   pastry 페이스트리   mezzanine 메자닌, 중2층(다른 층들보다 작게 두 층 사이에 지은 층)   founder 창립자   author 작가   required 필수의

---

[189]**수신:** 나디르 칼와르 〈kalwar.n@kdbuildingconcepts.com〉
발신: 올렉 드직 〈odzik.k@kdbuildingconcepts.com〉
날짜: 5월 12일
제목: 다가오는 마케팅 캠페인
첨부: 🔗 비디오 링크

나디르,

기업 마케팅 계획에 도움 주셔서 감사합니다. [188]**그라인드스톤 마케팅 그룹이 우리를 위해 제작한 동영상 링크를 첨부합니다.** 영상에서는 당사의 3D 프린팅 장비가 빠른 속도로 굳는 콘크리트를 층층이 쏟아붓는 모습을 보여 줍니다. 있는 그대로도 훌륭해 보인다고 생각하며, 특히 셰필드 하우스가 그때까지 매각된다면 6월 1일 출시의 가장 매력적인 측면이 될 것이라고 믿습니다.

혹시 못 들으셨을까 봐 말씀드리면, [189]**우리의 다음 공사 프로젝트는 당신의 사무실 건물에서 불과 몇 킬로미터 거리에 있는 주택이 될 예정입니다!**

올렉

어휘 corporate 기업의   attach 첨부하다   pour 붓다   fast-setting 빠르게 굳는   layer 층   as is 있는 그대로   compelling 매력적인, 강력한   aspect 측면   launch 출시

3D 기술로 건축한 주택 매물

셰필드 (5월 15일) — 혁신적인 건축 기술을 전문으로 하는 국제적인 건설사가 영국 최초의 3D 프린팅으로 지은 주택 중 하나를 완성했다. 새 건물은 셰필드의 모건 로에 위치해 있다.

사장인 올렉 드직에 따르면 KD 빌딩 콘셉츠가 콘크리트 벽을 프린팅하고 전기 및 배관 시스템을 설치하는 작업을 수반한 프로젝트의 첫 단계를 실행하는 데 2주가 채 걸리지 않았다고 한다. 190**단 두 달 만에 침실 두 개와 욕실 두 개를 갖추고 조경이 완비된 주택이 시장에 나올 준비가 되었다.**

"3D 프린팅 기술 덕분에 인건비가 절반으로 줄었습니다."라고 셰필드뿐 아니라 프랑스와 독일에 지사가 있는 기업의 소유주인 드직 씨는 말했다. "KD 빌딩 콘셉츠에서는 가격이 적당하면서도 고급스러운 주택을 짓는 데 전념하고 있습니다."

이 주택은 이번 주에 현지 부동산 중개인에 의해 매물로 등록되었다. 제시 가격은 15만 파운드이다.

189**향후 KD 빌딩 콘셉츠는 독일 함부르크에 주택을 건설할 예정이다.**

어휘 firm 회사 specialize in ~을 전문으로 하다 innovative 혁신적인 structure 건축물 execute 실행하다 phase 단계 entail 수반하다 electrical 전기의 plumbing 배관 landscape 조경을 하다 labour cost 인건비 as well as ~뿐 아니라 committed to ~에 전념하는 affordable 가격이 적당한 luxurious 고급스러운 real estate broker 부동산 중개인 asking price 제시 가격, 호가 on the horizon 곧 일어날

---

186 Not / True

번역 일정표에 언급된 것은?
(A) 학회 참가자들을 위한 무료 조식을 이용할 수 있다.
(B) 학회는 5일 동안 열린다.
(C) 기조연설은 첫날의 마지막 행사로 진행될 예정이다.
(D) 주요 연사가 교체되었다.

해설 일정표의 설명 첫 줄에 오전 친목회에 무료 오믈렛, 페이스트리, 커피, 차(Morning Social: Complimentary omelets ~ tea)가 제공된다고 나와 있으므로 (A)가 정답이다. 학회는 10월 23일-25일(23-25 October) 즉, 3일간 열리므로 (B)는 오답이고, 기조연설과 연사 교체에 대한 언급은 없으므로 (C)와 (D)도 정답이 될 수 없다.

어휘 participant 참가자 keynote address 기조연설 deliver (연설, 강연 등을) 하다 featured 주연의, 특집의

187 세부사항

번역 일정표에 따르면, 오전 10시 30분에 일어날 일은?
(A) 작가가 발표를 한 것이다.
(B) 로비에서 커피가 제공될 것이다.
(C) 점심 식사권이 10호실에서 판매될 것이다.
(D) 수정된 일정표가 배포될 것이다.

해설 일정표의 오전 10시 30분에서 정오(10:30 A.M. to noon)까지의 세션 설명에 클레어 송, 비즈니스 칼럼니스트 겸 베스트셀러 작가(Claire Song, business columnist and best-selling author)라고 나와 있으므로 클레어 송이라는 작가가 행사를 진행할 예정임을 알 수 있다. 따라서 (A)가 정답이다.

어휘 revised 수정된 distribute 배포하다

188 연계

번역 드직 씨에 대해 결론지을 수 있는 것은?
(A) 마케팅 동영상이 짧아지기를 원한다.
(B) 칼와르 씨에게 새로운 마케팅 계획을 요청했다.
(C) 런던에서 학회를 준비했다.
(D) 프로젝트를 위해 세카다 씨의 회사를 고용했다.

해설 일정표의 설명 중 두 번째 항목에서 마르코스 세카다, 그라인드스톤 마케팅 그룹 창립자 겸 최고 경영자(Marcos Secada, founder and CEO, Grindstone Marketing Group)라고 나와 있고, 이메일의 첫 단락 두 번째 문장에서 드직 씨가 그라인드스톤 마케팅 그룹이 제작한 동영상 링크를 첨부한다(Attached is a link to the video created for us by Grindstone Marketing Group)고 했다. 따라서 드직 씨는 세카다 씨의 회사인 그라인드스톤 마케팅 그룹을 고용해 동영상을 제작하도록 했음을 알 수 있으므로 (D)가 정답이다.

어휘 shorten 짧게 하다 organize 준비하다

189 연계

번역 칼와르 씨에 대해 암시된 것은?
(A) 동영상 제작자이다.
(B) 독일에서 일한다.
(C) 셰필드에 집을 살 계획이다.
(D) 건축 자재를 전문으로 한다.

해설 이메일의 수신자인 나디르 칼와르의 이메일 주소가 〈kalwar.n@kdbuildingconcepts.com〉이고 발신자인 올렉 드직의 이메일 주소가 〈odzik.k@kdbuildingconcepts.com〉으로, 이 둘의 이메일 도메인이 같은 점을 보아 칼와르 씨와 드직 씨 모두 KD 빌딩 콘셉츠에서 근무한다는 것을 알 수 있다. 이메일 마지막 문장에서 드직 씨가 칼와르 씨에게 다음 공사 프로젝트는 칼와르 씨의 사무실 건물에서 불과 몇 킬로미터 거리에 있는 주택이 될 예정(our next construction project will be a home ~ from your office building!)이라고 했고, 기사의 마지막 문장에서 향후 KD 빌딩 콘셉츠는 독일 함부르크에 주택을 건설할 예정(Next on the horizon for KD Building concepts is the construction of a home in Hamburg, Germany)이라고 했으므로, 칼와르 씨는 KD 빌딩 콘셉츠가 다음 프로젝트로 주택을 건설할 예정인 독일에서 근무하고 있음을 알 수 있다. 따라서 (B)가 정답이다.

어휘 videographer 동영상 제작자 material 자재

190 Not / True

번역 기사에서 3D 프린터로 만든 주택에 대해 명시한 것은?
(A) 건설하는 데 15만 파운드가 들었다.
(B) 두 달 만에 끝났다.
(C) 다음 주에 조경이 될 것이다.
(D) 침실이 모두 같은 크기이다.

해설 기사의 두 번째 단락 마지막 문장에서 단 두 달 만에 침실 두 개와 욕실 두 개를 갖추고 조경이 완비된 주택이 시장에 나올 준비가 되었다(In just two months, the fully landscaped house ~ was ready for market)고 했으므로 주택이 두 달 만에 완공되었음을 알 수 있다. 따라서 (B)가 정답이다.

191-195 구인 광고 + 전단 + 기사

---

¹⁹⁴ **크롬우드의 리차드 라히리 갤러리 매니저**

¹⁹¹ 이 전임직에 지원하는 지원자는 소매 예술 분야에 경험이 있고 예술품 진품 구매에 관심이 있는 고객을 성공적으로 유치해 본 입증된 이력을 갖추고 있어야 합니다. 소셜 미디어 계정을 관리한 경력 또한 요구됩니다. 해당 직무는 주로 현장 근무이지만 일부 원격 근무 시간도 주어질 수 있습니다. ¹⁹⁴ 채용 후보자는 4월 1일 또는 그전에 근무를 시작할 수 있어야 합니다. 자격을 갖춘 지원자들은 갤러리 관장 리차드 라히리에게 rlahiri@richardlahirigallery.com으로 연락 주시길 바랍니다.

어휘 retail 소매 established 입증된 history 이력, 내력 attract 유치하다 patron 고객 desire 원하다 primarily 주로 on-site 현장에서 remote 원격의 candidate 지원자, 후보자 qualified 자격을 갖춘

---

¹⁹², ¹⁹³ **여름 풍경 예술 프로그램**

¹⁹², ¹⁹⁴ 5월 1일부터 크롬우드에 있는 미술관 다섯 곳에서 5월부터 8월까지 매주 금요일에 공개 참관 행사를 개최할 예정입니다. 방문하여 크롬우드 데크 산책로에서 라이브 음악, 다과, 예술가 강연 등을 즐기세요. 행사는 오후 4시에 시작해서 저녁 9시 30분까지 날씨에 상관없이 계속됩니다. 참여 미술관 목록은 아래와 같습니다.

리타 블레이크 아트 • 시트바 갤러리 • 리차드 라히리 갤러리
패트리샤 돌리보 페인팅 • ¹⁹³ 애쉬랜드 도자기와 공예품

크롬우드 시의회와 리젠츠 은행에서 후원합니다.

어휘 scene 풍경 refreshments 다과 boardwalk 데크 산책로 rain or shine 날씨에 상관없이, 비가 오나 맑으나 participating 참여하는 pottery 도자기 craft 공예품 fund 자금을 후원하다 City Council 시의회

미들턴 카운티의 여름 활동
리사 유-시버 작성

크롬우드 아트 나이츠
엘름허스트, 멜브릿지, 크롬우드의 주민들은 이번 여름 크롬우드의 지역 예술 현장을 답사할 수 있도록 초대됩니다. ¹⁹³ 와이 강이 내려다보이는 데크 산책로에 있는 다섯 곳의 미술관은 여름 풍경 예술 프로그램의 일환으로 매주 금요일 특별 행사를 엽니다. ¹⁹⁴ 이번 주 금요일에는 리차드 라히리와 그의 갤러리 매니저인 지투 겔랑이 거대한 스크린을 사용하여 가상 예술을 만드는 소프트웨어를 시연할 예정입니다. 이 행사는 또한 공예품 노점상, 푸드 트럭, 라이브 음악을 포함합니다. www.cromwood.gov/things-to-do에서 자세한 내용을 확인하세요.

브래디 공원의 영화
¹⁹⁵ 헤론타운에서 인기 있는 여름 영화 시리즈가 6월 16일에 돌아옵니다! 매주 토요일 저녁, 브래디 공원의 그랜드 론에서 고전 영화가 상영될 것입니다. 소풍 바구니와 담요를 가져오셔서 편안하게 즐기세요! 영화 시간표는 www.bradypark.org/activites에서 확인할 수 있습니다.

어휘 compile 작성하다 resident 주민 explore 답사하다 overlook 내려다보다 giant 거대한 demonstrate 시연하다 virtual 가상의 feature 특별히 포함하다, 특징으로 하다 vendor 노점상 project (영상 등을) 상영하다[비추다]

---

191 Not / True

번역 구인 광고에서 관리직에 대해 언급된 것은?
(A) 전적으로 현장 근무이다.
(B) 라히리 씨의 현재 직업이다.
(C) 영업 경험을 요구한다.
(D) 4월 1일까지 파트타임 근무이다.

해설 구인 광고의 첫 문장에서 이 전임직에 지원하는 지원자는 소매 예술 분야에 경험이 있고 예술품 진품 구매에 관심이 있는 고객을 성공적으로 유치해 본 입증된 이력을 갖추고 있어야 한다(Applicants for this full-time position must have experience ~ attracting patrons interested in purchasing original works of art)고 했다. 따라서 구인 광고에서 구하는 관리직 지원자는 예술 작품 판매 경험이 있어야 하는 것이므로 (C)가 정답이다.

192 세부사항

번역 전단에 따르면, 5월 1일에 일어날 일은?
(A) 공공 예술 프로그램이 시작될 것이다.
(B) 시의회 회의가 열릴 것이다.
(C) 새로운 미술관이 개관식을 개최할 것이다.
(D) 리젠츠 은행이 당일 문을 닫을 것이다.

해설 전단의 제목이 여름 풍경 예술 프로그램(Summer Scene Arts Program)이고, 첫 문장에서 5월 1일부터 크롬우드에 있는 미술관 다섯 곳에서 5월부터 8월까지 매주 금요일마다 공개 참관 행사를 개최할 예정(Starting on May 1, five art galleries in Cromwood will be hosting open houses ~ through August)이라고 했다. 따라서 5월 1일은 크롬우드의 미술관 다섯 곳에서 예술 프로그램이 시작되는 첫날임을 알 수 있으므로 (A)가 정답이다.

193 연계

번역 애쉬랜드 도자기와 공예품에 대해 암시된 것은?
(A) 와이 강 근처에 위치해 있다.
(B) 가상 예술을 전문으로 한다.
(C) 매주 토요일에 도자기 워크숍을 연다.
(D) 여름 영화 시리즈를 후원하고 있다.

해설 전단의 제목이 여름 풍경 예술 프로그램(Summer Scene Arts Program)이고 참여 미술관 목록에 애쉬랜드 도자기와 공예품(Ashland Pottery and Crafts)이 나와 있으며, 기사의 첫 단락 두 번째 문장에서 와이 강이 내려다보이는 데크 산책로에 있는 다섯 곳의 미술관은 여름 풍경 예술 프로그램의 일환으로 매주 금요일 특별 행사를 연다(The five galleries on the boardwalk overlooking the Wye River ~ Summer Scene Arts Program)고 했다. 따라서 애쉬랜드 도자기와 공예품은 와이 강이 내려다보이는 데크 산책로에 위치하고 있다는 것을 알 수 있으므로 (A)가 정답이다.

어휘 specialize in ~을 전문으로 하다 sponsor 후원하다

194 연계

번역 지투 겔랑에 대해 암시된 것은?
(A) 지역 음악가이다.
(B) 5월 1일에 자신의 공예품을 판매할 것이다.
(C) 소셜 미디어 계정을 시작할 계획이다.
(D) 최근에 리차드 라히리 갤러리에 고용되었다.

해설 리차드 라히리 갤러리 매니저(Gallery manager at Richard Lahiri Gallery) 구인 광고의 네 번째 문장에서 채용 후보자는 4월 1일 또는 그 전에 근무를 시작할 수 있어야 한다(Candidates must ~ start work on or before April 1)고 했다. 전단의 첫 문장에서 5월 1일부터 크롬우드에 있는 미술관 다섯 곳에서 5월부터 8월까지 매주 금요일에 공개 참관 행사를 개최할 예정(Starting on May 1, five art galleries ~ August)이라고 했고, 기사의 크롬우드 아트 나이츠(Cromwood Art Nights)가 제목인 첫 단락 세 번째 문장에서 이번 주 금요일에는 리차드 라히리와 그의 갤러리 매니저인 지투 겔랑이 가상 예술을 만드는 소프트웨어를 시연할 예정(This Friday, Richard Lahiri and his gallery manager, Geetu Gelang ~ virtual art)이라고 했다. 따라서 5월 1일부터 열리는 미술관 공개 참관 행사에 참여하는 리차드 라히리 갤러리의 매니저인 지투 겔랑은 4월 1일 경 즉, 최근에 고용되었음을 알 수 있으므로 (D)가 정답이다.

195 세부사항

번역 기사에 따르면, 브래디 공원이 위치한 곳은?
(A) 크롬우드
(B) 엘름허스트
(C) 헤론타운
(D) 멜브릿지

해설 기사의 두 번째 단락 첫 문장에서 헤론타운에서 인기 있는 여름 영화 시리즈가 6월 16일에 돌아온다(The popular summer movie series in Herrontown ~ 16!)고 했고, 매주 토요일 저녁, 브래디 공원의 그랜드 론에서 고전 영화가 상영될 것(Each Saturday evening, a classic film ~ Brady Park's Grand Lawn)이라고 했다. 따라서 브래디 공원은 헤론타운에 있다는 것을 알 수 있으므로 (C)가 정답이다.

196-200 기사 + 회람 + 정책

세나노 디자인스, 6천만 달러에 젠달라 인수

로스앤젤레스 (3월 20일) — **196, 197 패션 강자 세나노 디자인스가 떠오르는 명품 브랜드 젠달라를 인수했다고 수요일에 발표했다.** 이번 인수는 디자이너 시계 라인으로 의류 제품을 보완하려는 세나노의 계획의 일환이다. 향후 2년 동안 회사는 향수와 여행 가방을 포함하여 제품을 확장하려는 추가 계획을 가지고 있다. 세나노의 최고 경영자인 리나 파체코는 다른 국제적인 패션 회사들에 뒤지지 않고 경쟁하려면 이러한 확장이 필수적이라고 말했다. **199 세나노는 로스앤젤레스에 본사를 두고 있지만** 최근 몇 년간 필라델피아, 시카고, 마이애미에 지사를 열었다. 파체코 씨는 1년 전 자동차 잡지에서 광고를 하나 봤을 때까지 젠달라 제품을 잘 알지 못했다고 말한다. "제품들이 독특하고 현대적인 스타일을 가지고 있으며, 세나노의 유행을 선도하는 의류와 잘 어울릴 것입니다."라고 파체코 씨는 말했다.

회람

발신: 회계부 오스카 요한슨
수신: 젠달라 전 직원
날짜: 3월 22일
제목: 출장 경비 정책
첨부: 정책

우리가 공식적으로 세나노 직원이 되는 3월 31일부터 시행될 세나노의 출장 경비 정책 사본을 첨부했습니다.

세나노의 정책은 몇 가지 면에서 젠달라의 정책보다 더 제한적이라는 점에 유의하십시오. 예를 들어, 직원들은 더 이상 경비 보고서를 제출하는 데 한 달의 기간을 갖지 않게 됩니다. 하지만 **200 새로운 정책으로 일부 절차는 훨씬 더 쉬워질 것이며, 특히 50달러 미만의 경비 제출에 대한 세나노의 요건은 현재 젠달라 정책에 따른 것보다 더 간단합니다.**

198, 199 세나노 본사에서 근무하는 회계 책임자 칼리 도슨이 198 3월 28일 목요일 오후 2시에 이를 포함한 기타 정책 관련 변경사항에 대한 설명회를 하기 위해 우리 뉴욕 사무실을 방문할 예정입니다. 여러분의 참석을 강력히 권장합니다.

**세나노 디자인스
출장 경비 정책**

- 업무 관련 출장에 대해 환급을 받기 위해 직원들은 출장 최소 2주 전에 출장 사유를 기재하고 모든 경비를 추산한 출장 요청서를 제출해야 합니다.
- **200 50달러 이상의 경비에 대해서는 원본 영수증을 제출해야 합니다. 그 미만의 경비에 대해서는 원본 영수증을 제출할 필요가 없습니다.**
- 모든 영수증과 경비 보고서는 출장이 완료된 후 3주 이내에 제출되어야 합니다. 이 시간 이후 제출되는 경비는 부장의 승인이 필요합니다.

1페이지

---

196 세부사항

번역 젠달라가 주로 생산하는 것은?
(A) 시계
(B) 여행 가방
(C) 의류
(D) 향수

해설 기사의 첫 문장에서 패션 강자 세나노 디자인스가 떠오르는 명품 브랜드 젠달라를 인수했다고 수요일에 발표했다(Fashion powerhouse Senano Designs ~ had acquired Gendalla, an up-and-coming luxury brand)고 했고, 이번 인수는 디자이너 시계 라인으로 의류 제품을 보완하려는 세나노의 계획의 일환(The acquisition is ~ to supplement its clothing products with a line of designer watches)이라고 했다. 따라서 젠달라는 명품 시계 브랜드임을 알 수 있으므로 (A)가 정답이다.

197 세부사항

번역 기사에 따르면, 세나노 디자인스가 젠달라를 인수한 이유는?
(A) 더 낮은 가격에 제품을 판매하려고
(B) 소셜 미디어 인지도를 넓히려고
(C) 더 다양한 제품을 제공하려고
(D) 일부 도시에서 감소하는 매출을 해결하려고

해설 기사의 첫 문장에서 패션 강자 세나노 디자인스가 떠오르는 명품 브랜드 젠달라를 인수했다고 수요일에 발표했다(Fashion powerhouse Senano Designs ~ had acquired Gendalla, an up-and-coming luxury brand)고 했고, 이번 인수는 디자이너 시계 라인으로 의류 제품을 보완하려는 세나노의 계획의 일환 (The acquisition is ~ to supplement its clothing products with a line of designer watches)이라고 했다. 따라서 세나노 디자인스는 제품 라인을 확장하려는 의도로 시계 브랜드인 젠달라를 인수했음을 알 수 있으므로 (C)가 정답이다.

어휘 expand 넓히다, 확장하다 presence 영향력, 존재감 diverse 다양한 a range of 다양한 address 해결하다 declining 하락하는

198 세부사항

번역 젠달라의 직원들이 3월 28일에 하라고 요청받은 일은?
(A) 출장 정책에 대한 변경 제안
(B) 오후 회의 참석
(C) 세나노 기업 본사 둘러보기
(D) 회계사와 일정 잡기

해설 회람의 마지막 단락 첫 문장에서 젠달라의 전 직원들에게 세나노 본사에서 근무하는 회계 책임자 칼리 도슨이 3월 28일 목요일 오후 2시에 기타 정책 관련 변경사항에 대한 설명회를 하기 위해 뉴욕 사무실을 방문할 예정(Carlie Dawson ~ policy-related changes on Thursday, March 28, at 2:00 P.M.)이라면서 전 직원들의 참석을 강력히 권장한다(I strongly encourage you to attend)고 했으므로 (B)가 정답이다.

어휘 corporate 기업 accountant 회계사

199 연계

번역 도슨 씨의 사무실은 어디에 있는가?
(A) 뉴욕
(B) 시카고
(C) 필라델피아
(D) 로스앤젤레스

해설 기사의 다섯 번째 문장에서 세나노는 로스앤젤레스에 본사를 두고 있지만(Although based in Los Angeles)이라고 했고, 회람의 마지막 단락 첫 문장에서 젠달라의 전 직원들에게 세나노 본사에서 근무하는 회계 책임자 칼리 도슨(Carlie Dawson, an accounting director who works at Senano's headquarters)이라고 했다. 따라서 도슨 씨는 세나노의 본사가 있는 로스앤젤레스에서 근무한다는 것을 알 수 있으므로 (D)가 정답이다.

200 연계

번역 젠달라의 현재 출장 경비 정책은 세나노의 정책과 어떻게 다른 것 같은가?
(A) 모든 경비에 대해 영수증을 제출해야 한다.
(B) 50달러 이상의 경비에 대해 사전 승인을 받아야 한다.
(C) 경비 보고서는 관리자의 서명을 받아야 한다.
(D) 직원들은 합동으로 경비 보고서를 제출할 수 있다.

해설 회람의 두 번째 단락 세 번째 문장에서 새로운 정책으로 일부 절차는 훨씬 더 쉬워질 것이며 특히 50달러 미만의 경비를 제출하는 데 대한 세나노의 요건은 현재 젠달라 정책에 따른 것보다 더 간단하다(the new policy ~ Senano's requirements for submitting expenses under $50 are simpler than those under current Gendalla policy)고 했고, 세나노의 출장 경비 정책의 두 번째 항목에서 50달러 이상의 경비에 대해서는 원본 영수증을 제출해야 한다(Original receipts ~ for expenses above $50)고 했고 그 미만의 경비에 대해서는 원본 영수증을 제출할 필요가 없다(Any expenses below that do not require the submission of original receipts)고 했다. 따라서 영수증을 제출할 필요가 없는 세나노의 50달러 미만 경비에 대한 정책과는 달리 젠달라에서는 모든 영수증을 제출해야 한다는 것을 알 수 있으므로 (A)가 정답이다.

어휘 preapproval 사전 승인 obtain 얻다 jointly 합동으로, 함께

101 (B)	**102** (B)	**103** (C)	**104** (C)	**105** (B)
106 (C)	**107** (C)	**108** (D)	**109** (A)	**110** (A)
111 (A)	**112** (A)	**113** (C)	**114** (C)	**115** (B)
116 (B)	**117** (D)	**118** (C)	**119** (C)	**120** (A)
121 (A)	**122** (D)	**123** (D)	**124** (D)	**125** (B)
126 (A)	**127** (D)	**128** (A)	**129** (C)	**130** (A)
131 (B)	**132** (A)	**133** (C)	**134** (B)	**135** (C)
136 (A)	**137** (C)	**138** (D)	**139** (A)	**140** (D)
141 (C)	**142** (B)	**143** (A)	**144** (B)	**145** (B)
146 (B)	**147** (C)	**148** (B)	**149** (C)	**150** (C)
151 (C)	**152** (D)	**153** (A)	**154** (B)	**155** (B)
156 (A)	**157** (C)	**158** (C)	**159** (B)	**160** (B)
161 (B)	**162** (D)	**163** (C)	**164** (D)	**165** (A)
166 (B)	**167** (A)	**168** (B)	**169** (D)	**170** (C)
171 (C)	**172** (B)	**173** (A)	**174** (A)	**175** (D)
176 (B)	**177** (D)	**178** (A)	**179** (A)	**180** (B)
181 (B)	**182** (C)	**183** (B)	**184** (B)	**185** (B)
186 (C)	**187** (B)	**188** (A)	**189** (A)	**190** (B)
191 (B)	**192** (A)	**193** (D)	**194** (D)	**195** (A)
196 (A)	**197** (B)	**198** (D)	**199** (A)	**200** (B)

PART 5

101 인칭대명사의 격 _ 소유격

해설 빈칸에는 to set의 목적어 역할을 하는 명사구 own working hours를 수식하는 말이 필요하므로 소유격 인칭대명사 (B) their가 정답이다.

번역 새로운 정책은 직원들이 특정 조건 하에서 자신의 근무 시간을 정할 수 있도록 허용한다.

어휘 policy 정책   certain 특정한   conditions 조건

102 전치사 자리

해설 빈칸 앞에 완전한 절(Paik Company increased ~ projections)이 있고 뒤에 명사구 the current year가 있으므로 빈칸은 전치사 자리이다. 문맥상 '올해에 대한 매출 전망치'라는 의미가 되어야 적절하므로 '~에 대한'이라는 뜻의 전치사 (B) for가 정답이다. (A) when, (C) if, (D) or는 접속사이므로 빈칸에 들어갈 수 없다.

번역 백 회사는 작년 자료를 바탕으로 올해 매출 전망치를 상향 조정했다.

어휘 projection 예상[추정]

103 전치사 어휘

해설 빈칸 뒤에 기간을 나타내는 명사구 standard business hours가 있고, 문맥상 '표준 영업시간 동안에'라는 의미가 되어야 자연스러우므로

'~ 동안'을 뜻하는 (C) during이 정답이다. (A) among은 '~ 사이에', (B) beside는 '~ 옆에', (D) onto는 '~ 위로'라는 의미이다.

번역 하비슨스 백화점은 표준 영업시간에 지원자 면접을 본다.

어휘 applicant 지원자

104 형용사 자리 _ 명사 수식 / 비교급

해설 빈칸에는 전치사 to의 목적어인 명사 areas를 수식하는 형용사나 areas와 복합명사를 이루는 명사가 들어갈 수 있다. 문맥상 '더 넓은 공간에 온기를 전달한다'라는 내용이 되어야 하므로 형용사 wide의 비교급인 (C) wider(더 넓은)가 정답이다. 명사 (A) wideness는 '넓이, 폭'을 의미하므로 areas와 복합명사를 이루기에 적절하지 않고, (B) widen은 동사, (D) widely는 부사이므로 빈칸에 들어갈 수 없다.

번역 테이컬롱 인더스트리스의 상업용 프로판 히터는 더 넓은 공간에 더 많은 온기를 전달한다.

어휘 commercial 상업의   propane 프로판(가스)   warmth 온기

105 부사 자리 _ 동사 수식

해설 빈칸은 동사구 has improved를 수식하는 부사 자리이므로 '크게'라는 뜻의 부사 (B) greatly가 정답이다. 참고로, great는 주로 형용사로 쓰이지만 부사로 쓰이는 경우도 있는데, 이때는 '아주 잘'이라는 뜻으로 보통 동사 뒤에 쓰고 improve와 문맥상 어울리지 않으므로 답이 될 수 없다.

번역 새로운 프로젝트 관리 소프트웨어로 전환함으로써 편집팀은 출판 과정을 크게 개선했다.

어휘 switch 전환하다   editorial 편집의   publication 출판   process 과정

106 동사 자리 _ 태

해설 The search committee가 주어인 문장에 동사가 보이지 않으므로 빈칸은 동사 자리이다. 빈칸 뒤에 목적어 three candidates가 있으므로 능동태가 와야 한다. 따라서 (C) has nominated가 정답이다. (A) nominating은 현재분사/동명사, (B) nomination 명사, (D) has been nominated는 현재완료 수동태이므로 빈칸에 들어갈 수 없다.

번역 인사 위원회는 최고 경영자 자리에 세 명의 후보를 지명했다.

어휘 search committee 인사 위원회   candidate 후보자   nominate 지명하다

107 전치사 자리

해설 명사구 a two-month delay를 목적어로 취하는 전치사 자리로, 문맥상 '두 달의 지연 이후에'라는 의미가 되어야 자연스러우므로 '~ 후에'라는 의미의 전치사 (C) After가 정답이다. (A) Additionally는 부사, (B) Although는 부사절 접속사, (D) Furthermore는 접속부사이므로 빈칸에 들어갈 수 없다.

번역 두 달의 지연 끝에 동쪽 회의실에 새로운 카펫이 깔렸다.

어휘 install 설치하다

108 명사 자리 _ to부정사의 목적어

해설 빈칸은 to부정사구 to boost의 목적어 역할을 하는 명사 자리이므로 '등록'이라는 뜻의 명사 (D) enrollment가 정답이다. (A) enroll은 동사, (B) enrolled는 동사/과거분사이므로 품사상 답이 될 수 없고, (C) enrolling을 동명사로 볼 경우 구조상으로는 빈칸에 들어갈 수 있으나, 등록하는 행위를 나타내므로 의미상 boost의 목적어로 적절하지 않다.

번역 메이크업 아티스트 아카데미는 등록을 늘리기 위해 신입생들에게 입문자용 무료 키트를 제공하고 있다.

어휘 boost 늘리다   offer 제공하다   kit (도구) 세트

109 동사 어휘

해설 문맥상 확실한 호텔 개관일을 확정할 수 있었던 이유가 와야 하므로 '가구 회사가 배송 시간을 보장해 주기 때문에'라는 의미가 되어야 적절하다. 따라서 '보장하다'를 뜻하는 (A) guarantees가 정답이다. (B)의 advise는 '조언하다', (C)의 require는 '요구하다', (D)의 delay는 '연기하다'라는 의미이다.

번역 렉툴라 가구 회사가 배송 시간을 보장해 주기 때문에 우리는 새 호텔의 개관 날짜를 확정할 수 있었다.

어휘 firm 확실한

110 형용사 어휘

해설 빈칸은 주어인 The computer technician을 보충 설명하는 주격 보어 자리로, '기술자'를 꾸미기에 적절한 형용사를 골라야 한다. 빈칸 뒤에 '그가 문제를 해결하지는 못했다'라는 절이 접속사 but으로 연결되었으므로 빈칸 앞은 상반되는 내용이 되어야 한다. 따라서 '친절한'이라는 뜻의 (A) friendly가 정답이다. (B) neutral은 '중립의', (C) possible은 '가능한', (D) frequent는 '빈번한'이라는 의미이다.

번역 그 컴퓨터 기술자는 매우 친절했지만 나의 문제를 해결하지 못했다.

111 형용사 자리 _ 명사 수식

해설 빈칸에는 명사 visitors를 수식하는 형용사 또는 visitors와 복합 명사를 이루는 명사가 들어갈 수 있다. 문맥상 '정기적인 방문객들'이 되어야 자연스러우므로 형용사 (A) regular(정기적인)가 정답이다. (B) regularly는 부사, (C) regularize는 동사이고, 명사 (D) regularity는 '질서, 규칙적임'을 의미하기 때문에 visitors와 복합 명사를 이루기에 적절하지 않으므로 빈칸에 들어갈 수 없다.

번역 회의 참석자를 위한 공간을 마련하기 위해, 사무실 건물의 정기 방문객들은 내일 뒤쪽 주차장을 이용해야 한다.

어휘 room 공간   attendee 참석자   rear 뒤쪽의

112 부사 어휘

해설 빈칸 뒤 형용사 visible을 수식하기에 적절한 부사를 고르는 문제이다. 문맥상 '분명히 알아볼 수 있는 방법'이라는 의미가 되어야 하므로 '분명히'라는 뜻의 (A) clearly가 정답이다. (B) recently는 '최근에', (C) evenly는 '고르게', (D) secretly는 '비밀리에, 몰래'라는 의미이다.

번역 직원들은 건물 내에 있을 때 분명히 알아볼 수 있는 방법으로 보안 배지를 착용해야 한다.

어휘 security 보안   visible 보이는, 알아볼 수 있는

113 접속부사 자리 / 어휘

해설 빈칸 앞의 세미콜론이 두 개의 완전한 문장을 연결하고 있으므로 빈칸에는 두 문장을 자연스럽게 연결할 접속부사가 들어가야 한다. 개관식 참석을 원했다는 앞 문장과 악천후로 불가능했다는 뒤 문장이 상반된 내용이므로 역접 관계를 나타내는 (C) however가 정답이다. 접속부사 (A) therefore는 '그러므로', (D) for example은 '예를 들어'이므로 문맥상 어울리지 않고, (B) following은 '~ 후에'라는 뜻의 전치사로 품사상 빈칸에 들어갈 수 없다.

번역 폰 씨는 갤러리 개관식에 참석하기를 원했지만 악천후로 인해 참석할 수 없었다.

어휘 attend 참석하다   inclement 궂은[좋지 못한]

114 동사 어휘   동영상 강의

해설 빈칸 뒤 목적어 them 뒤로 목적격 보어 역할을 하는 to부정사가 있고, '그들이 더 생산적으로 작업하도록 동기를 부여해 준다'라는 내용이 되어야 적절하므로 '동기를 부여하다'라는 뜻의 (C) motivates가 정답이다. motivate는 「motivate + 목적어 + to부정사」의 5형식 구조로 '…이 ~하도록 동기를 부여하다'라는 의미를 나타낸다. (A)의 adopt는 '채택하다', (B)의 reinforce는 '강화하다', (D)의 attract는 '끌어들이다'라는 의미이다.

번역 창고 소포 담당자들에게 리더십 과제를 주는 것은 종종 그들이 더 생산적으로 작업하도록 동기를 부여해 준다.

어휘 handler 처리[취급]하는 사람   productively 생산적으로

115 부사 자리 _ 동사 수식

해설 works는 목적어가 필요 없는 자동사로, 빈칸이 없어도 완전한 절이 이루어지므로 빈칸에는 동사 works를 수식하는 부사가 들어가야 한다. 따라서 '오로지; 독점적으로'라는 뜻의 부사 (A) exclusively가 정답이다. (B) exclusive는 형용사/명사, (C) exclusivity는 명사, (D) exclusives는 명사이므로 빈칸에 들어갈 수 없다.

번역 케이빙 건설은 뉴펀들랜드 지역에서 대형 상업 프로젝트만 전담하고 있다.

어휘 commercial 상업의   exclusive 독점적인; 독점권

116 to부정사 vs. 동명사 / 시제

해설 동사 plans는 to부정사를 목적어로 취하는 동사이므로 보기에서 (B) to resign과 (D) to have resigned 중 하나를 선택해야 한다. 동사 plan은 앞으로 할 일을 계획하는 것이므로 (B) to resign이 정답이다. (D) to have resigned는 완료 부정사로 주절의 시제인 현재 시제보다 앞선 과거 시제를 나타내므로 미래 계획의 의미를 지닌 plan의 목적어로 쓰일 수 없다. (A) resigning은 현재분사/동명사, (C) resigns는 동사이므로 품사상 빈칸에 들어갈 수 없다.

TEST 6

번역 칼리 로건이 사임할 계획이어서 앨런 질은 우표 클럽의 다음 회계 담당자가 되기를 자청했다.

어휘 volunteer 자청하다   treasurer 회계 담당자   resign 사임하다

117 전치사 자리

 동영상 강의

해설 빈칸 앞에 부사절 접속사 Although가 이끄는 완전한 절(the housing market slowed)이 있고 뒤에 명사구 the summer months가 있으므로 빈칸에는 전치사가 들어가야 한다. 따라서 기간 명사와 함께 쓰여 '~ 동안'을 의미하는 전치사 (D) over가 정답이다. (A) apart는 형용사/부사, (B) even은 형용사/부사/동사, (C) only는 형용사/부사이므로 빈칸에 들어갈 수 없다.

번역 여름 몇 달간 주택 시장이 주춤했지만 가을에 매매가 다시 살아나기 시작했다.

어휘 housing 주택   pick up 회복되다, 나아지다

118 부사 어휘

해설 빈칸 앞의 be cleaned를 수식하여 '정기적으로 청소되어야 한다'라는 의미가 되어야 적절하므로 '정기적으로, 일상적으로'라는 뜻의 (C) routinely가 정답이다. (A) rather는 '다소', (B) almost는 '거의', (D) openly는 '공공연히'라는 의미이다.

번역 완전한 기능을 유지하려면 운동 기계를 정기적으로 청소해야 한다.

어휘 remain (~인 상태로) 있다   functional 기능을 하는

119 복합관계사

해설 빈칸 앞에 완전한 절(The extended warranty is good ~)이 있고, 빈칸 뒤에 동사가 있으므로 접속사가 필요하다. 문맥상 '(10년과 10만 마일 중) 어느 것이 먼저 오든지'라는 의미가 되어야 자연스러우므로 '어느 쪽이든 ~한 것'이라는 뜻으로 주어 역할을 하면서 절을 연결할 수 있는 복합관계대명사 (C) whichever가 정답이다. 이때, whichever는 부사절 접속사로 쓰여 콤마 앞의 주절을 수식하고 있다. 복합관계대명사 (A) whoever는 '누가 ~하든지'라는 의미로 문맥상 적절하지 않고, (B) either와 (D) another는 부정대명사/수량형용사로, 접속사 역할을 할 수 없으므로 빈칸에 들어갈 수 없다.

번역 연장 보증은 10년 또는 10만 마일 중 먼저 도달하는 것에 적용됩니다.

어휘 extended 연장된   warranty 품질 보증(서)   good 유효한

120 동사 어휘

 동영상 강의

해설 온라인 쇼핑 옵션을 제공해야 하고 그렇지 않으면(or) '고객을 잃을 위험을 감수하다'라는 의미가 되어야 적절하므로 '위험을 감수하다'를 뜻하는 (A) risk가 정답이다. (B) protect는 '보호하다', (C) cancel은 '취소하다', (D) hold는 '개최하다, 잡다'라는 의미이다.

번역 애틀랜틱 식료품점은 온라인 쇼핑 옵션을 제공해야 하고, 그렇지 않으면 다른 슈퍼마켓에 고객을 빼앗길 위험을 감수해야 한다.

어휘 grocer 식료품점   lose 잃다

121 수량 형용사

 동영상 강의

해설 빈칸 뒤에 가산 단수명사인 client가 있으므로 (A) Each가 정답이다. (B) All, (C) Some, (D) Most는 뒤에 복수명사 또는 불가산명사가 와야 하므로 답이 될 수 없다.

번역 각 고객은 문의사항을 받게 되는 개인 재무 자문가에게 배정된다.

어휘 assign 배정하다   inquiry 문의   address to ~에게 보내다

122 명사 어휘

 동영상 강의

해설 to form(구성하다)의 목적어 자리에 들어가기에 적합한 명사를 골라야 하므로 구성할 수 있는 대상이어야 한다. 문맥상 '조사를 위한 위원회를 구성하기를 원한다'라는 내용이 되어야 자연스러우므로 '위원회'를 의미하는 (D) committee가 정답이다. (A) supervisor는 '관리자, 감독', (B) suggestion은 '제안, 의견', (C) notification은 '알림, 통지'라는 의미이다.

번역 싱 씨는 몇몇 직원 보상 프로그램을 알아보기 위해 위원회를 구성하고자 한다.

어휘 explore 알아보다, 조사하다   reward 보상

123 접속사 자리 _ 부사절 접속사 / 어휘

해설 빈칸 뒤에 the delivery driver가 주어, needs가 동사인 완전한 절이 왔으므로 부사절 접속사가 필요하고, 문맥상 '기사가 연락해야 할 경우에 대비하여'라는 내용이 되어야 하므로 '~한 경우에 대비해서'를 뜻하는 부사절 접속사 (D) in case가 정답이다. 부사절 접속사 (A) whereas는 '반면에'라는 의미로 문맥상 적절하지 않고 (B) despite는 전치사, (C) if not은 접속부사이므로 품사상 빈칸에 들어갈 수 없다.

번역 배달 기사가 연락해야 할 경우에 대비해 전화번호를 알려주십시오.

124 명사 어휘

해설 문맥상 빈칸에 들어갈 주어는 매달 임대료를 지불해야 하는 사람이므로 '세입자'를 뜻하는 (D) Tenants가 정답이다. (A)의 owner는 '주인, 소유자', (B)의 buyer는 '구매자', (C)의 tourist는 '관광객'이라는 의미이다.

번역 폰드뷰 타워의 세입자는 매월 1일 또는 그 전에 임대료를 지불해야 한다.

125 형용사 자리 _ 명사 수식

해설 빈칸에는 명사 impact를 수식하는 형용사 또는 impact와 복합명사를 이루는 명사가 들어갈 수 있다. 문맥상 '상당한 영향을 미친다'라는 내용이 되어야 자연스러우므로 형용사 (B) considerable(상당한)이 정답이다. (A) considerably는 부사이므로 빈칸에 들어갈 수 없고, impact는 consider(고려하다)의 주체가 아니므로 능동의 의미를 나타내는 현재분사 (C) considering은 답이 될 수 없다. 명사 (D) consideration은 '고려'를 의미하기 때문에 impact와 복합명사를 이루기에 문맥상 적절하지 않다.

번역 몸바사에서 가장 큰 회사 중 하나인 리코니 호스피탤리티 그룹은 지역 경제에 상당한 영향을 미친다.

어휘 hospitality 접객(업) employer 회사, 고용주 impact 영향

126 전치사 자리

해설 빈칸은 명사구 best sellers를 목적어로 취하는 전치사 자리로, 문맥상 '베스트셀러 이외에도'라는 의미가 되어야 자연스럽다. 따라서 '~ 이외에도'라는 의미의 전치사 (A) Besides가 정답이다. (B) Somewhat은 부사/명사, (C) Whose는 관계대명사/의문사이고, 현재분사 (D) Becoming은 부사절의 주어가 주절의 주어 Booksters와 일치하지 않기 때문에 분사구문으로 쓰일 수 없으므로 정답이 될 수 없다.

번역 베스트셀러 이외에도, 북스터스는 다양한 고전 문학과 전기를 제공한다.

어휘 a selection of 다양한 biography 전기 somewhat 다소

127 동명사 _ 동사의 주어 ▶ 동영상 강의

해설 빈칸은 that절의 동사 can be의 주어 자리이므로 명사나 동명사가 들어갈 수 있다. 빈칸 뒤에 목적어 undercooked meat가 있어 '덜 익은 고기를 먹는 것'이라는 내용이 되어야 하므로 동명사 (D) consuming이 정답이다. (A) consumer와 (B) consumption은 명사이므로 뒤에 목적어를 취할 수 없고, (C) consumes는 동사이므로 빈칸에 들어갈 수 없다.

번역 새로운 식품 규정은 모든 딘스 버거스 포장에 덜 익은 고기를 섭취하는 것이 해로울 수 있다는 공지문을 포함할 것을 요구한다.

어휘 regulation 규정 packaging 포장 contain 포함하다 notice 공지 undercooked 설익은 harmful 해로운 consume 먹다, 마시다

128 전치사 어휘

해설 빈칸 뒤의 명사구 the fat and cholesterol을 앞의 부정대명사 none에 연결하여 '지방과 콜레스테롤 중 아무것도 없이'라는 의미가 되어야 하므로 '~ 중, ~의'를 뜻하는 (A) of가 정답이다. (B) by는 '~에 의해, ~ 옆에', (C) out은 '~ 밖으로', (D) minus는 '~을 제외한[뺀]'이라는 의미이다.

번역 각각의 제누트리아 스낵바에는 지방과 콜레스테롤 없이 달걀 두 개만큼의 단백질이 들어 있다.

어휘 contain ~이 들어 있다, 함유하다 protein 단백질

129 명사 어휘

해설 형용사 various의 수식을 받는 명사 자리로, 뒤에 전치사 including과 함께 '원형, 사각형, 타원형'이라는 모양의 예시가 언급된 것으로 보아 '안경테가 다양한 모양으로 제공된다'라는 내용이 되어야 자연스럽다. 따라서 '모양'을 뜻하는 (C) shapes가 정답이다. (A)의 sight는 '시력', (B)의 method는 '방법', (D)의 material은 '자재, 재료'라는 의미이다.

번역 피스코 안경테는 원형, 사각형, 타원형을 포함해 다양한 모양으로 제공된다.

어휘 frame 틀, 뼈대 oval 타원형

130 동사 어휘

해설 동사 wants의 목적격 보어 자리로, 목적어인 명사구 a greater portion of next year's budget을 보충 설명하기에 적절한 과거분사형의 동사 어휘를 고르는 문제이다. 빈칸 뒤에 '~에'라는 의미를 지닌 to와 함께 예산이 쓰일 사용처가 온 것이 주요 단서로, '예산이 연구 개발에 할당되기를 원한다'라는 내용이 되어야 자연스러우므로 '할당하다'라는 동사의 과거분사형 (A) allocated가 정답이다. (B)의 imprint는 '각인하다', (C)의 economize는 '절약하다', (D)의 rationalize는 '합리화하다'라는 의미이다.

번역 CEO는 내년 예산의 더 많은 부분을 연구 개발에 할당하기를 원한다.

어휘 portion 부분

PART 6

131-134 광고

에스텔라 기타 강습: 최고와 연주하세요.

어쿠스틱 기타를 연주¹³¹**하든** 전자 기타를 연주하든, 에스텔라 기타 선생님과 함께하는 수업은 여러분의 능력을 향상시키는 최고의 방법입니다. 연주 기술을 다듬어온 다년간의 경험을 가진 ¹³²**우리의** 자격을 갖춘 강사들이 여러분이 세부 조정을 원하는 기술에 초점을 두어 맞춤 수업을 제공합니다. 목표를 설정하고 많은 연주자들을 낙담시키는 어려움을 극복하기 위한 맞춤형 학습 계획을 받아 보세요. ¹³³**학습자로서 여러분에게 가장 좋은 자원은 여러분의 발전 과정을 지도해 주는 전문가입니다.** 에스텔라 기타 선생님이 자신감을 높이도록 도와드릴 것입니다.

에스텔라 기타에서는 음악을 연주하는 것이 자신을 표현하는 방법이라고 믿습니다. ¹³⁴**이를 염두에 두고,** 익숙한 화음과 리프를 넘어 음악가로서 자신만의 정체성을 개발할 수 있도록 도와드리겠습니다. 시작할 준비가 되셨나요? www.estellaguitar.com/lessons를 방문하셔서 여러분에게 맞는 강사를 찾으세요!

어휘 craft 공들여 만들다 qualified 자격을 갖춘 instructor 강사 tailor 맞추다[조정하다] fine-tune 세부[미세] 조정을 하다 customized 맞춤형의 overcome 극복하다 discourage 낙담시키다 boost 신장시키다 confidence 자신감 express 표현하다 familiar 익숙한 chord 화음 riff 리프, 반복 악절 identity 정체성

131 접속사 자리 _ whether A or B

해설 Whether는 부사절 접속사로 쓰일 때 등위접속사 or가 뒤따라야 하며, 'whether A or B'의 형태로 쓰여 'A이든 B이든 상관없이'라는 의미를 나타낸다. Whether가 이끄는 부사절에 빈칸이 있고, 문맥상 '어쿠스틱 기타를 연주하든 전자 기타를 연주하든'이라는 의미가 되어야 하므로 (B) or이 정답이다.

132 인칭대명사의 격 _ 소유격

해설 빈칸에는 뒤에 온 명사구 qualified instructors를 수식하는 인칭대명사가 들어가야 한다. 따라서 명사 앞에 쓰여 한정사 역할을 할 수 있는 소유격 인칭대명사 (A) our가 정답이다.

133 문맥에 맞는 문장 고르기

번역 (A) 수리에 대한 문의는 기술자에게 연락하세요.
(B) 고품질의 악기가 최고의 연주를 할 수 있도록 도와줄 것입니다.
(C) 학습자로서 여러분에게 가장 좋은 자원은 여러분의 발전 과정을 지도해 주는 전문가입니다.
(D) 그들이 악기를 마스터하는 데는 몇 년이 걸렸습니다.

해설 앞 문장에서 강사들이 학생이 조정하고 싶어 하는 기술에 초점을 두어 수업을 맞춰주는 맞춤형 학습 계획을 제공한다(qualified instructors can tailor lessons ~ to fine-tune)고 했고, 뒤 문장에는 선생님이 자신감을 높이도록 도와준다(An Estella Guitar teacher will help boost your confidence)며 기타 연주 실력을 습득하는 데 있어 강사의 역할을 강조하고 있다. 따라서 빈칸에는 학습자에게 가장 좋은 자원은 지도 전문가, 즉, 강사라고 언급하는 내용이 들어가야 앞뒤 연결이 자연스러우므로 (C)가 정답이다.

어휘 technician 기술자 instrument 악기 resource 자원 expert 전문가 progress 발전, 진행

134 접속부사

해설 앞 문장에는 에스텔라 기타에서는 음악을 연주하는 것이 자신을 표현하는 방법이라고 믿는다(a way of expressing yourself)고 했고, 뒤 문장에는 음악가로서 자신만의 정체성을 개발할 수 있도록 도와준다(develop your own identity as a musician)고 했다. 두 문장이 인과 관계를 나타내고 있으므로 '그 점을 염두에 두고'를 뜻하는 (B) With that in mind가 정답이다. (A) So far는 '지금까지', (C) On a different note는 '그런데, 주제를 바꿔서', (D) At that point 는 '그 시점에서'라는 의미이다.

135-138 정책

> 자택 배송은 주문이 창고에서 발송된 후 약 일주일이 걸립니다. 실제 시간은 135 **거주지**의 위치 및 물품 수령 가능 여부에 따라 달라질 수 있습니다. 베르니코 가구는 귀하에게 편리한 시간을 136 **잡기 위해** 운송 회사와 협력할 것입니다. 일반적인 시간은 월요일부터 금요일까지 오전 8시부터 오후 5시 사이137 **이지만**, 저녁 예약도 종종 가능합니다. 주문 상품은 집에 도착하는 즉시 원하시는 위치에 놓입니다. 138 **포장재는 모두 제거됩니다.** 조립 서비스도 포함되어 있습니다.
>
> 어휘 approximately 대략 warehouse 창고 actual 실제의 vary 다르다 carrier 운송 회사 convenient 편리한 typical 일반적인, 전형적인 desire 원하다 assembly 조립

135 명사 어휘

해설 빈칸 앞 문장에서 주문이 창고에서 발송된 후 자택 배송에 걸리는 대략적인 시간을 언급하였으므로, 집의 위치에 따라 실제 배송 시간

이 달라질 수 있다는 내용이 되어야 적절하다. 따라서 '주택, 거주지'를 뜻하는 (C) residence가 정답이다. (A) garden은 '정원', (B)의 record는 '기록', (D) organization은 '조직, 단체'라는 의미이다.

136 to부정사 _ 부사적 용법

해설 빈칸 앞에 완전한 절(Vernico Furniture will work ~ carrier)이 있고 빈칸 뒤에 명사구 an appointment를 목적어로 취할 수 있어야 하므로 부사 역할을 하는 to부정사가 와야 한다. 문맥상 '편리한 시간을 잡기 위해'라는 의미가 되어야 적절하므로 '~하기 위해서'라는 목적의 의미를 가진 (A) to schedule이 정답이다. (D) that scheduled는 '약속을 (과거에) 잡은'이라는 의미가 되어 문맥에 적합하지 않다.

137 접속사 자리 _ 부사절 접속사 / 어휘

해설 빈칸 뒤에 완전한 절(evening appointments can often be arranged)이 왔으므로 부사절 접속사가 들어가야 한다. 문맥상 '일반적인 시간은 오전 8시부터 오후 5시 사이이지만 저녁 예약도 가능하다'라는 내용이 되어야 자연스러우므로 '~이지만'이라는 의미의 (C) though가 정답이다.

138 문맥에 맞는 문장 고르기

번역 (A) 집을 살 때 위치는 매우 중요합니다.
(B) 가구를 새로이 손질하는 것은 예술의 한 형태입니다.
(C) 가구가 갖춰진 아파트는 온라인에서 찾을 수 있습니다.
(D) 포장재는 모두 제거됩니다.

해설 빈칸 앞 문장에서 주문 상품은 도착 즉시 원하는 위치에 놓인다(Upon arrival at your home, the item will be placed in the location you desire)고 했고, 빈칸 뒤 문장에서는 조립 서비스도 포함되어 있다(Assembly is included as well)며 가구가 배송되었을 때 제공되는 서비스를 열거하고 있다. 따라서 두 문장 사이에도 마찬가지로 가구 배송 시 제공되는 서비스 내용이 들어가야 적합하므로 포장재를 제거한다고 언급하는 (D)가 정답이다.

어휘 refinish 표면을 새로 다시 손질하다 furnished 가구가 갖춰진

139-142 이메일

> 수신: 타오 팜 〈thaopham@amail.com〉
> 발신: 리나 몬토야 〈lmontoya@academemedia.com〉
> 날짜: 4월 17일
> 제목: 구독
>
> 팜 씨께,
>
> 139 **귀하의 요청을 처리하였습니다.** 〈분기별 의료 혁신〉의 구독이 취소되었습니다. 5월 1일140 **부터**, 더 이상 인쇄본을 받지 않게 되실 겁니다.
>
> 귀하께서 저희 출판물의 141 **독자**가 되는 것을 다시 한번 고려해 주시기를 바랍니다. 아카데미 미디어는 〈분기별 의료 혁신〉 외에도 많은 고품질 과학 저널을 발행하고 있습니다. 5월 31일까지 구독을 희망하실 경우, 귀하께 연간 요금으로 2년 구독을 제공해 드릴 수 있습니다. www.academemedia.com/shop을 방문하셔서 결제 142 **시** 코드

DOUBLE을 입력하십시오.

제품이나 서비스 개선에 도움이 될 수 있는 의견이 있으시면 212-555-0122로 직접 전화 주십시오.

리나 몬토야
고객 서비스 관리자, 아카데미 미디어

어휘 subscription 구독 innovation 혁신 quarterly 분기의 publication 출판(물) journal 학술지, 잡지 subscribe 구독하다 rate 요금 checkout 결제, 계산(대)

139 문맥에 맞는 문장 고르기

번역 (A) 적시에 주문해 주셔서 감사합니다.
(B) 귀하의 요청을 처리하였습니다.
(C) 이것은 지불 독촉장입니다.
(D) 귀하의 정보를 업데이트하시려면 저희에게 연락 주세요.

해설 빈칸 뒤 문장에서 잡지의 구독이 취소되었다(Your subscription ~ canceled)며 5월 1일부터 더 이상 잡지를 받지 않게 될 것(Starting May 1, you will no ~ print edition)이라고 했으므로, 빈칸에는 잡지 구독을 취소했다는 내용이 들어가야 적절하다. 따라서 '귀하의 요청(구독 취소)을 처리했다'고 언급하는 (B)가 정답이다.

어휘 timely 때맞춘 process 처리하다

140 분사구문

해설 빈칸은 쉼표 뒤의 완전한 절(you will no longer receive the print edition)에 시간 부사구 May 1를 연결하는 자리이다. 문맥상 '5월 1일부터 인쇄본을 받지 않게 될 것이다'라는 내용이 들어가야 자연스러우므로 '~부터, ~부터 시작해서'라는 의미를 나타내는 분사구문 관용 표현 (D) Starting이 정답이다.

141 명사 어휘

해설 빈칸 앞에서 귀하의 요청을 처리하여 출판물의 구독이 취소되었다고 했으므로, 해당 문장은 출판물의 구독자가 되는 것을 다시 고려해 달라고 요청하는 내용이 되어야 적절하다. 따라서 '독자'를 뜻하는 (C) reader가 정답이다. (A) distributor는 '유통업자', (B) producer는 '생산자', (D) teacher는 '선생님'이라는 의미이다.

142 전치사 자리 / 어휘

해설 명사 checkout을 목적어로 취하는 전치사 자리로, '결제 시 코드를 입력하라'는 내용이 되어야 하므로 '~ 즉시, ~하자마자'를 뜻하는 (B) upon이 정답이다.

143-146 정보

상업용 주방에서는 모든 냉장고에 0°F(-18°C)에서 220°F(104°C) 143범위의 온도계가 있어야 합니다. 세균이 자라는 것을 막기 위해 냉장 식품은 41°F(5°C) 이하에서 보관되어야 합니다. 수석 주방장은 주방이

항상 규정을 준수하는 상태일 수 있도록 하루 종일 이 온도계들을 점검할 책임이 있습니다.

144배치 또한 고려해야 할 중요한 사안입니다. 온도계는 항상 냉장고에서 가장 따뜻한 지점에 위치해야 합니다. 145이곳은 보통 문 안쪽입니다. 이 위치는 문을 열자마자 온도계를 쉽게 146볼 수 있기 때문에 적합한 점도 있습니다.

어휘 commercial 상업의 refrigerator 냉장고 thermometer 온도계 prevent 막다 store 보관하다 in compliance (규정 등에) 준수하여 at all times 항상 appropriate 적합한

143 동사 자리 _ 시제

해설 빈칸은 선행사 a thermometer를 수식하는 관계사절(that ~ (104°C))의 동사 자리이다. 상업용 주방에 필요한 온도계의 온도 범위를 설명하는 내용이므로 현재 시제를 써야 한다. 따라서 (A) ranges가 정답이다.

144 명사 어휘

해설 빈칸 앞에서 냉장고에 들어갈 온도계의 적정 온도 규정을 설명하고 있고, 빈칸 뒤 문장에서는 온도계가 있어야 할 위치를 설명하고 있다. 따라서 빈칸이 있는 문장은 온도계의 온도 외에도 위치 또한 고려해야 할 사항이라는 내용이 되어야 뒤 문장과의 연결이 자연스러우므로 '배치'를 뜻하는 (D) placement가 정답이다. (A) size는 '크기', (B) safety는 '안전', (C) reliability는 '신뢰성'이라는 의미이다.

145 문맥에 맞는 문장 고르기

번역 (A) 그것들을 조심스럽게 제거하세요.
(B) 이곳은 보통 문 안쪽입니다.
(C) 그것은 항상 시원하게 유지되어야 합니다.
(D) 그것들은 또한 대량으로 구매할 수 있습니다.

해설 빈칸 앞 문장에서 온도계는 냉장고에서 가장 따뜻한 곳에 위치해야 한다(Thermometers ~ in the warmest spot in the refrigerator)고 했고, 뒤 문장에서는 이 위치는 문을 열자마자 쉽게 볼 수 있어 적합하다(This location is also appropriate ~ opened)고 했다. 따라서 빈칸에는 냉장고의 위치에 대한 내용이 들어가야 자연스러우므로 이곳은 냉장고 문 안쪽이라고 언급하는 (B)가 정답이다.

어휘 typically 보통 in bulk 대량으로

146 동사 어휘

해설 동사 allows의 목적어 the thermometer를 보충 설명하는 목적격 보어 to부정사 to be 뒤에 수동 형태로 들어갈 동사 어휘를 고르는 문제이다. 앞 문장에서 온도계의 냉장고 속 적정 위치를 언급했으므로 이 위치는 냉장고 문을 열면 온도계가 '쉽게 보이므로' 적합하다는 내용이 되어야 연결이 자연스럽다. 따라서 (B) seen이 정답이다. (A)의 sell은 '팔다', (C)의 repair은 '수리하다', (D)의 remove는 '제거하다'라는 의미이다.

PART 7

147-148 이메일

수신: 〈m_castillo@rapidonet.com.ph〉
발신: 〈no-reply@rapidonet.com.ph〉
날짜: 6월 19일
제목: 라피도 넷

고객님의 계정에서 몇 가지 활동이 발견되었습니다. ¹⁴⁷ **비밀번호 복구를 위한 비밀 질문 옵션이 오늘 오후 3시 16분에 업데이트되었습니다. 고객님께서 이 업데이트를 실행시키셨다면 추가적인 작업은 필요하지 않습니다.** 그렇지 않은 경우, 저희가 계정 보호를 도와드릴 수 있습니다. 919-555-1066으로 전화하셔서 계정 담당자와 통화하십시오.

비밀 질문 암호 복구 옵션을 제거하고 싶으시면, 인증된 이메일 주소 또는 전화번호를 대신 사용하여 계정에 접속하실 수 있습니다. ¹⁴⁸ **2단계 인증을 설정하여 절차를 훨씬 더 안전하게 하십시오.** 저희 담당자에게 방법을 문의해 주십시오.

라피도 넷을 인터넷 서비스 제공 업체로 신뢰해 주셔서 감사합니다.

어휘 account 계정 recovery 복구 initiate 개시하다 further 추가의 secure 확보하다; 안전한 representative 담당자, 직원 verified 인증된 verification 인증, 검증

---

147 주제 / 목적

번역 이메일의 목적은?
(A) 라피도 넷의 신규 사용자를 환영하기 위해서
(B) 사용자에게 잊어버린 비밀번호에 대해 상기시키기 위해서
(C) 사용자 계정이 변경되었음을 확인하기 위해서
(D) 새 회사 정책에 대해 사용자에게 알리기 위해서

해설 첫 단락의 두 번째 문장에서 비밀번호 복구를 위한 비밀 질문 옵션이 오늘 오후 3시 16분에 업데이트되었다(Your secret-question option ~ was updated at 3:16 P.M. today)고 했고, 고객이 이 업데이트를 실행했다면 추가적인 작업은 필요하지 않다(If you initiated this update, no further action is necessary)고 확인하고 있으므로 (C)가 정답이다.

Paraphrasing 지문의 **was updated**
→ 정답의 **a change was made**

---

148 Not / True

번역 라피도 넷에 대해 명시된 것은?
(A) 경쟁사들보다 더 빠른 인터넷 속도를 제공한다.
(B) 2단계 인증을 통한 추가 보안을 제공한다.
(C) 고객을 위한 복잡한 비밀번호를 자동으로 생성한다.
(D) 월 사용료를 인상했다.

해설 두 번째 단락의 두 번째 문장에서 2단계 인증을 설정하여 절차를 훨씬 더 안전하게 하라(Make the process even more secure ~ setting up two-step verification)고 안내하고 있으므로 (B)가 정답이다.

어휘 competitor 경쟁사 security 보안 automatically 자동으로 generate 생성하다 complex 복잡한

Paraphrasing 지문의 even more secure
→ 정답의 extra security

149-150 이메일

수신: 〈lduberville@futuremail.co.uk〉
발신: 〈support@globaltech.co.uk〉
날짜: 3월 23일
제목: 주거 서비스

더버빌 씨께,

주문해 주셔서 감사합니다. ^{149, 150} **귀하를 새로운 고객으로 모시게 되어 매우 기쁘며, 저희 직원이 귀하의 댁에 글로벌 테크 모뎀을 설치하려면 예약을 하셔야 해서 연락드립니다.** ¹⁵⁰ 온라인에서 귀하의 계정에 게시해 드린 네 가지 창 중 30분 창을 선택하십시오.

저희가 방문할 것을 대비하여 모뎀 설치를 원하시는 벽면을 치워주십시오. 모뎀을 설치하는 데 몇 분만 소요되고 그 후에 서비스를 이용하실 수 있습니다.

예약 당일 오전에 귀하의 계정에 기재된 전화번호로 방문을 확인할 예정입니다. 문의사항이 있으시면 이때 알려주시기 바랍니다.

고든 맥키
고객 서비스, 글로벌 테크

어휘 residential 주거의 install 설치하다 in preparation for ~을 대비하여 clear 치우다 confirm 확인하다

---

149 추론 / 암시

번역 더버빌 씨가 계약했을 것 같은 서비스 종류는?
(A) 창문 설치
(B) 집 청소
(C) 바닥 전체를 덮는 카펫 설치
(D) 인터넷 이용

해설 두 번째 문장에서 더버빌 씨에게 새로운 고객으로 모시게 되어 매우 기쁘며 직원이 더버빌 씨 자택에 글로벌 테크 모뎀을 설치하려면 예약을 해야 해서 연락드린다(We are very pleased to have you as a new customer ~ to install a Global Tech modem at your home)고 했으므로 더버빌 씨는 인터넷 서비스 업체와 계약했음을 알 수 있다. 따라서 (D)가 정답이다.

어휘 installation 설치 wall-to-wall 바닥을 완전히 덮는

---

150 세부사항

번역 더버빌 씨가 선택한 시간에 일어날 일은?
(A) 사무실에서 장비를 가져갈 것이다.
(B) 새로운 글로벌 테크 휴대폰을 받을 것이다.
(C) 글로벌 테크 직원이 방문할 것이다.
(D) 고객 만족도 조사를 이메일로 받을 것이다.

해설 두 번째 문장에서 더버빌 씨에게 귀하를 새로운 고객으로 모시게 되어 매우 기쁘며 직원이 더버빌 씨 자택에 글로벌 테크 모뎀을 설치하려면 예약을 해야 해서 연락드린다(We are very pleased to have you as a new customer ~ to install a Global Tech modem at your home)고 했고, 세 번째 문장에서 온라인에서 귀하의 계정에 게시해 드린 네 가지 창 중 30분 창을 선택하라(Please go online and select a 30-minute window ~ your account)고 했으므로 더버빌 씨가 온라인으로 선택한 시간에 모뎀 설치를 위해 글로벌 테크 직원이 집으로 올 것임을 알 수 있다. 따라서 (C)가 정답이다.

어휘 equipment 장비 satisfaction 만족

Paraphrasing 지문의 install ~ at your home
→ 정답의 be visited

151-152 온라인 채팅

카트리나 핀튼 (오후 1시 46분)
안녕하세요, 스티븐. 제가 곧 새 아파트로 이사를 가려고 하는데, 집주인이 저의 직장과 소득을 입증하는 서류를 요구하고 있습니다. 제가 서류는 작성을 했습니다. 제가 여기 카리노 에이전시에서 근무하고 있다는 증거로 오늘 이 서류에 서명을 좀 해 주시겠습니까?

스티븐 켄 (오후 1시 48분)
151 아리아나 셀처에게 먼저 다시 확인하세요. 인사부에 보통 당신에게 줄 수 있는 양식이 있습니다.

카트리나 핀튼 (오후 1시 49분)
제가 알아봤습니다. 정해진 양식은 없습니다.

스티븐 켄 (오후 1시 50분)
그럼 문제없습니다. 서류를 가져오세요.

스티븐 켄 (오후 1시 51분)
그런데, 제인 컴퍼니 웹사이트에 대한 회의가 오후 3시로 변경되었습니다. 152 이미 그들의 웹사이트를 위한 당신의 디자인을 전부 준비해 놓으셨죠?

카트리나 핀튼 (오후 1시 52분)
준비해 놓았습니다.

어휘 landlord 집주인 verify 입증하다 employment 직장, 고용 income 소득 be willing to 기꺼이 ~하다 proof 증거, 증명 form 양식 set 정해진; 준비된

151 의도 파악

번역 오후 1시 49분에 핀튼 씨가 "제가 알아봤습니다"라고 쓴 의도는?
(A) 임대 계약서에 서명했다.
(B) 소득 증명서를 제출했다.
(C) 셀처 씨에게 연락했다.
(D) 양식을 작성했다.

해설 1시 48분에 켄 씨가 아리아나 셀처에게 먼저 다시 확인해 보라 (Double-check with Ariana Seltzer first)고 하자 1시 49분에 핀튼 씨가 제가 알아봤다(I tried that)고 대답했으므로, 핀튼 씨는 셀처 씨에게 이미 연락해서 확인해 봤다는 의도로 한 말임을 알 수 있다. 따라서 (C)가 정답이다.

어휘 agreement 계약(서) fill out (양식 등을) 작성하다

152 추론 / 암시

번역 핀튼 씨의 직책은 무엇일 것 같은가?
(A) 아파트 관리인
(B) 사무 관리자
(C) 인사 담당자
(D) 웹 디자이너

해설 1시 51분에 켄 씨가 핀튼 씨에게 그들의 웹사이트를 위한 디자인을 전부 준비해 놓았는지(You already have all your designs for their Web site ready, right?) 확인하는 것으로 보아 핀튼 씨는 웹사이트를 디자인하는 사람임을 알 수 있으므로 (D)가 정답이다.

153-155 웹페이지

http://www.marilisprofessionalcoaching.com

153 마릴리스 직업 코칭: 1월 행사

1월 15일 오후 4시 30분 - 153 구직 지원
보람 있는 신입직을 찾는 데 도움이 되는 최신 도구 및 기술에 대해 배워 보세요. 주제에는 최고의 구직 공고 웹사이트와 구직 기회를 잡기 위해 전문 조직을 활용하는 방법이 포함됩니다.

1월 16일 오후 4시 30분 - 153 스스로를 마케팅하는 방법
다른 구직자들로부터 스스로를 눈에 띄게 하려면, 회사에 가져다 줄 가치를 효과적으로 전달해야 합니다. 이 세션은 대면으로나 소셜 미디어를 통해 잠재적 고용주에게 자신을 성공적으로 홍보하는 데 도움이 될 것입니다.

154 1월 17일 오후 4시 30분 - 153 면접 전략
면접 규칙, 일반적인 질문, 그리고 면접 도중 및 전후에 해야 할 일에 대한 절차와 관련해 조언을 얻어 가세요. 154 이 세션은 참석자들과의 모의 면접을 포함해 대화식으로 진행됩니다.

이 저렴한 행사에 등록하시려면 www.marilisprofessionalcoaching. com/register를 방문하세요. 155 1월의 모든 행사는 온라인으로 진행됩니다.

어휘 rewarding 보람 있는 entry-level 초급의 lead 단서, 실마리 set ~ apart ~을 눈에 띄게 하다 candidate 지원자 effectively 효과적으로 value 가치 strategy 전략 potential 잠재적인 employer 고용주, 회사 process 절차 interactive 대화형의 mock 모의의 attendee 참석자 low-cost 저렴한 virtual 온라인의; 가상의

153 주제 / 목적

번역 웹페이지의 목적은?
(A) 진로 지원 서비스를 홍보하려고
(B) 최근 졸업생을 위한 지역 취업 박람회를 발표하려고
(C) 소셜 미디어 회사의 일자리를 광고하려고
(D) 웹 디자인 및 창작 분야의 보람 있는 직업을 설명하려고

해설 웹페이지의 제목이 마릴리스 직업 코칭: 1월 행사(Marilis Professional Coaching: January Events)이고, 행사 목록이 구직 지원(Job Search Support), 스스로를 마케팅하는 방법(How to Market Yourself), 면접 전략(Interview Strategies)인 것으로 보아 구직 지원 서비스를 홍보하려는 목적임을 알 수 있다. 따라서 (A)가 정답이다.

어휘 job fair 취업 박람회 graduate 대학 졸업자 creation 창작

154 세부사항

번역 웹페이지에 따르면, 1월 17일에 일어날 일은?
(A) 기업들이 취업 기회를 공시할 것이다.
(B) 고용주들이 채용 결정을 내릴 것이다.
(C) 구직자들이 단체 면접에 참석할 것이다.
(D) 참가자들이 면접관들에게 대답하는 것을 연습할 것이다.

해설 세 번째 행사 목록에 1월 17일 오후 4시 30분에 면접 전략(January 17 at 4:30 P.M.-Interview Strategies) 코칭을 한다고 나와 있고, 이 세션은 참석자들과의 모의 면접을 포함해 대화식으로 진행된다(This session will be interactive, featuring mock interviews with attendees)고 했으므로 (D)가 정답이다.

어휘 post 게시하다 participant 참가자

Paraphrasing 지문의 attendees → 정답의 Participants

155 Not / True

번역 행사에 대해 명시된 것은?
(A) 매달 열린다.
(B) 온라인에서 열린다.
(C) 상급 전문가들을 위한 것이다.
(D) 무료이다.

해설 마지막 문장에서 1월의 모든 행사는 온라인으로 진행된다(Note that all January events are virtual)고 했으므로 (B)가 정답이다. 첫 단락의 첫 문장에서 보람 있는 신입직을 찾는 데 도움이 되는 최신 도구 및 기술에 대해 배워보라(Learn about the latest ~ entry-level job)고 했으므로 (C), 마지막 단락의 첫 문장에서 이 저렴한 행사에 등록하려면 www.marilisprofessionalcoaching.com/register를 방문하라(Go to ~ any of these low-cost events)고 했으므로 (D)는 오답이고, (A)는 언급되지 않았다.

어휘 occur 일어나다 take place 열리다 senior 상급의 free of charge 무료의

Paraphrasing 지문의 virtual → 정답의 online

156-158 후기

> **볼만한 가치가 있는 에스톤 개발**
>
> 작성: 마커스 와타나베
>
> "이상적인 주거지 개발은 21세기의 편리함과 소도시의 매력을 결합합니다." 이는 에스톤 시 바로 외곽에 최근 완성된 주거 개발 구역인 홈스테드의 안내 책자에서 볼 수 있는 철학입니다.
>
> 이 소도시에는 넓은 대로, 인도, 그리고 중앙 광장을 둘러싸고 있는 세 개의 작은 공원이 있습니다. 광장에는 카페와 식당, 여러 가게들이 있습니다. 156개발 구역의 북동쪽 모퉁이에는 체육관, 극장, 수영장을 포함한 활동 단지가 있습니다. "이는 원하지 않는 한 도시를 떠날 필요가 없다는 것을 의미합니다."라고 마조리 솔로몬 영업 이사는 말했습니다. "일단 방문해 보시면 왜 이렇게 많은 사람들이 이곳에 집을 구입하는지 깨닫게 되실 겁니다."

개발 구역을 떠나지 않는다는 것이 이상한 생각처럼 느껴지기는 했지만, 158홈스테드 계획자들은 살기에 매우 매력적인 장소를 만든 것에 대해 칭찬받을 만합니다. 하지만 홈스테드는 단지 예쁜 장소 그 이상입니다. 158계획자들은 확실히 환경에 우선순위를 두었습니다. 자연 서식지는 조심스럽게 보존되었고, 집과 다른 건축물들은 물과 에너지를 아낄 수 있도록 설계되었습니다.

157모델 하우스는 현재 투어가 가능합니다. 주택 공개 행사는 토요일과 일요일 오후 12시 30분에서 4시 사이에 열립니다. 또는 856-555-0129로 전화하여 예약하실 수 있습니다.

어휘 worth ~할 가치가 있는 residential 주택지의 combine 결합하다 convenience 편리함 charm 매력 philosophy 철학 surround 둘러싸다 square 광장 feature ~을 특징으로 하다 complex (건물) 단지 realize 깨닫다 strike ~한 인상을 주다 odd 이상한 deserve ~을 받을 만하다 praise 칭찬 attractive 매력적인 obviously 분명히 prioritize 우선시하다 habitat 서식지 preserve 보존하다 structure 건축물 conserve 아끼다 alternatively 또는, 아니면

156 추론 / 암시

번역 활동 단지에 대해 암시된 것은?
(A) 다양한 유익한 시설들이 있다.
(B) 현재 공사 중이다.
(C) 회비가 저렴하다.
(D) 중앙 광장에 있다.

해설 두 번째 단락의 세 번째 문장에서 개발 구역의 북동쪽 모퉁이에는 체육관, 극장, 수영장을 포함한 활동 단지가 있다(In the northeast corner ~ there is an activity complex that includes a gym, theater, and swimming pool)고 했고, 이는 원하지 않는 한 도시를 떠날 필요가 없다는 것을 의미한다(This means you never have to leave the community unless you want to)면서 일단 방문해 보면 왜 이렇게 많은 사람들이 이곳에 집을 구입하는지 깨닫게 될 것(Once you visit, you'll realize why so many people are purchasing homes here)이라고 했다. 따라서 활동 단지의 유익한 시설 덕분에 인기가 있다는 것을 알 수 있으므로 (A)가 정답이다.

어휘 desirable 바람직한 feature 특징, 인기거리

157 세부사항

번역 예비 거주자는 어떻게 에스톤의 홈스테드에 대해 더 자세히 알 수 있는가?
(A) 온라인으로 모델 하우스를 봄으로써
(B) 안내 책자를 요청함으로써
(C) 커뮤니티를 방문함으로써
(D) 현재 주택 소유자에게 전화함으로써

해설 마지막 단락의 첫 문장에서 모델 하우스는 현재 투어가 가능하다(Model homes are currently available for tours)고 했고, 주택 공개 행사는 토요일과 일요일 오후 12시 30분에서 4시 사이에 열린다(Open houses take place ~ and Sundays)고 했으므로 (C)가 정답이다.

158 문장 삽입

번역 [1], [2], [3], [4]로 표시된 위치 중에서 다음 문장이 들어가기에 가장 적합한 곳은?

"하지만 홈스테드는 단지 예쁜 장소 그 이상입니다."

(A) [1]
(B) [2]
(C) [3]
(D) [4]

해설 주어진 문장에서 반전의 뜻을 가진 however를 사용해 '하지만 홈스테드는 예쁜 장소 그 이상'이라고 했으므로, 문장 앞에는 홈스테드를 예쁜 장소라고 묘사하는 내용이 와야 하고 문장 뒤에는 홈스테드가 단순히 예쁘기만 한 장소가 아니라는 것을 뒷받침할 수 있는 근거가 제시되어야 한다. 따라서 홈스테드를 살기에 매우 매력적인 장소라고 묘사한 문장과 환경에 우선순위를 두고 계획되었다고 언급하는 문장 사이에 들어가면 적절하므로 (C)가 정답이다.

159-160 이메일

발신: 스테판 폰스만 〈sfonsman@kaybunconstruction.ca〉
수신: 리타 팔로어 〈rpalore@palorecement.ca〉
제목: 팔로어 시멘트
160 **날짜: 3월 2일**

팔로어 씨께,

159 **스미스빌에서의 아파트 프로젝트에 대한 시멘트 작업 견적서를 보내 주셔서 감사합니다. 입찰에 수반된 귀하의 설명은 우리의 모든 질문에 답변이 되었고, 우리 팀은 귀사의 이전 작업과 추천서에 깊은 인상을 받았습니다.** 귀사는 제가 프로젝트를 맡길 1순위 선택입니다.

그럼에도 불구하고, 저는 여전히 저희 이사님인 애니타 조의 예산 승인이 필요합니다. 귀하가 제시한 가격은 예상했던 것보다 조금 높습니다. 160 **내일 아침에 이 건과 관련해 조 이사님과 이야기할 예정입니다.** 귀사의 뛰어난 작업에 대한 명성에 근거하여 이사님이 귀사의 입찰을 승인할 것이라고 확신합니다.

3월 4일까지 소식을 전할 수 있을 것으로 예상합니다.

스테판 폰스만
케이분 건설

어휘 estimate 견적서 narrative 설명, 이야기 accompany 수반하다 bid 입찰 impress 감명을 주다 previous 이전의 reference 추천서 budget 예산 approval 승인 director 이사 steep 너무 비싼 anticipate 예상하다 reputation 명성 outstanding 뛰어난 sign off ~을 승인하다

159 주제 / 목적

번역 이메일의 목적은?

(A) 새로운 소유주를 소개하려고
(B) 견적서 수령을 알려주려고
(C) 프레젠테이션에 팀원들을 초대하려고
(D) 추가 작업 추천서를 요청하려고

해설 첫 문장에서 스미스빌에서의 아파트 프로젝트에 대한 시멘트 작업 견적서를 보내 주어 감사하다(Thank you for sending your estimate ~ in Smithville)며, 입찰에 수반된 귀하의 설명은 우리의 모든 질문에 답변이 되었고 우리 팀은 귀사의 이전 작업과 추천서에 깊은 인상을 받았다(The narrative ~ previous work and references)고 했으므로 (B)가 정답이다.

어휘 acknowledge (편지 등을) 받았음을 알리다 receipt 수령

160 세부사항

번역 폰스만 씨는 언제 조 씨를 만날 예정인가?

(A) 3월 2일
(B) 3월 3일
(C) 3월 4일
(D) 3월 5일

해설 이메일을 작성한 날짜가 3월 2일(Date: March 2)이고, 두 번째 단락 세 번째 문장에서 폰스만 씨가 내일 아침에 이 건과 관련해 조 이사님과 이야기할 예정(I will be speaking with Ms. Cho about this tomorrow morning)이라고 했으므로 (B)가 정답이다.

161-163 공고

알타메사 시가 선거 운동원을 모집합니다.

<u>누가 선거 운동원이 될 자격이 있나요?</u> 주부, 전문직 종사자뿐만 아니라 실업자, 자영업자, 은퇴자를 포함한 거의 모든 분들이 가능합니다.

<u>요건:</u>

• 3월 5일, 6월 7일, 11월 1일 오전 6시부터 오후 1시까지 또는 오후 1시부터 오후 8시까지 근무 가능한 자
• 정치인이 아니며 정치인과 함께 살거나 일하고 있지 않은 자
• 18세 이상인 자
• 162 **시민들과 편하게 소통하는 자**
• 체계적이고 꼼꼼한 자

163 **운동원들은 3월 4일에 진행되는 4시간짜리 사전 선거 교육 워크숍에 참석해야 하며,** 직함에 따라 보상을 받게 됩니다:
161 **선거 보조원, 시간당 18달러**
161 **선거 사무원, 시간당 20달러**
161 **선거 관리 위원장, 시간당 22달러**

세부사항이나 지원을 원하시면 www.altamesaelections.gov/apply를 방문하세요.

어휘 seek 구하다 election 선거 qualified 자격이 있는 homemaker 주부 professional 전문가 unemployed 실업자인 self-employed 자영업자인 retired 은퇴한 politician 정치인 comfortable 편안한 interact 소통하다 organized 체계적인 detail-oriented 꼼꼼한 compensate 보상하다 apply 지원하다

161 세부사항

번역 공고에 포함된 정보는?

(A) 급여율
(B) 근무지 위치
(C) 지원 마감일
(D) 교육 워크숍의 시작 시간

해설 세 번째 단락에 선거 보조원, 시간당 18달러(Election Assistant, $18/hour), 선거 사무원, 시간당 20달러(Election Clerk, $20/hour), 선거 관리 위원장, 시간당 22달러(Election Chief, $22/hour)라고 직함에 따른 급여율이 제시되어 있으므로 (A)가 정답이다.

어휘 rate 비율

162 세부사항

번역 공고에서 제시하는 채용 요건은?
(A) 정치에 대한 관심
(B) 고등학교 졸업장
(C) 유권자 등록증
(D) 뛰어난 의사 소통 기술

해설 두 번째 단락에 제시된 요건 중 네 번째 항목에 시민들과 편하게 소통하는 자(Is comfortable interacting with the public)라고 나와 있으므로 (D)가 정답이다.

어휘 politics 정치 diploma 졸업장 voter 유권자 registration 등록

Paraphrasing 지문의 interacting → 정답의 communication

163 Not / True

번역 교육 워크숍에 대해 언급된 것은?
(A) 일 년에 세 번 제공된다.
(B) 경험 있는 선거 공무원이 주도한다.
(C) 모든 선거 운동원들에게 요구된다.
(D) 온라인과 대면 참여 둘 다 가능하다.

해설 세 번째 단락의 첫 문장에서 운동원들은 3월 4일에 진행되는 4시간짜리 사전 선거 교육 워크숍에 참석해야 한다(Workers must attend ~ workshop on March 4)고 했으므로 (C)가 정답이다.

어휘 experienced 경험 있는 official 공무원 in person 대면으로

Paraphrasing 지문의 must → 정답의 required

164-167 이메일

수신. 이지향 〈jlee@myemail.com〉
발신: 로버트 왕 〈rwang@frontstreetbank.com〉
날짜: 4월 7일
제목: VIS는 귀하를 위한 것입니까?

이 씨께:

164,165귀하께서는 이제 프런트 스트리트 은행의 새로운 음성 인식 시스템(VIS)에 등록하실 수 있습니다. VIS는 휴대폰으로 귀하의 은행 계좌에 접속하고 제어할 수 있는 빠르고 편리하며 안전한 방법입니다. 귀하는 다양한 특정 업무를 수행하실 수 있습니다. 167예를 들어, "대출금 지불"이라고 말하면 프런트 스트리트 은행 대금을 지불할 수 있습니다. "최근 거래"라고 말하면 신용카드 거래 내역을 확인할 수 있습니다. 심지어 "이체"라고 말하면 계좌 간에 돈을 이체할 수도 있습니다. www. frontstreetbank.com/VIS에서 VIS가 귀하의 은행 업무를 간편하게 해 주는 모든 방법을 확인하십시오.

귀하의 음성 인식 정보는 프런트 스트리트 은행에 의해 안전하게 저장되며 프런트 스트리트 은행에서만 사용될 수 있습니다. 615-555-0189로 전화하셔서 귀하의 계좌에 VIS를 설정하십시오. 166향후 VIS를 사용하여 계좌에 접속하는 것을 원치 않게 되실 경우, 저희 고객 서비스 담당자에게 전화하셔서 귀하의 신원 확인 정보 파일을 삭제하도록 요청하시기만 하면 됩니다.

프런트 스트리트 은행의 소중한 고객이 되어 주셔서 감사합니다.

로버트 왕, 지점장

어휘 enroll in ~에 등록하다 identification 신원 확인 secure 안전한 loan 대출(금) transaction 거래 transfer 이체하다; 이체 simplify 간소화하다 store 저장하다 delete 삭제하다 valued 소중한

164 주제 / 목적

번역 이메일의 목적은?
(A) 신규 고객을 환영하기 위해서
(B) 계정 오류를 보고하기 위해서
(C) 대출 승인을 확인하기 위해서
(D) 신규 서비스를 홍보하기 위해서

해설 첫 문장에서 이제 프런트 스트리트 은행의 새로운 음성 인식 시스템(VIS)에 등록할 수 있다(You are now able to enroll ~ Identification System (VIS))고 했고, VIS는 휴대폰으로 은행 계좌에 접속하고 제어할 수 있는 빠르고 편리하며 안전한 방법(VIS is a fast, convenient, and ~ accounts by phone)이라고 은행의 새로운 시스템을 고객에게 홍보하고 있으므로 (D)가 정답이다.

165 Not / True

번역 VIS에 대해 명시된 것은?
(A) 계좌에 음성 접속을 제공한다.
(B) 다양한 금융 기관에서 사용될 수 있다.
(C) 고객들에게 수수료 지불을 요구한다.
(D) 지정된 시간에만 이용할 수 있다.

해설 첫 문장에서 이제 프런트 스트리트 은행의 새로운 음성 인식 시스템(VIS)에 등록할 수 있다(You are now able to enroll ~ Identification System (VIS))고 했고, VIS는 휴대폰으로 은행 계좌에 접속하고 제어할 수 있는 빠르고 편리하며 안전한 방법(VIS is a fast, convenient, and ~ accounts by phone)이라고 했으므로 (A)가 정답이다.

어휘 institution 기관 designated 지정된

166 세부사항

번역 고객이 VIS를 취소하기 위해 해야 할 일은?
(A) 지역 은행 지점 방문하기
(B) 전화 통화하기
(C) 온라인 양식 작성하기
(D) 고객 서비스에 이메일 보내기

해설 마지막 문장에서 향후 VIS를 사용하여 계좌에 접속하는 것을 원치 않

게 될 경우, 고객 서비스 담당자에게 전화해서 신원 확인 정보 파일을 삭제하도록 요청하기만 하면 된다(If in the future you no longer wish to use VIS to access your account, simply call to have one of our customer-service representatives delete your identification file)고 했으므로 (B)가 정답이다.

Paraphrasing 지문의 call → 정답의 Make a telephone call

---

167 문장 삽입

번역 [1], [2], [3], [4]로 표시된 위치 중에서 다음 문장이 들어가기에 가장 적합한 곳은?

"귀하는 다양한 특정 업무를 수행할 수 있습니다."

(A) [1]
(B) [2]
(C) [3]
(D) [4]

해설 주어진 문장에서 다양한 특정 업무를 수행할 수 있다는 점을 홍보하고 있으므로, '예를 들어(For example)'로 시작해 대출금 지불, 거래 내역 확인, 이체와 같이 VIS를 통해 실제로 수행할 수 있는 여러 가지 업무들을 구체적인 예시를 통해 제시하는 문장 앞에 들어가면 글의 흐름이 자연스럽다. 따라서 (A)가 정답이다.

어휘 numerous 많은 specific 특정한

168-171 광고

섬네일 출판사

엔터프라이즈 시리즈 중 4권의 새로운 도서가 방금 출간되었습니다. [168]11월 30일까지 저희 웹사이트에서 구매하시고, 한 권 구매 시 한 권은 50퍼센트를 할인받으세요(배송비 제외). 오늘 주문하세요!

크리스틴 메논의 〈거장〉
[169,170]유명한 경영자 하루토 야마다의 전기로, 그의 경력이 기업 관리에 어떻게 영향을 미쳤는지에 대한 통찰이 담겨 있다. 페이퍼백 14.99유로

진창호의 〈달빛 아래 근무〉
[170]전직 무역회사 직원들과의 인터뷰를 통해 조명된 20세기 한국의 교역. 양장본 22.99유로로, 오디오북 8.99유로

[171]마이 쿠앙 빈의 〈보이지 않는 연결〉
[170,171]40년 경력의 경영학 교수 글로리아 드 레온이 강의한 내용의 필사와 기록 사진이 있는 전집. 양장본 25.99유로

잭 올리비에의 〈회상〉
[170]전직 호주 무역 사무관은 이 매력적인 회고록에서 자신의 외교 경력 중 겪었던 기복을 회상한다. 페이퍼백 14.99유로로, 다운로드 가능한 전자책 9.99유로

어휘 title 책, 출판물 release 출간하다 exclude 제외하다 biography 전기 executive 경영자 insight 통찰력 influence 영향을 미치다 governance 관리, 통치 paperback 페이퍼백(종이 표지 책) moonbeam 달빛 commerce 교역, 상업 illuminate (이해하기 쉽게) 밝히다 former 이전의 hardcover

---

양장본 connection 연결 transcribe 기록하다 archival 기록의 business administration 경영학 flashback 회상 trade commissioner 무역 사무관 recall 회상하다 highs and lows 기복 diplomatic 외교의 engaging 매력적인 memoir 회고록

---

168 세부사항

번역 회사에서 고객들에게 제공하고 있는 것은?
(A) 특정 작가의 책에 대한 쿠폰
(B) 온라인으로 책 두 권 주문 시 할인
(C) 배송료 할인
(D) 출판사의 무료 카탈로그

해설 첫 단락의 두 번째 문장에서 11월 30일까지 웹사이트에서 구매하고, 한 권 구매 시 한 권은 50퍼센트를 할인받으라(Buy one, get one 50 percent off when you purchase from our Web site by November 30)고 했으므로 (B)가 정답이다.

어휘 specific 특정한

Paraphrasing 지문의 50 percent off → 정답의 discount

---

169 세부사항

번역 야마다 씨는 누구인가?
(A) 정부 요원
(B) 직업 상담사
(C) 전기 작가
(D) 기업 임원

해설 두 번째 단락의 책 설명에 유명한 경영자 하루토 야마다의 전기로, 그의 경력이 기업 관리에 어떻게 영향을 미쳤는지에 대한 통찰이 담겨 있다(A biography of famous executive Haruto Yamada ~ business governance)고 했으므로 야마다 씨는 기업 경영자임을 알 수 있다. 따라서 (D)가 정답이다.

Paraphrasing 지문의 executive → 정답의 A company leader

---

170 세부사항

번역 광고에 설명된 모든 책들의 공통적인 특징은?
(A) 동일 작가가 썼다.
(B) 디지털 형식으로 읽을 수 있다.
(C) 비즈니스 주제에 초점을 두고 있다.
(D) 여러 언어로 번역되었다.

해설 첫 번째 책 설명에 유명한 경영자 하루토 야마다의 전기로 그의 경력이 기업 관리에 어떻게 영향을 미쳤는지에 대한 통찰이 담겨 있다(A biography of famous executive ~ business governance)고 했고, 두 번째 책 설명에 전직 무역회사 직원들과의 인터뷰를 통해 조명된 20세기 한국의 교역(Commerce in twentieth-century ~ trade company employees)에 관한 것이라고 했고, 세 번째 책 설명에 40년 경력의 경영학 교수 글로리아 드 레온이 강의한 내용의 필사와 기록 사진이 있는 전집(A collection of transcribed lectures ~ business administration)이라고 했으며, 마지막 책

설명에 전직 호주 무역 사무관이 이 매력적인 회고록에서 자신의 외교 경력 중 겪었던 기복을 회상한다(A former Australian trade commissioner ~ engaging memoir)고 했다. 따라서 네 책은 모두 비즈니스에 관한 내용을 다루고 있으므로 (C)가 정답이다.

어휘 author 작가 translate 번역하다

171 세부사항

번역 역사적 이미지가 포함된 책은?
(A) 〈거장〉
(B) 〈달빛 아래 근무〉
(C) 〈보이지 않는 연결〉
(D) 〈회상〉

해설 네 번째 단락의 책 설명에 마이 쿠앙 빈의 〈보이지 않는 연결〉은 40년 경력의 경영학 교수 글로리아 드 레온이 강의한 내용의 필사와 기록 사진이 있는 전집(A collection of transcribed lectures and archival photos ~ business administration)이라고 나와 있으므로 (C)가 정답이다.

Paraphrasing 지문의 archival photos
→ 질문의 historic images

172-175 문자 메시지

프리얀카 카푸어 [오전 9시 41분]
172, 173 곧 런던에서 열리는 가정의학 전문의 학회에 대해 이야기해야 합니다. 지금 어떤 상태죠?

알론소 곤잘레스 [오전 9시 44분]
172, 173, 174 이미 우리 모두를 위한 항공권을 구입했습니다.

프리얀카 카푸어 [오전 9시 47분]
좋습니다. 스콧 해리스가 런던 공항에서 학회 장소로 가는 셔틀을 마련할 것입니다. 우리 휴대폰이 와이파이 구역 밖에서 작동이 될까요?

알론소 곤잘레스 [오전 9시 50분]
우리 휴대폰 공급업체의 국제 요금 서비스를 알아봤습니다. 통화와 문자 기능은 되지만 다운로드 속도가 느린 제한된 데이터 옵션을 제공합니다.

브라이언 킴 [오전 9시 53분]
175 출발하기 전에 국제 심 카드를 삽시다. 초고속 데이터와 무제한 통화 및 문자 서비스를 제공하는 선불카드를 살 수 있습니다. 175 와이파이에 연결되는지를 걱정할 필요가 없을 겁니다.

프리얀카 카푸어 [오전 9시 57분]
그러면 문제가 해결되겠네요.

알론소 곤잘레스 [오전 9시 57분]
좋은 생각입니다, 브라이언. 감사합니다. 이제 식사를 위해 만나는 것에 대해 이야기합시다.

프리얀카 카푸어 [오전 9시 59분]
학회는 매일 로비에서 유럽식 아침 식사와 함께 시작됩니다. 아침에 그곳에서 만납시다. 제가 저녁 식사하기에 좋은 장소를 알고 있으니 첫날 저녁은 오후 6시로 계획을 잡읍시다. 다른 식사는 나중에 결정하면 됩니다.

어휘 upcoming 다가오는 physician 의사 arrange 마련하다 venue 장소 functional 작동되는 research 조사하다 plan (자금 등의) 제도; 계획하다 prepaid 선불된 unlimited 무제한의 continental 유럽식의

172 추론 / 암시

번역 메시지 작성자들이 근무할 것 같은 장소는?
(A) 여행사
(B) 병원
(C) 운송 회사
(D) 통신사

해설 9시 41분에 카푸어 씨가 곧 런던에서 열리는 가정의학 전문의 학회에 대해 이야기해야 한다(We need to talk ~ family physicians conference in London)고 했고, 9시 44분에 곤잘레스 씨가 이미 우리 모두를 위한 항공권을 구입했다(I've already ~ for all of us)고 했다. 따라서 메시지 작성자들은 가정의학 전문의 학회에 참석하는 의사들이라고 짐작할 수 있으므로 (B)가 정답이다.

어휘 transportation 운송 telecommunications 통신

173 의도 파악

번역 오전 9시 41분에 카푸어 씨가 "지금 어떤 상태죠?"라고 쓴 의도는?
(A) 여행 준비에 대한 업데이트를 요청하고 있다.
(B) 행사에 참석하는 동료들의 관심 정도를 가늠하고 싶어 한다.
(C) 동료들의 주말 활동에 대해 문의하고 있다.
(D) 직원들이 학회를 주최할 준비가 되어 있는지를 확인하고 있다.

해설 9시 41분에 카푸어 씨가 곧 런던에서 열리는 가정의학 전문의 학회에 대해 이야기해야 한다(We need to talk ~ conference in London)면서 지금 어떤 상태인지(Where do we stand?)를 묻자, 9시 44분에 곤잘레스 씨가 이미 우리 모두를 위한 항공권을 구입했다(I've already ~ for all of us)고 대답했다. 따라서 카푸어 씨는 학회 참석 준비가 어느 정도 진행되었는지를 물으려는 의도로 한 말임을 알 수 있으므로 (A)가 정답이다.

어휘 preparation 준비 assess 평가하다 colleague 동료 inquire 문의하다 readiness 준비(가 되어 있음) host 주최하다

174 추론 / 암시

번역 메시지 작성자들에 대해 결론지을 수 있는 것은?
(A) 함께 여행할 것이다.
(B) 발표를 준비 중이다.
(C) 새로운 휴대폰 서비스를 가지고 있다.
(D) 각각 처음으로 회의에 참석한다.

해설 9시 44분에 곤잘레스 씨가 이미 우리 모두를 위한 항공권을 구입했다(I've already ~ for all of us)고 한 것으로 보아 메시지 작성자들은 모두 함께 여행할 것임을 알 수 있다. 따라서 (A)가 정답이다.

175 세부사항

번역 킴 씨가 심 카드를 제안하는 이유는?
(A) 국제 요금 서비스보다 덜 비싸다.
(B) 모든 장치에 사용될 수 있다.
(C) 근처 전자제품 매장에 재고가 있다.
(D) 와이파이 연결이 필요하지 않다.

해설 9시 53분에 킴 씨가 출발하기 전에 국제 심 카드를 사자(Let's buy international SIM cards before we leave)고 제안하면서, 와이파이에 연결되는지에 대해 걱정할 필요가 없을 것(We won't have to worry about being connected to Wi-Fi)이라고 했으므로 (D)가 정답이다.

어휘 in stock 재고가 있는

176-180 구인 광고 + 이메일

행복한 마구간

176(A) 말에게 먹이를 주고, 말을 씻기고 손질해 줄 시간제 근로자를 구합니다. 때때로 주말 시간을 포함하여 일주일에 최소 8시간을 일할 수 있어야 합니다. 교육은 제공되지만 말과 함께 일한 경험이 있는 지원자를 우대합니다. 180 지원하려면 도로시 루에게 dlu@blissfulhorsestables.com.au로 이력서를 첨부하여 이메일을 보내 주세요.

행복한 마구간은 이 지역에서 가장 큰 말 관리 177 시설입니다. 176(D) 1988년부터 한 가족이 소유하고 운영해 왔습니다. 저희 회사는 단기 및 장기 관리 계약을 모두 제공합니다. 176(C) 우리의 말 친구들을 위한 최첨단 실내외 운동장과 5에이커의 방목 초원도 있습니다. 수의사는 상시 대기 중입니다.

어휘 blissful 행복한   stable 마구간   feed 먹이를 주다   groom 손질하다   occasional 가끔의   applicant 지원자   prefer 선호하다   attach 첨부하다   region 지역   horse-boarding 호스 보딩(말 관리)   facility 시설   operate 운영하다   contract 계약(서)   state-of-the-art 최첨단의   acre 에이커(약 4,050평방미터)   grazing 방목   pasture 초원   equine 말의   veterinarian 수의사   on call 대기 중인

발신: ota_kyle@opalmail.com.au
180 수신: dlu@blissfulhorsestables.com.au
제목: 시간제 일자리
날짜: 8월 1일
첨부: ⬛ota.rfg

180 루 씨께,

178 이 이메일은 〈콜비 투데이〉 어제 판에 실린 광고를 보고 보내는 것입니다. 179 현재 저는 네스 대형 동물 병원에서 기술 보조로 일하고 있지만 일주일에 3일뿐입니다. 180 귀사에서 광고하고 있는 시간제 일자리로 저는 근무 시간을 늘리면서도 제가 좋아하는 일을 할 수 있습니다. 요청하시는 즉시 기꺼이 추천서를 제공해 드리겠습니다.

카일 오타

어휘 in response to ~에 대한 회신으로   appear 나오다   edition (간행물의) 판, 호   technician 기술자   enable 할 수 있게 하다   reference 추천서

176 Not / True

번역 행복한 마구간에 대해 명시되지 않은 것은?
(A) 손질 서비스를 제공한다.
(B) 최소 3일간 체류해야 한다.
(C) 방목을 위해 크고 풀이 무성한 들판을 가지고 있다.
(D) 가족 경영 사업체이다.

해설 구인 광고의 첫 문장에서 말에게 먹이를 주고 말을 씻기고 손질할 시간제 근로자를 구한다(Part-time worker ~ and groom horses)고 했으므로 (A), 두 번째 단락의 네 번째 문장에서 우리의 말 친구들을 위한 최첨단 실내외 운동장과 5에이커의 방목 초원도 있다(We have ~ grazing pasture for our equine friends)고 했으므로 (C), 두 번째 단락의 두 번째 문장에서 1988년부터 한 가족이 소유하고 운영해 왔다(It has been ~ family since 1988)고 했으므로 (D)는 모두 언급된 사실이다. 체류 기간에 대한 언급은 없으므로 (B)가 정답이다.

어휘 grassy 풀이 무성한   field 들판   family-run 가족 경영의

Paraphrasing 지문의 operated by one family → 보기 (D)의 family-run

177 동의어 찾기

번역 광고에서 두 번째 단락 1행의 "facility"와 의미가 가장 가까운 단어는?
(A) 단순함
(B) 기회
(C) 개방성
(D) 센터

해설 의미상 행복한 마구간은 지역에서 가장 큰 '시설'이라는 뜻으로 쓰였으므로 '센터, 종합 시설'을 뜻하는 (D) center가 정답이다.

178 추론 / 암시

번역 〈콜비 투데이〉는 무엇일 것 같은가?
(A) 지역 신문
(B) 말 소유자를 위한 소식지
(C) 텔레비전 프로그램
(D) 관광 안내 책자

해설 이메일의 첫 문장에서 이 이메일은 〈콜비 투데이〉 어제 판에 실린 광고를 보고 보내는 것(This e-mail is in response ~ edition of the Colby Today)이라고 한 것으로 보아 〈콜비 투데이〉는 지역 일간지임을 짐작할 수 있다. 따라서 (A)가 정답이다.

어휘 regional 지역의

179 추론 / 암시

번역 오타 씨에 대해 암시된 것은?
(A) 동물들과 일한 경험이 있다.
(B) 지역 학교를 졸업했다.
(C) 기자가 되고 싶어 한다.
(D) 주말에 근무할 수 없다.

해설 이메일의 두 번째 문장에서 오타 씨가 현재 네스 대형 동물 병원에서 기술 보조로 일하고 있다(At this time, I work for Ness Large Animal Clinic as a technician's assistant)며 동물들이 있는 장소에서 근무하고 있다고 했으므로 (A)가 정답이다.

180 연계

번역 오타 씨는 이메일에 무엇을 첨부했을 것 같은가?
(A) 졸업장
(B) 이력서
(C) 추천서
(D) 말 관리에 대한 기사

해설 구인 광고의 첫 단락 마지막 문장에서 지원하려면 도로시 루에게 dlu@blissfulhorsestables.com.au로 이력서를 첨부하여 이메일을 보내 달라(To apply, send an e-mail to Dorothy Lu ~ attach your résumé)고 했고, 오타 씨가 루 씨에게(Dear Ms. Lu) 보내는 이메일의 수신 주소가 dlu@blissfulhorsestables.com.au 이고, 세 번째 문장에서 귀사가 광고하는 시간제 일자리로 근무 시간을 늘리면서 자신이 좋아하는 일을 할 수 있다(The part-time position you ~ increasing my working hours)며 일자리에 지원하고 있으므로 오타 씨가 첨부한 것은 이력서임을 알 수 있다. 따라서 (B)가 정답이다.

181-185 온라인 양식 + 이메일

https://www.pinkferngardens.co.nz/contact

| 소개 | 온라인 쇼핑 | 위치 | 연락 |

뉴질랜드 픽턴에 위치한 핑크 펀 가든스는 다양한 식용 및 장식용 식물을 판매합니다. 아래 양식을 사용하여 질문 및 의견을 제출해 주세요.

이름: 미아 딕슨

이메일: mdixon@sunmail.co.nz

남기는 글:

181 귀사의 소셜 미디어 피드에서 지역 재배자들을 향한 요청 글을 보았습니다. 182 몇 년 전, 저는 여기 헬렌스빌의 이웃들과 함께 여가 시간에 보살필 커다란 마을 먹거리 정원을 시작했습니다. 올해는 우리가 먹을 수 있는 것보다 식물이 더 많이 남았습니다. 구체적으로, 185 수십 개의 민트와 카타멈 묘목 화분뿐만 아니라 다른 희귀한 허브들도 가지고 있는데, 귀사에서 제공하는 허브 제품을 늘리는 것에 관심이 있는지 궁금합니다. 우리는 또한 2~3피트 높이의 2년 된 레몬 나무 묘목 여섯 그루를 가지고 있습니다.

어휘 edible 식용의 decorative 장식용의 callout 요청 grower 재배자 neighbour 이웃 tend 보살피다 consume 먹다, 소비하다 specifically 구체적으로 dozens of 수십의 potted 화분에 심은 seedling 묘목 uncommon 희귀한 expand 확장하다 offering 제품 sapling 묘목

수신: mdixon@sunmail.co.nz
발신: purchasing@pinkferngardens.co.nz
날짜: 1월 12일

제목: 귀하가 남기신 글

딕슨 씨께,

핑크 펀 가든스는 항상 희귀 식물을 찾고 있습니다. 183 **귀하의 감귤류 묘목과 관련해서는, 현재 저희는 허가받은 재배자들에게서만 구매하고 있습니다. 특정 품종에 영향을 미치는 질병이 있어서 주의해야 합니다. 작년 가을에 이와 관련된 교훈을 얻었습니다!**

저희는 묘목이 화분에 담겨 있고 시장에 내놓을 준비가 되어 있다면 자영업 재배자들에게서 다른 식물들을 구입합니다. 185 **저희가 구입하는 묘목의 종류와 각 식물에 지불하는 도매가격은 양치식물(8달러), 덩굴식물(6달러), 일년생 화초(5달러), 그리고 요리용 허브로, 특히 오레가노, 민트, 로즈메리(2달러)입니다.** 184 **편하실 때 귀하께서 제공하는 물건의 샘플을 가지고 방문해 주시면 저희가 필요한 것들에 대해 직접 더 자세히 논의할 수 있습니다.**

켄 요네다

구매 담당, 핑크 펀 가든스

어휘 as for ~에 관해 말하자면 citrus 감귤류 licensed 허가를 받은 disease 질병 affect 영향을 미치다 certain 특정한 variety 품종 cautious 조심스러운 regarding ~에 관하여 independent 독자적인 market ready 시장에 나올 수 있는 wholesale 도매 fern 양치식물 vine 덩굴식물 in person 직접

181 세부사항

번역 딕슨 씨가 핑크 펀 가든스에 연락하게 된 동기는?
(A) 고객의 긍정적인 평가
(B) 핑크 펀 가든스의 온라인 게시물
(C) 핑크 펀 가든스에 대한 기사
(D) 요네다 씨로부터 온 전화 메시지

해설 온라인 양식의 남기는 글 첫 문장에서 딕슨 씨가 귀사의 소셜 미디어 피드에서 지역 재배자들을 향한 요청 글을 보았다(I saw the callout to local growers on your social media feed)고 한 것으로 보아 딕슨 씨는 핑크 펀 가든스에서 올린 온라인 게시글을 보고 글을 남기고 있음을 알 수 있다. 따라서 (B)가 정답이다.

Paraphrasing 지문의 on your social media feed
→ 정답의 online post

182 Not / True

번역 딕슨 씨에 대해 명시된 것은?
(A) 자신의 취미를 전업으로 돌리고 싶어 한다.
(B) 핑크 펀 가든스에서 시간제 근무를 하고 싶어 한다.
(C) 이웃들과 함께 마을 정원을 만들었다.
(D) 헬렌스빌에 있는 원예 클럽의 회장이다.

해설 온라인 양식의 남기는 글 두 번째 문장에서 딕슨 씨가 몇 년 전, 여기 헬렌스빌의 이웃들과 함께 여가 시간에 보살필 커다란 마을 먹거리 정원을 시작했다(A few years ago, I started a large community food garden with my neighbours ~ tend in our free time)고 했으므로 (C)가 정답이다.

어휘 turn ~ into ... ~을 ...으로 바꾸다 found 설립하다 gardening 원예

183 세부사항

번역　요네다 씨에 따르면, 작년에 일어난 일은?
(A) 직원들 중 일부가 사직했다.
(B) 회사에서 구입한 나무 일부가 병약했다.
(C) 회사에서 감귤나무 수출 허가를 획득했다.
(D) 회사에서 팔 과일나무가 다 소진되었다.

해설　이메일의 첫 단락 두 번째 문장에서 요네다 씨가 귀하의 감귤류 묘목과 관련해서는 현재 허가를 받은 재배자들에게서만 구매하고 있다(As for your citrus ~ from licensed growers only)면서, 특정 품종에 영향을 미치는 질병이 있어서 주의해야(There is a disease ~ be cautious)하고 작년 가을에 이와 관련된 교훈을 얻었다(We learned our lesson regarding this last autumn!)고 했다. 따라서 작년에 구입한 일부 나무에 질병이 있었다는 것이므로 (B)가 정답이다.

어휘　resign 사직하다　obtain 얻다　export 수출하다　run out of (물건이) 바닥나다

Paraphrasing　　지문의 a disease → 정답의 unhealthy

184 세부사항

번역　요네다 씨가 딕슨 씨에게 요청하는 것은?
(A) 물품 목록을 보내 줄 것
(B) 자영업 재배자에게 연락할 것
(C) 핑크 펀 가든스에서 씨앗을 구입할 것
(D) 핑크 펀 가든스에 식물들을 가져올 것

해설　이메일의 마지막 문장에서 요네다 씨는 딕슨 씨에게 편할 때 제공하는 물건의 샘플을 가지고 방문하면 필요한 것들에 대해 직접 더 자세히 논의할 수 있다(Please stop by at your convenience with samples of your offerings ~ in person)고 했으므로 (D)가 정답이다.

어휘　supplies 물품　seed 씨앗

185 연계

번역　요네다 씨는 딕슨 씨에게 화분에 담긴 그녀의 묘목 하나 당 얼마를 지불하겠는가?
(A) 8달러
(B) 6달러
(C) 5달러
(D) 2달러

해설　온라인 양식의 남기는 글 네 번째 문장에서 딕슨 씨가 수십 개의 민트와 카다멈 묘목 화분뿐만 아니라 다른 희귀한 허브들도 가지고 있다(we have dozens of potted mint ~ other uncommon herbs)고 했고, 이메일의 두 번째 단락 두 번째 문장에서 요네다 씨가 구입하는 묘목의 종류와 각 식물에 지불하는 도매가격은 양치식물(8달러), 덩굴식물(6달러), 일년생 화초(5달러), 그리고 요리용 허브들로, 특히 오레가노, 민트, 로즈메리(2달러)(Here are the types of seedlings ~ herbs for cooking, especially oregano, mint, and rosemary ($2))라고 했다. 딕슨 씨가 가지고 있는 식물은 민트, 카다멈을 비롯한 허브이고 요네다 씨는 요리용 허브에 2달러를 지불한다고 했으므로 (D)가 정답이다.

186-190 웹페이지 + 이메일 + 후기

https://www.elektroproofrepair.com/about

**컴퓨터를 다시 정상적으로 작동시키려면
일렉트로프루프 리페어에 맡겨 주세요!**

일렉트로프루프 리페어의 반전 없는 정책은 세 가지 가격대인 145달러, 200달러, 350달러의 정액 요금을 제시합니다. 이 수수료에는 소프트웨어나 교체 부품 비용은 포함되지 않습니다. 대부분의 수리는 200달러의 수수료가 발생합니다.

참고: 186 급격한 수요의 증가로 인해 현재 모든 서비스에 예약이 필요합니다. 당사의 우수한 기술자와 초기 상담을 하시려면 저희 일정 페이지에서 가능한 시간대를 선택하시면 됩니다. 예약 시, 환불되지 않는 보증금 60달러를 지불하셔야 하며, 이 보증금은 제시된 서비스 비용에 적립됩니다.

질문이 있으시면 inquiries@elektroproofrepair.com으로 이메일을 보내 주세요. 가능하면 당일 또는 다음 영업일에 연락드리겠습니다. 190 대부분의 수리는 영업일 기준 3~5일 이내에 완료됩니다.

어휘　policy 정책　flat fee 정액[균일] 요금　labor 작업, 노동　replacement 교체　the majority of 대부분의, 대다수의　incur 발생시키다　dramatic 급격한　demand 수요　initial 초기의　consultation 상담　qualified 자격을 갖춘　time slot 시간대　nonrefundable 환불이 안 되는　deposit 보증금　credit 적립하다, 입금하다　render 제시하다　business day 영업일

수신: 제시카 넬슨 〈jnelson17@saffronmail.com〉
188 발신: 아서 자케 〈ajacquet@elektroproofrepair.com〉
날짜: 1월 14일
제목: 회신: 차를 쏟았습니다. 도와주세요!

넬슨 씨께,

188 일렉트로프루프 리페어에 연락 주셔서 감사합니다. 187 내일 1월 15일에 검사를 위해 노트북을 가지고 와도 되는지 문의하셨습니다. 안타깝게도 현재 1월 18일까지 예약이 완전히 다 찼습니다. 187 예약 가능한 가장 빠른 시간대는 1월 19일 오전 8시입니다. 이 시간대로 예약하기를 원하시거나 질문이 있으시면 알려주십시오.

아서 자케, 일렉트로프루프 리페어

어휘　spill 엎지름, 쏟아냄　inspection 검사　solid 완전히

https://www.buyertobuyerintel.com/repair_services/electronics/computer_devices

★★★★★
일렉트로프루프 리페어

오랫동안 믿고 잘 사용하던 노트북 키보드에 차를 쏟았고, 금세 꽤 빨리 말렸지만 189 **내부 부품이 망가졌을까 봐 걱정했습니다.** 다행스럽게도 일렉트로프루프 리페어가 구조에 나섰습니다! 웹사이트에 상담을 예약한 후, 초조하게 답변을 기다렸습니다. 188 **한 시간 이내로 사장님으로부터 직접 이메일을 받았습니다.** 제가 요청한 시간대는 불가능했지만, 얼마나 급하게 노트북이 필요한지를 호소하려고 그의 이메일에 답장을 보냈을 때 사장님은 갑작스러운 취소가 생겼다면서 바로 그날 아침에 노트북을 가져올 수 있는지 물었고, 저는 그렇게 했습니다. 사고가 일어났을 때 컴퓨터가 켜져 있지 않았기 때문에 일렉트로프루프 리페어 기사님이 컴퓨터의 내부를 건조하고 하드 드라이브나 내부 회로의 손상을 막을 수 있었습니다. 새 배터리 외에는 다른 부품이 필요하지 않았으며, 190 **일렉트로프루프 리페어에서 노트북이 제대로 작동하게 하여 24시간 이내에 저에게 돌려주었습니다.**

-제시카 넬슨

어휘 faithful 믿을 만한, 신뢰할 수 있는 exterior 외부 rather 꽤 internal 내부의 component 부품 ruin 망가뜨리다 rescue 구조 anxiously 초조하게 urgently 긴급하게 unexpected 예상치 못한 cancellation 취소 prevent 방지하다 damage 손상 circuit 회로 functional 작동하는

186 Not / True

번역 웹페이지에 따르면, 일렉트로프루프 리페어에 대해 사실인 것은?
(A) 최근에 가격을 인상했다.
(B) 더 많은 수리 기사를 고용하고 있다.
(C) 급격한 사업 상승세를 경험했다.
(D) 작업을 시작하기 전에 전액을 지불해야 한다.

해설 웹페이지의 두 번째 단락 첫 문장에서 급격한 수요의 증가로 인해 현재 모든 서비스에 예약이 필요하다(Because of a dramatic increase in demand ~ require appointments for all services)고 했으므로 (C)가 정답이다. 같은 단락 마지막 문장에서 예약 시, 환불되지 않는 보증금 60달러를 지불해야 하며, 이 보증금은 제시된 서비스 비용에 적립된다(When you schedule your appointment, we require a $60 ~ cost of services rendered)고 했으므로 (D)는 오답이고, (A)와 (B)에 대한 언급은 없으므로 답이 될 수 없다.

어휘 raise 올리다 sudden 갑작스러운

Paraphrasing 지문의 a dramatic increase in demand → 정답의 a sudden increase in business

187 세부사항

번역 이메일에 따르면, 넬슨 씨가 서비스를 위해 노트북을 가져올 수 있는 가장 빠른 날짜는?
(A) 1월 14일
(B) 1월 15일
(C) 1월 18일
(D) 1월 19일

해설 이메일의 두 번째 문장에서 내일 1월 15일에 검사를 위해 노트북을 가지고 와도 되는지 문의했는데(You asked if you could ~ tomorrow, January 15), 예약 가능한 가장 빠른 시간대는 1월 19

일 오전 8시(The earliest available time slot is 8:00 A.M. on January 19)라고 했다. 따라서 넬슨 씨가 수리를 위해 노트북을 가지고 방문할 수 있는 가장 빠른 날짜는 1월 19일이므로 (D)가 정답이다.

188 연계

번역 자케 씨에 대해 사실일 것 같은 것은?
(A) 사업체를 소유하고 있다.
(B) 기술자이다.
(C) 접수원이다.
(D) 수리된 장비를 배달한다.

해설 이메일의 첫 문장에서 발신인인 아서 자케 씨(From: Arthur Jacquet)가 넬슨 씨에게 일렉트로프루프 리페어에 연락 주셔서 감사하다(Thank you for contacting Elektroproof Repair)고 했고, 후기의 네 번째 문장에서 넬슨 씨가 한 시간 이내로 사장님으로부터 직접 이메일을 받았다(Within an hour, I got an e-mail directly from the owner)고 했다. 따라서 넬슨 씨에게 이메일을 보낸 자케 씨는 일렉트로프루프 리페어의 사장이므로 (A)가 정답이다.

189 세부사항

번역 후기에 따르면, 넬슨 씨가 노트북에 대해 가장 걱정했던 것은?
(A) 내부 부품이 손상될 수 있다는 점
(B) 수리하기에 연식이 너무 오래되었다는 점
(C) 반응이 너무 느리다는 점
(D) 운영 체제에 바이러스가 있다는 점

해설 후기의 첫 문장에서 넬슨 씨가 내부 부품이 망가졌을까 봐 걱정했다(I was afraid the internal components might have been ruined)고 했으므로 (A)가 정답이다.

어휘 operating system 운영 체제

Paraphrasing 지문의 the internal components → 정답의 the parts inside
지문의 ruined → 정답의 damaged

190 연계

번역 넬슨 씨의 컴퓨터 수리에 대해 암시된 것은?
(A) 새로운 운영 소프트웨어 설치가 수반되었다.
(B) 광고된 것보다 더 빨리 완료되었다.
(C) 내부 회로의 교체가 있었다.
(D) 하드 드라이브에 업그레이드를 해야 했다.

해설 웹페이지의 마지막 문장에서 대부분의 수리는 영업일 기준 3~5일 이내에 완료된다(Most repairs are completed within three to five business days)고 했고, 후기의 마지막 문장에서 넬슨 씨가 일렉트로프루프 리페어에서 노트북이 제대로 작동하게 하여 24시간 내에 돌려주었다(Elektroproof Repair had my laptop ~ within 24 hours)고 했다. 따라서 넬슨 씨의 노트북은 웹페이지에 제시된 기간보다 훨씬 더 짧은 시간 내에 수리되었으므로 (B)가 정답이다.

어휘 involve 수반하다, 포함하다

191-195 광고 + 이메일 + 영수증

---

191 알렉시스 인스트루먼츠에서 기타 연주를 배우세요!

알렉시스 인스트루먼츠는 4월 2일부터 그룹 및 개인 기타 교습을 제공할 예정입니다. **192 저희의 각 지점이 신축 교실과 연습실로 새로워졌습니다.** 저희 강사들은 전문 음악가로서 수년간 가르치고 연주한 경험이 있습니다. 지금 바로 알렉시스 인스트루먼츠 매장에 전화하셔서 수강 가능한 과정과 가격을 알아보세요.

> 어휘 instrument 악기 individual 개인의 instruction 교육, 지도 availability 이용 가능함

수신: 루시아 리베라 〈luciarivera@rapidonet.com〉
발신: 크리스타 타워스 〈ktowers@alexisinstruments.com〉
날짜: 4월 26일 오전 8시 30분
제목: TS1058293 주문

리베라 씨께,

4월 23일에 주문하신 건에 대해 말씀드릴 것이 있습니다. **193 고객님께서 원하시는 모델의 기타는 재고가 한 대 밖에 없습니다.** 이 기타는 여기 산타 바바라에 있는 저희 판매장 바닥에 전시용으로 사용된 것입니다. 이는 기타가 상자 밖에 나와 있었고 매장을 둘러보는 손님들에 의해 연주되었다는 것을 뜻합니다. 저희의 사내 현악기 제작자가 기타를 철저히 검사했고 아직 상태도 훌륭합니다. 긁힌 자국이나 흠집, 찌그러진 부분도 전혀 없습니다. 기타가 새 제품이라고 생각하고 구매하셨기 때문에 다음 두 가지 옵션을 제공해 드리고자 합니다.

1. 진열용 상품을 원하지 않을 경우, 주문을 취소하고 즉시 전액 환불을 받으실 수 있습니다.
2. **194 진열용 상품을 원하실 경우, 즉시 배송해 드리고 원래 소매가에서 10퍼센트를 할인해 드립니다.**

후자를 선택하신다면 기타가 내일 첫 수업에 늦지 않게 고객님 지역의 매장으로 배달되도록 하겠습니다. 불편을 드려 죄송합니다.

192 크리스타 타워스
알렉시스 인스트루먼츠

> 어휘 follow up on ~에 대해 후속 조치를 하다 in stock 재고가 있는 browse 둘러보다 in-house (조직) 내부의 luthier 현악기 제작자 thoroughly 철저히 inspect 검사하다 scuff 흠집 dent 찌그러진 곳 whatsoever (no, nothing 등과 함께 쓰여) 전혀 floor model 진열용 상품 immediate 즉각적인 immediately 즉시 retail 소매 latter 후자 in time 늦지 않게, 일찍

알렉시스 인스트루먼츠

주문 번호: TS1058293
날짜: 4월 26일

설명	가격
도밍고 313 풀바디 어쿠스틱 기타	450달러
194 기타 10퍼센트 할인	**-45달러**
195 알렉시스 인스트루먼츠 전 지점에서 유효한	75달러
3년 수리 및 유지 관리 서비스	
판매세	34.8달러

총액	514.8달러

배송지	194 청구 대상
알렉시스 인스트루먼츠, 23번 매장 조셉 드라이브 3914 치코, 캘리포니아 95926	**194 루시아 리베라** 셰이디 그로브 레인 11437 치코, 캘리포니아 95926

> 어휘 description 설명 maintenance 유지 관리 good 유효한

---

191 주제 / 목적

번역 광고의 목적은?
(A) 기타를 판매하려고
(B) 수업을 홍보하려고
(C) 음악 교사를 유치하려고
(D) 새로운 지점을 발표하려고

해설 광고의 제목에서 알렉시스 인스트루먼츠에서 기타 연주를 배우라(Learn to play guitar at Alexis Instruments!)고 제안하고 있으므로 기타 연주 수업을 홍보하는 광고임을 알 수 있다. 따라서 (B)가 정답이다.

---

192 연계

번역 타워스 씨가 일하는 매장에 대해 사실일 것 같은 것은?
(A) 개조되었다.
(B) 새로운 직원을 채용하고 있다.
(C) 다른 지점보다 재고가 많다.
(D) 영업시간이 연장되었다.

해설 이메일의 하단에 크리스타 타워스(Krista Towers)는 알렉시스 인스트루먼츠(Alexis Instruments)에서 근무하는 것으로 나와 있고, 광고의 두 번째 문장에서 저희(알렉시스 인스트루먼츠)의 각 지점이 신축 교실과 연습실로 새로워졌다(Each of our locations has been updated with newly constructed classrooms and practice rooms)고 했다. 따라서 타워스 씨가 일하는 알렉시스 인스트루먼츠의 전 지점이 개조되었다는 것을 알 수 있으므로 (A)가 정답이다.

어휘 renovate 개조하다 inventory 재고 extend 연장하다

> Paraphrasing 지문의 newly constructed
> → 정답의 renovated

---

193 Not / True

번역 이메일에서 기타에 대해 명시한 것은?
(A) 수리가 필요하다.
(B) 치코에 있는 매장의 선반에 있었다.
(C) 이전에 알렉시스 인스트루먼츠 고객이 소유했다.
(D) 해당 모델 중 현재 구입 가능한 유일한 기타이다.

해설 이메일의 두 번째 문장에서 고객이 원하는 모델의 기타는 재고가 한 대 밖에 없다(We have only one guitar of the model you want in stock)고 했으므로 (D)가 정답이다. 이메일의 세 번째 문장에서 이 기타는 여기 산타 바바라에 있는 판매장 바닥에 전시용으로 사용된

것(It was used as a display sample on the floor ~ here in Santa Barbara)이라고 했으므로 (B)는 오답이며, (A)와 (C)는 언급되지 않았다.

어휘 previously 이전에

Paraphrasing 지문의 have only one ~ in stock
→ 정답의 the only one ~ available

194 연계

번역 리베라 씨에 대해 추론될 수 있는 것은?
(A) 기타를 손상시켰다.
(B) 환불을 요청했다.
(C) 이전에 온라인 수업에 등록했다.
(D) 진열용 상품을 구입했다.

해설 이메일의 두 가지 옵션 중 2번에서 리베라 씨에게 진열용 상품을 원할 경우, 즉시 배송하고 원래 소매가에서 10퍼센트를 할인해 주겠다(If you would like the floor model ~ offer you a 10 percent discount off the original retail price)고 했고, 영수증의 설명 부분 두 번째 항목에 기타가 10퍼센트 할인되어 45달러가 공제되었으며(10% discount on guitar, -$45.00), 표에 청구 대상(Bill To)이 루시아 리베라(Lucia Rivera)라고 나와 있다. 따라서 리베라 씨가 이메일의 옵션 2번에 제시된 조건으로 진열되었던 기타를 구입했음을 알 수 있으므로 (D)가 정답이다.

어휘 damage 손상을 주다   enroll in ~에 등록하다

195 Not / True

번역 영수증에 따르면, 알렉시스 인스트루먼츠에 대해 사실인 것은?
(A) 매장에서 악기를 수리한다.
(B) 산타 바바라에 두 개의 매장이 있다.
(C) 연례 정기 세일 행사 중이다.
(D) 전문 음악가에 의해 설립되었다.

해설 영수증의 설명 부분 세 번째 항목에 알렉시스 인스트루먼츠 전 지점에서 유효한 3년 수리 및 유지 관리 서비스(Three-year repair ~ at any Alexis Instruments location)라고 나와 있는 것으로 보아 알렉시스 인스트루먼츠에서는 매장에서 악기 수리 서비스를 제공하고 있음을 알 수 있다. 따라서 (A)가 정답이다.

어휘 found 설립하다

Paraphrasing 지문의 location → 정답의 stores

196-200 이메일 + 청구서 + 이메일

수신: 모든 강사
발신: 최지영
제목: 신규 수수료 표
날짜: 8월 15일

---

196 강사님들께,

196 미라벨 미술관에 예술가이자 교육자로서의 능력을 제공해 주셔서 감사합니다. 월별 청구서를 작성하실 때 아래의 업데이트된 수수료 표를 사용하십시오.

항목	설명	소요 시간	수수료
투어	196 그룹 투어 인솔	60분	50달러
투어	그룹 투어 인솔	90분	75달러
강좌	미술 수업 지도	75분	65달러
198 강좌	미술 수업 지도	120분	110달러
200 개발	새로운 강의 내용 계획	미정	200달러
교육	전문적인 주제에 관한 미술관 직원 교육	미정	시간당 25달러

전자 지불은 청구서 제출 후 영업일 기준 10일 이후에 제공됩니다.

최지영, 교육 진행 담당

어휘 instructor 강사   schedule 표, 명세서   lend (도움을) 제공하다[주다]   educator 교육자   invoice 청구서   description 설명   duration 기간   vary 달라지다   instruct 교육하다   specialized 전문적인   submission 제출   coordinator 진행 담당자

데본트 메리웨더
d.merriweather@camail.ca

청구서 00278번
대상: 미라벨 미술관 서비스
발신 날짜: 9월 30일

날짜	설명	수수료
9월 22일	투어: 특별 전시회	50달러
9월 22일	197 강좌: 입문자를 위한 그림 그리기	65달러
9월 25일	197,198 강좌: 점토로 조각하기	198 110달러
	합계	225달러

어휘 exhibit 전시회   sculpt 조각하다

수신: 데본트 메리웨더 〈d.merriweather@camail.ca〉
발신: 최지영 〈jy.choi@mirabelmuseumofart.ca〉
제목: 지급
날짜: 10월 6일

메리웨더 씨께,

9월 청구서를 제출해 주셔서 감사합니다. 9월 25일에 처음 가르치신 200 조각 수업의 커리큘럼을 개발하신 일에 대해 저희 측에 청구를 빠뜨리신 것을 발견했습니다. 199 캐럴 스완에게 확인해 보니 00278번 청구서는 이미 지불이 되었기 때문에, 개발 건에 대해 두 번째 청구서를 제출하시는 것이 가장 좋다고 합니다. 제가 그것을 받으면 그녀에게 빨리 처리해 달라고 요청하겠습니다.

학생들의 피드백이 매우 긍정적이었다는 것을 알게 되시면 기뻐하실 것 같습니다. 오늘 중으로 그들의 피드백 양식 스캔본을 이메일로 보내 드리 겠습니다.

최지영, 교육 진행 담당

어휘 neglect ~하는 것을 잊다 charge 청구하다 process 처리하다 positive 긍정적인 form 양식

196 추론 / 암시

번역 첫 번째 이메일에서 미라벨 미술관에 대해 암시된 것은?
(A) 투어를 이끌 미술 선생님을 고용한다.
(B) 미술관 회원들에게 개인 투어를 제공한다.
(C) 미술 수업은 시민들에게 무료이다.
(D) 다음 직원 교육은 10일 후에 실시된다.

해설 첫 번째 이메일에서 강사님들께(Dear Teachers)라며 인사하고, 첫 문장에서 미라벨 미술관에 예술가이자 교육자로서의 능력을 제공해 주어 감사하다(Thank you for lending ~ the Mirabel Museum of Art)며 월별 청구서를 작성할 때 아래의 업데이트된 수수료 표를 사용하라(Please use the updated ~ your monthly invoices) 고 했고, 표의 첫 항목에 그룹 투어 인솔(Lead group tour)이 나와 있다. 따라서 미술관에서 강사들을 고용해 강사들이 제공하는 서비스 에 따라 급여를 지불하고 있으며 그 서비스에는 그룹 투어 인솔이 포 함되어 있음을 알 수 있으므로 (A)가 정답이다.

197 추론 / 암시

번역 청구서에서 메리웨더 씨에 대해 암시하는 것은?
(A) 9월 30일에 미술관에서 근무했다.
(B) 하나 이상의 미술 양식에 전문 지식이 있다.
(C) 그의 미술 수업 중 하나가 취소되었다.
(D) 그의 작품 중 일부가 9월에 전시되었다.

해설 청구서의 표에 따르면 메리웨더 씨가 입문자를 위한 그림 그리기 강 좌(Class: Drawing for Beginners)와 점토로 조각하기 강좌 (Class: Sculpting with Clay)를 가르쳤다고 나와 있다. 따라서 메 리웨더 씨는 회화와 조소 두 가지 분야에 전문성이 있음을 알 수 있으 므로 (B)가 정답이다.

어휘 expertise 전문 지식 exhibit 전시하다

198 연계

번역 메리웨더 씨가 가르친 조각 수업의 소요 시간은?
(A) 60분
(B) 75분
(C) 90분
(D) 120분

해설 청구서의 표에 따르면 메리웨더 씨가 가르친 점토로 조각하기 강좌 (Class: Sculpting with Clay)의 수수료는 110달러($110)이고, 첫 이메일의 수수료 표에 따르면 수수료가 110달러($110)인 미술 수업 지도 강좌(Teach art class)의 소요 시간은 120분(120 minutes) 이다. 따라서 메리웨더 씨가 가르친 조각 수업은 120분짜리였음을 알 수 있으므로 (D)가 정답이다.

199 추론 / 암시

번역 두 번째 이메일에 따르면, 스완 씨는 누구일 것 같은가?
(A) 경리
(B) 미술 선생님
(C) 메리웨더 씨의 조수
(D) 미라벨 미술관 관장

해설 두 번째 이메일의 세 번째 문장에서 캐럴 스완에게 확인해 보니 00278번 청구서는 이미 지불이 되었기 때문에 개발 건에 대해 두 번째 청구서를 제출하는 것이 가장 좋다고 한다(I checked with Carol Swann ~ a second invoice for the development)고 했 고, 그것을 받으면 그녀에게 빨리 처리해 달라고 요청하겠다(I will ask her to process it quickly when I receive it)고 했다. 따라 서 스완 씨는 급여 처리 회계를 담당하는 경리임을 알 수 있으므로 (A)가 정답이다.

어휘 bookkeeper 경리

200 연계

번역 최 씨에 대해 결론지을 수 있는 것은?
(A) 학생들의 피드백 양식을 읽는 것을 잊었다.
(B) 메리웨더 씨가 200달러를 받아야 한다고 믿는다.
(C) 한 달에 한 번 선생님들과 만난다.
(D) 메리웨더 씨의 10월 청구서를 거절했다.

해설 두 번째 이메일의 두 번째 문장에서 최 씨가 메리웨더 씨에게 조각 수 업의 커리큘럼을 개발한 일에 대해 청구를 빠뜨린 것을 발견했다(I noticed that you neglected to charge us for developing the curriculum for your sculpting class)고 했고, 첫 이메일의 수수 료 표의 개발(Development) 항목에 새로운 강의 내용 계획(Plan new course content)을 하면 200달러($200)를 청구할 수 있다고 나와 있다. 따라서 최 씨는 메리웨더 씨에게 조각 수업의 커리큘럼을 개발한 일에 대한 수수료인 200달러를 지급받지 않았다고 알리고 있 으므로 (B)가 정답이다.

어휘 owe (특정 금액을) 지불해야 하다 reject 거절하다

101 (A)	**102** (A)	**103** (B)	**104** (A)	**105** (C)
106 (D)	**107** (B)	**108** (D)	**109** (B)	**110** (C)
111 (A)	**112** (D)	**113** (B)	**114** (A)	**115** (C)
116 (A)	**117** (C)	**118** (A)	**119** (A)	**120** (A)
121 (C)	**122** (C)	**123** (D)	**124** (A)	**125** (D)
126 (B)	**127** (C)	**128** (C)	**129** (B)	**130** (A)
131 (B)	**132** (D)	**133** (A)	**134** (C)	**135** (C)
136 (A)	**137** (B)	**138** (D)	**139** (B)	**140** (C)
141 (D)	**142** (D)	**143** (B)	**144** (A)	**145** (D)
146 (A)	**147** (D)	**148** (C)	**149** (C)	**150** (B)
151 (D)	**152** (A)	**153** (B)	**154** (C)	**155** (C)
156 (A)	**157** (B)	**158** (C)	**159** (C)	**160** (A)
161 (D)	**162** (D)	**163** (C)	**164** (B)	**165** (D)
166 (D)	**167** (C)	**168** (A)	**169** (D)	**170** (C)
171 (C)	**172** (A)	**173** (C)	**174** (C)	**175** (B)
176 (C)	**177** (B)	**178** (D)	**179** (A)	**180** (D)
181 (C)	**182** (D)	**183** (C)	**184** (B)	**185** (D)
186 (A)	**187** (B)	**188** (D)	**189** (B)	**190** (C)
191 (B)	**192** (D)	**193** (A)	**194** (A)	**195** (D)
196 (B)	**197** (D)	**198** (D)	**199** (A)	**200** (C)

PART 5

101 소유격 대명사 어휘

해설 동사 must keep의 목적어인 명사구 boarding passes and luggage를 수식하는 자리이므로 소유격 인칭대명사가 들어가야 한다. 빈칸 앞에 주어로 쓰인 복수명사 Passengers를 대신해 '그들의 탑승권과 수하물'이라는 내용이 되어야 하므로 3인칭 복수 인칭대명사 (A) their가 정답이다.

번역 승객들은 그들의 탑승권과 수하물을 항상 지니고 있어야 한다.

어휘 passenger 승객　boarding pass 탑승권　luggage 수하물　at all times 항상

102 상관접속사

해설 빈칸 뒤 train과 airplane 사이에 and가 있으므로, and와 함께 상관접속사 구문을 이루어 'A와 B 둘 다'라는 뜻을 완성하는 (A) both가 정답이다. (B) either는 or와 상관접속사를 이루어 'A 또는 B 둘 중 하나'를 뜻하고, (C) further는 '추가의'라는 의미의 형용사로 문맥상 적절하지 않으며, (D) hardly는 부사이므로 명사를 수식하는 자리에 들어갈 수 없다.

번역 회사의 정책은 출장에 기차와 비행기를 이용하여 가는 것을 둘 다 허용합니다.

103 형용사 자리 _ 주격 보어

해설 빈칸은 be동사 뒤 주격 보어 자리이므로 형용사나 명사가 들어갈 수 있다. '장비를 관리할 책임을 맡고 있다'라는 내용이 되어야 하므로 전치사 for와 함께 '~을 책임지는, ~을 담당하는'을 뜻하는 형용사 (B) responsible이 정답이다. 주어인 technicians와 동격이 아니므로 '책임, 책무'를 뜻하는 명사 (C) responsibility와 (D) responsibilities는 답이 될 수 없으며, 부사인 (A) responsibly는 품사상 빈칸에 들어갈 수 없다.

번역 생산 기술자들은 공장 장비를 유지 관리할 책임을 맡고 있다.

어휘 production 생산　technician 기술자, 기사　maintain 유지하다

104 형용사 어휘

해설 「주어(The team)+동사(found)+목적어(Ms. Dietrich's advice)+목적격 보어(to be especially ------)」 구조의 5형식 문장이다. 따라서 빈칸에는 to be의 보어 역할을 하며, 목적어인 '디트리히 씨의 조언(Ms. Dietrich's advice)'을 보충 설명하기에 적절한 형용사를 골라야 한다. '조언이 특히 도움이 된다'라는 내용이 되어야 자연스러우므로 '도움이 되는'이라는 의미의 (A) helpful이 정답이다. (B) thankful은 사람이 주체로 쓰여 '고맙게 여기는'이라는 의미를 나타내고, (C) regular는 '정기적인', (D) extra는 '추가의'라는 뜻으로 문맥에 적합하지 않다.

번역 그 팀은 사무실 직원 관리에 관한 디트리히 씨의 조언이 특히 도움이 된다고 생각했다.

105 동사 자리

해설 The film crew가 주어인 문장에 동사가 보이지 않으므로 빈칸은 동사 자리이다. 따라서 정답은 (C) arrived이다. (A) to arrive는 to부정사, (B) having arrived와 (D) arriving은 동명사/분사이므로 동사 자리에 들어갈 수 없다.

번역 촬영 팀이 홍보용 관광 캠페인을 준비하기 위해 이번 주 초 나미비아에 도착했다.

어휘 crew (함께 일하는) 팀　promotional 홍보의　tourism 관광업

106 전치사 어휘   동영상 강의

해설 문맥상 '협상이 오후 4시까지 끝난다'는 의미가 되어야 적절하므로 특정 시점을 나타내는 표현과 함께 쓰여 '~까지'를 뜻하는 (D) by가 정답이다. 참고로, (B) until(~까지)은 어느 시점까지 계속되는 상태를 의미할 때 쓰이므로 '~까지 끝나다'와 같이 행위의 완료를 나타내는 문장에는 어울리지 않는다.

번역 위원회는 협상이 오후 4시까지 끝날 것으로 예상한다.

어휘 committee 위원회　negotiation 협상

107 형용사 자리 _ 명사 수식

해설 앞에 부정관사 an, 뒤에 명사 panel이 있으므로 빈칸에는 panel을 수식하는 형용사나 복합명사를 이루는 명사가 들어갈 수 있다. 문맥상

으로 '전문가 패널'이라는 의미가 되어야 자연스러우므로 '전문가의'라는 뜻의 형용사 (B) expert가 정답이다. 명사인 (A) expertise(전문 지식)와 (C) expertness(숙달)는 panel과 복합명사를 이룰 수 없고, (D) expertly(능숙하게)는 부사이므로 품사상 빈칸에 들어갈 수 없다.

번역 유나이티드 메디컬 보드는 병원 개선을 위한 권고안을 제시하는 의사 전문가 위원단이다.

어휘 panel 위원단, 패널(특정 문제에 대해 조언을 제공하는 전문가 집단) physician 의사 improvement 개선

108 부사 어휘

해설 빈칸 앞의 be동사 are가 현재 시제이고, 문맥상 '이제 디지털 결제가 가능하다'라는 의미가 되어야 적합하므로 '이제, 지금'을 뜻하는 (D) now가 정답이다.

번역 이제 모든 서던 코치 버스 정류장에서 디지털 결제가 가능합니다.

어휘 payment 결제 accept 받아들이다, 수락하다

109 접속사 자리 _ 부사절 접속사

해설 빈칸 뒤 완전한 절(the author's reading was canceled)을 이끄는 접속사 자리이므로 '비록 ~이지만'이라는 뜻의 부사절 접속사 (B) though가 정답이다. (A) seldom, (C) rarely, (D) secondly 모두 부사이므로 오답이다.

번역 작가의 낭독회는 취소되었지만 도서관을 위한 모금 행사는 성공적이었다.

어휘 fund-raising 모금(의) author 작가 reading 낭독회

110 동사 어휘

해설 부사적 역할을 하는 to부정사의 to 뒤에 들어갈 동사 어휘를 고르는 문제이다. the status를 목적어로 취해 '배송 상태를 확인하기 위해'라는 내용이 되어야 하므로 '확인하다'라는 뜻의 타동사 (C) check가 정답이다. (A) place는 '배치하다', (B) want는 '원하다'라는 뜻으로 문맥상 어울리지 않고, (D) look은 자동사로 목적어를 취할 수 없다.

번역 배송 상태를 확인하려면 드롭다운 메뉴에서 주문 추적 옵션을 선택하세요.

어휘 status 상태 select 선택하다 track 추적하다 drop-down menu (컴퓨터의) 드롭다운 메뉴

111 목적격 보어 _ to부정사

해설 「enable + 목적어(executives with limited time) + 목적격 보어」의 5형식 문장 구조에서 목적격 보어에 해당하는 자리로, 뒤에 오는 명사구 junior staff를 목적어로 취한다. 5형식 동사 enable의 목적격 보어로는 to부정사가 와야 하므로 (A) to counsel이 정답이다. 본동사인 (B) should counsel, 동명사/현재분사인 (C) counseling, 동사/과거분사인 (D) counseled는 enable의 목적격 보어 자리에 들어갈 수 없다.

번역 우리의 프로젝트 기반 멘토링 접근법은 한정된 시간을 가진 임원들이 후배 직원들에게 상담을 제공할 수 있게 해 줍니다.

어휘 based on ~에 기반을 둔 approach 접근법 enable ~을 할 수 있게 하다 executive 임원 counsel 상담하다

112 명사 어휘

해설 빈칸에는 sales와 함께 복합명사를 이루어 동사 is updating의 목적어 역할을 하는 단어가 들어가야 한다. 분기별로 업데이트할 대상으로 적절한 것은 판매 수치이므로 '수치'라는 뜻의 (D) figures가 정답이다. 참고로, (A)의 measure는 '조치', (B)의 ground는 '근거', (C)의 instruction은 '지시'라는 뜻으로 문맥상 적절하지 않다.

번역 여키스 씨는 보스턴 사무소로부터 최종 보고서를 받은 뒤 우리의 분기별 판매 수치를 업데이트하고 있다.

어휘 quarterly 분기별의

113 동사 어형 _ 명령문의 동사원형

해설 문장에서 주어와 동사가 보이지 않으므로 빈칸은 주어 You가 생략된 명령문의 동사 자리이다. 따라서 동사원형인 (B) Brighten이 정답이다. (A) Brightens는 3인칭 단수동사, (C) Brightened는 동사/과거분사, (D) Brightening은 동명사/현재분사이므로 명령문의 동사 자리에 들어갈 수 없다.

번역 노리미 문구의 아름다운 종이 제품으로 여러분의 책상에 활기를 주세요.

어휘 brighten 활기를 주다, 밝게 하다 stationery 문구류

114 동사 어휘

해설 동사 allows의 목적격 보어로 쓰인 to부정사의 to 뒤에 들어갈 동사 어휘를 고르는 문제이다. room temperature를 목적어로 취해 '사용자가 실내 온도를 원격으로 조절할 수 있게 해 준다'라는 의미가 되어야 하므로 '조절하다'라는 뜻의 (A) control이 정답이다. (B) impose는 '(세금 등을) 부과하다', (C) announce는 '발표하다', (D) encourage는 '장려하다'라는 의미이다.

번역 사용자가 실내 온도를 원격으로 조절할 수 있게 해 주는 애플리케이션 얼티템프는 현재 아시아에서만 이용 가능합니다.

어휘 application 애플리케이션, 응용 프로그램 allow 할 수 있게 하다 room temperature 실내 온도 remotely 원격으로

115 전치사 자리 / 어휘

해설 빈칸은 명사구 the cost of travel과 함께 콤마 뒤 완전한 절(the cost ~ is reasonable)을 수식하는 자리이므로 전치사가 들어가야 한다. 또한 '이동 경비를 제외하면 비용이 합리적이다'라는 내용이 되어야 적절하므로 '~을 제외하고, ~외에는'을 뜻하는 전치사 (C) Aside from이 정답이다. (A) Along은 '~을 따라'라는 뜻의 위치 전치사로 의미상 부적절하고, '비록 ~일지라도'의 의미인 (B) Even if와 '~이기 때문에'라는 뜻의 (D) Because는 부사절 접속사로 뒤에 완전한 절이 와야 하므로 오답이다.

번역 여행 경비를 제외하면 학회 참석 비용은 합리적이다.

어휘 conference 학회 reasonable 합리적인

116 부사 어휘
▶ 동영상 강의

해설 동사 are anticipating을 수식하여 '고객들이 간절히 기다리고 있다'는 의미가 되어야 자연스러우므로 '간절히'를 뜻하는 (A) eagerly가 정답이다. (B) sharply는 '날카롭게', (C) voluntarily는 '자발적으로', (D) rapidly는 '빠르게'라는 뜻으로 문맥상 어울리지 않는다.

번역 고객들은 아스키오 자동차의 최신 모델 픽업트럭을 간절히 기다리고 있다.

어휘 anticipate 기대하다, 고대하다   latest 최신의

117 명사 자리 _ 동사의 목적어

해설 동사 have의 목적어 자리로, 빈칸은 소유격 Mr. Garcia's의 수식을 받는 명사 자리이다. 따라서 '승인'이라는 의미의 명사 (C) approval이 정답이다. (A) approve와 (B) approves는 동사이므로 품사상 빈칸에 들어갈 수 없고, (D) approving은 동명사로 쓰일 경우 명사 자리에는 가능하나 뒤에 목적어가 와야 하므로 답이 될 수 없다.

번역 가르시아 씨의 승인을 받는 대로 늘 이용하는 웹사이트들에 구인 목록을 게시해 주세요.

어휘 post 게시하다   job listing 구인 목록   usual 늘 하는

118 형용사 어휘
▶ 동영상 강의

해설 빈칸 앞에 '고객층을 넓혔다(broadened its customer base)'는 내용이 온 것으로 보아, 빈칸에는 이를 뒷받침하며 change를 수식하기에 알맞은 형용사가 들어가야 한다. '광범위한 변화'라는 의미가 되어야 적합하므로 '광범위한, 폭넓은'이라는 뜻의 (A) extensive가 정답이다. (B) precious는 '귀중한', (C) commercial은 '상업의', (D) accurate은 '정확한'이라는 의미이다.

번역 다비 레스토랑은 메뉴에 광범위한 변화를 줌으로써 고객층을 넓혔다.

어휘 broaden 넓히다   customer base 고객층

119 부사 자리 _ 동사 수식

해설 주어 The redesigned intersection과 동사 shortens 사이에서 동사를 수식하는 부사 자리이다. 따라서 '효과적으로'라는 뜻의 부사 (A) effectively가 정답이다. (B) effects는 동사/명사, (C) effective는 형용사, (D) effected는 동사/과거분사이므로 빈칸에 들어갈 수 없다.

번역 재설계된 교차로는 보행자용 건널목 거리를 효과적으로 단축하여 더 안전하다.

어휘 redesigned 재설계된   intersection 교차로   shorten 단축하다   distance 거리   pedestrian 보행자

120 동사 어휘
▶ 동영상 강의

해설 「be asked+to부정사」의 수동태 구문에서 to부정사의 to 뒤에 들어갈 동사 어휘를 고르는 문제로, 빈칸 뒤에 목적어가 없는 것으로 보아 전치사 from과 함께 쓸 수 있는 자동사를 골라야 한다. '질문을 자제해 줄 것을 요청받는다'는 내용이 되어야 자연스러우므로 전치사 from과 함께 쓰여 '~을 자제하다, ~을 삼가다'를 뜻하는 (A) refrain이 정답이다. (B) forbid(금하다)는 타동사로 뒤에 목적어가 필요하고, 자동사 (C) retreat(후퇴하다)와 (D) hesitate(망설이다)는 문맥상 어울리지 않으므로 답이 되지 않는다.

번역 워크숍 참석자들은 공식 프레젠테이션이 끝날 때까지 질문을 자제해 달라는 요청을 받는다.

어휘 attendee 참석자   formal 공식의

121 명사 자리 _ 동사의 목적어 / 복합명사

해설 빈칸은 grant와 함께 복합명사를 이루어 동사 accepts의 목적어 역할을 하는 명사 자리로, '보조금 제안'이라는 복합명사를 만드는 '제안'이라는 뜻의 명사 (C) proposals가 정답이다. (A) proposes는 동사, (B) proposed는 동사/과거분사, (D) proposing은 동명사/현재분사이므로 빈칸에 적합하지 않다.

번역 타마노 재단은 다양한 과학 연구와 관련된 보조금 제안을 접수한다.

어휘 foundation 재단   accept 접수하다, 받아들이다   grant 보조금   related to ~와 관련된   a range of 다양한

122 전치사 어휘
▶ 동영상 강의

해설 빈칸 뒤 기간을 나타내는 시간 표현 five days와 함께 '5일 이내에'라는 의미를 나타내야 적절하므로 (C) within이 정답이다. (B) during은 특정 기간을 나타내는 명사와 함께 쓰여 '~ 동안에'라는 의미를 나타내며, 바로 뒤에 숫자 표현이 오지 않으므로 오답이다.

번역 게이트웨이 전자는 5일 이내에 찾아가지 않는 주문은 취소할 것이다.

어휘 pick up ~을 찾아가다

123 대명사 어휘
▶ 동영상 강의

해설 빈칸은 주격 관계대명사 who의 선행사 자리로, 사람을 나타내는 동시에 관계사절의 단수동사 arrives와 수 일치하는 대명사가 들어가야 한다. 따라서 '누구나[든지]'를 뜻하는 (D) Anyone이 정답이다. (A) Each는 관계사 who절의 수식을 받지 않고, (B) Those는 복수대명사이므로 관계사절에 복수동사 arrive가 쓰여야 하며, (C) Everything은 사물을 뜻하므로 사람 선행사를 수식하는 관계사 who 앞에 올 수 없다.

번역 오전 10시 이후 회사 주차장에 도착하는 사람은 누구나 출입 코드를 위해 보안실에 연락해야 한다.

어휘 parking garage 주차장   security 보안 부서   access 출입

124 부사 어휘

해설 빈칸 뒤 시간 전치사구 after passing the employee cafeteria와 함께 '직원 식당을 지나자마자'라는 의미가 되어야 자연스럽다. 따라서 시간 전치사 after나 before 앞에 쓰여 각각 '~한 직후', '~하기 직전'이라는 의미를 나타내는 '즉시'라는 뜻의 (A) immediately가 정답이다. (B) recently와 (D) lately는 '최근에'라는 뜻으로 주로 과거나 현재완료 동사를 수식하며, (C) originally는 '원래'라는 뜻으로 문맥상 어울리지 않는다.

번역 회의실로 가려면 직원 식당을 지나자마자 바로 왼쪽으로 도세요.

어휘 get to ~에 가다[도착하다]

125 명사 자리 _ 동사의 주어 / 복합명사

해설 빈칸 앞의 wellness와 함께 복합명사를 이루어 동사 led의 주어 역할을 하는 명사 자리이다. 따라서 '계획, (사업) 활동'이라는 뜻의 명사 (D) initiative가 정답이다. (A) initiate는 동사, (C) initiated는 동사/과거분사로 품사상 빈칸에 들어갈 수 없고, (B) initiator는 '개시자'라는 뜻의 명사로 문맥상 어울리지 않는다.

번역 트레이어 미디어 그룹의 건강 관리 계획은 곧바로 회사에 대한 더 높은 직원 만족으로 이어졌다.

어휘 wellness 건강 관리 directly 곧바로, 직접적으로 lead to ~으로 이어지다 satisfaction 만족 initiate 착수시키다

126 접속사 자리 _ 부사절 접속사

해설 빈칸 뒤 완전한 절(there is demand for them)을 이끌어 앞의 주절(We will keep ~ shoe designs)을 수식하는 부사절 접속사 자리이다. '수요가 있는 한'이라는 의미가 되어야 적절하므로 '~하는 한'이라는 의미의 부사절 접속사 (B) as long as가 정답이다. (A) or else는 '그렇지 않으면'이라는 뜻으로 주로 명령문 뒤에서 절을 연결할 때 쓰이고, (C) as well as는 '~에 더하여'라는 상관접속사이며, (D) in between은 '중간에'라는 뜻의 구전치사로 절을 연결할 수 없다.

번역 우리는 수요가 있는 한 우리의 대표 신발 디자인을 계속 생산할 것입니다.

어휘 demand 수요

127 부사 자리 _ 동사 수식

해설 주어 Regular applications of fertilizer에 두 개의 동사구 improve ~와 enhance ~가 등위접속사 and로 연결된 문장으로, 빈칸은 두 번째 동사 enhance를 수식하는 부사 자리이다. 따라서 '급격하게, 극적으로'라는 뜻의 부사 (C) dramatically가 정답이다. (A) drama는 명사, (B) dramatic은 형용사, (D) dramatize는 동사로 품사상 빈칸에 들어갈 수 없다.

번역 정기적인 비료의 사용은 묘목의 건강을 증진시키고 잎이 많은 채소의 성장을 급격하게 향상시킨다.

어휘 regular 정기적인 application 적용, 이용 fertilizer 비료 seedling 묘목 enhance 향상시키다 leafy 잎이 많은 dramatic 극적인 dramatize 극화하다

128 명사 어휘

해설 빈칸이 전치사 in과 of 사이에 있고, '사람 중심의 직장 환경을 인정받아 수상했다'라는 의미가 되어야 자연스러우므로 in recognition of의 형태로 쓰여 '~을 인정하여'를 뜻하는 (C) recognition(인정)이 정답이다. (B) accordance(일치, 부합)는 in accordance with의 형태로 쓰여 '~에 따라서'라는 뜻으로 쓰이고, (D) dedication(헌신)은 뒤

에 전치사 to와 어울려 쓰여 '~에 헌신'이라는 의미를 나타낸다.

번역 원트너 제조는 사람 중심의 직장 환경을 인정받아 올해 최고 고용주 상을 수상했다.

어휘 manufacturing 제조(업) employer 고용주 people-centered 사람 중심의 workplace 직장, 업무 현장 environment 환경

129 형용사 자리 _ 명사 수식

해설 빈칸 앞에 한정사 some, 뒤에 명사 content가 있으므로 명사를 수식하는 '반복되는'이라는 뜻의 형용사 (B) repetitious가 정답이다. (A) repetition과 (D) repetitiousness는 명사로 content와 복합명사를 만들기에 적절하지 않고, (C) repetitiously는 부사이므로 형용사 자리에 들어갈 수 없다.

번역 편집자는 일부 반복되는 내용을 발견하고 삭제되어야 할 글에 표시했다.

어휘 note 알아채다 content 내용 mark 표시하다 text 글 delete 삭제하다 repetitiously 자꾸 되풀이하여

130 형용사 어휘

해설 빈칸 뒤에 '회원 전용 활동(members-only activities)'이라는 내용이 온 것으로 보아, '독점적으로 이용할 수 있다'는 의미가 되어야 일관성 있는 문장을 완성할 수 있다. 따라서 '독점적인, 전용의'라는 뜻의 (A) exclusive가 정답이다. (B) unknown은 '알려지지 않은', (C) creative는 '창조적인', (D) previous는 '이전의'라는 의미이다.

번역 베이 시티 동물원 회원은 운영 시간 외 가이드 투어와 같은 회원 전용 활동을 독점 이용할 수 있다.

어휘 access 이용, 접근 such as ~와 같은 after-hours 근무[영업] 시간 외의 guided 가이드가 안내하는

PART 6

131-134 이메일

수신: 나오미 리히터 〈naomirichter@mailcurrent.com〉
발신: 와타나 사카모토 〈wsakamoto@RHNimports.com〉
날짜: 11월 23일
제목: 후속 제안
첨부: 물류 담당자 설명

리히터 씨께,

지난주에 수입 관리 대리직 면접을 위해 저희 사무실을 방문해 주셔서 감사합니다. 우리는 귀하의 자질과 열정에 깊은 인상을 받았습니다. **131 비록** 다른 지원자로 추진 중이기는 하지만, 지금 막 자리가 난 물류 담당직을 귀하에게 제안드리고 싶습니다.

132 귀하의 경험과 기량은 귀하를 훌륭한 적임자로 만듭니다. 첨부된 문서에는 상세한 직무 설명과 급여율이 포함되어 있습니다. 이 **133 기회는**

아직 공개적으로 게시되지 않았습니다. ¹³⁴**관심 있으시면** 이번 주말까지 알려 주십시오.

와타누 사카모토
인사부 부장, RHN 임포츠

131 접속사 자리 _ 부사절 접속사

해설 빈칸 뒤에 오는 완전한 절(we are moving ahead with another candidate)을 콤마 뒤 주절에 연결하는 자리이므로, 빈칸에는 부사절 접속사가 들어가야 한다. 따라서 '비록 ~하지만'이라는 뜻의 접속사 (B) Although가 정답이다. (A) Rather는 '오히려', (C) Similarly는 '비슷하게', (D) Consequently는 '결과적으로'라는 뜻의 부사로 절을 연결할 수 없다.

132 문맥에 맞는 문장 고르기

번역 (A) 다른 내부 지원자가 여러 명 있습니다.
(B) 안타깝게도 그 자리는 더 이상 지원 가능하지 않습니다.
(C) 제 조수가 귀하의 두 번째 면접 일정을 잡을 것입니다.
(D) 귀하의 경험과 기량은 귀하를 훌륭한 적임자로 만듭니다.

해설 앞 문장에서 지금 막 자리가 난 물류 담당직을 제안하고 싶다(we would like to offer you a different position ~ logistics coordinator)고 했고, 뒤 문장에서 첨부된 문서에는 직무 설명과 급여율이 포함되어 있다(The attached document contains the detailed job description and pay rate)며 물류 담당직에 지원할 것을 권하고 있다. 따라서 빈칸에는 경험과 기량으로 보아 훌륭한 적임자라고 설득하는 내용이 들어가야 자연스러우므로 (D)가 정답이다.

어휘 internal 내부의 applicant 지원자 schedule 일정을 잡다 skill set 기량, 역량 a great fit 적임자, 적합한 사람

133 명사 어휘

해설 앞에서 물류 담당직(logistics coordinator)을 제안하고 싶다며 일자리에 대해 설명하고 있으므로, 빈칸에는 이 일자리, 즉 취직 기회를 지칭할 수 있는 단어가 들어가야 적절하다. 따라서 '기회'를 뜻하는 (A) opportunity가 정답이다. (B) authorization은 '허가', (C) application은 '지원', (D) capacity는 '수용력'이라는 뜻이다.

134 형용사 자리 _ 주격 보어

해설 be동사 뒤에서 주어인 you를 보충 설명하는 주격 보어 자리로, 문맥상 사람이 느끼는 감정을 나타내는 형용사가 들어가야 자연스럽다. 따라서 '관심[흥미] 있어 하는'이라는 뜻의 과거분사 (C) interested가 정답이다. (D) interesting은 감정을 유발하는 대상을 묘사할 때 쓰이므로 문맥상 적절하지 않다.

135-138 공지

오크빌 원예 클럽에서 9월 9일 토요일에 화초 판매 행사를 ¹³⁵**엽니다.** 판매 행사는 오전 9시부터 오후 4시까지 힐 가 478에 있는 오크빌 커뮤니티 센터에서 열릴 예정입니다. 매대는 꽃바구니, 잔디, 허브를 크게 할인해 드립니다. ¹³⁶**가장 좋은 물건을 고르시려면 일찍 오세요.** ¹³⁷**또한** 다양한 맛있는 과일과 채소도 판매합니다. 하루 ¹³⁸**종일** 라이브 간담회와 시연을 즐기세요. 더 많은 정보를 원하시면 오크빌 원예 웹사이트 www.oakvillehorticultureclub.co.uk/events를 방문하세요.

135 동사의 시제

해설 빈칸이 있는 문장에서 판매 행사의 일정을 공지하고 있고, 뒤 문장에서 '판매 행사가 열릴 예정(The sale will be held)'이라며 미래 시제로 표현하고 있는 것으로 보아 행사는 미래에 일어날 일임을 알 수 있다. 현재진행 시제는 가까운 미래에 정해진 일정을 나타낼 때도 쓰이므로 (C) is hosting이 정답이다.

136 문맥에 맞는 문장 고르기

번역 (A) 가장 좋은 물건을 고르시려면 일찍 오세요.
(B) 식물은 여러분의 집안을 아름답게 만드는 데 도움을 줍니다.
(C) 지역 정원 관광에 할인을 받기 위해 클럽에 가입하세요.
(D) 커뮤니티 센터가 최근 새로 단장했습니다.

해설 앞 문장에서 판매 행사가 열리며 일정 상품들을 많이 할인해 준다(There will be great deals on ~ and herbs)고 했으므로, 마음에 드는 물건을 골라 살 수 있으려면 물건이 많이 남아 있을 때 오는 것이 좋다고 권하는 내용이 들어가야 자연스럽다. 따라서 좋은 물건을 고르려면 일찍 오라고 권장하고 있는 (A)가 정답이다.

어휘 renovate 새롭게 하다, 개조[보수]하다

137 부사 어휘

해설 앞 문장에서 여러 상품들을 크게 할인(great deals)해 준다며 행사의 특징을 언급하고 있고, 빈칸이 있는 문장에서 다양한 맛있는 과일과 채소도 살 수 있다(a delicious selection ~ available for purchase)며 행사의 또 다른 특징을 언급하고 있다. 따라서 비슷한 내용을 추가로 언급할 때 쓰는 부사가 들어가야 적절하므로 '또한'을 뜻하는 (B) also가 정답이다. (A) later는 '나중에', (C) nearly는 '거의', (D) merely는 '그저'라는 뜻으로 문맥상 어울리지 않는다.

138 전치사 자리 / 어휘

해설 빈칸은 명사구 the day를 목적어로 취하여, 빈칸 앞의 명령문(Enjoy live talks and demonstrations)을 수식하는 전치사 자리이다. '하루 종일 즐기라'는 내용이 되어야 자연스러우므로 '~ 내내, ~ 동안'이라는 뜻으로 the day와 함께 '하루 종일'이라는 의미를 만드는 전치사 (D) throughout이 정답이다. (A) within은 '~ 이내에', (C)

following은 '~ 후에'라는 뜻으로 의미상 부적절하고, (B) forward 는 부사/형용사/동사로 품사상 빈칸에 들어갈 수 없다.

어휘 forward 앞으로; (우편물, 정보 등을) 전달하다

139-142 편지

7월 2일

아라카키 씨께:

브릭스 가에 예정된 도로 정비에 대해 알려드리기 위해 글을 씁니다. 7월 15일부터 브릭스 가는 엘름 가에서 베이 로까지 1차선으로 축소 **139 될 것입니다.** **140 동봉된 해당 지역의 지도를 참조하십시오.** 귀하의 **141 사 업체**가 브릭스 가의 이 구간에 위치하고 있지는 않지만, 작업이 진행되 는 동안 이 도로 대부분의 차량은 평소보다 더 느리게 이동할 것입니다. **142 그러므로** 이 기간 동안 직원들에게 대체 출근 경로를 이용하도록 권 고하는 것을 고려해 보셔야 할 것입니다. 이 작업은 10월 22일 또는 그 이전에 끝날 것으로 예상됩니다. 귀하의 협조와 도움에 감사드립니다.

아말리아 빌라로보스
교통국장
동봉물

어휘 inform 알리다   scheduled 예정된, 일정이 잡힌
maintenance 정비, 유지 관리   reduce 줄이다   lane 차선
section 구간, 부분   advise 권고하다   alternate 대안이 되는
cooperation 협조   assistance 도움   enclosure 동봉된 것

139 동사의 시제

해설 편지의 작성일이 7월 2일(July 2)인데, 7월 15일부터 시작되는 (Beginning on July 15) 도로 정비(road maintenance)를 알리고 있으므로 미래의 일을 나타내는 (B) will be가 정답이다. (C) can be 도 미래의 가능성이나 추측을 나타낼 수 있지만 이미 정해진 일정 안 내에는 적절하지 않다.

140 문맥에 맞는 문장 고르기

번역 (A) 브릭스 가는 겨우 2마일 거리에 있습니다.
(B) 이 행사는 엘름 가에서 열릴 것입니다.
(C) 동봉된 해당 지역의 지도를 참조하십시오.
(D) 하지만 이 기간 동안 모든 도시 서비스가 중단될 것입니다.

해설 앞 내용에서 브릭스 가의 도로 정비(road maintenance on Briggs Avenue)로 인해 7월 15일부터 일정 구간이 1차선으로 축소될 것 (reduced to one lane)이라고 했고, 뒤 문장에서는 정비 작업이 업 체가 위치한 인근 도로까지 미치게 될 영향을 안내하고 있다. 따라서 빈칸에는 도로 정비 작업이 이루어지는 구간 안내와 관련된 내용이 들 어가야 글의 흐름이 자연스럽게 연결되므로, 도로 작업 구간을 확인할 수 있는 지도를 참고하라고 안내하고 있는 (C)가 정답이다.

어휘 refer to ~을 참조하다   enclosed 동봉된   affected 영향을 받는   close 중지하다

141 명사 어휘

해설 뒤 문장에서 공사 기간 동안 직원들에게 대체 출근 경로를 이용하도록 권고하는 것을 고려해 보라(consider advising your employees to take alternate routes to work)고 조언하고 있으므로, 빈칸 에는 직원들이 출근하는 장소를 나타낼 수 있는 단어가 들어가야 한다. 따라서 '사업체, 회사'를 뜻하는 (D) business가 정답이다. (A) mailbox는 '우편함', (B) school은 '학교', (C) signage는 '신호 체 계'라는 의미로 빈칸에 적절하지 않다.

142 접속부사

해설 앞 문장에는 사업체가 공사 구역에 있지는 않지만 작업이 진행되는 동 안 해당 도로의 차량 이동이 느려질 것(traffic ~ will move more slowly)이라고 했고, 뒤 문장에는 공사 기간 동안 직원들에게 대체 출 근 경로를 이용하도록(to take alternate routes to work) 권고하 는 것을 고려해 보라고 했다. 두 문장이 도로 정비 작업으로 차량 이 동이 느려질 것이므로 다른 도로를 이용하는 편이 낫다는 인과 관계 를 나타내고 있으므로 '그러므로, 따라서'를 뜻하는 (D) therefore가 정답이다. (A) fortunately는 '운이 좋게도', (B) instead는 '대신에', (C) likewise는 '마찬가지로'라는 의미이다.

143-146 기사

프랭클린 천문관, 도심으로 이전

(6월 3일) — 프랭클린 천문관이 메이필드 남쪽에 있는 현재 위치에서 48년 만에 새로운 곳으로 이전한다. 새 자연사 박물관을 포함하는 복합 단지의 일부인 도심 시설에 공사가 진행 중이다. 두 **143 건물** 모두 내년 9월에 시민들에게 공개될 예정이다.

현재 천문관의 주요 즐길 거리는 300석 규모의 극장으로, 방문객들은 위 쪽 돔에서 별과 행성의 투영을 볼 수 있다. 새로운 천문관은 더 큰 규모 의 극장 **144 외에도**, 업그레이드된 디지털 투영 시스템으로 특색을 갖출 것이다. **145 또한 세 개의 단기 전시물을 위한 공간도 있을 것이다.** 방문 객들은 밤하늘을 더 선명하게 **146 보고** 새로운 쌍방향 전시물을 통해 다 른 행성과 은하를 탐험할 수 있게 될 것이다.

어휘 planetarium 천문관, 천체 투영관   present 현재의
location 위치   underway 진행 중인   facility 시설   complex
(복합) 단지   the public 일반 사람들, 대중   attraction 즐길 거리,
명소   projection 투영, 영상   planet 행성   dome 돔, 반구형 지붕
galaxy 은하   interactive 쌍방향의, 상호적인

143 명사 어휘

해설 앞 문장에서 새로운 천문관과 자연사 박물관을 위한 공사가 진행 중 (Construction is underway ~ a complex that includes the new Natural History Museum)이라고 했으므로, 빈칸이 있는 문 장에서 내년 9월에 공개될 예정이라고 안내하는 대상은 천문관과 박 물관을 지칭하는 건물임을 알 수 있다. 따라서 '건물'을 뜻하는 (B) buildings가 정답이다. (A)의 trail은 '산책로', (C)의 campus는 '(대 학) 교정', (D)의 performance는 '공연'을 의미한다.

144 전치사 자리 / 어휘

해설 빈칸은 명사구 a larger theater를 목적어로 취해, 콤마 뒤 완전한 절(the new planetarium will feature an upgraded digital projection system)을 수식하는 전치사 자리이다. 새 천문관의 특징으로 '더 큰 규모의 극장' 뒤에 업그레이드된 디지털 투영 시스템을 추가로 언급하므로 '~ 외에도, ~에 더하여'라는 뜻의 전치사 (A) In addition to가 정답이다. (C) In agreement with도 전치사이지만 '~와 일치하여'라는 뜻으로 문맥상 어울리지 않고, (B) In particular(특히)와 (D) For instance(예를 들어)는 부사 역할을 하므로 명사구를 절에 연결할 수 없다.

145 문맥에 맞는 문장 고르기

번역 (A) 메이필드 지역에는 현재 세 개의 다른 박물관이 있다.
(B) 천문관의 관람객 수는 최근 몇 년간 증가해 왔다.
(C) 새로운 천문관에 대한 계획은 5년 전 시작되었다.
(D) 또한 세 개의 단기 전시물을 위한 공간도 있을 것이다.

해설 앞 문장에서 새로운 천문관은 더 큰 규모의 극장(a larger theater)과 업그레이드된 디지털 투영 시스템(an upgraded digital projection system)을 갖게 될 것이라고 했고, 뒤 문장에서 방문객들이 밤하늘을 더 선명하게 보고 새로운 전시물을 통해 다른 행성과 은하를 탐험할 수 있을 것(Visitors will ~ explore other planets and galaxies through new, interactive displays)이라며 새로운 천문관의 시설과 그로 인해 누릴 수 있는 혜택을 나열하고 있다. 따라서 빈칸에도 새 천문관에 추가될 시설에 관한 내용이 들어가야 자연스러우므로 단기 전시 공간도 갖출 것이라고 안내하는 (D)가 정답이다.

어휘 attendance 참석자 수, 참석률 planning 계획, 기획 room 공간 exhibit 전시(품) as well 또한, 마찬가지로

146 to부정사

해설 빈칸 앞에 형용사 able이 있고 뒤에 명사구 the night sky가 있으므로, the night sky를 목적어로 취하면서 형용사 able을 수식할 수 있는 준동사가 들어가야 한다. 형용사 able은 to부정사의 수식을 받아 'be able + to부정사'의 형태로 쓰여 '~을 할 수 있다'를 뜻하므로 to부정사 (A) to see가 정답이다.

PART 7

147-148 공지

공지

147 셀리노 아파트의 정기적인 유지 보수의 일환으로, 우리 건물의 모든 공공 구역은 다음 일정에 따라 페인트칠 될 예정입니다:

- 148 계단, 1층과 2층: 4월 12일
- 복도, 1층 및 2층: 4월 13일
- 148 계단, 3층과 4층: 4월 14일
- 복도, 3층 및 4층: 4월 15일

이 기간 동안 엘리베이터는 이용 가능합니다. 주의해 주시고, 마르지 않은 페인트에 손대지 마십시오.

셀리노 아파트 관리소

어휘 routine 정기적인 maintenance 유지 보수 following 다음의 stairwell 계단 hallway 복도 use caution 주의하다

147 추론 / 암시

번역 공지는 누구를 대상으로 하는 것 같은가?
(A) 페인트칠 시공업체
(B) 엘리베이터 수리 작업자
(C) 그래픽 아티스트
(D) 아파트 주민

해설 첫 문장에서 셀리노 아파트의 정기적인 유지 보수의 일환으로 건물의 모든 공공 구역은 다음 일정에 따라 페인트칠 될 예정(As part of our routine maintenance of Selino Apartments, all public areas of our building will be painted according to the following schedule)이라고 공지하고 있는 것으로 보아 아파트 주민들에게 알리는 글임을 알 수 있다. 따라서 정답은 (D)이다.

148 세부사항

번역 모든 층의 계단에 대한 작업은 언제 완료될 것 같은가?
(A) 4월 12일
(B) 4월 13일
(C) 4월 14일
(D) 4월 15일

해설 페인트칠 일정의 첫 항목에 1층과 2층 계단이 4월 12일(Stairwells, first and second floors: 12 April), 세 번째 항목에 3층과 4층 계단이 4월 14일(Stairwells, third and fourth floors: 14 April)에 작업한다고 나와 있다. 따라서 계단에 대한 모든 작업이 완료되는 때는 4월 14일이므로 (C)가 정답이다.

149-150 쿠폰

진화 그릴

북부 캘리포니아에서 30년 넘게 최고급 한국 요리를 제공하고 있습니다.

레이크사이드 로에서 새롭게 단장한 레스토랑의 재개점을 축하하러 오세요! 149 5월 한 달 동안 저녁 식사 2인분을 드시고 무료 애피타이저 플래터를 즐기세요.

150 캘리포니아주 오클랜드 레이크사이드 로 4104, 진화 그릴에서만 사용 가능합니다. 쿠폰은 테이크아웃 주문에는 적용되지 않습니다. 150 전 지점 목록, 영업시간, 메뉴를 보시려면 www.jin-hwagrill.com을 방문하세요.

어휘 finest 최고급의 cuisine 요리 celebrate 축하하다 complimentary 무료의 platter 큰 접시, (큰 접시에 담긴) 모둠 요리 entire 전체의 valid 유효한 apply 적용되다 operation 영업

149 세부사항

번역 쿠폰으로 혜택을 받을 수 있는 방법은?
(A) 테이크아웃 주문을 함으로써
(B) 최소 금액을 씀으로써
(C) 두 끼의 식사를 주문함으로써
(D) 개점식 축하 행사에 참석함으로써

해설 첫 단락의 두 번째 문장에서 5월 한 달 동안 저녁 식사 2인분을 드시고 무료 애피타이저 플래터를 즐기라(Purchase any two dinners and enjoy a complimentary ~ May)고 했다. 따라서 쿠폰을 사용하려면 식사 2인분을 주문해야 하므로 (C)가 정답이다.

어휘 minimum 최소한의

Paraphrasing 지문의 Purchase any two dinners
→ 정답의 ordering two meals

150 Not / True

번역 진화 그릴에 대해 언급된 것은?
(A) 기념일을 축하하고 있다.
(B) 여러 지점을 가지고 있다.
(C) 최근에 한국 음식을 제공하기 시작했다.
(D) 운영 시간을 늘렸다.

해설 두 번째 단락의 첫 문장에서 캘리포니아주 오클랜드 레이크사이드로 4104, 진화 그릴에서만 사용 가능하다(Valid only at Jin-Hwa Grill, 4104 Lakeside Drive, Oakland, CA)고 했고, 전 지점 목록, 영업시간, 메뉴를 보려면 www.jin-hwagrill.com을 방문하라(Visit www.jin-hwagrill.com for a list of all our locations, hours of operation, and menus)고 했다. 따라서 진화 그릴은 한 곳 이상의 여러 매장을 가지고 있음을 알 수 있으므로 (B)가 정답이다.

어휘 anniversary 기념일 expand 늘리다

151-152 이메일

수신: 빈두 길 〈bgil@opalmail.com〉
발신: 닐라 발레이 〈n_balay@celebrate.com〉
날짜: 6월 18일
제목: 후속 이메일

길 씨께,

151 오늘 오전 전화 통화와 관련하여, 152 토요일 배송에 변경하고 싶은 사항을 서면으로 알려드립니다.

152 사지 연회장 대신에 칼탄 호텔의 그랜드 다이닝 룸으로 꽃을 배송해 주실 것을 요청합니다. 이렇게 막바지에 변경하는 것이 죄송합니다만, 어젯밤 연회장 관리자로부터 주말에 수리가 필요한 전기 시스템 고장에 대해 연락을 받았습니다. 제가 계획하고 있는 사무실 파티는 연기할 수 없기 때문에 이 다른 장소를 예약해야 했습니다.

오후 4시까지 배송을 받을 수 있으면 감사하겠습니다.

닐라 발레이

어휘 regarding ~에 관한 banquet hall 연회장 last-minute 막바지의, 막판의 switch 변경 inform 알리다 electrical 전기의 malfunction 고장 postpone 연기하다 reserve 예약하다 venue 장소 appreciate 감사하다

151 주제 / 목적

번역 발레이 씨가 길 씨에게 이메일을 보낸 이유는?
(A) 주말 출장 일정을 변경하려고
(B) 사무실 파티에 초대하려고
(C) 전기 기사의 서비스를 요청하려고
(D) 몇 가지 구두 지침을 확인하려고

해설 첫 문장에서 발레이 씨가 길 씨에게 오늘 오전 전화 통화와 관련하여 토요일 배송에 변경하고 싶은 사항을 서면으로 알린다(Regarding our telephone conversation ~ here in writing is the change I would like to make to Saturday's delivery)고 한 것으로 보아, 전화 통화로 이야기했던 주문 관련사항을 서면으로 확인하기 위해 이메일을 보냈다는 것을 알 수 있다. 따라서 정답은 (D)이다.

어휘 reschedule 일정을 변경하다 electrician 전기 기사 spoken 구두의 instructions 지시

152 세부사항

번역 발레이 씨가 토요일 오후에 받기로 예상하는 것은?
(A) 꽃
(B) 입장권
(C) 서명된 계약서
(D) 업데이트된 비용 견적서

해설 첫 문장에서 발레이 씨가 토요일 배송에 변경하고 싶은 사항을 서면으로 알린다(here in writing is the change I would like to make to Saturday's delivery)면서, 사지 연회장 대신에 칼탄 호텔 그랜드 다이닝 룸으로 꽃을 배송해 줄 것을 요청한다(I am requesting that you now deliver the flowers ~ instead of the Saji Banquet Hall)고 했다. 따라서 발레이 씨가 토요일에 배송 받을 것은 꽃이라는 것을 알 수 있으므로 (A)가 정답이다.

어휘 estimate 견적(서)

153-154 온라인 채팅

김애차 (오전 9시 16분)
안녕하세요. 윈터 웨어 웹사이트에서 주문한 상품에 문제가 있습니다.

켈빈 롱 (오전 9시 18분)
안녕하세요. 무엇을 도와드릴까요?

김애차 (오전 9시 20분)
음, 153 2주 전에 장갑을 주문했는데 아직 도착하지 않았습니다.

켈빈 롱 (오전 9시 21분)
죄송합니다. 주문 번호는 받으셨나요?

김애차 (오전 9시 22분)
ADF193입니다.

켈빈 롱 (오전 9시 23분)
감사합니다.

켈빈 롱 (오전 9시 26분)
이번 일은 매우 드문 일입니다. ¹⁵⁴ 시스템에는 주문이 처리되었다고 나
오네요. 왜 물품이 아직 창고에서 출고되지 않았는지 모르겠습니다. 추가
요금 없이 다른 장갑을 급송으로 보내 드리겠습니다.

김애차 (오전 9시 27분)
그렇게 해 주시면 좋겠네요! 감사합니다!

어휘 issue 문제 unusual 드문, 이례적인 fulfill 이행하다
warehouse 창고 rush shipping 급송 charge 요금

153 세부사항

번역 김 씨가 가지고 있는 문제는?
(A) 주문품을 잘못 받았다.
(B) 주문품이 도착하지 않았다.
(C) 물품이 배송 중에 손상되었다.
(D) 물품이 주문에서 누락되었다.

해설 9시 20분에 김 씨가 2주 전에 장갑을 주문했는데 아직 도착하지 않
았다(I ordered some gloves two weeks ago, and they still
haven't arrived)고 했으므로 (B)가 정답이다.

어휘 damaged 손상된 in transport 운송 중에 missing 누락된

154 의도 파악

번역 오전 9시 26분에 롱 씨가 "이번 일은 매우 드문 일입니다"라고 쓴 의
도는?
(A) 느린 컴퓨터 시스템 때문에 짜증이 난다.
(B) 김 씨의 질문에 답하는 데 오래 걸린 것에 대해 미안해한다.
(C) 창고 문제에 대해 놀라워한다.
(D) 어떤 스타일의 장갑이 주문되었는지에 대해 혼란스러워한다.

해설 9시 26분에 롱 씨가 이번 일은 매우 드문 일(This is very unusual)
이라고 한 직후, 시스템에는 주문이 처리되었다고 나온다(The
system is showing that the order was fulfilled)면서 왜 물품
이 아직 창고에서 출고되지 않았는지 모르겠다(I'm not sure why it
hasn't left the warehouse yet)고 한 것으로 보아 창고에서 제품
이 제대로 출하되지 않은 예상하지 못한 문제에 대해 놀라움을 표현하
려는 의도로 한 말임을 알 수 있다. 따라서 (C)가 정답이다.

어휘 frustrated 짜증이 나는 confused 혼란스러워하는

155-157 이메일

수신: 제시카 유 〈jyu@myemail.com〉
발신: 고객 서비스 〈cs@velascobank.com〉
날짜: 7월 15일
제목: 고객 계정 보안

유 씨께,

¹⁵⁵,¹⁵⁷ 보안상의 이유로 벨라스코 은행 고객님께서는 은행에 기록된

연락처 정보를 매년 검토해 주셔야 합니다. 올해 연락처 정보 검토 마감
일은 7월 29일입니다. 이것은 두 가지 방법 중 하나로 수행될 수 있습
니다. ¹⁵⁷ 당사 웹사이트 www.velascobank.com에서 고객님의 정
보를 확인하시거나 벨라스코 은행 모바일 앱에서 확인하실 수 있습니다.
디지털 뱅킹 계정에 간편하게 로그인하시고 '설정'으로 이동한 다음 '연락
처'로 가시면 됩니다. 고객님의 전화번호와 이메일 주소를 확인하시고 모
두 최신 정보 상태로 해 주십시오. 그런 다음 기본 연락 방법으로 설정해
주십시오. ¹⁵⁶ 디지털 뱅킹에 아직 등록되지 않았다면 www.velas-
cobank.com/myaccount에서 온라인으로 등록해 주실 것을 권장
드립니다.

문의사항이 있으시면 월요일부터 금요일까지 오전 7시부터 오후 5시까
지 저희 지점을 방문하시거나 410-555-0156으로 전화 주십시오.

감사합니다.

벨라스코 은행 고객 서비스

어휘 security 보안 review 검토하다 app 애플리케이션
up-to-date 최신의 select 선택하다 primary 기본적인, 주요한
method 방법 enroll 등록하다 branch 지점

155 주제 / 목적

번역 이메일의 목적은?
(A) 계좌 폐쇄를 문의하려고
(B) 고객에게 은행 업무 시간 변경을 알리려고
(C) 고객에게 개인 정보를 확인해 달라고 요청하려고
(D) 은행 예금에 대한 정보를 제공하려고

해설 첫 문장에서 보안상의 이유로 벨라스코 은행 고객들은 은행에 기록된
연락처 정보를 매년 검토해 주어야 한다(For security reasons we
need our customers to review their contact information
with Velasco Bank every year)고 했고, 올해 연락처 정보 검토
마감일은 7월 29일(This year, the deadline ~ is July 29)이라며
연락처를 확인해야 하는 만기일까지 알려 주고 있으므로 고객에게 은
행에 제공하는 연락처 정보를 검토해 줄 것을 요청하기 위해 이메일을
보냈음을 알 수 있다. 따라서 (C)가 정답이다.

어휘 inquire 문의하다 closure 폐쇄 deposit 예금

156 세부사항

번역 이메일에 따르면, 고객이 디지털 뱅킹에 등록하기 위해 해야 할 일은?
(A) 은행 웹사이트 방문
(B) 고객 서비스 담당자에게 문의
(C) 지역 은행 지점 방문
(D) 모바일 앱 설치

해설 첫 단락의 마지막 문장에서 디지털 뱅킹에 아직 등록되지 않았다면
www.velascobank.com/myaccount에서 온라인으로 등록할 것
을 권장한다(If you are not yet enrolled in digital banking,
we recommend doing so online at www.velascobank.com/
myaccount)고 했으므로 (A)가 정답이다.

어휘 representative 직원 install 설치하다

번역 [1], [2], [3], [4]로 표시된 위치 중에서 다음 문장이 들어가기에 가장 적합한 곳은?

"이것은 두 가지 방법 중 하나로 수행될 수 있습니다."

(A) [1]

(B) [2]

(C) [3]

(D) [4]

해설 주어진 문장에서 이것(This)은 두 방법 중 하나로 할 수 있다고 했으므로, 주어진 문장 앞에 '이것', 즉 해야 할 일에 대한 내용이 나와 있어야 하고 뒤에는 두 가지 방법에 대한 설명이 나와야 한다. [2] 앞에 은행에 기록된 연락처 검토(to review their contact information with Velasco Bank)라는 할 일이 언급되어 있고, 뒤에 웹사이트에서 확인(check your information on our Web site at www.velascobank.com)하거나 모바일 앱에서 확인할 수 있다(do so on the Velasco Bank mobile app)는 두 가지 방법을 안내하고 있으므로 주어진 문장은 이 사이에 들어가는 것이 알맞다. 따라서 (B)가 정답이다.

158-160 안내책자

섬너 우드크래프팅

¹⁵⁸테네시주 멤피스의 섬너 우드크래프팅은 고품질의 수제 가구를 찾는 고객들에게 맞춤형 서비스를 제공하는 것을 목표로 약 45년 전 키란 섬너에 의해 설립되었습니다. 현재 반쯤 은퇴한 상태이지만, 섬너 씨는 여전히 목요일과 금요일에 회사의 고객 서비스 전화 라인인 901-555-0185를 통해 직접 주문을 받고 문의에 응답합니다. 섬너 우드크래프팅은 다양한 맞춤 제작 침실 세트, 탁자, 책상, 수납장 등을 제공하며, 이는 모두 고품질의 견고한 목재로 만들어집니다.

수공예 가구의 가격은 공장에서 대량 생산되는 가구보다 당연히 더 높습니다. ¹⁶⁰우리의 장인 공예가들이 아주 ¹⁵⁹훌륭한 작업을 하기 때문에, 고객들은 세대를 넘어서 지속될 가구에 조금 더 많은 비용을 들이는 것을 후회하지 않습니다.

주문 후 가구 한 점을 제작하는 데 최대 두 달이 걸릴 수 있다는 점에 유의해 주십시오. 배송비는 작업장과의 거리를 기준으로 합니다. 포장을 풀고 물품을 배치하는 작업은 추가 50달러의 비용으로 이용 가능합니다.

우리 작업장의 사진, 장인 약력, 고객 후기 및 주문 정보를 확인하시려면 온라인으로 www.sumnerwoodcrafting.com을 방문하십시오.

어휘 woodcraft 목공예 establish 설립하다 personalized 맞춤형의 semiretired 반쯤 퇴직한 take an order 주문을 받다 a selection of 다양한 custom-made 맞춤 제작한 cabinetry 수납장 solid 견고한 handcrafted 수공예품인, 수제의 mass-produce 대량 생산하다 crafter 공예가 exceptionally 특별히 fine 훌륭한, (질) 좋은 regret 후회하다 generation 세대 distance 거리 workshop 작업장 place 배치[설치]하다 artisan 장인 biography 약력, 전기

번역 섬너 우드크래프팅에 대해 언급된 것은?

(A) 가격 경쟁력이 매우 높다.

(B) 멤피스에서 무료 배송을 제공한다.

(C) 창립자가 전화 문의를 처리한다.

(D) 고객들이 작업장을 둘러볼 수 있다.

해설 첫 번째 단락의 첫 문장에서 테네시주 멤피스의 섬너 우드크래프팅은 고품질의 수제 가구를 찾는 고객들에게 맞춤형 서비스를 제공하는 것을 목표로 약 45년 전 키란 섬너에 의해 설립되었다(Sumner Woodcrafting of Memphis, Tennessee, was established nearly 45 years ago by Kiran Sumner ~ customers seeking high-quality, handmade furniture)고 했고, 두 번째 문장에서 현재 반쯤 은퇴한 상태이지만 섬너 씨는 여전히 목요일과 금요일에 회사의 고객 서비스 전화 라인인 901-555-0185를 통해 직접 주문을 받고 문의에 응답한다(Now semiretired, Mr. Sumner still takes orders and responds to questions himself through the company's customer-service telephone ~ Fridays)고 했으므로 섬너 우드크래프팅의 창립자인 섬너 씨가 전화 문의를 직접 처리하고 있음을 알 수 있다. 따라서 정답은 (C)이다.

어휘 competitive 경쟁력 있는 founder 창립자 handle 처리하다 inquiry 문의

159 동의어 찾기

번역 두 번째 단락 2행의 "fine"과 의미가 가장 가까운 단어는?

(A) 작은

(B) 날카로운

(C) 잘 만들어진

(D) 동의할 만한

해설 의미상 공예가들이 '훌륭한' 작업을 한다는 의미로 쓰였으므로 '잘 만들어진, 전문가가 만든'을 뜻하는 (C) skillful이 정답이다.

160 추론 / 암시

번역 섬너 우드크래프팅 제품에 대해 암시된 것은?

(A) 매우 오래간다.

(B) 천연 및 인공 재료가 모두 들어간다.

(C) 종종 배송 후 조립이 필요하다.

(D) 보통 사무실용으로 주문된다.

해설 두 번째 단락의 두 번째 문장에서 우리의 장인 공예가들이 아주 훌륭한 작업을 하기 때문에 고객들은 세대를 넘어서 지속될 가구에 비용을 더 들이는 것을 후회하지 않는다(Because our master crafters do exceptionally fine work, our customers never regret spending a bit more for pieces built to last for generations)고 한 것으로 보아 섬너 우드크래프팅 제품은 비싼 대신 내구성이 매우 좋다는 것을 알 수 있다. 따라서 정답은 (A)이다.

어휘 extremely 극히 long-lasting 오래가는 contain ~이 들어 있다 human-made 인공의 material 재료 assembly 조립

Paraphrasing 지문의 last for generations → 정답의 long-lasting

161-163 기사

어휘 decade 10년 instability 불안정 raw material 원자재 concern 관심사, 우려 manufacturer 제조업체 surpass 뛰어넘다 recruitment 채용 rank (순위를) 차지하다 respectively 각각 electronics 전자 제품, 전자 기술 typically 일반적으로 represent (~에) 해당하다 processed 가공 처리한 dramatically 극적으로, 크게 affect 영향을 미치다 bottom line 손익, 수지타산 predict 예측하다 temper 완화시키다 volatility 변동성 forecasting 예측 anticipate 예상하다

161 주제 / 목적

번역 기사의 주요 내용은?
(A) 제조 방법의 개선
(B) 소비자 선호도의 최근 변화
(C) 환경 규제의 도입
(D) 생산자가 직면한 비용의 변화

해설 첫 문장에서 지난 10년 동안 원자재 가격의 불안정성이 제조업체들의 가장 큰 관심사가 되어 왔다(Over the last decade, instability in the pricing of raw materials has become the biggest concern for manufacturers)고 했고, 현재 이 문제는 이전에 기업들이 각각 상위 두 개의 관심사로 꼽았던 채용과 기술을 넘어선다(The issue now surpasses recruitment ~ respectively)고 했다. 따라서 기사가 제조업체들이 직면한 생산 원가의 불안정성 문제를 주로 다루고 있음을 알 수 있으므로 정답은 (D)이다.

어휘 improvement 개선 manufacturing 제조 method 방법 shift 변화, 전환 consumer 소비자 preference 선호도 regulation 규제 face 직면하다

Paraphrasing 지문의 instability in the pricing
→ 정답의 The changes in costs

162 세부사항

번역 기사 작성자가 전자제품 제조업체를 언급하는 이유는?
(A) 10년 이상 동안의 혁신을 설명하려고
(B) 세계 무역의 영향을 보여 주려고
(C) 최근의 인력난을 설명하려고
(D) 산업 간 비교를 하려고

해설 두 번째 단락의 두 번째 문장에서 전자제품 제조업체의 경우 일반적으로 전체 비용의 20퍼센트를 자재가 차지하는 반면, 가공식품 제조업

체는 원자재에 40에서 60퍼센트 사이의 비용을 지출할 수 있다(For electronics manufacturers, materials typically represent 20 percent of all expenses, while makers of processed food can spend anywhere between 40 and 60 percent on materials)고 했다. 따라서 전자제품 제조업체와 가공식품 제조업체 간 원자재에 드는 비용의 차이를 비교하기 위해 전자제품 업체를 언급했다는 것을 알 수 있으므로 정답은 (D)이다.

어휘 illustrate 설명하다 innovation 혁신 impact 영향 staffing 인력 채용 comparison 비교 industry 산업

163 동의어 찾기

▶ 동영상 강의

번역 두 번째 단락 9행의 "temper"와 의미가 가장 가까운 단어는?
(A) 설정하다
(B) 강화하다
(C) 완화하다
(D) 결합하다

해설 시장 변동성의 영향을 '완화시킨다'는 뜻으로 쓰였으므로 '완화하다, 누그러뜨리다'라는 의미의 (C) moderate가 정답이다.

164-167 발표

어휘 feature 특별히 포함하다, 출연시키다 grind 갈다 gear 기어, 장비 latest 최신의 adventure 모험 inspector 수사관 beloved 총애[사랑]받는 investigate 조사하다 malfunction 고장 physics 물리학 laboratory 연구소 background 배경 follow 뒤를 잇다, 뒤따르다 attendee 참석자 register 등록하다 in advance 미리

164 주제 / 목적

번역 발표되고 있는 것은?
(A) 새로운 서점의 개점
(B) 도서 작가의 프레젠테이션
(C) 연구 프로젝트를 설명하는 책
(D) 책을 바탕으로 한 곧 개봉될 영화

해설 첫 문장에서 미션 베이에 있는 로웬스타인 서점에서 힐다 플로레스 작가가 출연하는 이달의 책 토론에 초대한다(The Lowenstein Bookstore in Mission Bay invites you to this month's book discussion featuring author Hilda Flores)고 했으므로 (B)가 정답이다.

어휘 describe 설명하다 upcoming 곧 있을

165 세부사항

번역 〈기어 갈아엎기〉는 어떤 종류의 책인가?
(A) 논픽션 이야기
(B) 과학자의 전기
(C) 단편 모음
(D) 미스터리 소설

해설 첫 번째 단락의 마지막 문장에서 인기 있는 수사관 스벤슨 시리즈의 최신 모험인 〈기어 갈아엎기〉는 총애 받는 수사관이 국립 물리학 연구소에서 수상한 장비 고장을 조사하는 내용(The latest adventure in the popular Inspector Svensson series, *Grinding the Gears* finds ~ strange equipment malfunctions at a national physics research laboratory)이라고 책을 설명하는 것으로 보아 〈기어 갈아엎기〉는 미스터리 소설임을 알 수 있다. 따라서 정답은 (D)이다.

어휘 biography 전기 collection 모음집, 작품 전집

166 Not / True

번역 등록에 대해 명시된 것은?
(A) 4월 9일에 마감한다.
(B) 수수료를 지불해야 한다.
(C) 선택사항이지만 권장된다.
(D) 온라인으로 할 수 없다.

해설 첫 번째 단락의 두 번째 문장에서 이 행사는 4월 10일 목요일 오후 7시부터 8시 30분까지 열릴 예정(The event will be held on Thursday, April 10, from 7:00 P.M. to 8:30 P.M.)이라고 했고, 두 번째 단락의 마지막 문장에서 서점에서는 참석자들이 적어도 하루 전에 등록해야 한다고 규정한다(The bookstore requires that attendees register at least one day in advance)고 했다. 따라서 등록은 행사일인 4월 10일 하루 전인 4월 9일까지 해야 하므로 (A)가 정답이다.

어휘 fee 수수료 optional 선택의 encourage 권장하다

167 문장 삽입

번역 [1], [2], [3], [4]로 표시된 위치 중에서 다음 문장이 들어가기에 가장 적합한 곳은?

"그녀의 진상 파악 조사 일부에는 정부 과학자들과의 인터뷰도 포함되었습니다."
(A) [1]
(B) [2]
(C) [3]
(D) [4]

해설 주어진 문장은 그녀(Ms. Flores)가 실시한 진상 파악 조사에 포함된 내용을 설명하고 있다. 따라서 플로레스 씨의 진상 파악 조사 즉, 그녀가 수행한 배경 조사(the background research she performed)를 언급하는 문장 뒤, 즉 [3]에 들어가는 것이 글의 흐름상 자연스러우므로 (C)가 정답이다.

어휘 fact-finding 진상 파악, 사실 조사 involve 포함하다 government 정부

168-171 이메일

수신: 고객 서비스 〈customerservice@kishintech.com〉
발신: 드미트로 페트로프 〈d.petrov@silkmail.com〉
날짜: 11월 5일
제목: 키신 XT20 디지털 녹음기 지원

관계자 귀하:

저는 며칠 분량의 학회 프레젠테이션을 녹음하기 위해 키신 XT20 디지털 녹음기를 구입했습니다. **168** 지금 행사 첫날을 마치고 오디오 파일을 노트북으로 전송하려고 하는데 운이 따라 주지 않네요. **169** 사용자 설명서에 있는 모든 지침뿐 아니라 제품 웹페이지의 FAQ 섹션에서 찾을 수 있는 팁들도 따라 해 봤습니다. 심지어 호텔 비즈니스 센터에서 대체 코드와 노트북을 사용해 보았고, 그래서 컴퓨터 하드웨어가 문제라고 생각되지는 않습니다.

171 저는 업무를 위해 이 학회의 남은 이틀을 **170** 취재하기로 되어 있습니다. **171** 제 사업 파트너들은 제가 최대한 많은 정보를 가지고 돌아올 것으로 기대하고 있습니다. 파일을 제대로 공유할 수 없다면 키신 XT20 디지털 리코더는 저에게 쓸모가 없습니다. 도와주실 수 있을까요?

드미트로 페트로프

어휘 to whom it may concern (편지를 시작하며) 관계자 귀하, 담당자께 worth ~만큼의 분량, (얼마) 어치 transfer 전송하다 instructions 지시, 설명 manual 설명서 FAQ 자주 묻는 질문 (frequently asked questions) section 부분 alternative 대체[대안]의 be supposed to ~하기로 되어 있다 remaining 남아 있는 of no use 쓸모없는, 도움이 안 되는 properly 제대로

168 세부사항

번역 페트로프 씨의 장치에 어떤 문제가 있는가?
(A) 오디오 파일을 컴퓨터로 옮길 수 없다.
(B) 외관이 마음에 들지 않는다.
(C) 파일 이름을 바꿀 수 없다.
(D) 음질에 만족하지 않는다.

해설 첫 번째 단락 두 번째 문장에서 페트로프 씨가 행사 첫날을 마치고 오디오 파일을 노트북으로 전송하려고 하는데 운이 따라 주지 않는다(Now, ~ I am trying to transfer the audio files to my laptop, but I am not having any luck)고 했으므로 (A)가 정답이다.

어휘 appearance 외관 rename 이름을 다시 짓다 unsatisfied 불만족스러워 하는

Paraphrasing 지문의 transfer ~ to my laptop
→ 정답의 move ~ to his computer

169 세부사항

번역 페트로프 씨가 웹페이지를 언급한 이유는?
(A) 이미지에 오해의 소지가 있다는 것을 암시하려고
(B) 추가적인 정보를 확인했다는 것을 설명하려고
(C) 제품 설명 변경을 권유하려고
(D) 호환되는 부속품에 대해 문의하려고

해설 첫 단락 세 번째 문장에서 페트로프 씨가 사용자 설명서에 있는 모든 지침뿐 아니라 제품 웹페이지의 FAQ 섹션에서 찾을 수 있는 팁들도 따라 해 봤다(I have followed all the instructions ~ the tips found in the FAQ section of the product's Web page)고 했으므로, 페트로프 씨는 설명서 외에도 추가적인 제품 관련 설명을 이미 확인했다는 것을 알리기 위해 웹페이지를 언급했음을 알 수 있다. 따라서 정답은 (B)이다.

어휘 suggest 암시하다 misleading 오해의 소지가 있는 obtain 입수하다 description 설명 inquire 문의하다 compatible 호환이 되는 accessories 부속품

Paraphrasing 지문의 the tips found in ~ Web page
→ 정답의 additional information

170 동의어 찾기

번역 두 번째 단락 1행의 "cover"와 의미가 가장 가까운 단어는?
(A) 보호하다
(B) ~이 들어 있다
(C) 위로 뻗다
(D) ~에 대해 보고하다

해설 업무를 위해 학회를 '취재하다'라는 뜻으로 쓰였으므로 '~에 대해 보고하다'를 뜻하는 (D) report on이 정답이다.

171 Not / True

번역 페트로프 씨에 대해 사실인 것은?
(A) 자진해서 일부 장비를 시험해 보았다.
(B) 현재 사업 파트너들과 함께 출장 중이다.
(C) 동료들과 학회 자료를 공유할 것이다.
(D) 곧 회사에서 새 노트북을 받을 것이다.

해설 두 번째 단락의 첫 문장에서 페트로프 씨가 업무를 위해 이 학회의 남은 이틀을 취재하기로 되어 있다(I am supposed to cover the remaining two days of this conference for work)면서 사업 파트너들은 페트로프 씨가 최대한 많은 정보를 가지고 돌아올 것으로 기대하고 있다(My business partners expect me to return with as much information as I can)고 했다. 따라서 페트로프 씨는 학회에서 취득한 정보를 동료들과 공유할 계획임을 알 수 있으므로 (C)가 정답이다.

어휘 volunteer to 자진해서[자발적으로] ~하다 material 자료 colleague 동료

Paraphrasing 지문의 business partners
→ 정답의 colleagues

172-175 온라인 채팅

크리스틴 버튼 (오전 8시 16분)
이 중소기업 토론방에 글을 올리는 것은 이번이 처음입니다. 여기 계신 분들 중에 아틀라라의 신용카드 리더기 중 하나를 주문할 때 문제를 겪으신 분 있나요?

마르코스 멘케 (오전 9시 4분)
172 휴대폰에 부착하는 작은 장치를 말씀하시는 건가요, 아니면 더 큰 독립형 태블릿 모델을 말씀하시는 건가요?

크리스틴 버튼 (오전 9시 30분)
전화기 장치요. 173 아틀라라 웹 호스팅 서비스를 사용해 온라인 매장을 시작했고 제가 만든 목걸이와 반지 사진을 추가했습니다. 하지만 대부분의 판매가 여전히 대면으로 이루어지고 있습니다. 그래서 박람회나 시장에 나갈 때 대면 결제를 받을 수 있는 방법만 필요합니다.

마르코스 멘케 (오전 10시 19분)
www.atlara.com/pos/hardware에 가셔서 원하는 것을 장바구니에 추가하시면 됩니다.

크리스틴 버튼 (오전 11시 21분)
그게 문제예요. 시스템에서 주문을 할 수 없습니다. "귀하의 계정을 확인할 수 없습니다."라는 오류 메시지가 나와요.

수잔 슈뢰어 (오전 11시 42분)
제가 알 것 같습니다. 174 사업자 등록증, 정부 발급 사진 신분증, 사업자 은행 계좌 명세서의 스캔 사본을 업로드하셔야 합니다.

크리스틴 버튼 (오후 12시 23분)
이미 전부 해 봤는데, 여전히 오류 메시지가 뜹니다.

수잔 슈뢰어 (오후 12시 33분)
그런 경우라면, 재로그인하고 절차를 다시 따라가 보세요.

신디 아코스타 (오후 1시 5분)
175 아마 지원 라인에 전화하셔야 할 것 같습니다. 몇 달 전 제 문제에는 매우 도움이 되었습니다.

크리스틴 버튼 (오후 1시 10분)
이미 세 분과 통화해 보았습니다.

어휘 post 게시하다 forum (온라인 커뮤니티의) 토론방[포럼] refer to ~을 언급[지칭]하다 unit (작은) 장치[기구] attach 부착하다, 붙이다 stand-alone 독립형의 in person 직접, 대면으로 fair 박람회 account 계정 verify 확인하다 registration 등록 statement 명세서 process 절차

172 세부사항

번역 멘케 씨가 버튼 씨에게 명확히 해달라고 요청한 것은?
(A) 구입하려는 장치의 유형
(B) 웹사이트에서 겪은 경험
(C) 휴대폰을 충전하는 방법
(D) 서비스에 대해 청구받은 금액

해설 9시 4분에 멘케 씨가 휴대폰에 부착하는 작은 장치를 말하는 것인지 아니면 더 큰 독립형 태블릿 모델을 말하는 것인지(Are you referring to the little unit ~ or the larger, stand-alone tablet model?)를 묻고 있는 것으로 보아 버튼 씨에게 장치의 종류를 명확히 알려 달라는 것임을 알 수 있다. 따라서 정답은 (A)이다.

어휘 device 장치 charge 충전하다; 청구하다

173 세부사항

번역 버튼 씨가 판매하는 것은?
(A) 미술용품
(B) 보드게임
(C) 보석류
(D) 가구

해설 9시 30분에 버튼 씨가 아틀라라 웹 호스팅 서비스를 사용해 온라인 매장을 시작했고 직접 만든 목걸이와 반지 사진을 추가했다(I started an online shop ~ added pictures of the necklaces and rings I create)고 설명하고 있으므로 버튼 씨가 판매하는 것은 목걸이와 반지, 즉 보석류임을 알 수 있다. 따라서 정답은 (C)이다.

174 세부사항

번역 슈뢰어 씨가 제안하는 것은?
(A) 서비스 요청서 작성
(B) 카드 리더기의 설정 조정
(C) 일부 서류 제출
(D) 별도의 사업자 계정 생성

해설 11시 42분에 슈뢰어 씨가 사업자 등록증, 정부 발급 사진 신분증, 사업자 은행 계좌 명세서의 스캔 사본을 업로드해야 한다(You have to upload scans ~ a statement from your business bank account)고 제안하고 있으므로 (C)가 정답이다.

어휘 fill out ~을 작성하다 adjust 조정하다 setting 설정 documentation 서류, 문서 separate 별도의

Paraphrasing 지문의 upload scans of your business registration, a government photo ID, and a statement from your business bank account → 정답의 Submitting some documentation

175 의도 파악

번역 오후 1시 10분에 버튼 씨가 "이미 세 분과 통화해 보았습니다"라고 쓴 의도는?
(A) 회사의 응대에 감명받았다.
(B) 이전에 지원 라인에 전화했다.
(C) 일부 사양을 철저히 조사했다.
(D) 제품이 배송된 것을 확인했다.

해설 1시 5분에 아코스타 씨가 아마 지원 라인에 전화해야 할 것 같다(You probably need to call the support line)고 제안하자 1시 10분에 버튼 씨가 이미 세 사람과 통화해 보았다(I've spoken with three people already)고 대답하고 있으므로, 버튼 씨는 이미 지원 라인에 전화했음을 알리려는 의도로 한 말임을 알 수 있다. 따라서 정답은 (B)이다.

어휘 impressed 감명받은 thoroughly 철저히 specifications 사양

176-180 웹페이지 + 이메일

https://www.sunnywelcomehotel.co.in

콜카타의 써니 웰컴 호텔에서는 여러분의 숙박이 즐거울 수 있도록 최선을 다하고 있습니다.

유의사항:

- 177 (A)각 객실에는 커피 메이커와 무료 커피 및 차가 마련되어 있습니다. 투숙객은 각 층에 위치한 자판기에서 스낵 및 기타 음료를 구입할 수 있습니다.
- 어린 자녀를 동반한 투숙객은 객실에 추가 요금 없이 바퀴가 달린 간이 침대 또는 유아용 침대를 요청할 수 있습니다.
- 비즈니스 센터는 매일 오전 9시부터 오후 5시까지 운영됩니다.
- 177 (D)수영장과 어린이 놀이터는 낮 시간 동안 이용 가능합니다. 어린이는 항상 성인의 감독하에 있어야 합니다.
- 객실 예약 보장을 위해 보증금이 필요합니다. 179도착 24시간 이전에 예약이 취소되거나 변경된 경우에만 보증금이 환불됩니다.
- 투숙객은 이르면 오후 2시에 체크인할 수 있습니다. 출발 당일 정오 이후 체크아웃 시 추가 요금이 부과됩니다.
- 176투숙객은 체크인 시 여권 또는 운전면허증을 제시해야 합니다.
- 177 (C)공항까지 무료 셔틀 서비스를 제공합니다. 투숙객은 프런트에서 예약할 수 있습니다.
- 저희 접수처에는 24시간 직원이 상주합니다.

어휘 note 유의하다 complimentary 무료의 beverage 음료 vending 자판기 rollaway bed 바퀴가 달린 간이 침대 crib 유아용 침대 charge 요금 supervise 감독하다 deposit 보증금 guarantee 보장하다 reservation 예약 refund 환불하다 be subject to ~에 해당하다 present 제시하다 make arrangements 예약하다, 준비하다 staff 직원을 제공[배치]하다

수신: generalmanager@sunnywelcomehotel.co.in
발신: samuelramon@myemail.co.uk
날짜: 5월 13일
제목: 예약 번호 EX52417

안녕하세요,

178작년에 우리 가족과 저는 콜카타의 써니 웰컴 호텔의 패밀리 스위트룸에서 매우 편안했고, 179올해는 4월 17일부터 일주일간의 재방문을 기대하고 있었습니다. 안타깝게도, 179갑자기 6월로 여행을 연기해야 해서 예약 날짜를 바꾸기 위해 4월 17일 아침에 호텔에 전화했습니다. 모든 것이 정상적으로 처리된 것으로 생각했지만, 이번 달에 신용카드 명세서를 확인했을 때 써니 웰컴 호텔로부터 추가 요금이 청구된 것을 발견했습니다.

이 문제에 대해 알아봐 주시겠습니까? 180제 생각에는 오류가 발생했고 금액을 상환받아야 한다고 생각합니다. 제 계좌로 그 금액을 입금해 주시면 감사하겠습니다. 우리는 여전히 올해 말에 콜카타로 다시 갈 계획이며 귀하의 호텔에서 즐거운 시간을 기대하고 있습니다.

새뮤얼 라몬

어휘 suite (호텔의) 스위트룸 postpone 연기하다 in order
정상적인, 제대로 된 statement 명세서 discover 발견하다
look into ~을 살펴보다, 조사하다 reimburse 상환하다, 배상하다
credit 입금하다 anticipate 기대하다, 예상하다 enjoyable
즐거운

176 세부사항

번역 웹페이지에 따르면, 호텔 투숙객이 체크인 시 제공해야 하는 것은?
(A) 집 주소
(B) 선결제
(C) 신분 증명
(D) 확인 번호

해설 웹페이지의 유의사항 중 일곱 번째 항목에서 투숙객은 체크인 시
여권 또는 운전면허증을 제시해야 한다(Guests are required
to present a passport or driver's license at the time of
check-in)고 했으므로 (C)가 정답이다.

어휘 in advance 사전에 proof 증명 identification 신분 증명
confirmation 확인

Paraphrasing 지문의 a passport or driver's license
→ 정답의 Proof of identification

177 Not / True

번역 써니 웰컴 호텔 투숙 시 포함되지 않는 것은?
(A) 따뜻한 음료
(B) 가벼운 아침식사
(C) 공항 셔틀 서비스
(D) 수영장 이용

해설 웹페이지의 유의사항 첫 항목에서 각 객실에는 커피 메이커와 무료 커
피 및 차가 마련되어 있다(Each room has a coffeemaker and
complimentary coffee and tea)고 했으므로 (A), 네 번째 항목
에서 수영장과 어린이 놀이터는 낮 시간 동안 이용 가능하다(The
swimming pool and children's playground are open during
daylight hours)고 했으므로 (D), 여덟 번째 항목에서 공항까지 무
료 셔틀 서비스를 제공한다(We offer free shuttle service to the
airport)고 했으므로 (C)는 호텔에서 제공되는 것이고, 아침식사에 대
한 내용은 없으므로 (B)가 정답이다.

Paraphrasing 지문의 coffee and tea
→ 보기 (A)의 beverages

178 Not / True

번역 라몬 씨가 이메일에 명시한 것은?
(A) 보통 혼자 여행을 한다.
(B) 콜카타에 사는 가족이 있다.
(C) 콜카타로 이사할 계획이다.
(D) 전에 써니 웰컴 호텔에 머문 적이 있다.

해설 이메일의 첫 단락 첫 번째 문장에서 라몬 씨는 작년에 그의 가족과 그
는 콜카타의 써니 웰컴 호텔의 패밀리 스위트룸에서 매우 편안했다
(My family and I were very comfortable in the family suite
at the Sunny Welcome Hotel in Kolkata last year)고 했다. 따
라서 라몬 씨가 작년에 써니 웰컴 호텔에서 숙박했다는 것을 알 수 있
으므로 (D)가 정답이다.

179 연계

번역 써니 웰컴 호텔이 라몬 씨에게 수수료를 청구한 이유는 무엇일 것 같
은가?
(A) 도착까지 하루도 채 남지 않은 날 예약을 취소했다.
(B) 객실에 바퀴가 달린 간이 침대를 요청했다.
(C) 정오 이후에 객실 체크아웃을 했다.
(D) 비즈니스 센터에 작업 공간을 예약했다.

해설 웹페이지의 다섯 번째 항목에서 도착 24시간 이전에 예약이 취소되거
나 변경된 경우에만 보증금이 환불된다(The deposit will only be
refunded if the reservation is cancelled or changed more
than 24 hours prior to arrival)고 했는데, 이메일의 첫 문장에
서 라몬 씨가 지난해의 써니 웰컴 호텔 방문을 언급하며 올해는 4
월 17일부터 일주일간의 재방문을 기대하고 있었지만(we were ~
returning this year for a week starting on 17 April) 갑자기
6월로 여행을 연기해야 해서 예약 날짜를 바꾸기 위해 4월 17일 아
침에 호텔에 전화했다(we suddenly ~ so I called the hotel on
the morning of 17 April to change our reservation dates)
고 했다. 따라서 라몬 씨는 도착 예정일인 4월 17일 당일에 연락하여,
도착일로부터 24시간이 남지 않았을 때 예약을 취소 및 변경한 경우
에 해당하여 보증금을 환불받지 못했음을 알 수 있으므로 (A)가 정답
이다.

어휘 midday 정오 work space 작업 공간

180 세부사항

번역 라몬 씨가 요청하는 것은?
(A) 자신의 계좌로 입금
(B) 향후 호텔 숙박 할인
(C) 패밀리 스위트룸으로 객실 업그레이드
(D) 호텔 숙박 기간 연장

해설 이메일의 두 번째 단락 두 번째 문장에서 라몬 씨가 오류가 발생했고
금액을 상환받아야 한다고 생각한다(I believe that an error has
been made and that I should be reimbursed)며 자신의 계좌
로 그 금액을 입금해 주면 감사하겠다(I would appreciate having
the money credited to my account)고 했다. 따라서 라몬 씨는
배상 금액을 자신의 계좌로 입금해 달라고 요청하고 있으므로 (A)가
정답이다.

어휘 extension (기간의) 연장

181-185 이메일 + 웹페이지

발신: 덱스터 애벗
수신: 니나 소사
날짜: 8월 20일
제목: 다음 단계

소사 씨께,

좋은 소식이 있습니다. **181 새로운 파운틴 로드 사무실 건물의 배치 계획이 방금 본사의 란페이 찬에 의해 승인되었습니다.** **181, 184 이제는 건물 3층에 있는 주요 개방형 사무실 구역에 설치할 미술 작품에 대해 생각해 봐야 합니다.** 이는 사무실이 10월에 문을 열기 전에 우리가 마지막으로 해야 할 작업 중 하나입니다.

182 레드 스탈링 아트가 사무실 인테리어를 도와주는 데 있어 좋은 평판을 가지고 있다고 들었습니다. 오늘 그 회사의 웹사이트를 보시고 업체의 서비스 중에 우리에게 어떤 것이 적합할지 알아봐 주시겠습니까? **184 저는 사진이나 그림이 그 공간에 가장 잘 어울릴지 궁금합니다.** 어떻게 생각하십니까? **183 아직 미술품 예산과 관련해 재무부의 맥스웰 윌리스로부터 답변을 기다리고 있으니**, 더 자세히 알게 될 때까지는 레드 스탈링 아트와 어떤 것에도 합의하지 말아 주십시오.

덱스터 애벗, 시설 관리자
KLX 회계

어휘 layout 배치 approve 승인하다 corporate office 본사 artwork 미술[예술] 작품 open-plan 오픈 플랜식의, 건물 내부가 벽으로 나뉘지 않은 task 업무 reputation 평판 suitable 적합한 facility 시설 accountancy 회계 업무

---

https://www.redstarlingart.co.uk/offices/

| 홈 | 소개 | **서비스** | 연락처 |

레드 스탈링 아트는 사무실 건물을 위한 다양한 컨설팅 서비스를 제공합니다:

- **리메이크**: 사무실 내부를 완전히 재디자인하고자 하는 고객을 위해, 고객과 함께 협업하여 고객의 요구에 맞는 배치 및 장식 설계를 세워드립니다.

- **184 얼라인**: 새로운 사무실에 미술품을 설치하려는 고객을 위해, 고객의 공간에 적합한 작품(그림, 사진, 판화 또는 조각품)을 찾도록 도와드립니다.

- **커넥트**: 사무실에 현지 감각을 더하려는 고객을 위해, 지역 예술가 및 사진작가와 협력하여 그들의 독특한 시각을 불어넣습니다.

- **리프레임**: 기존 미술품을 유지하고 싶지만 업데이트를 원하는 고객을 위해, 새로운 분위기를 위한 새로운 액자나 새로운 조명 또는 새로운 배치를 제안합니다.

저희 작업은 항상 고객의 특정한 요구에 맞추어 진행되기 때문에 고정된 가격을 제공할 수 없습니다. **185 무료 상담을 예약하시려면 비르기트 로웬브루크에게 blowenbruck@redstarlingart.co.uk로 이메일을 보내 주십시오.** 상담 후, 그녀가 합의된 서비스에 대한 견적서를 보내 드릴 것입니다.

어휘 a range of 다양한 consultancy 자문, 조언 remake 새로 만들다 interior 실내 decoration 장식 scheme 설계, 계획 align 조정하다, 정렬하다 incorporate ~ into ~을 …에 집어넣다 print 판화 sculpture 조각 collaborate 협력하다 perspective 시각, 관점 reframe (틀을) 다시 만들다, 재구성하다 exiting 기존의 framing 액자, 틀 arrangement 배치 be tailored to ~에 맞추어지다 specific 특정한 fixed 고정된 consultation 상담 estimate 견적(서) agreed-upon 합의된

181 추론 / 암시

번역 파운틴 로드 사무실 건물에 대해 암시된 것은?
(A) 지난 10월에 문을 열었다.
(B) KLX 회계의 본사이다.
(C) 층이 여러 개 있다.
(D) 회의장이 있다.

해설 이메일의 첫 단락 두 번째 문장에서 새로운 파운틴 로드 사무실 건물의 배치 계획이 방금 본사의 란페이 찬에 의해 승인되었다(The plans for the layout of the new Fountain Road office building ~ our corporate office)며, 이제는 건물 3층에 있는 주요 개방형 사무실 구역에 설치할 미술 작품에 대해 생각해 봐야 한다(We now need ~ on the third floor of the building)고 했다. 따라서 파운틴 로드 사무실 건물에 3층, 즉 최소 3층 이상의 여러 층이 있다는 사실을 알 수 있으므로 (C)가 정답이다.

어휘 headquarters 본사

182 세부사항

번역 이메일에서, 애벗 씨가 소사 씨에게 요청하는 것은?
(A) 지난주에 시작한 업무를 완료할 것
(B) 사무실 배치 계획을 승인할 것
(C) 미술품 구매 가격에 동의할 것
(D) 온라인으로 인테리어 디자인 옵션을 조사할 것

해설 이메일의 두 번째 단락 첫 문장에서 애벗 씨가 소사 씨에게 레드 스탈링 아트가 사무실 인테리어를 도와주는 데 있어 좋은 평판을 가지고 있다고 들었다(I have heard that Red Starling Art has a good reputation ~ office interiors)면서, 오늘 그 회사의 웹사이트를 보고 업체의 서비스 중에 어떤 것이 적합할지 알아봐 달라(Could you look at the company's Web site today and find out ~ suitable for us?)고 요청하고 있으므로 (D)가 정답이다.

어휘 task 업무 research 조사하다

183 세부사항

번역 미술품에 대한 예산을 책임지는 사람은?
(A) 애벗 씨
(B) 찬 씨
(C) 윌리스 씨
(D) 소사 씨

해설 이메일의 두 번째 단락 마지막 문장에서 미술품 예산과 관련해 재무부의 맥스웰 윌리스로부터 답변을 기다리고 있다(I am still waiting to hear back from Maxwell Willis in Finance about the budget for art)고 한 것으로 보아 미술품에 대한 예산 담당자는 윌리스 씨임을 알 수 있다. 따라서 정답은 (C)이다.

184 연계

번역 파운틴 로드 사무실 건물에 가장 적합한 레드 스탈링 아트 서비스는?
(A) 리메이크
(B) 얼라인
(C) 커넥트
(D) 리프레임

해설 이메일의 첫 단락 세 번째 문장에서 이제는 건물(새로운 파운틴 로드 사무실 건물) 3층에 있는 주요 개방형 사무실 구역에 설치할 미술 작품에 대해 생각해 봐야 한다(We now need to start thinking about the artwork for ~ the building)고 한 뒤, 두 번째 단락의 세 번째 문장에서 사진이나 그림이 그 공간에 잘 어울릴지 궁금하다(I am wondering whether photography or paintings would look best in the space)고 언급했다. 한편 레드 스탈링 아트 사의 웹페이지를 보면 두 번째 서비스 항목에서 얼라인(Align) 서비스가 새로운 사무실에 미술품을 설치하려는 고객을 위해 고객의 공간에 적합한 작품(그림, 사진, 판화 또는 조각품)을 찾도록 도와준다(For clients looking to incorporate artwork into a new office, we help you find the right pieces ~ for your space)고 나와 있다. 따라서 고객의 새로운 사무실에 알맞은 그림, 사진 등을 찾는 데 도움을 주는 얼라인 서비스가 파운틴 로드 사무실 건물에 적합하므로 (B)가 정답이다.

185 세부사항

번역 웹페이지에 따르면, 레드 스탈링 아트의 서비스 비용은 어떻게 알 수 있는가?
(A) 연락처 페이지를 통해 정보를 제출함으로써
(B) 비용 정보가 있는 웹페이지를 방문함으로써
(C) 로웬브루크 씨에게 서류를 제출함으로써
(D) 로웬브루크 씨와의 상담에 참석함으로써

해설 웹페이지의 마지막 단락 두 번째 문장에서 무료 상담을 예약하려면 비르기트 로웬브루크에게 blowenbruck@redstarlingart.co.uk로 이메일을 보내라(Please e-mail Birgit Lowenbruck ~ to book a free consultation)고 했고, 상담 후 그녀가 합의된 서비스에 대한 견적서를 보내 준다(After the consultation, she will provide you with an estimate for the agreed-upon services)고 했다. 따라서 로웬브루크 씨와 무료 상담 후 서비스 비용에 대해 알 수 있으므로 정답은 (D)이다.

186-190 이메일 + 회람 + 회람

수신: jdixon@milkalenterprises.com
발신: humanresources@milkalenterprises.com
날짜: 4월 28일
제목: 직원 설문 조사 응답

딕슨 씨께,

반년마다 하는 직원 설문 조사의 모든 응답을 읽고 나서 반복적으로 제기된 몇몇 사항을 강조하고 싶습니다. 이 제안 목록을 사용하면 우리의 우선순위를 정하는 데 도움이 될 것입니다.

제안 1. 재택근무에 대한 보다 유연한 정책
187 **제안 2. 확장된 사내 재활용 전략**
제안 3. 우수한 업무에 대한 더 큰 금전적 보상
제안 4. 기술 교육에 더 많은 기회

또한, 186 승인해 주신다면 다시 시행하기 전에 설문 조사 양식을 간소화하고 싶습니다. 개방형 질문은 데이터 분석을 어렵게 만듭니다. 직원이 진술에 얼마나 동의하거나 동의하지 않는지를 알아보기 위해 186 **더 많은 네-아니오 질문 또는 평가 척도를 포함시킬 것을 제안합니다.**

인사부 주디스 해서웨이

어휘 response 응답 read through ~을 다 읽다 semiannual 반년마다의 highlight 강조하다 repeatedly 반복적으로 raise 제기하다 determine 결정하다 priority 우선순위 flexible 유연한 expanded 확장된 in-office 사내의 recycling 재활용 strategy 전략 reward 보상 technical 기술적인, 전문적인 simplify 간소화하다 administer 시행[집행]하다 open-ended 개방형의 analyze 분석하다 incorporate 포함하다 rating scale 평가 척도 colleague 직장 동료 statement 진술

회람

수신: 전 직원
발신: 제나 딕슨, 총괄 매니저
날짜: 5월 8일
제목: 자원봉사자 모집

187 **사무실 재활용 프로그램을 시작할 위원회를 구성하기 위한 자원봉사자를 모집하고 있습니다.** 이러한 프로그램 운영은 최근 직원 설문 조사에서 가장 빈번하게 언급된 요구사항 중 하나였습니다. 이 프로그램은 플라스틱, 유리, 금속, 종이 및 판지를 포함한 재활용품이 쓰레기 매립지로 가게 되는 것을 방지할 것입니다.

또한, 이 위원회의 운영자가 될 자원봉사자가 필요합니다. 저는 이 운영자와 기꺼이 만나서 첫 단계를 논의할 것입니다. 조정 업무에 소요되는 시간은 정규 업무 외에 추가적인 것임을 유념해 주세요. 189 **프로그램 설정 비용으로 쓰일 소액의 자금이 지원될 것입니다.**

어휘 form 구성하다 committee 위원회 launch 시작하다 frequently 자주 identified 확인된 need 요구사항 prevent 방지하다 recyclables 재활용품 cardboard 판지, 골판지 end up (결국) ~하게 되다 landfill 쓰레기 매립지 coordinator 진행자 coordination 조정, 조직 duty 업무, 직무 fund 자금, 기금 setup 설정

회람

수신: 전 직원
발신: 모하마드 아스가리
날짜: 6월 13일
제목: 재활용 수거함이 준비되었습니다.

사내 재활용 위원회의 위원장으로서, 주방에 유리병, 탄산음료 캔, 판지 및 종이용 재활용 수거함이 구비되었다는 것을 알리게 되어 기쁩니다. ¹⁸⁸문과 냉장고 사이에 세 개를 넣기에 충분히 폭이 좁은 수거함을 찾기가 어려웠기 때문에 이 프로그램을 시작하는 데 시간이 좀 걸렸습니다. 그래도 ¹⁸⁹마침내 구입하게 되었습니다.

¹⁹⁰우리가 협력하는 재활용 시설에서 수용하는 물품에 엄격한 지침을 가지고 있어서, 삽화를 넣은 지침서를 각 수거함 위에 걸어 두기 위해 제작하고 있습니다. 그것들은 내일 게시될 예정이며, 위원회 회원들이 프로그램이 순조롭게 진행될 수 있도록 수거 시스템을 모니터링할 것입니다. 질문, 우려사항 또는 의견이 있으시면 저에게 연락 주세요.

어휘 bin 수거함, 통 chairperson 위원장 container 용기 narrow 좁은 squeeze (좁은 공간에) 밀어 넣다, (억지로) 들어가다 refrigerator 냉장고 prove ~임이 드러나다[판명되다] challenging 힘든, 어려운 facility 시설 stringent 엄격한, 까다로운 guideline 지침 accept 수용하다 illustrated 삽화를 넣은 instruction 지시, 설명 collection 수거 go 진행되다 smoothly 순조롭게

186 세부사항

번역 이메일에서, 해서웨이 씨가 제안하는 향후 설문 조사 개선 방안은?
(A) 일부 질문 형식을 변경하는 것에 의해
(B) 응답을 익명으로 수집하는 것에 의해
(C) 더 자주 실시하는 것에 의해
(D) 전문 소프트웨어를 활용하는 것에 의해

해설 이메일의 세 번째 단락 첫 문장에서 해서웨이 씨가 승인해 준다면 다시 시행하기 전에 설문 조사 양식을 간소화하고 싶다(if you approve, I would like to simplify the survey form ~ again)고 했고, 개방형 질문으로 인해 데이터 분석이 어렵다(The open-ended questions make the data difficult to analyze)며 더 많은 네-아니오 질문 또는 평가 척도를 포함시킬 것을 제안한다(I propose incorporating more yes-no questions or rating scales)고 했다. 따라서 정답은 (A)이다.

어휘 format 형식 anonymously 익명으로 conduct (특정 활동을) 하다 specialized 전문적인

187 연계

번역 딕슨 씨는 설문 조사 결과 중 어떤 제안에 대해 조치를 취하고 있는가?
(A) 제안 1
(B) 제안 2
(C) 제안 3
(D) 제안 4

해설 직원 설문 조사 응답과 관련하여 해서웨이 씨가 딕슨 씨에게 보낸 이메일에 제안 목록이 나열되어 있고, 딕슨 씨가 전 직원에게 보낸 첫 번째 회람의 첫 문장에서 그는 사무실 재활용 프로그램을 시작할 위원회를 구성하기 위한 자원봉사자를 모집하고 있다(I am seeking volunteers to form a committee that will launch an office recycling program)고 했다. 따라서 딕슨 씨는 이메일에 제시된 제안들 중 두 번째에 있는 사내 재활용 전략(Suggestion 2. An expanded in-office recycling strategy)을 수용하여 조치를 취하고 있으므로 (B)가 정답이다.

188 세부사항

번역 아스가리 씨에 따르면, 새로운 프로그램이 지체된 이유는?
(A) 일부 주문을 처리하는 데 시간이 오래 걸렸다.
(B) 일부 장비를 옮겨야 했다.
(C) 운영자의 승인이 필요했다.
(D) 방에 공간 제약이 있었다.

해설 두 번째 회람의 첫 단락 두 번째 문장에서 아스가리 씨가 문과 냉장고 사이에 세 개를 넣기에 충분히 폭이 좁은 수거함을 찾기가 어려웠기 때문에 이 프로그램을 시작하는 데 시간이 좀 걸렸다(It took us some time to get this program started because finding containers narrow enough ~ proved challenging)고 했으므로 (D)가 정답이다.

어휘 process 처리하다 limitation 제약

189 연계

번역 아스가리 씨에 대해 암시된 것은?
(A) 재활용에 대한 교육 시리즈를 이끌어 왔다.
(B) 회사의 자금을 사용해 몇몇 물건을 결제했다.
(C) 딕슨 씨를 일주일 간격으로 만난다.
(D) 회사 소식지에서 노고를 인정을 받았다.

해설 첫 회람의 두 번째 단락 마지막 문장에서 프로그램 설정 비용으로 쓰일 소액의 자금이 지원될 것(A small amount of funds ~ to be spent on program setup costs)이라고 했고, 두 번째 회람의 첫 단락 세 번째 문장에서 아스가리 씨가 마침내 (수거함을) 구입하게 되었다(I was finally able to purchase some)고 했다. 따라서 아스가리 씨는 사내 재활용 프로그램을 위해 마련된 자금으로 재활용 수거함을 구입했다는 것을 알 수 있으므로 (B)가 정답이다.

어휘 on a weekly basis 주 단위로 acknowledge 인정하다

Paraphrasing 지문의 funds → 정답의 money

190 세부사항

번역 아스가리 씨가 계획 중인 것은?
(A) 자원봉사자 모집
(B) 공급업체 연락
(C) 표지판 게시
(D) 재고 조사

해설 두 번째 회람의 두 번째 단락 첫 문장에서 아스가리 씨가 협력하는 재활용 시설에서 수용하는 물품에 엄격한 지침을 가지고 있어서, 삽화를 넣은 지침서를 각 수거함 위에 걸어 두기 위해 제작 중(Please note that the recycling facility we are working with has stringent guidelines ~ so I am creating illustrated instructions to hang above each bin)이며 내일 게시될 예정(Those will be up tomorrow)이라고 했다. 따라서 정답은 (C)이다.

어휘 take inventory 재고 조사를 하다

Paraphrasing 지문의 illustrated instructions → 정답의 signs

191-195 구인 광고 + 웹페이지 + 후기

쿠퍼스 비전에서 안경 부서를 위한 안경사를 구하고 있습니다. 유효한 매사추세츠 안경사 면허와 최소 3년 이상의 관련 경력이 있어야 합니다. 이 직책은 뛰어난 고객 서비스 기술과 업계의 최신 패션 트렌드에 대한 높은 인식이 요구됩니다. 업무에는 고객이 안경테를 고르는 것을 돕고, 안경을 주문하고, 보험금 청구를 신청하는 것이 포함됩니다.

193 이 정규직 자리는 댄버스 몰에 있는 쿠퍼스 비전에서 구합니다. 매장 관리자 타니샤 모슬리에게 978-555-0101로 연락하세요. **191** 8월 마지막 주에 근무를 시작할 수 있어야 합니다.

어휘 optician 안경사 eyewear 안경류 valid 유효한 license 면허 relevant 관련된 awareness 인식, 의식 industry 업계 frame 테 file (서류 등을) 제출하다 insurance claim 보험금 청구

---

https://www.koopersvision.com

댄버스 몰의 쿠퍼스 비전

시간:

월요일	오전 10시 - 오후 7시
화요일	오전 10시 - 오후 7시
수요일	오전 10시 - 오후 7시
목요일	오전 10시 - 오후 7시
금요일	오전 10시 - 오후 7시
토요일	오전 10시 - 오후 6시
일요일	오전 10시 - 오후 4시

195 8월 한 달간 두 번째 안경을 50퍼센트 할인된 가격으로 즐기세요.

쿠퍼스 비전은 매사추세츠주 댄버스에 있는 여러분의 눈 관리에 필요한 모든 것들을 위한 지역 시력 센터입니다. 댄버스 몰 위층 에잇데이즈 스포츠용품 옆에 위치하고 있습니다. **192** 오늘 978-555-0101로 전화하셔서 연례 눈 검진 일정을 잡으세요. 검진은 예약제로만 진행됩니다.

어휘 optical 시력의, 시각적인 goods 제품 schedule 일정을 잡다 exam 검진 appointment 약속

시력 센터 후기

평점: 별 5개 ★★★★★

저는 10살 때부터 안경을 썼습니다. 지금은 다섯 명의 아이가 있고 그중 네 아이가 안경을 써서, 수년간 많은 안경점을 방문해 왔습니다. **195** 최근 8월 31일에 방문한 쿠퍼스 비전은 단연 최고였습니다.

193 팔머 씨는 제가 쿠퍼스 비전의 수많은 안경 제품에 압도된 것을 보고 도움을 주었습니다. **194** 그녀는 저의 얼굴형을 보고 저에게 꼭 맞는 안경 몇 개를 보여 주었습니다! 그녀는 어떤 것이 저에게 가장 잘 어울리는지 정확히 알았고, 제가 고려하는 안경테의 크기, 색상, 품질, 가격에 대해 조언해 주었습니다. 팔머 씨는 또한 다양한 유형의 렌즈와 이용 가능한 렌즈 코팅도 설명해 주었습니다! **195** 어떤 안경이 가장 마음에 드는지 결정할 수 없어서 두 개를 구매했습니다. **193** 그녀가 그 매장에서 근무하는 첫날이라고 말했을 때 믿기지 않았고, 그녀는 제가 여태

껏 만나본 안경사 중 최고였습니다!

멜빈 드레이크

어휘 by far 단연코 overwhelmed 압도된 selection 선정된 제품 shape 모양 steer (특정 방향으로) 이끌다, 안내하다 incredulous 믿기지 않는

191 Not / True

번역 구인 광고에 따르면, 모집 중인 일자리에 대해 사실인 것은?
(A) 건강 보험이 제공된다.
(B) 8월 말에 시작한다.
(C) 세련된 회사 유니폼이 나온다.
(D) 지원자들이 팀으로 일할 것을 요구한다.

해설 구인 광고의 마지막 문장에서 8월 마지막 주에 근무를 시작할 수 있어야 한다(Must be available to start during the last week of August)고 했으므로 (B)가 정답이다.

어휘 candidate 지원자

Paraphrasing 지문의 during the last week of August
→ 정답의 at the end of August

192 Not / True

번역 웹페이지에서 쿠퍼스 비전에 대해 명시된 것은?
(A) 토요일에는 늦게까지 문을 연다.
(B) 쇼핑몰의 아래층에 위치해 있다.
(C) 다양한 스포츠 안경을 제공한다.
(D) 눈 검진은 예약이 필요하다.

해설 웹페이지의 마지막 단락 세 번째 문장에서 오늘 978-555-0101로 전화하여 연례 눈 검진 일정을 잡으라(Call 978-555-0101 today to schedule your annual eye exam)면서 검진은 예약제로만 진행된다(Exams by appointment only)고 명시했으므로 (D)가 정답이다.

어휘 stay ~인 채로 있다 a selection of 다양한

193 연계

번역 팔머 씨에 대해 사실일 것 같은 것은?
(A) 모슬리 씨와 함께 일한다.
(B) 이전에 패션 매장에서 일했다.
(C) 2년 전 안경사 면허를 취득했다.
(D) 쿠퍼스 비전의 새로운 소유주이다.

해설 구인 광고의 두 번째 단락 첫 문장에서 이 정규직 자리는 댄버스 몰에 있는 쿠퍼스 비전에서 구한다(This full-time position is available at Kooper's Vision at Danvers Mall)며 매장 관리자 타니샤 모슬리에게 연락하라(Contact store manager Tanisha Mosley)고 했다. 후기의 두 번째 단락 첫 문장에서 팔머 씨는 드레이크 씨가 쿠퍼스 비전의 수많은 안경 제품에 압도된 것을 보고 도움을 주었다(Ms. Palmer offered her help ~ the eyeglass selection at Kooper's Vision)고 한 뒤, 마지막 문장에서 그녀(=팔머 씨)가

그 매장에서 근무하는 첫날이라고 말했을 때 믿기지 않았다(I was incredulous ~ it was her first day working at the store)고 했다. 따라서 팔머 씨는 댄버스 몰의 쿠퍼스 비전에서 매장 관리인인 모슬리 씨와 함께 근무하고 있다는 것을 알 수 있으므로 (A)가 정답이다.

194 세부사항

번역　후기에 따르면, 팔머 씨가 드레이크 씨를 도운 방법은?
(A) 얼굴에 맞는 안경테를 추천함으로써
(B) 예약 시간을 연장함으로써
(C) 아이들을 위해 안경을 골라 줌으로써
(D) 안경 렌즈의 코팅을 업그레이드함으로써

해설　후기의 두 번째 단락 두 번째 문장에서 드레이크 씨는 그녀(=팔머 씨)가 자신의 얼굴형을 보고 꼭 맞는 안경 몇 개를 보여 주었다(She looked at the shape of my face and steered me ~ glasses that were perfect for me!)고 설명하고 있으므로 (A)가 정답이다.

어휘　extend 연장하다　length 시간, 길이

Paraphrasing　지문의 steered me toward a few pairs of glasses → 정답의 recommending frames

195 연계

번역　드레이크 씨에 대해 암시된 것은?
(A) 안경 도수가 바뀌었다고 생각한다.
(B) 최근에 안경을 쓰기 시작했다.
(C) 댄버스 몰에서 쇼핑을 자주 한다.
(D) 구매에 대해 할인을 받았다.

해설　웹페이지의 두 번째 단락에서 8월 한 달간 두 번째 안경을 50퍼센트 할인된 가격으로 즐기라(During ~ enjoy 50 percent off the second pair of eyeglasses)고 나와 있고, 후기의 첫 단락 마지막 문장에서 드레이크 씨가 최근 8월 31일에 방문한 쿠퍼스 비전은 최고였다(My recent visit to Kooper's vision ~ the best)고 했으며, 두 번째 단락 다섯 번째 문장에서 가장 마음에 드는 안경을 결정할 수 없어서 두 개를 구매했다(I could not decide ~ so I bought two pairs!)고 했다. 따라서 드레이크 씨가 8월 구매 할인 혜택을 받아 두 번째 안경을 50퍼센트 할인된 가격에 구매했다는 사실을 추론할 수 있으므로 (D)가 정답이다.

어휘　prescription 안경 도수　frequently 자주

Paraphrasing　지문의 50% off the second pair of eyeglasses → 정답의 a discount on his purchase

196-200 웹페이지 + 이메일 + 이메일

https://www.hellosnackvending.com/services

우리의 서비스

헬로 스낵 밴딩은 회사 휴게실과 자판기를 위한 다양한 자판기 및 커피 서비스를 제공합니다.

---

196 **서비스 1 (마이크로마켓)** — 귀사의 휴게실에 개방형 선반 위에 맞춤형 상품들로 채워진 작은 마켓을 만들어 드립니다. 196 **마이크로마켓은 셀프서비스이며 전자 결제를 지원합니다.** 선반 및 고정 장치가 제공됩니다.

서비스 2 (팬트리) — 귀사의 휴게실 캐비닛을 선택하신 다양한 제품들로 채워 드립니다. 팬트리 서비스는 선불이며 이용자가 품목마다 지불해야 하는 번거로움을 없애 드립니다.

서비스 3 (커피) — 귀사의 휴게실에 커피, 차 및 관련 필수품들을 계속 채워드립니다. 그룹용 커피 메이커와 커피, 개별 크기의 크리머와 설탕 종류를 제공합니다.

200 **서비스 4 (전통 자판기)** — 정기적으로 귀사의 자판기를 맞춤 주문 탄산음료, 주스, 물로 채워 드립니다.

서비스 5 (건강 자판기) — 정기적으로 귀사의 자판기를 다양한 건강 간식으로 채워 드립니다.

어휘　set up ~을 마련하다　customized 맞춤형의　feature 특색을 갖추다　electronic 전자의　payment 결제　shelving 선반　fixture 고정물, 붙박이 설비　pantry 식료품 저장실　stock (물품을) 채우다, 비축하다　pay in advance 선불하다　free (번거로움, 불쾌함 등을) 없애 주다　related 관련의　essentials 필수품　individually 개별적으로　variety 종류　carbonated 탄산이 든

수신: customercare@hellosnackvending.com
발신: dlewis@kivowitzcompany.com
날짜: 11월 14일
제목: 자판기 서비스

안녕하세요,

197 저희 회사는 최근 깨끗하게 사용된 비냉장 자판기를 구입해 직원 휴게실에 비치했습니다. 직원들이 사용하기 시작할 수 있도록 저희 자판기에 물품을 구비해 줄 서비스 업체를 찾고 있습니다.

귀사는 소유하고 있는 자판기에만 물품을 채워 주시나요, 아니면 다른 기계에도 서비스를 제공하시나요? 저희 기계에도 서비스를 제공하실 수 있다면 199 자판기에 채워 넣을 만한 귀사의 제공 간식에 대해 더 알고 싶습니다. 귀사에서 제공하는 제품 목록을 보내 주실 수 있을까요?

도움에 감사드립니다.

데니키아 루이스
키보위츠 사

어휘　gently 조심스럽게, 살살　nonrefrigerated 비냉장의　fill 채우다　service 서비스를 제공하다　assistance 도움

수신: 데니키아 루이스 〈dlewis@kivowitzcompany.com〉
발신: 고객 관리 〈customercare@hellosnackvending.com〉
날짜: 11월 15일
제목: 회신: 자판기 서비스
첨부: @ 목록

루이스 씨께,

귀하의 이메일에 감사드립니다. 저희 회사 소유 기계가 아니더라도 귀사의 자판기에 기꺼이 물품을 채워드릴 수 있습니다. 하지만 귀사의 기계가 오래되면 부품을 구하기가 어려울 수 있고 오래된 기계는 고장도 더 잦습니다. 수리 비용이 높아질 수 있어 저희 자판기 중 하나를 사용하시는 것이 비용 면에서 더 효율적일 수 있습니다. **198 모델 번호를 알려 주시겠습니까?**

199 요청하신 목록을 첨부했습니다. 특별한 요청이 있을 경우 맞춤드릴 수 있습니다. **200 또한 직원들이 보통 간식과 함께 차가운 음료를 즐긴다는 점을 알기에 저희로부터 음료 자판기를 대여할 것도 권장드립니다.**

추가 문의사항이 있으시면 저에게 연락 주십시오.

도미닉 샤이블러
고객 관리 담당자

어휘   obtain 구하다   break 고장나다   cost-effective 비용 효율적인   accommodate 맞추다, 수용하다

196 Not / True

번역 서비스 1에 대해 언급된 것은?
(A) 정해진 제품 구성이 제공된다.
(B) 사용자가 전자 결제를 할 수 있다.
(C) 연간 계약을 해야 한다.
(D) 추가 수수료를 내는 선반이 포함되어 있다.

해설 웹페이지의 첫 번째 서비스 품목인 서비스 1(마이크로마켓)(Service 1 (Micromarket))에 마이크로마켓은 셀프서비스이며 전자 결제를 지원한다(Micromarkets ~ feature electronic payments)고 나와 있으므로 (B)가 정답이다.

어휘 fixed 정해진   electronically 전자로

197 추론 / 암시

번역 루이스 씨가 자신의 회사 자판기에 대해 암시하는 것은?
(A) 상태가 좋지 않다.
(B) 최근에 점검을 받았다.
(C) 가격이 너무 비쌌다.
(D) 현재 비어 있다.

해설 첫 번째 이메일의 첫 문장에서 루이스 씨는 회사가 최근 깨끗하게 사용된 비냉장 자판기를 구입해 지원 휴게실에 비치했다(My company recently bought a gently used nonrefrigerated vending machine ~ break room)며, 직원들이 사용하기 시작할 수 있도록 자판기에 물품을 구비해 줄 서비스 업체를 찾고 있다(I am looking for a stocking service to fill it ~ using it)고 했다. 따라서 루이스 씨의 회사 자판기는 물품이 채워져 있지 않은 상태임을 알 수 있으므로 (D)가 정답이다.

어휘 service (기계를) 점검하다   overpriced 너무 비싼

198 세부사항

번역 샤이블러 씨가 루이스 씨에게 보내 달라고 요청하는 것은?
(A) 서명된 서비스 계약서
(B) 자판기 사진
(C) 필요한 부품 목록
(D) 모델 번호

해설 두 번째 이메일의 첫 단락 마지막 문장에서 샤이블러 씨가 루이스 씨에게 모델 번호를 알려 줄 수 있는지(Can you provide me with the model number?)를 묻고 있으므로 (D)가 정답이다.

199 연계

번역 샤이블러 씨가 이메일에 첨부한 목록에 포함된 것은?
(A) 그의 회사에서 제공하는 간식
(B) 그의 회사에서 배달할 수 있는 날짜
(C) 그의 회사에서 사용하는 자판기 브랜드
(D) 자판기 서비스와 관련된 비용

해설 첫 이메일의 두 번째 단락 두 번째 문장에서 루이스 씨가 자판기에 채워 넣을 만한 제공 간식에 대해 더 알고 싶다(I would like to know more about the snacks you have available to fill the machine)면서 샤이블러 씨 회사에서 제공하는 제품의 목록을 보내 줄 수 있는지(Could you please send me a list of the products you offer?)를 물었고, 두 번째 이메일의 두 번째 단락 첫 문장에서 샤이블러 씨가 루이스 씨에게 요청하신 목록을 첨부했다(I have attached the list you requested)고 했다. 따라서 샤이블러 씨가 이메일에 첨부한 것은 루이스 씨가 요청한 간식 제품 목록임을 알 수 있으므로 (A)가 정답이다.

200 연계

번역 샤이블러 씨가 제안하는 추가 서비스는?
(A) 서비스 2
(B) 서비스 3
(C) 서비스 4
(D) 서비스 5

해설 두 번째 이메일의 두 번째 단락 세 번째 문장에서 샤이블러 씨는 직원들이 보통 간식과 함께 차가운 음료를 즐긴다는 점을 알기에 음료 자판기를 대여할 것도 권장한다(I also recommend renting a drink machine ~ employees usually enjoy having a cold drink with their snacks)고 했고, 웹페이지의 네 번째 서비스 품목인 서비스 4(전통 자판기)에 정기적으로 자판기를 맞춤 주문 탄산음료, 주스, 물로 채워 준다(Service 4 (Traditional Vending) – We regularly stock your vending machine with a customized selection of carbonated beverates, juice, and water)고 나와 있다. 따라서 샤이블러 씨가 제안하는 서비스는 음료를 제공하는 서비스 4이므로 (C)가 정답이다.

기출 TEST 8

동영상 강의

101 (A)	102 (D)	103 (A)	104 (C)	105 (B)
106 (C)	107 (C)	108 (C)	109 (A)	110 (B)
111 (B)	112 (C)	113 (D)	114 (A)	115 (B)
116 (A)	117 (C)	118 (A)	119 (B)	120 (A)
121 (C)	122 (B)	123 (B)	124 (D)	125 (D)
126 (D)	127 (A)	128 (C)	129 (B)	130 (D)
131 (B)	132 (A)	133 (D)	134 (D)	135 (D)
136 (C)	137 (D)	138 (D)	139 (C)	140 (D)
141 (B)	142 (D)	143 (D)	144 (B)	145 (A)
146 (D)	147 (C)	148 (B)	149 (C)	150 (D)
151 (D)	152 (C)	153 (A)	154 (C)	155 (D)
156 (A)	157 (B)	158 (B)	159 (C)	160 (B)
161 (D)	162 (A)	163 (D)	164 (B)	165 (D)
166 (A)	167 (C)	168 (B)	169 (A)	170 (C)
171 (B)	172 (D)	173 (C)	174 (A)	175 (B)
176 (B)	177 (B)	178 (A)	179 (C)	180 (D)
181 (C)	182 (D)	183 (A)	184 (B)	185 (B)
186 (C)	187 (A)	188 (B)	189 (D)	190 (C)
191 (D)	192 (D)	193 (C)	194 (A)	195 (A)
196 (C)	197 (A)	198 (B)	199 (B)	200 (D)

PART 5

101 전치사 어휘

해설 빈칸 뒤에 특정 시점을 나타내는 명사구 November 15가 있고, '11월 15일까지 도착한다'라는 완료의 의미가 되어야 하므로 '~까지'를 뜻하는 (A) by가 정답이다. (B) until(~까지)은 계속적인 상태를 나타내는 동사와 쓰이므로 arrive와 어울리지 않는다. (C) at은 November 15가 날짜이므로 '11월 15일에'를 의미하기 위해서는 on이 와야 하므로 답이 될 수 없다. (D) down은 전치사로 쓰일 때 '~의 아래쪽으로'라는 의미로 문맥상 어울리지 않는다.

번역 주문은 11월 15일까지 도착할 것으로 추정된다.

어휘 estimate 추정하다

102 인칭대명사의 격 _ 소유격

해설 that이 이끄는 절의 주어인 명사구 personal belongings를 한정 수식하는 자리이므로 소유격 인칭대명사 (D) your가 정답이다.

번역 개인 소지품은 보이지 않는 곳에 안전하게 보관해 주십시오.

어휘 belongings 소지품   store 보관하다   out of sight 보이지 않는 곳에

103 부사 어휘

▶ 동영상 강의

해설 to fold를 수식하여 '옷을 깔끔하게 개다'라는 의미가 되어야 자연스러우므로 '깔끔하게, 단정히'를 의미하는 (A) neatly가 정답이다. (B) deeply는 '깊이', (C) highly는 '매우', (D) surely는 '확실히'라는 의미이다.

번역 고객들을 위해 옷을 가방에 넣기 전에 모두 깔끔하게 개세요.

어휘 fold (옷 등을) 개다   place 놓다

104 명사 자리 _ 동사의 목적어

해설 빈칸은 동사 take의 목적어 자리로, '사진을 찍으면 안 된다'라는 의미가 되어야 자연스럽다. 따라서 동사 take와 함께 '사진을 찍다'라는 의미를 만드는 '사진'이라는 뜻의 명사 (C) photographs가 정답이다. (A) photographic은 형용사, (D) photographed는 동사/과거분사이므로 품사상 빈칸에 들어갈 수 없고, (B) photographing은 현재분사/동명사로 보통 뒤에 목적어를 수반하므로 오답이다.

번역 방문객들은 시설의 제한 구역을 둘러보는 동안 사진을 찍어서는 안 됩니다.

어휘 restricted 제한된   facility 시설   photographic 사진(술)의   photograph 사진; ~의 사진을 찍다

105 형용사 어휘

해설 주어 The new novel을 보충 설명하는 주격 보어 자리로, 문맥상 '신작 소설은 서점에서 구입할 수 있다'라는 의미가 되어야 하므로 '구할 수 있는'을 의미하는 (B) available이 정답이다. (A) regular는 '정기적인', (C) convenient는 '편리한'이라는 뜻으로 The new novel을 보충 설명하기에 부적절하고, (D) completed는 '완성된'이라는 뜻으로 The new novel과는 어울리지만 전체 문맥상 적합하지 않다.

번역 미스터리 작가 메레디스 델가도의 새로운 소설은 7월 9일에 전국 서점에서 구입할 수 있다.

어휘 nationwide 전국적으로

106 형용사 자리 _ 명사 수식

해설 빈칸 앞에는 부정관사 an, 뒤에는 명사 cashier가 있으므로 빈칸에는 명사 cashier를 수식하는 형용사 또는 복합명사를 이루는 명사가 들어갈 수 있다. 문맥상 '추가 계산원'이라는 내용이 되어야 자연스러우므로 형용사 (C) additional(추가적인)이 정답이다. 명사 (A) addition과 (B) additions는 cashier와 복합명사를 이루기에 문맥상 적절하지 않고, (D) additionally는 부사로 품사상 답이 될 수 없다.

번역 계산원은 세 명 이상의 고객이 줄을 서 있을 때 추가 계산원을 요청해야 한다.

어휘 call for ~을 요청[요구]하다

107 명사 어휘

해설 빈칸에는 '(일·책임 등을) 맡다'라는 뜻의 동사 take on의 목적어 역할을 하는 명사가 들어가야 하고, '영업 관리자인 은가 호 씨가 새로운

역할을 맡을 것이다'라는 내용이 되어야 적절하므로 '역할'을 뜻하는 (C) role이 정답이다. (A) view는 '전망', (B) access는 '접근', (D) session은 '(특정 활동) 기간'이라는 의미이다.

번역   현재 남부 사업부의 영업 관리자인 은가 호는 2월에 트랑 미디어 그룹 내에서 새로운 역할을 맡을 예정이다.

어휘   southern 남부의   division 사업부, 부서   take on a role 역할을 맡다

108   부사 자리 _ 동사 수식

해설   stir가 동사, it이 목적어인 명령문에서 stir를 수식할 부사가 들어가야 하므로, '계속해서'를 뜻하는 부사 (C) continuously가 정답이다. (A) continues와 (B) continue는 동사, (D) continuous는 형용사이므로 품사상 답이 될 수 없다.

번역   소스가 가열되는 동안 눌어붙는 것을 방지하기 위해 나무 숟가락으로 계속 저으세요.

어휘   prevent 방지하다   scorch (불에) 눋게 하다   stir 젓다

109   동사 어휘

해설   be동사 뒤에서 현재분사 형태로 experienced guides를 목적어로 취해 '경험 많은 가이드를 구하고 있다'라는 내용이 되어야 자연스러우므로 '구하다'라는 뜻의 (A) seeking이 정답이다. (B)의 spread는 '펼치다', (C)의 work는 '일하다', (D)의 focus는 '집중하다'라는 의미이다.

번역   나이토 여행사는 일본에서 여행을 인솔할 경험 많은 가이드를 구하고 있습니다.

110   접속사 자리 _ 부사절 접속사

해설   빈칸 뒤의 완전한 절과 콤마 뒤의 완전한 절을 연결해야 하므로 부사절 접속사가 들어가야 한다. 따라서 '~ 후에'를 뜻하는 부사절 접속사 (B) After가 정답이다. (A) That은 명사절 접속사/관계대명사, (C) How는 의문사/관계부사, (D) Every는 한정사이므로 빈칸에 들어갈 수 없다.

번역   근처에서 미네랄이 풍부한 온천이 발견된 후, 호텔 덴잘리는 인기 있는 관광지가 되었다.

어휘   mineral-rich 미네랄이 풍부한   spring 온천, 샘   discover 발견하다   tourist destination 관광지

111   전치사 자리 / 어휘

해설   빈칸에는 arriving을 동명사로 볼 경우 전치사가, 분사로 볼 경우 분사구문을 이끄는 접속사가 들어갈 수 있다. 완전한 절(download ~ phone)에 arriving at the venue를 연결해야 하고, arriving과 함께 쓰여 '도착하기 전에'라는 의미가 되어야 하므로 (B) before가 정답이다. (A) since(~ 이래로)는 완료 시제와 함께 쓰이므로 답이 될 수 없고, 부사절 접속사 (C) although는 '비록 ~하지만', 전치사 (D) without은 '~ 없이'라는 의미로 문맥상 적절하지 않다.

번역   시간을 절약하기 위해 행사장에 도착하기 전에 휴대폰에 표를 다운로드하세요.

어휘   venue 행사장

112   동사 어형 _ 현재완료

해설   빈칸은 have와 함께 현재완료 동사를 이루는 과거분사가 와야 한다. 따라서 (C) submitted가 정답이다. have 뒤에 동사원형인 (A) submit, 현재분사인 (D) submitting은 올 수 없고, 빈칸 뒤에 이미 목적어 bids가 있으므로 명사인 (B) submission도 들어갈 수 없다.

번역   이미 여러 회사들이 우리 배달 트럭에 로고를 칠하기 위한 입찰서를 제출했다.

어휘   bid 입찰(서)

113   명사 어휘   동영상 강의

해설   패션 컬렉션에 등장한 소재와 그 효과를 묘사하는 문장이므로 '원단이 의류에 고급스러운 분위기를 주었다'라는 의미가 되어야 자연스럽다. 따라서 '의류'를 의미하는 (D) garments가 정답이다. (A)의 mark는 '표시', (B)의 portion은 '부분', (C)의 type은 '유형'이라는 의미이다.

번역   노퍽 패션의 봄 컬렉션에 등장하는 보석 색감의 원단은 의류를 고급스럽게 보이도록 했다.

어휘   jewel-toned 보석 색감의   fabric 원단   feature ~의 특징을 이루다   luxurious 고급스러운

114   대명사 어휘

해설   빈칸은 전치사 with의 목적어 자리로, 현재분사구(living in ~ Apartments)의 수식을 받아 '아버 힐 아파트 이외의 지역에 거주하는 누구와도'라는 의미가 되어야 하므로 '누구(든)'을 뜻하는 (A) anyone이 정답이다. (B) either는 '(둘 중의) 어느 한 쪽', (C) most는 '대부분', (D) each는 '각각'을 뜻하므로 의미상 적절하지 않다.

번역   아버 힐 아파트 이외의 지역에 거주하는 누구와도 주민 출입 코드를 공유하지 마세요.

어휘   resident 주민   access 출입   other than ~ 이외의

115   형용사 어휘

해설   빈칸은 명사 ways를 수식하는 to make의 목적격 보어 자리로, more와 함께 목적어 people을 보충 설명한다. 빈칸 뒤에 전치사 of가 있고 '사람들이 브랜드를 더 잘 알도록 만드는 방법'이라는 의미가 되어야 하므로, 전치사 of와 함께 쓰여 '~을 아는'이라는 뜻을 나타내는 (B) aware가 정답이다. (A) concise는 '간결한', (C) precious는 '귀중한', (D) defined는 '정의된'이라는 의미이다.

번역   소셜 미디어 전문가는 항상 사람들이 진타만 브랜드를 더 잘 알게 할 방법을 찾아야 한다.

116   동사 자리 _ 태

해설   문장에 동사가 보이지 않으므로 빈칸에는 동사가 들어가야 한다. 또

한 빈칸 뒤에 목적어 their unwanted appliances가 있으므로 능동태가 와야 한다. 따라서 (A) can discard가 정답이다. (B) have been discarded는 수동태이므로 목적어를 취할 수 없고, (C) to be discarding은 to부정사, (D) discarding은 동명사/현재분사이므로 동사 자리에 들어갈 수 없다.

번역 모든 테이튼 주민은 소정의 수수료를 내고 원치 않는 가전제품을 공공사업 시설에 폐기할 수 있다.

어휘 appliances 가전제품 facility 시설 fee 수수료 discard 폐기하다

117 부사 어휘

해설 문맥상 수많은 고객 요청에 따른 결과로 이루어진 일을 나타낼 수 있어야 하므로 '마침내 채식주의자 옵션을 추가했다'라는 의미가 되어야 적절하다. 따라서 '마침내'를 뜻하는 (C) finally가 정답이다. (A) extremely는 '극히', (B) typically는 '전형적으로', (D) closely는 '면밀히'라는 의미이다.

번역 고객들의 수많은 요청에 따라 마닐라 런치 박스는 마침내 채식주의자 옵션을 메뉴에 추가했다.

어휘 numerous 수많은 add 추가하다

118 형용사 자리 _ 명사 수식

해설 빈칸에는 명사 manufacturers를 수식하는 형용사 또는 manufacturers와 복합명사를 이루는 명사가 들어갈 수 있다. 문맥상 '업계 최고의 제조업체'라는 내용이 되어야 자연스러우므로, 분사형 형용사 (A) leading(최고의, 선두의)이 정답이다. (B) leader는 명사, (C) leads는 동사/명사, (D) leadership은 명사로 모두 manufacturers와 복합명사를 이루기에 문맥상 적절하지 않다.

번역 크러치필드 냉난방은 업계 최고 제조업체들의 가스, 석유 및 전기 보일러를 설치합니다.

어휘 install 설치하다 furnace 보일러 industry 업계 manufacturer 제조업체

119 동사 어휘

해설 등위접속사 and로 연결된 to부정사구에서 to가 생략된 자리에 들어갈 동사 어휘를 고르는 문제이다. productivity를 목적어로 취해 '생산성을 높이기 위해'라는 의미가 되어야 자연스러우므로 '신장시키다, 북돋우다'를 뜻하는 (B) boost가 정답이다. (A) distribute는 '분배하다', (C) sweat는 '땀 흘리다', (D) tone은 '(신체를) 탄탄하게 하다'라는 의미이다.

번역 스트레스를 줄이고 생산성을 높이기 위해 시알로 사는 직원들에게 무료 점심시간 피트니스 강좌를 제공한다.

어휘 reduce 줄이다 productivity 생산성

120 동사 자리

해설 문장에 동사가 보이지 않으므로 빈칸은 동사 자리이다. 따라서 (A) are guaranteed가 정답이다. (B) to guarantee는 to부정사, (C)

guaranteeing은 동명사/현재분사, (D) having guaranteed는 동명사/현재분사이므로 동사 자리에 들어갈 수 없다.

번역 요시미 패션 고객들은 안전한 온라인 쇼핑 경험을 보장받는다.

어휘 secure 안전한 guarantee 보장하다

121 전치사 어휘   동영상 강의

해설 동사 invest와 명사구 a new grocery service를 적절히 이어주는 전치사를 선택해야 한다. '새로운 식료품 배달 서비스에 투자한다'라는 내용이 되어야 자연스러우므로, 동사 invest와 함께 쓰여 '~에 투자하다'라는 의미를 나타내는 전치사 (C) in이 정답이다.

번역 샤카르 씨는 작년의 기록적인 이익을 활용해 새로운 식료품 배달 서비스에 투자할 수 있었다.

어휘 record 기록적인 profit 이익 invest 투자하다 grocery 식료품

122 명사 자리 _ 동사의 목적어

해설 빈칸은 동사 must renew의 목적어 자리이고, 앞에 정관사 the가 있으므로 명사가 들어가야 한다. '계약을 갱신해야 한다'라는 의미가 되어야 하므로 '계약'을 뜻하는 명사 (B) contract가 정답이다. 명사 (A) contractor(시공사)는 문맥상 적절하지 않고, (C) contracting은 동명사/현재분사로 정관사 the와 쓰일 수 없으며, (D) contracted는 동사/과거분사이므로 품사상 답이 될 수 없다.

번역 센트럴 오리건 파워는 현재 계약이 만료되기 최소 30일 전에 계약을 갱신해야 한다.

어휘 renew 갱신하다 expire 만료되다

123 접속사 자리 _ 부사절 접속사 / 어휘   동영상 강의

해설 빈칸은 두 개의 완전한 절을 연결하는 부사절 접속사 자리이다. 문맥상 '입구 근처 주차 공간은 고객이 이용할 수 있도록'이라는 의미가 되어야 자연스러우므로 '~할 수 있도록'을 뜻하는 부사절 접속사 (B) so that이 정답이다. (A) instead of(~ 대신에), (C) resulting from(~으로 인한)은 구전치사이고, 부사절 접속사 (D) as if(마치 ~인 것처럼)는 가정법 시제와 쓰이므로 답이 될 수 없다.

번역 입구와 가까운 주차 공간은 고객이 이용할 수 있도록 건물 서편에 주차하세요.

어휘 entrance 입구

124 부사 자리 _ 동사 수식

해설 The report가 주어, was authored가 동사인 완전한 절에서 동사구 was authored를 수식하여 '공동으로 쓰였다'라는 의미가 되어야 하므로 '공동으로'라는 뜻의 부사 (D) jointly가 정답이다. (A) joint는 형용사/명사/동사, (B) joints는 명사/동사, (C) jointed는 동사/과거분사로 품사상 답이 될 수 없다.

번역 그 보고서는 연구부의 손채원과 마케팅 부장 레이 한에 의해 공동으로 작성되었다.

TEST 8 (세로 탭)

어휘 author 작성하다 joint 공동의; 관절; 접합하다

125 형용사 어휘

해설 빈칸 뒤의 명사 activities를 수식하기에 적절한 형용사를 골라야 한다. '다양한 활동'이라는 의미가 되어야 자연스러우므로 '다양한'을 뜻하는 (D) numerous가 정답이다. (A) capable은 '유능한', (B) dense는 '빽빽한', (C) absent은 '없는; 결석한'이라는 의미이다.

번역 티슨 리조트는 어린이와 어른을 위한 다양한 활동을 하루 종일 제공합니다.

126 부사 어휘

해설 앞에서 박물관이 후한 기부금을 받는다고 했으므로 '입장권 가격을 좀처럼 올리지 않는다'라는 내용이 되어야 연결이 자연스럽다. 따라서 '좀처럼 ~하지 않다'를 뜻하는 (D) rarely가 정답이다. (A) nearly는 '거의', (B) likely는 very나 most를 앞에 붙여 '아마', (C) generally는 '일반적으로'라는 의미이다.

번역 그 박물관은 후한 기부금을 받기 때문에 입장권 가격을 좀처럼 올리지 않는다.

어휘 generous 후한 donation 기부 raise 올리다 admission 입장

127 형용사 자리

해설 빈칸 앞에 완전한 절(Global Data LLC will promote Hae-In Ahn ~ Officer)이 있고, 뒤에 시점을 나타내는 명사구 June 1가 나왔으며, 문맥상 '6월 1일부터'라는 의미가 되어야 한다. 따라서 「effective+시점 표현」의 형태로 '~부터 (시행되어)'를 뜻하는 형용사 (A) effective가 정답이다. '(어떤 결과를) 가져오다'라는 뜻의 동사 effect에서 파생된 동명사/현재분사 (B) effecting은 의미상 June 1을 목적어로 취하기에 부적절하고, (C) effected는 동사/과거분사, (D) effect는 동사/명사로 품사상 답이 될 수 없다.

번역 글로벌 데이터 LLC는 6월 1일부터 안해인을 최고 재무 책임자로 승진시킬 예정이다.

어휘 promote 승진시키다 Chief Financial Officer 최고 재무 책임자(CFO)

128 전치사 + 관계대명사

해설 빈칸 앞에 전치사 during이 있고 뒤에는 each participant가 주어, can join이 동사인 완전한 절이 있다. 따라서 빈칸에는 전치사와 함께 쓰여 선행사를 수식할 수 있는 관계대명사가 들어가야 한다. 선행사가 사물 명사인 an online meeting이고, 빈칸은 전치사 during의 목적어가 들어갈 자리이므로 목적격 관계대명사인 (C) which가 정답이다. (A) through는 전치사, (B) there는 부사/명사, (D) who는 사람 선행사를 수식하는 관계대명사이므로 오답이다.

번역 곧 있을 포커스 그룹은 각 참가자가 화상 회의 프로그램을 통해 참여할 수 있는 온라인 회의가 될 것이다.

어휘 upcoming 곧 있을 participant 참가자 via ~을 통해

129 명사 어휘

해설 빈칸에 들어갈 명사는 문맥상 유기 세정 화합물 제품을 위해 개발한 것이어야 하므로 '~ 제품을 위한 제조법을 개발했다'라는 내용이 되어야 적절하다. 따라서 '제조법'을 뜻하는 (B) formula가 정답이다. (A) menu는 '메뉴', (C) article은 '기사', (D) decision은 '결정'이라는 의미이다.

번역 패트리샤 박은 100퍼센트 유기 세정 화합물인 스프레이즈의 독자적인 제조법을 개발했다.

어휘 proprietary 독자적인, 전매특허의 organic 유기의 compound 화합물

130 명사 자리 _ 전치사의 목적어 ▶ 동영상 강의

해설 빈칸은 전치사 of의 목적어 자리이며, 앞에 소유격 its가 있으므로 명사가 들어가야 한다. 또한 뒤에 나온 복수대명사 their가 지칭하는 명사가 앞에 없는 것으로 보아, 빈칸의 명사를 가리켜야 적절하므로 이에 수 일치하는 복수명사가 필요하다. 따라서 '연구원들'이라는 뜻의 복수 가산명사 (D) researchers가 정답이다. (A) research는 '연구'라는 뜻의 불가산명사이므로 their와 수 일치되지 않고, (B) researching은 동명사/현재분사, (C) researched는 동사/과거분사로 품사상 답이 될 수 없다.

번역 라옐 제약은 웹사이트에 자사의 연구원들과 그들의 소속 목록을 제공한다.

어휘 pharmaceutical 제약 affiliation 소속 (기관)

PART 6

131-134 이메일

수신: mnandy@gmantcs.com
발신: jblaire@blaireaccounting.ca
회신: 자동 응답
날짜: 1월 9일, 오전 10시 34분

안녕하세요, 블레어 회계에 연락 주셔서 감사합니다. 저는 1월 31일까지 사무실에 없을 예정입니다. 제가 **131 돌아오면** 메시지에 답변해 드리겠습니다. **132 즉각적인** 도움이 필요하시면 저의 행정 비서인 수잔 루이스에게 slewis@blaireaccounting.ca로 연락하십시오. **133 또한** 그녀에게 416-555-0193으로 직접 전화하셔도 됩니다. **134 루이스 씨는 평일 오전 9시부터 오후 5시까지 사무실에 있습니다.**

장 블레어, 사장

어휘 automatic 자동의 accounting 회계 assistance 도움 administrative 행정상의 directly 직접

131 동사 어휘

해설 빈칸 앞 문장에서 1월 31일까지 사무실에 없을 예정(I will be out of the office until 31 January)이라고 했으므로, 문맥상 '(사무실에) 돌아왔을 때 답변하겠다'라는 내용이 되어야 자연스럽다. 따라서 '돌

아오다'라는 뜻의 (B) return이 정답이다. (A) recover는 '회복하다', (C) begin은 '시작하다', (D) finish는 '끝내다'라는 의미이다.

132 형용사 자리 _ 명사 수식

해설 빈칸에는 명사 assistance를 수식하는 형용사 또는 assistance와 복합명사를 이루는 명사가 들어갈 수 있다. 문맥상 '즉각적인 도움'이라는 내용이 되어야 자연스러우므로 형용사 (A) immediate(즉각적인)가 정답이다. 명사 (C) immediacy와 (D) immediacies는 '즉각성'을 의미하기 때문에 assistance와 복합명사를 이루기에 적절하지 않고, (B) immediately는 부사이므로 품사상 빈칸에 들어갈 수 없다.

133 부사 어휘

해설 빈칸 앞에서 도움이 필요할 경우 수잔 루이스에게 연락하라(contact Susan Lewis)며 이메일 주소를 알려 주었는데, 빈칸 뒤에 수잔에게 연락할 수 있는 방법으로 전화번호를 추가적으로 알려 주고 있다. 따라서 비슷한 내용을 추가할 때 쓰는 '또한'이라는 부사 (A) also가 정답이다. (B) lightly는 '가볍게', (C) similarly는 '비슷하게', (D) again은 '다시'라는 의미이다.

134 문맥에 맞는 문장 고르기

번역 (A) 블레어 씨는 예상보다 일찍 사무실로 돌아올 것입니다.
(B) 토론토에 오시게 되면 꼭 저희를 방문해 주십시오.
(C) 유능한 급여 및 세금 담당 회계사를 고용하는 것이 필수입니다.
(D) 루이스 씨는 평일 오전 9시부터 오후 5시까지 사무실에 있습니다.

해설 빈칸 앞에서 도움이 필요할 경우 수잔 루이스에게 연락하라(contact Susan Lewis)며 연락처를 알려 주고 있다. 앞 내용에서 비상시 연락할 수 있는 직원의 연락처를 알려 주었으므로, 이 직원에게 연락이 가능한 시간을 안내하는 내용이 연결되어야 자연스럽다. 따라서 루이스 씨의 근무 시간을 언급하고 있는 (D)가 정답이다.

어휘 expect 예상하다 essential 필수적인 competent 유능한 payroll 급여 accountant 회계사 weekday 평일

135-138 공지

메트로 커피 고객님께 알립니다:

두 번째 메트로 커피 매장을 ¹³⁵열었다는 소식을 발표하게 되어 기쁩니다! 아시다시피, 최근에 커피뿐 아니라 제과 제품까지 포함시켜 판매 제품을 확대했습니다. 그 결과, ¹³⁶사업은 상당히 커졌습니다. 수요를 따라잡기 위해, 저희는 두 번째 매장이 필요하다고 결정했습니다. ¹³⁷그 매장은 사적지에서 2마일 떨어진 곳에 위치해 있습니다. 새로운 공간은 상당히 ¹³⁸더 크지만, 기존과 동일한 다양한 상품을 제공합니다. 오늘 꼭 들르셔서 저희의 새로운 매장을 확인하세요!

어휘 expand 확대하다 offering 판매[취급] 제품 significantly 상당히, 현저하게 keep up with ~을 따라잡다 demand 수요 substantially 상당히 stop by ~에 들르다

135 동사 어형 _ 시제 ▶ 동영상 강의

해설 마지막 문장에서 꼭 새 매장을 방문하고 확인하라(stop by and check out our new location today)고 권유하고 있으므로 새로운 매장이 이미 영업 중이라는 것을 알 수 있다. 따라서 두 번째 매장을 연 것은 이미 완료된 일이므로 현재완료 시제인 (D) have opened가 정답이다.

136 명사 어휘

해설 빈칸 앞에서 최근에 판매 제품의 종류를 확대했다(we recently expanded our offerings)고 했고, 빈칸이 있는 문장은 '그 결과(As a result)'로 초래된 일을 언급하는 내용이 되어야 한다. 또한 빈칸 뒤에서 수요를 따라잡기 위해 두 번째 매장이 필요하다고 결정했다(we decided that a second store was necessary)며 사업 규모가 확대되었음을 시사하고 있으므로, 빈칸이 있는 문장은 '사업이 커졌다'라는 의미가 되어야 적절하다. 따라서 '사업'을 뜻하는 (C) business가 정답이다. (A) debt는 '빚', (B) payroll은 '급여', (D) investment는 '투자'라는 의미이다.

137 문맥에 맞는 문장 고르기

번역 (A) 메트로 커피는 9년 동안 지역 사회의 일부였습니다.
(B) 저희는 바로 여기 현장에서 커피 원두를 볶습니다.
(C) 많은 사람들이 커피를 마시면서 페이스트리 먹는 것을 즐깁니다.
(D) 그 매장은 사적지에서 2마일 떨어진 곳에 위치해 있습니다.

해설 빈칸 앞에서 두 번째 매장이 필요하다고 결정했다(we decided that a second store was necessary)고 했고, 빈칸 뒤에서 새로운 공간(Our new space) 즉, 두 번째 매장의 특징을 설명하고 있다. 따라서 빈칸에는 새로운 매장에 대한 내용이 들어가야 연결이 자연스러우므로 새 매장의 위치를 설명하는 (D)가 정답이다.

어휘 roast (콩 등을) 볶다 on-site 현장에서 historic district 사적지, 역사 지구

138 형용사 자리 _ 주격 보어 / 비교급 ▶ 동영상 강의

해설 빈칸은 주어 Our new space를 보충 설명하는 자리로, 형용사가 들어가야 한다. 문맥상 기존 매장과 새로운 매장을 비교하는 내용이고, 비교급을 강조하는 부사인 'substantially(상당히)'의 수식을 받고 있으므로 비교급 형용사 (B) larger가 정답이다. (A) large는 원급 형용사, (C) largely(주로)는 부사, (D) largest는 최상급 형용사이므로 빈칸에 들어갈 수 없다.

139-142 회람

수신: 페레스 호텔 전 직원
발신: 세르지오 프리에토, 호텔 관리자
날짜: 7월 4일 월요일
제목: 글로벌 배송 협력사 콘퍼런스

페레스 호텔은 다음 주 화요일부터 일요일까지 글로벌 배송 협력사 콘퍼런스를 개최할 예정입니다. ¹³⁹따라서 경영진은 호텔 레스토랑과 기념

품점에서 더 많은 고객을 볼 수 있을 것으로 기대하고 있습니다. ¹⁴⁰ **비즈니스 센터 또한 평소보다 더 바쁠 것입니다.** ¹⁴¹ **우리가** 이러한 수요 증가를 충족시킬 수 있도록 임시 직원을 채용할 예정입니다. 그들이 이곳에 있을 때 우리의 ¹⁴² **일상 업무**를 배울 수 있도록 시간을 내어 도와주십시오. 그렇게 하면 콘퍼런스가 열리는 동안 모든 운영이 순조롭게 진행될 것입니다.

> 어휘   partner 협력사   host 개최하다   management 경영진
> temporary 임시의   ensure 보장하다   demand 수요
> operation 운영   smoothly 순조롭게   take place 일어나다

139 접속부사

해설   앞 문장에서 호텔에서 다음 주에 콘퍼런스를 개최한다(will be hosting the Global ~ Conference next week)고 했고, 뒤 문장에서는 일부 호텔 시설에 더 많은 고객이 올 것으로 기대한다(expects to see many more customers ~ gift shops)고 했다. 두 문장이 행사가 열리므로 손님이 늘 것이라는 인과 관계를 나타내고 있으므로 '그러므로, 따라서'를 뜻하는 (C) Therefore가 정답이다. (A) If not은 '그렇지 않으면', (B) After all은 '결국', (D) In the meantime은 '그동안에'라는 의미이다.

140 문맥에 맞는 문장 고르기

번역   (A) 레스토랑 보수 공사가 거의 완료되었습니다.
(B) 콘퍼런스 등록 양식이 온라인에 게시되어 있습니다.
(C) 지원서는 이번 주 말에 검토될 예정입니다.
(D) 비즈니스 센터 또한 평소보다 더 바쁠 것입니다.

해설   빈칸 앞에서 호텔에서 다음 주에 콘퍼런스를 개최해 레스토랑과 선물 가게에 더 많은 고객이 올 것으로 기대한다고 했으므로, 사람이 많을 것으로 예상되는 시설에 대한 내용이 연결되면 자연스럽다. 따라서 (D)가 정답이다.

어휘   renovation 보수, 개조   registration 등록   form 양식   post 게시하다   application 지원서

141 대명사 어휘

해설   해당 글은 호텔 관리자가 호텔 전 직원들에게 보내는 회람이며, 빈칸은 can meet의 주어 자리로 호텔의 전 직원들이 해야 할 업무를 언급하고 있으므로 자신을 포함한 함께 일하는 호텔 직원 모두를 지칭하는 주격 인칭대명사 (B) we가 정답이다.

142 명사 어휘

해설   앞 문장에서 호텔의 수요 증가를 충족시킬 수 있도록 임시 직원을 채용할 예정(will be hiring temporary staff)이라고 했으므로, 빈칸에는 호텔 업무와 관련해 그들(임시 직원)이 배워야 하는 것이 들어가야 적절하다. 따라서 '일상 업무, 규칙적으로 하는 일'을 뜻하는 (D) routines가 정답이다. (A)의 line은 '줄', (B)의 step은 '단계', (C)의 name은 '이름'이라는 의미이다.

143-146 기사

> 댈러스 (7월 28일) — 주라 테크놀로지 솔루션스(ZTS)는 오늘 이곳 댈러스의 밴 커크 가 425에 위치한 사무실 건물 ¹⁴³**매입**을 완료했다고 발표했다. 가장 최근에 브릭홀 보험의 본사였던 이 건물은 ZTS의 ¹⁴⁴**주요** 사업 거점 역할을 할 예정이다. 포트워스로부터의 회사 이전은 올해 말까지 완료될 것으로 예상된다. ¹⁴⁵**ZTS의 지도부는 이번 이전을 전략적인 것으로 보고 있다.** "우리의 건물 인수 결정은 댈러스 지역에 대한 ZTS의 지속적인 노력을 반영하는 것이며, 우리가 고객, 사업 파트너 및 주주들에게 더 나은 서비스를 제공할 수 있도록 해 줄 것입니다."라고 ZTS의 최고 경영자인 글로리아 루비로사는 말했다. "댈러스의 새로운 본거지에서 전 세계에 있는 고객 한 분 한 분의 요구를 충족시키기 위해 ¹⁴⁶**계속해서** 열심히 일할 것입니다."

> 어휘   complete 완료하다; 완료[완성]된   headquarters 본사
> insurance 보험   serve as ~으로서 역할을 하다   base 근거지
> operation 사업   relocation 이전   acquire 인수하다   reflect
> 반영하다   ongoing 계속 진행 중인   commitment 헌신   enable
> ~ to ... ~가 …할 수 있게 하다   stakeholder 주주

143 명사 어휘

해설   뒤 문장에서 브릭홀 보험의 본사였던 이 건물(The building, most recently the headquarters of Brickhall Insurance)은 ZTS의 사업 거점(base of operations) 역할을 할 예정이라고 했고, 후반부에서 ZTS의 최고 경영자가 건물 인수(acquire the building) 결정을 언급하고 있다. 따라서 빈칸이 있는 문장은 ZTS가 '건물 매입을 완료했다'라는 내용이 되어야 하므로 '매입'을 뜻하는 (D) purchase가 정답이다. (A) construction은 '건설', (B) cleaning은 '청소', (C) inspection은 '점검'이라는 의미이다.

144 형용사 어휘

해설   앞에서 ZTS가 건물을 매입했다고 했으며, 뒤에서 건물을 인수한 것은 해당 지역에 대한 지속적 노력을 반영(reflects ZTS's ongoing commitment)하며 이 새로운 본거지(home)에서 전 세계의 고객을 위해 계속해서 열심히 일할 것이라고 했다. 따라서 이 건물은 '주요한 사업 거점'으로서 역할을 할 것이라는 내용이 되어야 자연스러우므로 '주요한, 기본적인'을 뜻하는 (B) primary가 정답이다. (A) voluntary는 '자발적인', (C) short-term은 '단기의', (D) occasional은 '가끔의'라는 의미이다.

145 문맥에 맞는 문장 고르기

번역   (A) ZTS의 지도부는 이번 이전을 전략적인 것으로 보고 있다.
(B) 예를 들어, 그것은 중소기업에 다양한 서비스를 제공한다.
(C) 메인 가 구역에는 이용 가능한 부지가 몇 곳 밖에 없다.
(D) 전 세계적으로 15,000명 이상의 사람들이 ZTS에 고용되어 있다.

해설   빈칸 앞은 회사 이전이 올해 말까지 완료될 것이라며 회사 이전 일정을 안내하고 있고, 빈칸 뒤에서는 회사 이전의 이유 및 의의에 대한 경영진의 언급을 인용하고 있다. 따라서 빈칸에도 회사 이전에 대한 설명이 들어가야 내용이 일관성 있게 연결되므로, 회사 이전에 관한 ZTS 지도부의 견해를 간략하게 제시하고 있는 (A)가 정답이다.

어휘 strategic 전략적인 site 부지

146 동사 자리 _ 시제

해설 빈칸은 주어 we의 동사 자리이다. 앞에서 댈러스로의 회사 이전이 올해 말까지 완료될 것이라고 했으므로 빈칸이 있는 문장은 댈러스의 새로운 본거지로 이전을 완료한 뒤 앞으로의 계획을 제시하는 내용임을 알 수 있다. 따라서 미래 시제 (D) will continue가 정답이다. (A) continued는 과거형, (C) would have continued는 가정법 과거완료형이고, (B) continuing은 동명사/현재분사로 품사상 답이 될 수 없다.

PART 7

147-148 광고

조야스 바스켓

뉴저지주 테나플라이 틸튼 가 12, 07670

www.zoyasbasket.com

조야스 바스켓의 모든 제품이 마음에 드시나요? 여기 그것들이 더 마음에 들게 될 이유가 있습니다! **147 저희 보상 프로그램에 가입하시고 조야스의 모든 제품에 최대 5퍼센트를 돌려받으세요!** 현금 보상 포인트를 매장이나 온라인에서 사용하세요.

- 비타민 및 보충제
- 견과 및 씨앗 버터
- 잼, 젤리, 과일 스프레드
- 통곡물 및 시리얼
- 건강 및 건강 관리 제품

저희는 뉴저지 전역에 배송합니다. 배송은 최소 35달러 구매 시 무료입니다. **148 배송에는 최대 3일이 걸릴 수 있습니다.**

어휘 sign up for ~에 가입하다 reward 보상 supplement 보충제 seed 씨앗 spread 스프레드(빵에 발라 먹는 식품) whole grain 통곡물 wellness 건강 관리

147 주제 / 목적

번역 광고의 목적은?
(A) 단종된 제품에 대한 판매를 알리려고
(B) 소비자에게 좋아하는 제품에 대한 의견을 물으려고
(C) 소비자들이 보상 프로그램에 가입하도록 장려하려고
(D) 신선한 과일과 채소에 대한 특가 판매를 광고하려고

해설 첫 단락의 세 번째 문장에서 조야스의 고객들에게 보상 프로그램에 가입하고 조야스의 모든 제품에 최대 5퍼센트를 돌려받으라(Sign up for our reward program and get up to 5% on everything Zoya's offers!)고 권유하고 있으므로 (C)가 정답이다.

어휘 discontinued 단종된 consumer 소비자 special offer 특가 판매

Paraphrasing 지문의 Sign up for → 정답의 join

148 Not / True

번역 배송에 대해 명시된 것은?
(A) 서명이 필요하다.
(B) 3일 이내에 도착한다.
(C) 쿠폰 코드가 있으면 무료이다.
(D) 주문을 할 때 일정을 잡아야 한다.

해설 마지막 문장에서 배송에는 최대 3일이 걸릴 수 있다(Please allow up to three days for delivery)고 했으므로 (B)가 정답이다.

어휘 signature 서명 place an order 주문하다

Paraphrasing 지문의 up to three days
→ 정답의 within three days

149-150 광고

그리션 테라스 호텔

149 아름다운 메세니안 만에 위치한 5성급 호텔에서 다음 비즈니스 컨퍼런스를 개최하십시오. 150 저희 시설은 바다와 그림 같은 해변이 내려다보이는 넓은 회의실을 갖추고 있습니다. 149 저희 호텔은 귀사의 직원을 위한 회사 야유회에 완벽한 장소입니다. 고급 식사, 멋진 전망, 최고의 엔터테인먼트를 이용하면서 팀의 유대를 쌓는 경험을 즐기십시오.

연락처: 헬레나 사마라스, 호텔 매니저
hsamaras@grecianterrace.com.gr
+30 2721 093365

어휘 Grecian 그리스풍의 gulf 만 facility 시설 spacious 넓은 overlook 내려다보다 picturesque 그림 같은 corporate 회사의, 기업의 retreat 야유회 bonding 유대 take advantage of ~을 이용하다 gourmet 고급 음식의, 미식가의 first-rate 최고의 hospitality 접객(업)

149 추론 / 암시

번역 광고는 누구를 대상으로 하는 것 같은가?
(A) 칼라마타 주민
(B) 휴가 중인 해외 방문객
(C) 기업 출장 기획자
(D) 현지 출장 요리 업체

해설 첫 문장에서 아름다운 메세니안 만에 위치한 5성급 호텔에서 다음 비즈니스 컨퍼런스를 개최하라(Host your next business conference at our five-star hotel on the beautiful Messenian Gulf)고 했고, 세 번째 문장에서 해당 호텔은 직원을 위한 회사 야유회에 완벽한 장소(The hotel is the perfect setting for a corporate retreat for your staff)라고 한 것으로 보아 기업 행사를 기획하는 사람을 대상으로 하는 광고임을 알 수 있다. 따라서 (C)가 정답이다.

어휘 resident 주민 overseas 해외의 catering 출장 요리

150 추론 / 암시

번역 그리션 테라스 호텔에 대해 암시된 것은?
(A) 최근에 식당을 개조했다.
(B) 새로운 경영진 하에 있다.
(C) 여러 지점이 있다.
(D) 해변에 인접해 있다.

해설 두 번째 문장에서 시설은 바다와 그림 같은 해변이 내려다보이는 넓은 회의실을 갖추고 있다(Our facility has spacious meeting rooms overlooking the sea and the picturesque beach)고 했으므로 호텔이 해변과 가까이 있음을 알 수 있다. 따라서 (D)가 정답이다.

어휘 renovate 개조하다 management 경영진 seaside 해변

Paraphrasing 지문의 overlooking the sea and ~ beach
→ 정답의 near the seaside

151-152 보고서

<table>
<tr><td colspan="2" align="center">151 코질레 슬리퍼스
12월 소셜 미디어 보고서</td></tr>
<tr><td align="center">측정 기준</td><td align="center">결과</td></tr>
<tr><td>이달 게시글 수</td><td>8</td></tr>
<tr><td>각 게시글당 평균 조회 수</td><td>223,648</td></tr>
<tr><td>152 각 게시글을 본 평균 개인 수</td><td>152 87,122</td></tr>
<tr><td>151 게시글당 코질레 슬리퍼스의 평균 광고 수</td><td>1</td></tr>
<tr><td>151 게시글의 광고 링크가 클릭된 평균 횟수</td><td>24,015</td></tr>
<tr><td>게시글당 평균 총 반응(좋아요, 공유 및 댓글 수)</td><td>674</td></tr>
<tr><td colspan="2" align="center">151 기업 내부 전용 데이터</td></tr>
</table>

어휘 metric 측정 기준 post 게시글 average 평균의 individual 개인 per ~당 interaction (대화형) 반응, 상호 작용 comment 댓글, 의견 corporate 기업의 internal 내부의

151 추론 / 암시

번역 보고서는 누구를 대상으로 하는 것 같은가?
(A) 코질레 슬리퍼스의 공급업체
(B) 코질레 슬리퍼스의 마케팅팀
(C) 코질레 슬리퍼스의 배송부
(D) 코질레 슬리퍼스의 가장 충실한 고객들

해설 보고서의 제목이 코질레 슬리퍼스(Cozilete Slippers) 12월 소셜 미디어 보고서(Social Media Report for December)이고 표의 측정 기준 네 번째, 다섯 번째 칸에 각각 평균 광고 수(Average number of advertisements)와 게시글의 광고 링크가 클릭된 평균 횟수(Average number ~ clicked)라고 광고 관련 정보가 나와 있으며, 보고서 하단에 기업 내부 전용 데이터(Data for corporate internal use only)라고 명시되어 있으므로 회사 외부와는 공유할 수 없는 마케팅 관련 보고서임을 알 수 있다. 따라서 (B)가 정답이다.

어휘 supplier 공급업체 loyal 충실한

152 Not / True

번역 보고서에 명시된 것은?
(A) 모든 게시글에는 코질레 슬리퍼스 광고가 하나 이상 포함되었다.
(B) 대부분의 사람들이 조회한 각각의 게시글에 댓글을 달았다.
(C) 평균 약 87,000명이 각각의 게시글을 보았다.
(D) 게시글을 한 번 이상 본 사람은 거의 없다.

해설 표의 세 번째 칸에 각 게시글을 본 평균 개인 수(Average number of individuals who viewed each post)가 87,122명이라고 나와 있으므로 (C)가 정답이다. 게시글당 코질레 슬리퍼스의 평균 광고 수(Average number of advertisements for Cozilete Slippers per post)가 1이므로 (A), 각 게시글을 본 평균 사람 수는 87,122명인데 게시글당 평균 총 반응은 674회이므로 (B), 각 게시글을 본 평균 개인 수는 87,122명인데 게시글당 평균 조회 수는 223,648회이므로 (D)는 오답이다.

어휘 contain 포함하다

153-154 문자 메시지

케리 모한 (오후 12시 40분)
보석 주문의 배송 준비 작업을 거의 끝냈습니다. 153 각 상자에 포장 전표와 명함을 넣었습니다. 밀봉해서 우체국에 가져가기 전에 포함시켜야 할 것이 또 있나요?

수제이 리시 (오후 12시 42분)
각 상자에 리시 젬스톤스 자석을 넣어 주시겠어요?

케리 모한 (오후 12시 43분)
물론이죠! 지금 바로 하겠습니다.

케리 모한 (오후 12시 50분)
그리고 154 배송 라벨이 모자랍니다. 제가 좀 더 주문하겠습니다.

수제이 리시 (오후 12시 54분)
사실, 통째로 한 통 있어요. 154 비품 창고를 확인해 보세요. 못 찾으면 알려 주세요.

어휘 ready 준비하다 insert 넣다 packing slip 패킹 슬립 (상품, 출하지 정보가 기재된 전표) business card 명함 seal up ~을 밀봉하다 drop off ~을 가져다 놓다 gemstone 보석 magnet 자석 run low on ~이 부족해지다 entire 전체의 bin 통 supply closet 비품 창고

153 세부사항

번역 모한 씨가 문의하는 것은?
(A) 상자에 포함시킬 물건
(B) 주문 발송 시기
(C) 보석을 안전하게 포장하는 방법
(D) 명함이 보관된 장소

해설 12시 40분에 모한 씨가 각 상자에 포장 전표와 명함을 넣었다(I've inserted a packing slip and business card in each box)면서 밀봉해서 우체국에 가져가기 전에 포함시켜야 할 것이 또 있는지(Should anything else be included before I seal them up ~ at the post office?)를 묻고 있으므로 (A)가 정답이다.

어휘 package 포장하다 store 보관하다

154 의도 파악

번역 오후 12시 54분에 리시 씨가 "사실, 통째로 한 통 있어요"라고 쓴 의도는?
(A) 모한 씨는 자석을 나눠줄 수 있다.
(B) 모한 씨는 비품 창고를 다시 정리할 수 있다.
(C) 모한 씨는 추가 라벨을 주문해서는 안 된다.
(D) 모한 씨는 우체국에 가서는 안 된다.

해설 12시 50분에 모한 씨가 배송 라벨이 모자라다(we're running low on shipping labels)면서 좀 더 주문하겠다(I can order some more)고 하자, 12시 54분에 리시 씨가 사실 통째로 한 통 있다(Actually, we have an entire bin of them)고 대답하며 비품 창고를 확인해 보고(Check the supply closet), 못 찾으면 알려달라(Let me know if you can't find them)고 했다. 따라서 리시 씨는 비품 창고에 라벨이 충분히 있으니 주문을 할 필요가 없다는 의도로 한 말임을 알 수 있다. 따라서 (C)가 정답이다.

어휘 give away 나누어 주다 reorganize 다시 정리하다

155-157 공지

> ### 155, 157 트윈 레이크스
> *틸러즈버그에서 가장 살기 좋은 장소!*
>
> **월례 주민 정보 회의에 트윈 레이크스 직원들과 함께해 주세요.**
>
> **일시:** 3월 21일 화요일 오후 7시 ~ 8시 30분
> **장소:** 주민센터 회의실 (임대 사무소 맞은편)
>
> **안건 및 발표자:**
> 1. 156 부지 개선: 울타리 보수 및 수영장 구역의 새로운 조경 계획에 대한 개요 — 압가리안 씨, 부지 관리 및 유지 감독관
> 2. 공동체 정원: 정원 부지 계약 및 연례 최대 토마토 콘테스트에 대한 세부 정보 — 칸터 씨, 행사 및 활동 진행 담당자
> 3. 157 휴론 가의 수도관 공사: 진행 상황 업데이트 — 카터 씨, 틸러즈버그 시 공공사업부
> 4. 공과금: 시에서 트윈 레이크스 부지 관리에 부과하는 분기별 공과금 인상에 대한 논의 — 언더우드 씨, 총괄 관리자
> 5. 신규 사업: 주민 자문 위원회 신설 — 데이비스 씨, 임대 및 주민 관계 관리자
> 6. 질문 및 의견
> 7. 휴회

어휘 resident 주민 rental 임대 agenda 안건 presenter 발표자 property 건물, 부지 enhancement 개선 overview 개요 fence 울타리 landscaping 조경 groundskeeping 부지 관리 maintenance 유지 supervisor 감독관 plot 부지, 작은 땅 sign-up 계약, 등록 annual 연례의 coordinator 진행 담당자 water main 수도관 progress 진행 utility rate 공과금 quarterly 분기별의 general 종합적인 creation 단지 advisory board 자문 위원회 leasing 임대 relation 관계 adjournment 휴회

155 추론 / 암시

번역 트윈 레이크스는 무엇일 것 같은가?
(A) 상가
(B) 원예 센터
(C) 놀이공원
(D) 주택 단지

해설 제목에 트윈 레이크스(Twin Lakes)는 틸러즈버그에서 가장 살기 좋은 장소(The best place to live in Tielersburg!)라고 했으므로 트윈 레이크스는 주거 지역임을 알 수 있다. 따라서 (D)가 정답이다.

어휘 housing 주택 complex 단지

Paraphrasing 지문의 place to live
→ 정답의 A housing complex

156 세부사항

번역 회의에서 압가리안 씨의 역할은?
(A) 예정된 개량 공사 대한 정보 제공
(B) 연례 콘테스트에 대한 세부 정보 설명
(C) 고장 난 수도관의 수리 계획
(D) 사람들이 지불할 요금 책정

해설 안건 및 발표자(Agenda items and presenters)의 첫 항목에서 부지 개선 관련 울타리 보수 및 수영장 구역의 새로운 조경 계획에 대한 개요를 부지 관리 및 유지 감독관인 압가리안 씨(Property enhancements: overview of plans for fence repair ~ Mr. Abgarian, groundskeeping and maintenance supervisor)가 발표한다고 나와 있으므로 (A)가 정답이다.

어휘 improvement 개량 (공사), 개선

Paraphrasing 지문의 enhancements
→ 정답의 improvements

157 세부사항 ▶ 동영상 강의

번역 트윈 레이크스 외부 업무 담당자는?
(A) 칸터 씨
(B) 카터 씨
(C) 언더우드 씨
(D) 데이비스 씨

해설 제목에 트윈 레이크스(Twin Lakes)는 틸러즈버그에서 가장 살기 좋은 장소(The best place to live in Tielersburg!)라고 했고, 안건 및 발표자(Agenda items and presenters)의 세 번째 항목에서 휴론 가의 수도관 공사 관련 진행 상황 업데이트를 틸러즈버그 시 공공사업부의 카터 씨(Water main work on Huron Street: progress update – Mr. Carter, Department of Public Works, City of Tielersburg)가 발표한다고 나와 있다. 따라서 트윈 레이크스는 틸러즈버그에 속하는 일부 주거 단지이고, 카터 씨는 틸러즈버그 시 전체의 공공사업을 담당하는 부서의 직원이므로 (B)가 정답이다.

158-160 공지

> **158 링게이트 화학 기업**
> **실험실 안전 규칙**
>
> **158** 다음은 실험실에 있는 동안 따라야 할 규칙의 일부 목록입니다. **158, 159** 실험실에서 작업을 시작하기 전에 또한 모든 직원은 최신 안전 규정을 읽고 기본 안전 과정을 이수해야 합니다. **159** 이러한 전제 조건을 완수해야 할 경우 강 씨에게 연락하십시오.
>
> - **160(A)** 실험실 가운, 고글, 신발 의무 착용
> - 사고에 대비하여 게시된 표지판의 지시사항 준수
> - 모든 안전 장비(소화기, 눈 세척기 등)의 올바른 작동법 숙지
> - 모든 비상구의 위치 파악
> - **160(C)** 실험실에서 음식 및 음료 섭취 삼가
> - **160(D)** 안전하지 않은 상황, 사고 또는 유출을 관리자에게 즉시 보고
> - 위급 상황 시 즉시 대피, 긴급 서비스 호출 후 관리자에게 연락
>
> ---
>
> 어휘 chemical 화학의 corporation 기업 laboratory 실험실 partial 일부의 manual 규정 prerequisite 전제 조건 mandatory 의무적인 directions 지시 in case of ~에 대비하여 accident 사고 properly 제대로 operate 작동하다 safety equipment 안전 장비 fire extinguisher 소화기 emergency exit 비상구 refrain from ~을 삼가하다 spill 유출 immediately 즉시 supervisor 관리자

158 추론 / 암시

번역 공지의 대상은 누구일 것 같은가?
(A) 학생
(B) 직원
(C) 청소부
(D) 구급 요원

해설 공지의 제목이 링게이트 화학 기업(Lingate Chemical Corporation)의 실험실 안전 규칙(Laboratory Safety Rules)이고, 첫 문장에서 다음은 실험실에 있는 동안 따라야 할 규칙의 일부 목록(The following is ~ must follow while in the laboratory)이고 실험실에서 작업을 시작하기 전에 모든 직원은 최신 안전 규정을 읽고 기본 안전 과정을 이수해야 한다(Before beginning work in the lab, all workers are also required to read ~ complete our basic safety course)고 설명하고 있다. 따라서 화학 기업의 실험실에서 일하는 직원들을 대상으로 하는 공지임을 알 수 있으므로 (B)가 정답이다.

어휘 crew 작업팀 personnel 직원

Paraphrasing 지문의 workers → 정답의 Employees

159 세부사항

번역 강 씨가 연락을 받게 될 이유는?
(A) 안전 장비를 입수하기 위해
(B) 안전하지 않은 상황을 보고하기 위해
(C) 과정 이수를 준비하기 위해
(D) 안전 규정에 대한 수정사항을 제출하기 위해

해설 두 번째 문장에서 실험실에서 작업을 시작하기 전에 모든 직원은 최신 안전 규정을 읽고 기본 안전 과정을 이수해야 한다(Before beginning work in the lab, all workers are also required to ~ complete our basic safety course)면서 이러한 전제 조건을 완수해야 할 경우 강 씨에게 연락하라(Please contact Mr. Kang if you need to complete these prerequisites)고 했다. 따라서 기본 안전 과정을 이수해야 할 경우 강 씨에게 연락해야 하는 것이므로 (C)가 정답이다.

어휘 obtain 얻다 arrange 준비하다 revision 수정

160 Not / True

번역 실험실 작업을 위해 명시된 규칙이 아닌 것은?
(A) 고글을 착용해야 한다.
(B) 출구가 열려 있어야 한다.
(C) 음식을 먹어서는 안 된다.
(D) 사고는 반드시 보고되어야 한다.

해설 실험실 안전 규칙 목록의 첫 항목에서 실험실 가운, 고글, 신발 의무 착용(Wear mandatory lab coat, goggles, and footwear)이라고 했으므로 (A), 다섯 번째 항목에서 실험실에서 음식 및 음료 섭취 삼가(Refrain from eating or drinking in the laboratory)라고 했으므로 (C), 여섯 번째 항목에서 안전하지 않은 상황, 사고 또는 유출을 관리자에게 즉시 보고(Report any unsafe conditions, accidents, or spills immediately to your supervisor)하라고 했으므로 (D)는 규칙으로 명시되었다. 출구가 열려 있어야 한다는 내용은 없으므로 (B)가 정답이다.

Paraphrasing 지문의 Refrain from eating
→ 보기 (C)의 must not be eaten

161-163 이메일

> 수신: 전 직원
> 발신: 리자 추, IT 부서
> 날짜: 6월 8일 오후 1시 13분
> **161** 제목: 네트워크 문제
>
> 안녕하세요 여러분.
>
> **161, 162** 오늘 오전 10시에 정보 기술 팀이 네트워크 유지 보수 작업을 한 결과, 건물 전체에 일련의 문제들이 발생했습니다. **162** 프린터 오작동, 누락된 네트워크 드라이브, 이메일 메시지 로딩이 잘 안되는 것을 비롯한 기타 문제들에 대해 신속하게 보고를 받았습니다.
>
> 저희가 현재 상황을 진정시켰으나 **163** 아직도 이러한 문제나 유사한 문제를 겪으실 경우 먼저 컴퓨터를 다시 시작하여 문제를 해결해 보십시오. 그렇게 한 뒤에도 문제가 지속될 경우, 저희에게 전화하십시오.
>
> ---
>
> 어휘 maintenance 유지 보수 result in ~을 초래하다 malfunction 오작동 missing 누락된 stabilize 안정시키다 encounter 맞닥뜨리다 attempt 시도하다 address 해결하다

161 주제 / 목적

번역 이메일은 무엇에 관한 것인가?
(A) 팀 회의 일정 잡기
(B) 새 이메일 계정 설정
(C) 웹 브라우징 보안에 관한 우려
(D) 컴퓨터 네트워크 관련 문제

해설 이메일의 제목이 네트워크 문제(Subject: Network issues)이고, 첫 문장에서 오늘 오전 10시에 정보 기술 팀이 네트워크 유지 보수 작업을 한 결과, 건물 전체에 일련의 문제들이 발생했다(At 10:00 this morning, the Information Technology team did some network maintenance, resulting in a series of issues across the building)고 했으므로 컴퓨터 네트워크 관련 문제에 관한 이메일임을 알 수 있다. 따라서 (D)가 정답이다.

어휘 account 계정 security 보안

Paraphrasing 지문의 issues → 정답의 Problems

162 추론 / 암시

번역 추 씨가 이메일을 보내기 전에 발생했을 것 같은 일은?
(A) 직원들이 IT 부서에 지원을 요청했다.
(B) 회사 계정에 대한 로그인 절차가 변경되었다.
(C) 컴퓨터 장비가 건물에서 제거되었다.
(D) 일부 직원들이 새 프린터를 받았다.

해설 첫 번째 단락 첫 문장에서 추 씨가 오늘 오전 10시에 정보 기술 팀이 네트워크 유지 보수 작업을 한 결과 건물 전체에 일련의 문제들이 발생했다(At 10:00 this morning, the Information Technology team did some network maintenance, resulting in a series of issues across the building)고 했고, 프린터 오작동, 누락된 네트워크 드라이브, 이메일 메시지 로딩이 잘 안되는 것을 비롯한 기타 문제들에 대해 신속하게 보고를 받았다(We quickly received reports of printer malfunctions, missing network drives, difficulty loading e-mail messages, and other problems)고 했다. 따라서 추 씨가 이메일을 보내기 전에 직원들이 IT 부서에 네트워크 문제를 보고하고 도움을 요청했다는 것을 알 수 있으므로 (A)가 정답이다.

어휘 assistance 도움, 지원 procedure 절차 remove 제거하다

163 문장 삽입

번역 [1], [2], [3], [4]로 표시된 위치 중에서 다음 문장이 들어가기에 가장 적합한 곳은?

"그렇게 한 뒤에도 문제가 지속될 경우, 저희에게 전화하십시오."
(A) [1]
(B) [2]
(C) [3]
(D) [4]

해설 주어진 문장의 after doing so가 문제 해결의 단서이다. '그렇게 한 뒤에도 문제가 지속될 경우 전화하라'는 지침을 전달하고 있으므로 주어진 문장 앞에는 'doing so'에 해당하는 문제에 대한 해결책이 제시되어 있어야 한다. 따라서 아직도 이러한 문제나 유사한 문제를 겪을 경우 먼저 컴퓨터를 다시 시작하여 문제를 해결하라(if you should

still encounter these or similar issues, please attempt first to address them by restarting your computer)는 문장 뒤인 (D)가 정답이다.

164-167 문자 메시지

수니사 소머 (오후 1시 30분)
안녕하세요 라파엘 그리고 하메드. 164 평소 B 회의실에 있는 노트북이 어디에 있는지 아는 분 계세요? 프로젝터가 놓인 카트에 없군요.

라파엘 루옹고 (오후 1시 32분)
월요일에 제가 발표에 사용하기는 했지만 회의실에 두고 나왔습니다.

하메드 가브르 (오후 1시 32분)
165, 166 노트북이 제대로 작동이 안 돼서 마틴 다블리즈가 IT 부서의 누군가에게 살펴봐 달라고 요청하려고 했던 것 같습니다.

수니사 소머 (오후 1시 34분)
알겠습니다. 수리 요청이 제출되었는지 아시나요?

하메드 가브르 (오후 1시 35분)
166 마틴이 IT 절차를 전부 알지는 못할 것 같습니다. 근무한 지 일주일밖에 안 됐거든요.

수니사 소머 (오후 1시 37분)
그렇군요. 직원 오리엔테이션 자료에 반드시 그 정보를 포함해야겠습니다.

라파엘 루옹고 (오후 1시 41분)
IT 사이트에 요청 내용이 보이지 않습니다. 167 지금 IT에 연락해서 처리하겠습니다.

어휘 properly 제대로, 적절히 repair ticket 수리 요청(서) submit 제출하다 procedure 절차 material 자료 reach out to ~에 연락을 취하다

164 주제 / 목적

번역 소머 씨가 동료들에게 메시지를 보낸 이유는?
(A) 프로젝터가 고장 났다고 알리기 위해서
(B) 컴퓨터가 어디에 있는지 묻기 위해서
(C) 프레젠테이션을 만드는 데 도움을 요청하기 위해서
(D) 회의실이 이용 가능한지 알아보기 위해서

해설 1시 30분에 소머 씨가 평소 B 회의실에 있는 노트북이 어디에 있는지 알려달라(Can either of you tell me where I can find the laptop that's usually in Conference Room B?)고 요청하고 있으므로 (B)가 정답이다.

어휘 alert (문제, 위험 등을) 알리다

Paraphrasing 지문의 laptop → 정답의 computer

165 의도 파악

번역 오후 1시 34분에 소머 씨가 "알겠습니다"라고 쓴 의도는?
(A) 수리 요청서를 찾았다.
(B) 이제 웹사이트에 접속할 수 있다.
(C) 따라야 할 올바른 절차를 알고 있다.
(D) 무슨 일이 있었는지 이해한다.

해설 1시 32분에 가브르 씨가 노트북이 제대로 작동이 안 돼서 마틴 다블리즈가 IT 부서의 누군가에게 살펴봐 달라고 요청하려고 했던 것 같다(I believe Martin Dabliz was going to ask ~ because it wasn't working properly)고 하자 1시 34분에 소머 씨가 '알겠습니다(Got it)'라고 했다. 따라서 소머 씨가 가브르 씨의 상황 설명을 이해했음을 표현하기 위해 한 말임을 알 수 있으므로 (D)가 정답이다.

어휘 access 접근

166 추론 / 암시

번역 다블리즈 씨에 대해 암시된 것은?
　(A) 최근에 고용되었다.
　(B) 가브르 씨의 상사이다.
　(C) 최고 기술 책임자이다.
　(D) 월요일에 면접을 봤다.

해설 1시 32분에 가브르 씨가 노트북이 제대로 작동이 안 돼서 마틴 다블리즈가 IT 부서의 누군가에게 살펴봐 달라고 요청하려고 했던 것 같다(I believe Martin Dabliz was going to ask ~ because it wasn't working properly)고 했고, 1시 35분에 가브르 씨가 마틴이 IT 절차를 전부 알지는 못할 것 같다(I don't think Martin knows all the IT procedures)며 근무한 지 일주일 밖에 안 됐다(He's only in his first week)고 했다. 따라서 마틴 다블리즈는 최근에 입사했다는 것을 알 수 있으므로 (A)가 정답이다.

어휘 supervisor 상사　chief technology officer 최고 기술 경영자

167 추론 / 암시

번역 루옹고 씨는 다음에 무엇을 할 것 같은가?
　(A) 회사 정책 수정하기
　(B) 직접 노트북 수리하기
　(C) IT 부서에 연락하기
　(D) 교육 자료 업데이트하기

해설 1시 41분에 루옹고 씨가 지금 IT에 연락해서 처리하겠다(I'll reach out to IT and take care of that now)고 한 것으로 보아 루옹고 씨는 곧바로 IT 부서에 연락할 것임을 알 수 있다. 따라서 (C)가 정답이다.

어휘 revise 수정하다　policy 정책

Paraphrasing 지문의 reach out to → 정답의 Contact

168-171 이메일

수신: 린지 갤러웨이 〈lgalloway@sportsupplies.com〉
발신: 새뮤얼 베인스 〈samuelbains@exertreks.com〉
날짜: 8월 16일
제목: 겨울 활동을 위한 엑서트렉스 부츠

안녕하세요 갤러웨이 씨,

168 **오늘 아침에 전화를 받지 못해서 죄송합니다. 귀하의 문의에 대한 답변은 아래와 같습니다.**

저희 엑서트렉스는 최근에 윈터 하이커스의 개발을 완료했습니다. 다른 모델과 마찬가지로 윈터 하이커스도 방수이지만 극한 추위에서 사용하기에 가장 적합합니다. 169(D) **이 부츠는 체온 유지에 매우 효과적인 전매특허 소재로 안감을 댔습니다.** 169(B), (C) **이 부츠는 또한 내구성이 좋으며 가볍고 편안합니다.** 윈터 하이커스를 50켤레 이상 주문하실 경우 한 켤레당 도매가는 65달러입니다. 권장 소매가격은 89달러입니다. 주문품은 2주 후에 배송해 드릴 수 있습니다.

아웃도어 스포츠 전문가들의 부츠에 대한 사전 판매 평가는 열광적입니다. 올해 귀하의 고객들에게 큰 170 **인기**를 끌 것으로 예상하셔도 됩니다. 171 **곧 연락 주셔서 다른 문의사항에 답변을 드리거나 첫 주문을 도와드리게 되길 기대합니다.**

새뮤얼 베인스

어휘 waterproof 방수(의)　appropriate 적합한　extreme 극한의　line 안감을 대다　proprietary 전매특허의　material 소재　effective 효과적인　retain 유지하다　durable 내구성이 있는　wholesale 도매의　per ~당　retail 소매　presale 사전 특별 판매　expert 전문가　enthusiastic 열광적인

168 추론 / 암시

번역 베인스 씨의 이메일에 암시된 것은?
　(A) 갤러웨이 씨가 그녀의 최근 주문을 확인해 달라고 요청했다.
　(B) 갤러웨이 씨가 그에게 정보를 요청하는 메시지를 남겼다.
　(C) 갤러웨이 씨에게 전날 했던 전화에 회신을 해 달라고 요청했다.
　(D) 갤러웨이 씨와 당일 오전에 만났다.

해설 첫 문장에서 베인스 씨가 갤러웨이 씨에게 오늘 아침에 전화를 받지 못해서 죄송하다(I am sorry I missed your call this morning)며 귀하의 문의에 대한 답변은 아래와 같다(The answers to your questions are given below)고 했다. 따라서 갤러웨이 씨가 오늘 아침 베인스 씨에게 문의사항이 포함된 전화 메시지를 남겼음을 알 수 있으므로 (B)가 정답이다.

169 Not / True

번역 부츠에 대해 언급되지 않은 것은?
　(A) 색깔
　(B) 무게
　(C) 내구성
　(D) 따뜻함

해설 두 번째 단락의 네 번째 문장에서 이 부츠는 내구성이 좋으며 가볍고 편안하다(They are also durable, light, and comfortable)고 했으므로 (B)와 (C), 세 번째 문장에서 이 부츠는 체온 유지에 매우 효과적인 전매특허 소재로 안감을 댔다(The boots are lined with a proprietary material that is highly effective at retaining body heat)고 했으므로 (D)는 언급이 되었다. 따라서 언급되지 않은 (A)가 정답이다.

170 동의어 찾기

번역 세 번째 단락 2행의 "hit"와 의미가 가장 가까운 단어는?

(A) 맞수

(B) 도착

(C) 성공

(D) 요청

해설 의미상 고객들에게 큰 '인기'를 끌 것이라는 뜻으로 쓰였으므로 '성공'을 뜻하는 (C) success가 정답이다.

171 세부사항

번역 베인스 씨가 갤러웨이 씨에게 원하는 것은?

(A) 온라인에서 부츠에 좋은 평가를 해 주는 것

(B) 부츠 배송을 준비해 달라고 연락하는 것

(C) 고객에게 부츠 한 켤레당 65달러를 청구하는 것

(D) 부츠에 사용될 단열재를 파는 것

해설 마지막 문장에서 베인스 씨가 갤러웨이 씨에게 곧 연락을 주어서 다른 문의사항에 답변을 하거나 첫 주문을 도와주게 되길 기대한다(I look forward to hearing from you soon to answer any other questions and to help you with your first order)고 했으므로 베인스 씨는 갤러웨이 씨가 부츠를 주문하기 위해 자신에게 연락하기를 바란다는 것을 알 수 있다. 따라서 (B)가 정답이다.

어휘 arrange 준비하다   insulation 단열

172-175 웹페이지

---

https://www.hurnhamhistoricalsociety.org/news

화요일 저녁 강연 시리즈

[172] 저희의 세 번째 연례 강연 시리즈가 헌햄 헤리티지 박물관에서 향후 6주에 걸쳐 화요일 저녁마다 개최될 것임을 알려드리게 되어 기쁩니다. [173, 175] 각각의 초청 연사는 박물관 소장품에 있는 물건들에 초점을 둘 것입니다. 여기에는 가구, 자수, 일기, 악기 및 의류와 같은 물건들이 포함됩니다. [173] 6월 15일 저녁 7시에 열리는 첫 강연에는 노울즈 아트 갤러리의 수석 큐레이터인 조지아 하인즈가 출연합니다. [174] 하인즈 씨는 글쓰기 책상, 서랍장, 그리고 가정용 탁자를 이용하여 200년 이상 전의 헌햄 초기 주민들의 삶에 대해 가구가 우리에게 무엇을 보여줄 수 있는지를 논의할 것입니다.

강연 시리즈는 일반인이 참여할 수 있으며 헌햄 헤리티지 박물관 무료 입장권이 포함됩니다. 박물관 옆에 있는 파셀러 카페는 강연 참석자와 일반 시민들이 이용할 수 있도록 화요일 늦게까지 문을 열 예정입니다.

6월 8일 게시

어휘 lecture 강연   heritage 유산   object 물건, 객체   permanent collection (영구) 소장품   feature 특별히 포함하다   chest 서랍장   household 가정의   reveal 보여 주다, 드러내다   resident 주민   public 일반 사람들, 대중   admission 입장   accommodate 수용하다   attendee 참석자   general 일반적인   post 게시하다

---

172 Not / True

번역 강연 시리즈에 대해 사실인 것은?

(A) 현대 미술과 공예를 강조한다.

(B) 월별로 행사를 잡는다.

(C) 지역 미술관들의 후원을 받는다.

(D) 3년째 제공되고 있다.

해설 첫 문장에서 세 번째 연례 강연 시리즈가 헌햄 헤리티지 박물관에서 향후 6주에 걸쳐 화요일 저녁마다 개최될 것임을 알리게 되어 기쁘다(We are pleased to announce that our third annual lecture series will be hosted ~ over the next six weeks)고 했으므로 강연 시리즈가 매년 3년째 열리고 있다는 것을 알 수 있다. 따라서 (D)가 정답이다.

어휘 highlight 강조하다   craft 공예   on a monthly basis 월별로, 월 단위로   sponsor 후원하다

> **Paraphrasing** 지문의 **third annual**
> → 정답의 **for the third year**

173 세부사항

번역 하인즈 씨가 강연할 물건의 소유자는?

(A) 헌햄 역사학회

(B) 노울즈 아트 갤러리

(C) 헌햄 헤리티지 박물관

(D) 파셀러 카페

해설 첫 단락 두 번째 문장에서 각각의 초청 연사는 박물관 소장품에 있는 물건들에 초점을 둘 것(Each guest speaker will focus on objects from the museum's permanent collection)이라고 했고, 네 번째 문장에서 6월 15일 저녁 7시에 열리는 첫 강연에는 노울즈 아트 갤러리의 수석 큐레이터인 조지아 하인즈가 출연한다(The first lecture, on June 15 at 7:00 P.M., features Georgia Hinds, head curator of the Knowles Art Gallery)고 했다. 따라서 초청 연사인 하인즈 씨가 강연에서 다루게 될 물품은 헌햄 헤리티지 박물관의 영구 소장품임을 알 수 있으므로 (C)가 정답이다.

어휘 historical 역사학의   society 학회, 협회

174 추론 / 암시

번역 헌햄 지역에 대해 암시된 것은?

(A) 100년 이상 전에 설립되었다.

(B) 노령 인구가 살고 있다.

(C) 많은 예술가들을 끌어들인다.

(D) 가구 생산의 중심지였다.

해설 첫 단락 다섯 번째 문장에서 하인즈 씨는 글쓰기 책상, 서랍장, 그리고 가정용 탁자를 이용하여 200년 이상 전의 헌햄 초기 주민들의 삶에 대해 가구가 무엇을 보여 줄 수 있는지를 논의할 것(Ms. Hinds will use ~ the lives of the first Hurnham residents over 200 years ago)이라고 했다. 따라서 헌햄 초기 주민들의 삶이 200년 이상 전에 시작되었다는 것으로 보아 헌햄 마을은 100년보다 더 전에 설립되었음을 알 수 있으므로 (A)가 정답이다.

어휘 found 설립하다   aging 노령의, 고령화의   population 인구   production 생산, 제작

175 문장 삽입

번역 [1], [2], [3], [4]로 표시된 위치 중에서 다음 문장이 들어가기에 가장 적합한 곳은?

"여기에는 가구, 자수, 일기, 악기 및 의류와 같은 물건들이 포함됩니다."

(A) [1]

(B) [2]

(C) [3]

(D) [4]

해설 주어진 문장에서 여기(These)에 가구, 자수, 일기, 악기 및 의류와 같은 물건들이 포함된다고 했으므로, 앞에는 '이것들' 즉, 가구, 의류 등의 물품을 총칭할 수 있는 명사가 복수 형태로 있어야 한다. 따라서 박물관 소장품에 있는 물건들(objects from the museum's permanent collection)이 복수명사로 언급되어 있는 문장 뒤인 (B)가 정답이다.

어휘 needlework 자수 musical instrument 악기

176-180 목차 + 서평

<리더십: 위대한 리더가 되는 것에 관한 에세이>
176 스카이밀 출판
176 조안 크리스토프 선임 편집장

목차

어휘 senior 선임의 introduction 서문 agenda 의제 matter 중요하다 low-tech 수준이 낮은[저차원적] 기술

서평: <리더십: 위대한 리더가 되는 것에 관한 에세이>

177 사업가로서, 저는 비즈니스에만 초점을 두고 있는 출판사가 있다는 점이 기쁩니다. 스카이밀 출판의 최신 도서는 모든 산업의 리더들에게 훌륭한 책입니다. 조안 크리스토프는 독자들에게 독특한 관점을 제공할 이 책을 위해 에세이를 집필할 세계 최고의 지성들을 찾았습니다. 178 자신이 쓴 서문에서 그녀는 비즈니스에 있어 더 유능한 리더에 대한 필요성이 그 어느 때보다 크다고 주장합니다.

크리스토프는 각 저자의 목소리가 서로 보완될 수 있도록 이 모음집 속 에세이들을 노련하게 배열합니다. 샤오핑 리의 에세이는 이것의 완벽한 예시입니다. 이것은 프란치스카 콩데의 행동하는 리더십과 세부적인 것에 초점을 맞춘 론 블레이크의 에세이 사이에 전략적으로 삽입되었습

니다. 180 로데릭 뮬러의 에세이는 179 유일하게 실망스러운 부분입니다. 180 놀랍게도 이 글에는 새로운 정보나 통찰력이 거의 제시되지 않았으며 문체는 다소 평이합니다. 이 외에는, 모음집은 훌륭하며 여러 다른 상황의 리더십에 관심이 있는 독자들은 그 안에서 유용한 지혜와 비전을 발견할 것입니다.

어휘 sole 유일한 latest 최신의 industry 산업 seek out ~을 찾다 mind (지성이 뛰어난) 사람, 지성(인) perspective 관점 argue 주장하다 effective 유능한 expertly 노련하게 arrange 배열하다 complement 보완하다 one another 서로 strategically 전략적으로 sandwich 사이에 끼우다 disappointment 실망 insight 통찰력 flat 평이한 nugget 작지만 가치 있는 정보 wisdom 지혜

176 세부사항

번역 목차에 따르면, 크리스토프 씨는 누구인가?

(A) 스카이밀 출판의 소유주

(B) 도서 편집자

(C) 지역 사업가

(D) 업계 선두주자

해설 목차의 상단에 스카이밀 출판(Skymill Publishing)의 조안 크리스토프 선임 편집장(Joan Cristophe, Senior Editor)이라고 나와 있으므로 크리스토프 씨는 출판사 편집자임을 알 수 있다. 따라서 (B)가 정답이다.

177 Not / True

번역 스카이밀 출판에 대해 명시된 것은?

(A) 최근에 상을 받았다.

(B) 비즈니스 도서 전문이다.

(C) 현재 채용 중이다.

(D) 첫 번째 도서를 출간할 예정이다.

해설 서평의 첫 문장에서 사업가로서 비즈니스에만 초점을 두고 있는 출판사가 있다는 점이 기쁘다(As a businessperson, I am glad there is a publisher whose sole focus is on business)며 스카이밀 출판의 최신 도서는 모든 산업의 리더들에게 훌륭한 책(Skymill Publishing's latest book is a great one for leaders in all industries)이라고 언급했다. 따라서 스카이밀 출판은 비지니스 분야를 전문으로 하는 출판사임을 알 수 있으므로 (B)가 정답이다.

어휘 specialize in ~을 전문으로 하다 release 출간하다, 발매하다

Paraphrasing 지문의 sole focus is on
→ 정답의 specializes in

178 세부사항

번역 서평에 따르면, 책 서문의 주제는?

(A) 강력한 비즈니스 리더십에 대한 현재의 필요성

(B) 유명한 비즈니스 리더들에게 배울 점

(C) 기업에서 인기 있는 교육 프로그램

(D) 효과 있는 절차 개선

해설 서평의 첫 단락 마지막 문장에서 크리스토프 씨는 서문에서 비즈니스에 있어 더 유능한 리더에 대한 필요성이 그 어느 때보다 크다고 주장한다(In her own introduction, she argues that there is a greater need than ever before for more effective leaders in business)고 했다. 따라서 유능한 비즈니스 리더의 필요성에 대한 내용이 책 서문에 다뤄지고 있는 것이므로 (A)가 정답이다.

어휘 corporation 기업 process 절차 improvement 개선

179 동의어 찾기

번역 서평에서 두 번째 단락 5행의 "sole"과 의미가 가장 가까운 단어는?
(A) 근본적인
(B) 전체의
(C) 유일한
(D) 보통의

해설 의미상 뮬러의 에세이가 '유일한' 실망이었다는 뜻으로 쓰였으므로 '유일한'을 뜻하는 (C) only가 정답이다.

180 연계 ▶ 동영상 강의

번역 새로운 정보가 눈에 띄게 적은 에세이가 시작하는 페이지는?
(A) 34페이지
(B) 51페이지
(C) 83페이지
(D) 119페이지

해설 서평의 두 번째 단락 네 번째 문장에서 로데릭 뮬러의 에세이는 유일하게 실망스러운 부분(Roderick Muller's essay is the sole disappointment)이라며 놀랍게도 이 글에는 새로운 정보나 통찰력이 거의 제시되지 않았으며 문제는 다소 평이하다(Surprisingly little new information or insight is offered on its pages, and the writing style is rather flat)고 했고, 목차의 하단에 로데릭 뮬러(Roderick Muller)의 미래 리더십 모델(Future Leadership Models)이 119 페이지부터 시작한다고 나와 있다. 따라서 새로운 정보가 거의 없는 에세이는 로데릭 뮬러의 에세이로 119 페이지부터 시작하므로 (D)가 정답이다.

어휘 notably 눈에 띄게 minimal 아주 적은

181-185 정책 + 이메일

타냐로그 인더스트리스 정책 4-02

구내식당(3층)은 오전 8시부터 오후 2시 30분까지 모든 직원과 손님들에게 열려 있습니다. 185 **구내식당의 음식은 그곳에서 먹거나 쟁반에 담아 체스트넛 실(1층), 번사이드 실(2층), 스미스 실(3층), 댄빌 실(4층) 등의 회의실로 가져갈 수 있습니다.**

점심시간에 이 회의실들을 이용하는 데는 예약이 필요하지 않습니다. 그러나 업무 회의를 위해 직원들이 이미 사용 중인 경우에는 회의실에 들어가지 마십시오. 181 **회의실 일정은 각 회의실 문 옆 디지털 패널에 표시됩니다.**

182 **사용 후 모든 음식물 및 쓰레기는 회의실에서 치워야 합니다.** 쓰레기통은 각 회의실 바로 바깥에 있습니다.

185 **에섹스 실(3층) 또는 마티넬리 실(4층)에서는 음식이나 음료가 허용되지 않습니다.**

어휘 industry 산업 reservation 예약 occupied (공간 등을) 사용 중인 display 보여 주다 remove 치우다 directly 바로

발신: 유진 라식
수신: 확장 위원회 전 위원
제목: 타냐로그 인더스트리스 확장 회의
날짜: 9월 10일

위원회 회원께,

9월 17일 월요일 확장 위원회의 첫 회의에 참석해 주십시오. 모든 참석자는 오전 10시에 마티넬리 실에 도착해야 합니다. 그리고 나서 12시에 점심 식사를 위해 쉴 것이고, 183 **무료 식사를 하기 위해 구내식당을 방문하시면 됩니다.** 184 **4번 창구에서 방문자 배지를 보여 주시기만 하면 됩니다.** 185 **모든 위원들은 구내식당 바로 옆 3층 회의실로 쟁반을 가지고 오셔야 하며, 이곳에서 오후 12시 45분부터 오후 4시까지 회의를 계속할 것입니다.**

감사합니다. 회의에서 당신의 의견을 기대합니다.

유진 라식, 확장 위원회 위원장
타냐로그 인더스트리스

어휘 expansion 확장 committee 위원회 attendee 참석자 complimentary 무료의 input 의견

181 세부사항

번역 정책에 따르면, 디지털 패널에 표시되는 것은?
(A) 곧 있을 회의의 의제
(B) 회의실 사용 규칙
(C) 회의실 이용 가능 여부에 대한 상세 정보
(D) 회의실 장비에 대한 지침

해설 정책의 두 번째 단락 마지막 문장에서 회의실 일정은 각 회의실 문 옆 디지털 패널에 표시된다(The room schedule is displayed on a digital panel by the door of each conference room)고 했으므로 (C)가 정답이다.

어휘 agenda 의제 upcoming 곧 있을 availability 이용 가능성 instruction 지침 device 장치

Paraphrasing 지문의 The room schedule
→ 정답의 a room's availability

182 세부사항

번역 회의실 사용자가 회의실을 나가기 전에 해야 할 일은?
(A) 출석부에 서명하기
(B) 문 닫기
(C) 불 끄기
(D) 청소하기

TEST 8

해설 정책의 세 번째 단락 첫 문장에서 사용 후 모든 음식물 및 쓰레기는 회의실에서 치워야 한다(All food items and trash must be removed from the conference room after use)고 했으므로 (D)가 정답이다.

어휘 attendance sheet 출석부

Paraphrasing 지문의 All food items and trash must be removed → 정답의 Clean up

183 동의어 찾기

번역 이메일에서 첫 번째 단락 4행의 "complimentary"와 의미가 가장 가까운 단어는?
(A) 무료의
(B) 건강한
(C) 호의적인
(D) 균형 잡힌

해설 의미상 '무료의' 식사라는 뜻으로 쓰였으므로 '무료의'를 뜻하는 (A) free가 정답이다.

184 세부사항

번역 위원회 위원들이 4번 창구에서 해야 할 일은?
(A) 회의 자료 수령
(B) 신분 증명서 제시
(C) 음식 주문서 제출
(D) 사용한 쟁반 반납

해설 이메일의 첫 단락 네 번째 문장에서 4번 창구에서 방문자 배지를 보여주기만 하면 된다(Just show your visitor's badge at Window 4)고 했으므로 (B)가 정답이다.

어휘 material 자료 proof 증명(서) identification 신원 확인

Paraphrasing 지문의 visitor's badge → 정답의 proof of identification

185 연계

번역 위원회 위원들이 오후 1시에 있을 것 같은 장소는?
(A) 구내식당
(B) 스미스 실
(C) 에섹스 실
(D) 마티넬리 실

해설 이메일의 첫 단락 마지막 문장에서 모든 위원들은 구내식당 바로 옆 3층 회의실로 쟁반을 가지고 와야 하며, 이곳에서 오후 12시 45분부터 오후 4시까지 회의를 계속할 것(All committee members should bring their trays to the conference room on the third floor ~ where we will continue our meeting from 12:45 P.M. until 4:00 P.M.)이라고 했고, 정책의 첫 단락 두 번째 문장에서 구내식당의 음식은 그곳에서 먹거나 쟁반에 담아 체스트넛 실(1층), 번사이드 실(2층), 스미스 실(3층), 댄빌 실(4층) 등의 회의실로 가져갈 수 있다(Food from the cafeteria may be eaten there or brought on trays to ~ Smith Room (3rd floor), and

Danville Room (4th floor))고 했으며, 마지막 문장에서 에섹스 실(3층) 또는 마티넬리 실(4층)에서는 음식이나 음료가 허용되지 않는다(No food or drink is allowed in the Essex Room (3rd floor) or the Martinelli Room (4th floor))고 했다. 따라서 위원회 위원들은 오후 1시에 음식 쟁반을 가지고 들어갈 수 있는 3층 회의실인 스미스 실에 있을 것임을 알 수 있으므로 (B)가 정답이다.

186-190 기사 + 이메일 + 이메일

업턴 공원 등산 허가증 필요

업턴 (1월 8일) — **186 5월 25일부터 등산객들은 업턴 공원의 특정 등산로에서 등산을 하는 날마다 허가증을 받아야 한다.** 지정된 등산로에는 이 지역에서 가장 인기 있는 등산 장소 중 일부가 포함된다. 허가증은 무료이며, 등산객들은 www.uptonparks.org에서 온라인으로 또는 업턴 공원 부서 사무실에서 등록하기만 하면 된다. 등록하자마자 등산객들은 출력할 수 있거나 휴대 장치로 보여 줄 수 있는 허가증을 받게 된다.

186 이 조치는 가장 많이 이용되는 등산로의 도보 통행량을 줄이기 위한 노력의 일환이지만, 일부 등산객들은 우려하고 있다. "제가 가고 싶을 때 등록증이 소진되었을 경우 가장 좋아하는 등산로에 대한 허가증을 받지 못할 수도 있어요."라고 업턴 공원 등산객인 레지나 파로니는 말한다. **188 "게다가 저는 종종 아침에 날씨를 확인하고 나서 등산하기 좋은 날인지를 결정합니다."라고 그녀는 말한다.** 허가증을 신청해야 한다면 그녀는 즉흥적으로 등산을 나서지 못할 것이다. "다른 한편으로는 특정 등산로의 등산객 수를 줄일 수 있을 겁니다."라고 파로니는 인정한다.
— EJ 하르조, 〈업턴 다이제스트〉

어휘 hiking 등산 permit 허가증 obtain 얻다 trail 등산[산책]로 designated 지정된 free of charge 무료인 register 등록하다 device 장치 move 조치 effort 노력 reduce 줄이다 foot traffic 도보 통행량 concerned 걱정하는 apply for ~을 신청하다 prevent ~ from ...ing ~이 ...을 못하게 하다[막다] spontaneous 즉흥적인 admit 인정하다

발신: 알로 고메스 〈arlog@uptonhikingclub.org〉
수신: 업턴 공원 부서 〈info@uptonparks.org〉
제목: 등산 허가증
날짜: 1월 22일

관계자 귀하,

〈업턴 나이제스트〉에서 등산객들이 곧 특정 등산로에서 등신하기 위해 허가증을 등록해야 한다고 읽었습니다. **187 업턴 등산 클럽의 운영자로서, 이것이 저희 클럽에 어떤 영향을 미칠지 더 자세히 알고 싶습니다.** 예를 들면 허가증이 필요한 등산로 목록이 있습니까? 귀하의 웹사이트를 확인했지만 찾지 못했습니다.

발급되는 허가증의 수가 등산로마다 다를 수도 있나요? **189 저희 단체 등산에는 대략 17명에서 20명 정도의 클럽 회원들이 참가합니다.** 함께 등산하려는데 허가증을 충분히 받지 못할까 걱정됩니다. 대규모 단체에 대한 특별한 배려가 있나요?

마지막으로, **188 허가증 요건으로 저희 클럽 회원들이 즉흥적으로 모여 등산을 하지 않게 될까 봐 걱정입니다.** 저희는 종종 여러 회원들이 쉬는 날이라는 것을 알게 되면 계획에 없던 등산을 합니다.

저희는 이미 봄과 여름 등산을 계획 중이기 때문에 빠른 시일 내에 답변

주시기를 바랍니다.

알로 고메스
운영자, 업턴 등산 클럽

어휘 concern 관련되다 organizer 기획자 affect 영향을
미치다 issue 발급하다 vary 다르다 participate in ~에
참가하다 consideration 배려 requirement 요건 on the
spur of the moment (계획없이) 즉흥적으로, 순간적인 기분으로

발신: 업턴 공원 부서 〈info@uptonparks.org〉
수신: 알로 고메스 〈arlog@uptonhikingclub.org〉
제목: 회신: 등산 허가증
날짜: 1월 23일
첨부: ⬗ 허가증_정보_초안

안녕하세요, 고메스 씨,

이메일 주셔서 감사합니다. 저희 웹사이트가 검색하신 정보와 관련해 아
직 업데이트되지 않았으며, 〈업턴 다이제스트〉의 기사가 명확하지 않은
점에 대해 사과드립니다. 허가증이 필요한 제안된 열두 개의 등산로 목록
과 각 등산로에 하루에 발급될 허가증의 수를 첨부했습니다. 이 목록은
다음 달에 최종 결정될 예정입니다.

허가증은 최대 2주 전까지 예약할 수 있으며 189 **대부분의 등산로에서
이용 가능한 허가증의 수는 단체 등산에 참여하는 업턴 등산 클럽 회원
수보다 훨씬 더 많습니다.** 당일 허가증을 받으실 수도 있습니다.

190 **아직 가입하지 않으셨다면 저희의 주간 소식지를 위해 저희 웹사이
트에 가입하실 수 있습니다. 그렇게 하시면 저희 정책 업데이트에 대한
사전 알림을 받으실 수 있습니다.**

제니 그리브, 홍보팀, 업턴 공원부

어휘 draft 초안 search for ~을 찾다 proposed 제안된
finalize 완결하다 reserve 예약하다 in advance 사전에
substantially 훨씬, 상당히 public relations 홍보

186 세부사항

번역 기사에 따르면, 일부 등산로에 허가증이 필요하게 될 이유는?
(A) 공원 유지를 위한 돈을 모으기 위해서
(B) 방문객들이 등산 이외의 공원 활동을 경험하도록 장려하기 위해서
(C) 등산로가 너무 붐비지 않도록 하기 위해서
(D) 가장 자주 이용되는 등산로를 알아보기 위해서

해설 기사의 첫 문장에서 5월 25일부터 등산객들은 업턴 공원의 특정 등산
로에서 등산을 하는 날마다 허가증을 받아야 한다(Starting on May
25, hikers will be required to obtain a permit ~ in Upton
parks)고 했고, 두 번째 단락 첫 문장에서 이 조치는 가장 많이 이용
되는 등산로의 도보 통행량을 줄이기 위한 노력의 일환(The move
is part of an effort to reduce foot traffic on the most used
trails)이라고 했으므로 (C)가 정답이다.

어휘 raise 모으다 maintain 유지하다 other than ~ 이외의
determine 알아내다 frequently 자주

Paraphrasing 지문의 reduce foot traffic
→ 정답의 not too crowded

---

187 주제 / 목적

번역 고메스 씨가 업턴 공원 부서에 연락한 이유는?
(A) 정보를 요청하기 위해서
(B) 등산로 지도를 획득하기 위해서
(C) 단체 허가증을 신청하기 위해서
(D) 멤버십 선택사항을 논의하기 위해서

해설 첫 번째 이메일의 두 번째 문장에서 고메스 씨가 업턴 등산 클럽의 운
영자로서 이것이 클럽에 어떤 영향을 미칠지 더 자세히 알고 싶다(As
the organizer of the Upton Hiking Club, I would like more
details on how this will affect our club)고 했다. 따라서 고메스
씨가 이메일을 쓴 이유는 좀 더 세부적인 정보를 문의하기 위한 것이
므로 (A)가 정답이다.

188 연계

번역 고메스 씨가 〈업턴 다이제스트〉 독자와 공유하는 걱정은?
(A) 너무 많은 등산로에 허가증이 필요할 것이다.
(B) 갑작스러운 허가증 입수가 불가능할 수도 있다.
(C) 등산 허가증을 받는 것이 비싸다.
(D) 야간 허가증은 단체에만 허용될 것이다.

해설 기사의 두 번째 단락 세 번째 문장에서 파로니 씨는 종종 아침에 날
씨를 확인하고 나서 등산하기 좋은 날인지를 결정한다(In addition,
I often check the weather in the morning and then decide
if it's a good day to hike)고 했고, 허가증을 신청해야 한다면 즉흥
적으로 등산을 나서지 못할 것이다(Having to apply for a permit
could prevent her from taking spontaneous hikes)고 했으며,
첫 번째 이메일의 세 번째 단락 첫 문장에서 고메스 씨는 허가증 요건
으로 클럽 회원들이 즉흥적으로 모여 등산을 하지 않게 될까 봐 걱정(I
am concerned that the permit requirement will not allow
our club members to get together for a hike on the spur
of the moment)이라고 했다. 따라서 고메스 씨와 〈업턴 다이제스
트〉 독자는 즉흥적으로 갑자기 등산을 가고 싶을 때 허가증을 못 받을
수도 있는 점을 공통적으로 걱정하고 있으므로 (B)가 정답이다.

어휘 last-minute 막판의, 마지막 순간의 overnight 야간의

189 연계

번역 대부분의 등산로에 제공될 것 같은 허가증의 수는?
(A) 12개 미만
(B) 12개에서 17개 사이
(C) 18개에서 20개 사이
(D) 20개 이상

해설 두 번째 이메일의 두 번째 단락 첫 문장에서 대부분의 등산로에서 이
용 가능한 허가증의 수는 단체 등산에 참여하는 업턴 등산 클럽 회
원 수보다 훨씬 더 많다(the number of permits available for
most trails is substantially higher than the number of
Upton Hiking Club members who join your group hikes)고
했고, 첫 이메일의 두 번째 단락 두 번째 문장에서 단체 등산에는 대략
17명에서 20명 정도의 클럽 회원들이 참가한다(About seventeen
to twenty club members participate in our group hikes)고
했다. 따라서 대부분의 등산로 허가증은 업턴 등산 클럽의 단체 등산
참여 회원 수인 20명보다 많이 발급된다는 것이므로 (D)가 정답이다.

TEST 8

190 세부사항

번역 두 번째 이메일에 따르면, 소식지가 제공하는 것은?
(A) 업턴 등산 클럽이 작성한 기사
(B) 등산로 상태에 대한 세부정보
(C) 정책 변경에 대한 정보
(D) 추가 허가증 입수

해설 두 번째 이메일의 마지막 단락의 첫 문장에서 아직 가입하지 않았다면 주간 소식지를 위해 웹사이트에 가입할 수 있다(If you have not already done so, you can sign up on our Web site for our weekly newsletter)며 그렇게 하면 정책 업데이트에 대한 사전 알림을 받을 수 있다(Doing so will ensure that you get advance notice of any updates to our policies)고 했으므로 (C)가 정답이다.

Paraphrasing 지문의 updates → 정답의 changes

191-195 예약 내역 + 이메일 + 이메일

유어 무브 차량 대여 회사

예약 번호: 15288242

인수 장소: 인디애나주 먼시 센테니얼 로 2833, 47303

191, 192 일시: 10월 31일 오전 10시

반납 장소: 인수 장소와 동일

191 일시: 10월 31일 오후 6시 30분

차량 설명: 5미터 이삿짐 밴

192 예약을 변경해야 할 경우, 예정된 인수일로부터 3일 전까지 고객님의 온라인 계정을 통해 하실 수 있습니다. 그 이후에는 reservations@yourmove.com의 고객 지원 센터로 연락 주세요. 이메일 제목에 고객님의 예약 번호를 입력해 주세요.

어휘 reservation 예약 drop-off (사물을) 가져다 놓는 것 description 설명 via ~을 통해 support 지원 subject 제목

수신: reservations@yourmove.com
발신: selina_os@chestnutmail.com
192 날짜: 10월 29일
제목: 예약 15288242

안녕하세요,

195 온라인으로 이삿짐 밴을 예약했는데 150달러의 견적 가격을 받았습니다. 그런데 제가 실수로 인수와 반납 모두 같은 장소로 잘못 기재했습니다. 컴벌랜드에 있는 저의 목적지에 더 가까운 반납 장소가 있는지 알고 싶습니다. 만약 있다면, **192 예약 변경을 도와 주실 수 있을까요?**

셀리나 오스만

어휘 estimated 견적의 mistakenly 실수로, 잘못하여 destination 목적지

수신: selina_os@chestnutmail.com
발신: reservations@yourmove.com
날짜: 10월 30일
193 제목: 회신: 예약 15288242

오스만 씨께,

저희는 컴벌랜드로부터 차로 약 10분 거리인 인디애나폴리스 바로 외곽에 대여 사무소를 두고 있습니다. 그곳이 반납 장소라면 먼시의 출발 지점에서부터 약 90km를 운전하게 될 것입니다. 이에 근거하여 **195 다음과 같이 귀하의 가격 견적서를 업데이트하였습니다.**

194 대여: 5미터 이삿짐 밴 1일 = 39.99달러

194 대여: 바퀴 달린 가구 카트 = 6.99달러

대여: 가구 완충재 (12개 세트) = 9.99달러

거리: 1km당 1.05달러 = 94.5달러 (90km 추정)

차량 손해 보험 = 19.99달러

195 총액 = 171.46달러

이 총액에는 세금이 포함되지 않았다는 점에 유의해 주십시오. 최종 가격은 실제 주행 거리에 따라 달라질 수 있으며 차량이 반납 장소에 반환되면 계산됩니다. 그때까지 접수된 귀하의 신용 카드에는 대여 장비에 대해서만 청구됩니다.

193 알리스테어 먼
유어 무브 차량 대여 회사

어휘 based on ~에 근거하여 price estimate 가격 견적(서) as follows 다음과 같이 wheeled 바퀴 달린 pad 완충재 distance 거리 damage 손해 insurance 보험 vary 다르다 actual 실제의 calculate 계산하다 on file 기록된 charge 청구하다

---

191 세부사항

번역 차량이 대여될 시기는?
(A) 10월 28일
(B) 10월 29일
(C) 10월 30일
(D) 10월 31일

해설 예약 내역의 첫 단락 세 번째 항목에 인수 일시는 10월 31일 오전 10시(Date and Time: October 31, 10:00 A.M.), 다섯 번째 항목에 반납 일시는 10월 31일 오후 6시 30분(Date and Time: October 31, 6:30 P.M.)이라고 나와 있는 것으로 보아 차를 대여하는 날짜는 10월 31일이므로 (D)가 정답이다.

192 연계

번역 오스만 씨에 대해 결론지을 수 있는 것은?
(A) 이전에 같은 대여 회사를 이용한 적이 있다.
(B) 오랫동안 이사를 계획해 왔다.
(C) 대여 계약서를 꼼꼼히 읽지 않았다.
(D) 온라인으로 예약을 변경할 수 없었다.

해설 예약 내역의 첫 단락 세 번째 항목에 인수 일시가 10월 31일 오전 10시(Date and Time: October 31, 10:00 A.M.)라고 나와 있고 두 번째 단락 첫 문장에서 예약을 변경해야 할 경우 예정된 인수일로부터 3일 전까지 온라인 계정을 통해 할 수 있다(If you need to change your reservation, you can do so via your online account until three days before your scheduled pickup)며 그 이후에는 reservations@yourmove.com의 고객 지원 센터로 연락하라(After that point, contact customer support at reservations@yourmove.com)고 했고, 오스만 씨가 작성한 첫 이메일의 작성 날짜가 10월 29일(October 29)이고 마지막 문장에서 예약 변경을 도와줄 수 있는지(can you please help me update the reservation?)를 묻고 있다. 차량 인수 예정일인 10월 31일로부터 2일 전인 29일에 이메일이 작성된 것으로 보아 오스만 씨는 온라인으로 예약을 변경할 수 없었다는 것을 알 수 있으므로 (D)가 정답이다.

어휘 previously 이전에 agreement 계약서

193 세부사항

번역 먼 씨는 누구인가?
(A) 가구 운송업자
(B) 차량 보험 설계사
(C) 예약 담당자
(D) 보관 시설 관리자

해설 두 번째 이메일에서 회신 제목이 예약 15288242(RE: Reservation 15288242)이고, 하단 서명이 알리스테어 먼(Alistair Muhn), 유어 무브 차량 대여 회사(Your Move Vehicle Rental Company)라고 나와 있으므로 먼 씨는 유어 무브 차량 대여 회사 소속이며 예약 관련 문의 이메일에 회신하고 있는 것으로 보아 예약 담당 업무를 하고 있다는 것을 알 수 있다. 따라서 (C)가 정답이다.

어휘 storage 보관, 저장 facility 시설

194 Not / True

번역 가구 카트에 대해 명시된 것은?
(A) 대여료가 하루에 6.99달러이다.
(B) 반납할 필요가 없다.
(C) 쉽게 운반할 수 있도록 접힌다.
(D) 세트의 일부이다.

해설 두 번째 이메일의 두 번째 단락 첫 항목에서 5미터 이삿짐 밴 대여 가격이 1일 (Rental: 5-meter moving van for 1 day) 기준이라고 나와 있고, 두 번째 항목에 바퀴 달린 가구 카트 대여 비용이 6.99달러(Rental: wheeled furniture cart = $6.99)라고 나와 있다. 따라서 카트 대여는 1일간이며 그 비용은 6.99달러이므로 (A)가 정답이다.

어휘 fold up 접히다 transport 운송

195 연계

번역 새로운 비용 견적에 대해 사실인 것은?
(A) 원래 견적액보다 높다.
(B) 즉시 완납되어야 한다.
(C) 연료비가 포함되어 있다.
(D) 3일 후에 만료된다.

해설 두 번째 이메일의 첫 단락 마지막 문장에서 다음과 같이 가격 견적서를 업데이트하였다(we have updated your price estimate as follows)고 했고, 총액이 171.46달러(Total = $171.46)라고 나와 있으며, 첫 이메일의 첫 문장에서 온라인으로 이삿짐 밴을 예약했는데 150달러의 견적 가격을 받았다(I reserved a moving van online and was given an estimated price of $150)고 했다. 따라서 새로 업데이트된 견적 비용은 기존의 150달러보다 높은 금액이므로 (A)가 정답이다.

어휘 immediately 즉시 fuel 연료 expire 만료되다

196-200 이메일 + 이메일 + 웹페이지

수신: 김순이
발신: 프랭크 주비리
날짜: 2월 12일
제목: 환영합니다

김 씨께,

자코비 테크놀로지스의 영업팀에 합류하신 것을 환영합니다! **198 첫 근무일은 2월 28일 월요일입니다.** 오전 9시에 네이퍼빌에 있는 자코비 서클 1의 그린 빌딩으로 오세요. 당신의 팀장인 소피아 홀랜드가 첫날 동안 지도해 줄 것입니다. 다음은 예상 일정에 대한 개요입니다.

1. 고용 계약서에 서명하고 사원증을 받으세요.

2. 옐로 빌딩 4층에 있는 배정된 자리를 방문하세요.

3. **196 옐로 빌딩 회의실에서 팀원들과 함께하는 오찬에 참석하세요.**

4. **198 다른 신입 사원들과 캠퍼스 안내 투어에 참여하세요.** 며칠 안에 이에 관한 이메일을 확인하세요.

프랭크 주비리
선임 이사, 인사부

어휘 supervisor 관리자 outline 개요 employment 고용 contract 계약서 assigned 배정된 cubicle (칸막이로 된) 사무실 자리[구획] luncheon 오찬 new hire 신입 사원

수신: 신입 사원 배정 목록
발신: 토루 하다
날짜: 2월 15일
제목: 캠퍼스 투어 날짜

다음 투어 날짜는 2월 21일과 28일, 3월 7일과 14일입니다. 신청하시려면 이 이메일에 귀하의 이름과 시작일에 해당하는 날짜를 회신해 주십시오. **198 투어는 오후 3시에 시작하여 약 한 시간 동안 진행됩니다.** 오후 3시 몇 분 전에 블루 빌딩 로비에서 저를 만나세요. 블루 빌딩은 그린 빌딩과 옐로 빌딩 사이의 자코비 서클에 있습니다. **199 투어에는 실험실, 지속 가능한 발전소, 모든 직원 편의 시설 방문이 포함됩니다.**

197 시작일, 투어, 또는 신입 사원 교육 자료에 대한 문의사항이 있으시면 주저하지 말고 저에게 연락하세요.

어휘 distribution 배정 sign up 신청하다 corresponding to ~에 해당하는 last 지속되다 sustainable 지속 가능한 power plant 발전소 amenities 편의 시설 onboarding 신입 사원 적응 교육 과정 material 자료 hesitate 망설이다

자코비 테크놀로지스는 스마트 TV, 노트북 컴퓨터 및 기타 전자 기기에 전원을 공급하는 첨단 마이크로프로세서를 개발, 제조 및 판매합니다. 200 **일리노이 주 네이퍼빌에 8,000명 이상의 직원이 있고, 로드아일랜드의 프로비던스에 4,000명 이상의 직원을 더 두고 있습니다.**

자코비 테크놀로지스는 1950년에 900에이커 규모의 네이퍼빌 부동산을 인수했습니다. 그 이후로, 열 개의 친환경 건물과 폐자원 에너지 발전소를 포함한 지속 가능한 기반 시설을 건설하는 데 30억 달러 이상을 투자했습니다. 최첨단 연구실과 생산 시설 외에도, 199 **캠퍼스는 두 개의 카페, 체육관, 야외 농구장과 테니스장, 보육 센터를 포함하여 직원들을 위한 특별한 편의 시설을 자랑합니다.**

어휘 manufacture 제조하다 advanced 첨단의 power 동력을 공급하다 electronic device 전자 기기 acquire 인수하다 property 부동산 invest 투자하다 construct 건설하다 earth-friendly 환경[지구] 친화적인 infrastructure 기반 시설 waste-to-energy 폐자원 에너지화 state-of-the-art 최첨단의 facility 시설 boast 자랑하다 childcare 보육

196 세부사항

번역 첫 번째 이메일에 따르면, 김 씨가 근무 첫날 할 일 중 하나는?
(A) 회사 소프트웨어 사용법 배우기
(B) 신입 사원을 위한 동영상 보기
(C) 팀과 함께 식사하기
(D) 노트북 컴퓨터 받기

해설 첫 이메일의 예상 일정 개요의 세 번째 항목에서 김 씨에게 옐로 빌딩 회의실에서 팀원들과 함께하는 오찬에 참석하라(Attend a luncheon with members of your team in the Yellow Building conference room)고 했으므로 (C)가 정답이다.

Paraphrasing   지문의 luncheon → 정답의 meal

197 추론 / 암시

번역 하다 씨는 누구일 것 같은가?
(A) 인사부 직원
(B) 영업팀장
(C) 기술 전문가
(D) 카페 종업원

해설 두 번째 이메일의 마지막 문장에서 하다 씨가 시작일, 투어, 또는 신입 사원 교육 자료에 대한 문의사항이 있으면 주저하지 말고 본인에게 연락하라(Should you have any questions about your start day, the tour, or any of the employee onboarding materials, please do not hesitate to contact me)고 하는 것으로 보아 하다 씨는 신입 사원들의 출근 및 교육 등의 직원 관리 업무를 담당하는 인사부 직원임을 알 수 있다. 따라서 (A)가 정답이다.

198 연계

번역 김 씨는 2월 28일 오후 3시에 어디에 있을 것 같은가?
(A) 옐로 빌딩에 있는 그녀의 자리
(B) 블루 빌딩의 로비
(C) 옐로 빌딩 회의실
(D) 홀랜드 씨의 사무실

해설 첫 이메일의 첫 단락 두 번째 문장에서 김 씨에게 첫 근무일은 2월 28일 월요일(Your first day is Monday, February 28)이며, 예상 일정 개요의 네 번째 항목에서 다른 신입 사원들과 캠퍼스 안내 투어에 참여하라(Join other new hires for a guided tour of the campus)고 했고, 두 번째 이메일의 세 번째 문장에서 투어는 오후 3시에 시작하여 약 한 시간 동안 진행된다(Tours begin at 3:00 P.M. and last about an hour)며 오후 3시 몇 분 전에 블루 빌딩 로비에서 만나자(Please meet me in the Blue Building lobby a few minutes before 3:00 P.M.)고 했다. 따라서 김 씨는 첫 근무일인 2월 28일 오후 3시에 블루 빌딩 로비에서 투어에 참여할 예정이므로 (B)가 정답이다.

199 연계

번역 자코비 테크놀로지스의 안내 투어에 대해 암시된 것은?
(A) 직원과 직원이 아닌 사람 모두 참여할 수 있다.
(B) 실내와 실외 모두를 방문한다.
(C) 대략 두 시간 정도 진행된다.
(D) 연구원 한 명의 짧은 담화가 포함된다.

해설 두 번째 이메일의 첫 단락 마지막 문장에서 투어에는 실험실, 지속 가능한 발전소, 모든 직원 편의 시설 방문이 포함된다(The tour will include stops at the labs ~ and all employee amenities)고 했고, 웹페이지의 마지막 문장에서 캠퍼스는 두 개의 카페, 체육관, 야외 농구장과 테니스장, 보육 센터를 포함하여 직원들을 위한 특별한 편의 시설을 자랑한다(the campus boasts special amenities ~ outdoor basketball and tennis courts, and a childcare center)고 했다. 따라서 투어에서 방문하게 될 직원 편의 시설에는 실내 외에도 야외 농구장과 테니스장도 포함되므로 (B)가 정답이다.

어휘 approximately 대략 brief 짧은

200 Not / True

번역 웹페이지에 따르면, 자코비 테크놀로지스에 대해 사실인 것은?
(A) 곧 보육 시설을 열 것이다.
(B) 10년 전에 네이퍼빌 부동산을 인수했다.
(C) 직원들에게 회사 체육관 이용료를 청구한다.
(D) 두 곳 이상의 캠퍼스를 운영한다.

해설 웹페이지의 첫 단락 두 번째 문장에서 일리노이 주 네이퍼빌에 8,000명 이상의 직원이 있고 로드아일랜드의 프로비던스에 4,000명 이상의 직원을 더 두고 있다(The company has more than 8,000 employees in Naperville, Illinois, and another 4,000 in Providence, Rhode Island)고 했다. 따라서 두 지역에 캠퍼스가 있는 것이므로 (D)가 정답이다.

어휘 charge 청구하다

기출 TEST 9

동영상 강의

101 (B)	**102** (B)	**103** (D)	**104** (B)	**105** (B)
106 (D)	**107** (D)	**108** (C)	**109** (D)	**110** (A)
111 (C)	**112** (A)	**113** (A)	**114** (A)	**115** (B)
116 (A)	**117** (C)	**118** (C)	**119** (A)	**120** (C)
121 (A)	**122** (A)	**123** (D)	**124** (B)	**125** (A)
126 (D)	**127** (D)	**128** (D)	**129** (A)	**130** (A)
131 (C)	**132** (C)	**133** (B)	**134** (B)	**135** (D)
136 (D)	**137** (B)	**138** (C)	**139** (C)	**140** (A)
141 (B)	**142** (A)	**143** (A)	**144** (B)	**145** (C)
146 (D)	**147** (A)	**148** (D)	**149** (B)	**150** (D)
151 (B)	**152** (B)	**153** (C)	**154** (A)	**155** (A)
156 (B)	**157** (B)	**158** (D)	**159** (D)	**160** (B)
161 (C)	**162** (B)	**163** (D)	**164** (B)	**165** (C)
166 (B)	**167** (D)	**168** (A)	**169** (B)	**170** (C)
171 (A)	**172** (D)	**173** (D)	**174** (C)	**175** (C)
176 (D)	**177** (B)	**178** (C)	**179** (A)	**180** (C)
181 (B)	**182** (C)	**183** (B)	**184** (D)	**185** (D)
186 (D)	**187** (A)	**188** (B)	**189** (D)	**190** (C)
191 (C)	**192** (C)	**193** (C)	**194** (B)	**195** (D)
196 (C)	**197** (D)	**198** (B)	**199** (A)	**200** (A)

PART 5

101 부사 자리 _ 준동사 수식

해설 주어가 Mr. Liu, 동사가 is known인 완전한 문장에서 빈칸은 전치사 for의 목적어 역할을 하는 동명사 negotiating을 수식하는 부사 자리이므로 '차분하게'라는 의미인 부사 (B) calmly가 정답이다. (A) calm은 형용사, (C) calmest는 형용사 calm의 최상급, (D) calmness는 명사이므로 품사상 답이 될 수 없다.

번역 류 씨는 직원들의 분쟁을 차분하게 조정하는 것으로 유명하다.

어휘 negotiate 조정하다, 협상하다 dispute 분쟁 calm 차분한 calmness 고요, 침착

102 전치사 자리

해설 빈칸은 시간 명사구 January 25를 목적어로 취하는 전치사 자리이므로, '~까지'라는 의미의 전치사 (B) until이 정답이다. (A) when은 부사절 접속사, (C) a few는 수량 형용사/대명사, (D) whether는 명사절 접속사이므로 품사상 빈칸에 들어갈 수 없다.

번역 시는 1월 25일까지 오시다 공원의 재설계를 위한 기획안을 접수하고 있다.

어휘 accept 접수하다, 받다 proposal 제안 redesign 재설계

103 명사 자리 _ 동사의 주어

해설 동사 maintain과 provide의 주어 역할을 하는 명사 자리로, 빈칸 앞의 Sales와 함께 '판매 보조원'이라는 의미의 복합명사를 만들 수 있는 (D) assistants가 정답이다. (A) assists는 '돕다'라는 뜻의 동사, (B) assisted는 동사/과거분사이므로 품사상 답이 될 수 없다. (C) assisting은 동명사/현재분사 외에도 '보조'라는 뜻의 명사로 쓰일 수 있지만 단수동사를 취하므로 답이 될 수 없다.

번역 판매 보조원은 고객 파일을 관리하고 물류 지원을 제공한다.

어휘 maintain 유지하다 logistical 물류에 관한 support 지원

104 동사 어휘

해설 작가가 출연하는 도서관 행사를 설명하는 문장이므로 문맥상 '작가가 어린 시절 이야기를 나눌 것'이라는 내용이 되어야 자연스럽다. 따라서 '(자신의 생각, 경험 등을) 말하다, 함께 나누다'라는 의미의 (B) sharing이 정답이다. (A)의 divide는 '(여러 부분으로) 나누다', (C)의 use는 '사용하다', (D)의 award는 '수여하다'라는 의미이다.

번역 오늘 밤 하버 폴스 도서관에서 델로이 그린 작가는 자메이카에서의 어린 시절 이야기를 들려줄 예정이다.

어휘 childhood 어린 시절

105 인칭대명사의 격 _ 소유격

해설 빈칸은 to부정사 to attend의 목적어로 쓰인 복합명사 retirement party를 수식하는 자리이다. 따라서 명사 앞에 쓰여 한정사 역할을 할 수 있는 소유격 인칭대명사 (B) his가 정답이다.

번역 캠 씨는 그의 은퇴식에 직원 모두를 초대했다.

106 명사 어휘

해설 빈칸은 four plays와 and로 연결되어 동사 will produce의 목적어 역할을 하는 명사 자리이므로 문맥상 '연극(plays)'처럼 극장에서 제작하는 공연의 종류가 와야 한다. 따라서 '뮤지컬'을 뜻하는 (D) musicals가 정답이다. (A)의 actor는 '배우', (B)의 audience는 '청중', (C)의 ticket은 '입장권'을 의미한다.

번역 디트로이트 시내에 있는 스탠리 포인트 극장은 다음 시즌에 연극 네 편과 뮤지컬 세 편을 제작할 예정이다.

107 현재분사

▶ 동영상 강의

해설 빈칸 앞에 There is enough money라는 완전한 절이 있고, 빈칸부터 budget까지는 money를 수식하는 수식어구이다. 따라서 '남아 있는'이라는 의미로 명사 money를 뒤에서 수식할 수 있는 현재분사 (D) remaining이 정답이다. (A) remains는 동사이므로 품사상 빈칸에 들어갈 수 없고, (B) remainder는 '나머지'를 뜻하는 명사로 money와 함께 복합명사를 이루기에 어색하며, 자동사인 remain은 수동형이 없기 때문에 과거분사 형태로 명사를 수식하지 않으므로 (C) remained는 답이 될 수 없다.

번역 여행 경비를 충당할 돈이 예산에 충분히 남아 있다.

어휘   budget 예산   cover (비용을) 충당하다, 대다   expense 비용

108   전치사 자리 / 어휘

해설   빈칸은 명사구인 the same day를 목적어로 취하는 전치사 자리
이다. 문맥상 '같은 날에'라는 내용이 되어야 자연스러우므로 날이나
날짜, 요일 앞에 쓰여 '~에'를 뜻하는 전치사 (C) on이 정답이다. 전
치사 (B) into(~ 속으로)와 (A) as(~로서, ~같이)는 문맥상 적절하
지 않고, (D) once는 접속사/부사이므로 품사상 답이 될 수 없다.

번역   롬 인더스트리스 직원들은 같은 날 고용된 아홉 명의 새로운 직장 동
료들을 교육했다.

어휘   associate (직장) 동료

109   전치사 자리 / 어휘

해설   빈칸은 명사구 his 40-year career를 목적어로 취해 빈칸 앞
의 완전한 절(Taylor Kanagawa wrote several books ~
management)을 수식하는 전치사 자리이다. his 40-year
career가 기간을 나타내는 명사이고, 문맥상 '그가 40년 근무하는
동안'이라는 의미가 되어야 자연스러우므로 '~ 동안'을 뜻하는 (D)
during이 정답이다. during과 같은 의미를 지닌 (B) while은 부사절
접속사로 완전한 절이 뒤따라야 하므로 오답이고, (A) between은 '둘
사이에'라는 뜻으로 두 시점 사이를 나타내며, (C) beside는 '~ 옆에'
라는 의미로 시간 명사와 어울리지 않으므로 답이 될 수 없다.

번역   테일러 카나가와는 샙 출판사에서 40년 근무하는 동안 효과적인 팀
운영에 관한 책을 여러 권 집필했다.

어휘   effective 효과적인   publisher 출판사

110   명사 어휘

해설   to부정사 to improve의 목적어 역할을 하는 명사 자리로, 빈칸 앞
의 명사 health와 함께 쓰여 '건강 상태[결과]'라는 의미의 복합명사
를 만들 수 있는 '결과'라는 뜻의 (A) outcomes가 정답이다. (B)의
reason은 '이유', (C)의 correction은 '정정', (D)의 grade는 '등급'
이라는 의미이다.

번역   지역 사회 진료 사업은 고립된 지역의 건강 상태를 향상시키기 위해
고안되었다.

어휘   clinic 진료, 병원   project 사업, 프로젝트   improve
향상[개선]하다   isolated 고립된

111   형용사 자리 _ 명사 수식

해설   빈칸은 동사 will be hiring의 목적어 역할을 하는 명사 employees
를 수식하는 형용사 자리이다. '200명의 추가 직원'이라는 의미가 되
어야 자연스러우므로 '추가의'라는 뜻의 형용사 (C) additional이 정
답이다. (A) add는 동사, (D) additionally는 부사이므로 품사상 답
이 될 수 없고, 동명사/현재분사인 (B) adding은 현재분사로 쓰이는
경우 주로 목적어를 취해 '~을 더하는'이라는 뜻으로 명사를 뒤에서
수식하므로 빈칸에 적절하지 않다.

번역   징쎈 항공은 내년에 200명의 추가 직원을 채용할 예정이라고 발표
했다.

어휘   announce 발표하다   additionally 추가적으로

112   부사 어휘

해설   의문부사 how가 이끄는 명사절에서 동사 operated를 수식하여 적
절한 문맥을 완성하는 부사를 고르는 문제이다. '기계를 능숙하게 조
작하는 것에 감탄하다'라는 의미가 되어야 자연스러우므로 '능숙하게'
라는 뜻의 (A) skillfully가 정답이다. (B) primarily는 '주로', (C)
obviously는 '분명히', (D) richly는 '풍부하게'라는 의미이다.

번역   고객은 슈미드 씨가 복잡한 기계를 능숙하게 조작하는 것에 감탄
했다.

어휘   impressed 감명받은   operate 조작하다   complicated 복잡한
machinery 기계

113   명사 어휘

해설   문맥상 '일련의 행사에 참여한다'는 내용이 되어야 자연스러우므로, 부
정관사 a와 전치사 of와 함께 관용어구 a series of를 만드는 '일련,
연속'이라는 뜻의 (A) series가 정답이다. a series of(일련의) 형태
로 암기해 두자. (B) status는 '지위, 상태', (C) theory는 '이론', (D)
guest는 '손님'이라는 의미이다.

번역   직원들은 5월 첫째 주 동안 일련의 친목 행사에 참여하도록 초대받
는다.

어휘   participate in ~에 참여하다   social 친목[사교]를 위한

114   형용사 어휘

해설   빈칸은 that절의 주어 Solcus Corporation을 보충 설명하는 보어
자리로, 문맥상 '비용을 책임진다'는 내용이 되어야 자연스럽다. 따라
서 빈칸 뒤의 전치사 for와 함께 쓰여 '~에 대해 책임이 있는'이라는
뜻을 나타내는 (A) accountable이 정답이다. (B) manageable은
'관리할 수 있는', (C) knowledgeable은 '많이 아는', (D) flexible은
'유연한'이라는 뜻으로 문맥상 적절하지 않다.

번역   계약서에는 솔커스 사가 업무 지연으로 인한 비용을 책임진다고 명시
되어 있다.

어휘   state 명시하다   result from ~이 원인이다   delay 지연

115   부사 자리 _ 동사 수식

해설   동사구 was influenced를 수식하는 부사 자리이므로 '(정도 등이)
많이, 심하게'라는 뜻의 부사 (B) heavily가 정답이다. (A) heavy는
형용사, (C) heaviest는 heavy의 최상급, (D) heavier는 비교급으로
품사상 빈칸에 들어갈 수 없다.

번역   민 판 작가의 최신 소설은 베트남 민간 설화의 영향을 많이 받았다.

어휘   latest 최신의   influence 영향을 미치다   folk story 민간 설화

116 부사 자리 / 어휘 _ 동사 수식

해설 빈칸은 주어 it과 자동사 opens로 이루어진 완전한 절 뒤에서 동사 opens를 수식하는 자리이므로 부사가 들어가야 한다. 문맥상 앞으로 일어날 일을 예상하는 것으로 '박물관이 곧 개관하면'이라는 내용이 되어야 하므로 '곧'이라는 뜻의 부사 (A) soon이 정답이다. (B) as는 전치사/접속사, (D) initial은 '초기의'라는 뜻의 형용사로 품사상 답이 될 수 없고, (C) almost는 부사로 동사나 형용사를 주로 앞에서 수식하므로 빈칸에 적절하지 않다.

번역 홋카이도 미카사에 있는 소라치 디스커버리 박물관이 곧 개관하면 관광객들이 몰릴 것으로 예상된다.

어휘 flock to ~에 몰려 들다

117 형용사 어휘

해설 명사 sections를 수식하기에 적절한 형용사를 골라야 한다. 동사 is divided into와 함께 '네 개의 뚜렷이 다른 구역으로 나뉜다'는 내용이 되어야 자연스러우므로 '뚜렷이 다른, 별개의'라는 뜻의 (C) distinct가 정답이다. (A) previous는 '이전의', (B) eligible은 '적격의', (D) installed는 '설치된'이라는 뜻으로 의미상 어울리지 않는다.

번역 공장의 작업 현장은 제품 조립의 각 단계별로 네 개의 뚜렷이 다른 구역으로 나뉜다.

어휘 divide 나누다 section 구획 stage 단계 assembly 조립

118 전치사 어휘

해설 빈칸 뒤에 시간을 나타내는 명사 the lunch break가 있고, 문맥상 '점심시간 전에 준비되어야 한다'라는 의미가 되어야 자연스러우므로 '~ 전에'를 뜻하는 전치사 (C) before가 정답이다. (A) down(~ 아래로), (B) beside(~ 옆에), (D) off(~에서 떨어져)는 장소 명사와 어울리는 전치사로 문맥상 빈칸에 적절하지 않다.

번역 오후 세미나를 위한 유인물은 점심시간 전에 준비되어야 한다.

어휘 handout 유인물, 인쇄물

119 명사절 접속사

해설 빈칸에는 동사 will determine의 목적어 역할을 하는 명사절을 이끄는 접속사가 들어가야 한다. 빈칸 뒤에 완전한 절(the company will open ~ stores)이 있고, 문맥상 '추가 점포를 열지 말지를 결정할 것'이라는 내용이 되어야 하므로 '~인지 아닌지'라는 뜻의 명사절 접속사 (A) whether가 정답이다. (B) who는 의문사로 명사절 접속사 역할을 할 수 있지만 주어가 빠진 불완전한 문장을 이끄므로 오답이고, (C) since는 전치사/부사절 접속사이므로 빈칸에 들어갈 수 없다. (D) that은 완전한 절을 이끄는 명사절 접속사이기는 하지만 '~한 것'이라는 뜻으로 확정된 사실을 나타낼 때 쓰이므로 미확정 상황인 will determine의 목적어로 적절하지 않다.

번역 챗 모바일은 연말 매출액에 근거해 추가 점포를 열지 여부를 결정할 것이다.

어휘 determine 결정하다 based on ~에 근거하여

120 동사 어형 _ 조동사 + 동사원형

해설 조동사 will 뒤에는 동사원형이 와야 하므로 (C) make가 정답이다. (A) made는 동사의 과거형/과거분사, (B) makes는 3인칭 단수동사, (D) making은 동명사/현재분사로 조동사 뒤에 들어갈 수 없다.

번역 레드 라인은 주말에 핀 로에서 분 로까지 급행 정차만 할 것이다.

어휘 make a stop 정차하다 express 급행의

121 부사 자리 _ 동사 수식

해설 수동태로 쓰인 완전한 절(The company's latest video game ~ has been praised) 뒤에서 동사구 has been praised를 수식하는 자리이므로 부사가 들어가야 한다. 따라서 '열렬히, 열광적으로'라는 뜻의 부사 (A) enthusiastically가 정답이다. (B) enthusiastic은 형용사, (C) enthusiasm과 (D) enthusiast는 명사이므로 품사상 오답이다.

번역 이 회사의 최신 비디오 게임인 〈보물 사냥〉은 평가단으로부터 열렬히 찬사를 받았다.

어휘 latest 최신의 treasure 보물 praise 칭찬하다 reviewer 평가자, 논평가 enthusiasm 열정 enthusiast 열심히 하는 사람

122 형용사 어휘

해설 빈칸은 뒤의 명사 hours를 수식하는 형용사 자리로, '(비수기에는) 단축된 시간으로 운영된다'는 의미가 되어야 자연스러우므로 '단축된, 감소된'을 뜻하는 분사형 형용사 (A) reduced가 정답이다. (B) employed는 '고용된', (C) slow는 '느린', (D) busy는 '바쁜'이라는 의미로 문맥에 어울리지 않는다.

번역 그레이트 마운틴 놀이공원은 비수기 동안 단축된 시간으로 운영된다.

어휘 off-season 비수기 amusement park 놀이공원

123 동사 자리 _ 조동사 + 동사원형

해설 조동사 will 뒤에는 동사원형이 와야 하고, 빈칸 뒤에 동사가 따로 보이지 않으므로 빈칸은 동사 자리이다. 따라서 보기 중 유일한 동사인 '포함하다'라는 뜻의 (D) include가 정답이다. (A) overall은 형용사/부사, (B) first는 형용사/부사/명사, (C) about은 전치사/부사이므로 품사상 답이 될 수 없다.

번역 이 건설 사업은 주거용 30세대와 열 개의 상업용 공간을 포함한다.

어휘 residential 주거의 unit (공동 주택의) 세대 commercial 상업의

124 부사절 접속사 어휘

해설 빈칸 앞뒤에 모두 주어와 동사를 갖춘 완전한 절이 왔으므로 빈칸에는 이 두 절을 연결시키는 부사절 접속사가 들어가야 한다. 문맥상 '초봉이 아직 협상 중이기 때문에'라는 내용이 되어야 자연스러우므로 '~ 때문에'라는 의미의 (B) because가 정답이다. (A) once는 '~하자마자', (C) after는 '~한 뒤에', (D) until은 '~까지'라는 의미이므로 문맥상 적절하지 않다.

번역 팜 씨의 초봉이 아직 협상 중이기 때문에 고용 계약이 확정될 수 없다.

어휘 | employment 고용 contract 계약 finalize 마무리 짓다 negotiate 협상하다

125 대명사 어휘

해설 | 빈칸은 전치사 for의 목적어 역할을 하는 동시에 관계대명사 who의 선행사 역할을 하는 대명사 자리이다. 관계사절의 동사가 단수동사 needs이고, 사람을 선행사로 취하는 who의 선행사 자리이므로 단수이면서 사람을 나타내는 대명사가 들어가야 한다. 문맥상 '사무용품이 필요한 사람은 누구나'라는 의미가 되어야 하므로 '누구든지, 누구나'라는 뜻의 (A) anyone이 정답이다. (B) whichever는 선행사를 포함하고 있는 복합관계대명사로 사물을 나타내고, (C) such는 앞서 나온 명사를 대신하여 '그러한 것[사람]'을 의미하며, (D) more는 '더 많은 사람들'을 뜻할 때 복수동사와 써야 하므로 답이 될 수 없다.

번역 | 사무용품이 필요한 사람은 누구나 우리의 물품 보관함에서 사무용품을 이용할 수 있습니다.

어휘 | office supplies 사무용품 resources 자재, 자원

126 동사 어휘

해설 | 동사 intends의 목적어 역할을 하는 to부정사에 들어갈 적절한 동사 어휘를 고르는 문제이다. 문맥상 '임대업 부문에 혁신을 일으키고자 한다'는 의미가 되어야 자연스러우므로 '혁신을 일으키다'라는 뜻의 (D) revolutionize가 정답이다. (C) participate는 '참가하다'라는 뜻의 자동사이므로 빈칸에 들어갈 수 없고, (A) exercise는 '발휘하다', (B) indicate는 '나타내다'라는 의미로 문맥상 적절하지 않다.

번역 | 신생 주택 공급 업체인 필로세니아는 지역 중개인 네트워크를 통해 임대업 부문에 혁신을 일으키고자 한다.

어휘 | agent 중개상 housing 주택 (공급) start-up 신생[신규] 업체 intend to ~하고자 하다, ~할 작정이다 sector 부문, 분야

127 to부정사 _ 목적격 보어

해설 | 빈칸은 분사구문을 이끄는 현재분사 allowing의 목적어인 users를 보충 설명하는 목적격 보어 자리이다. allow는 주로 to부정사를 목적격 보어로 취하는 5형식 동사이므로 (D) to send가 정답이다. (A) sent는 동사의 과거형/과거분사, (B) have sent는 현재완료 동사, (C) sending은 동명사/현재분사로 품사상 빈칸에 들어갈 수 없다.

번역 | 래피드 북스는 모든 회사가 필요로 하는 급여 솔루션을 갖추고 있어 사용자로 하여금 손쉬운 3단계로 청구서를 보낼 수 있게 해 준다.

어휘 | payroll 급여 allow 가능하게[수월하게] 하다 invoice 청구서

128 전치사 어휘

해설 | 빈칸 뒤에 기간을 나타내는 명사구 the next two years가 있고, 문맥상 '향후 2년 안에'라는 의미가 되어야 자연스러우므로 '~ 안에, ~ 이내에'를 뜻하는 기간의 전치사 (D) within이 정답이다. (A) above는 '~보다 위에', (B) behind는 '~ 뒤에', (C) about은 '~에 대한, ~ 정도'라는 뜻으로 빈칸에 적절하지 않다.

번역 | 엡키 전자는 향후 2년 안에 여덟 곳의 소매점을 추가로 열 예정이다.

어휘 | retail store 소매점

129 명사 자리 _ 복합명사

해설 | 빈칸은 전치사 on의 목적어 역할을 하는 동시에 관계대명사 that의 선행사 역할을 하는 명사 자리이다. 따라서 빈칸 앞의 명사구 public speaking과 함께 '대중 연설 전략'이라는 의미의 복합명사를 만들 수 있는 '전략'이라는 뜻의 명사 (A) strategies가 정답이다. (B) strategized는 동사/과거분사, (C) strategically는 부사, (D) strategic은 형용사이므로 품사상 답이 될 수 없다.

번역 | 3일간의 워크숍은 기억에 남을 만한 발표를 하는 데 핵심이 되는 대중 연설 전략에 초점을 둔다.

어휘 | focus on ~에 초점[중점]을 두다 central to ~에 핵심[중심]적인 deliver (연설, 강연 등을) 하다 memorable 기억에 남을 만한 strategize 전략을 짜다 strategically 전략상

130 부사 어휘

해설 | 동사 combines를 수식하여 적절한 문맥을 완성하는 부사를 고르는 문제이다. 문맥상 '컴퓨터 이미지와 라이브 액션을 매끄럽게 결합한다'는 의미가 되어야 자연스러우므로 '매끄럽게'라는 뜻의 (A) seamlessly가 정답이다. (B) collectively는 '집단적으로', (C) factually는 '사실상', (D) distantly는 '멀리'라는 의미이다.

번역 | 비평가들은 영화 〈색다른 소개〉가 컴퓨터 생성 이미지와 라이브 액션을 매끄럽게 결합한다는 점에 동의한다.

어휘 | critic 비평가 unusual 색다른 combine 결합하다 computer-generated 컴퓨터로 생성된

PART 6

131-134 공지

> **스카이 에어 퍼스트 패스**
>
> 항공 여행을 131 **우리** 스카이 에어 퍼스트와 함께해 주셔서 감사합니다. 즐거운 비행이 되시기 바랍니다.
>
> 스카이 에어 퍼스트 패스를 구매132 **함으로써** 향후 항공편을 최저가로 이용하실 수 있습니다. 133 **저렴한** 연회비로 특별 할인, 좌석 업그레이드, 전용 여행자 라운지 이용을 즐길 수 있습니다. 134 **또한 우선 탑승 혜택도 제공됩니다.** 추가 정보 및 신청서는 승무원에게 문의하십시오
>
> 어휘 | fly (특정 항공사를) 이용하다 take advantage of ~을 이용하다 exclusive 전용의 flight attendant 승무원 application 신청서

131 인칭대명사의 격 _ 목적격 / 어휘

해설 | 빈칸은 전치사 with의 목적어 자리로, 문맥과 어울리는 인칭대명사가 필요하다. 해당 글은 스카이 에어 퍼스트 항공사가 고객에게 전하는 공지문으로 빈칸 뒤 문장에서 즐거운 비행이 되길 바란다(We hope you enjoy your flight)고 한 것으로 보아 빈칸이 있는 문장은 항공 여행을 우리(=스카이 에어 퍼스트)와 함께해 주어 감사하다는 내용이 되어야 적절하다. 따라서 '우리'의 목적격인 (C) us가 정답이다.

132 전치사 어휘

해설 빈칸은 동명사구 purchasing a Sky Air First Pass를 목적어로 취하는 전치사 자리이다. 문맥상 '패스를 구매함으로써 최저가를 이용할 수 있다(You can take advantage of our best prices)'는 의미가 되어야 적절하므로 '~함으로써'라는 수단의 의미를 지닌 전치사 (C) by가 정답이다.

133 형용사 자리 _ 명사 수식

해설 부정관사 a와 명사구 annual fee 사이에서 annual fee를 수식하는 자리로, '저렴한 연회비'라는 의미가 되어야 적절하므로 '저렴한'을 뜻하는 형용사 (B) low가 정답이다. (C) lowly는 '~ly'로 끝나는 형용사로 '(지위 등이) 낮은, 하찮은'을 뜻하므로 의미상 부적절하고, (D) lowest도 형용사이지만 최상급 앞에 있어야 하는 소유격이나 the가 없으므로 빈칸에 들어갈 수 없다. (A) lowers는 '낮추다'라는 뜻의 동사이므로 품사상 답이 될 수 없다.

134 문맥에 맞는 문장 고르기

번역 (A) 스카이 에어 퍼스트를 다시 이용해 주시기를 바랍니다.
(B) 또한 우선 탑승 혜택도 제공됩니다.
(C) 즉시 좌석을 찾아 주십시오.
(D) 비행기 지연은 최소화될 것입니다.

해설 앞에서 스카이 에어 퍼스트 패스를 구매하면 저렴한 연회비로 특별 할인(special discounts), 좌석 업그레이드(seat upgrades), 전용 여행자 라운지 이용(the use of our exclusive travelers' lounge)을 즐길 수 있다며 패스 구매에 따른 특혜를 열거하고 있으므로 이와 관련된 내용이 연결되어야 자연스러운 문맥을 완성할 수 있다. 따라서 우선 탑승 혜택도 받을 수 있다며 추가적인 혜택을 언급하는 (B)가 정답이다.

어휘 priority 우선(권) boarding 탑승 immediately 즉시 delay 지연 minimal 최소의

135-138 기사

CJOK 라디오 쇼 신입 스태프 영입

퀸즈빌 (7월 7일) — 지역 라디오 방송국 CJOK는 인기 프로그램인 〈아웃 앤 어바웃 인 퀸즈빌〉의 새로운 제작자로 캐서린 디즈를 발표했다. 디즈 씨는 이제 스케줄 편성, 프로그램을 위한 출연자 섭외, 그리고 미디어 관계 관리를 135 담당한다.

136 또한, 방송국은 새로운 임무를 맡은 디즈 씨를 지원할 음향 편집자 버지니아 태커와 제작 보조 레지 디트리히를 고용했다. 137 이 신규 채용은 제작자 에드 에번스의 은퇴에 따른 것이다.

30년간 방영 중인 〈아웃 앤 어바웃 인 퀸즈빌〉은 퀸즈빌 시내 오르페움 극장에서 9월부터 5월까지 매주 생방송으로 진행된다. 음악 게스트, 작가, 이야기꾼들이 매주 한 시간으로 편성된 프로그램에 138 출연한다.

어휘 coordinate 편성[조정]하다 relations 관계 production 제작 support 지원하다 role 임무, 역할 air 방송하다 weekly 매주, 주 1회의 programming 방송 프로그램 편성

135 형용사 자리 _ 주격 보어

해설 빈칸은 be동사 is 뒤 주격 보어 자리이므로 형용사나 분사, 또는 명사가 들어갈 수 있다. 빈칸 뒤에 전치사 for가 있고 문맥상 '디즈 씨는 ~을 담당한다'는 의미가 되어야 하므로 전치사 for와 함께 쓰여 '~을 담당하는, ~을 책임지고 있는'을 뜻하는 형용사 (D) responsible이 정답이다. (A) responsive는 '응답[반응]하는'이라는 뜻으로 주로 전치사 to와 함께 쓰이고, (B) responsibly는 '책임감 있게'라는 의미의 부사이며, (C) responding은 '응답하다'라는 뜻의 동사 respond의 현재분사로 의미상 빈칸에 적절하지 않다.

136 접속부사

해설 앞 단락에서 방송국이 새로운 제작자로 캐서린 디즈(Katherine Dees as the new producer)를 임명했다고 했고, 빈칸이 있는 문장에서 디즈 씨를 지원할 음향 편집자와 제작 보조도 고용했다(the station hired sound editor ~ to support Ms. Dees)고 했다. 앞에서 언급된 직원 임용 내용과 유사하게 직원을 새로 고용했다는 문장이 추가적으로 이어지고 있으므로, '또한, 게다가'라는 뜻의 접속부사 (D) In addition이 정답이다. (A) Even so는 '그렇다 하더라도', (B) In fact는 '사실', (C) For example은 '예를 들어'라는 의미이다.

137 문맥에 맞는 문장 고르기

번역 (A) CJOK는 60년 전에 설립되었다.
(B) 이 신규 채용은 제작자 에드 에번스의 은퇴에 따른 것이다.
(C) 디즈 씨는 시더버그에서 태어나고 자랐다.
(D) CJOK 편성 프로그램에는 인기 있는 프로그램이 여럿 있다.

해설 앞에서 프로그램의 새로운 제작자로 캐서린 디즈(Katherine Dees as the new producer)를 임명했고 디즈 씨를 지원할 음향 편집자와 제작 보조를 추가로 고용했다(the station hired sound editor ~ to support Ms. Dees)고 했다. 따라서 이렇게 새로운 인사를 단행하게 된 이유를 부연 설명하는 문장이 뒤따르는 것이 자연스러우므로 이 신규 채용은 제작자의 은퇴에 따른 것이라고 언급하는 (B)가 정답이다.

어휘 found 설립하다 hire 채용, 고용 follow ~에 뒤따르다 raise (아이를) 기르다 lineup 편성, 구성

138 동사 어휘

해설 빈칸이 있는 문장은 쇼를 구성하는 음악 게스트, 작가, 이야기꾼들(musical guests, writers, and storytellers)이라는 출연진에 대한 소개를 하고 있으므로, 빈칸에는 이 출연진들을 목적어로 취하는 알맞은 동사가 와야 한다. 따라서 '음악 게스트, 작가, 이야기꾼들이 출연한다'라는 의미를 만드는 '출연시키다, 특별히 포함하다'라는 뜻의 (C) features가 정답이다. (A)의 give는 '주다', (B)의 mark는 '표시하다', (D)의 hold는 '잡다; 개최하다'라는 의미이다.

TEST 9

139-142 이메일

수신: 산드라 바르가 ⟨sbarga97@hjmail.ca⟩
발신: 아티 로망쉬 ⟨service@northwestbags.ca⟩
날짜: 7월 12일
제목: 주문 번호 71280

바르가 씨:

클라마스 쿨 핸드백에 이름을 바느질로 새겨달라는 고객님의 최근 주문을 받았습니다. 저희는 139**당연히** 고객님의 주문을 완수하기를 바랍니다. 안타깝게도, 개인 맞춤 서비스 주문을 담당하는 재봉사가 앞으로 3일간 휴가를 갈 예정입니다. 그녀의 140**부재**로 인해 고객님의 가방 배송이 지연될 수 있음을 알려드리고자 합니다.

기다리시는 동안의 불편을 141**보상해 드리기 위해**, 이번에 주문하신 상품에 10퍼센트 할인을 제공해 드리고자 합니다. 아니면, 원하실 경우 다음 주문 시 무료 개인 맞춤 서비스를 선택하실 수 있습니다. 142**고객님께서 선택하시면 됩니다.** 노스웨스트 백스에서는 고객 만족 100퍼센트를 위해 노력합니다!

아티 로망쉬
노스웨스트 백스, 고객 서비스 담당자

어휘 stitch 바느질하다 be eager to ~을 하고 싶어 하다
seamstress 재봉사 fulfil 이행하다 personalisation 개인
맞춤 서비스 requirement 요구 on leave 휴가 중인 cause
야기하다 opt for ~을 선택하다 strive 노력하다

---

139 접속부사

해설 빈칸의 앞 문장에서 핸드백에 이름을 새겨달라는 주문을 받았다(We received your recent order ~ handbag)고 했고, 빈칸이 있는 문장에서 고객의 주문을 완수하고 싶다(eager to complete your order)고 했다. 업체에서 주문을 받으면 주문을 이행하는 것이 당연한 일이므로 당위성을 나타내는 '당연히, 물론'이라는 의미의 (C) of course가 정답이다. (A) still은 '여전히', (B) besides는 '게다가', (D) nevertheless는 '그럼에도 불구하고'라는 의미로 문맥상 적절하지 않다.

140 명사 어휘

해설 앞 문장에서 개인 맞춤 서비스를 담당하는 재봉사가 3일간 휴가를 떠난다(our seamstress ~ on leave for the next three days)고 했고, 빈칸이 있는 문장은 이로 인해 배송이 지연될 것(will cause a delay in shipping your bag)이라고 언급하고 있다. 따라서 재봉사가 휴가를 떠나고 없을 것이라는 내용과 관련 있는 명사가 알맞으므로 '부재'라는 뜻의 (A) absence가 정답이다. (B) arrival은 '도착', (C) request는 '요청', (D) investigation은 '조사'라는 의미이다.

141 to부정사의 부사적 용법

해설 빈칸 뒤의 전치사구 for the wait을 콤마 뒤의 완전한 절(we would like to offer you ~ order)에 적절하게 이어줄 연결어가 필요하다. 문맥상 '기다리는 동안의 불편을 보상해 드리기 위해'라는 내용이 되어야 자연스러우므로 '~하기 위해'라는 목적의 의미를 지닌 부

사적 용법의 to부정사 (B) To compensate가 정답이다. (C) For compensating은 미래의 의미를 지닌 to부정사와 달리, 이미 행해진 일을 이유로 설명할 때, 또는 사물의 기능이나 용도를 나타낼 때 쓰이므로 빈칸이 있는 문장에서처럼 앞으로 할 일에 대한 목적을 나타낼 때는 사용하지 않는다. (A) Compensated는 동사/과거분사로, 과거분사로 쓰일 경우 '보상된, 보상되어서'를 뜻하므로 의미상 적절하지 않고, (D) It is compensation은 절이므로 콤마 뒤의 절과 접속사 없이 연결될 수 없다.

142 문맥에 맞는 문장 고르기

번역 (A) 고객님께서 선택하시면 됩니다.
(B) 검토해 주셔서 감사합니다.
(C) 고객님의 이니셜이 새겨진 가방은 근사해 보일 겁니다.
(D) 저희는 맞춤 서비스를 제공하는 유일한 지역 소매업체입니다.

해설 빈칸 앞에서 기다리는 동안의 불편을 보상하기 위해 이번 주문에 10퍼센트 할인(a 10 percent discount on your current order)을 제공해 주거나, 또는 다음 주문 시 무료 개인 맞춤 서비스(free personalisation on your next order)를 선택할 수 있다고 했다. 따라서 '앞서 제시한 두 가지 옵션 중 선택은 고객이 한다'라는 내용이 연결되어야 자연스러우므로 (A)가 정답이다.

어휘 appreciate 고맙게 여기다 initial 이니셜, 이름의 첫 글자 retailer 소매업체 custom 맞춤의

143-146 기사

세헬렉, 풍력-태양광 하이브리드 프로젝트를 발표하다

뭄바이 (3월 15일) — 세헬렉 유한 회사는 인도 방갈로르 외곽에 500 메가와트 규모의 풍력-태양광 하이브리드 143**발전소** 건설을 시작한다고 발표했다. 144**이 시설은 태양 전지판과 풍력 터빈이 혼합된 형태로 조성될 것이다.** 세헬렉은 24개월 이내에 가동을 시작할 것으로 예상하며, 인도의 거대 에너지 기업인 노바선 인더스트리스에 전력을 판매할 예정이다.

"노바선과의 145**재생 가능한** 전력 공급 계약으로 우리의 장기적인 기업 목표에 더 가까워지고 있습니다."라고 세헬렉의 최고 경영자인 수미트 바르마는 말했다. "우리의 목표는 5년 내에 20기가와트 용량을 달성하는 것입니다. 그렇게 함으로써 우리는 인도에서 가장 큰 친환경 전력 회사 중 하나가 될 것입니다. 그리고 그것은 결국 인도가 탄소 저감 목표에 146**도달하는** 데 도움이 될 것입니다."

어휘 megawatt 메가와트(전력 단위. 100만 와트) solar 태양광을
이용한 hybrid 하이브리드의, 혼성의 operation 가동
long-term 장기적인 corporate 기업의 objective 목표
achieve 달성하다 capacity 용량 gigawatt 기가와트(10억 와트)
in turn 결국 carbon-reduction 탄소 저감[감축]

---

143 명사 자리 _복합 명사

▶ 동영상 강의

해설 전치사 on의 목적어 역할을 하는 명사 자리로, 앞의 복합명사 wind-solar hybrid power와 함께 적절한 복합명사를 만들어야 한다. 따라서 빈칸 앞의 power와 함께 '발전소'라는 의미를 만드는 '공장'이라는 뜻의 (A) plant가 정답이다. (B) planter는 '농장주', (C)

planting은 '(나무 등을) 심기'라는 뜻이므로 의미상 어울리지 않고, (D) planted는 동사/과거분사이므로 품사상 빈칸에 들어갈 수 없다.

144 문맥에 맞는 문장 고르기 ▶ 동영상 강의

번역 (A) 바람이 부는 환경은 고층 건물에 손상을 일으킬 수 있다.
(B) 이 시설은 태양 전지판과 풍력 터빈이 혼합된 형태로 조성될 것이다.
(C) 전기 자동차는 다른 자동차보다 배기가스가 적다.
(D) 올해 인도 전력망 업그레이드 속도가 약간 느려졌다.

해설 앞 문장에서 풍력-태양광 하이브리드 발전소 건설을 시작한다고 발표했다(Sehelec Ltd. announced it will begin construction on a 500-megawatt wind-solar ~ India)고 했으므로 발전소와 관련된 설명이 뒤따르면 자연스럽다. 따라서 하이브리드 발전소를 '이 시설(The facility)'로 받아 태양 전지판과 풍력 터빈이 혼합된 형태로 조성될 것이라고 발전소가 건설되는 방식을 설명하는 (B)가 정답이다.

어휘 damage 손상 facility 시설 consist of ~으로 구성되다 turbine 터빈 emission 배기가스 pace 속도 power grid 전력망

145 형용사 자리 _ 명사 수식

해설 빈칸은 to부정사 to provide의 목적어 역할을 하는 명사 power를 수식하는 자리이므로 형용사 또는 복합명사를 만드는 명사가 들어가야 한다. 따라서 '재생 가능한'이라는 뜻의 형용사 (C) renewable이 정답이다. (A) renew는 '갱신하다'는 뜻의 동사, (D) to renew는 to부정사이므로 품사상 답이 될 수 없고, (B) renewers는 '갱신자'라는 뜻의 명사로 power와 복합명사를 이루지 않으므로 오답이다.

146 동사 어휘

해설 앞 문장에서 우리의 목표는 5년 내에 20기가와트 용량을 달성(Our objective is to achieve a capacity ~ five years)하여 인도에서 가장 큰 친환경 전력 회사 중 하나가 되는 것(one of India's largest green power companies)이라고 설명하고 있다. 따라서 빈칸이 있는 문장은 회사가 목표를 달성하게 되면 궁극적으로 '인도가 탄소 저감 목표(its carbon-reduction target)에 도달하는 데 도움이 될 것'이라는 내용이 되어야 자연스러우므로 '도달하다'는 뜻의 (D) reach가 정답이다. (A) understand는 '이해하다', (B) explain은 '설명하다', (C) block은 '막다'라는 의미이다.

PART 7

147-148 메뉴

카리나스 카페 런치 스페셜
월요일부터 금요일, 오전 11시부터 오후 3시까지

147 **단돈 8달러에 오늘의 수프를 다음 음식 항목 중 하나와 함께 드세요:**

칠면조 샌드위치 - 밀빵 위에 칠면조, 아보카도, 토마토, 양상추, 마요네즈

채소 파니니 - 토마토, 오이, 시금치, 마요네즈로 채운 사워도우 빵을 구운 것

버섯 치킨 카바타피 - 버섯, 셀러리, 양파 소스와 치킨을 S자 모양 파스타에 올린 것

148 **채소 랩** - 신선한 토마토, 오이, 당근과 함께 후무스(우리 가게 비법으로 만듦)를 바른 납작한 빵

어휘 combine 결합하다 turkey 칠면조 lettuce 양상추 wheat 밀 sourdough (발효시켜) 시큼한 맛이 나는 반죽[빵] fill 채우다 spinach 시금치 grill 굽다 hummus 후무스 (병아리콩으로 만들어진 스프레드 형태의 중동 음식)

147 세부사항

번역 각각의 런치 스페셜 메뉴에 포함된 것은?
(A) 수프
(B) 당근
(C) 토마토
(D) 음료

해설 두 번째 줄에서 단돈 8달러에 오늘의 수프를 다음 음식 항목 중 하나와 함께 드세요(For only $8, combine the soup of the day with one of the following items)라고 했다. 따라서 런치 스페셜 메뉴에 수프가 제공된다는 것을 알 수 있으므로 (A)가 정답이다.

148 세부사항

번역 카리나스 카페에서만 이용할 수 있는 재료가 들어있는 품목은?
(A) 칠면조 샌드위치
(B) 채소 파니니
(C) 버섯 치킨 카바타피
(D) 채소 랩

해설 마지막 줄에서 채소 랩은 신선한 토마토, 오이, 당근과 함께 후무스(우리 가게 비법으로 만듦)를 바른 납작한 빵(Vegetable Wrap - Fresh tomato, cucumber, and carrots with hummus (made with our secret recipe) on flatbread)이라고 했다. 따라서 채소 랩에는 카리나스 카페의 비법으로 만든 후무스가 들어가므로 (D)가 정답이다.

149-150 광고

공인 아쿠아 강사 워크숍

이 워크숍은 도전적이고 효과적인 수중 수업을 149 **설계하는** 방법을 시연함으로써 피트니스 전문가들이 공인 아쿠아 강사가 되도록 도와 드립니다. 150 **디숀트 스미스 강사와 종일 과정을 함께하며 학생들에게 동기를 부여해 줄 일련의 수영장 기반 운동을 배우십시오.** 스미스 씨는 밸리 플로어 피트니스에서 수업을 들으며 강사 자격증 취득을 위한 과정을 시작했습니다. 그는 윌킨슨 대학의 교수이기도 합니다.

워크숍 비용은 99달러이며 미줄라의 밸리 플로어 피트니스에서 8월 27일 오전 9시부터 오후 5시까지 열립니다. 자세한 정보 및 등록을 원하시면 마야 크레이머에게 certification@valleyfloorfitness.com으로 이메일을 보내십시오.

---

149 동의어 찾기

번역 첫 번째 단락 2행의 "design"과 의미가 가장 가까운 단어는?
(A) 찾다
(B) 만들다
(C) 그리다
(D) 이름을 짓다

해설 의미상 수업을 '설계한다'는 뜻으로 쓰였으므로 '만들다, 제작하다'를 뜻하는 (B) create가 정답이다.

150 Not / True

번역 워크숍에 대해 명시된 것은?
(A) 윌킨슨 대학교의 수영장에서 열릴 예정이다.
(B) 다른 두 날짜에 제공된다.
(C) 8월에는 할인된 요금으로 이용할 수 있다.
(D) 밸리 플로어 피트니스의 예전 학생이 가르칠 것이다.

해설 첫 단락의 두 번째 문장에서 디숀트 스미스 강사와 종일 과정을 함께 하며 학생들에게 동기를 부여해 줄 일련의 수영장 기반 운동을 배우라(Join instructor Deshonte Smith for a full-day course ~ motivate your students)고 했고, 스미스 씨는 밸리 플로어 피트니스에서 수업을 들으며 강사 자격증 취득을 위한 과정을 시작했다(Mr. Smith started his journey to instructor certification by taking classes at Valley Floor Fitness)고 했다. 따라서 디숀트 스미스 강사는 밸리 플로어 피트니스의 학생이었다는 것을 알 수 있으므로 (D)가 정답이다.

어휘 rate 요금 former 이전의

151-152 문자 메시지

조현준 (오후 3시 27분)
151 제가 토요일 오전 7시부터 오후 3시까지 프런트에서 근무하기로 되어 있어요. 그날 제 친구가 오기로 했는데, 하루만 있다가 갈 예정이에요. 151 저와 근무 시간을 바꿔 주실 수 있을지 궁금해요. 저는 일요일에 근무할 수 있어요.

스테파니 두쉬민 (오후 3시 29분)
토요일 괜찮아요. 지난주 같은 일요일은 겪지 않으셔야 할 텐데요. 너무 바빴거든요. 152 의료 콘퍼런스에 참석한 의사들 전원이 프런트에서 체크인을 했어요.

조현준 (오후 3시 31분)
152 그리고 동시에 다른 콘퍼런스에 참석하는 회계사들도 모두 프런트에서 객실 요금을 확인했다고 들었어요!

스테파니 두쉬민 (오후 3시 32분)
로비가 정말 북적거렸어요.

조현준 (오후 3시 34분)
도와줘서 고마워요. 대학교 졸업 이후로 제 친구 카이를 처음 보는 거예요.

어휘 wonder 궁금하다 switch 바꾸다 shift (교대) 근무 시간 accountant 회계사 charge 요금 bustling 북적거리는

151 의도 파악

번역 오후 3시 29분에 두쉬민 씨가 "토요일 괜찮아요"라고 쓴 의도는?
(A) 아침 근무 시간에 일하는 것을 선호한다.
(B) 조 씨의 부탁을 들어줄 수 있다.
(C) 콘퍼런스에 참석할 것이다.
(D) 조 씨의 친구를 만나고 싶어 한다.

해설 3시 27분에 조 씨가 토요일 오전 7시부터 오후 3시까지 프런트에서 근무하기로 되어 있다(I'm scheduled to work the front desk on Saturday from 7 A.M. to 3 P.M.)고 했고, 두쉬민 씨에게 근무 시간을 바꿔 줄 수 있을지 궁금하다(I was wondering if I could switch shifts with you)면서 일요일에 근무할 수 있다(I can work on Sunday)고 하자 3시 29분에 두쉬민 씨가 토요일 괜찮다(Saturday is good for me)고 대답했다. 따라서 두쉬민 씨는 조 씨가 근무 시간을 바꿔달라고 한 제안을 수락하려는 의도로 한 말임을 알 수 있으므로 (B)가 정답이다.

어휘 do a favor 부탁을 들어주다

152 추론 / 암시

번역 조 씨와 두쉬민 씨가 근무할 것 같은 곳은?
(A) 호텔
(B) 대학교
(C) 의료 센터
(D) 회계 법인

해설 3시 29분에 두쉬민 씨가 의료 콘퍼런스에 참석한 의사들 전원이 프런트에서 체크인을 했다(All the doctors ~ checking in at the front desk)고 했고, 3시 31분에 조 씨가 그리고 동시에 다른 콘퍼런스에 참석하는 회계사들도 모두 프런트에서 객실 요금을 확인했다고 들었다(And I heard that all the accountants ~ at the front desk reviewing their room charges at the same time!)고 했다. 프런트에서 손님들이 체크인을 하거나 객실 요금을 확인한 상황을 이야기하는 것으로 보아 두 사람은 호텔 직원임을 알 수 있으므로 (A)가 정답이다.

153-154 이메일

수신: 마달레나 나바스 〈mnavas@cordovacreations.com〉
발신: 휴고 존스 〈hkjones@sunmail.com〉
날짜: 4월 2일
제목: 감사합니다

나바스 씨께,

지난주에 부매니저 자리에 대해 이야기하게 되어 즐거웠고, 말씀드린 대

로 코르도바 크리에이션스에서 귀하와 함께 일할 수 있다는 가능성에 무척 흥분됩니다. 153 제가 다른 회사로부터 일자리 제안을 받았다는 점을 알려드리고자 하며, 그 채용 담당자에게 곧 답변을 해야 합니다. 154 면접을 본 지 불과 며칠밖에 지나지 않았다는 것을 알고 있지만 이번 주가 끝나기 전에 저의 지원 상황에 대해 조금이라도 알려주실 수 있다면 무척 도움이 될 것입니다. 저는 코르도바 크리에이션스를 오랫동안 동경해 왔고, 진심으로 일원이 되고 싶습니다. 귀하로부터 긍정적인 소식을 듣기를 바랍니다.

감사합니다,

휴고 존스

어휘 associate (직함에 쓰여) 부~ respond 답변하다 realize 알다 status 상황 application 지원 admire 동경하다, 존경하다 positive 긍정적인

153 Not / True

번역 존스 씨가 이메일에 명시한 것은?
(A) 나바스 씨와 함께 일했었다.
(B) 그는 부매니저이다.
(C) 다른 회사에서 그를 고용하고 싶어 한다.
(D) 면접이 다음 주로 잡혀 있다.

해설 두 번째 문장에서 존스 씨가 다른 회사로부터 일자리 제안을 받았다는 점을 알려드리고자 하며, 그 채용 담당자에게 곧 답변을 해야 한다 (I wanted to let you know that I have received a job offer from another company, and I have to respond to that hiring manager soon)고 했으므로 (C)가 정답이다.

154 세부사항

번역 존스 씨가 주말까지 알고 싶어 하는 것은?
(A) 중요한 결정이 이루어졌는지
(B) 나바스 씨가 회의에 참석할 수 있는지
(C) 나바스 씨가 새 직책에 지원하고 싶어 하는지
(D) 회사가 제품을 확대할지

해설 세 번째 문장에서 존스 씨가 면접을 본 지 불과 며칠밖에 지나지 않았다는 것을 알고 있지만 이번 주가 끝나기 전에 자신의 지원 상황에 대해 조금이라도 알려줄 수 있다면 무척 도움이 될 것(I realize ~ if it is at all possible for you to update me on the status of my application before the end of the week, that would be very helpful)이라고 했다. 따라서 존스 씨는 주말까지 자신의 채용 여부가 결정되었는지를 알고 싶어 하는 것이므로 (A)가 정답이다.

어휘 expand 확대하다 offering 제품, 제공되는 것

155-157 기사

히비스커스 서플라이, 자체 컨테이너선 운영

부산 (10월 15일) — 국제선 운항이 지속적으로 증가함에 따라 대륙 간 상품을 운송하는 기업들은 컨테이너선의 비싼 공간을 두고 경쟁을 벌이고 있다. 공장 및 상점으로의 상품 배송 지연은 더욱 흔한 일이 되었다.

155 국내 최대 주택 건설용품 수출업체 중 하나로서 히비스커스 서플라이는 특히 이 문제에 취약하다. 발생 가능성이 있는 운송 문제를 피하기 위해, 157 히비스커스 서플라이는 제품을 해외로 수출하는 데에 자체 컨테이너선을 운영하기로 결정했다. 새로 인수한 선박은 이달 말부터 운항을 시작할 예정이다.

156 히비스커스 서플라이의 제임스 고 사장에 따르면, 회사 자체 선박을 운영하는 것은 항구에서의 효율성을 높이고 전반적인 운송 비용을 줄여 줄 것이다. "화물 업체를 이용한 운송 비용은 지난해 두 배가 되었습니다. 우리 제품을 직접 운송함으로써 고객들에게 운송과 관련된 가격 상승을 전가하는 일을 피할 수 있을 것입니다."라고 고 씨는 말한다.

어휘 run 운영하다 transport 운송하다 continent 대륙 compete 경쟁하다 delay 지연 common 흔한 exporter 수출업체 building supplies 건축 자재 particularly 특히 vulnerable to ~에 취약한 avoid 피하다 potential 발생 가능성이 있는 operate 운영하다 export 수출하다 overseas 해외로 efficiency 효율(성) port 항구 decrease 줄이다 overall 전반적인 freight 화물 pass ~ on to ~을 …에게 전가하다

155 추론 / 암시

번역 히비스커스 서플라이가 판매할 것 같은 제품은?
(A) 건축 자재
(B) 베개와 시트
(C) 도매 식료품
(D) 예비 자동차 부품

해설 두 번째 단락의 첫 문장에서 국내 최대 주택 건설용품 수출업체 중 하나로서 히비스커스 서플라이는 특히 이 문제에 취약하다(As one of the biggest exporters of home building supplies in the country, Hibiscus Supply is ~ issues)고 했으므로 히비스커스 서플라이는 주택 건설용품을 취급하는 업체임을 알 수 있다. 따라서 (A)가 정답이다.

어휘 wholesale 도매의 spare 예비용의

Paraphrasing 지문의 home building supplies
→ 정답의 Construction materials

156 세부사항

번역 히비스커스 서플라이가 자체 컨테이너선을 운영하고자 하는 이유는?
(A) 다른 회사에 운송 서비스를 제공하려고
(B) 제품을 신속하고 저렴하게 운송하려고
(C) 제품을 일반적이지 않은 장소로 배송하려고
(D) 대부분의 화물 업체가 처리할 수 있는 것보다 더 많은 제품을 운송하려고

해설 세 번째 단락의 첫 문장에서 히비스커스 서플라이의 제임스 고 사장에 따르면, 회사 자체 선박을 운영하는 것은 항구에서의 효율성을 높이고 전반적인 운송 비용을 줄여 줄 것(According to Hibiscus Supply ~ operating the company's own ship should improve efficiency at ports and decrease overall shipping costs)이라고 했다. 따라서 히비스커스 서플라이가 자체 선박을 운영하려는 이유는 효율적이고 저렴한 운송을 위한 것이므로 (B)가 정답이다.

Paraphrasing   지문의 improve efficiency → 정답의 quickly

지문의 decrease overall shipping costs
→ 정답의 ship ~ cheaply

157 문장 삽입

번역   [1], [2], [3], [4]로 표시된 위치 중에서 다음 문장이 들어가기에 가장 적합한 곳은?

"새로 인수한 선박은 이달 말부터 운항을 시작할 예정이다."

(A) [1]

(B) [2]

(C) [3]

(D) [4]

해설   주어진 문장에서 새로 인수한 선박이 언제부터 운항을 시작할지를 언급하고 있는 것으로 보아 그 앞에는 선박을 새로 인수하게 된 일과 관련된 내용이 와야 적절하다. 따라서 히비스커스 서플라이가 자사 제품의 해외 수출에 자체 컨테이너선을 운영하기로 결정했다(Hibiscus Supply has decided to operate its own container ship to export products overseas)며 선박을 구입하기로 한 소식을 알려 주는 문장 뒤인 (D)가 정답이다.

158-160 회람

회람

수신: 모든 회계 직원

발신: 제니퍼 스노, 선임 관리자

날짜: 1월 8일

제목: 페드로 아옌데

158 페드로 아옌데가 우리 회계부에서 전임 행정 보조원으로서 새로운 역할을 맡기 위해 159 준비하고 있으니 저와 함께 축하해 주세요. 160 아옌데 씨는 우리 우편물실에서 근무하는 파트타임 직원으로 지난달 랜더 직업 훈련소에서 컴퓨터 지원 분야의 자격증 과정을 수료했습니다. 그는 처음에 우리 회사에 배달 기사로 채용되어 2년 동안 근무하다가 우편물실로 옮겼습니다.

아옌데 씨가 회계부에서 근무하는 첫날은 1월 11일 월요일입니다. 우리 모두 그에게 행운을 빕시다!

어휘   accounting 회계   administrative 행정[관리]의   clerk 직원   certificate 자격증   vocational 직업과 관련된   institute 기관   transfer 옮기다   wish ~ well ~의 행운[성공]을 기원하다

158 주제 / 목적

번역   스노 씨가 회람를 보낸 이유는?

(A) 사무실 파티에 직원들을 초대하려고

(B) 직원의 업무 변경을 발표하려고

(C) 근무시간 단축에 대해 직원들에게 공지하려고

(D) 부서 정책에 대해 직원 의견을 요청하려고

해설   첫 문장에서 스노 씨가 페드로 아옌데가 회계부에서 전임 행정 보조원으로서 새로운 역할을 맡기 위해 준비하고 있으니 함께 축하해 달라(Please join me in congratulating Pedro Allende

as he prepares to enter his new role as a full-time administrative assistant in our accounting department)고 한 것으로 보아 페드로 아옌데라는 직원의 업무가 바뀌는 것을 알리기 위해 회람을 보낸 것이므로 (B)가 정답이다.

어휘   inform 통지하다   reduction 축소   departmental 부서의   policy 정책

Paraphrasing   지문의 enter ~ new role
→ 정답의 a change to ~ job

159 동의어 찾기

번역   첫 번째 단락 1행의 "prepares"와 의미가 가장 가까운 단어는?

(A) 모이다

(B) 돌아오다

(C) 연락을 취하다

(D) 준비하다

해설   의미상 새 역할을 맡기 위해 '준비하고 있다'라는 뜻으로 쓰였으므로 '준비하다'를 뜻하는 (D) gets ready가 정답이다.

160 Not / True

번역   아옌데 씨에 대해 명시된 것은?

(A) 현재 배달 기사로 일하고 있다.

(B) 최근에 교육 과정을 마쳤다.

(C) 이전에 다른 부서에서 스노 씨를 보조했다.

(D) 다음 주부터 파트타임 근무를 시작한다.

해설   첫 단락의 두 번째 문장에서 아옌데 씨는 우편물실에서 근무하는 파트타임 직원으로 지난달 랜더 직업 훈련소에서 컴퓨터 지원 분야의 자격증 과정을 수료했다(Mr. Allende, a part-time clerk in our mail room, completed a certificate program ~ last month)고 했으므로 (B)가 정답이다.

어휘   previously 이전에   assist 돕다

161-163 광고

구인: 기계 기술자

161 뉴질랜드 네이피어의 캐멀리 사에 다양한 산업을 위한 맞춤형 공구 및 기계 부품을 생산하는 15,000평방미터 규모의 제조 공장에서 근무할 숙련된 기계 기술자를 위한 일자리가 있습니다. 이 직책에 필요한 요건은 다음과 같습니다:

• 엔지니어와 협업하여 공구 및 기계 부품을 제작할 수 있는 능력

• 전문 장비에 대한 숙지

• 기술 도면에 근거해 정밀 작업을 수행하는 기술

• 162 금속, 목재 및 플라스틱과 같은 다양한 재료를 편하게 다룰 수 있는 능력

• 163 독립적으로도, 또는 팀의 일원으로서도 일할 수 있는 능력

지원하려면 이력서와 두 장의 추천서를 jobs@camerleycorp.co.nz
로 보내세요.

161 세부사항

번역 광고를 게재한 업체의 종류는?
(A) 토지 개발업체
(B) 자동차 수리점
(C) 공장
(D) 철물점

해설 첫 문장에서 뉴질랜드 네이피어의 캐멀리 사에 다양한 산업을 위한 맞
춤형 공구 및 기계 부품을 생산하는 15,000평방미터 규모의 제조 공
장에서 근무할 숙련된 기계 기술자를 위한 일자리가 있다(Camerley
Corp. of Napier, New Zealand, has ~ fabrication plant,
which produces custom tools and machine parts for a
variety of industries)고 했다. 따라서 광고를 낸 캐멀리 사는 공구
및 기계 부품을 생산하는 공장을 운영하는 업체임을 알 수 있으므로
(C)가 정답이다.

Paraphrasing 지문의 our ~ fabrication plant
→ 정답의 A factory

162 Not / True

번역 광고에 명시된 재료가 아닌 것은?
(A) 금속
(B) 유리
(C) 목재
(D) 플라스틱

해설 직책에 필요한 네 번째 요건에서 금속, 목재 및 플라스틱과 같은 다
양한 재료를 편하게 다룰 수 있는 능력(Comfort working with
metal and various other materials, such as wood and
plastics)을 명시하고 있고, 유리는 언급된 적이 없으므로 (B)가 정답
이다.

163 세부사항

번역 직무에 필요한 요건으로 나열된 것은?
(A) 기업 간 영업 관련 교육
(B) 공학 분야의 대학 학위
(C) 기술 도면 작성 경험
(D) 혼자 일하고 다른 사람과 협력하는 능력

해설 직책에 필요한 다섯 번째 조건에서 독립적으로도, 또는 팀의 일원으로
서도 일할 수 있는 능력(Ability to work both independently and
as part of a team)을 언급하고 있으므로 (D)가 정답이다.

어휘 business to business 기업 간의 degree 학위

Paraphrasing 지문의 work both independently and as
part of a team
→ 정답의 work alone and with others

164-167 문자 메시지

래니 맥기니스 (오전 7시 16분)
좋은 아침입니다, 켈리 그리고 마티유. 164, 166 제가 공원 입구에서 펀
페어 사전 등록 표지판을 치웠는데 북문에 있는 하나를 깜빡한 것 같아
요. 166 두 분 중에 한 분이 혹시 그게 아직 거기 있는지 확인해 주실 수
있을까요?

켈리 센 (오전 7시 18분)
안녕하세요, 래니. 164, 165 메인 텐트에 있는 환영 테이블에 팸플릿과
다른 자료들을 갖다 놓는 걸 도우려고 오늘 아침 일찍 자전거를 타고 공
원에 왔어요. 그런데 여기는 일을 마무리할 수 있는 다른 자원봉사자들
이 있어서 제가 지금 그쪽 입구로 갈 수 있어요.

래니 맥기니스 (오전 7시 19분)
그러면 좋겠네요. 저는 당분간 공원 반대편에 있는 남쪽 입구에 있을 거
라서요. 도시 공원 부서의 담당자들을 만날 예정이에요.

마티유 허먼 (오전 7시 21분)
제가 할게요, 켈리. 166 방금 북쪽 입구에 도착했으니 여기 걸어 둔 표지
판을 내릴게요. 래니, 167 이걸 어떻게 하면 좋을까요?

래니 맥기니스 (오전 7시 22분)
완벽하네요! 167 메인 텐트에 있는 환영 테이블 뒤에 다른 것들과 함께
두실 수 있을까요? 오늘 중으로 가지러 갈게요. 날짜를 바꿔서 내년에
다시 사용할 수 있어요.

마티유 허먼 (오전 7시 23분)
그럴게요. 164 성공적인 박람회를 위하여!

164 추론 / 암시

번역 메시지 작성자들에 대해 사실일 것 같은 것은?
(A) 자전거로 출근하기 프로그램에 사람들을 등록시키고 있다.
(B) 공공 행사를 준비하고 있다.
(C) 도시 공원 부서에서 일한다.
(D) 공원에서 걷는 동아리의 회원이다.

해설 7시 16분에 맥기니스 씨가 공원 입구에서 펀페어 사전 등록 표지판
을 치웠는데 북문에 있는 하나를 깜빡한 것 같다(I removed the
Funfair preregistration signs from the park entrances ~
the north gate)고 했고, 7시 18분에 센 씨가 메인 텐트에 있는 환영
테이블에 팸플릿과 다른 자료들을 갖다 놓는 걸 도우려고 오늘 아침
일찍 자전거를 타고 공원에 왔다(I rode my bike to the park ~ to
help put pamphlets and other materials on the welcome
table in the main tent)고 했으며, 7시 23분에 허먼 씨가 성공적인
박람회를 위하여(Here's to a successful fair!)라고 했다. 따라서
메시지 작성자들은 공원에서 열리는 펀페어라는 박람회를 준비하고
있다는 것을 알 수 있으므로 (B)가 정답이다.

어휘 register 등록하다   coordinate 조직화[편성]하다

165 세부사항

번역 센 씨가 하고 있던 일은?
(A) 텐트 치기
(B) 팸플릿 디자인하기
(C) 환영 테이블에 물품 배치하기
(D) 공원 입구에 표지판 부착하기

해설 7시 18분에 센 씨가 메인 텐트에 있는 환영 테이블에 팸플릿과 다른 자료들을 갖다 놓는 걸 도우려고 오늘 아침 일찍 자전거를 타고 공원에 왔다(I rode my bike to the park ~ to help put pamphlets and other materials on the welcome table in the main tent)고 했으므로 (C)가 정답이다.

어휘 erect 세우다   attach 붙이다

Paraphrasing 지문의 put pamphlets and other materials
→ 정답의 Placing items

166 의도 파악

번역 오전 7시 21분에 허먼 씨가 "제가 할게요, 켈리"라고 쓴 의도는?
(A) 이미 표지판을 뗐다.
(B) 맥기니스 씨가 요청한 일을 수행할 것이다.
(C) 사용하지 않은 자료를 사무실로 반납할 것이다.
(D) 센 씨가 도움이 필요하지 않다는 것을 알고 있다.

해설 7시 16분에 맥기니스 씨가 공원 입구에서 펀페어 사전 등록 표지판을 치웠는데 북문에 있는 하나를 깜빡한 것 같다(I removed the Funfair preregistration signs ~ I forgot one at the north gate)며 두 사람 중에 한 사람이 혹시 표지판이 아직 거기 있는지 확인해 줄 수 있을지(Could one of you check to see if it is still there?)를 물었고, 7시 21분에 허먼 씨가 '제가 할게요, 켈리(I've got it, Kelly)'라면서 방금 북쪽 입구에 도착했으니 여기 걸어 둔 표지판을 내리겠다(I just arrived at the north entrance and will take down the sign we hung here)고 했다. 따라서 허먼 씨는 맥기니스 씨가 북문에 있는 표지판이 아직 붙어 있는지 확인해 달라고 한 요청을 수행하겠다는 의도로 한 말임을 알 수 있으므로 (B)가 정답이다.

어휘 take down 치우다   task 일

167 세부사항

번역 맥기니스 씨가 허먼 씨에게 하라고 지시한 것은?
(A) 그녀가 메인 텐트를 찾을 수 있도록 도울 것
(B) 남쪽 입구에서 그녀와 만날 것
(C) 참가자의 정보를 적을 것
(D) 환영 테이블 뒤에 물건을 둘 것

해설 7시 21분에 허먼 씨가 맥기니스 씨에게 이걸 어떻게 하면 좋을지(what would you like me to do with it?)를 묻자, 7시 22분에 맥기니스 씨가 메인 텐트에 있는 환영 테이블 뒤에 다른 것들과 함께 둘 수 있는지(Can you put it ~ behind the welcome table in the main tent?) 요청하고 있으므로 (D)가 정답이다.

어휘 locate (위치를) 찾아내다   participant 참가자

Paraphrasing 지문의 put it → 정답의 Leave an object

168-171 보고서

6월 30일 종료되는 회계 연도의 질란디아 항공 보고서

서비스 수준 및 수용력: 질란디아 항공은 4개 도시 간 지역 서비스를 제공합니다. 각 경우, 평균 항공 수용력이 회사 목표인 85퍼센트를 [168]넘어섰습니다.

[169]**정시 실적(OTP):** 정시 실적을 측정하기 위해 항공편이 예정된 도착 시간으로부터 15분 이내에 목적지에 도착하면 "정시에 온" 것으로 간주됩니다. 지역 항공사는 OTP가 50퍼센트 미만으로 떨어질 경우 벌금이 부과됩니다. [169]다음 차트는 최근 회계 연도에 있어 질란디아의 칭찬받을 만한 OTP율을 보여줍니다.

도시	[169]OTP
켈튼폴스	52퍼센트
그랜저턴	68퍼센트
새처빌	79퍼센트
바버시티	64퍼센트

확장 제안: [170]질란디아 항공은 지역 승객들에게 항공 서비스를 제공하며, 상업용 항공 화물 배송을 시작하기 위해 항공기 보유 대수를 늘리고자 합니다. 이 서비스를 구축하는 일은 항공사의 성장 계획 및 기업 비전의 한 요소입니다. 항공사는 현재 선택지를 모색하기 위해 항공 당국과 협상 중입니다.

터미널 및 서비스 개선: [171]질란디아 항공은 공항 경영진과 승객 라운지 및 카페의 종합적인 개조와 관련한 논의에 참여 중이며, 예산 중에서 500만 달러를 프로젝트에 투입하겠다고 제안했습니다. 회사 경영진은 또한 계획을 마무리 짓고 보상 프로그램을 개편하기 위한 자금을 투입했습니다. 이 계획은 유사한 항공사들 사이에서 선도적인 서비스 제공 업체가 되고 시장 점유율을 늘리고자 하는 목표를 지원합니다.

어휘 fact sheet 보고서, 사실 자료표   fiscal year 회계 연도 capacity 수용력   regional 지역의   average 평균의   exceed 넘어서다   on-time 정시의   for the purpose of ~을 위해 measure 측정하다   destination 목적지   be subject to ~의 대상이다   fine 벌금   following 다음의   commendable 칭찬받을 만한   rate 비율   expansion 확장   passenger 승객 expand 확장하다   fleet (한 기관이 보유한 전체 차량, 비행기 등의) 무리   commercial 상업의   airfreight 항공 화물   establish 구축하다   component 요소   growth 성장   negotiation 협상 aviation 항공   authorities 당국   explore 모색하다 participate in ~에 참여하다   comprehensive 종합적인 renovation 보수[개조]   commit (돈·시간을) 쓰다   executive 경영진, 임원   fund 자금   overhaul 개편하다   reward 보상 initiative (목적 달성 등을 위한) 계획   leading 선도적인   capture 차지하다   market share 시장 점유율

168 동의어 찾기

번역 첫 번째 단락 2행의 "exceeded"와 의미가 가장 가까운 단어는?
(A) 넘어섰다
(B) 탁월했다
(C) 완벽하게 했다
(D) 결정했다

해설 의미상 회사 목표인 85퍼센트를 '넘어섰다'는 뜻으로 쓰였으므로 '(범위·한계점 등을) 넘었다, 초월했다'라는 뜻의 (A) surpassed가 정답이다.

169 Not / True

번역 보고서에 따르면, 질란디아 항공에 대해 사실인 것은?
(A) 경영진이 항공 수용력을 향상하는 것을 목표로 하고 있다.
(B) 대부분의 항공편이 정시에 목적지에 도착한다.
(C) 지역 항공사의 85퍼센트보다 규모가 더 크다.
(D) 항공 당국으로부터 벌금이 부과되었다.

해설 두 번째 단락의 첫 문장에서 정시 실적(OTP)(On-Time Performance)을 설명하며, 정시 실적을 측정하기 위해 항공편이 예정된 도착 시간으로부터 15분 이내에 목적지에 도착하면 '정시에 온' 것으로 간주된다(For the purpose of measuring OTP, flights are considered "on time" when they reach their destination ~ scheduled arrival time)고 했다. 세 번째 문장에서 다음 차트는 최근 회계 연도에 있어 질란디아의 칭찬받을 만한 OTP율을 보여 준다(The following chart shows Zealandia's commendable OTP rates for the recent fiscal year)고 했으며, 차트에 따르면 도시별 OTP가 52퍼센트, 68퍼센트, 79퍼센트, 64퍼센트로 모두 50퍼센트를 넘었음을 알 수 있다. 따라서 질란디아 항공은 대부분의 항공편이 정시에 목적지에 도착하고 있다는 것을 알 수 있으므로 (B)가 정답이다.

170 세부사항

번역 질란디아 항공이 향후 제공하기를 원하는 것은?
(A) 전용 전세기
(B) 고급 관광
(C) 상업 운송
(D) 항공기 임대

해설 세 번째 단락의 첫 문장에서 질란디아 항공은 지역 승객들에게 항공 서비스를 제공하며 상업용 항공 화물 배송을 시작하기 위해 항공기 보유 대수를 늘리고자 한다(Zealandia Airlines provides ~ is seeking to expand its fleet to begin providing commercial airfreight delivery)고 했으므로 앞으로 상업용 운송 서비스를 제공할 계획임을 알 수 있다. 따라서 (C)가 정답이다.

어휘 charter (항공기 등의) 전세   aircraft 항공기   leasing 임대업

Paraphrasing 지문의 airfreight delivery → 정답의 shipping

171 세부사항

번역 질란디아 항공은 승객을 위한 서비스를 어떻게 개선하기를 바라는가?
(A) 승객 대기 구역을 개조함으로써
(B) 터미널 내의 새로운 위치로 이동함으로써
(C) 항공기 내부의 좌석을 업그레이드함으로써
(D) 모든 항공편에 개선된 식사 서비스를 제공함으로써

해설 네 번째 단락의 첫 문장에서 질란디아 항공은 공항 경영진과 승객 라운지 및 카페의 종합적인 개조와 관련한 논의에 참여 중이며, 예산 중에서 500만 달러를 프로젝트에 투입하겠다고 제안했다(Zealandia Airlines is participating in discussions with airport management about comprehensive renovations to its passenger lounge and café ~ budget to the project)고 했다. 따라서 승객 라운지 및 카페, 즉 승객 대기 장소를 개조하여 서비스를 개선할 계획임을 알 수 있으므로 (A)가 정답이다.

어휘 remodel 개조하다

Paraphrasing 지문의 renovations → 정답의 remodeling

172-175 보도 자료

> ### 동북 철도의 새로운 열차
>
> 173 동북 철도는 65대의 여객 열차를 교체하는 데 56억 달러를 지출할 것으로 예상하고 있으며, 이 열차 중 다수는 40년 이상 되었습니다.
>
> 172, 174 회사는 로지엔스 운송과 새로운 열차 차량에 대한 계약을 맺었으며, 이 열차는 전동 선로 시스템을 이용할 수 있을 때는 그 위에서 운행하고 그 외에는 경유로 운행할 예정입니다. 이 열차들은 최대 시속 130킬로미터의 속도로 운행할 수 있으며 현재 열차보다 훨씬 적은 공해를 배출할 것입니다.
>
> 로지엔스는 또한 향상된 승객 경험을 약속합니다. 175 열차는 파노라마 창, 개선된 환기구, 그리고 더 넓은 통로를 갖출 것입니다. 각 리클라인 좌석에는 개별 전원 공급 장치와 USB 포트가 있을 것입니다.
>
> 또한 172 동북 철도와 로지엔스의 계약에는 장비 및 교체 부품이 포함되며 장기 정비 서비스 계약을 제공합니다.
>
> 어휘 fleet (차량, 열차) 무리, 차단   enter into a contract 계약을 맺다   operate 운행[가동]되다   electrified 전기화된   diesel fuel 경유   capable 할 수 있는   pollution 공해   enhanced 향상된   ventilation 환기   aisle 통로   replacement 교체   long-term 장기의   agreement 계약

172 세부사항

번역 로지엔스 운송의 역할은?
(A) 공해를 줄이는 방법을 추천하는 것
(B) 구매를 위한 자금 조달을 받는 것
(C) 열차 엔지니어들에게 새로운 기술을 교육하는 것
(D) 교체 열차를 제조 및 정비하는 것

해설 두 번째 단락의 첫 문장에서 회사는 로지엔스 운송과 새로운 열차 차량에 대한 계약을 맺었다(The company has entered into a contract with Logiens Transport for a new fleet of trains)고 했고, 마지막 단락에서 동북 철도와 로지엔스의 계약에는 장비 및 교

TEST 9

체 부품이 포함되며 장기 정비 서비스 계약을 제공한다(Northeast's contract with Logiens also includes equipment and replacement parts and provides a long-term service agreement)고 했다. 따라서 로지엔스 운송은 열차를 생산하고 사후 관리 서비스까지 제공하는 업체라는 것을 알 수 있으므로 (D)가 정답이다.

어휘 acquire 얻다 financing 자금 조달 familiarize 익숙하게 하다 service 정비[점검]하다

173 세부사항

번역 보도 자료에 포함된 내용은?
(A) 열차가 인도되는 날짜
(B) 현재 열차를 교체하기 위한 예산
(C) 부품 및 서비스에 대한 연간 비용
(D) 각 열차 칸의 승객 좌석 수

해설 첫 문장에서 동북 철도는 65대의 여객 열차를 교체하는 데 56억 달러를 지출할 것으로 예상하고 있다(Northeast Railways expects to spend $5.6 billion to replace its fleet of 65 passenger trains)고 했으므로 (B)가 정답이다.

174 추론 / 암시

번역 동북 철도가 이용하는 선로에 대해 암시된 것은?
(A) 정부 소유이다.
(B) 화물 열차와 공유하지 않는다.
(C) 대부분은 긴급한 수리가 필요하다.
(D) 일부는 전동화되지 않았다.

해설 두 번째 단락의 첫 문장에서 회사는 로지엔스 운송과 새로운 열차 차량에 대한 계약을 맺었으며, 이 열차는 전동 선로 시스템을 이용할 수 있을 때는 그 위에서 운행하고 그 외에는 경유로 운행할 예정(The company has entered into a contract with Logiens Transport for a new fleet of trains that will operate on electrified tracks when those track systems are available and on diesel fuel at all other times)이라고 한 것으로 보아 동북 철도가 이용하는 선로 중 일부는 아직 전동 주행이 불가능하다는 것을 알 수 있으므로 (D)가 정답이다.

어휘 government 정부 freight 화물 (운송) urgent 긴급한

175 문장 삽입

번역 [1], [2], [3], [4]로 표시된 위치 중에서 다음 문장이 들어가기에 가장 적합한 곳은?
"각 리클라인 좌석에는 개별 전원 공급 장치와 USB 포트가 있을 것입니다."
(A) [1]
(B) [2]
(C) [3]
(D) [4]

해설 주어진 문장에서 리클라인 좌석(Each reclinable seat)에는 개별 전원 공급 장치 및 USB 포트가 있을 것이라고 특정 품목에 갖추어질 편의성을 설명하고 있다. 따라서 이 문장은 파노라마 창, 개선된 환기구,

더 넓은 통로(panoramic windows, improved ventilation, and wider aisles) 등 새로운 열차에 포함될 승객 편의 시설을 열거한 문장 뒤에 연결하면 자연스러우므로 (C)가 정답이다.

어휘 reclinable 뒤로 젖힐 수 있는

176-180 이메일 + 양식

수신: headquartersstaff@seonwulawfirm.com
발신: iqalandar@seonwulawfirm.com
날짜: 10월 1일 오전 9시 39분
제목: 원격 작업 설정
첨부: ⬛ 장비 요청서

임직원 여러분께,

176, 178 **12월 3일, 우리 본사는 보수 공사를 위해 한 달간 문을 닫을 예정입니다.** 176 **여러분 모두 보통 샌프란시스코에 있는 이 사무실에서 근무하므로,** 12월 1일 이전에 외부에서 일할 계획을 세우고 필요한 모든 것(노트북, 서류철 등)을 챙기시기 바랍니다. 그날 이후에는 건물 출입이 제한될 것입니다.

179 **산호세 사무실에 임시 공간을 원할 경우, 저에게 이메일을 보내시면 자리를 마련해 두겠습니다.** 177, 179 **재택근무를 할 계획으로 추가 장비(프린터 등)가 필요한 경우, 기술 부서의 첨부 양식을 작성하여 저에게 반송해 주십시오. 해당 부서의 직원이 집 주소로 장비를 보내 드릴 것입니다.**

178 **이 건물 공사가 업무에 지장이 된다는 점을 알고 있지만, 비수기에 맞춰 진행하는 것이 상황을 좀 더 쉽게 만들 것입니다.** 건물이 1월 5일에 다시 문을 열면 여러분이 변화에 만족하실 것이라고 생각합니다. 문의 사항이 있을 경우 저에게 연락해 주십시오.

이안 칼란다르, 관리자
선우 법률회사
(415) 555-0177

어휘 remote 원격의 equipment 장비 request form 요청[신청]서 associate (직장) 동료 headquarters 본사 renovation 보수, 개조 normally 보통 off-site 부지 밖에서 entry 출입 restrict 제한하다 temporary 임시의 reserve 따로 잡아 두다, 예약하다 additional 추가의 fill out ~을 작성하다 representative 직원, 담당자 realize 인식하다 disruption 지장, 혼란 reach out to ~에게 연락을 취하다

선우 법률회사 ― 장비 요청서

179 **사원명: 제이슨 강**

사원 ID: 102899

이메일: jkang@seonwulawfirm.com

수령일: 11월 30일

179 **장비: 데스크톱 모니터, 프린터**

───────────────

180 **(이 부분은 기술 부서에서 작성합니다.)**

요청 이행: ✓네 아니오

180 **요청 이행자: 오브리 스미스**

장비 일련번호: VN3902556, MXE96400

발송일: 11월 27일 익일 배송

어휘 fill (주문대로) 이행하다 serial number 일련번호
overnight mail 익일 배송

176 Not / True

번역 선우 법률회사에 관해 명시된 것은?
(A) 부동산법에 중점을 둔다.
(B) 광고 예산이 크다.
(C) 전국의 고객들에게 서비스를 제공한다.
(D) 본사가 샌프란시스코에 있다.

해설 이메일의 첫 단락 첫 문장에서 12월 3일, 본사는 보수 공사를 위해 한 달간 문을 닫을 예정(On December 3, our headquarters will close for a month for renovation)이며 이 이메일을 받는 직원들 모두는 보통 샌프란시스코에 있는 이 사무실에서 근무한다(As all of you normally work out of these offices in San Francisco)고 언급했다. 따라서 선우 법률회사의 본사가 샌프란시스코에 있다는 사실을 알 수 있으므로 (D)가 정답이다.

어휘 focus on ~에 초점을 두다, 주력하다 advertising 광고 budget 예산 headquarter ~에 본사를 두다

177 세부사항

번역 이메일에 따르면, 기술 부서에서 할 일은?
(A) 직원 노트북에 업데이트 설치
(B) 직원들에게 사무실 장비 발송
(C) 직원들에게 새 소프트웨어 사용 교육
(D) 보수된 사무실에 장비 설치

해설 이메일 두 번째 단락의 두 번째 문장에서 재택근무를 할 계획으로 추가 장비(프린터 등)가 필요할 경우 기술 부서의 첨부 양식을 작성하여 반송해 달라(If you plan to work from home ~, fill out the attached form from our technology department and return it to me)고 한 뒤, 해당 부서 직원이 집 주소로 장비를 보낼 것(A representative of that department will mail the equipment to your home address)이라고 했다. 따라서 기술 부서에서 사무 장비가 필요한 직원에게 장비를 보내 주는 일을 할 것임을 알 수 있으므로 (B)가 정답이다.

어휘 install 설치하다 place 설치[배치]하다 renovated 보수[개조]된

Paraphrasing 지문의 mail → 정답의 Send

178 추론 / 암시

번역 선우 법률회사에 대해 이메일에 암시된 것은?
(A) 사업을 확장할 계획이다.
(B) 주로 원격 근무자를 고용한다.
(C) 12월에는 보통 바쁘지 않다.
(D) 세간의 이목을 끄는 사건을 많이 다룬다.

해설 이메일의 첫 단락 첫 문장에서 12월 3일, 본사는 보수 공사를 위해 한 달간 문을 닫을 예정(On December 3, our headquarters will close for a month for renovation)이라고 했고, 세 번째 단락의 첫 문장에서 이 건물 공사가 업무에 지장이 된다는 점을 알고 있지만 비수기에 맞춰 진행하는 것이 상황을 좀 더 쉽게 만들 것(We realize ~, but timing it with our slow season should make the situation easier)이라고 했다. 따라서 공사가 진행되는 12월은 선우 법률회사의 비수기라는 것을 짐작할 수 있으므로 (C)가 정답이다.

어휘 expand 확장하다 operation 사업, 운영 high-profile 세간의 이목을 끄는, 눈에 띄는

Paraphrasing 지문의 slow season → 정답의 not busy

179 연계

번역 강 씨에 대해 결론지을 수 있는 것은?
(A) 산호세 사무실에서 근무하지 않기로 했다.
(B) 선우 법률회사에서 선임 파트너이다.
(C) 11월 이후에 휴가를 갈 예정이다.
(D) 더 큰 사무실을 요청했다.

해설 이메일의 두 번째 단락 첫 문장에서 칼란다르 씨가 산호세 사무실에 임시 공간을 원할 경우 이메일을 보내면 자리를 마련해 주겠다(If you would like a temporary space at our San Jose offices ~ I will reserve one for you)고 하고, 두 번째 문장에서 재택근무를 하기로 계획하여 추가 장비(프린터 등)가 필요할 경우 기술 부서의 첨부 양식을 작성하여 반송해 달라(If you plan to work from home and need additional equipment (such as a printer), fill out the attached form from our technology department and return it to me)고 했다. 한편, 양식(장비 요청서)의 첫 줄에 사원명이 제이슨 강(Employee name: Jason Kang)이고, 요청하는 장비는 데스크톱 모니터와 프린터(Equipment: desktop monitor, printer)라고 나와 있다. 따라서 강 씨가 장비를 요청하는 양식을 작성한 것으로 보아 산호세 사무실에서 일하지 않고 재택근무를 하기로 한 것을 알 수 있으므로 (A)가 정답이다.

어휘 senior 선임의, 상위의

180 추론 / 암시

번역 스미스 씨의 직업은 무엇일 것 같은가?
(A) 변호사
(B) 사무장
(C) 기술 지원부 직원
(D) 행정 보조원

해설 선으로 구분된 양식의 하단부에서 이 부분은 기술 부서에서 작성한다(This section is to be completed by the technology department)고 했고, 두 번째 항목에 요청 이행자는 오브리 스미스(Request filled by: Aubrey Smith)라고 나와 있다. 기술 부서에서 작성하는 부분에 요청을 이행한 사람이 오브리 스미스라고 기재되어 있으므로 스미스 씨는 기술 부서 직원임을 알 수 있다. 따라서 (C)가 정답이다.

어휘 technical support 기술 지원부 administrative 행정[관리]상의

TEST 9

181-185 기사 + 이메일

시설 투어 계획하기
디디아네 레사드 작성

공장 투어는 많은 공장에서 흔히 있는 일이지만, 모든 투어가 최대한 효과적으로 진행되는 것은 아니다. **181 너무 많은 회사들이 유용성을 극대화하는 맞춤형 투어보다는 일률적인 방식을 채택하는 실수를 범한다.** 잠재적 투자자와 일반 관람객은 아마도 같은 것에 감명을 받지 않을 것이므로 투어의 목적을 초기에 분명히 하는 것이 최선이다. 여기 각 투어를 가능한 한 효과적으로 만들기 위한 몇 가지 지침이 있다.

선택적으로 하라. 184 **투어가 안전 점검을 목적으로 하는 것이 아닌 이상, 손님들은 공장의 모든 부분을 볼 필요가 없다(원하지도 않는다).** 손님들의 관심을 끌고 당신의 제품을 보다 잘 알게 해주는 구역을 몇 곳 선택하라. 예를 들어, 기자들은 공장에 대한 이야기를 쓰고 싶어 할 것이므로 그들에게는 회사의 초기 생산 장비가 전시된 공간과 같이 공장에서 역사적으로 중요한 의미가 있는 부분을 보여 주어라.

시간 관리가 전부이다. 투어의 체력적 부담을 항상 염두에 두어라. 가장 체력이 좋은 손님도 장시간 서 있거나 걷는 데에 지칠 것이다. 한 시간 이상 지속되는 투어에는 휴식 시간을 일정에 넣는 것이 좋다. 한 구역에서 보내는 시간도 중요하다. **182 손님들을 한 구역에서 5분만 있게 한다면 그들은 곧 그곳을 잊을 것이다.** 반면, 가장 인상적인 공간조차도 30분이 지나면 지루해진다.

성격이 전부는 아니다. 183 (A) **용모가 단정하고 친절한 현장 가이드가 필수적이지만,** 손님들은 당신의 제품을 만드는 데 무엇이 들어가는지 보러 온다. 현장 가이드는 다양한 질문을 받고, 일부 예상 밖의 질문도 있으므로 183 (C) **생산 공정에 대한 종합적인 지식이 중요하다(점검 중에는 절대적인 필수사항이다).** 또한 183 (D) **방문객들은 정시에 시작하고 끝마치는 투어를 좋아할 것이므로 투어를 계속 움직이게 할 사람이 필요하다.**

어휘 commonplace 아주 흔한 adopt 채택하다 one-size-fits-all 일률적인, 두루 적용되게 만든 approach 접근법 tailor 맞추다 maximize 극대화하다 usefulness 유용성 potential 잠재적인 investor 투자자 casual 평상시의 be impressed by ~에 감명받다 selective 선택적인 safety inspection 안전 점검 significance 의의, 중요성 be mindful of ~을 유념하다 physical 신체의 demands 부담, 요구 hardy 튼튼한 tire 지치다 last 지속되다 impressive 인상적인 personable 용모가 단정한, 매력적인 essential 필수적인 comprehensive 종합적인 process 공정 vital 필수적인

수신: 마스미 토다 〈mt978@vidatechsystems.com〉
발신: 아나 미프타로스키 〈am680@vidatechsystems.com〉
날짜: 5월 1일
제목: 다가오는 공장 투어
첨부: 📎 레사드_기사

안녕하세요, 마스미

이달 말에 진행 예정인 투어를 계획하는 데 도움이 될 만한 디디아네 레사드의 4월 15일자 기사를 첨부했습니다. 저는 특히 시간 관리에 대한 부분에 동의합니다. 184 **이번 투어는 필요에 의해 공장 전체를 돌아야 하기 때문에 가능한 한 효율적으로 진행되어야 합니다.** 185 **네이선 자라테를 가이드로 추천하려고 했지만, 그는 5월 21일에 출장을 갈 예정입니다.** 아마 마자 클라우센도 가능할 겁니다. 그녀도 이곳에서 여러 해 근

무해서 우리의 시설, 공정, 정책, 절차를 아주 잘 알고 있습니다. 그녀가 방문객들이 문의할 수 있는 각종 질문을 잘 처리할 수 있을 것이라고 확신합니다.

아나 미프타로스키, 운영 부사장

어휘 attach 첨부하다 especially 특히 by necessity 필요해서 cover 다루다, 포함하다 entire 전체의 conduct (특정 활동을) 하다 efficiently 효율적으로 as for ~에 관해서는 knowledgeable 많이 아는 policy 정책 procedure 절차

181 세부사항

번역 기사에서 공장 투어에 관해 언급된 한 가지 문제는?
(A) 막판에 일정이 변경되는 경우가 종종 있다.
(B) 모든 유형의 방문객들에게 같은 정보를 제공한다.
(C) 모두에게 맞는 보호 장비를 제공하지 못한다.
(D) 너무 큰 규모의 단체를 허용한다.

해설 기사의 첫 단락 두 번째 문장에서 너무 많은 회사들이 유용성을 극대화하는 맞춤형 투어보다는 일률적인 방식을 채택하는 실수를 범한다(Too many companies make the mistake of adopting a one-size-fits-all approach rather than tailoring tours to maximize their usefulness)고 했으므로 (B)가 정답이다.

어휘 at the last minute 마지막 순간에 protective gear 보호 장비 fail to ~하지 못하다 fit 맞다

Paraphrasing 지문의 adapting a one-size-fits-all approach → 정답의 give the same information

182 세부사항

번역 기사에 따르면, 투어가 한 구역에서 지속되어야 하는 최대 시간은?
(A) 10분
(B) 20분
(C) 30분
(D) 60분

해설 기사의 세 번째 단락 여섯 번째 문장에서 손님들이 한 구역에서 5분만 있게 한다면 그들은 곧 그곳을 잊을 것(If you allow guests only five minutes in an area, they will soon forget it)이라고 한 뒤, 반면 가장 인상적인 공간조차도 30분이 지나면 지루해진다(On the other hand, even the most impressive room gets boring after half an hour)고 했다. 따라서 투어 중 한 구역에서 머무는 시간은 최대 30분을 넘지 말아야 한다는 의미이므로 (C)가 정답이다.

Paraphrasing 지문의 half an hour → 정답의 30 minutes

183 Not / True

번역 좋은 현장 가이드의 특징으로서 기사에 명시된 것이 아닌 것은?
(A) 친절한 성격
(B) 오래 서 있을 수 있는 능력
(C) 공정에 대한 심층 지식
(D) 시간에 세심한 주의를 기울이는 능력

해설　기사의 마지막 단락 두 번째 문장에서 용모가 단정하고 친절한 현장 가이드가 필수(having a personable and friendly tour guide is essential)라고 했으므로 (A), 세 번째 문장에서 생산 공정에 대한 종합적인 지식이 중요하다(a comprehensive knowledge of the production processes is important)고 했으므로 (C), 방문객들은 정시에 시작하고 끝마치는 투어를 좋아할 것이므로 투어를 계속 움직이게 할 사람이 필요하다(You also ~ visitors will appreciate a tour that begins and ends on time)고 했으므로 (D)는 좋은 현장 가이드의 자질로서 명시되어 있다. 오래 서 있을 수 있는 능력에 대한 언급은 없으므로 (B)가 정답이다.

어휘　pay attention to ~에 주의를 기울이다

Paraphrasing　지문의 comprehensive knowledge
→ 보기 (C)의 deep knowledge
지문의 begins and ends on time
→ 보기 (D)의 pay close attention to time

184　연계

 동영상 강의

번역　토다 씨는 누구를 위해 투어를 준비하는 것 같은가?
(A) 일반 관람객
(B) 신입 사원
(C) 잠재적 투자자
(D) 안전 검사관

해설　기사의 두 번째 단락 두 번째 문장에서 투어가 안전 점검을 목적으로 하는 것이 아닌 이상, 손님들은 공장의 모든 부분을 볼 필요가 없다(원하지도 않는다)(Unless your tour is for a safety inspection, your guests do not need ~ every part of your factory)고 했고, 이메일의 세 번째 문장에서 이번 투어는 필요에 의해 공장 전체를 돌아야 하기 때문에 가능한 한 효율적으로 진행되어야 한다(Since the tour, by necessity, will have to cover the entire plant, it ~ as possible)고 했다. 이를 종합해 볼 때, 토다 씨가 계획하는 투어는 공장 전체를 돌아봐야 하는 안전 점검일 가능성이 가장 높으므로 (D)가 정답이다.

185　세부사항

번역　투어는 언제 진행될 예정인가?
(A) 4월 15일
(B) 4월 21일
(C) 5월 1일
(D) 5월 21일

해설　이메일의 네 번째 문장에서 네이선 자라테를 가이드로 추천하려고 했지만, 그는 5월 21일에 출장을 갈 예정(As for a guide, I would have recommended Nathan Zarate, but he will be traveling on May 21)이라고 한 것으로 보아 자라테 씨가 출장을 가는 5월 21일에 투어가 진행될 것임을 알 수 있다. 따라서 (D)가 정답이다.

186-190　웹페이지 + 일정표 + 추천 글

https://www.zonecatering.com/home

홈	메뉴	추천 글	연락

존 케이터링은 캘리포니아 전역의 영화 및 TV 제작 현장에 푸드 트럭을 제공합니다. 푸드 트럭이 필요한 곳과 식사 인원수만 알려 주시면 됩니다. 전체 출연진과 제작진에게 음식을 제공할 수 있습니다. 저희 트럭은 또한 촬영 장소가 다양할 경우 귀하의 팀과 함께 이동 가능합니다.

존 케이터링에서는 다양한 요리를 제공합니다. 189 메뉴에 사용하는 모든 과일과 채소는 이곳 캘리포니아에서 재배됩니다. 저희 메뉴는 식이 제한사항을 수용하기 쉽게 조정됩니다. 편의를 위해 저희 푸드 트럭은 정식 및 개별 음식을 모두 제공합니다. 뷔페식으로 식사를 제공할 수도 있고, 트럭에서 바로 주문할 수도 있습니다.

귀하의 제작 활동에 필요한 음식 공급을 저희에게 맡겨 주세요. 음식이 맛있으며, 서비스가 친절하고 편리하다는 것을 알게 되실 겁니다. 186 저희가 귀하의 현장에 있는 동안 문제가 발생할 경우를 대비해 24시간 지원도 제공합니다. 곧 귀하에게 서비스할 수 있게 되기를 바랍니다!

어휘　testimonial 추천 글　production (영화 등의) 제작　feed 음식을 먹이다　entire 전체의　cast 출연진　crew 작업팀　shoot 촬영하다　scene 장면　cuisine 요리　adapt 조정하다　accommodate 수용하다　dietary 식이 요법의　restriction 제한, 제약　individual 개별의　directly 바로　arise 발생하다

존 케이터링 푸드 트럭

일정 날짜: 187 6월 10일

영화	촬영 장소	연락 담당자
187 〈트래핑스〉	하핀 로트	187 에린 베그
188 〈메이크 더 미팅〉	188 라레도 가 192	마크 릴로
〈튜터스 앤 턱시도스〉	탠더 필즈	길준서
〈제이템 앤 더 스톰〉	스펙트럼 홀	도나 가와슨

https://www.zonecatering.com/testimonials

홈	메뉴	추천 글	연락

6월 10일—저는 25년 넘게 연기를 해왔고 때때로 영화 제작 현장의 푸드 트럭에 실망하기도 합니다. 188 오늘 〈메이크 더 미팅〉 촬영 때는 그렇지 않았습니다. 푸드 트럭은 커피도 훌륭했고, 189 커다란 과일 샐러드 속 딸기도 아주 신선하고 맛있었습니다! 190 무덥고 불쾌한 날씨에 손님들 줄이 길었는데도 서버는 모두의 음식을 신속하게 준비해 주었습니다. 그녀는 또한 친절하고 여유로웠습니다! 심지어 푸드 트럭조차 보기 좋았는데, 트럭 옆면에 그려진 그림도 아름다웠습니다! 다음 영화 촬영 장소에서 존 케이터링 푸드 트럭을 볼 수 있기를 희망합니다.

—로버트 키오도

어휘　film 촬영하다　uncomfortable 불쾌한　easygoing 느긋한　pleasant-looking 보기 좋은　mural 벽화, 벽면 장식

186 Not / True

번역 존 케이터링에 대해 웹페이지에서 명시한 것은?
(A) 음악 콘서트에서의 음식 제공을 전문으로 한다.
(B) 경쟁사보다 가격이 낮다.
(C) 최근 캘리포니아로 회사 사무실을 이전했다.
(D) 24시간 고객 지원을 제공한다.

해설 웹페이지의 마지막 단락 세 번째 문장에서 현장에 있는 동안 문제가 발생할 경우를 대비해 24시간 지원도 제공한다(We even offer 24-hour support in case any issues arise ~ at your location)고 했으므로 (D)가 정답이다. 첫 번째 단락 첫 문장에서 영화 및 TV 제작 현장에 푸드 트럭을 제공한다(Zone Catering provides food trucks at film and television production sites)고 했으므로 (A)는 오답이고, (B)와 (C)에 대해서는 언급된 바가 없다.

어휘 specialize in ~을 전문으로 하다   competitor 경쟁사

187 세부사항

번역 일정표에 따르면, 6월 10일 〈트래핑스〉 촬영의 연락 담당자는 누구였는가?
(A) 에린 베그
(B) 마크 릴로
(C) 길준서
(D) 도나 가와슨

해설 일정표를 보면, 일정 날짜(scheduled date)가 6월 10일이고, 첫 번째에 영화 〈트래핑스〉(Trappings)의 연락 담당자가 에린 베그(Erin Begg)라고 나와 있으므로 (A)가 정답이다.

188 연계

번역 키오도 씨가 방문한 푸드 트럭이 있었던 곳은?
(A) 하핀 로트
(B) 라레도 가 192
(C) 탠더 필즈
(D) 스펙트럼 홀

해설 추천 글에서 키오도 씨는 연기를 하면서 영화 제작 현장의 푸드 트럭에 실망하기도 했지만 오늘 〈메이크 더 미팅〉 촬영 때는 그렇지 않았다(That was not the case today ~ filming *Make the Meeting*)고 했으므로, 키오도 씨가 방문한 푸드 트럭은 영화 〈메이크 더 미팅〉의 촬영 현장에 있었음을 알 수 있다. 일정표를 보면, 두 번째에 영화 〈메이크 더 미팅〉(Make the Meeting)의 촬영 장소가 라레도 가 192(192 Laredo Street)라고 나와 있으므로 (B)가 정답이다.

189 연계

번역 키오도 씨가 주문한 샐러드에 대해 아마도 사실인 것은?
(A) 특이한 맛이 났다.
(B) 다 먹기에 너무 컸다.
(C) 여러 종류의 베리가 들어 있었다.
(D) 캘리포니아에서 재배된 과일이 들어 있었다.

해설 추천 글의 세 번째 문장에서 키오도 씨는 커다란 과일 샐러드 속 딸기가 아주 신선하고 맛있었다(the strawberries in the large fruit salad were so fresh and tasty!)고 했는데, 웹페이지의 두 번째 단락 두 번째 문장을 보면 메뉴에 사용하는 모든 과일과 채소는 이곳 캘리포니아에서 재배된다(All the fruits and vegetables we use in our menus are grown here in California)고 나와 있다. 따라서 키오도 씨가 주문한 샐러드 속 과일은 캘리포니아에서 재배된 것임을 알 수 있으므로 (D)가 정답이다.

어휘 unusual 특이한   contain ~이 들어 있다

190 Not / True

번역 추천 글에서 푸드 트럭 서버에 관해 명시된 것은?
(A) 더위 속에서 일하는 것을 힘들어했다.
(B) 여가 시간에 벽화를 그린다.
(C) 주문 음식을 빨리 마련한다.
(D) 업계에서 25년 동안 일했다.

해설 추천 글의 네 번째 문장에서 무덥고 불쾌한 날씨에 손님들 줄이 길었는데도 서버는 모두의 음식을 신속하게 준비해 주었다(Even though there was ~ the server was able to get everyone's food ready quickly)고 했으므로 (C)가 정답이다.

어휘 heat 더위   spare time 여가 시간   prepare 마련[준비]하다

Paraphrasing 지문의 get everyone's food ready
→ 정답의 prepares orders

191-195 이메일 + 목록 + 이메일

수신: 정해원
발신: 줄리아 로랑
날짜: 7월 28일
제목: 댈러스 호텔
첨부: 🔗 시내 숙소 목록

해원에게,

저는 10월에 전국 디지털 마케팅 콘퍼런스에 참석할 계획입니다. 당신이 댈러스에서 열리는 이 콘퍼런스에 여러 번 참석한 것으로 알고 있습니다. 191 저는 이번이 처음 참석하는 건데, 어느 호텔을 예약할지 잘 모르겠습니다. 컨벤션 센터 근처에 있는 숙소 목록을 첨부했습니다. 193 지금은 보니타 스위츠 호텔 쪽으로 마음이 기울고 있지만 191 당신이 어떤 숙소를 추천해 줄지 알고 싶습니다.

디지털 마케팅 부서에서의 새로운 직책에 적응하셨기를 바랍니다. 콘퍼런스가 기대되며 그곳에서 다시 뵙기를 바랍니다.

줄리아 로랑
이메일 마케팅 전문가
더 3R 마케팅 회사

어휘 accommodation 숙소   lean toward (마음이) ~으로 기울다   property 건물   settle into ~에 적응하다, 자리 잡다

시내 숙박 시설 목록

(출처: www.topbusinesshotels.com/search/Dallashotels)

호텔	요금	설명
194 오크트리 호텔	194 204달러/1박	시내 중심부에 위치한 고급 호텔 컨벤션 센터와 가까움 야외 수영장, 호텔 내 레스토랑 3곳 쇼핑 구역과 가까움
알레시 댈러스 호텔	155달러/1박	댈러스 시내에 위치한 고풍스러운 부티크 호텔 조식 및 석식이 가능한 로비 레스토랑 컨벤션 센터, 역사 박물관과 가까움
192 보니타 스위츠 호텔	125달러/1박	시내 컨벤션 센터 지역의 신규 호텔 각 스위트룸 내 사무실 및 주방 구비 192 로비에 위치한 프린터를 갖춘 컴퓨터 센터 192 단체 이용 가능한 회의 공간 무료 현장 주차

어휘 description 설명 on-site 현장에 있는 quaint 고풍스러운, 예스러운

수신: 줄리아 로랑

발신: 정해원

날짜: 7월 29일

제목: 회신: 댈러스 호텔

줄리아에게,

저는 올해도 전국 디지털 마케팅 콘퍼런스에 참석할 예정입니다! 훌륭한 네트워크 형성 기회라서 매년 이 콘퍼런스를 위해 댈러스로 출장 가는 것을 좋아합니다. 195 이번이 처음 참석하는 것이니 첫째 날 밤에 처음 참석하는 분들을 위해 마련된 환영회에 가 보시기를 권합니다. 콘퍼런스 운영 기획 위원회에서 이 행사를 진행하고 있으며, 다른 콘퍼런스 참가자들과 어울릴 수 있는 좋은 기회가 될 것입니다.

저는 알레시 댈러스 호텔에 머물 예정입니다. 컨벤션 센터와 가장 가깝고 객실도 편안합니다. 193 당신에게는 이미 선호하시는 것 같은 그 호텔을 추천드립니다. 마침 새로운 참석자들을 위한 환영회도 그곳의 행사장 중 한 곳에서 진행될 예정입니다. 약간 더 멀지만 역시 편리합니다. 참고로 알려 드리자면, 194 우리는 회사 한도인 1박당 175달러를 초과하는 요금의 호텔을 예약하지 말라는 권고를 받습니다.

10월에 뵙기를 기대합니다. 만나서 이야기할 수 있으면 좋겠습니다.

정해원

디지털 마케팅 이사

더 3R 마케팅 회사

어휘 networking 인적 네트워크 형성 newcomer 새로 온 사람 reception 환영회 executive 운영의 committee 위원회 put on (행사 등을) 준비하다 occasion 기회 socialize with ~와 어울리다 goer ~에 (자주) 다니는 사람 comfortable 편안한 it so happens that 우연히, 마침 farther 더 먼 convenient 편리한 reminder 상기시키는 것 exceed 초과하다 catch up (그간의 소식, 정보 등을) 이야기하다

---

191 주제 / 목적

번역 첫 이메일의 목적은?
(A) 고객과의 회의 일정을 잡으려고
(B) 프로젝트에 도움을 요청하려고
(C) 동료의 제안을 구하려고
(D) 승진한 동료를 축하하려고

해설 첫 이메일의 첫 단락 세 번째 문장에서 이번이 처음 참석하는 건데 어느 호텔을 예약할지 잘 모르겠다(This will be my first time attending, and I'm not sure which hotel to book)고 했고, 첫 단락의 마지막 문장에서 당신이 어떤 숙소를 추천해 줄지 알고 싶다(I would like to know which property you would recommend)고 했다. 따라서 호텔 예약과 관련해 동료의 의견을 구하려고 이메일을 쓴 것이므로 (C)가 정답이다.

어휘 assistance 도움, 지원 seek 구하다, 찾다 be promoted 승진[진급]하다

Paraphrasing 지문의 would like to know which ~ recommend → 정답의 seek a suggestion

---

192 추론 / 암시

번역 목록에 따르면, 보니타 스위츠 호텔에 대해 암시된 것은?
(A) 역사적인 건물에 위치해 있다.
(B) 출장자들을 위한 자원을 갖추고 있다.
(C) 많은 시내 관광 명소와 가깝다.
(D) 일일 주차 요금을 부과한다.

해설 목록의 마지막에 있는 보니타 스위츠 호텔(Bonita Suites Hotel)에 대한 설명 중에 로비에 위치한 프린터를 갖춘 컴퓨터 센터(Computer center with printers located in lobby)와 단체 이용 가능한 회의 공간(Meeting space available for groups)이 있다고 나와 있다. 따라서 보니타 스위츠 호텔에 출장자들이 이용할 수 있는 시설이 있음을 알 수 있으므로 (B)가 정답이다.

어휘 resources 자원 tourist attraction 관광 명소

Paraphrasing 지문의 Computer center ~ for groups → 정답의 resources for business travelers

---

193 연계

번역 정 씨에 대해 사실인 것은?
(A) 마케팅 콘퍼런스에 전에 참석한 적이 없다.
(B) 레스토랑 때문에 알레시 댈러스 호텔을 선호한다.
(C) 로랑 씨가 보니타 스위츠 호텔에 묵어야 한다고 생각한다.
(D) 로랑 씨와 다른 회사에서 근무한다.

해설 첫 이메일의 다섯 번째 문장에서 로랑 씨가 지금은 보니타 스위츠 호텔 쪽으로 마음이 기울고 있다(Right now, I am leaning toward the Bonita Suites Hotel)고 했고, 두 번째 이메일의 두 번째 단락 두 번째 문장에서 정 씨가 로랑 씨에게는 이미 선호하는 것 같은 그 호텔을 추천하겠다(For you, I would suggest the one you already seem to prefer)고 했다. 따라서 정 씨는 로랑 씨가 마음에 든다고 한 보니타 스위츠 호텔에 숙박할 것을 추천하고 있으므로

(C)가 정답이다. 두 번째 이메일 첫 문장에서 정 씨는 올해도 콘퍼런스에 참석할 예정이라고 했으므로 (A), 두 번째 단락에서 알레시 댈러스 호텔에 대해 컨벤션 센터와 가장 가깝고 객실이 편안하다고 언급하고 있으므로 (B), 첫 번째 로랑 씨의 이메일과 두 번째 정 씨의 이메일 끝에 서명을 보면 두 사람 모두 더 3R 마케팅 회사 소속이므로 (D)는 오답이다.

194 연계

번역 정 씨는 왜 로랑 씨에게 오크트리 호텔을 피하라고 제안할 것 같은가?
(A) 호텔 내 레스토랑이 없다.
(B) 객실 요금이 회사 한도를 초과한다.
(C) 고객들이 대부분 시끄러운 관광객이다.
(D) 회의 장소에서 너무 멀다.

해설 두 번째 이메일의 두 번째 단락 마지막 문장에서 정 씨는 회사 한도인 1박당 175달러를 초과하는 요금의 호텔을 예약하지 말라는 권고를 받는다(we are advised not to book hotels with rates that exceed our company's limit of $175/night)고 했는데, 숙박 시설 목록 첫 번째에 오크트리 호텔(The Oaktree Hotel)의 요금은 1박당 204달러($204/night)로 나와 있다. 따라서 회사 한도를 초과하는 숙박비 때문에 오크트리 호텔을 피해야 한다고 제안할 가능성이 높으므로 (B)가 정답이다.

195 Not / True

번역 두 번째 이메일에서 전국 디지털 마케팅 콘퍼런스에 대해 명시한 것은?
(A) 장소가 매년 다른 도시로 바뀐다.
(B) 작년에는 알레시 댈러스 호텔에서 개최되었다.
(C) 정 씨는 운영 기획 위원회에 속해 있다.
(D) 최초 참석자를 위한 행사가 포함되어 있다.

해설 두 번째 이메일의 첫 단락 세 번째 문장에서 이번이 처음 참석하는 것이니 첫째 날 밤에 처음 참석하는 사람들을 위해 마련된 환영회에 가 보기를 권한다(Since this is your first time attending, I recommend you go to the newcomers' reception on the first night)고 한 뒤, 콘퍼런스 운영 기획 위원회에서 이 행사를 진행하고 있으며 다른 콘퍼런스 참가자들과 어울릴 수 있는 좋은 기회가 될 것(The conference executive planning committee is putting it on, ~ socialize with other conference goers)이라고 언급했다. 따라서 콘퍼런스에는 처음 참석하는 사람들을 위한 행사가 있다는 것을 알 수 있으므로 (D)가 정답이다.

Paraphrasing 지문의 the newcomers' reception
→ 정답의 an event for first-time attendees

196-200 편지 + 이메일 + 이메일

도버 상수도
로드니 대로 7400, 도버, DE 19904

3월 12일

나리 캠 씨
파밍 가 361
도버, DE 19902

캠 씨께,

196 이 편지는 도버 상수도가 4월 6일 수요일에 귀하의 주소지에서 서비스를 시작할 것임을 확인하기 위함입니다. 귀하의 고객 계정 번호는 귀하의 수도 계량기 번호와 동일한 DWS4289입니다.

청구는 매월 이루어지며 197 납부 기한은 매월 15일입니다. 고지서는 본사 주소로 수표를 보내거나 www.doverwatersupply.com/billing의 보안 페이지에서 귀하의 계정 번호와 지불 정보를 입력하여 납부할 수 있습니다.

4월 4일 월요일에 귀하 지역의 배관에 대한 시스템 세척을 실시할 예정입니다. 고객들은 일시적으로 그 시간대에 물에서 변색이나 침전물을 발견할 수 있습니다. 자세한 정보는 저희 웹사이트를 방문해 주십시오. questions@doverwatersupply.com으로 고객 지원팀에 연락하시거나 (302) 555-0135로 전화하실 수도 있습니다.

매튜 엔사인
계정 담당, 도버 상수도

어휘 water supply 상수도 account 계정 billing 청구서 발부 due 지불 기일이 된 bill 고지서, 청구서 secure 안전한, 보안된 perform 실시하다 flush (물로) 씻어 내림 temporarily 일시적으로 discoloration 변색 sediment 침전물

수신: questions@doverwatersupply.com
발신: 나리 캠 〈n.cam@mailcurrent.com〉
날짜: 3월 17일
제목: 계정 번호 DWS4289

안녕하세요,

저는 도버에 있는 새집으로 이사를 하고 있습니다. 4월 6일에 수도 서비스가 시작된다는 편지를 받았습니다. 또한 4월 4일에 배관을 세척한다는 내용도 있었습니다. 제가 물을 사용하기 시작할 때 변색이 나타날 것을 예상해야 할까요? 제가 취해야 하는 조치가 있습니까?

또한, 197, 200 귀사의 보안 페이지를 사용하려고 했는데 제 계정 번호가 유효하지 않다는 오류 메시지가 떴습니다. 5월 15일 만기일까지 온라인 접속을 하는 데 도움이 필요합니다.

귀하께서 제공해 주는 어떤 정보라도 감사드립니다.

나리 캠

어휘 be in the process of ~을 하는 중이다 flush 씻어 내리다 take a step 조치를 취하다 valid 유효한 due date 만기일

수신: 나리 캠 〈n.cam@mailcurrent.com〉
발신: 고객 지원 〈questions@doverwatersupply.com〉
날짜: 3월 18일
제목: 회신: 계정 번호 DWS4289

캠 씨께,

메시지를 보내 주셔서 감사합니다. 198 4월 6일에 수도꼭지를 처음 틀면 물이 탁해 보일 수 있습니다. 사용하시기 전에 물이 맑아질 때까지 틀어

두실 것을 권합니다. 199 물은 어떤 식으로든 해롭지 않다는 것을 보장합니다. 변색의 원인이 되는 미네랄은 자연적으로 발생하며, 최근 수질 검사는 매우 높은 품질을 보여 주었습니다.

200 말씀하신 문제에 대해 사과드립니다. 이를 해결했으니 더 이상의 문제는 없을 것입니다.

다른 문의사항이 있으시면, 주저하지 마시고 다시 연락해 주십시오.

라모나 하이즌
고객 지원, 도버 상수도

어휘 cloudy 탁한 faucet 수도꼭지 assure 보장하다, 장담하다 harmful 해로운 occur 발생하다 water analysis 수질 검사[분석] describe 말하다, 서술하다 further 더 이상의

196 주제 / 목적

번역 편지를 쓴 한 가지 목적은?
(A) 고객 혜택을 나열하려고
(B) 고객에게 가격 변경을 알리려고
(C) 서비스 시작을 확인하려고
(D) 웹사이트 변경사항을 설명하려고

해설 편지의 첫 문장에서 이 편지는 도버 상수도가 4월 6일 수요일에 고객의 주소지에서 서비스를 시작할 것임을 확인하기 위함(This letter is to confirm that Dover Water Supply will begin service ~ April 6)이라고 명시하고 있으므로 (C)가 정답이다.

어휘 list 열거하다 benefit 혜택 alert 알리다

197 연계

번역 캠 씨는 5월 15일에 온라인으로 무엇을 하고 싶어 할 것 같은가?
(A) 새 수도 계량기 요청
(B) 고객 설문 작성
(C) 누수관 신고
(D) 수도 요금 지불

해설 편지의 두 번째 단락에서 납부 기한은 매월 15일(payment is due on the fifteenth of each month)이며 고지서는 본사 주소로 수표를 보내거나 보안 페이지에서 계정 번호와 지불 정보를 입력하여 납부할 수 있다(Bills can be paid ~ by entering your account number and payment information on our secure page)고 했고, 첫 번째 이메일의 두 번째 단락에서 캠 씨는 보안 페이지를 사용하려고 했는데 계정 번호가 유효하지 않다는 오류 메시지가 떴다(I tried to use your secure page, but ~ my account number was not valid)면서 5월 15일 만기일까지 온라인 접속을 하는 데 도움이 필요하다(I will need your help in getting online access by the May 15 due date)고 했다. 따라서 캠 씨는 5월 15일까지 온라인으로 요금 납부하기를 원하는 것이므로 (D)가 정답이다.

어휘 complete (서식을) 작성하다 leaking (물, 가스 등이) 새는

198 세부사항

번역 두 번째 이메일에 따르면, 캠 씨가 4월 6일에 해야 할 일은?
(A) 식수를 5분 동안 끓일 것
(B) 얼마 동안 물을 흘러보낼 것
(C) 이웃들에게 연락할 것
(D) 서비스 방문을 요청할 것

해설 두 번째 이메일의 두 번째 문장에서 캠 씨에게 4월 6일에 수도꼭지를 처음 틀면 물이 탁해 보일 수 있다(Your water might look cloudy ~ turn on your faucets)며 사용하기 전에 물이 맑아질 때까지 틀어 둘 것을 권한다(We recommend that you keep the water running ~ before you use it)고 했으므로 (B)가 정답이다.

199 Not / True

번역 두 번째 이메일에서, 도버 상수도의 물에 대해 명시된 것은?
(A) 사용하기에 안전하다.
(B) 매달 측정된다.
(C) 많은 도시로 급수된다.
(D) 자연적으로 미네랄이 없다.

해설 두 번째 이메일의 첫 단락 네 번째 문장에서 물은 어떤 식으로든 해롭지 않다는 것을 보장한다(I assure you that the water is not harmful in any way)고 한 뒤, 변색의 원인이 되는 미네랄은 자연적으로 발생하며 최근 수질 검사는 매우 높은 품질을 보여 주었다(The minerals ~ occur naturally, and our latest water analysis showed very high quality)고 했으므로 도버 상수도에서 제공하는 물은 안전하다는 것을 알 수 있다. 따라서 (A)가 정답이다.

어휘 measure 측정하다 distribute 분배하다 free of ~이 없는

Paraphrasing   지문의 not harmful → 정답의 safe

200 연계

번역 하이즌 씨에 대해 결론지을 수 있는 것은?
(A) 캠 씨의 계정 문제를 해결했다.
(B) 수질 검사 사본을 캠 씨에게 보냈다.
(C) 캠 씨에게 신규 고객 할인을 제공할 것이다.
(D) 캠 씨의 지역에 살고 있다.

해설 첫 이메일의 두 번째 단락 첫 문장에서 캠 씨가 보안 페이지를 사용하려고 했는데 계정 번호가 유효하지 않다는 오류 메시지가 떴다(I tried to use your secure page, but ~ my account number was not valid)며 온라인 계정의 문제를 보고했고, 두 번째 이메일의 두 번째 단락에서 하이즌 씨가 캠 씨에게 문제에 대해 사과하고 이를 해결했으니 더 이상의 문제는 없을 것(I have fixed it, so you should not have any further trouble)이라고 했다. 따라서 하이즌 씨가 캠 씨의 온라인 계정 문제를 해결했다는 것을 알 수 있으므로 (A)가 정답이다.

어휘 resolve 해결하다

Paraphrasing   지문의 fixed → 정답의 resolved

101 (B)	**102** (A)	**103** (C)	**104** (D)	**105** (C)
106 (C)	**107** (B)	**108** (C)	**109** (C)	**110** (A)
111 (B)	**112** (D)	**113** (A)	**114** (D)	**115** (D)
116 (B)	**117** (D)	**118** (C)	**119** (B)	**120** (A)
121 (D)	**122** (C)	**123** (D)	**124** (B)	**125** (B)
126 (D)	**127** (C)	**128** (A)	**129** (A)	**130** (A)
131 (D)	**132** (B)	**133** (B)	**134** (A)	**135** (D)
136 (C)	**137** (A)	**138** (C)	**139** (B)	**140** (C)
141 (A)	**142** (D)	**143** (C)	**144** (C)	**145** (C)
146 (B)	**147** (D)	**148** (A)	**149** (C)	**150** (B)
151 (D)	**152** (B)	**153** (A)	**154** (B)	**155** (D)
156 (D)	**157** (A)	**158** (A)	**159** (C)	**160** (C)
161 (C)	**162** (C)	**163** (A)	**164** (B)	**165** (B)
166 (B)	**167** (D)	**168** (D)	**169** (D)	**170** (C)
171 (B)	**172** (D)	**173** (B)	**174** (C)	**175** (D)
176 (B)	**177** (D)	**178** (A)	**179** (B)	**180** (C)
181 (C)	**182** (D)	**183** (A)	**184** (D)	**185** (A)
186 (C)	**187** (A)	**188** (B)	**189** (D)	**190** (C)
191 (B)	**192** (B)	**193** (C)	**194** (A)	**195** (D)
196 (C)	**197** (C)	**198** (B)	**199** (A)	**200** (B)

PART 5

101 인칭대명사의 격 _ 주격

해설 빈칸은 동사 are의 주어 자리이고, '우리는 준비가 되었다'는 의미가 되어야 하므로 주격 인칭대명사 (B) we가 정답이다. (D)의 소유대명사 ours도 주어로 쓰일 수 있지만 문맥상 적절하지 않다.

번역 부서장에 따르면, 우리는 아르보니교 프로젝트에 대한 작업을 시작할 준비가 되었다.

102 부사 어휘

해설 동사구 must be followed를 수식하는 부사 자리로, 문맥상 '엄격히 준수되어야 한다'는 의미가 되어야 적절하다. 따라서 '엄격히'라는 뜻의 (A) strictly가 정답이다. (B) bitterly는 '몹시; 비통하게', (C) sizably는 '상당히 크게', (D) colorfully는 '다채롭게'라는 뜻이다.

번역 방문자의 실험실 출입을 금지하는 방침은 엄격히 준수되어야 한다.

어휘 policy 방침, 정책 prohibit 금지하다 access 출입, 접근 laboratory 실험실 follow 준수하다, 따르다

103 형용사 자리 _ 명사 수식

해설 빈칸 앞에 정관사 the, 뒤에 명사 graduate가 있으므로 명사를 수식하는 형용사 자리이다. 따라서 '첫 졸업생'이라는 의미를 완성하는 형

용사 (C) first가 정답이다. (A) most는 형용사 many의 최상급으로 정관사 the와 함께 '가장 많은'이라는 의미를 나타내며 뒤에 가산 복수 명사 또는 불가산명사가 와야 한다. (B) for는 전치사, (D) nearly는 부사로 품사상 답이 될 수 없다.

번역 김윤희는 포천 500대 기업을 이끄는 첫 세리카 대학 졸업생이다.

어휘 graduate 졸업생 Fortune 500 포천 500대 기업(경제지 〈포천〉이 매년 발표하는 상위 500개 사 리스트)

104 접속사 자리 _ 부사절 접속사

해설 빈칸 앞 명령문과 뒤에 오는 완전한 절(you have any problems ~ software)을 연결하는 접속사 자리로, 등위접속사인 (A) and와 (C) but, 부사절 접속사인 (D) if가 빈칸에 들어갈 수 있다. 문맥상 '만약 문제가 있으면'이라는 내용이 되어야 하므로 '(만약) ~하면'이라는 뜻의 부사절 접속사 (D) if가 정답이다. 명령문 뒤에서 '그러면'을 뜻하는 (A) and와 대조적인 내용을 연결하는 (C) but은 문맥상 적합하지 않고, (B) then은 부사로 품사상 빈칸에 들어갈 수 없다.

번역 만약 새로운 데이터베이스 소프트웨어에 문제가 있으면 IT 부서의 프랭크 마릴리에게 연락하십시오.

105 형용사 자리 _ 명사 수식

해설 빈칸 앞에 부정관사 a, 뒤에 복합명사 efficiency expert가 있으므로 명사를 수식하는 형용사 자리이다. 따라서 '선도하는, 일류의'라는 의미의 형용사 (C) leading이 정답이다. (A) led는 동사/과거분사, (B) leader는 명사, (D) leads는 동사/명사로 빈칸에 적합하지 않다.

번역 선도적인 효율성 전문가가 11월 초에 우리 작업 현장을 방문할 예정이다.

어휘 efficiency 효율성 expert 전문가 site 현장

106 명사 어휘 _ 복합명사

해설 빈칸은 be동사 are의 주어 자리로, 앞의 customer와 함께 복합명사를 이루어 자연스러운 문맥을 만드는 명사를 골라야 한다. 매장에서 영업시간 내에 '고객 주문이 접수된다'는 내용이 되어야 적절하므로 '주문'을 의미하는 (C) orders가 정답이다. (A)의 behavior는 '행동', (B)의 relation은 '관계', (D)의 type은 '유형'이라는 뜻으로 customer와 복합명사를 이룰 수는 있으나 문맥상 어울리지 않는다.

번역 갤런츠 펫 스토어에서 고객 주문은 오전 9시부터 오후 6시 사이에 접수됩니다.

어휘 accept 받다

107 부사 자리 / 어휘

해설 빈칸 뒤의 동사 values를 수식하여 '매우 중요하게 여기다'라는 의미가 되어야 적절하므로 '매우, 대단히'라는 뜻의 부사 (B) highly가 정답이다. (A) high, (C) highest, (D) higher가 부사로 쓰일 경우, 위치나 수치가 '높게, 높이'를 뜻하므로 동사 value를 수식하기에 문맥상 적절하지 않다.

번역 카레트 인더스트리스의 경영진은 연구팀의 업무를 매우 중요하게 여긴다.

어휘 value 가치 있게 여기다, 중요시하다

108 동사 어휘 동영상 강의

해설 「be able＋to부정사」 구문의 to 뒤에 들어갈 동사 어휘를 고르는 문제이다. 빈칸 뒤의 most prescriptions와 함께 '대부분의 처방약을 조제할 수 있다'는 의미를 나타내야 자연스러우므로 '조제하다'라는 뜻의 (C) fill이 정답이다. (A) care는 '보살피다', (B) earn은 '(돈을) 벌다', (D) lifts는 '들어올리다'의 의미로 문맥상 적절하지 않다.

번역 펜트렉사 약국은 영업일 기준 1일 이내에 대부분의 처방약을 조제할 수 있습니다.

어휘 prescription 처방약, 처방전 business day 영업일

109 명사 자리 _ 동사의 주어

해설 동사 will begin의 주어 자리로, 앞에 정관사 The가 있고 뒤에 전치사 of가 있으므로 빈칸에는 명사가 들어가야 한다. 따라서 '공사, 건설'이라는 뜻의 명사 (C) construction이 정답이다. 주로 동사로 쓰이는 (A) construct와 (D) constructs는 명사로도 쓰이지만 '(구조적인) 생각, 개념'이라는 의미이므로 문맥상 어울리지 않고, (B) constructed는 동사/과거분사이므로 품사상 답이 될 수 없다.

번역 휴런 종합병원의 주차 건물 공사는 6월 1일에 시작될 것이다.

어휘 structure 건축물 general hospital 종합병원

110 전치사 어휘

해설 the recent rainstorm을 목적어로 취하는 자리로, '최근의 폭우 이후에 화단이 다시 심어졌다'는 내용이 되어야 자연스러우므로 '~ 후에'를 뜻하는 (A) after가 정답이다. (B) among은 '~ 중에', (C) opposite은 '~ 건너편에', (D) beside는 '~ 옆에'라는 뜻이다.

번역 데일 밸리 로지를 둘러싼 화단의 일부는 최근의 폭우 이후에 다시 심어져야 했다.

어휘 flower bed 화단 surround 둘러싸다 lodge 오두막, 산장 replant 다시 심다 rainstorm 폭우

111 동사 자리 _ 태

해설 Several water stations가 주어인 문장에 동사가 보이지 않으므로 빈칸은 동사 자리이고, install은 타동사인데 빈칸 뒤에 목적어가 없으므로 수동태가 와야 한다. 따라서 정답은 (B) will be installed이다. 동사의 과거형인 (D) installed는 뒤에 목적어를 필요로 하는 능동태이므로 답이 될 수 없다.

번역 다음 주에 있을 마라톤의 경로를 따라 여러 개의 급수대가 설치될 예정이다.

어휘 water station 급수대

112 형용사 어휘

해설 빈칸 뒤의 명사 view를 수식하여 '도시의 근사한 전망'이라는 의미가 되어야 자연스러우므로 '경치가 좋은'이라는 뜻의 (D) scenic이 정답이다. (A) valid는 '유효한', (B) recent는 '최근의', (C) modern은 '현대의'라는 뜻이다.

번역 크라운 라군 호텔은 각각 도시의 근사한 전망을 갖춘 150개의 객실을 보유하고 있다.

113 접속사 자리 _ 부사절 접속사

해설 빈칸 앞에 주어 charitable donations와 동사 rose를 갖춘 완전한 절이 있고, 뒤에 또 다른 완전한 절(specific dollar amounts are not yet available)이 왔으므로, 이들을 이어주는 접속사가 필요하다. 부사절 접속사인 (A) although와 (C) whenever, 등위접속사인 (D) so가 들어갈 수 있는데, 문맥상 '기부는 증가했지만, 금액은 공개되지 않았다'는 내용이 되어야 적절하므로 '비록 ~이지만'을 뜻하는 부사절 접속사 (A) although가 정답이다. (B) neither는 nor와 함께 neither A nor B(A도 아니고 B도 아닌)의 형태로 쓰여야 절을 연결할 수 있다.

번역 전반적으로 지난해에 자선 기부는 증가했지만, 아직 구체적인 달러 금액은 공개되지 않았다.

어휘 overall 전반적으로 charitable 자선의 donation 기부 specific 구체적인

114 전치사 자리

해설 빈칸은 뒤에 오는 turning it in과 함께 앞에 나온 완전한 절(We strongly advise you ~ electronic device)을 수식하는 자리로, '맡기기 전에'라는 의미가 되어야 적절하므로 (D) before가 정답이다. (A) once는 부사(한 번)/접속사(일단 ~하면), (B) both는 한정사(둘 다의)/대명사(둘 다), (C) then은 부사(그 다음에)이므로 품사상 빈칸에 들어갈 수 없다. 참고로, before -ing(~하기 전에)와 after -ing(~한 후에)는 빈출 표현으로 암기해 두자.

번역 수리를 위해 맡기기 전에 전자 기기에 저장된 데이터를 백업할 것을 강력히 권고합니다.

어휘 advise 권고하다 store 저장하다 electronic device 전자 기기 turn in ~을 제출하다

115 부사 자리 _ 동사 수식

해설 빈칸은 주어 her supervisor와 동사 asks 사이에서 동사를 수식하는 부사 자리이다. 따라서 '자주, 빈번히'라는 뜻의 부사 (D) frequently가 정답이다. (A) frequent는 형용사/동사, (B) frequents는 동사, (C) frequenting은 동명사/현재분사로 품사상 답이 될 수 없다.

번역 가르시아 씨가 도표와 그래프 만드는 것을 즐겨 하기 때문에 상사는 그녀에게 프레젠테이션 자료를 만들어 줄 것을 자주 요청한다.

어휘 chart 도표 supervisor 상사, 감독관 material 자료 frequent 잦은; 자주 다니다

116 명사 어휘

해설 소비자들이 물건을 덜 구매한다는 내용으로 보아 남는 제품을 처리해야 한다는 의미가 되어야 적절하므로, 빈칸 앞의 형용사 excess와 함께 '과잉 재고'라는 의미를 나타내는 명사 (B) inventory가 정답이다. (A) confidence는 '자신감', (C) capacity는 '수용력', (D) energy는 '활기, 에너지'라는 의미로 문맥상 적절하지 않다.

번역 소비자들이 사치품을 덜 구매함에 따라 고급 제품 제조업체들은 과잉 재고를 처리하고 있다.

어휘 manufacturer 제조업체 high-end 고급의 deal with ~을 처리하다 excess 과잉의, 초과한 consumer 소비자

117 관계대명사 _ 주격

해설 빈칸이 있는 절은 문장의 주어이자 선행사인 The Hayle Group과 동사 advocates 사이에서 선행사를 보충 설명하는 관계사절로, 빈칸 뒤에 동사 consists가 있으므로 주격 관계대명사가 들어가야 한다. 따라서 (D) which가 정답이다. (A) themselves는 재귀대명사, (B) someone은 대명사, (C) whoever는 부사절/명사절을 이끄는 복합 관계대명사로 빈칸에 들어갈 수 없다.

번역 비즈니스 컨설턴트와 변호사로 구성된 헤일 그룹은 조세 정책 개혁을 지지한다.

어휘 consist of ~로 구성되다 advocate 지지하다 reform 개혁

118 동사 어휘

해설 명사 applicants를 뒤에서 수식하는 분사구 being p.p.의 과거분사 자리에 들어갈 알맞은 동사 어휘를 고르는 문제이다. 문맥상 '프랜차이즈를 감독할 것으로 고려되고 있는 지원자들'이라는 내용이 되어야 하므로 '고려하다'라는 뜻의 동사 consider의 과거분사형 (C) considered가 정답이다. (A)의 decide는 '결정하다', (B)의 correct는 '정정하다', (D)의 practice는 '실행하다'라는 뜻으로 문맥상 적합하지 않다.

번역 다이시 아사야마는 킹스턴 프랜차이즈를 감독하는 일에 고려되고 있는 세 명의 지원자 중 한 명이다.

어휘 applicant 지원자 oversee (작업 등을) 감독하다

119 형용사 자리 _ 주격 보어

해설 빈칸은 be동사 뒤 주격 보어 자리이므로 형용사나 분사, 또는 명사가 들어갈 수 있다. '그녀의 연구가 인상적이었다'는 내용이 되어야 자연스러우므로 '인상적인'이라는 뜻의 형용사 (B) impressive가 정답이다. 형용사 (A) impressed는 '감명받은'이라는 뜻으로 사람의 감정을 설명하고, 동사 (C) impress는 주격 보어 자리에 들어갈 수 없으며, 명사 (D) impression은 주어 her research와 동격이 아니므로 답이 될 수 없다.

번역 첸 씨 책의 평론가는 그녀의 연구가 인상적이었다고 언급했다.

어휘 reviewer 평론가 note 언급하다 research 연구, 조사 impression 인상, 감명

120 전치사 어휘

해설 빈칸 뒤의 명사구 his transfer를 목적어로 취해 '전근한 이래로 법무 부서에서 근무해 왔다'는 내용이 되어야 자연스러우므로 '~ 이래로'를 뜻하는 (A) since가 정답이다. (B) between은 '~ 사이에', (C) without은 '~ 없이', (D) like는 '~처럼'이라는 뜻이다. 참고로, 전치사 since는 현재완료 시제와 자주 쓰인다.

번역 페레이라 씨는 10년 전 애틀랜타 사무실로 전근한 이래로 우리 법무 부서에서 근무해 왔다.

어휘 legal department 법무 부서 transfer 전근, 이동

121 명사 자리 _ 복합명사

해설 빈칸은 앞의 its largest, 뒤의 center와 함께 전치사 on의 목적어 역할을 하는 명사구를 이루는 자리이다. 문맥상 '가장 큰 유통 센터'라는 의미가 되어야 자연스러운데 center의 용도, 목적을 나타내는 '유통[물류] 센터'는 복합명사로 나타내므로 (D) distribution(유통)이 정답이다. 형용사인 (A) distributive(분배의, 유통의)와 (C) distributable(분배 가능한)도 명사 앞에서 수식할 수 있지만 쓰임이 적절하지 않고, (B) distribute(유통시키다)는 동사이므로 품사상 답이 될 수 없다.

번역 페니팩 마켓츠는 곧 이 지역에서 가장 큰 유통 센터를 착공할 계획이다.

어휘 break ground 착공하다

122 부사 어휘

해설 빈칸 뒤의 동사 welcomed를 수식하여 '짧게[간단히] 환영했다'는 의미가 되어야 적절하므로 '짧게, 간단히'라는 뜻의 (C) briefly가 정답이다. (A) accessibly는 '접근하기 쉽게', (B) abundantly는 '풍부하게', (D) momentarily는 '곧, 순간적으로'라는 뜻이다. 참고로, briefly welcome은 자주 쓰이는 표현이므로 암기해 두자.

번역 밀러 씨는 워크숍을 이끌 발표자들을 짧게 환영했다.

123 동사 어형 _ 시제

해설 Mr. Nayar가 주어, the need가 목적어인 문장의 동사 자리이므로 (A), (C), (D) 중에서 선택해야 한다. before 부사절의 동사 issued가 과거 시제이고, 문맥상 정부가 과거에 보고서를 발표한 이전의 일을 나타내야 하므로 과거보다 앞선 일을 나타내는 과거완료 시제가 들어가야 한다. 따라서 (D) had stressed가 정답이다.

번역 나야르 씨는 정부가 해당 주제에 대한 보고서를 발표하기 훨씬 이전에 강화된 안전 규약의 필요성을 강조했다.

어휘 enhanced 강화된 protocol 규약 long before 훨씬 이전에, 오래 전에 government 정부 issue 발표하다

124 형용사 어휘

해설 빈칸 뒤의 명사 changes를 수식하기에 적절한 형용사를 고르는 문제이다. 선행사 changes to its benefits package를 수식하는 관

계사절이 직원들의 열렬한 환영을 받았다(that were greeted ~ by its staff)는 긍정적인 내용인 것으로 미루어 보아, '상당한 변화'라는 의미가 되어야 자연스러우므로 (B) substantial이 정답이다. (A) judgmental은 '비판적인', (C) magnetic은 '자성의; 매력 있는', (D) chaotic은 '혼란스러운'이라는 의미이다.

번역　안젤리아 파이낸셜은 최근 복리 후생 제도에 직원들의 열렬한 환영을 받은 상당한 변화를 발표했다.

어휘　benefits package 복리 후생 제도　greet 환영하다
enthusiastically 열렬하게

125　형용사 자리 _ 명사 수식

해설　빈칸은 poems가 주어, are included가 동사인 문장에서 주어인 poems를 수식하는 형용사 자리이다. 따라서 '몇몇의'라는 뜻의 형용사 (B) Several이 정답이다. (A) Whichever는 명사절/부사절을 이끄는 복합관계대명사이고, (C) Something과 (D) None은 대명사이므로 명사를 수식하는 자리에 들어갈 수 없다.

번역　마이크 하노버가 쓴 몇몇 시들이 〈머윈의 문집〉의 개정판에 포함되어 있다.

어휘　poem 시　edition (출판물의) 판　anthology 문집

126　동사 어휘

해설　빈칸은 please로 시작하는 명령문의 동사 자리로, 뒤에 전치사 to가 있으므로 to와 함께 쓰이는 자동사가 들어가야 한다. 문맥상 '명단을 원하면 협회 웹사이트를 참조하라'는 의미가 되어야 하므로 전치사 to와 함께 '~을 참조하다'라는 뜻을 나타내는 (D) refer가 정답이다. 자동사로 쓰일 경우 (A) elect는 '선거하다', (C) present는 '(증상 등이) 나타나다'라는 뜻이고, 특히 (B) adapt는 '~에 적응하다'라는 뜻으로 전치사 to와 자주 쓰이지만 문맥상 적합하지 않다.

번역　식당에 식품을 공급하는 지역 농장의 명단을 원하시면 휴랜드 농장 협회 웹사이트를 참조하십시오.

어휘　supply 공급하다　association 협회

127　명사 자리 _ 동명사의 목적어 / 복합명사

해설　전치사 of 뒤의 동명사 improving의 목적어 자리로, 빈칸 앞의 명사 employee와 함께 복합명사를 이루는 명사가 들어가야 적절하므로 (C) productivity가 정답이다. (A) produced는 동사/과거분사, (B) productive는 형용사, (D) productively는 부사이다. 참고로, employee는 가산 단수명사로 앞에 한정사 없이 쓸 수 없으므로 해당 문장에서 복합명사의 앞자리 명사임을 알 수 있다.

번역　사미두 커뮤니케이션즈는 직원 생산성을 향상시킬 방법에 대한 직원들의 제안을 수렴하고 있다.

어휘　solicit 간청하다, 얻으려고 하다　productive 생산적인

128　접속사 자리 _ 부사절 접속사

해설　빈칸은 뒤에 오는 완전한 절(the sales team has a holiday event)을 이끌어 앞의 주절을 수식하는 부사절 접속사 자리로, 문맥

상 '영업팀이 휴일 기념 행사를 할 때마다'라는 의미가 되어야 자연스럽다. 따라서 '~할 때마다'라는 뜻으로 부사절을 이끄는 복합관계부사 (A) whenever가 정답이다. (B) regarding(~에 관하여)과 (D) besides(~ 외에도)는 전치사이므로 절을 연결할 수 없고, (C) whether는 부사절 접속사로 쓰일 경우 보통 or와 함께 '~이든 아니든'이라는 의미를 나타내므로 문맥상 적절하지 않다.

번역　벤모셰 씨는 영업팀이 휴일 기념 행사를 할 때마다 항상 사이토미스 키친에 연회장을 예약한다.

어휘　reserve 예약하다　banquet room 연회장

129　동사 자리 _ 시제

해설　Annika Dulin이 주어, the marketing department가 목적어인 문장의 동사 자리이다. 문장 끝에 미래를 나타내는 tomorrow가 있으므로 미래 시제를 나타내는 (A) will represent가 정답이다.

번역　아니카 둘린은 내일 톨라슨 인더스트리스의 기획 회의에서 마케팅 부서를 대표할 예정이다.

어휘　planning 기획　represent 대표하다

130　명사 어휘

해설　문맥상 '사전 승인 없이'라는 내용이 되어야 자연스러우므로 '승인, 허가'라는 뜻의 (A) authorization이 정답이다. (B) supplement는 '보충', (C) consequence는 '결과', (D) responsibility는 '책임'이라는 뜻이다.

번역　사전 승인 없이 소셜 미디어에 회사에 대한 어떠한 발언도 게시하지 마십시오.

어휘　post 게시하다　statement 발표, 성명　prior 사전의

PART 6

131-134　기사

그랜드 오프닝을 기념하는 크레이 빌라 박물관

디어필드 (5월 2일) — 5월 29일 오전 10시에 크레이 빌라 박물관의 공식 개관식이 열릴 예정이다. 이 행사를 기념하기 위해 다양한 축제 행사가 하루 종일 열린다. 131 **입장료는 무료이지만 기부가 권장된다.** 자세한 내용은 www.krayvillamuseum.org를 방문하면 된다.

박물관은 1800년대 후반부터 한때 영향력 있던 크레이 가의 자택이었 132 **던 웅장한 건축물에** 자리하고 있다. 지난 30년간 방치되어 있던 이 건축물은 2년 전 디어필드 역사 협회에 의해 매입되었다. 그 뒤, 정원은 크레이 가 1세대가 빌라에 입주했을 당시처럼 보이도록 복원되었다. 133 **또한,** 가족에 의해 사용되었을 법한 가구들이 전시되어 있다.

박물관의 개관 기념행사 기간 동안 라이브 밴드가 19세기 후반에 유행한 음악을 134 **연주할 것이다.**

어휘　celebrate 기념하다　opening 개관, 개장　official 공식적인　mark 기념[축하]하다　occasion 행사　various

다양한 festivity 축제 행사 house 수용하다 imposing 웅장한, 인상적인 structure 건물, 건축물 influential 영향력 있는 late ~ 말[후반]의 lay 두다 abandoned 버려진, 유기된 property 건물, 소유지 society 협회, 단체 subsequently 그 뒤에, 이어서 restore 복원하다 generation 세대 furnishings 가구, 세간 on display 전시된

131 문맥에 맞는 문장 고르기

번역 (A) 올해의 기념행사는 일주일 동안 열리는 전국 캠페인의 일부이다.
(B) 설문 조사 결과는 오후 6시에 발표될 예정이다.
(C) 프로그램은 다음 회의에서 배포될 것이다.
(D) 입장료는 무료이지만 기부가 권장된다.

해설 빈칸 앞에서 박물관의 개관 소식(The official opening ~ will take place)을 전하며 개관식 일정 및 행사에 대해 언급하고 있으므로, 개관식 행사와 관련된 소식을 안내하는 내용이 이어져야 자연스럽다. 따라서 개관식의 입장료는 무료이지만 기부가 권장된다고 언급하고 있는 (D)가 정답이다. 참고로, 박물관 개관식은 반복되는 행사가 아니므로 (A)는 답이 되지 않는다.

어휘 weeklong 일주일에 걸친 distribute 배포하다 admission 입장(료) donation 기부

132 관계대명사 _ 주격

해설 빈칸 이하는 선행사 the imposing structure를 수식하는 관계사절로, 빈칸 뒤에 동사 was가 나오므로 주격 관계대명사인 (B) that이 정답이다. (A) such와 (D) all은 한정사/대명사로 절을 이끌 수 없고, (C) what은 선행사를 포함하는 관계대명사로 앞에 선행사가 올 수 없다.

133 접속부사

해설 앞 문장에서 정원이 크레이 가족이 입주했을 당시처럼 보이도록 복원되었다고 한 뒤, 빈칸이 있는 문장에서 가족이 사용했을 법한 가구들이 전시되어 있다며 크레이 가족이 살던 당시 모습의 재현 요소를 언급하고 있다. 따라서 '게다가, 또한'을 뜻하는 (B) Additionally가 정답이다. (A) Conversely는 '반대로', (C) In the meantime은 '그동안에', (D) To this end는 '이를 위하여'라는 뜻이다.

134 동사 어형 _ 시제

해설 빈칸이 있는 문장은 박물관의 개관 기념행사 기간 동안의 일에 대해 언급하고 있는데, 기사의 첫 문장에서 박물관 개관식이 5월 29일에 열릴 예정(will take place)이라고 했으므로 박물관 개관식은 미래에 일어날 일임을 알 수 있다. 따라서 빈칸에는 미래 시제가 쓰여야 자연스러우므로 (A) will perform이 정답이다.

135-138 이메일

수신: 전 직원
발신: 세실 라두, 정보기술 관리자
날짜: 4월 8일

회신: 네트워크 경고

당사의 로컬 네트워크에 몇몇 문제가 발생하고 있습니다. 영향을 받은 서비스 중에는 135 내부 회사 웹사이트와 급여 데이터베이스가 있습니다. 또한 네트워크 데이터가 손상되고 파일이 제대로 저장되지 않는다는 것 136 에 대한 정보도 받았습니다. 그러므로 어떠한 작업도 유실되지 않도록 저희 팀이 이 137 문제를 해결하는 동안 오늘 오전에 네트워크 사용을 피해 주십시오. 오늘 오후까지는 시스템이 완전히 작동될 것으로 예상합니다. 138 양해해 주셔서 감사합니다.

어휘 alert 경고 experience 겪다 affected 영향을 받은 payroll 급여 corrupted (데이터가) 손상된 properly 제대로 ensure 확실하게 하다 avoid 피하다 address 해결하다 anticipate 예상하다, 기대하다 functional 작동을 하는

135 형용사 자리 _ 명사 수식

해설 빈칸은 정관사 the와 복합명사 company Web site 사이에서 명사를 수식하는 자리이므로, 현재분사 (A) internalizing과 형용사 (D) internal 중 하나를 선택해야 한다. '내부의 회사 웹사이트'라는 내용이 되어야 하므로 '내부의'를 뜻하는 형용사 (D) internal이 정답이다. 현재분사인 (A) internalizing은 '내면화하는'이라는 뜻이므로 웹사이트를 수식하기에 적절하지 않고, (B) internalize는 동사, (C) internally는 부사이므로 품사상 답이 될 수 없다.

136 전치사 어휘

해설 빈칸 뒤 동명사구 network data becoming corrupted and files not saving properly를 이끌어 앞에 있는 명사 information을 수식하는 전치사 자리로 문맥상 '네트워크 데이터가 손상되고 파일이 제대로 저장되지 않는다는 것에 대한 정보'라는 내용이 되어야 적절하므로 '~에 대한'이라는 뜻의 (C) about이 정답이다. (A) as는 '~로서', (B) in은 '~에', (D) with는 '~와 함께'라는 뜻이다.

137 명사 어휘

해설 빈칸에는 동사 address(해결하다)의 대상이 들어가야 하고, 앞 내용에서도 회사 네트워크에 발생한 문제에 대해 설명하고 있으므로 문제를 해결한다는 내용이 되어야 적절하다. 따라서 '문제'를 뜻하는 (A) issues가 정답이다. (B)의 client는 '고객', (C)의 article은 '기사', (D) proposal은 '제안'이라는 뜻이다.

138 문맥에 맞는 문장 고르기

번역 (A) 네트워크 서버는 비용이 많이 들 것입니다.
(B) 컴퓨터가 손상되었을 수 있습니다.
(C) 양해해 주셔서 감사합니다.
(D) IT 지원 데스크로 문의하십시오.

해설 빈칸 앞에서 문제를 해결하는 동안 오전에 네트워크 사용을 피해 달라(avoid using the network this morning)고 요청하면서 오후까지는 시스템이 작동될 것으로 예상한다(the systems will be fully functional by this afternoon)고 설명하고 있다. 따라서 문제 해결을 위한 협조 및 인내에 감사를 전하는 말로 글을 마무리하는 것이 자

연스러우므로 양해해 주셔서 감사하다고 언급하고 있는 (C)가 정답이다.

어휘 patience 인내

139-142 공지

4월 2일

TP&G 고객님께,

타코라디 전력&가스(TP&G)는 모든 고객에게 믿을 수 있는 전력 서비스를 제공하는 데 전념하고 있습니다. 이를 위해, 저희는 **139 시스템**을 일부 개선해야 합니다. 정비팀이 4월 22일 경에 오전 10시부터 고객님 지역의 변압기를 업그레이드할 예정입니다. **140 유감스럽게도**, 해당 날짜에 대략 오전 10시부터 오후 1시까지 고객님 지역의 거주지에 전력을 차단해야 합니다. **141 일시적으로 불편을 끼쳐 드려 죄송합니다.** 이 공지문을 **142 보냄**으로써 계획된 정전으로 인한 차질이 최소화되기를 바랍니다.

어휘 be committed to ~에 전념하다 dependable 믿을 수 있는 electricity 전력 to this end 이를 위해 make improvements 개선하다 maintenance 유지 관리 crew 작업팀 transformer 변압기 neighbourhood 지역, 동네 shut off ~을 차단하다, 끄다 residence 거주지, 주택 approximately 대략 disruption 차질, 방해 outage 정전 minimize 최소화하다

139 명사 어휘

해설 문맥상 빈칸에는 우리(TP&G)가 개선해야(make some improvements) 하는 대상이 들어가야 적절하다. 빈칸 뒤 문장에서 개선을 위한 작업 내용으로 정비팀이 변압기를 업그레이드할 예정이라고 설명하고 있으므로, 빈칸이 있는 문장은 TP&G에서 전력을 공급하는 '시스템을 개선한다'는 내용이 되어야 적절하다. 따라서 '시스템'을 뜻하는 (B) system이 정답이다. (A) office는 '사무실', (C)의 vehicle은 '차량', (D)의 record는 '기록'을 뜻한다.

140 접속부사

해설 빈칸 앞 문장에서 고객의 지역에 있는 변압기를 업그레이드할 것이라고 한 뒤, 빈칸이 있는 문장에서 지역 거주지에 전력을 차단해야한다며 앞 문장의 작업 내용으로 인해 초래될 불편함에 대해 언급하고 있다. 따라서 불편함을 주기에 앞서 사과나 유감의 뜻을 전달하기위해 사용하는 '유감스럽게도'라는 뜻의 (C) Unfortunately가 정답이다. (A) If not은 '그렇지 않다면', (B) Nonetheless는 '그렇더라도', (D) On the other hand는 '반면에'라는 뜻이다.

141 문맥에 맞는 문장 고르기

번역 (A) 일시적으로 불편을 끼쳐 드려 죄송합니다.
(B) 저희는 대부분의 서비스 요청에 24시간 이내로 응대합니다.
(C) 다른 회사들은 조명 설치를 전문으로 합니다.
(D) 에너지 요금을 줄이기 위한 몇 가지 팁이 여기 있습니다.

해설 빈칸 앞에서 정비팀이 변압기를 업그레이드할 예정으로 작업 당일 거주지에 공급되는 전력을 차단해야 한다(we will need to shut off the electricity)고 했다. 따라서 작업으로 인해 일상생활에 지장을 준점에 대해 사과하는 내용이 뒤따르는 것이 자연스러우므로, 일시적으로 불편을 끼쳐 죄송하다고 언급하고 있는 (A)가 정답이다.

어휘 temporary 일시적인 inconvenience 불편 specialize in ~을 전문으로 하다 lighting 조명 installation 설치 reduce 줄이다 bill 청구서

142 동명사 _ 전치사의 목적어

해설 빈칸은 전치사 by의 목적어 역할을 하는 동명사 자리이다. 따라서 (D) sending이 정답이다. (A) sent는 동사/과거분사, (B) to send는 to부정사, (C) will send는 동사로 구조상 빈칸에 들어갈 수 없다.

143-146 이메일

수신: hanna.kalita@netmail.co.uk
발신: patientoutreach@ebmp.co.uk
날짜: 6월 12일
제목: 환자 포털에 초대합니다

칼리타 씨께,

이스트 버버리 병원은 최근 환자 포털인 버메드 커넥트를 출시했습니다. 이 서비스는 귀하께서 편리하실 때 의료 서비스를 관리할 수 있도록 돕기 **143 위한 것입니다.** 포털에 접속하는 계정을 만드실 수 있도록 초청드립니다. 등록되면 의료 기록을 보고 처방전을 요청할 수 있을 뿐 아니라 의사와의 진료 예약도 할 수 있습니다. **144 뿐만 아니라,** 담당 의사에게 메시지를 보내기 위해 버메드 커넥트를 이용할 수도 있습니다. 귀하와 담당 의사만이 두 사람 사이에 주고받는 메시지를 확인할 수 있습니다. **145 귀하의 개인 정보를 보호하는 것은 저희가 중대하게 여기는 책임입니다.**

계정을 만드시려면, www.eastburberrymedicalpractice/patient-portal.co.uk로 이동하십시오. **146 등록** 절차에 어려움이 있을 경우, 20 5550 0169로 전화 주십시오.

엠마 리처드슨, 환자 지원 담당자

어휘 patient 환자 medical practice 병원, 의료업 roll out ~을 출시하다 at one's convenience 편리한 시간에 account 계정 access 접속하다, 이용하다 enroll 등록하다 as well as ~뿐 아니라, 게다가 prescription 처방전 exchange 교환하다 process 절차 outreach 지원 활동 coordinator 담당자, 조정자

143 동사 어형 _ 시제 ▶ 동영상 강의

해설 앞에서 최근 환자 포털을 출시했다고 발표한 데 이어서 빈칸이 있는 문장은 포털 서비스를 출시한 목적에 대해 설명하고 있으므로, '편리할 때 의료 서비스를 관리하도록 돕기 위한 것이다'라며 현재 시제로 나타내는 것이 자연스럽다. 따라서 정답은 (D) is intended이다.

어휘 be intended to ~하기 위한 것이다, ~할 목적이다

144 접속부사

해설 앞 문장에서 포털에 등록되면 의료 기록을 보고 처방전을 요청할 수 있으며 진료 예약을 할 수 있다고 한 뒤, 빈칸 뒤에서 담당 의사에게 메시지를 보낼 수 있다고 했다. 즉, 포털을 통해 할 수 있는 일을 추가적으로 나열하고 있으므로 '뿐만 아니라, 더욱이'라는 뜻의 (A) Furthermore가 정답이다. (B) Instead는 '대신에', (C) However 는 '하지만', (D) Otherwise는 '그렇지 않으면'이라는 뜻이다.

145 문맥에 맞는 문장 고르기 ▶ 동영상 강의

번역 (A) 이전 포털은 더 이상 업데이트되지 않을 것입니다.
(B) 건강 앱은 저희 웹사이트에서 다운로드하실 수 있습니다.
(C) 귀하의 개인 정보를 보호하는 것은 저희가 중대하게 여기는 책임입니다.
(D) 세 번째 시도가 실패하면 귀하의 계정이 잠기게 됩니다.

해설 빈칸 앞에서 담당 의사에게 메시지를 보낼 수 있으며 이 메시지는 환자와 담당 의사 두 사람만 확인할 수 있다(Only you and your doctor will be able to see ~ between the two of you)고 설명하고 있는 것으로 보아, 개인 정보 보호를 철저히 한다는 점을 강조하는 내용이 연결되어야 자연스럽다. 따라서 개인 정보를 보호하는 것은 중대하게 여겨지는 책임이라고 언급하고 있는 (C)가 정답이다.

어휘 previous 이전의 no longer 더 이상 ~않다
take ~ seriously ~을 중대[심각]하게 여기다 failed 실패한
attempt 시도

146 명사 어휘

해설 앞 문장에서 계정을 만들기 위해 할 일에 대해 안내하고 있으므로, 빈칸이 있는 문장은 앞서 언급한 계정을 만드는 일과 관련되어야 적절하다. 따라서 '등록'을 뜻하는 (B) registration이 정답이다. (A) selection은 '선택', (C) invention은 '발명', (D) deletion은 '삭제'를 뜻한다.

PART 7

147-148 안내판

¹⁴⁷ 갤러웨이 오피스 파크

빌딩 1
해리스 토드먼, ¹⁴⁸의학 박사
랜신 ¹⁴⁸진단 연구소
스마일리 ¹⁴⁸치과

빌딩 2
프릴 ¹⁴⁸1차 진료 의사
랠리 스타 ¹⁴⁸물리치료 협회

빌딩 3
리 앤 어소시에이츠, ¹⁴⁸내과 전문의
카레 ¹⁴⁸의료 서비스

빌딩 4
루리에 ¹⁴⁸제약회사

¹⁴⁷트럭 출입 금지
잡상인 출입 금지
무단출입 금지

어휘 MD 의학 박사(Doctor of Medicine) diagnostic 진단의 primary care 1차 진료 physician 의사 physical therapy 물리치료 internist 내과 전문의 pharmaceuticals 제약회사 solicit 호객 행위를 하다 trespass 무단 출입하다

147 추론 / 암시

번역 안내판을 찾을 수 있을 것 같은 장소는?
(A) 사무실 책상 위
(B) 병원 대기실
(C) 부동산 중개소 로비
(D) 사무실 단지 입구 근처

해설 안내판의 제목이 갤러웨이 오피스 파크(Galloway Office Park)인 것으로 보아 사무실 단지의 이름임을 짐작할 수 있다. 또한 각 빌딩마다 입주해 있는 업체가 나열되어 있고, 마지막 단락에 트럭 출입 금지(No Truck Access), 잡상인 출입 금지(No Soliciting), 무단출입 금지(No Trespassing)라고 출입 관련 규정들이 적혀 있는 것으로 보아 안내판은 사무실 단지의 입구에 있을 것으로 추정할 수 있다. 따라서 (D)가 정답이다.

어휘 entrance 입구 complex (건물) 단지

148 세부사항

번역 안내판에 적혀 있는 사업체의 종류는?
(A) 의료
(B) 법률 서비스
(C) 제조
(D) 금융

해설 각 빌딩에 입주한 업체로 의학 박사(MD), 진단 연구소(Diagnostic Labs), 치과(Dental Offices), 1차 진료 의사(Primary Care Physicians), 물리치료 협회(Physical Therapy Associates), 내과 전문의(Internists), 의료 서비스(Medical Services), 제약회사(Pharmaceuticals)가 안내되어 있으므로 정답은 (A)이다.

149-150 문자 메시지

다리온 게인즈 [오전 11시 16분]
소니아, 3층 휴게실 싱크대가 막혔어요.

소니아 핑커턴 [오전 11시 20분]
또요? 이번 달에만 두 번째예요.

다리온 게인즈 [오전 11시 22분]
지난번에 우리 영업 사원 중 한 명이 뚫어주었는데, 이번에는 전문가를 불러야 할 것 같아요. ¹⁴⁹그린 씨에게 연락해서 알려야 할까요?

소니아 핑커턴 [오전 11시 23분]

149 사무실 관리자요? 150 제 생각에는 유지보수 팀장인 타미 토스카에게 전화하는 편이 가장 좋을 것 같아요. 아마도 누군가를 보내서 빨리 고칠 수 있을 거예요.

다리온 게인즈 [오전 11시 24분]

좋아요. 150 제가 그녀에게 연락해 보겠습니다.

소니아 핑커턴 [오전 11시 25분]

그렇게 하세요. 그동안 저는 모두에게 싱크대를 사용하지 말라는 공지를 붙이겠습니다.

어휘 sink 싱크대 clog 막다; 막히다 associate 직원, 동료 professional 전문가 maintenance 유지 (관리) reach out to ~에게 연락을 취하다 in the meantime 그동안에

149 추론 / 암시

번역 그린 씨는 누구일 것 같은가?
(A) 관리인
(B) 배관공
(C) 관리자
(D) 영업 사원

해설 11시 22분에 게인즈 씨가 그린 씨에게 연락해서 알릴지(Should I contact Mr. Green and let him know?)를 묻자, 11시 23분에 핑커턴 씨가 사무실 관리자(The office manager?)를 말하는 것인지 되물으며 확인하는 것으로 보아 정답은 (C)이다.

어휘 custodian 관리인, 수위

150 의도 파악

번역 오전 11시 25분에 핑커턴 씨가 "그렇게 하세요"라고 쓴 의도는?
(A) 게인즈 씨가 휴게실에 들어갈 수 있다.
(B) 게인즈 씨가 토스카 씨에게 연락해야 한다.
(C) 게인즈 씨가 공지를 게시해야 한다.
(D) 게인즈 씨가 싱크대를 수리해 볼 수 있다.

해설 11시 23분에 핑커턴 씨가 유지보수 팀장인 타미 토스카에게 전화하는 편이 가장 좋을 것 같다(I think it might be best to call the head of maintenance, Tammy Toska)고 하자 11시 24분에 게인즈 씨가 그녀에게 연락해 보겠다(I could reach out to her)고 했고, 11시 25분에 핑커턴 씨가 그렇게 하세요(Go ahead)라고 했다. 따라서 타미 토스카에게 연락해 보겠다고 한 게인즈 씨의 제안을 핑커턴 씨가 수락하려는 의도로 한 말임을 알 수 있으므로 (B)가 정답입니다.

151-152 이메일

151 수신: 람데오 켐라즈 〈rkhemradj@topofthehill.jm〉
발신: 케렌사 메인 〈kmayne@topofthehill.jm〉
날짜: 8월 17일
제목: 정보
152 첨부: 🔗 최신 시안

안녕하세요, 람데오.

152 최신 시안을 보시고 어떻게 생각하는지 알려 주세요. 제가 배치를 바꿔서 이제 디저트가 뒤표지 안쪽에 있고, 151,152 당신과 당신의 주방 직원들이 다음 달에 선보일 추가 저녁 요리에 대한 설명을 넣었습니다.

가격은 아직 업데이트하지 않았는데, 일부를 인상해야 할지 결정하지 못했기 때문입니다.

디자인 회사가 주방을 업그레이드하고 식당을 더 밝고 매력적으로 만드는 작업을 훌륭하게 해냈다는 데 동의하실 거라고 확신합니다.

케렌사

어휘 latest 최신의 draft 시안, 초안 layout 배치 description 설명 additional 추가적인 introduce 선보이다 firm 회사 dining room 식당 bright 밝은 inviting 유혹[매력]적인

151 추론 / 암시

번역 켐라즈 씨는 누구일 것 같은가?
(A) 실내 장식가
(B) 식당 주인
(C) 건축가
(D) 주방장

해설 이메일의 수신인이 람데오 켐라즈(To: Ramdeo Khemradj)이고 첫 단락 두 번째 문장에서 메인 씨가 켐라즈 씨와 그의 주방 직원들이 다음 달에 선보일 추가 저녁 요리에 대한 설명을 넣었다(provided descriptions of the additional dinner dishes that you and your kitchen staff will be introducing next month)고 했다. 따라서 켐라즈 씨가 주방을 책임지고 있는 사람이라는 것을 알 수 있으므로 정답은 (D)이다.

어휘 architect 건축가

152 추론 / 암시

번역 이메일에 첨부되어 있을 것 같은 것은?
(A) 가격표
(B) 수정된 메뉴
(C) 음식 사진
(D) 식당 조명 설계도

해설 첨부 파일명이 최신 시안(Attachment: Latest draft)이고, 첫 문장에서 최신 시안을 보고 어떻게 생각하는지 알려 달라(Please take a look at the latest draft and let me know what you think)며 배치를 바꿔서 이제 디저트가 뒤표지 안쪽에 있고, 다음 달에 선보일 추가 저녁 요리에 대한 설명을 넣었다(I changed the layout — desserts are now on the inside back cover — and provided descriptions of the additional dinner dishes)고 한 것으로 보아 첨부 파일은 메인 씨가 디저트 목록 위치와 요리 설명을 수정한 식당 메뉴임을 알 수 있다. 따라서 (B)가 정답이다.

어휘 revised 수정된 lighting 조명 plan 도면, 설계도

153-154 지원서

페이지 터너 서점
입사 지원서

지원 날짜: 9월 1일

개인 정보

이름: 아르투로 라미	주소: 비미쉬 가 10, 웨리비, VIC 3030
이메일: arturo.rami@amail.com.au	전화번호: 03 9555 3744

고용 희망

희망 직책	부지점장		
근무 시작 가능일	9월 20일		
¹⁵³선호 지점	☐ 시홈	☒ 웨리비	☐ 포트 멜버른
선호 근무 형태	☒ 풀타임	☐ 파트타임	☐ 임시직

학력

교육 기관	졸업장/자격증/취득 학위
사우스뱅크 고등학교	고등학교 졸업장
다이목스 대학교	학사 학위

고용 이력

고용주	직책	근속 기간
가먼트 반	^{154(C)}판매 사원	2년
알토나 마케팅	대리	3년

직책에 대한 관심 설명

^{154(D)} 저는 속도가 빠르고 힘든 근무 환경에 잘 적응하는데, 제 최근 근무지들이 그런 환경으로 잘 알려져 있습니다. 상당히 분주해 보이는 페이지 터너 서점도 마찬가지일 것이라고 예상합니다. 게다가 ^{154(A)}저는 소매 경영학에 학사 학위를 가지고 있어서 이 직책에 매우 적합하다고 믿습니다.

어휘 employment 고용 application 지원 form 양식 desired 희망하는 assistant 부-, 보조의 status 상태 temporary 임시의 education 교육 institution 기관 diploma 졸업장 certificate 자격증 degree 학위 Bachelor 학사 employer 고용주 duration 기간 sales associate 판매 사원 explanation 설명 flourish 잘 지내다, 활약하다 fast-paced 빠른 속도의 demanding 힘든, 까다로운 retail 소매 be suited for ~에 적합하다

153 추론 / 암시

번역 페이지 터너 서점에 대해 암시된 것은?
(A) 지점이 여러 곳에 있다.
(B) 사우스뱅크 고등학교 근처에 있다.
(C) 9월 20일에 새로운 매장을 열 예정이다.
(D) 현재 상근직만 지원 가능하다.

해설 고용 희망 작성란의 세 번째에 선호 지점 선택지가 시홈, 웨리비, 포트 멜버른(Preferred location: Seaholme, Werribee, Port Melbourne)이라고 나와 있다. 따라서 이 세 지역에 페이지 터너 서점 지점들이 있다는 것을 알 수 있으므로 (A)가 정답이다.

어휘 multiple 다수의

154 Not / True

번역 라미 씨에 대해 명시된 것이 아닌 것은?
(A) 소매 경영학을 공부했다.
(B) 최근 웨리비로 이사했다.
(C) 판매직에서 일한 경험이 있다.
(D) 바쁜 환경에서 근무하는 것을 선호한다.

해설 고용 이력 작성란의 두 번째에 라미 씨가 판매 사원(Sales associate)으로 근무한 경력이 나와 있으므로 (C), 직책에 대한 관심 설명란의 첫 문장에서 라미 씨가 속도가 빠르고 힘든 근무 환경에 잘 적응한다(I flourish in a fast-paced and demanding work environment)고 했으므로 (D), 세 번째 문장에서 소매 경영학에 학사 학위를 가지고 있다(with my bachelor's degree in retail management)고 했으므로 (A)는 지문에 명시된 사실이다. 라미 씨가 최근에 웨리비로 이사했는지에 대해서는 언급된 바가 없으므로 정답은 (B)이다.

어휘 setting 환경

Paraphrasing 지문의 a fast-paced and demanding work environment
→ 보기 (D)의 a busy setting

155-157 광고

도노반 오토 루브

도노반 오토 루브(DAL)는 원활한 자동차 ¹⁵⁵운행을 원하는 넵워스 주민들에게 최우선의 선택입니다. 저희는 오일 교환, 타이어 위치 교환, 정기 점검을 제공합니다. 공인 자동차 정비사들로 이루어진 팀에서 모든 차량 제조사 제품과 모델을 정비할 수 있습니다. ¹⁵⁶고객님은 예약을 하시거나 월요일부터 토요일 오전 8시부터 오후 8시까지, 그리고 일요일 오전 11시부터 오후 5시까지 영업시간 중에 어느 DAL 지점으로든 차량을 그냥 가지고 오시면 됩니다.

¹⁵⁷올여름 DAL은 5쿼트 오일 교환, 오일 필터 교체 및 종합 정비 검사를 단돈 15파운드에 제공하는 특별 판촉 행사를 진행합니다. 이 행사는 허포드셔 전역의 모든 DAL 지점에서 이용하실 수 있지만 다른 판촉 행사와는 결합할 수 없습니다. 제시된 가격에는 부가가치세가 포함되지 않으며 차량 검사에서 요구될 수 있는 추가 정비, 수리 및 부품에 대한 비용은 포함되지 않습니다.

귀하의 자동차에 필요한 모든 것을 위해 DAL을 방문하십시오.

어휘 run 운행하다, 작동하다 smoothly 원활하게 rotation 교대, 회전 routine 정기적인 inspection 점검 certified 공인의 auto technician 자동차 정비사 service 정비하다 make 제품, -제 promotion 판촉 (활동) quart 쿼트(액량 단위: 약 1.14리터) replacement 교체 comprehensive 종합적인 maintenance 정비 combine 결합하다 promotional 판촉의 quoted 제시된, 인용된 value-added tax 부가가치세 cover (비용을) 대다 call for 요구하다 automotive 자동차의

155 동의어 찾기

번역 첫 번째 단락 2행의 "running"과 의미가 가장 가까운 단어는?
(A) 흐르는
(B) 속력을 내는
(C) 통제하는
(D) 작동을 하는

해설 의미상 자동차가 원활하게 '운행하다'라는 뜻으로 쓰인 것이므로 정답은 '작동[기능]을 하는'을 뜻하는 (D) functioning이다.

156 세부사항

번역 고객이 도노반 오토 루브에서 정비를 받을 수 있는 때가 아닌 것은?
(A) 월요일 오전 8시
(B) 수요일 오후 6시
(C) 토요일 오후 4시
(D) 일요일 오후 6시

해설 첫 단락의 마지막 문장에서 고객은 예약을 하거나 월요일부터 토요일 오전 8시부터 오후 8시까지, 그리고 일요일 오전 11시부터 오후 5시까지 영업시간 중에 어느 DAL 지점으로든 차량을 그냥 가지고 오면 된다(Customers ~ simply drive up to any DAL location during our business hours of 8:00 A.M. to 8:00 P.M., Monday to Saturday, and 11:00 A.M. to 5:00 P.M. on Sunday)고 했다. 따라서 일요일 오후 5시 이후로는 서비스를 받을 수 없으므로 (D)가 정답이다.

157 Not / True

번역 판촉 행사에 대해 사실인 것은?
(A) 넵워스 밖에서는 유효하지 않다.
(B) 필터 교체가 포함된다.
(C) 정비 검사에는 적용되지 않는다.
(D) 모든 세금이 포함되어 있다.

해설 두 번째 단락 첫 문장에서 올여름 DAL은 5쿼트 오일 교환, 오일 필터 교체 및 종합 정비 검사를 단돈 15파운드에 제공하는 특별 판촉 행사를 진행한다(This summer, DAL offers a special promotion: a 5-quart oil change, oil filter replacement, and comprehensive maintenance check for just £15)고 했다. 따라서 판촉 행사에 필터 교체가 포함되어 있으므로 (B)가 정답이다. 허포드셔 전역의 모든 지점에서 이용할 수 있다(This offer is available at all DAL locations throughout Herfordshire)고 했으므로 (A), 특별 판촉 행사에 종합 정비 검사(comprehensive maintenance check)가 포함되어 있으므로 (C), 제시된 가격에 부가가치세가 포함되지 않는다(The quoted price does not include value-added tax)고 했으므로 (D)는 오답이다.

어휘 valid 유효한 apply to ~에 적용되다

158-160 전기

> 카셈 응암은 태국 논타부리 주 출신의 유명한 연사이자 작가이다. 방콕에 있는 상수완 대학을 졸업하자마자, ¹⁵⁸**그는 찬타라 가스&일렉트릭(CG&E)에 입사했다.** ¹⁶⁰**25년의 기간 동안, 그는 CG&E에 가장**

> 헌신적이고 존경받는 직원 중 한 명으로 명성을 떨쳤고, 심지어 국내외의 인정을 받았다. 그가 이 회사에서 마지막으로 맡은 직책은 연구개발이사였다.

> ¹⁵⁸,¹⁵⁹**현재 응암 씨는 기업들이 현대 사회에 동력을 제공할 혁신적인 신기술을 개발하는 것을 돕기 위해 4년 전 시작한 컨설팅 회사를 운영하고 있다.** 그는 태양 전지판, 수소 동력 자동차를 포함해 다양한 주제에 관한 수많은 글의 저자이다. 그의 영예에는 여러 언어로 번역된 바이오 연료에 관한 그의 저서 〈미래의 연료〉가 받은 팍스 혁신상이 포함된다. 그의 차기 도서 〈에너지 가격 책정: 새로운 그린 에너지에 대한 자금 지원〉은 5월에 출판될 것이다.

어휘 renowned 유명한 author 작가 province (행정 단위) 주, 도 immediately 즉시 make a name 명성을 떨치다 dedicated 헌신적인 respected 존경받는 gain 얻다 recognition 인정, 표창 run 운영[경영]하다 firm 회사 innovative 혁신적인 power 동력을 공급하다; 동력 numerous 수많은 solar panel 태양 전지판 hydrogen-powered 수소 동력의 honor 영광(스러운 것) innovation 혁신 fuel 연료 translate 번역하다 forthcoming 다가오는 fund 자금을 제공하다

158 추론 / 암시

번역 응암 씨가 종사할 것 같은 업계는?
(A) 에너지
(B) 여행
(C) 금융
(D) 언론

해설 첫 단락의 두 번째 문장에서 응암 씨가 찬타라 가스&일렉트릭에 입사했다(he joined Chanthara Gas&Electric (CG&E))고 했고, 두 번째 단락 첫 문장에서 현재 기업들이 현대 사회에 동력을 제공할 혁신적인 신기술을 개발하는 것을 돕기 위해 4년 전 시작한 컨설팅 회사를 운영하고 있다(Mr. Ngam currently runs a consulting firm ~ to help businesses develop innovative new technologies to power the modern world)고 했다. 응암 씨가 에너지 회사에서 근무했고, 현재도 에너지 신기술 개발을 돕는 컨설팅 회사를 운영하고 있는 것으로 보아 에너지 분야에 종사하고 있음을 알 수 있으므로 정답은 (A)이다.

Paraphrasing 지문의 **Gas & Electric** → 정답의 **Energy**

159 Not / True

번역 응암 씨에 대해 명시된 것은?
(A) 그의 첫 책을 쓰고 있다.
(B) 여러 언어를 알고 있다.
(C) 자신의 사업을 운영하고 있다.
(D) 최근에 대학을 졸업했다.

해설 두 번째 단락 첫 문장에서 현재 응암 씨는 4년 전 시작한 컨설팅 회사를 운영하고 있다(Mr. Ngam currently runs a consulting firm)고 했으므로 (C)가 정답이다.

어휘 operate 운영하다 graduate 졸업생

160 문장 삽입

번역 [1], [2], [3], [4]로 표시된 위치 중에서 다음 문장이 들어가기에 가장 적합한 곳은?

"그가 이 회사에서 마지막으로 맡은 직책은 연구개발 이사였다."

(A) [1]

(B) [2]

(C) [3]

(D) [4]

해설 주어진 문장에서 '이 회사에서 마지막으로 맡은 직책(The last position he held at the company)'이라고 했으므로, 문장 앞에는 그가 근무했던 회사에 대한 언급이 있어야 한다. [2] 앞에서 응암 씨가 CG&E에 입사했으며(he joined Chanthara Gas & Electric), 25년 동안 가장 헌식적이고 존경받는 직원으로 명성을 떨쳤다(Over a period of 25 years, he made a name ~ most dedicated and respected employees)고 소개하고 있으므로, 주어진 문장은 [2]에 들어가는 것이 가장 적절하다. 따라서 (B)가 정답이다.

161-163 기사

윌렛빌에 생기는 일자리

161 윌렛빌 (3월 8일) — 테니스 할인 마트(TDM)는 이달 말 윌렛빌에서 채용 박람회를 개최할 것이라고 오늘 발표했다. 161 인근 리터시티에 본사를 둔 이 회사는 다음 달 이곳에 문을 열 예정인 새로운 물류 센터에 300개의 일자리를 충원하고자 한다. 162(A) 기술자와 관리자를 구하는 것 외에도 이 회사는 물류 처리, 재고 검사 및 유지 관리 부서의 일자리를 충원하기를 바란다.

"TDM의 물류 센터는 현대적인 자동화 시스템을 사용하며, 이로 인해 특히 자격을 갖춘 기술 직원이 많이 필요합니다."라고 TDM의 사장인 켄트 사일러는 채용 박람회를 발표하는 보도 자료에서 말했다.

162(B) 이 행사는 3월 20일 목요일 오전 9시 30분부터 오후 6시 30분까지 트윈 리지스 호텔의 연회장에서 열릴 예정이다. 162(D) 자세한 내용은 tdm.com/careers를 방문해 확인할 수 있다.

"이번 채용 행사는 우리 상품에 대해 예상되는 수요 증가를 맞추기 위해 필요한 직원들을 찾는 데 도움이 될 것입니다."라고 사일러 씨는 말했다. 163 "TDM은 할인 소매업에서 입지를 지속적으로 확대하고 있습니다. 올해 지금까지 세 개의 매장을 열었으며 내년 말까지 다섯 개의 매장을 추가로 개점할 계획입니다." 사일러 씨는 또한 TDM이 풀타임 및 시간제 고용직에 경쟁력 있는 급여를 제공한다고 언급했다.

어휘 job fair 채용 박람회 headquartered 본사를 둔 look to ~하기를 바라다 fill 채우다 distribution 유통 set to ~할 예정인 seek 구하다 processing 처리, 가공 stock 재고 inspection 검사 maintenance 유지 관리 automated 자동화된 qualified 자격이 있는, 적임의 in particular 특히 press release 보도 자료 recruiting 채용 anticipated 예상되는 growth 증가 demand 수요 expand 확대하다 retail 소매 so far 지금까지 slate (일정을) 계획하다 competitive 경쟁력 있는 wage 급여, 임금 employment 고용

161 Not / True

번역 TDM의 새로운 물류 센터에 대해 언급된 것은?

(A) 자동화 시스템을 사용하는 회사의 첫 번째 물류 센터이다.

(B) 회사가 건설한 것 중 가장 큰 시설이다.

(C) 4월에 문을 열 예정이다.

(D) 윌렛빌에 있는 건축 회사에 의해 설계되었다.

해설 도입부에 기사 작성일이 3월 8일(March 8)로 나와 있는데, 기사 두 번째 문장에서 인근 리터시티에 본사를 둔 이 회사는 다음 달 이곳에 문을 열 예정인 새로운 물류 센터에 300개의 일자리를 충원하고자 한다(The company, ~ at its new distribution center, set to open here next month)고 했다. 따라서 새로운 물류 센터는 기사가 작성된 3월의 다음 달, 즉 4월에 문을 열 예정이므로 (C)가 정답이다.

어휘 facility 시설 architectural 건축(학)의

162 Not / True

번역 채용 박람회에 대해 언급된 것이 아닌 것은?

(A) 제안되는 일자리 종류

(B) 개최 요일과 날짜

(C) 제공되는 다과 종류

(D) 자세한 정보의 출처

해설 첫 단락의 마지막 문장에서 기술자와 관리자를 구하는 것 외에도 이 회사는 처리, 재고 검사 및 유지 관리 부서의 일자리를 충원하기를 바란다(In addition to seeking technicians and supervisors, the company wants to fill positions in the processing, stock inspection, and maintenance departments)고 했으므로 (A), 세 번째 단락의 첫 문장에서 이 행사는 3월 20일 목요일 오전 9시 30분부터 오후 6시 30분까지 트윈 리지스 호텔의 연회장에서 열릴 예정(The event will be held ~ on Thursday, March 20, in the ballroom of the Twin Ridges Hotel)이라고 했으므로 (B), 뒤이어 자세한 내용은 tdm.com/careers을 방문해 확인할 수 있다(Details can be found by visiting tdm.com/careers)고 했으므로 (D)는 기사에 언급되어 있다. 제공되는 다과에 대해서는 언급된 바가 없으므로 (C)가 정답이다.

어휘 refreshments 다과 source (자료의) 출처

163 Not / True

번역 사일러 씨가 TDM에 대해 명시하는 것은?

(A) 성장하고 있는 업체이다.

(B) 매년 열리는 채용 박람회를 후원한다.

(C) 대부분 시간제 근로자들로 직원이 구성되어 있다.

(D) 온라인 판매에 크게 의존한다.

해설 마지막 단락의 두 번째 문장에서 사일러 씨가 TDM은 할인 소매업에서 입지를 지속적으로 확대하고 있고(TDM continues to expand its position in discount retail) 올해 지금까지 세 개의 매장을 열었으며 내년 말까지 다섯 개의 매장을 추가로 개점할 계획(So far this year, we have opened three stores, and we have five more slated to open by the end of next year)이라고 언급했으므로 정답은 (A)이다.

어휘 growing 성장[증가]하는 sponsor 후원하다 staff 직원을 두다;
직원으로 일하다 rely on ~에 의존하다 heavily 크게

Paraphrasing 지문의 continues to expand its position
→ 정답의 growing

164-167 온라인 채팅

> **라샨 리틀 (오후 5시 40분)**
> 안녕하세요, 아만다 그리고 데스몬드. 164 오늘 아침 시에서 등대를 철거
> 하기 위해 우리 회사를 고용했다는 것을 알았습니다.
>
> **아만다 리처즈 (오후 5시 43분)**
> 저도요. 그렇지만 그 구조물을 철거하는 데 대해 여러 감정이 드네요.
>
> **데스몬드 윌리엄스 (오후 5시 43분)**
> 저는 그 일에 대해 지금 처음 들었습니다. 오늘 하루 종일 사무실을 비웠
> 거든요.
>
> **라샨 리틀 (오후 5시 44분)**
> 아만다, 어째서 그런가요?
>
> **아만다 리처즈 (오후 5시 46분)**
> 165 최근 들어 사업이 상당히 부진한 것을 고려하면 우리 회사는 이 일을
> 해야 해요. 그렇긴 한데 166 이 등대는 100년 동안 벌링게이트의 주요
> 랜드마크였다는 역사적인 가치가 있습니다.
>
> **라샨 리틀 (오후 5시 48분)**
> 알고 있습니다. 그렇지만 말씀하신 이유로 회사에서 이 기회를 놓칠 여유
> 는 없습니다. 게다가 등대는 대체로 구식이 되었습니다.
>
> **데스몬드 윌리엄스 (오후 5시 49분)**
> 꼭 그런 것은 아니에요. 선박들은 항상 위험한 곳에 대한 경고를 받아야
> 합니다. 등대는 오랫동안 그 기능을 수행해 왔습니다.
>
> **라샨 리틀 (오후 5시 51분)**
> 맞는 말이지만 지금은 항해를 단순하고 등대를 점점 과거의 유물로 만
> 드는 현대 기술 장비가 존재합니다. 어쨌든 167 내일 오전 10시에 만나
> 서 이 일을 어떻게 진행할 것인지 논의합시다.

어휘 learn 알게 되다 demolish 철거하다 lighthouse 등대
take down ~을 철거하다 structure 구조물 given that ~을
고려하면 slow 부진한, 침체된 historic 역사적인 major 주요한
realize 인식하다 can't afford to ~할 여유가 없다 pass up
(기회를) 놓치다 opportunity 기회 besides 게다가 largely
주로 outdated 구식인 function 기능 technological
기술적인 simplify 간소화하다 navigation 항해 increasingly
점점 더 carry out ~을 수행하다

164 추론 / 암시

번역 채팅 작성자들이 근무할 것 같은 업종은?
(A) 건물 철거
(B) 해운 기술
(C) 기업 회계
(D) 역사 보존

해설 5시 40분에 리틀 씨가 오늘 아침 시에서 등대를 철거하기 위해 회
사를 고용했다는 것을 알았다(Earlier today I learned that the
town has hired our company to demolish the lighthouse)고
한 것으로 보아 채팅 작성자들이 철거 회사에서 근무하고 있다는 것을
알 수 있으므로 (A)가 정답이다.

어휘 demolition 철거 corporate 기업의 accounting 회계
historical 역사와 관련된 preservation 보존

165 Not / True

번역 채팅 작성자들이 근무하는 회사에 대해 명시된 것은?
(A) 최근에 초현대식 장비를 구입했다.
(B) 사업상 하락을 겪었다.
(C) 시 의회에 의해 정기적으로 고용된다.
(D) 100년 동안 사업을 해 왔다.

해설 5시 46분에 리처즈 씨가 최근 들어 사업이 상당히 부진한 것을 고려
하면 회사는 이 일을 해야 한다(given that business has been
quite slow lately, our company needs the work)고 했으므로
회사의 사업이 최근 하락세임을 알 수 있다. 따라서 (B)가 정답이다.

어휘 ultramodern 초현대적인 decline 하락 regularly 정기적으로

Paraphrasing 지문의 business has been ~ slow
→ 정답의 a decline in business

166 의도 파악

번역 오후 5시 48분에 리틀 씨가 "알고 있습니다"라고 쓴 의도는?
(A) 윌리엄스 씨가 부재중이었던 이유를 알고 있다.
(B) 시에 있어 등대의 중요성을 인식하고 있다.
(C) 회사가 시에 얼마나 중요한지 이해한다.
(D) 리처즈 씨가 시의 역사에 대해 많이 안다는 것을 알고 있다.

해설 5시 46분에 리처즈 씨가 이 등대는 100년 동안 벌링게이트의 주요 랜
드마크였다는 역사적인 가치가 있다(the lighthouse has historic
value: it has been a major landmark of Burlingate for 100
years)고 하자 5시 48분에 리틀 씨가 알고 있다(I realize that)고 대
답했다. 따라서 리틀 씨는 시에서 등대가 차지하는 의의에 대해 인식
하고 있음을 전하려는 의도로 한 말임을 알 수 있으므로 (B)가 정답
이다.

어휘 absent 부재의 recognize 인식하다 significance 중요성
aware 알고 있는

167 추론 / 암시

번역 채팅 작성자들은 내일 오전에 무엇을 할 것 같은가?
(A) 새로운 구인 광고
(B) 시의회 회의 참석
(C) 등대 관람
(D) 곧 있을 프로젝트에 대한 계획 시작

해설 5시 51분에 리틀 씨가 내일 오전 10시에 만나서 이 일을 어떻게 진
행할 것인지 논의하자(let's meet tomorrow at 10:00 A.M. to
discuss how we'll carry out this job)고 했으므로 정답은 (D)
이다.

TEST 10

어휘 advertise 광고하다 upcoming 곧 있을

Paraphrasing 지문의 discuss how we'll carry out
정답의 planning

168-171 안내 책자

**컨템포 스페이시스
창문 처리 패키지**

거실, 다이닝 공간 또는 침실의 창문을 새로 장식하는 것을 고려하고 계시다면, 컨템포 스페이시스가 귀하를 위한 완벽한 처리 디자인 패키지를 가지고 있습니다. 귀하의 창문에 맞춰 완벽하게 맞춤 제작되는 셰이드, 패널, 커튼, 밸런스의 적절한 조합 구성을 도와드립니다.

168 진행 방식은 다음과 같습니다:

• 먼저 저희 스타일 담당자 한 명이 고객님 댁을 방문하여 각 방의 창문을 측정하고 사진을 찍습니다.

• 방문하는 동안 **171 담당자가 저희 제품 라인에서 이용할 수 있는 다양한 스타일의 직물 및 금속 부속품 샘플을 보여드립니다.** 당사의 전체 스타일 컬렉션은 저희 웹사이트에서 보실 수 있습니다. 또는 가정 방문 후 저희 쇼룸에 오셔서 제품을 선택하실 수 있습니다.

• **169 창문 처리를 결정하고 1~2일 후에 자재, 설치 및 인건 비용이 기재된 청구서를 보내 드립니다. 견적 가격은 30일간 유효합니다.** 대금을 받는 즉시 자재가 발주됩니다. 자재가 저희 매장에 도착하는 데는 보통 7일에서 14일이 걸립니다.

• 마지막으로 설치 날짜와 시간을 잡기 위해 저희가 연락을 드립니다. **170 작업 규모에 따라 설치하는 데 두 시간에서 여덟 시간이 걸릴 수 있습니다.**

어휘 window treatment 창문 처리[장식](창문에 차양, 블라인드, 커튼 등을 이용해 기능적·장식적으로 처리하는 것) redecorate 새로 장식하다 combination 조합 shade 셰이드, 차양 drape 드레이프, (두꺼운) 커튼 valance 밸런스, 장식용 천 tailor 맞춤 제작하다 fit 맞다, 적합하다 representative 담당자 measure 측정하다 fabric 직물 opt to ~하기로 선택하다 selection 선택 invoice 청구서 material 자재 installation 설치 labor 노동 quoted 견적된, 제시된 valid 유효한 receipt 받음, 수령 payment 대금 reach 도달하다 depending on ~에 따라

168 주제 / 목적

번역 안내 책자의 목적은?
(A) 새로운 정책을 설명하기 위해서
(B) 인기 제품을 설명하기 위해서
(C) 특별 할인을 광고하기 위해서
(D) 표준 절차를 설명하기 위해서

해설 두 번째 단락에서 진행 방식은 다음과 같다(Here's how it works)고 한 뒤, 아래에서 창문 측정, 제품 선택, 대금 결제, 설치 등 진행 방식에 대해 순서대로 설명하고 있다. 따라서 안내 책자의 글은 업체의 서비스가 이루어지는 기본 절차를 설명하기 위한 것이므로 (D)가 정답이다.

어휘 describe 설명하다 standard 표준의

169 세부사항

번역 청구서에 기재된 총비용은 며칠 뒤에 변경될 수도 있는가?
(A) 2일
(B) 7일
(C) 14일
(D) 30일

해설 진행 방식을 설명하는 세 번째 항목의 첫 문장에서 창문 처리를 결정하고 1~2일 후에 자재, 설치 및 인건 비용이 기재된 청구서를 보낸다(One or two days after you've made your window treatment decisions, we will send you an invoice ~ and labor)고 했고, 견적 가격은 30일간 유효하다(The quoted price is valid for thirty days)고 했다. 따라서 청구서에 기재된 견적 비용은 30일이 지나면 변경될 수 있으므로 (D)가 정답이다.

170 추론 / 암시

번역 안내 책자에 설치에 관해 암시된 것은?
(A) 모든 창문 처리에 가능한 것은 아니다.
(B) 고객의 책임이다.
(C) 완료하는 데 8시간을 넘지 않는다.
(D) 외부 업체에 하도급을 준다.

해설 진행 방식을 설명하는 마지막 항목의 마지막 문장에서 작업 규모에 따라 설치하는 데 두 시간에서 여덟 시간이 걸릴 수 있다(Depending on the size of the project, installation can take two to eight hours)고 했으므로 설치를 완료하는 데 8시간은 넘지 않는다는 것을 알 수 있다. 따라서 (C)가 정답이다.

어휘 subcontract 하도급을 주다 vendor 판매 업체

Paraphrasing 지문의 take two to eight hours
→ 정답의 no more than eight hours

171 문장 삽입

번역 [1], [2], [3], [4]로 표시된 위치 중에서 다음 문장이 들어가기에 가장 적합한 곳은?

"당사의 전체 스타일 컬렉션은 저희 웹사이트에서 보실 수 있습니다."
(A) [1]
(B) [2]
(C) [3]
(D) [4]

해설 주어진 문장에서 '당사의 전체 스타일 컬렉션은 웹사이트에서 볼 수 있다(Our entire style collection can be viewed on our Web site.)'고 했으므로, 앞에는 일부 스타일에 대해 확인하는 것과 관련된 내용이 와야 적절하다. [2] 앞에서 고객의 집을 방문한 담당자가 다양한 스타일의 직물 및 금속 부속품 샘플을 보여 준다(our representative will show you samples of the many styles ~ in our product line)고 했으므로, 그 뒤에 주어진 문장이 들어가는 것이 글의 흐름상 자연스럽다. 따라서 (B)가 정답이다.

수신: 모건 테벨레 〈mtebele@newsom.com.na〉
발신: 에스메 무카야 〈emukaya@skyleopard.com.na〉
날짜: 8월 21일
제목: 제안

테벨레 씨께,

172 대출을 재융자하든, 직원을 교육하든, 금융 서비스를 온라인으로 마케팅하든, 빠르고 믿을 수 있는 인터넷 이용은 고객님과 같은 은행 관리자에게 필수입니다. 스카이 레오파드 커뮤니케이션즈는 고도로 발전된 네트워크와 헌신적인 인력 덕분에 바로 그것을 제공해 드립니다.

실제로, **173** 나미비아 소상공인 협회(NASO)가 실시한 최근 설문 조사에 따르면 회원의 75퍼센트가 경쟁사의 서비스보다 저희 서비스를 선호한다고 합니다.

그 이유는 최첨단 인터넷 기반 시설과 **174** 뛰어난 기술자 인력 외에도 고속 인터넷 연결(HIVIA) 서비스 요금제를 통해 프리미엄 인터넷 연결을 제공하기 때문입니다. HIVIA는 가장 근접한 경쟁사보다 3배 더 빠른 다운로드 및 업로드 속도를 제공합니다.

175 스카이 레오파드 커뮤니케이션즈는 신규 고객 및 당사의 다른 서비스 요금제 중 하나를 사용 중인 고객들에게 30일 동안 무료로 HIVIA를 사용할 수 있는 기회를 제공합니다. 가입하시려면 www.skyleopard.com.na를 방문하시거나 061-987-555로 전화 주십시오. **175** 한 달간의 체험 기간 동안 이 요금제에 만족하지 않으실 경우 언제든지 무료로 서비스 가입을 취소하실 수 있습니다.

에스메 무카야, 영업부

어휘 refinance 재융자하다 loan 대출 personnel 직원 reliable 믿을 수 있는 essential 필수적인 advanced 발전된 dedicated 헌신적인 workforce 인력 conduct 실시하다 association 협회 reveal 드러내다, 보여 주다 competitor 경쟁사 state-of-the-art 최첨단의 infrastructure 기반 시설 outstanding 뛰어난 pool 이용 가능 인력 connectivity 연결 velocity 속도 plan 요금제 subscribe 가입하다 trial period 체험 기간 satisfied 만족하는 unsubscribe 등록을 취소하다

172 추론 / 암시

번역 테벨레 씨가 종사할 것 같은 업종은?
(A) 웹 디자인
(B) 접객
(C) 마케팅
(D) 은행

해설 첫 단락의 첫 번째 문장에서 테벨레 씨에게 대출을 재융자하든, 직원을 교육하든, 금융 서비스를 온라인으로 마케팅하든, 빠르고 믿을 수 있는 인터넷 이용은 테벨레 씨와 같은 은행 관리자에게 필수(Whether you are refinancing a loan, training personnel ~ is essential for bank managers like you)라고 한 것으로 보아 테벨레 씨는 은행 관리자로 근무하고 있음을 알 수 있다. 따라서 (D)가 정답이다.

173 Not / True

번역 스카이 레오파드 커뮤니케이션즈에 대해 명시된 것은?
(A) NASO 회원들에게 할인을 제공한다.
(B) 소상공인들에게 인기 있다.
(C) 최근에 새로운 서비스 요금제를 출시했다.
(D) 인력을 늘리려 하고 있다.

해설 두 번째 단락에서 나미비아 소상공인 협회(NASO)가 실시한 최근 설문 조사에 따르면 회원의 75퍼센트가 경쟁사의 서비스보다 자사의 서비스를 선호한다(a recent survey conducted by the Namibian Association of Small-Business Owners (NASO) revealed that 75 percent of its members prefer our services over those of our competitors)고 했으므로 스카이 레오파드 커뮤니케이션즈는 소상공인들에게 인기 있다는 것을 확인할 수 있다. 따라서 (B)가 정답이다.

어휘 launch 출시하다

Paraphrasing 지문의 75 percent of its members prefer our services → 정답의 popular

174 동의어 찾기

번역 세 번째 단락 1행의 "outstanding"과 의미가 가장 가까운 단어는?
(A) 다양한
(B) 이용 가능한
(C) 탁월한
(D) 남아 있는

해설 의미상 '뛰어난' 기술자들이라는 뜻으로 쓰인 것이므로 정답은 '훌륭한, 탁월한'을 뜻하는 (C) excellent이다.

175 추론 / 암시

번역 HIVIA 서비스 요금제에 대해 결론지을 수 있는 것은?
(A) 다른 요금제보다 비싸다.
(B) 고객 설문 조사 후에 만들어졌다.
(C) 특수 장비 구입이 필요하다.
(D) 첫 달 이내에 무료로 취소할 수 있다.

해설 네 번째 단락의 첫 문장에서 스카이 레오파드 커뮤니케이션즈는 신규 고객 및 당사의 다른 서비스 요금제 중 하나를 사용 중인 고객들에게 30일 동안 무료로 HIVIA를 사용할 수 있는 기회를 제공한다(Sky Leopard Communications offers ~ the opportunity to try HIVIA for free for 30 days)고 했고, 마지막 문장에서 한 달간의 체험 기간 동안 이 요금제에 만족하지 않을 경우 언제든지 무료로 서비스 가입을 취소할 수 있다(If at any time during the one-month trial period ~ you can unsubscribe from the service at no cost to you)고 했다. 따라서 HIVIA 서비스 요금제는 한 달간의 무료 체험 중 언제든 취소할 수 있으므로 (D)가 정답이다.

어휘 following ~ 후에, ~에 이어 at no charge 무료로

Paraphrasing 지문의 unsubscribe ~ at no cost → 정답의 be canceled ~ at no charge

TEST 10

프로젝트 관리 입문
온라인 웨비나
180 **1월 18일 오전 9시 - 오후 2시**
발표자: 슈리야나 파텔
비용: 45유로
(1월 10일까지 등록하고 10퍼센트 할인을 받으세요!)

이 라이브 웨비나는 참석자들에게 프로젝트 관리가 조직에서 하는 역할을 개선하는 방법에 대한 더 나은 이해를 제공합니다. 발표는 프로젝트와 작업자를 관리하는 기초를 제공할 것입니다. 참가자들은 프로젝트를 효과적으로 감독하고 주요 관계자들로부터 동의를 촉진하기 위한 전략과 모범 사례를 배우게 됩니다.

176 **참가자들은 프로젝트를 관리하기 위한 간단한 단계별 과정을 살펴보고 범위 기술서와 커뮤니케이션 계획서 같은 툴과 문서 사용법을 학습하게 됩니다.** 발표자는 또한 프로젝트의 비즈니스 사례 개발 및 생산적인 팀 회의 조성 같은 주제들도 177 **다룰** 것입니다.

어휘 introduction 입문; 설명 webinar 인터넷상의 세미나 presenter 발표자 register 등록하다 attendee 참석자 participant 참가자 best practice 모범 운영 사례 effectively 효과적으로 oversee 감독하다 foster 촉진하다, 조성하다 buy-in 받아들임, 승인 explore 탐구하다 tool (컴퓨터) 툴, 도구 scope 범위 statement 기술(서) cover 다루다 facilitate 가능하게 하다 productive 생산적인

수신: 마야 리우
발신: 레너드 청
제목: 웨비나
날짜: 1월 2일

리우 씨께:

웨비나 안내문을 보내 주셔서 감사합니다. 178, 179 **초보 관리자로서 가능한 한 모든 교육을 받아야 하는데 이 특정한 제의를 이용할 수 있을지 확신할 수 없습니다.** 178, 180 **저는 같은 날 회사의 분기별 부서 회의에서 상세 프로젝트 업데이트를 발표할 예정**인데, 팀원 중 저를 대신할 만한 사람이 아무도 없을 것 같습니다.

웨비나가 녹화될 예정인지, 아니면 나중에 유사한 웨비나가 있을지 아시는지요? 1월 29일 이후에는 겹치는 일정이 없습니다.

레너드 청

어휘 novice 초보자 supervisor 관리자, 감독관 take advantage of ~을 이용하다 particular 특정한 detailed 상세한 quarterly 분기별의 division 부서 take one's place ~의 자리를 대신하다[채우다] schedule conflict 겹치는 일정

176 Not / True

번역 웨비나에 대해 명시된 것은?
(A) 취업 면접 준비에 대한 세션이 포함되어 있다.
(B) 참가자들에게 특정 툴의 사용법을 보여줄 것이다.
(C) 참가자들에게 드는 비용이 없다.
(D) 등록은 1월 10일에 마감된다.

해설 웨비나 설명의 두 번째 단락 첫 문장에서 참가자들은 프로젝트를 관리하기 위한 간단한 단계별 과정을 살펴보고 범위 기술서와 커뮤니케이션 계획서 같은 툴과 문서 사용법을 학습한다(Participants will explore ~ and learn how to use tools and documents such as scope statements and communication plans)고 했다. 따라서 (B)가 정답이다.

어휘 session (특정 활동) 기간 specific 특정한 registration 등록

177 동의어 찾기

번역 웨비나 설명에서, 두 번째 단락 3행의 "cover"와 의미가 가장 가까운 단어는?
(A) 보호하다
(B) 펼치다
(C) 요청하다
(D) ~에 대해 이야기하다

해설 의미상 주제를 '다루다'라는 뜻으로 쓰인 것이므로 정답은 '~에 대해 이야기하다'를 뜻하는 (D) talk about이다.

178 주제 / 목적

번역 이메일의 목적은?
(A) 일정이 겹치는 것을 설명하려고
(B) 기한 연장을 요청하려고
(C) 행사에 늦게 도착한 데 대해 사과하려고
(D) 발표 준비에 도움을 요청하려고

해설 이메일의 첫 단락 두 번째 문장에서 초보 관리자로서 가능한 한 모든 교육을 받아야 하는데 이 특정한 제의를 이용할 수 있을지 확신할 수 없다(As a novice supervisor ~ I'm not sure whether I will be able to take advantage of this particular offering)면서, 같은 날 회사의 분기별 부서 회의에서 상세 프로젝트 업데이트를 발표할 예정(I am scheduled to present a detailed project update ~ on the same day)이라고 했다. 따라서 웨비나 강좌와 자신의 발표 일정이 겹친다는 것을 설명하기 위해 이메일을 썼다는 것을 알 수 있으므로 (A)가 정답이다.

어휘 extension 연장 ask for ~을 요청하다

179 추론 / 암시 ▶ 동영상 강의

번역 청 씨에 대해 암시된 것은?
(A) 자신의 발표를 녹화할 계획이다.
(B) 종종 새로운 프로젝트 관리자들을 교육한다.
(C) 정기적으로 웨비나에 참석한다.
(D) 관리자로서 경험이 비교적 적다.

해설 이메일의 첫 단락 두 번째 문장에서 청 씨가 자신은 초보 관리자로서 가능한 한 모든 교육을 받아야 한다(As a novice supervisor, I need to get all the training I can)고 한 것으로 보아 관리자 경력이 많지 않다는 것을 알 수 있다. 따라서 (D)가 정답이다.

Paraphrasing 지문의 a novice → 정답의 has relatively little experience

번역　청 씨가 발표할 예정인 날짜는?
　　　(A) 1월 2일
　　　(B) 1월 10일
　　　(C) 1월 18일
　　　(D) 1월 29일

해설　웨비나 설명의 세 번째 줄에 1월 18일 오전 9시 – 오후 2시(18 January, 9 A.M. – 2 P.M.)라고 웨비나 일정이 나와 있고, 이메일의 첫 단락 세 번째 문장에서 같은 날 회사의 분기별 부서 회의에서 상세 프로젝트 업데이트를 발표할 예정(I am scheduled to present ~ on the same day)이라고 했다. 따라서 청 씨가 발표할 날짜는 웨비나가 열리는 1월 18일임을 알 수 있으므로 (C)가 정답이다.

181-185 기사 + 후기

골웨이 (3월 4일) — 181 **아델 로지에는 3세대 비누 제조업자로 8년 전 골웨이에 매장을 열었다.** 레이븐 테라스의 에글린턴 고메 마켓 뒤에 자리 잡은 그녀의 사업체인 로지에 앤 핀치는 호황을 맞고 있다.

로지에 씨는 이 성공을 그녀가 평생 학습에 전념한 덕이라 말한다. "네, 저의 수공예 비누, 샴푸, 그리고 로션은 고급스럽습니다."라고 그녀는 말했다. "하지만 고급 스킨케어 제품들은 시장에 허다합니다. 그래서 가족들로부터 이 일을 배운 뒤, 182 **저는 기업 대 기업(B2B) 마케팅 온라인 강좌를 수강해 영업 지식을 늘려 왔습니다.**"

183 **로지에 씨는 그 강좌들이 자신의 제품을 호텔에 직접 판매하는 데 자신감을 키워 주었다고 덧붙인다.** "B2B 전략 강좌에서 제가 배운 것들 덕분에 저의 제품을 사용해 보도록 유럽의 많은 부티크 호텔들을 설득할 수 있었습니다." 그리하여 184 **로지에 앤 핀치 스킨케어 제품들은 예를 들어 골웨이의 브루아데어 호텔, 포르투갈 리스본의 플로린다 그랜드, 아이슬란드 레이캬비크의 제라 인과 같은 호텔 객실에서 이용 가능하다.**

게다가 로지에 씨는 많은 고객들이 그녀의 제품을 호텔 숙박 중에 처음 접하게 된다고 언급한다. 그 후, 그들은 직접 매장을 방문하거나 온라인에서 스스로 상품을 구입한다.

로지에 앤 핀치는 레이븐 테라스 12에 위치해 있으며 온라인 www.rosierandfinch.co.ie에서 찾을 수 있다.

어휘　generation 세대　nestle 자리 잡다　boom 호황을 맞다　credit A to B A를 B의 공으로 돌리다　commitment 전념, 헌신　lifelong 평생의　handcrafted 수공예의　luxurious 고급스러운, 호화로운　knowledge 지식　strategy 전략　manage to ~을 해내다, 성공하다　persuade 설득하다　for instance 예를 들어　further 더 나아가　point out ~을 언급하다, 지적하다　afterward 그 후에　in person 직접

---

https://www.florindagrand.pt/en/guest_reviews

저는 회사의 포르투갈 사무실로 갑작스럽게 출장을 준비해야 했고, 제가 평소 예약하는 호텔은 완전히 만실이었습니다. 184 **몇몇 온라인 추천에 따라 저는 플로린다 그랜드에 머물기로 결정했습니다.** 이 매력적인 호텔은 제가 평소 묵는 곳보다 훨씬 작지만 출장 중 누구나 원할 만한 모든 편안함을 갖추고 있습니다. 고상하게 꾸며진 편안한 객실 외에도, 184 **베개 위에는 고급 간식이 있었고 최고급 비누, 샴푸, 그리고 다른 세면도**

구들이 즐길 수 있게 준비되어 있었습니다. 185 **유일하게 유감스러운 것은 제가 리스본에 단 3일만 있었다는 점입니다.** 다음번에 리스본 사무실을 방문할 때는, 더 오래 머물면서 플로린다 그랜드에 방을 예약할 것입니다.

— 애시턴 우 게시, 6월 7일

어휘　arrange 준비하다　last-minute 마지막 순간의, 임박하여　completely 완전히　recommendation 추천　charming 매력적인　comfort 안락　tastefully 고상하게　decorated 꾸며진, 장식된　gourmet (미식가용) 고급의　treat 간식　pillowcase 베갯잇　finest 최고급의　toiletries 세면도구　regret 후회, 유감　post 게시하다

181 주제 / 목적

번역　기사의 목적은?
　　　(A) 연간 호텔 등급을 제공하기 위해서
　　　(B) 매장 개점을 발표하기 위해서
　　　(C) 소상공인의 프로필을 소개하기 위해서
　　　(D) 온라인 쇼핑 트렌드에 대해 논하기 위해서

해설　기사의 첫 번째 문장에서 아델 로지에는 3세대 비누 제조업자로 8년 전 골웨이에 매장을 열었다(Adelle Rosier, a third-generation soap maker, opened her shop in Galway eight years ago)고 했고, 레이븐 테라스의 에글린턴 고메 마켓 뒤에 자리 잡은 그녀의 사업체인 로지에 앤 핀치는 호황을 맞고 있다(Nestled behind Eglinton Gourmet Market on Raven Terrace, her business, Rosier and Finch, is booming)며 로지에 앤 핀치라는 업체를 운영하고 있는 아델 로지에에 대해 소개하고 있다. 그 뒤로도 로지에 씨와 그녀의 사업체에 대한 내용이 계속 이어지고 있으므로 (C)가 정답이다.

어휘　annual 연례의　rating 등급　profile 프로필을 알려 주다

182 세부사항

번역　로지에 씨가 마케팅 기술을 향상시킨 방법은?
　　　(A) 해외에 있는 가족을 방문함으로써
　　　(B) 전문 협회에 가입함으로써
　　　(C) 호텔 업계에 근무함으로써
　　　(D) 온라인 수업에 참여함으로써

해설　기사의 두 번째 단락 마지막 문장에서 로지에 씨가 기업 대 기업(B2B) 마케팅 온라인 강좌를 수강해 영업 지식을 늘렸다(I have increased my sales knowledge by taking online courses in business-to-business (B2B) marketing)고 했으므로 (D)가 정답이다.

어휘　overseas 해외에　association 협회　industry 업계, 산업　participate in ~에 참여하다

Paraphrasing　지문의 taking online courses
　　　　　　　정답의 participating in online classes

183 Not / True

번역 로지에 앤 핀치에 대해 언급된 것은?

(A) 다른 사업체에 제품을 판매한다.

(B) 전 세계 도시에 매장을 가지고 있다.

(C) 전자 상거래 사이트를 재설계하고 있다.

(D) 비누 제조 강좌를 제공한다.

해설 기사의 세 번째 단락 첫 문장에서 로지에 씨는 그 강좌들이 자신의 제품을 호텔에 직접 판매하는 데 자신감을 키워 주었다고 덧붙인다 (Ms. Rosier adds that those courses built her confidence in selling her products directly to hotels)고 언급했다. 따라서 로지에 앤 핀치는 제품을 호텔에 납품하고 있다는 것을 알 수 있으므로 (A)가 정답이다.

어휘 e-commerce 전자 상거래 soapmaking 비누 제조

184 연계

번역 우 씨에 대해 암시된 것은?

(A) 에글린턴 고메 마켓을 관리한다.

(B) 온라인에서 로지에 앤 핀치 제품을 구입했다.

(C) 출장 중에 로지에 씨를 만났다.

(D) 로지에 앤 핀치 제품을 좋아한다.

해설 기사의 세 번째 단락 마지막 문장에 따르면 로지에 앤 핀치 스킨케어 제품들은 골웨이의 브로아데어 호텔, 포르투갈 리스본의 플로린다 그랜드, 아이슬란드 레이캬비크의 제라 인과 같은 호텔 객실에서 이용 가능하다(Rosier and Finch skin-care products are available in guest rooms at ~ the Florinda Grand in Lisbon, Portugal, and the Zerra Inn in Reykjavik, Iceland)고 했고, 후기의 두 번째 문장에서 우 씨는 몇몇 온라인 추천에 따라 플로린다 그랜드에 머물기로 결정했다(Based on some online recommendations, I decided to stay at Florinda Grand)고 한 뒤, 네 번째 문장에서 베개 위에는 고급 간식이 있었고 최고급 비누, 샴푸, 그리고 다른 세면도구들이 즐길 수 있게 준비되어 있었다(there were gourmet treats on my pillowcase and the finest soap, shampoo, and other toiletries available for me to enjoy)고 했다. 따라서 우 씨가 플로린다 그랜드 호텔에 납품된 로지에 앤 핀치 제품을 써 보고 마음에 들어했다는 것을 알 수 있으므로 (D)가 정답이다.

185 세부사항

번역 후기에 따르면, 우 씨가 아쉬워하는 것은?

(A) 여행 기간

(B) 객실 장식

(C) 베개의 편안함

(D) 호텔의 규모

해설 후기의 다섯 번째 문장에서 우 씨가 유일하게 유감스러운 것은 리스본에 단 3일만 있었다는 점(My only regret is that I was in Lisbon for just three days)이라고 했다. 따라서 우 씨는 짧았던 여행 기간을 아쉬워하는 것이므로 (A)가 정답이다.

어휘 length 길이, 기간

186-190 판매 보고서 + 회람 + 기사

187 마고의 아이스크림 하우스
매출 비율에 따른 맛 구매
7월

맛	퍼센트
초콜릿	22
바닐라	18
딸기	11
186 쿠키 앤 크림	8
186 버터 피칸	8
민트 초콜릿 칩	7
기타	26

어휘 flavor 맛 percentage 비율

회람

수신: 모든 점장

발신: 준 윌콕스, 최고 경영자, 마고의 아이스크림 하우스

제목: 신규 매장

날짜: 10월 5일

188 마고의 아이스크림 하우스는 다음의 신규 매장을 맞이하게 되어 자랑스럽습니다.

매장 번호	위치	개점일	점장
66	미국 매사추세츠 프레이밍햄	9월 1일	잉가 슬라빈
67	미국 위스콘신 애플턴	9월 7일	정 통
68	호주 뉴사우스웨일스 울런공	9월 14일	제프리 플랫
189 69	뉴질랜드 로토루아	9월 15일	케힌데 이로구
70	캐나다 온타리오 그레이터서드베리	9월 29일	할리 스트래포드

188 향후 6개월 동안, 우리는 이 매장들의 현지 미디어 시장 광고를 지원할 예정입니다.

12월에 우리는 이탈리아와 스위스에 매장을 열 계획입니다. 우리의 고품질 제품에 대한 수요가 그 어느 때보다 높고, 우리의 시장 점유율은 상승하고 있으며, 확장은 아직 끝나지 않았습니다! 더 많은 정보를 위해 계속 지켜봐 주세요!

어휘 following 다음의 support 지원하다 demand 수요 quality 고급[양질]의 market share 시장 점유율 expand 확장하다 stay tuned 지켜봐라, 계속 주목하라

인기 아이스크림 공급업체가 뉴질랜드에 오다

이사이 멘데즈 작성

로토루아 (11월 2일) — 마고의 아이스크림 하우스가 뉴질랜드에 첫 매장을 연 카길 가로 로토루아 주민들이 몰려들고 있다.

"비결이 무엇인지는 모르겠지만 그들의 아이스크림은 정말 특별합니다."라고 며칠 전 오후에 가족과 함께 아이스크림콘을 즐기던 학교 교사 제레미 프랭크는 말했다. "매장이 문을 연 이후로 이미 여러 번 왔습니다. 우리는 단골이 될 것 같습니다."

190 "저는 딸기를 정말 좋아하는데 이곳의 딸기는 제가 먹은 것 중 최고예요."라고 그의 열 살짜리 딸 올리비아 프랭크가 덧붙였다.

마고의 아이스크림 하우스는 예전에 화학 전공자였던 마고 서머스가 5년 전 샌프란시스코에서 창립했다. 187 이 회사의 아이스크림에는 적어도 11퍼센트의 유지방이 들어 있다. 회사 최고 경영자인 준 윌콕스에 따르면, 생산에 사용되는 우유는 가능할 때마다 현지 지역에서 공급받는다.

로토루아 매장의 점장 케힌데 이로구는 방문객 수가 꾸준히 증가하고 있다고 말한다.

"한 달에 한 번 특별 행사를 가져 이 여세를 이어갈 계획입니다."라고 그는 말했다. "190 다음은 딸기 축제입니다. 189 뉴질랜드의 딸기 시즌이 시작될 것입니다. 우리의 훌륭한 아이스크림에 더하여 초콜릿에 찍어 먹는 딸기, 딸기 컵케이크, 딸기 밀크셰이크를 제공할 예정입니다. 우리는 로토루아에서 멋진 미래를 기대합니다."

어휘 purveyor 공급업자 resident 주민 flock 모이다
regular 단골 found 창립하다 former 예전의, 이전의
chemistry 화학 major 전공자 contain ~이 들어 있다
production 생산 be sourced (특정 장소에서) 얻다, 공급받다
regionally 지역에서 steadily 꾸준히 momentum 여세, 기세
superb 훌륭한 dip 살짝 적시다

186 세부사항

번역 판매 보고서에 따르면, 버터 피칸과 같은 비율로 구매되는 아이스크림 맛은?
(A) 초콜릿
(B) 바닐라
(C) 쿠키 앤 크림
(D) 민트 초콜릿 칩

해설 판매 보고서의 표에 쿠키 앤 크림(Cookies and cream)이 8%, 버터 피칸(Butter pecan)이 8%라고 나와 있으므로 버터 피칸과 같은 비율로 판매된 아이스크림은 쿠키 앤 크림이라는 것을 알 수 있다. 따라서 (C)가 정답이다.

187 연계

번역 판매 보고서에 기재된 제품에 대해 사실인 것은?
(A) 적어도 11퍼센트의 유지방이 포함되어 있다.
(B) 인공 향료로 만들어졌다.
(C) 곧 가격이 인상될 예정이다.
(D) 주로 샌프란시스코에서 판매된다.

해설 판매 보고서의 첫 줄에 마고의 아이스크림 하우스(Margot's House of Ice Cream)라고 나와 있고, 기사의 네 번째 단락 두 번째 문장에서 마고의 아이스크림 하우스의 아이스크림에는 적어도 11퍼센트의 유지방이 들어 있다(Its ice cream contains at least 11 percent milk fat)고 했으므로 (A)가 정답이다.

어휘 artificial 인공의 mainly 주로

188 Not / True

번역 회사의 새 점장들에 대한 회람에 명시된 것은?
(A) 이탈리아와 스위스에서 교육을 받았다.
(B) 6개월 동안 광고 지원을 받을 것이다.
(C) 그들의 매장이 12월에 수익이 날 것으로 예상한다.
(D) 개점일에 특별 판촉 행사를 제공했다.

해설 회람의 첫 번째 줄에 마고의 아이스크림 하우스는 다음의 신규 매장을 맞이하게 되어 자랑스럽다(Margot's House of Ice Cream is proud to welcome the following new stores)고 했고, 표 아래에서 향후 6개월 동안 이 매장들의 현지 미디어 시장 광고를 지원할 예정(For the next six months, we will be supporting these stores with advertisements in their local media markets)이라고 했다. 따라서 마고의 아이스크림 하우스 신규 매장의 점장들은 6개월간 광고 지원을 받을 것이므로 (B)가 정답이다.

어휘 profitable 수익이 나는 promotion 판촉 (활동)

Paraphrasing 지문의 supporting ~ with advertisements
→ 정답의 advertising support

189 연계

번역 69호점에서 곧 일어날 일은?
(A) 더 많은 아이스크림 맛이 메뉴에 추가될 것이다.
(B) 한 어린이의 생일을 축하할 것이다.
(C) 부점장이 채용될 것이다.
(D) 다양한 특별 간식이 판매될 것이다.

해설 회람의 신규 매장 중 69호점은 위치가 뉴질랜드 로토루아(Rotorua, New Zealand), 점장이 케힌데 이로구(Kehinde Ilogu)이다. 한편, 기사의 마지막 단락 세 번째 문장에서 이로구 씨는 뉴질랜드의 딸기 시즌이 시작될 것(New Zealand's strawberry season will be getting started)이고 아이스크림에 더하여 초콜릿에 찍어 먹는 딸기, 딸기 컵케이크, 딸기 밀크셰이크를 제공할 예정(In addition to our superb ice cream, we'll offer strawberries dipped in chocolate, strawberry cupcakes, and strawberry milkshakes)이라고 했다. 따라서 뉴질랜드 로토루아에 위치한 69호점은 다가오는 딸기 시즌에 아이스크림 외에도 여러 가지 간식 제품을 판매할 것임을 알 수 있으므로 (D)가 정답이다.

어휘 celebrate 축하하다 a range of 다양한 treat 간식

190 추론 / 암시

번역 딸기 축제를 즐길 것 같은 사람은?
(A) 멘데즈 씨
(B) 윌콕스 씨
(C) 프랭크 씨
(D) 서머스 씨

해설 기사의 세 번째 단락에서 올리비아 프랭크(Olivia Frank)는 딸기를 정말 좋아하는데 이곳, 즉 마고의 아이스크림 하우스 로토루아 매장의 딸기는 먹은 것 중 최고(I love strawberry, and their strawberry is the best I ever had)라고 했다. 따라서 기사의 마지막 단락에 언급된 로토루아 매장의 딸기 축제를 즐길 가능성이 높은 사람은 올리비아 프랭크이므로 (C)가 정답이다.

191-195 이메일 + 이메일 + 회람

수신: 에미 토쿠다 〈etokuda@paterradepartmentstores.com〉
발신: 폴 소더먼 〈p.soderman@galahadindustrialmachinery.com〉
날짜: 1월 25일
제목: 논의사항

토쿠다 씨께,

오늘 오전에 통화했던 내용을 확인하고자 글을 씁니다.

논의했던 대로 갤러해드 산업 기계는 해든필드의 파테라 백화점이 운영하는 4개 지점에 셀프서비스 무인 계산대를 각각 1대씩 설치하고 유지관리할 예정입니다. **192 각 무인 계산대의 설치 요금은 1대당 2,000달러입니다.** 설치 일정은 상호 합의된 날짜와 시간으로 예정될 것입니다.

4대의 무인 계산대를 모두 포함한 유지 관리 비용은 월 120달러입니다. **191 저희 기술자들이 하루 24시간, 주 7일 동안 무인 계산대 정비를 위해 대기할 것입니다.** 모든 장비는 국제 품질 기준을 충족하거나 넘어서며, 저희의 모든 작업은 보증됩니다.

정식 서면 계약서는 등기 우편으로 보내 드리겠습니다. 귀사와 함께 일하게 되기를 기대합니다.

폴 소더먼, 상무 이사
갤러해드 산업 기계

어휘 industrial 산업[공업]의 machinery 기계(류) install 설치하다 maintain 유지하다 checkout kiosk 무인 계산대 operate 운영[경영]하다 installation 설치 charge 요금 unit (상품의) 한 개[단위] mutually 상호 간에 agreed-upon 합의된, 절충된 maintenance 유지 관리 cover 포함하다, 다루다 service 정비하다 exceed 넘어서다 guarantee 보증하다, 보장하다 formal 정식의 agreement 계약(서), 합의(서) registered mail 등기 우편

수신: 폴 소더먼 〈p.soderman@galahadindustrialmachinery.com〉
발신: 에미 토쿠다 〈etokuda@paterradepartmentstores.com〉
193 날짜: 4월 2일
제목: 장비 철거 및 재설치

소더먼 씨께,

194 메이플 가 1506에 있는 자사 매장을 폐점하기로 결정했음을 알려드립니다. 재고와 모든 장비를 타운 스퀘어 플라자 3300의 새로운 지점으로 이전할 계획입니다. 이전은 6월 중순으로 계획되어 있지만 아직 날짜를 정하지는 않았습니다.

193 날짜를 확인하고 귀사의 작업팀이 무인 계산대를 설치하기에 편리한 시간을 잡기 위해 다음 달에 연락드리겠습니다. 192 1월 25일자 계약에 따라 귀사의 재설치 요금은 메이플 가 매장에서의 초기 설치 요금과 동일한 것으로 알고 있습니다.

에미 토쿠다, 상무 이사
파테라 백화점

어휘 removal 제거 reinstallation 재설치 transfer 이전하다; 이전 inventory 재고 equipment 장비 set 정하다, 결정하다 arrange 예정을 세우다 crew 작업팀 per ~에 의하여; ~당[마다] initial 초기의

회람

수신: 모든 파테라 직원
발신: 엘리너 비앙키, 지점장
날짜: 6월 5일
회신: 이전 업데이트

여러분의 노고 덕분에 타운 스퀘어 플라자에 있는 우리의 새 매장이 예정대로 6월 15일에 개점합니다. **194 우리가 현재 근무 중인 매장의 문제점 중 하나는 버스 노선이 없다는 점입니다.** 대조적으로, 우리가 이전할 장소에는 698번 버스가 운행하고 있어서 더 많은 고객이 지점을 찾을 것으로 기대합니다. **195 원예 부서에서 진열을 끝낼 수 있도록 창고에서 마지막 진열 선반이 배송되기만을 기다리고 있습니다.**

여러분의 노력에 감사하고자 아니카스 베이커리에서 페이스트리를 가져왔습니다. 휴게실 카운터에 이 간식들을 두었습니다. 맛있게 드세요!

어휘 on track 제대로 진행되고 있는 by contrast 대조적으로, 반대로 a number of 많은 warehouse 창고 in appreciation of ~에 감사하여 treat 간식, 대접

191 Not / True

번역 첫 번째 이메일에서, 갤러해드 산업 기계에 대해 언급된 것은?
(A) 하루 안에 수리를 마친다.
(B) 상시 유지 관리 서비스가 제공된다.
(C) 국제 업무 경험이 있는 기술자들을 보유하고 있다.
(D) 해든필드에 사무실이 있다.

해설 갤러해드 산업 기계의 소더먼 씨가 보낸 첫 번째 이메일의 세 번째 단락 두 번째 문장에서 자사 기술자들이 하루 24시간, 주 7일 동안 무인 계산대 정비를 위해 대기할 것(Our technicians will be available 24 hours a day, 7 days a week, to service the kiosks)이라고 했으므로 (B)가 정답이다.

어휘 complete 마치다, 끝내다 at all times 상시, 항상

Paraphrasing 지문의 24 hours a day, 7 days a week
→ 정답의 at all times

192 연계

번역 셀프서비스 무인 계산대의 재설치에 대해 사실인 것은?
(A) 소더먼 씨가 직접 할 것이다.
(B) 파테라 백화점에게 2,000달러의 비용이 들게 할 것이다.
(C) 월간 유지 관리비에 변화를 초래할 것이다.
(D) 새로운 계약에 서명해야 할 것이다.

해설 두 번째 이메일의 마지막 문장에서 파테라 백화점의 토쿠다 씨가 1월 25일자 계약에 따라 재설치 요금은 메이플 가 매장에서의 초기 설치 요금과 동일한 것으로 알고 있다(I understand that, ~ your charge for the reinstallation will be the same as for the initial installation at the Maple Street store)고 했고, 첫 번째 이메일의 두 번째 단락 두 번째 문장에서 각 무인 계산대의 설치 요금은 1대당 2,000달러(The installation charge for each kiosk will be $2,000 per unit)라고 했다. 따라서 계산대의 재설치 비용은 초기 설치 요금과 동일한 2,000달러이므로 (B)가 정답이다.

어휘 personally 직접

206

193 세부사항

번역 토쿠다 씨는 언제 소더먼 씨와 이전 계획에 대해 논의할 것인가?
(A) 3월
(B) 4월
(C) 5월
(D) 6월

해설 두 번째 이메일의 발신 날짜가 4월 2일(Date: April 2)이고, 두 번째 단락 첫 문장에서 토쿠다 씨가 날짜를 확인하고 작업팀이 무인 계산대를 설치하기에 편리한 시간을 잡기 위해 다음 달에 연락하겠다(I will contact you next month to confirm the date ~ for your work crew to install the self-service kiosk)고 했다. 따라서 토쿠다 씨는 이메일을 발송한 4월의 다음 달인 5월에 소더먼 씨에게 연락할 계획이므로 (C)가 정답이다.

194 연계

번역 메이플 가 1506에 있는 파테라 매장에 대해 암시된 것은?
(A) 버스로 갈 수 없다.
(B) 개조되어 재개장할 것이다.
(C) 창고에서 멀다.
(D) 베이커리 섹션이 있다.

해설 파테라의 토쿠타 씨가 작성한 두 번째 이메일의 첫 문장에서 메이플 가 1506에 있는 자사 매장을 폐점하기로 결정했음을 알린다(Please be advised that we have decided to close our store at 1506 Maple Street)고 했고, 파테라 직원에게 발송된 회람의 첫 단락 두 번째 문장에서 현재 근무 중인 매장의 문제점 중 하나는 버스 노선이 없다는 점(One of the problems with the store we are currently working out of is that it is not on a bus line)이라고 했다. 따라서 현재 운영 중인 메이플 가 1506에 위치한 매장은 버스를 이용하기 힘들다는 것을 알 수 있으므로 (A)가 정답이다.

어휘 accessible 접근할 수 있는, 이용 가능한 renovate 개조하다, 보수하다

Paraphrasing 지문의 not on a bus line
→ 정답의 not accessible by bus

195 세부사항

번역 회람에 따르면, 새 파테라 매장에서 여전히 마무리되어야 할 일은?
(A) 일부 제품의 가격이 책정되어야 한다.
(B) 일부 구역이 페인트칠 되어야 한다.
(C) 일부 문이 교체되어야 한다.
(D) 일부 선반이 배송되어야 한다.

해설 회람의 첫 단락 마지막 문장에서 원예 부서에서 진열을 끝낼 수 있도록 창고에서 마지막 진열 선반이 배송되기만을 기다리고 있다(We are only waiting for the last of our display shelves to be delivered ~ in the gardening department)고 했으므로 (D)가 정답이다.

어휘 price 가격을 책정하다 replace 교체하다

196-200 기사 + 초대장 + 이메일

설문 조사: 소비자는 실물 매장을 선호한다

최근 소비자 설문 조사는 응답자의 33퍼센트가 구입하고자 하는 제품을 만져 보는 것을 선호한다는 것을 보여 준다. 게다가 조사에 응한 사람들의 61퍼센트는 쇼핑을 할 때 온라인 상점보다 오프라인 상점에서 돈을 더 많이 쓰는 것 같다고 말했다.

196 다른 소비자 선호도 조사에서도 뒷받침되는 이 데이터로 인해 모든 수익을 온라인 판매에서 창출하는 많은 상인이 온라인상의 입지를 보완하기 위해 실물 상점을 개점하고 있다.

실물 공간의 장점은 소매점 주인들이 브랜드 충성도를 구축하는 데 도움이 된다는 것이다. "편리함에 있어서는 온라인이 최고입니다."라고 셀번에 아동 매장 토들스와 온라인 사이트 toddles.com을 소유하고 있는 말린 피츠로이는 말한다. "하지만 실물 공간은 지역 고객들을 재방문하게 하고 새로운 고객들을 끌어들이는 공동체 의식을 조성해 줍니다."

198 피츠로이 씨는 지역 비즈니스 행사에 자주 참여하는 강연자로, 고객 참여의 강력한 지지자이자 홍보일 뿐 아니라 자신이 전하는 대로 실천한다.

197 "1년에 네 번, 우리는 어린이들이 다양한 활동을 즐길 수 있는 특별 판매 행사를 주최합니다."라고 그녀는 말했다. "이 행사들은 어린이들과 부모님 모두에게 인기 만점입니다. 비록 부모들이 이런 행사에서 아무 것도 사지 않더라도 다음번에 아이들의 장난감, 게임, 책, 또는 퍼즐이 필요할 때 아마도 우리가 생각날 것입니다."

어휘 consumer 소비자 physical 실제의, 물리적인 respondent 응답자 intend 의도하다 brick-and-mortar 오프라인의 back up ~을 뒷받침하다 preference 선호도 merchant 상인 generate 발생시키다 revenue 수익, 소득 supplement 보충(물) presence 존재 advantage 장점 retail 소매 loyalty 충성 in terms of ~ 면에서 convenience 편리 beat 더 낫다, 능가하다 foster 조성하다 attract 끌어들이다 frequent 빈번한 promoter 홍보자 engagement 참여 preach 전하다, 설교하다 occasion 행사

셀번 비즈니스 연합(SBC)

10월 8일 셀번 컨벤션 센터에서 열리는 연례 비즈니스 정상 회의에 셀번 및 인근 지역 사업가들의 참석을 권합니다.

올해 우리의 기조 연설자는 윈터에덴 호텔리어스의 설립자이자 최고 경영자인 한스라지 데쉬판데 씨입니다. 198 그 외의 연사들은 모두 지역 사업주인 오모델 아킨조 씨, 말린 피츠로이 씨, 재스퍼 클링크하머 씨, 앨빈 리우 씨입니다. 다루어질 주제는 강력한 인력 구축, 신용 한도 설정, 고객과의 관계 형성, 벤처 자본 유치입니다.

199 이 행사에 등록하시면 저희 이메일 목록에 자동으로 추가됩니다. 전체 일정을 확인하시려면 웹사이트 www.shelburnbusinesscoalition.org 를 방문하세요.

어휘 coalition 연합 surrounding 인근의 summit 정상 회담 founder 설립자 cover 다루다 workforce 인력 establish 확립하다 line of credit 신용 한도 engage 관계를 맺다 venture capital 벤처 자본 register for ~에 등록하다

TEST 10

수신: 본 스가마토 〈vsgammato@opalmail.com〉
발신: 아이린 워가 〈irenewarga@shelburnbusinesscoalition.org〉
날짜: 9월 15일
제목: 등록 확인

스가마토 씨께,

199 셸번 비즈니스 연합은 귀하께서 비즈니스 정상 회의에 등록해 주신 데 대해 감사드립니다. 귀하의 확인 번호는 R56690입니다.

알려 드리자면, 200 컨벤션 센터 지하 주차장은 10월 8일에 유지 관리를 위해 폐쇄될 예정입니다. 그러므로 길 건너 공영 주차장에 주차해 주십시오. 정상 회의가 끝날 때 주차비를 충당할 수 있는 할인권을 드립니다.

만나 뵙기를 기대합니다. 문의사항이 있으시면 555-0138로 연락하십시오.

아이린 워가, 행사 진행자

어휘 confirmation 확인 reminder 상기시키는 것[주의] garage 주차장 maintenance 유지 관리 public 공영의 voucher 할인권 cover (비용을) 감당하다, 부담하다

196 세부사항

번역 기사에 따르면, 많은 온라인 판매자들에 의해 고려되고 있는 조치는?
(A) 웹사이트 재설계
(B) 광고 예산 증액
(C) 실물 매장 개점
(D) 새로운 제품 라인 개발

해설 기사의 두 번째 단락에서 다른 소비자 선호도 조사에서도 뒷받침되는 이 데이터로 인해 모든 수익을 온라인 판매에서 창출하는 많은 상인들이 온라인상의 입지를 보완하기 위해 실물 상점을 개점하고 있다(These data, ~ causing many merchants who generate all their revenue from online sales to open physical stores as a supplement to their online presence)고 했으므로 (C)가 정답이다.

어휘 redesign 재설계하다 line 제품군

197 세부사항

번역 피츠로이 씨가 자신의 고객에게 제공한다고 말하는 것은?
(A) 쇼핑하기 편리한 장소
(B) 아동복 할인
(C) 즐거운 쇼핑 경험
(D) 장난감 특가 상품

해설 기사의 다섯 번째 단락 첫 문장에서 피츠로이 씨(Ms. Fitzroy)는 1년에 네 번, 어린이들이 다양한 활동을 즐길 수 있는 특별 판매 행사를 주최한다(Four times a year, we host a special sales event during which children can enjoy themselves with a variety of activities)고 했으므로 (C)가 정답이다. 피츠로이 씨의 매장이 장난감을 취급하기는 하지만 특정 품목의 특가 상품을 제공한다는 언급은 없으므로 (D)는 답이 되지 않는다.

어휘 convenient 편리한 enjoyable 즐거운 special deal 특가 상품

198 연계

번역 고객과의 관계 형성 주제에 대해 연설할 것 같은 사람은?
(A) 아킨조 씨
(B) 피츠로이 씨
(C) 데쉬판데 씨
(D) 리우 씨

해설 초대장의 두 번째 단락 두 번째 문장에 소개된 지역 사업주 연설자 중에 말린 피츠로이(Ms. Marlene Fitzroy)가 있고, 뒤이어 다루어질 주제는 강력한 인력 구축, 신용 한도 설정, 고객과의 관계 형성, 벤처 자본 유치(Topics to be covered include ~ engaging with customers, and attracting venture capital)라고 했으며, 기사의 네 번째 단락에서 피츠로이 씨는 지역 비즈니스 행사에 자주 참여하는 강연자로 고객 참여의 강력한 지지자이자 홍보자일 뿐 아니라 자신이 전하는 대로 실천한다(Ms. Fitzroy, ~ is not only a strong supporter and promoter of customer engagement; she also practices what she preaches)고 했다. 따라서 고객 참여의 강력한 지지자이자 홍보자인 피츠로이 씨를 고객과의 관계 형성 주제에 관한 연설자로 추정할 수 있으므로 (B)가 정답이다.

199 연계

번역 스가마토 씨에 대해 사실일 것 같은 것은?
(A) 메일 목록에 추가되었다.
(B) 사업을 시작할 것이다.
(C) 등록비를 할인받았다.
(D) 전에 SBC 행사에 참석한 적이 없다.

해설 초대장의 마지막 단락 첫 문장에서 이 행사에 등록하면 우리의 이메일 목록에 자동으로 추가된다(By registering for this event, you will automatically be added to our e-mail list)고 했고, 이메일의 첫 문장에서 스가마토 씨에게 셸번 비즈니스 연합은 비즈니스 정상 회의에 등록해 주신 데 대해 감사드린다(Shelburn Business Coalition thanks you for registering for our Business Summit)고 했다. 따라서 행사에 등록한 스가마토 씨는 자동으로 메일 목록에 추가되었음을 알 수 있으므로 (A)가 정답이다.

Paraphrasing 지문의 e-mail list → 정답의 mailing list

200 세부사항

번역 스가마토 씨가 컨벤션 센터에 도착했을 때 해야 할 일은?
(A) 워가 씨와의 만남 요청하기
(B) 길 건너에 주차하기
(C) 확인 번호 받기
(D) 회의 자료 가져가기

해설 이메일의 두 번째 단락 첫 문장에서 스가마토 씨에게 컨벤션 센터 지하 주차장은 10월 8일에 유지 관리를 위해 폐쇄될 예정(please note that the convention center underground garage ~ on October 8)이니 길 건너 공영 주차장에 주차해 달라(Therefore, please park your car in the public parking area across the street)고 요청하고 있으므로 (B)가 정답이다.